Guide to the
SOLO HORN REPERTOIRE

Indiana Repertoire Guides

Guide to the

SOLO HORN REPERTOIRE

LINDA DEMPF *and*
RICHARD SERAPHINOFF

INDIANA UNIVERSITY PRESS
Bloomington & Indianapolis

This book is a publication of

INDIANA UNIVERSITY PRESS
Office of Scholarly Publishing
Herman B Wells Library 350
1320 E. 10th Street
Bloomington, IN 47405-3907

iupress.indiana.edu

Manufactured in the United States of America

Library of Congress Cataloging-in-Publication Data

Names: Dempf, Linda, compiler, editor. | Seraphinoff, Richard, compiler, editor.
Title: Guide to the solo horn repertoire / Linda Dempf and Richard Seraphinoff.
Other titles: Indiana repertoire guides.
Description: Bloomington ; Indianapolis : Indiana University Press, 2016. | 2016 | Series: Indiana repertoire guides | Includes indexes.
Identifiers: LCCN 2016006153| ISBN 9780253019295 (cloth : alkaline paper) | ISBN 9780253019356 (ebook)
Subjects: LCSH: Horn music—Bibliography. | Horn and keyboard instrument music—Bibliography. | Horn with instrumental ensemble—Bibliography.
Classification: LCC ML128.H67 D46 2016 | DDC 016.7889/4—dc23 LC record available at http://lccn.loc.gov/2016006153

1 2 3 4 5   21 20 19 18 17 16

To the memory of
Philip Farkas (1914–1992)

Contents

Preface

SCOPE

This book is meant to serve as a comprehensive guide to the music for solo horn that is significant and available. Our aim is to bring together information in one location for readers who want to know what solo music has been written for the horn, some basic information about the pieces, and where they can be obtained. It is intended for horn players and teachers, but we hope that it will be useful for conductors, composers, and scholars who may be interested in finding out more about the literature written for the horn.

The guide includes music written originally for the horn, so excludes arrangements, with the exception of piano reductions of works for horn and ensemble. We have included mostly published works that are available for purchase or available from libraries in the United States. In a few cases we have included unpublished works, either obtaining these directly from the composer or from a lending library, such as the Fleisher Collection at the Free Library of Philadelphia. We corresponded with several international music centers that serve as clearinghouses for music in other countries and included works that were of significance, our thought being that if we are able to obtain the music, you would be able to as well.

To identify the significant works for horn, we consulted many bibliographies, lists, and publications about horn repertoire, including Robin Gregory, *The Horn: A Comprehensive Guide to the Modern Instrument & Its Music;* Bernhard Brüchle and Kurt Janetzky, *The Horn;* Gunther Schuller, *Horn Technique;* Douglas Hill, *Collected Thoughts on Teaching and Learning, Creativity, and Horn Performance;* and Verne Reynolds, *The Horn Handbook.* Several dissertations were invaluable starting points, including Timothy Kerwin, *A Core Repertoire of Solo and Accompanied Works for the Horn: An Annotated Bibliography with Analysis;* Gayle Chesebro, *An Annotated List of Original Works for Horn Alone and for Horn with One Other Non-keyboard Instrument;* Karen Robertson Smith, *An Annotated Bibliography of Works for Unaccompanied Horn, 1975–1995;* and Lin Foulk, *Works for Horn and Piano by Female Composers: An Annotated Guide.* For information on composers and works, we consulted composers' and publishers' websites, Worldcat, music and recording reviews published in *The Horn Call* and other journals, plus many reference works and dissertations, particularly those written about works for horn by specific composers. We examined nearly every score that is included in the list; a few, however, were not obtainable, but determined significant enough for inclusion, so are listed with as much information as available. The focus of this guide is on the music itself, but there are occasional "see also" references when a source has been consulted or quoted extensively, or to point readers to a significant resource about a piece.

USING THE GUIDE

The guide is organized into three large sections: works for unaccompanied horn, works for horn and keyboard, and works for horn and ensemble. The appendix contains indexes for titles of works, names of soloists and dedicatees, and a list of the composers by country designation. We have also provided two ensemble indexes for locating solos with band, wind ensemble, brass band and smaller instrumental ensemble.

In each chapter, composers are listed alphabetically with dates and their primary country of residence. The title of the work appears in italics, with date of composition, when available, indicated in parentheses. We list publisher and date, and have made no attempt to include every published edition of a work, but instead list the major editions available and of interest to performers. For works for horn and ensemble, we indicate if a piece is available as an arrangement for horn and piano (piano reduction), or as a full score only. Annotations include a brief description of the form and character of a work, technical details of the horn writing, and information on dedication and premiere. Our goal is to let you know about a piece, give you guidance on its significance, and pique your curiosity, providing enough basic information in the event you are interested in finding out more. In a few entries we refer to *New Grove,* which is the *New Grove Dictionary of Music and Musicians,* second edition. Entries may include a composer's own words about a piece, and unless otherwise noted, quotations are from the preface of a score, or from a dedication on the title page. Range is for horn in F unless indicated otherwise. The system of octave designation for horn range is adapted from D. Kern Holoman's style guide, *Writing About Music: A Style Sheet,* as seen in figure 1. Durations, when included, have been taken from the printed music, from a commercial recording, or from the authors' own calculations.

Figure 1: Octave designation for horn range.

We have made no attempt to establish a grading system for individual works, but instead try to give some idea of the difficulties and appropriateness of each work for players of different skill levels through description in the text of the various techniques required and the challenges that each presents. This system has its own inherent problems, yet we hope that by doing this, each entry will give a fuller picture than an assigned grade and also be more specific in what makes a piece particularly challenging or accessible. We indicate when a work stands out as particularly suited to a certain level of player, such as a high-school player or a younger college player, or if a work is a good introduction to a specific technique or style for a certain level of player.

Acknowledgments

We would like to thank the many people who made this book possible. We are grateful to all of the composers who sent us their scores, recordings, and words of encouragement, continually reminding us that this was a worthwhile endeavor. Numerous publishers and distributors sent us music, including Theodore Presser, Solid Wood, Musik Fabrik, JOMAR Press, RM Williams, and Veritas Music. A special thanks to Robert King Music, who allowed us to peruse scores on site over two snowy days at their North Easton, Massachusetts, headquarters. The staff in the publishing rental departments at Schott/EAM, Boosey & Hawkes, Theodore Presser, Schirmer, and C.F. Peters were tireless in their efforts in tracking down music and helping us navigate the complex world of rental scores and distribution.

Many colleagues provided invaluable feedback and support. Special thanks to Tomoko Kanamaru, for her collegiality and her help with translations, and to Barry Tuckwell and faculty at the Barry Tuckwell Institute for inspiration and encouragement during early stages of the book. The horn faculty and horn students at Indiana University provided invaluable input by bringing pieces and composers to our attention, and talented graduate assistants in the horn department at Indiana, Katie Baker and Burke Anderson, provided helpful research assistance.

We are grateful to music librarians and staff at the libraries we visited and corresponded with, who came through time and again with their expertise and suggestions, including Eva Heater at Yale University, the music specialists at the Performing Arts Reading Room at the Library of Congress, Stu Serio at the Fleisher Collection of the Free Library of Philadelphia, and Darwin Scott at Princeton University. The ever efficient Interlibrary Loan departments at our home institutions, Indiana University Library, and The College of New Jersey Library, obtained literally hundreds of research materials for us, for which we are extremely thankful.

We would like to express our gratitude to Indiana University Press and to our editor Raina Polivka, for her wisdom, patience, guidance, and her firm belief in this project. This book would never have been possible without the unwavering support of our spouses, Celeste Holler-Seraphinoff and Peter McKhann. We are grateful for their continual cheering on, cheering up, last minute indexing skills, and their infinite patience. And finally, we are grateful to all of the horn soloists—of the past, and those in the present—who continue to inspire great works for our instrument.

Guide to the
SOLO HORN REPERTOIRE

1
Music for Unaccompanied Horn

INTRODUCTION

The literature for unaccompanied horn has come about for many different reasons. Horn teachers have written unaccompanied works as exam pieces for students. Performers intrigued by the possibilities of their own instrument have been inspired to write for horn alone, often to fulfill the need for more freely expressive pieces for their own performing. Contemporary composers interested in exploring the horn's different timbres and technical possibilities have written many works for horn alone and in recent years have succeeded in pushing the boundaries of the instrument's technical and expressive capabilities.

The beauty of the unaccompanied work—the range of expression available, the total freedom possible—is also what makes these works so challenging. The performer has complete responsibility for all aspects of the piece. And since there is no one else to carry the music forward or share in the expression, these works are not only some of the most taxing and technically difficult in the horn literature but they also require much individual musical thought in their preparation and presentation. Another challenge for both composer and performer is avoiding the monotony inherent in a work for one instrument. The same timbre heard for more than just a few minutes can wear on the listener, no matter how beautiful the line or how novel the gesture. However, when composed and performed effectively, the sparseness, immediacy, and expressiveness of an unaccompanied work can balance out a recital and add great variety to a program. Unaccompanied pieces also give the horn player the opportunity to perform in a more theatrical way than the average ensemble player may be used to, since the visual aspect in an unaccompanied performance can be just as important as the sound.

Since so many of these works push the technical and expressive boundaries of the horn, there are many extended techniques that require careful consideration, deciphering, and coordination. Unaccompanied works are an excellent pedagogical opportunity and can be used in conjunction with etudes. In addition to the great technical challenges, the complete musical responsibility that these works require make them a powerful teaching tool. As with the other sections of this book, we have made no attempt to establish a grading system for individual works, but instead try to give some idea of the difficulties and appropriateness of each work for players of different skill levels through description in the text of the various techniques required, and the challenges that each presents.

MUSIC FOR UNACCOMPANIED HORN

Adler, Samuel (1928–) United States, born in Germany

Canto XI for Solo Horn
Ludwig Music Publishing, 1986
Dedicated to Adler's Eastman colleague Verne Reynolds, "with a slight apology
to Richard Strauss." Adler wrote "cantos" for many different instruments
over a sixteen-year period, starting in 1970. The heroic nature of the horn
is developed in this work, and the listener will hear echoes of the famous
call of Richard Strauss' *Till Eulenspiegels Lustige Streiche*. In two contrasting sections: The first, "Slowly and quite freely" is unmeasured and features
beautiful, loud, legato playing, full of romantic sweeps reminiscent of great
orchestral horn writing. The second section is a fast § that echoes the familiar Strauss call. Agility and flexibility are needed, particularly for the second
half of this work.
Range: A♭–c³
Duration: 6:30

Agrell, Jeffrey (1948–) United States
Jeffrey Agrell is the former associate principal horn of the Lucerne Symphony Orchestra (Switzerland) and currently on the faculty at the University of Iowa.

Attitudes (2005)
RM Williams Publishing, 2005
    I. Exuberant
    II. Grieving
    III. Peevish
    IV. Fast Lane
Commissioned for the 2006 Midwest Horn Workshop Solo Competition and
dedicated to Patrick Miles. Each movement has an improvised cadenza.
Notes are included for the individual cadenzas, plus there are extensive instructions on how to approach improvising in general, and how to practice
it. This is a solid addition to the solo horn and pedagogical literature for
anyone interested in trying out improvisation through an unaccompanied
work. Suitable for the college-level player and above.
Range: E♭–a♭²
Duration: ca. 8:00

Meditation (1997)
JOMAR Press, 1997
A short, flowing, unaccompanied work with modest technical demands and
plenty of opportunity for expression. This would be a suitable introduction
to unaccompanied playing for the high school or early college player.
Range: a–e♭²
Duration: 2:30

Romp
Editions Marc Reift, 1996
A short, energetic and rhythmic work in $\frac{6}{8}$, to be played *with abandon*. Includes
 a few extended techniques. This was a required piece for horn players at all
 conservatories in France in 2003.
Range: G–b♭²
Duration: 2:00

Aho, Kalevi (1949–) Finland

Solo X (2010)
Fennica Gehrman, 2011
The composer wrote this as a preparatory work for his *Horn Concerto* to explore
 characteristics of the horn. A virtuosic work with a wide range of ideas,
 from expressive horn calls in the opening that alternate stopped and
 open gestures, to driving rhythmic motives. Contrasts abound, with swift
 changes in dynamics and quick leaps between extreme ranges of the horn.
 This is challenging and dramatic writing for the horn.
Range: E–c³
Duration: 7:00

Almila, Atso (1953–) Finland

Unicorno, op. 14 *for Solo Horn* (1976)
Warner/Chappell, 1995
Dedicated to Esa-Pekka Salonen. Four short movements, mostly unmeasured,
 with one section in $\frac{6}{8}$. The length of this work will vary, due to improvisational sections. The first movement has a recurring theme of twelve notes,
 interspersed with an angular sixteenth-note passage. The second movement is based on minor seconds and major sevenths and has fast chromatic
 slurs and passages of wide leaps. The third movement opens and closes
 with a twelve-note theme that goes through various permutations of more
 angular writing. The fourth movement is the most free in form, with many
 decisions left up to the performer. Challenges include alternating open and
 closed notes and negotiating wide leaps. The movements are short and well
 paced.
Range: f♯–c³
Duration: 6:10–8:35

Amram, David (1930–) United States
Horn player, composer, conductor, and jazz hornist. His works are infused with
elements of jazz and world music.

Blues and Variations for Monk (1982)
C. F. Peters, 1991
David Amram wrote this work "in memory of Thelonious Monk for his friend-
 ship and inspiration." It was premiered by Douglas Hill at the 1982 Interna-

tional Horn Workshop in Avignon, France. Containing a prelude, a theme, five short variations, a return to the theme, then ending with a coda, this is a highly accessible work in the jazz idiom. The theme and variations are a twelve-bar blues, except for variation IV which is fifteen measures in length. A good opportunity for the intermediate hornist and above to explore jazz rhythms and style.

Range: c–g^2
Duration: 6:00

Andriessen, Jurriaan (1925–1996) Netherlands

Serenade voor hoorn solo (1985)
Donemus, 1986
Featuring modal melodies with clever sections of contrapuntal writing within the framework of regular phrasing, and interesting intervallic combinations, this work is suitable for the early college player.

    I. Andante rubato: Begins with a horn call motive on fourths and fifths, increasing in rhythmic complexity and dynamic intensity before a return of the opening call motive.

   II. Allegro moderato: In ABA form with changing meters.

  III. Andante con moto: In ABA form, the middle section is piu mosso.

  IV. Allegro: A quick romp in $\frac{6}{8}$ with hemiolas and interesting contrapuntal writing. This movement opens with arpeggiated figures that become smaller intervals as the piece progresses.

   V. Valzer lento, Dolce grazioso, sempre espressivo: a slow and expressive waltz, felt in one.

Range: g♯–a♭^{2}
Duration: 12:00

Apostel, Hans Erich (1901–1972) Austria, born in Germany
Apostel was a pupil of Berg and Schoenberg and an active pianist, composer, accompanist, and private teacher in Vienna.

Sonatine, op. 39b (1964)
Universal Edition, 1965
This is an atonal work, based on a twelve-tone row, with interesting rhythmic and tone combinations. In three movements: Allegro moderato—Lento—Allegro giocoso. The first movement is a march with the form ABCBA, the middle C section being a study in the contrasting characters presented in the A and B sections. The second movement is a short theme with three variations of three or four bars each, marked espressivo. The third movement is a rondo that juxtaposes short staccato phrases, marked molto ritmico, with short legato phrases, alternating over changing $\frac{3}{8}$ and $\frac{5}{8}$. A challenging work in twelve-tone harmonic language.

Range: g♯–c^3
Duration: 5:00

Armstrong, John Gordon (1952–) Canada

Trotte Vieille, 13 Vignettes for Solo Horn
Canadian Music Centre, 1994
Dedicated to Janine Gaboury-Sly who first performed the piece on March 26, 1997
    at Michigan State University in East Lansing, Michigan. These vignettes,
    varying in length anywhere from six notes to three pages, can be played on
    their own or in different combinations and are of contrasting characters,
    such as "Disjointed, ragged," "Harsh, violent," and "Serene, contemplative."
    Moderately difficult writing for the horn, with fast technical passages that
    span the entire range of the instrument, extending up to c^3.
Range: $c–c^3$

Arnecke, Jörn (1973–) Germany

Bamberger Hörnchen, für Horn solo (2009–2010)
    Sikorski, 2010
Commissioned by the ARD International Music Competition in 2010. Based on
    two extended techniques for the horn: multiphonics (singing while playing
    the horn) and playing on the horn's naturally occurring harmonic series.
    The singing voice, notated in C, uses treble clef to take into account the
    difference between male range and female range, and both are indicated.
    The recurring upward passages that unify this work are notated with mi-
    crotones, indicating which notes reside outside of the tempered scale. A
    challenging work that fully explores these two extended techniques. The
    title is a humorous play on words—the piece was written in the town of
    Bamberg, and *Hörnchen* could mean "small horn," but it is also a sort of
    croissant which they bake in a special way in Bamberg.
Range: $F\sharp–b^2$
Duration: 9:00

Arnold, Malcolm (1921–2006) United Kingdom

Fantasy for Horn, op. 88 (1966)
Faber Music, 1966
Arnold wrote fantasies for different solo instruments throughout his career. The
    Fantasy for Horn was commissioned by the City of Birmingham Symphony
    Orchestra for the Birmingham International Wind Competition in 1966.
    It begins with a jaunty tune in $\frac{6}{8}$, followed by an espressivo section, in mi-
    nor marked Poco lento. A section of echoing fanfares contrasts open and
    stopped horn, followed by virtuosic sixteenth notes. The final section is a
    return to the jaunty opening material, and the piece ends with a flourish
    repeatedly going up to $b\flat^2$. This piece has earned a solid position in the horn
    repertoire, with its interesting character and tuneful writing that is well
    paced and idiomatic for the horn.
Range: $e–b\flat^2$
Duration: 3:50

Arter, Matthias (1964–) Switzerland
Arter is a composer and oboist and serves on the faculty of the Bern University of the Arts, Switzerland

Voice, for French Horn (1998)
Egge Verlag, 2000, also available from www.marterart.ch/en/kompositionen.html
Dedicated to Karl Fassler. Explores many different colors and techniques, including multiphonics, glissandi, quarter tones and playing several phrases with a "pale sound, like a Renaissance-cornett" with slide/slides removed. Challenges include a passage on repeated b^2, but judicious rests make this contemporary work well paced.
Range: G–b^2
Duration: 4:00

Babbitt, Milton (1916–2011) United States

Around the Horn (1993)
Smith Publications, 1994
Composed for William Purvis, this work is dedicated to the memory of Marjorie Schuller, the wife of Gunther Schuller. An acrobatic challenge, the horn line comes out of the emphasis on different notes as it jumps two or more octaves throughout the piece. Dynamics alternate suddenly between loud and soft, achieving a brilliant echo effect. Rhythmically complex, the piece is metered with continually changing time signatures. Grounded firmly in the twelve-tone tradition, this brilliant and challenging solo pushes the boundaries of the horn, both musically and technically.
Range: f♯–b^2
Duration: 9:30

Bach, Jan (1937–) United States

French Suite (1982)
Cimarron Music Press, 2012
Written for Doug Hill to perform at the 1982 International Horn Society Workshop in Avignon, France. Jan Bach was writing a horn concerto around this time and contacted Doug Hill who was writing *Extended Techniques for the Horn*. This piece uses several of the techniques in the book, and bears a loose resemblance to the baroque suite. The first movement, Fantaisie, is unmeasured and free, marked Leisurely, un poco rubato. The Courante consists of active sections of changing meters that alternate with a quiet stopped horn theme, echoing, or coming from afar. Sarabande features a cantabile horn line with a "soft shoe" effect, achieved by rubbing a hairbrush or sandpaper back and forth on a mute. The last movement, Fugue, is full of jazz inflections, with running eighth notes, crescendos, accents, and quick flutter tonguing.
Range: B♭–c^3
Duration: 12:40

Baldwin, Daniel (1978–) United States

Rashomon (2006)
Imagine Music, 2006
Commissioned and dedicated to Mike Keegan. The title refers to the ancient gate
    of Kyoto. This work is suitable for a strong high school player, with a section
    of slurred sixteenth notes and stopped and muted echo effects.
Range: A–g^2
Duration: 3:00

Barboteu, Georges (1924–2006) France
Barboteu was principal of the Orchestre de Paris and professor of horn at the Paris
Conservatoire. He composed many studies for the horn as well as chamber music
for horn and other brass instruments.

Cinq Pieces poetiques, pour cor en fa (1972)
Editions Choudens, 1974
These five movements are tuneful and flowing. The first movement is an easygo-
    ing $\frac{6}{8}$. The second, marked Mouvement tres libre, provides opportunity for
    freedom of expression with legato leaps and a cadenza like flourish up to
    a♭^{2} in the middle of the movement. The fourth movement is in ABA form,
    starting and finishing with an Allegro vivo in a steady $\frac{2}{4}$, mostly triadic
    writing, with flutter tonguing, sixteenth-note figures, and trills. The mid-
    dle section, in $\frac{12}{8}$, is reminiscent of the first movement. The final movement
    is expansive and free and is based on fourths and fifths. Suitable for the
    college player.
Range: d–c^3
Duration: 10:15

Fa 7, pieces pour cor seul
Editions Choudens, 1987
      1. Étrange
      2. Volubile
      3. Monologue
      4. Chanté
      5. Enjoué
Averaging one minute apiece, each movement explores contemporary horn tech-
    niques found in twentieth-century music, including wide vibrato, stopped
    notes, trills, flutter tonguing, and multiphonics. In addition, there are in-
    stances of pronouncing words into the horn. These sounds and techniques
    are all explored within the context of traditional metric notation.
Range: G–c^3
Duration: 6:00

Basler, Paul (1963–) United States

Cantos, for Solo Horn
RM Williams, 2003

For William Capps. Commissioned by and written for the 2004 Southeast Horn
   Workshop as the required first-round work for the collegiate solo horn competition. Short work in contrasting sections that gradually builds momentum, with a final return to the opening motive, this time played *fortissimo*
   and sustained. Quickly moves between different moods, and opportunities
   abound for expression in this very idiomatic work for horn. Features expressive wide legato leaps and some stopped writing. A very accessible work for
   the college-level student and above.

Range: B♭–b♭²
Duration: 3:50

Five Pieces for Solo Horn
RM Williams, 1998
Written for Michelle Stebleton, associate professor of music at Florida State University. The composer describes this work in the preface: "Descriptive in
   nature, each piece deals with a specific horn 'issue'—i.e. fast scalar passages, lyrical arpeggios, fingering exercises, etc." In five movements: Chop-
   buster—Rhapsodic—March—Song for Vitali—Auto pilot. These works
   have a pedagogical focus, yet are tuneful and interesting.

Range: b–b³
Duration: 10:00

Marathon, for Solo Horn (1997)
RM Williams, 1998
Written for Michelle Stebleton. The composer writes, "the piece combines supple,
   lyrical arches with fearless, athletic leaps in a 'marathon' of sorts for the
   horn player." Changing tempos and wide leaps through different ranges,
   with some stopped writing and flutter tonguing. A challenging work requiring good overall endurance, but with judicious rests for the performer.

Range: G♭–c³
Duration: 5:00

Son of Till (1989–1993)
RM Williams, 1998
Dedicated to William Capps, horn professor at Florida State University who was
   a mentor to the composer; movements are dedicated to different perform-
   ers. The work was "written as a showcase piece for the virtuoso hornist.
   The title implies a humorous link to the celebrated figure in German myth,
   Till—a rambunctious, likable prankster." It includes various extended
   techniques such as flutter tonguing, stopped horn, and half-valve glissandi.
   I. Phoenix rising: To Kathy Wood. Basler writes that this movement "is pri-
      marily concerned with a quick ascending gesture that travels through
      the better part of the horn's range."
   II. Arioso Dreams: To William Purvis. This movement "conjures up images
      of nightmares, illusions and a demented form of Chinese water torture
      in which a single, short note . . . appears regularly, sending the performer
      into even greater fits of demented athletic activity."

III. Electric Screwdriver: To D. Bruce Heim. "This last movement 'celebrates' our obsession with power tools, process music (minimalism) and mindless virtuosity for its own sake."

Range: G–c³

Duration: 7:30

Triathlon (2001)

RM Williams

Written for the 2001 American Horn Competition, this was the required piece for the second round of the professional division. In three movements: Aggressive—Apprehensive—Acrobatic.

Duration: 6:00

Báthory-Kitsz, Dennis (1949–) United States

Sweet Ovals for Solo Horn (2005)

Westleaf Edition, 2005 (also available from Frog Peak music and from the composer's website at maltedmedia.com/people/bathory/cat-solo.html)

Written for the 2005 Vermont Composers Festival for Lydia Busler-Blais. On his website, the composer describes this as a "lush piece, it explores the range and effects of the horn with a finely honed beauty." An exploration of the low to middle range of the horn, with a sweeping motive that begins in the middle range that swoops downward and upward. An accessible work due to its range, requiring good flexibility. Features proportional notation; contains some stopped and muted passages. This would also be a satisfying work to help develop flexibility and moving between ranges.

Range: F♯–c³

Duration: 6:00

Bauer, Robert P. (1950–) Canada

Episodes (1977)

Canadian Music Centre, 1977

Repeated rhythmic motives in atonal patterns drive this work, which is notated in straightforward common time. Of medium difficulty, with some taxing writing leading up to the highest note of the piece. Stopped low notes, including pedal notes, are difficult to project; straight mute may be a better choice for this passage.

Range: G♯–d♭³

Duration: 7:00

Baumann, Hermann (1934–) Germany

Elegia für Naturhorn (1984)

Bote & Bock, 1984

This work was written for the International Natural Horn Competition in Bad Harzburg, Germany in 1984. dedication is to "Franceso zum Andenken" ("In memory of Francesco"). Baumann played a large part in the natural

horn revival of the 1970s and 1980s, and founded the competition to further promote the natural horn. The crook, or key, that the horn should be
pitched in is unspecified and left up to the performer. Although written for
natural horn, it is in the contemporary idiom. It makes particular use of the
seventh and eleventh partials on the overtone series. Unmeasured and free,
with flutter tonguing, trills.
Range: c–b² (written range for natural horn in the chosen key)
Duration: 4:30

Le Rendez-vous de chasse
See: Rossini, Gioacchino, *Le rendez-vous de chasse*

Bentzon, Niels Viggo (1919–2000) Denmark

In the Forest, Suite for French Horn 1968, op. 239
W. Hansen, 2006
Dedicated to Barry Tuckwell. In eight short movements, each evoking a different mood: At the pond—Shadows—Two birds on a branch—Twilight—The
fox is hunting—Haunted spot—The frog—Sunset. Effects include stopped
writing, a *slapped tongue* (tsk-tsk-ing into the horn), muted passages, and
sospiro (playing like a sigh). The movements are short, and the piece is a
nice combination of traditional writing with contemporary effects. "The
frog" has the most experimental writing, with aleatoric sections, glissandi,
humming through the horn, and blowing air through the horn.
Range: F–c³
Duration: 12:00

Berge, Sigurd (1929–2002) Norway

Horn-Lokk (1972)
Norsk Musikforlag, 1973
Meaning "horn call," this piece is dedicated to hornist Frøydis Ree Wekre. Evocative, expressive, and well-paced for the hornist, it is widely performed and
has become a standard in the horn repertoire. It opens with a recitative that
sets up the recurring pattern of A, B♭, and G♯, followed by a cantabile section which evolves into a free cadenza-like variation on the three-note motive. The cantabile section returns, followed by a coda. This is an excellent
introduction to the unaccompanied-horn repertoire, suitable for the college-level player and above. There is a challenging passage in the cadenza
section that goes from d to b♭² followed by a *forte* section up to high b², however a college student could master this section with careful preparation.
Range: D–b² (with ossia A–b²)
Duration: 7:30

Berthomieu, Marc (1906–1991) France

Florilège musical No. 11 pour cor
Lido Melodies, 1973

Suitable for the advanced-beginner horn student, with nice melodies that venture beyond the basic beginner keys. In four short movements of different character, mostly cantabile writing with some interesting intervallic material.
Range: g–e^2
Duration: 3:15

Bieler, Helmut (1940–) Germany
Bieler attended the Munich Hochschule for Music and taught at the Universität Bayreuth from 1979–2004.

Nah und fern, Capriccio für Horn solo (2010)
Keturi Musikverlag, 2012
This short work is dedicated to Wilfried Krüger. It alternates a dotted gesture with longer expressive lines, often moving quickly between the two. The piece has a free character to it, while being notated in $\frac{4}{4}$. There are passages extending up into the high range, but there are sensible points of rest for the hornist.
Range: e♭–a♯^{2}
Duration: 3:45

Bischof, Rainer (1947–) Austria

Sonatine für Horn (F) Solo, op. 2
Doblinger, 1978
The form of this work is indicated in its preface:
    I. Satz: A-B-C (Durchf.)-B-A-Coda
    II. Satz: 9 Variationen über ein 12-Ton-Thema
    III. Satz: A-B-C-A-B-A-Coda
An interesting work, perhaps not as difficult as other atonal works for horn. The overall form is clearly notated, and there are frequent dynamic changes over short spans. The first movement is an Allegro, in $\frac{3}{4}$ and $\frac{4}{4}$. The second movement variations are short, one of which is a quasi-cadenza, played freely. The third movement changes character, moving from Allegro con fuoco to Tranquillo to Tempo di marcia, changing meters as well. This is a challenging and complex work with wide leaps and quick rhythmic figures, requiring solid technique.
Range: B–c^3
Duration: ca. 6:00

Bissill, Richard (1960–) United Kingdom
Hornist, composer, and arranger, Bissill has played with the London Symphony Orchestra and London Philharmonic Orchestra. Currently principal horn of the Orchestra of the Royal Opera House, Covent Garden and professor at London's Guildhall School of Music and Drama.

Lone Call and Charge (1994)
Warwick Music, 2003

Commissioned by Philip Jones, written as a test piece for the Charles Leggett Award in 1994. An opening rubato section, marked "Proudly," is followed by a rhythmic scherzando that takes the horn through wide leaps and quick passages in a § groove familiar to the hornist. Requires good flexibility and a solid low range.

Range: D♭–b♭^{2} (ossia G–b♭^{2})
Duration: 3:26

Nunc est bibendum
Richard Bissill, 2007
On his website, the composer describes this piece as "A musical depiction of a night on the tiles and its consequences!" Opens with a raucous motive of quick leaps in changing meters at a very fast tempo. A more relaxed middle section starts off "Slower & daintily," with a dance-like melody that is played with rubato, followed by contrasting sections in a moderate tempo, with extended techniques such as glissandi, pitch bends, alternating stopped and open writing, and a bit of flutter tonguing. The frenzied opening material returns for a bravura finish. A challenging and agile work.

Range: B–b♭^{2}
Duration: 4:20

Black, Daniel (1979–) United States

Soliloquy for Unaccompanied Horn in the Style of Mahler (2001)
Manduca Music, 2006
For Cara Sawyer. The four contrasting sections correspond to the four movements of a symphony. Moderately technical, with few breaks between sections, yet stays in the mid-to-low range of the horn, making this an accessible work for an intermediate player. A fun piece for exploring stylistic aspects of Mahler's writing.

Range: c–g^2
Duration: 7:00

Voyager for Solo Horn (2013)
Daniel Black, 2013 (available from J. W. Pepper)
Commissioned for the 2014 Southeast Horn Workshop, premiered by Boston Symphony hornist Rachel Childers. This work was "inspired by the news that NASA's Voyager space probe had left the boundaries of the solar system and entered open space." The music portrays the event in five sections: Liftoff—In orbit-debris field—Between planets—Passing Jupiter—Hymn to the beyond (Open space). Extended techniques include blowing air through the instrument, half-valve glissandi, smacking sounds, and multiphonics.

Range: B–b♭^{2}
Duration: 6:00

Blank, Allan (1925–2013) United States

Five Lines for Solo French Horn (1973)
Nichols Music Company, 1992

Many decisions are left up to the performer here, including choice for dynamics and optional mute. Five movements of contrasting character written in
contemporary harmonic language; the writing is unmeasured, with wide
ranges of expressive writing, such as flowing and lyrical phrases, complex
rhythmic figures, long sonorities, glissandi, wide leaps, alternating open
and closed writing, and large dynamic contrasts. The fourth movement is
notated only with noteheads grouped in sets, with lines above to indicate
groupings. Fast tempos require agility and lightness.
Range: F♯–c³ (ossia D–c³)
Duration: ca. 14:00

Bleuse, Marc (1937–) France

Corps à corps, trois cadences pour cor simple (1977)
Billaudot, 1981
    La chasse (Ton de ré)
    La guerre (Ton de fa)
    L'amour (Ton de ré)
Dedicated to Daniel Bourgue. In three intense movements; the two outer move-
ments are for horn in D. Moves into the extremes of the upper range of the
horn, with quick wide leaps, and extended techniques that include flutter
tonguing, trills, glissandi, accelerated tonguing.
Range: La chasse, c–d³ for horn in D
La guerre, g–c³ for horn in F
L'amour, c–e³ for horn in D
Duration: 5:30

Boisseau, Jean-Thierry (1949–) France

Clair-Obscur
Musik Fabrik, 2005
Flowing writing that makes use of the full range of the horn, with active sixteenth-note passages that often cover a wide range, and a few abrupt range
changes. Writing is not terribly chromatic, in a contemporary tonal language. The penultimate measure has a high c³ that pops up to a high e³
before landing on a low c to finish the piece.
Range: c–e³
Duration: 4:00

Booren, Jo van den (1935–) Netherlands

Strofa III per corno solo (1972)
Donemus, 1972
Made up of a series of four cadenzas, written using proportional notation and
indications such as *furioso, jazz stacc., burlesco,* and *delicato.* Flutter tongu-
ing, stopped and muted writing, and extremes in dynamics add color to
this highly improvisatory work.
Range: b♭–c³
Duration: 5:00

Bouchard, Rémi

In paradisum-Riel 1885, pour cor
Les éditions du Blé, 1985
In one movement. This well-paced work begins quietly in the low range. A section
of stopped-note interjections set up the legato moving lines of the middle
section. This would be suitable for the younger player; a nice introduction
to unaccompanied works for the horn.
Range: e–a♭²
Duration: ca. 5:30

Boulard, Frederic (1967–) France

Pile ou face, pour cor (1998)
Durand, 1999
Theatrical effects abound in this work, incorporating stage directions that have
the horn player facing the audience, then playing while turning away from
the audience, with a few full turns for good measure. The piece is centered
on a repeated g♯, to be played *mecanique*. Various open and stopped tones
and grace note pickups are added, in increasing complexity, as the "mecanique" motive continues to build. A slow and expressive middle section
has multiphonics, quarter tones, flutter tonguing, glissandi, and trills. An
interesting work; part of its challenge is coordinating all of the moving
pieces of theatre and music.
Range: G–b♭²
Duration: 5:30

Bourgeois, Derek (1941–) United Kingdom

Fantasy Pieces (1993)
Brass Wind Publications, 1996
Derek Bourgeois wrote *Fantasy Pieces* for every instrument of the orchestra as
test pieces for the National Youth Orchestra. Nine pieces are in this collection for horn, each emphasizing a different technical or musical aspect. The
preface includes instructions and guidance for each piece, including trans-
posing the pieces into different keys. These would be a good supplement to
etudes for the intermediate hornist.
Range: B♭–c³ (ossia A–c³)
Duration: 12:00

Boziwick, George (1954–) United States

Lament, for Solo Horn (1991)
Red Skies Music, 1991
For Kathy Canfield. Unmeasured and marked "Freely," this short work begins
with a horn-call motive, then develops expressive gestures of different char-
acter, before a return of the opening material. Stopped and open writing for
echo effects.
Range: g–g²
Duration: ca. 2:30

Braun, Gerhard (1932–) Germany

Hornrufe, 12 kleine Stücke für Horn (in F) solo (2009)
Edition Gamma, 2009
Dedicated to hornist Jan Schroeder. Premiered at the Hochschule und Institut
    für evangelische Kirchenmusik Bayreuth on February 6, 2010. Twelve very
    short pieces of contrasting character utilizing contemporary harmonic lan-
    guage and effects, such as hitting the mouthpiece with a flat hand, making
    a pizzicato sound into the mouthpiece, flutter tonguing, intense whispering
    into the mouthpiece, and stomping of the foot. The pieces may be performed
    as an entire set or grouped into sets of four movements of the performer's
    choosing.
Range: g–b^2
Duration: 6:00

Braun, Yehezkel (1922–2014) Israel

Twelve Preludes for Unaccompanied Horn (1976)
Israel Brass Woodwind Publications, 1985
These works are similar to etudes by Gallay or Reynolds, primarily instructional,
    but individually can stand alone in recital performance. Quite challenging,
    with demands on technique and endurance, leaps and arpeggiated pas-
    sages in the context of interesting modal harmonies.
Range: c–c^3
Duration: 25:00

Bredemeyer, Reiner (1929–1995) Germany

Ein-Horn-Musik (1988)
Deutsche Verlag fur Musik, 1988
    1. Lebhaft (e Erinnerung an Untermarchtal)
    2. paarhufig-märchenwaldig
    3. hornissenmässig, Steinig ('N Horn is' 'n Horn is' 'n Horn)
In three movements. The first is wide ranging, interspersing short gestures with
    interjections of flutter tonguing. The second movement is lyrical, alternat-
    ing open and muted passages. The third movement is more angular writ-
    ing, moving through different ranges of the horn.
Range: d–d♭^{3}
Duration: 6:00

Brevik, Tor (1932–) Norway
Tor Brevik studied violin and theory at the conservatory in Oslo, has worked with
amateur musicians in regional and school orchestras, and is largely self taught as
a composer.

Adagio religioso (1967)
Musikk-huset, 1980
This work begins slowly in the horn's low range, working its way to a quicker sec-
    tion of dotted eighth-sixteenth figures before returning to the slow, somber
    mood of the opening. Of medium difficulty, it would be a suitable work for

a younger player. It is unmeasured, leaving it up to the performer to work out musical phrasing and overall pacing of the work.

Range: d♯–g♯²
Duration: 5:00

Brings, Allen (1934–) United States
Composer and pianist, Brings is emeritus professor of music at the Aaron Copland School of Music at Queens College of the City University of New York.

Peroration for Solo Horn (1996)
Seesaw, 1996; also available at New Music USA, library.newmusicusa.org
Premiered by David Jolley on November 4, 1998, at Queens College. Contrasting
    sections, notated in ²₄ and ⁴₄, with fast sixteenth-note patterns followed by a
    slower section that returns at the end of the piece. The composer indicates
    on the New Music USA website that the piece "uses devices that can be
    thought of as rhetorical. It is like a speech delivered to a large crowd in
    which the speaker seeks at once to enthrall and to persuade."
Range: c–b♭²
Duration: 4:48

Brotons, Salvador (1959–) Spain

Ab origine for natural horn, op. 114bis
Brotons & Mercadal, 2011
Written for Javier Bonet and based on themes from the horn concerto of the same
    title. This piece brings together parts of the concerto that were written for
    natural horn, which are played by four different instruments in the con-
    certo version: the hora-gai (conch shell), the alpine horn, the natural horn
    and chromatic horn. The composer's preface states that this work "is an
    introduction to the study of the concerto, but also seeks to bring out the
    expressive possibilities of the natural horn." A challenging contemporary
    work in mixed meter, includes overtone singing and hand horn technique
    for a few closed E♭s, D♭s, and A♭s.
Range: B♭–c³ for F horn (can also be played on E or E♭ horn) (with ad lib C–c³)
Duration: 6:00

Brouwer, Margaret (1940–) United States
Margaret Brouwer's works are performed regularly by ensembles throughout the
United States, and she served as professor of composition at the Cleveland Insti-
tute of Music for many years.

SCHerZOid (1989)
Pembroke, 1994; available at www.margaretbrouwer.com
SCHerZOid premiered April 18, 1989, at the University of Idaho, Moscow, Idaho.
    The composer writes on her website that "SCHerZOid is a study in oppo-
    sites. It combines the contrasting sounds that the horn does so beautifully;
    the familiar, singing lyricism with the heroic and the aggressive. It also
    explores new sounds that are sometimes shocking and grotesque." Tech-

nical challenges include fast sixteenth-note runs requiring agility and flexibility.
Range: D♭–c³
Duration: 6:00

Bruns, Victor (1904–1996) Germany
Bruns grew up in Russia, studied bassoon and composition, and played in several orchestras before settling in with the Berlin State Orchestra from 1946–1969.

Vier Virtuose Stücke für Horn solo, op. 94 (1989)
Feja, 1994
This work is dedicated to German hornist Peter Damm, a close friend of the composer. Intended for "concert, competition, and studying purposes," these are similar to Reynolds' etudes, but are slightly easier, in both the technical material and the endurance required. These would be a good study for the college student starting to learn music that is more harmonically adventurous yet still very rhythmically traditional.
Range: A–b²
Duration: 14:00

Burdick, Richard O. (1961–) Canada, born in United States
Richard Burdick is a composer and principal horn with the Regina Symphony and Regina Chamber Players in Saskatchewan. He writes in a variety of styles, from tonal to improvisational to avant-garde, often using the *I Ching* as a foundation for his pieces. The following unaccompanied works are available from www.i-ching-music.com.

Infinite, op. 88d (1995)
I Ching Music
Imitates sound of tape loop delay, with echo effects.
Duration: 6:22

More than 64 Solos, op. 139 (2003–2004)
I Ching Music
Sixty-five movements one to three minutes long, based on I Ching scales. Written in the form of fantasies.

The Long & the Short for Solo Horn, op. 36a (1987)
I Ching Music
Duration: 1:30

The Planets (1984)
I Ching Music,
Nine short movements, each is a planet. Based on I Ching scales,
Duration: 15:54

Sculpture I–V, op. 49 (1980–89)
I Ching Music
Short works that explore extended techniques for horn, particularly multiphonics.

Buss, Howard J. (1951–) United States

A Day in the City, 7 Vignettes for Unaccompanied Clarinet, Trumpet, Horn or Baritone
Brixton publications, 1996
      I. Another sunrise
     II. Off to a busy day
    III. Lost key episode in §
    IV. The waitin' in line blues
     V. Romantic interlude
    VI. Sudden storm
   VII. Out on the town
A range of moods and characters; based on everyday themes.
Duration: ca. 9:30

Butler, Martin (1960–) United Kingdom

Hunding for Solo Horn (2003)
Oxford University Press, 2007
"To Anthony Gilbert at 70." Commissioned by the Endymion Ensemble, pre-
    miered by Steven Stirling. The composer writes that "Hunding is named af-
    ter the brutish and bitter woodsman in Wagner's Valkurie, memorable for
    the blood-curdling nature of his horn calls." A Wagnerian dotted-eighth
    triplet motive opens this work, and the listener is taken through permu-
    tations of this theme, with ever widening leaps at a fast tempo. There is an
    expressive middle section, before a return to the driving opening material.
    Effective and fun work based on a familiar motive.
Range: a♭–c³
Duration: 4:00

Butt, James (1929–2003) United Kingdom

A Horn Suite
Hinrichsen, 1961
     I. Hunting call
    II. Soliloquy
   III. Gigue
Can be performed with piano, orchestra, or unaccompanied. The three move-
    ments are relatively easy, the first features hunting horn figures and stopped
    horn; the second, a simple flowing melody; and the third, a spirited dance
    in §.
Range: d–g²
Duration: 3:40

Buyanovsky, Vitaly [Buianovskii, Vitalii] (1928–1993) Russia
Professor at the Leningrad Conservatory, principal horn of the Kirov Theater and
the Leningrad Philharmonic.

Ballade für Naturhorn in F (1987)

Bote & Bock, 1991

Commissioned for the International Natural Horn Competition in Bad Harzburg in 1987 by Hermann Baumann, to whom the work is dedicated. In five
sections; each has a different character, with the legato opening motive returning throughout. A few contemporary techniques appear, such as flutter
tonguing, glissandi, and stopped writing marked *cuivre*. This is a tradi-
tional-sounding work requiring modest hand horn technique. Challenges
include multiple tonguing, wide leaps, and quick passages.

Range: C–c^3 (for natural horn in F)

Duration: 5:19

Pieces for Horn Solo, Four Improvisations (from Traveling Impressions)
and Russian Song

McCoy's Horn Library

    Scandinavia

    Italy

    España

    Japan

    Russian Song

Includes helpful notes on performance by Frøydis Ree Wekre. These colorful
works are based on music characteristic of different countries. "Scandi-
navia" has several contrasting sections, including an opening fanfare and
a section marked cantabile espressivo, based on a Norwegian folk tune.
"Italy" evokes church bells throughout, played as pedal Fs, and a Chorale
di Palestrina. "España" is a brilliant movement in one, with trills and a cadenza. "Japan" evokes the Japanese koto. The "Russian song" is a melody in
ABA form. This work is a favorite for recitals, and different combinations of
movements are often performed, "España" being the most popular.

Range: F–b^2 (ossia E–b^2)

Duration: 10:36

Sonate für Horn Solo ("Baumann" Sonata)

Hans Pizka Edition, 1987 (published with the *Finnish Sonata*)

    I. Moderato espressivo—Andantino cantabile—Piu mosso—Andantino
       cantabile

    II. Allegretto

    III. Adagio—Andante espressivo—Adagio

    IV. Allegro vivace

Dedicated to Hermann Baumann. A flowing and expressive work in three movements of contrasting sections, written in a mostly tonal language, with
trills, quick grace notes, and flutter tonguing that provide colorful effects.

Duration: ca. 9:00

Sonata no. 2 "Finnish" (*Sonaatti no. 2 "Suomalainen"*)

Fazer, 1984; Hans Pizka Edition, 1987 (published with the *Sonate für Horn Solo,*
    (*"Baumann" Sonata*)

   I. Animato espressivo e molto rubato—Moderato grazioso—Maestoso—
      Tempo animato, espressivo
  II. Andantino—Poco animato, espressivo—Allegretto moderato, scherzan-
      do—Tempo di valse
 III. Allegro molto—Allegro molto vivace
Dedicated to Mikko Hynninen and the hornists of Finland. An extensive work
   in three movements that incorporates Finnish folk tunes. Each movement
   has contrasting sections. The second movement is a theme with variations.
   This is a lyrical and tuneful work, sometimes light, and at other times dra-
   matic. Fairly difficult, with technical passages, wide leaps, and plenty of
   music in the low range. There are judicious breaks, but long range endurance is needed. Notated in mixed meters and with old notation bass clef.
Range: C♯–c³ (ossia F–c³)
Duration: ca. 12:00

Cacioppo, Curt (1951–) United States
Cacioppo is currently professor of music at Haverford College in Pennsylvania.

of dark and bright, prelude for solo horn (1972)
Mobart Music Publishers, 1984 (In collection *Five Compositions for Solo Horn*)
Marked *very slowly, with quiet longing; much inflection throughout,* this work's
   legato lines increase in their intensity, building to a challenging entrance
   and a crescendo-decrescendo figure in the high b²–c³ range. Rhythmically
   straightforward in common time, with a few stopped notes. Atonal harmonic language that utilizes the horn's expressive legato makes this an interesting and accessible work, suitable for a college player with a strong
   high range.
Range: f–c³
Duration: 4:00

Campo, Régis (1968–) France
Marines, pour cor solo en fa (2006)
Henry Lemoine, 2007
Marines is dedicated to Vincent Robinot, who premiered the work on October
   15, 2006, at the conservatory in Marseille. This lively and rhythmic work
   explores the horn's harmonic series and is based on a driving rhythmic motive that develops throughout the piece. The horn plays in various "keys" by
   depressing the valves (horn in Fa, Re, Sol), then plays on the natural harmonic series of each fingering, instead of fingering each note. The resulting
   partials, which are all flat to equal temperament, are also clearly indicated
   in the score. The soloist has the option of playing into the soundboard of
   a piano while holding the pedal down throughout the piece (using a piano
   stool or other object). At certain points in the piece, the horn rests briefly
   while the resonance from the piano rings.
Range: G–b²
Duration: 5:00

Carter, Elliott (1908–2012) United States

Retracing II (2009)
Hendon Music: Boosey and Hawkes, 2009
This work is extracted from parts of Carter's 1991 *Quintet for Piano and Winds,*
  and assembles various expressive passages, ranging from long lyrical lines
  to quick-moving gestures with large leaps. With explosive dynamic contrasts, this is a challenging contemporary work requiring flexibility and
  solid technique. This is an excellent addition to the horn repertoire by one
  of America's most prolific and renowned composers.
Range: G–b^2
Duration: 2:35

Ceccarossi, Domenico (1910–1997) Italy
Renowned Italian hornist.

Dix Caprices pour cor
Alphonse Leduc, 1955
Ceccarossi wished to elevate the position of the horn to be on par as a solo instrument with the violin, piano, and voice. These caprices display the technical
  virtuosity of the horn, and can be considered solo works. Written in traditional harmonic language, with occasional changing meters, glissandi,
  flutter tonguing, and trills. Recorded by Ceccarossi on vinyl LP.
Range: F–c^3 (with ossias F–b♭^{2})

Charlton, Alan (1970–) United Kingdom

Étude, for Solo Horn in F (2003)
IHS Manuscript Press, 2003
Dedicated to Jeremy Bushell, fourth horn of the BBC Scottish Symphony, who
  gave the first performance at BBC Scotland on October 20, 2003. A finalist for the IHS Composition Contest 2003, this work explores the different
  aspects of the low range of the horn as well as other techniques such as
  stopped horn, flutter tonguing, multiple tonguing, trills, and muted horn.
  A challenging work for the hornist, the wide leaps and rapid passages require excellent flexibility and good facility in all ranges.
Range: c–a♭^{2}
Duration: 7:00

Chasalow, Eric (1955–) United States

Winding Up, for Solo Horn in F (1989, rev. 1992)
Editions BIM, 1991
Written for Bruno Schneider. Different sections of very fast passages, that gain
  momentum until the very end. In program notes on his website, the composer says these passages are "a kind of jazz solo mixed with the heroic fanfare . . . with a basic pulse over which the music constantly speeds up and
  slows down to articulate phrases" Detailed descriptions are in the music to

indicate the varying tempos and character. The last of the four pages stays in the high range, going up to a high d³.

Range: a–d³
Duration: 5:30

Childs, Barney (1926–2000) United States

Five Considerations for Solo Horn (1955)
American Composers Alliance, 1964
Five contrasting movements, unmeasured throughout but in traditional rhythmic notation. Occasional descriptions appear in the music, indicating the character. Only a few instances of extended techniques such as flutter tonguing and muted and stopped writing. The final movement is ripping fast, driven by continuously changing rhythmic figures.

Range: d–b♭²
Duration: ca. 9:00

Variations for David Racusen (1963)
Tritone Press, Theodore Presser sole selling agent, 1967
Consisting of a short theme, six variations, and a coda, with descriptive titles such as "Subdued and uneasy," "Very crisply," and "Spacious, evocative." The theme is based on a twelve-tone series, and there are extended techniques throughout. Variation 5 is marked *hand muted throughout* and has flutter tonguing and lipping notes upward, however none of these are very difficult or extreme.

Range: g–b²
Duration: 7:35

Chiti, Gian Paolo (1939–) Italy

Bagatelle (2004)
Musik Fabrik, 2005
For Luciano Giuliani. Much of this work exploits the horn's low register, with slow legato passages marked Lento alternating with staccato groups of five and six. Extended techniques include downward glissandi, flutter tonguing, trills.

Range: F–c³
Duration: 6:00

Cooman, Carson P. (1982–) United States

River song, Remembering Dennis Abelson (2007)
Musik Fabrik, 2007
Written in memory of Dennis Abelson, horn professor at Carnegie Mellon University. The music is based on the written pitches D and A, taken from Abelson's initials, and the piece develops in a flowing style, making reference to the three rivers of Pittsburgh, where Abelson spent his life. Contemporary harmonic language, with one stopped passage.

Range: a–b♭²
Duration: 4:00

Turning Sunwards (2003)

Music Fabrik, 2003

Written for and dedicated to hornist John Aubrey. The work is in ABA form, with two outer sections that are quite slow and legato, and a quicker middle section in ¾. Sustained writing in the high range, with dramatic dynamic contrasts.

Range: g♯–a♯²

Duration: 6:30

Cope, David (1941–) United States

BTRB for any Brass Instrument (1970)

Brass Music, 1974

Written for Tom Everett. Although *BTRB* stands for bass trombone, this can be played on any brass instrument. This is a theater piece, and most of it is the performer acting out an exploration of his/her relationship with their instrument, approaching it as if it were a brand-new, unknown entity—what is this horn, and what do I do with it? Interesting, sometimes humorous meditation on musical creation, the performer's role, and the tools used to create music. There are only three measures of actual music that are repeated, and instructions indicate that the performer may substitute a music excerpt of their own choice.

Range: a–d²

Duration: 20:00

Coppens, Claude A. (1936–) Belgium

Hornithography (1985)

CeBeDeM, 1997

For horn solo with ad lib piano. This is one movement in Coppens' "Taming of the Shrewd" series, which are compulsory works for all of the different instruments of the orchestra. The movements can be played separately or together as a set of movements, in any combination. Coppens uses humor, puns, and wordplay in titles and subtitles (for example, "filled with Satiesm"—a pun on Satie and satiety). There are ad lib notations for bass drum and hi-hat, which can be replaced by stamping the foot. Technical challenges include fast triplet passages and wide leaps. There are a few extended techniques, such as singing in the mouthpiece and multiphonics, but overall this is an accessible contemporary work. The instructions say that the piano part is never essential.

Range: F♯–g²

Duration: 6:00

Coulombe Saint-Marcoux, Micheline

See: Saint-Marcoux, Micheline Coulombe

Crawford, Paul (1947–) Canada

The Circle of Time
Canadian Music Centre, 2000
Flowing legato phrases of eighth notes and triplets in interesting harmonic se-
    quences, appropriate for the advanced-beginner horn student. Unmeasured,
    but in traditional rhythmic notation. The composer indicates that the piece
    looks to Gregorian chant of the past, with groups of two and three notes;
    and also to the future, with its nontraditional use of major triads.
Range: g–e♭²
Duration: 3:00 long version; 1:30 short version

Darbellay, Jean Luc (1946–) Switzerland

Espaces (1985)
Edition Modern, 1995
Composed for Hermann Baumann, there is also a version for horn and string
    orchestra. Marked Lent et rêveur, this mostly unmeasured work has long
    espressivo passages, with contrasting sections of quick gestures. Large leaps,
    stopped notes, and rhythmic indications in proportional notation. *Pianis-
    simo* writing and long phrases make for a dreamlike character.
Range: c–b♭²
Duration: 4:30
See: Horn and ensemble

Spectrum für Naturhorn (1993)
Edition Modern, 1995
For Hella and Hermann Baumann. Composed for the 1993 Natural Horn Com-
    petition in Bad Harzburg. The opening, marked Presto e brilliante, consists
    of fast passages on the open notes of the harmonic series. A middle section,
    marked Tranquillo, shows more of the colors of the natural horn and also
    shows off the soloist's hand-horn technique, with wide slurs that require
    a change of hand position. Flutter tonguing on a few notes and multiple
    tonguing in the final section.
Range: c–c³ (for natural horn in F, key is not specified)
Duration: 3:00

David, Avram (1930–2004) United States

Sonata for Horn Solo, op. 101 (1978)
Margun Music, 1981
Written in honor of Gunther Schuller for his fiftieth birthday, first performed at
    Tanglewood by Robert Ward, August 6, 1978. The composer indicates in the
    score preface that "the intervallic structure emerges organically in a net-
    work of interconnected, varied, and extended rhythmic cells. While devel-
    opment is constant, the most immediately audible feature is the continually
    wide-ranging melodic contour." In three movements, this work alternates
    between lyrical lines and declamatory outbursts. The first movement is the

most complex, with continually changing tempos and rhythmic groupings. There are no bar lines in the work, but dotted bar lines indicate groupings, and nearly every note has a performance indication for length, tempo, or style.

Range: F–c³

Duration: 14:10

Davies, Alison (1956–) United Kingdom

Four Studies

Broadbent & Dunn, 1994

    No. 1–Four note piece

    No. 2–One, two, three

    No. 3–Five note piece

    No. 4–Le Basquish

The first movement is an Andante that features large leaps; the second is in three, with an easygoing swing feel; the third movement features a few stopped notes and is marked *jauntily* in §; and the final movement is an Allegro in §. Short, tuneful works suitable for the intermediate student and above, these would be a good supplement to etudes and studies.

Range: c–g²

Duration: 6:30

Davies, Peter Maxwell (1934–) United Kingdom

Fanfare, Salute to Dennis Brain (2007)

Chester Music, 2007

Commissioned to mark the fiftieth anniversary of the death, in 1957, of horn virtuoso Dennis Brain. Michael Thompson first performed it at the East Midlands Horn Festival, University of Nottingham, March 25, 2007. The work is in six very short movements played without breaks. It has an overarching symmetry that places the third and fourth adagio movements—which are ruminations on the tragedy of Dennis Brain's early death—at the very center of the work. The fanfares of the opening and closing movements sound impish and virtuosic. In complete contrast to Davies' *Sea Eagle,* this work is accessible to players at the early-college level and above. There is also a version of this work scored for horn ensemble.

Range: e–g²

Duration: 3:00–5:00 (repeated phrases left to discretion of the performer)

Sea Eagle (1982)

Chester Music, 1983

In three movements. This is one of the most challenging works for horn, requiring great endurance, range and agility. The first movement is an Adagio with variations in tempo. The second movement is a Lento in § with contrasting dynamics and large legato leaps. The final movement is a Presto molto with alternating time signatures, requiring the utmost facility and finger dexterity. The work ends on a stopped high d³ that starts *sfzp* and is held as long as possible *a niente*.

Range: b♭–d³
Duration: 9:00

de Vienne, Bernard (1957–) France

Epure, pour cor seul (2003)
Zurfluh, 2003
A short work with a variety of rhythmic gestures in contrasting tempos and continuously changing meters. Extended techniques include flutter tonguing, stopped writing, trills. Flexibility required for quick legato runs and passages into the low range, but with its short length and writing that stays mostly in the midrange, this an approachable contemporary work.

Range: A–b²
Duration: 2:00

Oolithe (1996)
Henry Lemoine, 1996
Dedicated to Didier Velty.
Duration: 7:00

Deason, David (1945–) United States

Musica Sonante for Horn Solo (1978)
Faust Music, 1980
In two movements. The expressive and lyrical first movement, marked Mesto, flows nicely to exploit the horn's sonorities, often in wide, disjunct intervals. Some stopped playing in the low range could be a bit challenging. The second movement, marked Allegro, is quick and agile, built on an opening call motive. Written in a contemporary harmonic language, with mixed meters and some proportional notation. This is a very accessible work with its reasonable length and approachable technical demands.

Range: e♭–a♭²
Duration: ca. 3:30

Diethelm, Caspar (1926–1997) Switzerland

Sonate, op. 127 (1975)
Amadeus Verlag, 1975 (published with *Cappriccio*, op. 131)
In four movements: Ruhig bewegt—Lebhaft bewegt—Elegie, sehr langsam—Energisch bewegt. Each movement is measured throughout, notated in changing but traditional meters, in a harmonic language that could be described as freely tonal. Final movement is felt in one, and is the most challenging due to the fast tempo. Very accessible work, a potential supplement to etudes for the intermediate player and above.

Range: F–c³
Duration: ca. 12:00

Capriccio, op. 131 (1975)
Amadeus Verlag, 1975 (published with *Sonate* op. 127)
One movement, marked Schwungvoll, in $\begin{smallmatrix}6\\8\end{smallmatrix}$. Written in a freely tonal language. A
     few stopped notes and glissandi.
Range: F–b♭²
Duration: 3:00

Dodgson, Stephen (1924–2013) United Kingdom

Cor Leonis (1990)
Editions BIM, 1991
Composed for the 1991 Leggett Prize, a competition for younger players. The
     composer notes that the title refers to the brightest star in the constellation
     of Leo, and is a pun on the ancient riddle, "How did the lion lose his horn?
     (Answer: he lost it when he gained his heart.)" Composed to test younger
     players on technique, and to challenge them musically, with many oppor-
     tunities to evoke mood and color. It begins with a slow, wide ranging line
     that is interrupted by agitando gestures, becoming more animated as the
     piece progresses, and builds to a penultimate *fortissimo* Largamente be-
     fore ending calmly and quietly. There are a few instances of quick alter-
     nations of open and stopped notes. Well-paced work for the intermediate
     player.
Range: d–b♭²
Duration: 3:40

Donatoni, Franco (1927–2000) Italy

Till, due pezzi per corno in fa (1996)
Ricordi, 1996
Dedicated to the city of Verona. This unmeasured work opens with bits of the
     familiar horn calls from *Till Eulenspiegels lustige Streiche,* giving us just
     enough to recognize before reworking motives into new gestures based on
     the familiar. There are a few passages above the staff and fast chromatic
     writing that moves around the horn; this is a fun and approachable work,
     suitable for the advanced student or professional.
Range: e–c³
Duration: 9:00

Dubost, André (1935–) France

Coups de vent, quatre pièces pour cor seul (1986)
Alphonse Leduc, 1987
Dedicated to Georges Barboteu and André Cazalet, written as a Paris Conser-
     vatory exam piece. The title is taken from the first movement, with coups
     de vent ("gust of wind") expressed in rapid legato figures that crescendo
     from *forte* to *fortissimo.* This work includes many extended techniques:
     flutter tonguing, glissandi, stopped and half-stopped writing, explosive

dynamic contrasts, and continuously changing tempos and character. The work is unmeasured, carefully notated, and performance instructions are included.

Range: b–c³
Duration: 7:45

Dubrovay, László (1943–) Hungary

Solo No. 13 (1998)
Johann Kliment Verlag
In three movements: Lento con fuoco—Moderato—Presto. This is a very virtuosic work that explores a wide range of sounds and effects that are possible on the horn, with extended techniques of flutter tonguing, multiphonics, lip vibrato, stopped and muted effects, bending of pitches, trills, and glissandi, among others.

Range: F–d³
Duration: 9:00

Dünser, Richard (1959–) Austria

The Host of the Air (1988)
Doblinger Verlag, 1990
Dedicated to Dr. Herbert Vogg for his sixtieth birthday, the title comes from the poem of the same name by W. B. Yeats. In two short movements. The first movement is molto legato, marked *Rühig, elegisch, traümerisch,* with the text of the poem appearing throughout the movement, coinciding with different sections of the piece. The contrasting second movement, subtitled "The dance," marked *Aufgeregt, wild,* is short and furious, full of wide leaps and changing meters that are accentuated with *sforzandi* and *forte-pianos.*

Range: d–b²
Duration: 4:00

Durand, Philippe (1956–) France

Abysses pour cor en Fa solo
Alphonse Leduc, 2002
Begins Adagio espressivo then finishes in a quicker Andantino. Stopped writing, alternating open and closed pitches, using the hand in the bell, glissandi, and "fluttering" quickly with all three valves, make this a very good piece for introducing contemporary techniques for the developing player.

Range: e♭–a♭²
Duration: 2:50

Dzubay, David (1964–) United States

David Dzubay is on the music faculty at Indiana University, where he teaches composition and directs the New Music Ensemble.

Solus I (1990)

Thompson Edition, 1991

This work is based on a twelve-note row that is the basis for the "shapes" of different gestures throughout the piece. It begins slowly and quietly, only using a few pitches, then gradually increases in intensity and speed, with an occasional return to the slower opening material. This is a challenging work, with changing meters, interesting rhythmic combinations, and highly chromatic writing with complex technical passages that can contain large leaps. Although the final measure is demanding with repeated high b^2s at *fff*, this work is well paced overall.

Range: e–b^2

Duration: 7:00

Faust, Randall (1947–) United States

Call and Response for Solo Horn (1997)

Randall Faust, 1997

For John Heilman, dean of the College of Liberal Arts at Auburn University. The work was composed for a presentation at the Auburn University Research Council. It is a set of variations on "Amazing Grace," with the famous theme heard at the end of the piece. A mostly flowing work with some wide leaps, some stopped phrases, and a multiphonic chord for the final note.

Range: B♭–$b♭^2$

Duration: 5:51

Harmonielehre for Solo Horn (1996)

Randall Faust, 1997

Composed for Doug Campbell. In contrasting sections, marked by descriptive instructions, such as *gently, swiftly, relaxed, reflective,* and *expressive*. Explores playing on the natural harmonic series in different keys, indicating stopped and half-stopped notes for correcting the pitch (that is, for playing notes between the partials). Transpositions are indicated to put the horn in different keys. An interesting contemporary work that explores hand horn technique with valve horn. Would be a good piece for learning some basic concepts of hand horn technique.

Range: c–a^2

Duration: 7:10

Mazasha for Horn Solo (1985)

Randall E. Faust, 2002

Inspired by the composer's study of the chants and dance rhythms of Native Americans, this work was performed by the composer at the 1989 International Horn Symposium in Munich. The opening features alternating sections of Allegro con fuoco and Lento, with the hornist tapping rhythmically on the bell and singing multiphonics. The second section is a driving rhythmic Allegro scherzando in continuously changing meters, beginning *pianissimo*

in the low range, climbing higher and increasing in dynamic volume. This
  work includes glissandi, stopped writing, multiphonics. A challenging work
  with continually shifting rhythms and agile leaps through the ranges of the
  horn.
Range: G–b♭^{2}
Duration: 3:30

Prelude for Solo Horn (1974)
Randall E. Faust, 1977
Written for Marvin C. Howe, this piece was a solo horn selection for the Univer-
  sity Division of the American Horn Competition in 1991, 1994, 1997, and
  2001. According to Alan Mattingly, this work was "written as a compan-
  ion to the treatise on stopped horn that Howe published in the *Horn Call*
  in 1973." The piece is unmeasured, with continuous alternation between
  stopped and open notes.
Range: B–g^2
Duration: 4:10
See also: Alan Mattingly, "A performance guide to the solo horn works of Randall
  Faust." DMA thesis, Florida State University, 1998.

Ferrari, Giorgio (1925–2010) Italy

Improvvisazione per corno in fa solo, sul nome D. Ceccarossi (1990)
Pizzicato Verlag Helvetia, 2002
Based on notes spelling out Ceccarossi's name, this work in contemporary harmonic language is notated in $\frac{4}{4}$ with note groupings of five and seven in
  changing tempos. Dynamic contrasts, use of echo horn, and some technically demanding runs, but overall, an accessible work. Old notation bass
  clef.
Range: A–c^3
Duration: 3:40

Florentz, Jean-Louis (1947–2004) France

Lune de sang
Alphonse Leduc, 1983
The title means "blood moon." Short, flowing work that begins quietly, marked
  distant and mysterious, then grows more animated and impassioned, returning to the quiet opening mood before dying away. Modal harmonic
  language with effective use of stopped-horn color. Accessible and expressive, remains mostly in the staff.
Range: c^1–b^2
Duration: 4:00

Flory, Neil (1970–) United States
Neil Flory teaches composition and theory at Del Mar College in Corpus Christi,
Texas.

Rhapsody of Remembrance (1995, rev. 1999)
JOMAR Press, 1999
Composed for Paul Basler. In ABA form, this work has flutter tonguing, some
    stopped passages, and is well paced for endurance, with accessible and
    sensible horn writing. The composer notes in the score preface that "outer
    sections are rhapsodic and mostly lyrical, while the inner section is more
    percussive and forceful. The work is an expression of the power and mys-
    tery of recollection as a phenomenon in the composer's life and in the lives
    of all human beings."
Range: A♭–c³
Duration: 5:00

Flothuis, Marius (1914–2001) Netherlands

Diana's Dream, op. 76, no. 5 (1978)
Donemus, 1978
This work opens with a declamatory fanfare in ¹²⁄₈, with a contrasting lyrical sec-
    tion in ⁴⁄₄, then returns to the opening statement, repeated an octave lower
    than the opening.
Range: A♭–a²
Duration: 2:15

Romeo's Lament
Donemus, 1975
Short work with modal inflections, large dynamic contrasts, and dramatically
    quiet stopped passages.
Range: c¹–b²
Duration: 2:30

Fodi, John (1944–) Canada, born in Hungary
Composer and librarian John Fodi is on the faculty at the University of Toronto.

Scherzo for Horn, op. 72 (1984)
Canadian Music Centre, 1984
This work is in a light ⁶⁄₈ with hemiola figures, stopped writing, and explorations
    into the low and high ranges.
Range: A–b♭²
Duration: 4:30

Frackenpohl, Arthur (1924–) United States
A prolific composer, Frackenpohl studied at Eastman and with Darius Milhaud
at Tanglewood and Nadia Boulanger at Fountainebleau. He was on the faculty at
the Crane School of Music, Potsdam, New York.

Three Movements for Solo Horn
Almitra Music, sole selling agent Kendor Music, 1981
Written for Roy Schaberg. In three movements: March—Elegy—Rondo. Tradi-
    tional meters and harmonic language with a few stopped passages. The

first movement develops motives of a regal sounding fanfare in $\frac{4}{4}$. The second movement is a flowing elegy, with wide-ranging lyrical passages. The third movement is a lively $\frac{6}{8}$ rondo. Suitable for the intermediate horn player and above.

Range: c–c³ (ossia B–c³)
Duration: 5:35

Francis, Alun (1943–) United Kingdom
Francis played horn with the Halle and Bournemouth Symphony Orchestras before turning to a career in conducting and composing.

The Dying Deer, an Elegy for Natural Horn (1989)
Bote and Bock, 1990
Written for the 1990 International Natural Horn Competition at Bad Harzburg and dedicated to Hermann Baumann. The composer indicates that this piece "contrasts the nobility of the wounded animal in its dying moments with the frivolity of the hunt." This challenging work treats the natural horn as a fully chromatic instrument and utilizes the complete range of the instrument. Certain passages contain the naturally occurring notes of the overtone series, with instructions not to correct the pitches.

Range: G–c³ (for natural horn in F, key is not specified)
Duration: 4:20

Freedman, Harry (1922–2005) Canada, born in Poland
Freedman was a prolific composer, an educator, and English hornist with the Toronto Symphony for twenty-five years.

Mono . . . (1977)
Canadian Music Centre, 1977
Written for Bob Creech. Instead of time signatures, sections are indicated with dotted bar lines, and graphic notation indicates increasing speed of the notes, which creates sweeping gestures in the horn line. Lyric melodic sections alternate with playful groupings of rhythmic writing. Extended techniques include tapping rhythmic patterns on the horn, quarter tones, stopped horn, and flutter tonguing. Endurance is required for the last section of repeated g♯² leading up to a high c³, but otherwise this is a well-paced work.

Range: B♭–c³
Duration: 7:15

Freund, Don (1947–) United States
Composer, pianist, conductor, Don Freund is professor of composition at Indiana University.

Intermezzo for Solo Horn (1971)
Seesaw Music, 1977
Written in a contemporary harmonic language and marked *freely,* this work is full of sudden shifts in timbre. It begins with a heroic eighth-note motive

that is soon interrupted by short stopped-note interjections. A third element, flutter tonguing, is eventually introduced, which, as the composer describes on his website, creates a "three-way conversation which is more than a little combative in its schizophrenic climax," with repeated *fortissimo* high a^{2}s that alternate the open-stopped flutter character.

Range: g–b^2

Duration: 4:30

Fried, Alexej (1922–2011) Czech Republic

Drei charakteristische Etüden für Horn solo (1990)

Peer Musikverlag, 1997

In three movements: Die Betrachtung—Die Stimmung—Die Entscheidung. This
   work incorporates jazz idioms into traditional classical forms.

Range: b–g^2

Duration: 6:00

Friedman, Stanley (1951–) United States

Four Etudes for Trumpet (or Horn, or Clarinet) (1986)

Editions BIM, 1996

   I.   Allegro non troppo
   II. Poco adagio
   III. Tempo di menuetto
   IV. Allegro

Each etude is dedicated to a person: Jean-Pierre Mathez, Scott Moore, Marvin
   Stamm, and Jerry Boots, respectively. The composer notes that these can
   be for performance or for study, and they "present an introduction to contemporary musical language without sacrificing drama, lyricism and poi-
   gnancy. Although the pitch material is organized serially, the suggestions
   of tonality are emphasized deliberately. Interpretations featuring warmth
   and a gentle sense of humor are encouraged."

Range: f–c^3

Duration: 8:00

Topanga Variations (1981–1982)

Seesaw Music, 1984

Commissioned by and written for Frøydis Ree Wekre, who also recorded it on
   her *Songs of the Wolf* CD (Crystal Records, 1996). Four variations based on
   a three-note theme of a♭–e♭–f. This is a fairly challenging work that requires
   flexibility and dexterity as the horn jumps through different ranges, often
   at fast tempos. The second variation is in the swing style, with uneven
   eighth notes. Very well-paced and interesting writing for the horn.

Range: F♯–c^3

Duration: 8:30

Frischknecht, Hans Eugen (1939–) Switzerland

FanSolSi III (2003)
Edition Gamma, 2008
The composer refers to this as a fantasy piece, and it is built upon gestures of re-
  peated notes. It is unmeasured, notated in seconds of time noted spatially.
  Explanations are in the preface (in German). Extended techniques include
  stopped and half-stopped writing, quarter tones, and glissandi.
Range: F–c³
Duration: 12:00

Gallay, Jacques François (1795–1864) France
Renowned hornist, composer, and professor at the Paris Conservatory, Gallay
wrote chamber and solo works for horn, as well as studies and a method book.
His etudes are written for the natural horn and they show how it was seen as a
fully chromatic instrument. They also give us an idea of the outstanding hand
horn technique that players had (or aspired to) during this era. During this period, when Chopin, Paganini, and others were composing "concert worthy"
etudes, Gallay saw the same possibilities for the horn, and began writing some
of the first horn etudes that, in addition to addressing technical issues of the
natural horn, were also well composed, expressive pieces of music. These etudes
pose many challenges to the hand horn player and are as difficult as anything
written for the natural horn, venturing into written key areas that are far from
the home key. They are quite challenging on the valve horn as well, due to their
range, the endurance required, and musical thought that is needed, particularly
for the unmeasured preludes, op. 27. The following two sets of etudes are those
most often played as solos today, and many have been recorded.

12 Grand Caprices, op. 32
International Music, 1968, (James Chambers, ed.)

40 Preludes for Horn Solo, op. 27 (1839)
International Music, 1968
Twenty measured preludes and twenty unmeasured preludes.

Gardner, Randy C. (1952–) United States
Randy Gardner is the former second horn of the Philadelphia Orchestra and is
horn professor at University of Cincinnati College-Conservatory of Music.

Why?! (2000)
Thompson Edition, 2002
This work juxtaposes two very different musical ideas to depict the universal
  struggle to answer life's questions. Atonal music, marked *shocked, angry*
  and rising tritones marked *like a scream,* are pitted against very tonal motives that quote J. S. Bach. Extended techniques include vibrato effects, lip
  trills while using half valves, downward glissandi using the right hand,
  and wind sounds created by reversing the mouthpiece and blowing air

through horn. This is a very accessible work of moderate difficulty, not overly taxing.

Range: C♯–b♭²
Duration: 8:00

Garrop, Stacy L. (1969–) United States
Stacy Garrop is currently professor of composition at the Chicago College of the Performing Arts, Roosevelt University.

Sanskara for Solo Horn (1991)
Inkjar Publishing
Sanskara is a flowing work that builds on a haunting opening melody, explor-
  ing the low register of the instrument. Unmeasured and marked rubato, it
  offers the soloist great freedom of expression. Clearly notated with breath-
  marks to delineate sections and convey the composer's musical intentions.
Range: A–b²
Duration: 4:12

Gastinel, Gèrard (1949–) France

Comme une cadence pour cor
Editions J. M. Fuzeau, 1989
For André Fournier. This piece features extended techniques, yet the technical demands are not too difficult, making it suitable for a younger player. Graphic
  notation for long tones of varying durations and dynamics are notated in
  seconds. These alternate with active passages and colorful effects. Groups of
  notes are barred using graphic notation to indicate changes in speed. Also
  includes flutter tonguing, stopped notes, and a muted section. Pedal tones
  are featured at the start and finish of the piece, bass clef is old notation.
Range: F♯–g♯²
Duration: 3:00

Gellman, Steven (1947–) Canada
Gellman studied at the Paris Conservatory and is currently on the music faculty at the University of Ottawa.

Dialogue
Canadian Music Centre, 1978
This work is in three movements. The first movement, "Dialogue for one," explores different patterns and articulations, such as flutter tonguing, multiphonics, and staccato passages. The second movement, "Reflections," is in
  a cantabile style, with large leaps, and wind sound effects made by blowing
  through the horn. The third movement, "Toccata," is rhythmic with continuous sixteenth-note passages. This work is full of contemporary effects,
  with a recurring multiphonics passage, wide leaps, and writing that stays
  in the high range.
Range: B–b²
Duration: 10:00

Gentile, Ada (1947–) Italy

Ab imis, per corno in fa (1983)
Ricordi, 1983
This work explores timbre and color on the horn with closed, open, and echo
    sounds; flutter tonguing in the low register; sounds of blowing and tongu-
    ing through the horn, and a wide range of dynamics, many of them ex-
    tremely soft. Not terribly difficult compared to similar contemporary works,
    with an emphasis on interesting colors and timbre, rather than pushing the
    limits of horn technique.
Range: e–c³
Duration: 7:00

Ghezzo, Dinu (1941–2011) United States, born in Romania
Ghezzo won many awards and commissions, and was on the faculty at New York
University and other New York area schools.

Sound Shapes II, Five Pieces for Solo Brass (1982)
Seesaw, 1982
New Grove states that Ghezzo's "scores are an amalgamation of elements ranging
    from tonality, modality, jazz and folk music to electronic sounds, natural
    harmonics, repetitive cycles and improvisation. These diverse elements
    are combined to produce works of sincerity and powerful expression." The
    original version of *Sound Shapes II* is for bass trombone, but is written in
    movable "Do" system, and the composer indicates that this work may also
    be performed on horn, trumpet, or tuba. In five short movements: Night-
    song—Trios—What did she say?—Dithyramb—Collage. Notated graphi-
    cally and full of contemporary effects that are clearly described, such as dia-
    phragm spasms, jazz improvisation, multiphonics, and whinnying through
    the horn. A piano is needed, for playing into the resonance plate.
Range: left up to the performer
Duration: 7:08

Gillespie, Don (1942–)

Sonata for Solo Horn (1992)
Seesaw Music, 1992
Dedicated "To Kane." In four short movements of different and distinctive char-
    acter: Prelude—Dance—Improvisation—Fanfare. Moderately difficult, with
    fast angular passages in changing meters and expressive writing in a con-
    temporary harmonic language.
Range: a♭–b♭²
Duration: 5:45

Globokar, Vinko (1934–) Slovenia

Echanges für einen Blechbläser (1973)
C. F. Peters, 1975

For any brass instrument. This avant-garde work is in graphic notation, using various shapes and symbols to guide the soloist on what and how to play. A tone row is given in the preface, providing notes to choose from. Rhythm and articulation are left entirely up to the performer, with only shapes to indicate increasing and decreasing intensity, or force. Different mouthpieces are also called for: single reed, double reed, or pipe made of metal or plastic. A microphone and loudspeakers are used. Extended techniques include pitch bends, flutter tonguing, trills.

Range: at performer's discretion
Duration: at performer's discretion

Res/as/ex/ins-pirer für einen Blechbläser (1973)
C. F. Peters, 1975
For any brass instrument. In graphic notation, this piece is for a brass player who can circular breathe, as instructions are for both the "in" breath and "out" breath. Avant-garde work, graphically notated, using an intricate system of symbols. Performance instructions in German are included.

Range: at performer's discretion
Duration: ca. 5:00 (at performer's discretion)

Gomez, Alice (1960–) United States

La Calavera, Solo Horn
Potenza Music, 2014
La calavera is the name of the skull and crossbones card in loteria, a traditional card game in Mexico. In one movement, with scherzo-like figures that dart up and down in surprising and unexpected patterns. Good facility required for negotiating leaps at a quick tempo.

Range: g–a^2
Duration: 4:00

Goossen, Frederic (1927–2011) United States
After teaching at the University of Minnesota and Berea College, Kentucky Goossen joined the faculty of the University of Alabama, where he taught theory and composition and was director of graduate studies. He wrote over 150 musical works in a wide variety of genres.

Solo Music for Horn (1988)
Tritone Press, 1991
Written for Randall Faust, who premiered the work in 1989. The composer notes in this edition that his current compositional style is "a flexible chromaticism firmly based in tonality." Energetic sixteenth-note motives of the opening are developed, interspersed with slower sections of rising and falling eighth notes. Good endurance needed, as there are few opportunities for rest.

Range: A–a^2
Duration: 5:00

Gouders, Willy, Belgium

Trois Pièces pour cor seul (Three Pieces for Horn Solo)
McCoy's Horn Library, 1982
Dedicated to Francis Orval and Brigida Romano. This is a challenging and intricate work with large leaps, abruptly changing tempos, and mixed meters, with wide-ranging passages at fast tempos.
Range: F–d♯³
Duration: 7:30

Gough, Christopher (1991–) United Kingdom (Scotland)

Monuments
Edition db
For Jamie Shield. Hornist and composer Gough explains that this piece explores the different qualities and emotions that monuments can evoke. Different tone qualities of the horn are presented to create colors and atmosphere. In three movements. The two outer movements are slow and lyrical. The middle movement, marked *gentle pace,* is in a rhythmic ¾ with wide leaps and runs that move throughout the range of the horn.
Range: A–a²
Duration: 11:45

Grabois, Daniel (1964–) United States
Grabois is professor of horn at University of Wisconsin and hornist with the Meridian Arts Ensemble.

The Spikenard
Blue Bison Music, 2000, also available at www.danielgrabois.com
Grabois described this piece as "middle eastern chant meets rock and roll, for solo horn" (Q&A interview on Jacob Stockinger's blog, *The Well-Tempered Ear,* welltempered.wordpress.com.) Contrasting sections of "free" with "fast and energetic," this work includes multiphonics, wide leaps, and changing meters.
Range: B–b²
Duration: 4:00

Graef, Friedemann (1949–) Germany
Graef studied composition with Earle Browne and is an active composer and performer on saxophone with contemporary groups that specialize in improvised music, yet his compositions are rooted in the European classical tradition.

Dialect V für Horn solo
Ries & Erler, 1997
This work presents a variety of contrasting musical ideas that are interspersed with a recurring statement of the twelve-tone theme, which is played espressivo and stopped.
Range: c–a²
Duration: 7:00

Grant, James (1954–) United States

Stuff, Theme with Seven Variations for Unaccompanied French Horn
Potenza Music, 2012
One of four recital pieces that were commissioned by a group of seventy-eight
    tuba players who were part of the 2001 Solstice/Equinox Commissioning
    Consortium. As each solstice and equinox approached during the year 2001,
    a new piece was sent out to each of the tuba players in the consortium. The
    composer has arranged *Stuff* for other instruments, including horn. Con-
    sisting of a legato theme with moderately wide intervals, and seven vari-
    ations: Lullaby—Insistent—Cartoon music—Gregarious—Urgent—More
    urgent—Swing it. Medium difficulty, suitable for college student through
    professional.
Range: F–b² (ossia F–c³)
Duration: 5:28

Greer, Lowell (1950–) United States
Valve and natural horn soloist, orchestra musician, and teacher.

Musical Portraits, (Fopus), for Unaccompanied Horn (1977–78)
Veritas Music Publishing, 2011
Each short piece represents a horn player, including friends and former students:
    You're a brave man (to wear that hair) (Fofuz)—Peg of Chicopee (Fomeara)
    —Don't quit until you're done (Fogael)—Elliott of all trades (Foliot)—True
    friendship (Folikinriz)—Golden Faden (Fogimp)—Warmth and generosity
    (Fomoree)—The Viking hymn of conviviality (Feeb).
Each of these entertaining little solo pieces can be played by itself or in combina-
    tion with others. Technically straightforward and accessible.
Range: F♯–b♭²

The Crust Around Emptiness (1979–1980, rev. 1991)
Veritas Music Publishing, 2010
Written in memory of John Pierce. In six sections: The globus—The struggle—
    The premonition—Breaking the crust—Emptiness is fluid—Struggle of
    resignation. This work features plaintive horn calls, light scherzando play-
    ing with wide leaps, and stately double-dotted figures. This is an accessible
    work and a welcome addition to the unaccompanied repertoire.
Range: A–b♭²
Duration: 7:00

Het Valkhof
DWS Archive, 1991
    I. Prelude
    II. Frederick Barbarosa
Composed for the 1991 American Horn Competition-Natural Horn Division.
    Written for natural horn in E or F. In two short movements in a contempo-
    rary style. The first movement, marked Feroce, is unmeasured, and is based
    on a horn-call motive. The second movement, marked Presto-agitato, has

echoes of a traditional hunting-theme rondo, but changes meters between
$\frac{6}{8}$, $\frac{5}{8}$, and $\frac{9}{8}$. Well-paced and idiomatic in its writing for the natural horn.

Range: c^1–$a\flat^2$ (for natural horn in F)
Duration: 2:30

Grüger, Vincent (1962–) Germany

Brevi Loquens, Four Exercises for Natural Horn (1989)
Bote & Bock, 1990
Commissioned for the 1990 Bad Harzburg Natural Horn Competition. Each etude
is based on the breviary prayers: Vespers, Compline, Matins, and Prime.
Challenging writing for the hand horn player.

Range: B–$g\sharp^2$ (for natural horn in F, key is not specified)
Duration: ca. 5:00

Grunelius, Wilhelm von (1942–) Germany

*"Hermaphroditus und Salmacis" from Embrassing Ovid, Drei Soli
für Blechbläser*
Editions Marc Reift, 1996
For Stefan Dohr. In three movements that follow the form of a classical sonata.
The first movement is for horn, the second is for tuba, the third is for trombone. They can be played alone or as a set. The piece for horn is a musical
telling of the story from Ovid, propelled forward with varying rhythmic
gestures of quickly contrasting character, with clear indications of rubato
and accelerando. Extended techniques include stopped and muted writing,
flutter tonguing, trills.

Range: E–b^2
Duration: 6:50

Gryč, Stephen (1949–) United States

Reflections on a Southern Hymn for Horn Alone (1988)
Robert King Music, 1989
Intonation
Chant
Pastoral
Wondrous Love
Commissioned by Peter Landgren. The composer indicates that each movement
is "based on the hymn tune 'Wondrous Love' as published in a three-voice
setting in *The Sacred Harp* of 1859. All three voices of the choral arrangement are woven into the fabric of the piece." Opportunity abounds for
expression and rubato in this unmeasured work. The first movement has
wide-ranging eighth-note gestures. The second movement consists of quiet
murmuring triplets that crescendo into longer notes from the theme. The
third movement is very flexible, with expressive sixteenth-note motives
and groupings of seven and nine that give the movement a cadenza-like
feel. The final movement is a statement of the "Wondrous Love" hymn.

Well paced for the hornist, this is a suitable work for the intermediate student through professional.

Range: A–b♭²

Duration: 9:28

Guarnieri, Camargo (1907–1993) Brazil

Guarnieri was a prolific composer and important figure in the Brazilian national school during the first half of the twentieth century.

Etude for Horn Solo (1953)

Rongwen Music, 1958

The one-page *Etude for Horn Solo,* marked *unhurried,* consists of flowing legato lines, with stopped and echo horn. Glissandi finish this short work with a flourish.

Range: d–c³

Duration: 2:27

Guérinel, Lucien (1930–) France

Clameurs, d'après António Ramos Rosa (2001)

Symétrie, 2002

Commissioned for the Trévoux International Horn Competition, this three-movement work is based on writings by Portuguese poet António Ramos Rosa, which are included (in French) at the beginning of each movement. This intricate work is unmeasured, organized by varying groups of gestures that propel the music forward, with colorful contemporary effects throughout, such as quarter tones, tremolos, glissandi, flutter tonguing, and blowing air through the horn. Virtuosic and agile writing, with wide leaps.

Range: G♯–c³

Duration: 16:30

Haapanen, Perttu (1972–) Finland

Prism, for Horn Solo (2004, rev. 2005/06)

Uusinta Publishing Company, 2008 (dist. Theodore Front)

Dedicated to Tommi Hyytinen, who premiered and recorded the work. Partly funded by the International Horn Society Meir Rimon Commissioning Assistance Program. The material in this piece is "one melodic, one dynamic, and one rhythmic basic gesture," according to the Music Finland website (composers.musicfinland.fi). Highly virtuosic, rhythmic, and colorful, with multiple tonguing, stopped writing, wide leaps, and glissandi.

Range: A–d³

Duration: 6:23

Halstead, Anthony (1945–) United Kingdom

Valve and natural horn player, conductor, and pianist Anthony Halstead was principal horn with the English Chamber Orchestra and many other modern and period instrument orchestras.

Suite for Solo Horn (1978)
Dunster Music, 1978
    I. Allemande
    II. Aria
    III. Variants: theme, waltz, lament, gigue
In three movements. The first movement is a chromatic Allemande organized
    around sixteenth notes in changing meters. The second movement, Aria, is
    in flowing groups of sixteenths and triplets, notated in $\frac{3}{4}$. The third move-
    ment is a theme and short variations. Challenging work with writing that
    is angular, chromatic, and quite agile.
Range: f♯–c³
Duration: 5:30

Hartzell, Eugene (1932–2000) Austria, born in the United States
Hartzell attended Yale, then moved to Vienna and studied composition with Hans
Erich Apostel, whose teachers were Schoenberg and Berg. Most of his music is in
twelve-tone style, but is often infused with American elements such as jazz. He
wrote a series of "Monologues" for all of the orchestra instruments.

Monologue 10, Phrases for Horn (1977)
Doblinger, 1980
This contemporary atonal work opens with active and declamatory motives that
    cover the full range of the horn, played on natural tones (without valves)
    for the first twenty-eight bars. Contrasting sections of different character
    follow, including foot tapping steady eighth notes while playing a *swinging*
    motive; several bars of multiphonics over a held note in the horn; and a
    section of free rubato writing, with arrows that indicate accelerando and
    allargando. Expressive and challenging, with wide leaps and quick runs
    through different ranges of the horn,
Range: F♯–c3
Duration: 7:15

Monologue 18, Combinations for (Viennese) Horn (1987)
Doblinger, 1990
This piece does not put great demands on endurance and range, and is in a slow
    and thoughtful tempo, ♩=48, with motivic material that is interesting and
    varied, with echoes of Gershwin. Many phrases jump down into the low
    range for contrasting effect. The gestures culminate in a short, fast coda,
    wrapping things up with a flourish.
Range: G♭–a²
Duration: 7:00

Hedges, Anthony (1931–) United Kingdom
Composer and teacher, taught at the Royal Scottish Academy of Music in Glasgow
and the University of Hull.

3 Impromptus for Solo Horn, op. 102
Westfield Music, 1986 (also available from www.imslp.org)

The first movement, marked Andante ma con moto e molto flessibile, develops a sixteenth-note motive in a flowing $\frac{2}{4}$. The second movement is also flowing, with a folk-like tune of dotted-eighth rhythms in $\frac{6}{8}$. The third movement, marked Allegro moderato, has moving eighth-note patterns with playful metric shifts in phrasing, notated in $\frac{4}{4}$ and $\frac{7}{8}$.
Range: g–c^3
Duration: 7:00

Heider, Werner (1930–) Germany

12 Signale für Trompete (oder Horn) solo (1985)
Peters, 1986
Performance instructions indicate that each "Signal" can be played separately, consecutively from 1–12, in reverse order from 12–1, or in different combinations with optional repetitions. They should be performed while standing. These are twelve energetic calls in a contemporary style, full of wide leaps and quick passages, with flutter tonguing, glissandi, and echo playing. The range of performance options make this a flexible work.
Range: a–d♭^{3}
Duration: ca. 5:00–15:00, depending on performance option

Henderson, Moya (1941–) Australia

G'day USA 1, Not Instantaneous or Merciful (2003)
Henderson Music, 2003
Premiered November 2003 at the Sydney Conservatorium of Music by Carla Blackwood. In the composer's words, this "is a commemoration of the Columbia astronauts who lost their lives upon re-entering the hell-fire of Earth's atmosphere on Feb. 1 2003 . . . one of the NASA experts referred to the deaths of the astronauts as 'not instantaneous or merciful.'" Sections of contrasting character, written in a contemporary tonal language in changing meters, wide legato leaps.
Range: G–b♭^{2}
Duration: 7:00

Henry, Otto (1933–) United States
Otto Henry was professor of composition, history, and ethnomusicology at East Carolina University.

Capriccio for Solo Horn in F
Media Press, 2004
Henry calls this work a "rondo-capriccio in a snappy neo-classical style" in the score preface. He wrote it to play in his horn recital class while a student at Boston University. Written in a contemporary yet tonal harmonic language, based on an opening motive of eighths and sixteenths that propel the music forward. In $\frac{2}{4}$ throughout, with a short section of meno mosso.
Range: f–A♭^{2}
Duration: 2:30

Henslee, Kenneth C. (1941–) United States

Lament for Solo Horn
Pelican Music Publishing, 2004
Slow and expressive legato melody in written f minor for the horn, with several
    statements of the melody, one of them an octave lower than the others.
    Suitable for the advanced beginner through intermediate student inter-
    ested in expanding range and venturing into four flats in a minor key.
Range: c–a♭²
Duration: 2:15

Herchet, Jörg (1943–) Germany
Herchet studied in Dresden and East Berlin, and teaches composition at the Dresden Conservatory.

Einschwingen (1999)
Deutscher Verlag für Musik, 1999
For Peter Damm. Unmeasured, with traditional notation in the first section; the
    second section is mostly graphic notation with durations indicated in sec-
    onds. There are quick, angular passages with large leaps, and varying timbre
    changes at different dynamic levels, with slow and rapid vibrato glissandi that
    vary the pitch by quarter tones. The final section consists of long held notes
    that explore different effects, such as vibrato and flutter tonguing. A chal-
    lenging work that explores the many different colors possible on the horn.
Range: F–f³ (ossia F–c³)
Duration: 8:00

Hermanson, Åke (1923–1996) Sweden

Alarme, op. 11 (1969)
Wilhelm Hansen, 1971
Marked *Intensive molto (e quasi come una sirena)* and based on fourths and tri-
    tones, the startling "siren" motive of the opening is developed and carried
    throughout the piece, with wide intervals and long sustained gestures that
    crescendo dramatically. There are a few glissandi to high notes d³ and b♭²,
    indicated with an "x" in lieu of a notehead, perhaps suggesting an "airy"
    note, or the highest note possible. Otherwise, the actual range of the piece
    is not too demanding, but good endurance is required for the sustained
    forte and *fortissimo* gestures. Includes flutter tonguing and glissandi. Old
    notation bass clef.
Range: c–d³
Duration: 4:20

Hespos, Hans-Joachim (1938–) Germany
Chorna (1980)
Hespos, 1980
Hespos is known for avant-garde music that is quite demanding for the perform-
    ers. This work is notated in a combination of graphic symbols and tradi-

tional notes, with many explanations for execution. Time is indicated in seconds, and a separate set of instructions is included with the score that further explains the graphic notation for this complex and ultra-modern work.
Range: varies
Duration: 6:30

Heuser, David (1966–) United States
David Heuser is professor of music theory and composition at Potsdam's Crane School of Music, where he also serves as associate dean.

Dusty Red Sphere (2004)
Non Sequitur Music, 2003
This work was written the year of the scientific explorations of Mars, and was inspired by Ray Bradbury's *Martian Chronicles*. The piece evokes "both the real martian landscape with its dust storms, as well as the fictional dust collecting in the homes of Bradbury's ancient, dead civilizations," according to program notes on the publisher's website (www.nonsequiturmusic. com). The opening section is in a slow tempo, with contrasting dynamics and *subito fortissimos*, establishing the intervallic motive that is carried through the work. The second section, marked "Sneakily," moves between ⅝ and ⅜ with ornamental rips with large dynamic contrasts. This builds to a forceful declamatory statement, and then winds back down into the quiet motives of the opening. Most of this work is in the mid-to-low range of the horn, and there is ample use of space between notes and phrases, allowing the music (and the performer) to breathe.
Range: G–f♯²
Duration: 4:00

Hill, Douglas (1946–) United States
Former professor of horn at the University of Wisconsin and composer of numerous works for horn, many of which incorporate jazz elements. He has authored several important pedagogical books, including *Collected Thoughts on Teaching and Learning, Creativity, and Horn Performance* (Warner Brothers Publications, 2001), and *Extended Techniques for the Horn* (Warner Brothers Publications, 1996).

Character Pieces (1973–74)
Really Good Music, 1999
>   Whimsical
>   Restless
>   Quarrelsome
>   Foolish
Four contrasting movements, some in mixed meters, others unmeasured. Contains much angular writing, with wide leaps and colorful effects. The third movement, "Quarrelsome," is like a battle waged with extended techniques.
Duration: 8:50
Range: G–b²

Elegy for Horn Alone (1998)
Really Good Music, 1998
The composer writes that this work "was composed in the early summer after my
    mother died. The disjunct and wavering melodies, as well as the sudden si-
    lences were the natural results of my meditative improvisations." This work
    is played freely, like a recitative. It is mournful, with the opening-bar mo-
    tive returning several times. An unmeasured section, marked "Agitated," is
    followed by a return to the lamentful opening.
Range: g–b♭²
Duration: ca. 4:00

Five Little Songs and Dances for Solo Horn (2006)
>   1. Introit
>   2. Quadrille with Bebop
>   3. Ballad
>   4. Whimsical Waltz
>   5. Romp with Rumba

Based on melodic ideas from Hill's *A Set of Songs and Dances* for clarinet, horn,
    vibes, and bass. The composer had intended to write this in the style of a
    baroque suite with a touch of jazz, but "the jazz took over, and the 'suite'
    became a 'set' of congenial melodies and rollicking rhythms, in the hopes
    that 'fun will be had by all.'"
Range: d–c³
Duration: 12:00

Greens/Blues/Reds, Three Moods (2005)
Really Good Music, 2005
>   1. Joy (Greens)
>   2. Sorrow (Blues)
>   3. Aggravation (Reds)

Inspired by the composer's thoughts on nature and the way humanity is treating
    our natural world. The first movement is a "joyous celebration of the beauty
    and splendor" of our world, expressed in a rollicking ⁶⁄₈ and ⁹⁄₈ with a middle
    section in legato. The second movement, "Blues," marked *freely, contempla-
    tive,* expresses sorrow over our "reckless neglect" of our planet, intersperse-
    ing lyrical blues with more agitated writing. The third movement, "Reds,"
    is an energetic musical expression of the anger over the "greed that moti-
    vates and allows for this neglect," with driving intensity throughout. This
    work includes many extended techniques with clear explanations. Move-
    ments may be played as a set or individually, and there is also a version of
    this work for horn and string quartet.
Range: A–b♭²
Duration: ca. 13:00

Jazz Set for Solo Horn (1982–1984)
Margun Music, 1984
>   Lost and found
>   Cute 'n sassy

Lullaby waltz

Fussin' for Emily

Written using jazz idioms, rhythm, and style, these four contrasting movements are full of colorful extended techniques. Writing is agile and quick, as well as lyrical. Extended techniques include quarter tones, falling-off pitches, upward scoops, ¾ stopped notes, ghost tones, doinks, plops, and multiphonics, to name a few. Challenging low writing with pedal tones. The composer indicates that these may be played "as a unified set utilizing a rather traditional though freely modified four-movement design."

Range: Db–c^3

Duration: 12:30

Jazz Soliloquies for Horn (1978–1980)

Really Good Music, 1999

    1. Blues-like

    2. Mixin'

    3. Laid back

Hill writes in the preface: "These demanding little pieces were meant to challenge the hornist with a special style of music uncommon to our up-bringing and ultimately for the fun-of-it-all." Special effects such as glissandi, doinks, bends, are all carefully explained for each movement. Quarter tones include suggested fingerings. Trills on high c^3, large leaps, and moving quickly through different ranges make this a fun and challenging work. Hill was writing *Extended Techniques for the Horn* while he was writing this work. It is more of a contemporary classical work that incorporates jazz writing, while his *Jazz Set* is firmly written in a jazz style.

Range: Gb–c^3

Duration: 9:30

Oddities for Solo Horn (2004)

Really Good Music, 2004

    1. Ones

    2. Fives

    3. Threes

    4. Nines

    5. Sevens/Elevens

Also available as a horn quartet, Hill mentions that it may help to listen to the quartet version to learn about the harmonic complexities and rhythmic support he had in mind. Written in the jazz style, each work can be performed individually, or in groups of any combination. The entire work may be performed in any order. A fun work and a challenge to play convincingly in the jazz style.

Range: A–c^3

Duration: 17:15

Reflections for Horn Alone (1994)

Manduca Music, 2005

Hill writes that this "is meant as a theatrical soliloquy reflecting upon memories of (a) lost relationship(s)." It is based on music from his *Shared Reflections for Four Horns*. In this contemplative work, the opening, marked "Thoughtfully," begins with expressive eighth-note patterns. A middle section, "Lively (somewhat playfully)," builds in energy, arriving at a cadenza-like section, before returning to the contemplative material of the opening.

Range: f–c³
Duration: 6:00

Hjorth, Daniel (1973–) Sweden

Blo(t)t horn (2001)
Daniel Hjorth, 2001, available from danielhjorth.com
First performance by Erik Sandberg, 2001. The third slide is removed for the piece, to produce notes with an airy sound that comes out of the valve slide. Sixteenth notes and groups of five drive this work, with contrasting sections of lyrical playing. Each character is indicated in the music: *spasmodically restless, flowing, gentle, sentimentally, violently,* and *furious.* Includes wide dynamic contrasts and *sforzando* interjections, as well as extended techniques that include multiphonics, glissandi, trills, flutter tonguing, and stopped writing. Long-range endurance is required, however the majority of this work lies within the treble staff.

Range: e–a²
Duration: 8:30

Hlouschek, Theodor (1923–2010) Germany, born in Czech Republic
Born in Brno, resided for most of his career in Weimar, was professor of music at the Hochschule für Musik Franz Liszt Weimar.

Caprice pour cor
Hofmeister, 1998
This is a lively and energetic unmeasured work that moves between sections of contrasting character. Technical facility and flexibility required for legato passagework that travels quickly through the range of the horn.

Range: a–b♭²
Duration: 4:00

Hodkinson, Sydney (1934–) United States, born in Canada
Award-winning composer, served on the faculty at Eastman School of Music for many years.

Night Rounds (2010)
Theodore Presser, 2010
Written for Peter Kurau. This work exploits the full range of the horn, with running sixteenth-note gestures and legato leaps, and is full of dynamic contrasts and outbursts. Made up of three sections, Introduction, Scherzo, and Coda, each working their way up higher in the range of the horn as the piece progresses. There are varying tempos and gestures within each sec-

tion. The Coda has an extended stopped legato section. Other contemporary techniques include glissandi, echo horn, trills. Flexibility and command throughout the ranges is needed for this challenging work.
Range: F♯–c♭³ (ossia G–c♭³)
Duration: 7:00

Holab, William (1958–) United States

Soliloquy, Horn Solo (1983)
Henmar Press; Sole selling agents, C. F. Peters, 1986
Premiered by David Wakefield at the Composers Concordance on October 25th, 1984, in New York City. Dedicated to Dan Meier. In three movements. The first develops a continuous eighth-note motive in mixed meters, with abrupt changes in range and wide dynamic contrasts. The second is lyrical and flowing, and the third is marked Allegretto, quasi rubato, with light and quick legato phrases. This is a challenging work in contemporary harmonic language, agile, encompassing the entire range of the horn, and pushing its boundaries.
Range: C♯–e♭³ (ossia G–c♯³)
Duration: 10:00

Holley, Alan (1954–) Australia

Concorno, for Solo Horn
Kookaburra Music, 2010
Commissioned by the 42nd Horn Symposium for performance in Brisbane, July 2010, premiered by Robert Johnson. In three movements. The last movement of this work is from the "Lament" for solo horn from Holley's brass quintet, *Canzona for Ligeti,* written as a tribute to Ligeti in 2006. Holley expanded on the "Lament" and added the first two movements, which are lighter in character. The second movement includes cross-fingerings to create microtonality and tremolos.
Range: g♭–b²
Duration: 5:30

Holliger, Heinz (1939–) Switzerland

Cynddaredd—Brenddwyd (Fury—dream) (2001, rev. 2004)
Schott, 2005
This work for solo horn is a movement taken directly from Holliger's 2001 *COncErto . . . ? Certo!cOn soli pEr tutti (. . . perduti?. . .)* which consists of forty different pieces for solo instruments, small ensembles, and orchestral tuttis that the conductor selects from during the performance. Written for Jonathan Williams. Challenging and dramatic writing, made up almost completely of extended techniques for the horn. Unmeasured, the notation is at times graphic, with fast and extreme changes in dynamics, moving quickly between registers, with trills, quick changes from open, stopped and half-stopped notes, and multiphonics.

Range: F–c³
Duration: 6:00–6:30
See also: Virginia Thompson, "Music and Book Reviews: Heinz Holliger—'Cynddaredd-Brenddwyd' for Horn Solo," *The Horn Call* 38 (February 2008): 76–77.

Hummel, Bertold (1925–2002) Germany

Bertold Hummel was a student of Harald Genzmer. He was a cellist and composer, and taught at the State Conservatory in Würzburg.

Suite für Horn in F solo, op. 64 (1977)
Musikverlag Zimmerman, 1978
    I. Invocation
    II. Intermezzo
    III. Choral
    IV. Finale

The *Suite* was first performed by Philip Myers, June 24, 1981. It is in four movements: The first is based on a dotted eighth-sixteenth motive with an emphasis on fourths and fifths, reminiscent of Hindemith. The second is in changing meters, with quick passages based on a minor-second interval. The third is in a slow tempo, with quiet passages, some of them in the high tessitura, requiring good control. The last movement has driving triplet figures, changing dynamics, flutter tonguing, and rounds out the piece with a virtuosic flourish. This work is musically satisfying and technically challenging with well-paced writing for the horn.
Range: d–b♭²
Duration: 11:00

Ikebe, Shin'ichirō (1943–) Japan

A Horn Gets Angry, Yet He Chants, for Horn Solo (2003)
Zen-on Music, 2004
Premiered November 27, 2003, in Tsuda Hall, Tokyo, Hiroshi Matsuzaki, horn soloist. Energy abounds in this tour de force for horn alone, unified by a driving rhythmic figure that alternates with slow passages played with "hand technique" that explore the different colors of the horn. Notation is traditional, with clear and intuitive symbols that indicate *accelerando,* *ritardando,* and *a tempo.* Flutter tonguing, playing wind sound with the breath, glissandi, muted horn, and stopped horn add color to this contemporary work. Organized in eight sections, time may be taken between sections; the performer need not play all sections, and can choose which ones to play.
Range: C♯–c³
Duration: 15:16

Jarrell, Michael (1958–) Switzerland

Jarrell is professor of composition at the Geneva Conservatory.

Assonance IVb, pour cor solo
Henry Lemoine, 2009
This work was premiered October 8, 2009, in Paris, France, by the Ensemble In-
    tercontemporain. This is an intricate work that pushes the limits of tech-
    nique on the horn, with agile chromatic writing, alternating stopped and
    open notes, wide leaps, large dynamic contrasts, multiphonics.
Range: F♯–d^2
Duration: 8:00

Johnson, Tom (1939–) United States, resides in France

Tilework for Horn, Partitions (2002)
Editions 75, 2003
Johnson explains in his preface that "Tilework" refers to "fitting together little
    tiles to fill lines and loops. One can think of this as making mosaics in
    one dimension . . . In musical terms, the *Tilework* series is a collection of
    compositions in which individual tiles/rhythms fit together into musical
    sequences without simultaneities, often filling all the available points of a
    line or a loop." He wrote fourteen "Tilework" pieces for each instrument of
    the orchestra. This work consists of nine different combinations of a pat-
    tern of notes. Good legato is required, otherwise, technical demands are
    very modest, with an emphasis on the patterns that are created.
Range: a–e^2
Duration: 11:00

Kalabis, Viktor (1923–2006) Czech Republic
Leading Czech composer of the late twentieth century.

Invokace, op. 90
Bärenreiter Praha, 2001
This is a one movement work marked Allegro drammatico that features declam-
    atory writing in a driving § with occasional legato passages. There are few
    rests, making this a challenging work not only in endurance, but also in
    keeping the musical intensity going.
Range: e–b^2
Duration: 5:00

Kallstrom, Michael J. (1956–) United States
Kallstrom is on the composition faculty at Western Kentucky University.

Shining Moment
RM Williams, 2001
Written for Lorraine Fader, horn teacher at Western Kentucky University. In ABA
    form, with outer sections of energetic writing in changing meters and syn-
    copated rhythms. The contrasting slow and expressive middle section is
    played with rubato. This is a very good work for the intermediate student,
    with its middle-range tessitura and moderate technical demands.
Range: f–a♭^{2}
Duration: 4:23

Kaminsky, Laura (1956–) United States
Kaminsky is on the faculty at the Conservatory of Music at Purchase College/
SUNY, and was Artistic Director of Symphony Space in New York City until
2014.

Blast, for French Horn (2009)
Subito Music, 2010
For Ann Ellsworth. Begins quietly, exploring timbres of the horn with a slow
    half-step bend and *sforzando* punctuations. Lyrical gestures of wide leaps
    grow increasingly active and forceful before returning to material of the
    quiet opening. Good flexibility required, but the moderate range makes
    this an accessible work.
Range: g♭–a²
Duration: 5:00

Kanefzky, Franz (1964–) Germany
Kanefzky attended Augsburg Conservatory and is a hornist with the Munich
Radio Symphony Orchestra.

Präsentation und Idylle
Edition Hage, 1989
This piece is challenging yet accessible. "Präsentation" has many changing sec-
    tions and styles, alternating heroic writing with quick passages of slurred
    eighth notes. "Idylle" exploits the lyrical and singing qualities of the horn,
    beginning with an easygoing melody that grows in intensity, followed by
    a section of stopped writing before returning to the opening theme. Both
    movements are tonal, using traditional harmonic language interspersed
    with occasional extended techniques, such as flutter tonguing and stopped
    writing.
Range: F–a²
Duration: 4:30

Karkoff, Maurice (1927–2013) Sweden

Contrasts (1982)
Da Capo Music, 1995
    I. Libero
    II. Allegretto scherzando
    III. Adagio
    IV. Moderato maestoso
Contemporary harmonic language notated in traditional rhythms in changing
    meters. Lyrical and free writing, agile passages, an expressive adagio, and a
    final movement with dramatic glissandi and trills are some of the charac-
    teristics of this work. Karkoff notes in the preface that "the last movement
    has some nostalgic 'memories' of Chopin's Polanaise rhythms, reflecting
    my earlier career as a pianist." Old notation bass clef.
Range: A–c³
Duration: 12:00

Kauder, Hugo (1888–1972) Austria and United States, born in Czech Republic

Kleine Abendmusik
Seesaw Music, 1987
"Für Willem und Gertrud Valkenier." Written in traditional harmonic language consisting of an introductory prelude followed by a theme with short variations. Written without bar lines, it stays mostly in the midrange of the horn and is not very taxing or difficult.
Range: g–c³
Duration: 4:00

Three Melodies for Horn Solo
Seesaw Music, 1987
Three very short movements, written without bar lines, straightforward writing in a tonal/modal harmonic language.
Range: a–a²
Duration: 3:15

Kavanaugh, Patrick (1954–) United States

Debussy Variations, No. 11 for Solo Horn in F
Pembroke Music, 1977, sole selling agents Carl Fischer
Kavanaugh wrote fourteen *Debussy Variations* for different instruments. This work is full of extended techniques for the horn, including flutter tongue, wind sound only (blowing air through the instrument), humming into and outside of the horn, lip buzz, echo stop, half-valve fingerings, three-quarter stopping, removing slides to produce a percussive "pop," playing with slides removed. This work combines both graphic and traditional notation, and there are many aleatoric elements, leaving decisions, such as pitch and note duration, up to the player.
Range: varies
Duration: varies, approximately 6:00

Keegan, Mike, United States

Gloach corn (Irish Horn Call) (2005)
Imagine Music, 2006
This work opens with a characteristic horn call motive that recurs throughout the piece. With short, contrasting sections in changing meters and keys, it incorporates traditional Irish folk songs and quotes two contemporary horn works, Poulenc's *Elegy for Horn and Piano* and Kurt Atterberg's *Horn Concerto*. Extended techniques are modest, with a glissando and stopped notes, making this work suitable for the adventurous high school student or college player.
Range: E–b²

Kelterborn, Rudolf (1931–) Switzerland

Melodien für Solo-Horn (2007)
Tre Media, 2007

Written for Stefan Ruf. In four contrasting sections, with detailed instructions throughout. This work uses extended techniques for dramatic effect, including glissandi, half-valve glissandi, flutter tonguing, aleatoric sections of humming into the horn, and extensive stopped writing. Alternative notes are given for a section that goes above the staff, making this an accessible work for the college player or above.

Range: F–c³ (ossia to a²)
Duration: 7:00

Ketting, Otto (1935–) Netherlands
Prior to becoming a full-time composer, Ketting was a trumpet player with Residentie Orkest-The Hague Philharmonic.

Intrada for Trumpet or Horn (1958)
Donemus, 1977
Written for his own trumpet exam at the Royal Conservatoire in The Hague, this work was initially written for both horn and trumpet. The piece opens with a haunting, bluesy theme that develops and alternates with fanfare and signaling motives, returning several times to the opening material. Well paced and idiomatic, suitable for a college-level player and above, and is now considered a standard in the horn repertoire.

Range: e¹–b♭²
Duration: 3:30

Kibbe, Michael (1945–) United States
Michael Kibbe, composer and performer of wind instruments, studied composition at UCLA with Elaine Barkin, Roy Travis, Alden Ashforth, and Henri Lazarof.

Theme and Variations for Horn Alone, op. 32 (1976, rev. 1984)
Michael Kibbe, 1991; available from michaelkibbe.com
This work is a theme with five variations: Allegro—Arioso—Scherzo—Canto—Alla marcia. Of medium difficulty, with changing meters, some wide leaps, and phrases that move through the range of the horn, it is in a reasonable tessitura, suitable for college-level player and above.

Range: G–a²
Duration: 7:30

Kilpiö, Lauri (1974–) Finland

Black Joy (1999)
Uusinta Pub. Co., 2003
First performance March 10, 2001, Reeta Rossi, horn, at the Musica Nova Festival, Helsinki, Finland. This work begins Quasi misterioso, developing legato gestures in a cantabile style, followed by a brief section of scherzando writing, returning to the Quasi misterioso writing featuring the low-to-middle range of the horn. Continually changing meters give the piece a free, im-

provised feel. There are a few stopped-horn effects for color. With much of the piece in the low range and midrange tessitura, it is well paced for the hornist.
Range: A–a♭²
Duration: 4:00

Klein, Juliane (1966–) Germany

Aus der Wand die Rinne 9 (2009)
Edition Juliane Klein, 2011
For Juliane Baucke. This work is part of a series of pieces for solo instruments under the same title. The first *Aus der Wand die Rinne* was written in 1996 for solo cello as part of a sculpture by the visual artist Britta Brückner. Since then, the composer has written pieces in the series for violin, oboe, accordion, piano, clarinet, saxophone, electronics, theremin, video, and flute that can be played alone or in any possible combination. Highly improvisatory, the solo horn piece is full of contrasting effects: wide leaps, repeated high b♭² gestures, trills, quarter tones, half-stopped and stopped effects, and sections of molto espressivo writing.
Range: G–b♭²
Duration: 10:00

Klein, Lothar (1932–2004) Canada, born in Germany

Voluntaries for Horn Solo
Canadian Music Centre, 1984
Horn players may be familiar with Lothar Klein from his *Aoidoi* for horn and harp, recorded by Sören Hermansson. This work for solo horn is in three movements. The first has several contrasting sections. It opens with a distant legato horn call motive, followed by light and joyous scherzo-like writing, with wide leaps and grace-note embellishments on the top notes. The second movement, marked Calmo, ben canto, is lyrical, opening with a similar horn call motive to the first movement, becoming increasingly agitated with triplet figures, then relaxing again. The third movement is muted, and has the most virtuosic writing, with scherzo-like figures, and a brief return of the legato horn call opening. Requires agility and a light touch but is reasonable in range.
Range: c♯–g²
Duration: 6:48

Knüsel, Alfred (1941–) Switzerland

Niemandsland. Ort der Einsamkeit (2007)
Schweizer Musikedition, 2010
In four sections: Rezitativ I—Dialog—Aria—Rezitativ II. Includes explanations of symbols used throughout the piece for different types of articulations, flutter tonguing, multiphonics, hitting the fingernail on the bell, etc. Phrases with wide leaps that encompass the entire range of the horn. Explosive

dynamics. Unmeasured, the rhythmic notation is a combination of traditional notation with symbols that indicate pauses and duration.

Range: E–b²

Duration: 7:00

Koch, Erland von (1910–2009) Sweden

Monolog 6 (1975)
Carl Gehrmans Musikförlag, 1977
Koch wrote a series of "Monologs" for different wind instruments. In two short, contrasting movements, the first, *Andante espressivo, liberamente,* builds on an easygoing tune with a few jazz inflections. The second movement, *Allegro molto vivace,* is a spirited $. Liberal use of stopped writing for color contrasts and echo effects, as well as a few glissandi. This is a challenging work, but the composer presents alternatives for passages that go into the extreme high range.

Range: c–f³ (c³ if alternative passages played)

Duration: 6:00

Kocsár, Miklós (1933–) Hungary

Kocsár, known for his choral music and wind chamber music, was a professor at the Budapest Conservatory.

Echos No. 1 for Horn Solo (1984)
Editio Musica Budapest, 1987
Opens quietly with a repeated minor-third motive, then grows increasingly active, with contrasting sections of Allegretto. A busy Allegro of sixteenth-note gestures precedes a return to the quiet opening. This work has wide leaps, some intricate passages and several instances of stopped writing.

Range: e–b♭²

Duration: 6:00

Koechlin, Charles (1867–1950) France

Les Confidences d'un joueur de clarinette
    No. 4: L'appel du matin
    No. 7: Réveil
    No. 13: Sonnerie de Waldhorn à la fête d'Eckerswir avant le bal
Three short pieces for solo horn that are excerpts from a set of pieces written for a film score that Koechlin wrote in 1934 based on the novel *Confessions of a clarinet player* by Émile Erckmann and Alexandre Chatrian. The main characters of the story are Kasper (clarinet) and his friend Waldhorn. Averaging one minute each, these are all hunting horn music, written in $, in the written key of A.

Range: e–b²

Duration: ca. 3:00

Monodie pour cor seul, op. 218 bis (1948)
Billaudot, 1988

Composed for the competition of the music conservatory at Saint-Étienne, France. This short work opens heroically with a horn call motive, first in the mid-range, then moving into the high range. Contrasting sections present a variety of quickly changing moods, some heroic, some introspective. There are changes in color, with sections of stopped and muted horn. Challenging range, with several phrases above the staff and passages with wide leaps, making this a suitable work for a college-level hornist and above.

Range: c–d♭³
Duration: 3:00

Kogan, Lev (1927–2007) Israel, born in Russia

Kaddish for Horn Solo
Israel Brass Woodwind Publications
Dedicated to Meir Rimon. Kaddish is a hymn of praise in the Jewish prayer service and often refers specifically to a mourner's Kaddish. In $\frac{3}{4}$, marked larghetto, this flowing and soulful work stays mostly in the dark midrange of the horn and is in a minor/modal tonality throughout. There is one stopped passage. An intermediate work for advanced high school or early-college player and above. The piece is basically one mood/theme, so there are many opportunities for shaping phrases and keeping the line moving to keep things interesting for the listener.

Range: d–g²
Duration: 3:00

Kraft, William (1923–) United States
William Kraft was head of the composition department at University of California Santa Barbara, a percussionist and timpanist with the Los Angeles Philharmonic, and served as their assistant conductor and composer in residence from 1981–1985.

Evening Voluntaries (1980)
New Music West, 1981
This work was written for and dedicated to John Cerminaro, who also recorded it. It is organized into an introductory theme, three short variations, and a finale that brings back the slow introductory material. The range is extreme, and there are wide leaps—both slurred and tongued—and fast and angular technical passages; and quick triple tonguing. Most of the multiphonics are in major/minor tonality, and are quite effective, set against the contemporary harmonic language of the rest of the piece.

Range: C–g³ (ossia C–c³)
Duration: 6:00

Krol, Bernhard (1920–2013) Germany

Laudatio (1965)
Simrock, 1966
This colorful and dramatic work is a standard in the horn literature, and is an excellent introduction to the unaccompanied horn, suitable as a recital piece

for the college student through professional. In five sections. It is based on
a segment of the "Te deum laudamus" from the *Liber Usualis*. Expressive
and free, the half-step motive and the clear delineation of sections make it
musically accessible for both the player and the listener.

Range: d♭–b♭²
Duration: 3:30

Moment Musical, op. 103, for Natural Horn (1989)
Bote & Bock
Composed in 1989 for the second annual Natural Horn Competition in Bad Harzburg in 1990. A flowing work in contrasting sections, unmeasured, with
a recurrence of the two-measure opening motive. Moderately challenging
hand horn technique.

Range: c–c³ (for natural horn in F, key is not specified)
Duration: ca. 3:30

Kvam, Oddvar S. (1927–) Norway

Monofoni for horn, op. 43
Musikk-Huset, 1948
From the woodwind quintet *5 monofonier for blåsekvintett,* op. 43, this work may
be played individually or as a piece for woodwind quintet, with a solo for
each instrument. Appropriate for the intermediate student, it features dotted eighth-sixteenth motives and sixteenth-note gestures in an Allegretto
tempo. The second half is a Maestoso with sustained *forte* passages.

Range: c¹–a♭²
Duration: 2:00

Kvandal, Johan (1919–1999) Norway

Salmetone—Hymn Tune
Norsk Musikforlag, 1985
One page in length, this is a straightforward introduction to unaccompanied
horn literature. Marked Adagio solenne, the character is slow and somber
throughout, in a deliberate tempo. The range is not excessive, but a continuous amount of energy is required to keep the intensity of the piece going.
There is one brief passage of stopped writing.

Range: c¹–a²
Duration: 3:15

Lane, Liz (1964–) United Kingdom

Linear Lines, Five Soliloquies Based on the Chant "In Principio Omnes"
by Hildegard of Bingen (2009)
Available from the composer lizlane.co.uk
Commissioned by hornist Marlene Ford, this work is based on a chant from Hildegard's *Ordo Virtutum,* and explores the musical language of Hildegard of
Bingen with that of the present day. The composer's preface indicates that
the chant "is used as the basis of the piece which is split into five sections,

each a progressive soliloquy on the original musical material." The text is also presented, and could be read aloud if desired. Techniques include stopped writing, glissandi, changing meters, and a few wide intervals, with a technical level suitable for a college hornist.

Range: B–b^2

Duration: 5:00

Láng, István (1933–) Hungary

Monologue (1974)

Editio Musica Budapest, 1976

Dedicated to Ferenc Farjáni. Unmeasured throughout, with some graphical notation and instructions written over the music indicating tempo and character. Very wide leaps, abrupt dynamic changes, and many extended techniques, such as quarter tones, stopped writing, glissandi, trills. The high d♯^{3} is preceded by a glissando, making the range in other respects more reasonable.

Range: E♭–d♯^{3}

Duration: 9:00

Lang, Konrad (1943–) Germany

Monológos (2005)

Edition Tilo Medik, 2007

For Ela Nägele. In a driving $^{12}_8$ that moves quickly through the ranges of the horn, with wide leaps, stopped writing, flutter tonguing, glissandi, and dramatic dynamic contrasts. The leaps and high tessitura make this a challenging work. There are several points in the middle section where breaks are indicated.

Range: B–c^3

Duration: 4:00

Lázaro, José Villena (1941–) Spain

Juego no. 12

Piles, 1996

For Juan José Llimerá. The title means "Game number 12." In three movements: Andante—Adagio—Allegro. Contemporary harmonic language, written in traditional notation and meters, with fast switching between low and middle ranges, with a good amount of writing in the low range.

Range: G–c^3

Duration: ca. 15:00

Lazarof, Henri (1932–2013) United States, born in Bulgaria

Composer and educator Lazarof was a member of the music faculty at UCLA for many years.

Intrada for Solo Horn (1994)

Merion Music, 1995

For Robert Routch. Sections of contrasting character that push the limits of the
    horn's range and require flexibility and endurance. Full of rubato, contrast-
    ing dynamics, and opportunities for expression. A challenging work for
    the hornist.
Range: G–d³
Duration: 6:00

Lebic, Lojze (1934–) Slovenia

In voce cornus, pet miniatur za rog solo (five miniatures for French horn) (1990)
Edicije DSS, 2006
Commissioned by the Deutscher Verlag für Musik, Leipzig. Three of the five
    Miniatures were premiered by Jože Falout in Zagreb, March 5, 1990. The
    entire piece was premiered in 2000 by Boštjan Lipovšek in Ljubljana, who
    also recorded the work. These five miniatures explore a large variety of
    effects, colors, and sounds, with stopped writing, flutter tonguing, pitch
    bending, multiphonics, enharmonic fingerings, glissandi, and quarter
    tones. Among these colors is the beautiful sound of the horn. Instructions
    are clear and include a translation of the performance notes. The piece is
    notated both traditionally and proportionally, and all five miniatures may
    be performed as a set or individually in different combinations. Agility is
    required, but, with many decisions left up to the performer, this becomes
    an accessible work. Challenging, but could serve as a good introduction to
    contemporary techniques for the adventurous college player.
Range: G–c³
Duration: 11:00

Lefebvre, Claude (1931–2012) France

Vallée . . . pour cor solo (1987)
Editions Salabert, 1990
"En hommage à Maurice Ravel." Liner notes from the CD (Salabert Actuels/
    Harmonia Mundi) describe *Vallée* as "an acoustic reminiscence of the val-
    ley where the composer lives." The piece begins low and soft with long-
    held tones, then grows increasingly complex, culminating in a call of fifths
    up to a high c³, then returning to the quiet opening.
Range: c–c³
Duration: 4:00

Leitermeyer, Fritz (1925–2006) Austria

Leitermeyer was a composer and also a violinist for many years with the Vienna
Philharmonic.

Hornissimo, op. 76 (1981)
Doblinger, 1990
This piece begins in a virtuosic flourish, with many elements introduced in the
    first six bars: dramatic octave jumps from the highest range of the horn
    down to the lowest, multiple tonguing, stopped writing, and dynamics from

forte to *pianissimo*. The piece alternates quick legato figures and forceful marcato sixteenths, interspersed with a dotted-eighth motive. There is an opportunity for a cadenza, followed by furious repetitive sixteenths marked Presto possible. This is a challenging and virtuosic work requiring good endurance, flexibility and a flair for the dramatic.

Range: F–c^3

Duration: 5:00

Lejet, Edith (1941–) France

Emeritus professor at the Paris Conservatory and professor of composition at the Ecole Normale de Musique de Paris Alfred Cortot.

Deux soliloques (1992)

Editions Amphion, 1992

The first *Soliloque* was commissioned by the French Ministry of Culture; the second at the request of Jacques Adnet, as the exam piece for the 1993 class at the Paris Conservatory. Dedicated to Jacques Adnet, Bernard Le Pogam, and Andre Cazalet. This work is full of contemporary techniques. It is unmeasured, written in a combination of traditional notation, proportional notation, and detailed directions in French. Large dynamic contrasts, phrases on the harmonic series ("cor naturel"), stopped writing, flutter tonguing. The first soliloquy emphasizes long notes, contrasting colors, and extended techniques, the second is more virtuosic, with quick passages that require dexterity and flexibility.

Range: F♯–c^3

Duration: 6:00

Le Siege, Annette (1945–) United States

Shadow Dancer

Seesaw Music, 1993

Beginning with a somber lyrical opening followed by a faster sixteenth-note motive that recurs throughout the piece. Written in a contemporary tonal style with a few stopped passages. The piece lies mostly in the staff, and fast passages are in familiar key areas, making this a good work for the high school or early-college player.

Range: g–a^2

Duration: 6:00

Lewis, Robert Hall (1926–1996) United States

Composer and trumpet player, taught at Peabody Conservatory in Baltimore.

Monophony VI

Doblinger, 1984

    Andante con fuoco

    Adagio espressivo

    Andante marziale

Lewis wrote several "Monophony" for other wind instruments and for voice. In three contrasting movements, the first is unmeasured, with sections of rubato, the second is slow and lyrical, with murmuring 32nd notes that embellish legato lines. The last movement is rhythmic, in changing meters. Full of trills, dynamic contrasts, flutter tonguing, stopped writing, and fast chromatic passages.

Range: E♭–c³
Duration: 8:00

Lischka, Rainer (1942–) Germany

Steps and Leaps (1990)
Hofmeister, 1994
Published with Lischka's *A Jazzy Joke* for horn and piano. In two sections, an unmeasured, mostly legato Andante espressivo followed by an Allegro con brio that is full of syncopated rhythms in changing meters. There are a few wide leaps in legato, but overall tessitura is within the staff. A few instances of trills, stopped writing, and flutter tonguing.

Range: g–a♭²
Duration: 2:30

Lohse, Horst (1943–) Germany

Die Sirenen noch im Ohr . . . Hommage à Claude Debussy for Horn Solo (2004)
Edition Gravis, 2004
Dedicated to Wilfried Krüger. Begins quietly, then builds in the middle section, returning to the quiet opening. It is based on motives from "Sirènes," which is the third of Debussy's *Nocturnes* for orchestra and women's chorus. Not technically demanding, although it spans the full range of the horn.

Range: F♯–c³
Duration: 4:00

Pallas Athene für Horn solo (1991)
Edition Gravis, 2001
This work is from *Fünf Portraits für Bläsersoli* which was conceived as a set of five short pieces for each instrument of the woodwind quintet, written as part of a staged reading of the *Odyssey,* premiered by members of the Bamberger Symphony, June 24, 1991. Each piece is a portrait of a female character in Homer's epic. The pieces are unified by an "Odysseus motive" that appears in modified form throughout each. This is a challenging work that begins Energico maestoso, followed by a Piu vivo, full of energetic runs that burst above the staff, contrasting with slower phrases in the low range. Published separately, these can be performed individually or as a set.

Range: c–c³
Duration: 3:00

Louël, Jean (1914–2005) Belgium

Invention pour cor solo (1973)
CeBeDeM Brussels, 1974
For Andre Van Driessche. In three sections; the first two are unmeasured, the
third is an Allegro scherzando, alternating between $\frac{5}{8}$, $\frac{6}{8}$, and $\frac{3}{8}$. The piece
opens with a glissando up to high c^3 that jumps up to a trill on e^3, making
its way back down. Things continue at this level of difficulty and intensity,
with contrasting sections that present a wide variety of characters and gestures, using the expressive effects of glissandi trills, multiple tonguing, and
a range that extends beyond the traditional.
Range: A–e^3
Duration: 7:00

Lu, Wayne (1970–) United States

The Sea (1998)
Veritas Musica Publishing, 2009
    I. Waves
    II. The Discoverers
    III. Sea Winds
    IV. White Caps
Each movement depicts an aspect of the sea, inspired by a trip to the coast of
Maine and a fishing trip "in a much too small and fragile fishing boat during
heavy rains and winds." Contemporary techniques include multiphonics,
alternate fingerings, half-valve notes, stopped writing, and pitch bending.
Range: B–c^3
Duration: 11:00

Lucidi, Marco (1962–) Italy
Lucidi studied composition, piano, percussion and conducting at St. Cecilia Conservatory, Rome, and had additional training with Karlheinz Stockhausen.

Tre Studi per corno
Rai Trade, 2009
The first study is based on a perfect-fifth fanfare in a syncopated rhythm. The
second study is unified around a driving eighth-two-sixteenth figure, with
a free middle section of triplets. The third movement is very different from
the others, and explores the colors of the horn through long tones and half-
stopped writing. Approachable studies with only modest requirements in
range.
Range: b♭–b♭^{2}
Duration: 4:05

Lundberg, Staffan (1952–) Sweden

Two Moods for French Horn (1981)
Libitum Musik

Dedicated to Bengt Belfrage. In two short movements, the first is bold, notated
in changing meters that give it an improvisatory and dramatic character.
There are a few stopped phrases, glissandi, and trills. The second move-
ment shifts between $\frac{6}{8}$ and $\frac{9}{8}$, and centers around a motive of slurred groups
of quickly moving patterns on major triads, grouped into six notes per
beat.
Range: d–c³
Duration: 5:00

Lyon, David (1938–) United Kingdom

Partita for Solo Horn, op. 6
Schirmer, 1967
　　1. Introduction (Moderato)
　　2. Waltz (Lento)
　　3. Hornpipe (Allegro con spirito)
　　4. Aria (Adagio dolente)
　　5. Finale (Allegro non troppo)
Five character pieces written in traditional rhythmic notation and tonal harmonic language. Changing meters create interesting metric shifts. These
are intermediate-level pieces, and would work well as an addition to
etudes.
Range: d–a♭²
Duration: 7:45

Madsen, Trygve (1940–) Norway

The Dream of the Rhinoceros, op. 92 (1994)
Musikk-Husets Forlag A/S, 1994
Dedicated to Frøydis Ree Wekre, this is based on a Norwegian folk song traditionally used for herding. Liner notes from Frøydis' recording (Crystal Records) describe the story of this piece: "All mammals are having
dreams while sleeping, and this particular Rhinoceros always had the
same dream. In the dream he was able to play on his horn, and the horn
tune from the dream was this one." Two outer sections are slow and legato,
and a fast middle section is in a jazzy swing style, with syncopated figures
and flutter tonguing. Expression and style are packed into this short and
effective work, very accessible for a college-level player.
Range: c–g♯²
Duration: 3:37

Malmlöf-Forssling, Carin (1916–2005) Sweden

Orizzonte per corno (1981)
Gehrmans Musikförlag, 2004
Dedicated to Ib Lanzky-Otto. *Orizzonte* means "horizon" in Swedish. Long
lines for the horn, often plaintive in character, are interrupted with quick

gestures. The liberal use of multiphonics, stopped and half-stopped writing, glissandi, and flutter tonguing, all explore different timbres of the horn. Challenging contemporary work requiring endurance, flexibility, and strength for dramatic glissandi into the high range.

Range: B–c^3

Duration: 9:00

Maros, Miklós (1943–) Sweden, born in Hungary

Lur II, per corno in Fa (1989)

Svensk music, 1989

Dedicated to Peter Damm. This work explores several contemporary horn techniques. Much of this piece is played on the naturally occurring harmonic series, with smooth runs up the harmonic series in "keys" of F, E, and E♭. There is a middle section of tremolos in thirds and improvisatory trills, before a return of the opening harmonic series motive. Multiphonics with notes in the pedal range of the horn, plus phrases that stay consistently on or above the staff, make this a challenging work.

Range: C–c^3

Duration: 5:00

Marshall, Pamela (1954–) United States

Colored Leaves

Spindrift Music, 1994

      Crisp and cool

      Aria—whistling wind

The composer's intention here was to provide a musically interesting piece that doesn't emphasize the high register. The first movement, to be played *freely,* is unmeasured, with an upward-sweeping motive that runs throughout the first section. A middle section, marked *deliberato,* in changing meters, is more disjointed. The second movement, "Aria—whistling wind," is unmeasured with flowing chromatic passages.

Range: d–g♭^{2}

Duration: 6:00

Miniatures for Unaccompanied Horn (1973)

Seesaw Music, 1976

In five short movements. This work is an approachable introduction to extended techniques for horn. Free and flowing, leaving many decisions of pacing up to the performer; extended techniques include multiphonics, glissandi, open, stopped and half-stopped writing requiring alternate fingerings. The first-movement march requires a bit of coordination for tapping on the mute while playing.

Range: B–a^2

Duration: 7:30

Martin, Robert (1952–) United States

Regulus (1988)

Merion Music-Theodore Presser, 1998

The composer wrote a series of nine "stellar" solo wind pieces, and each one is
named for a bright star in a constellation. *Regulus* refers to the blue-white
star in the constellation Leo, and represents the heart of the lion. In five
contrasting sections marked Sonore—Andante—Cantabile—Misterioso—
Serioso. Written in changing meters with some proportional notation, the
piece stays mostly in the staff, however there are few breaks. Premiered by
William Purvis, who also recorded the work.

Range: c–b♭²

Duration: 6:15

Matchett, Steve (1957–) United States

Matchett, professional tubist, composer, and teacher working in the Houston area, has written original music and arrangements for brass, winds, and
strings.

Portrait for Solo Horn (1989)

RBC Publications, 1990

Dedicated to William C. (Bill) Jones, this work is in five contrasting movements: Andante—Allegro assai—Adagio—Veloce—Largo Misterioso. The
two slow movements are perhaps the most challenging, with wide leaps;
stopped writing; and sections of free, unmeasured writing providing opportunities for the soloist to develop expressive playing in a contemporary idiom. This is an accessible work, suitable for the college player and
above.

Range: e–a²

Duration: 9:10

Matthus, Siegfried (1934–) Germany

*Hoch willkommt das Horn, nach Motiven der Opernvision "Die Weise von Liebe
und Tod des Cornetts Christoph Rilke"*

Hofmeister, 1992

Composed in 1985 for Peter Damm, based on Matthus' opera of the same title.
Contrasting sections incorporate horn motives from the opera. The work
begins softly with a sextuplet figure that increases with intensity, leading
up to a high b♭². A blues section follows, with a return to the opening sextuplets. There are two sections of molto cantabile, called "Notturno I" and
"Notturno II," and the piece ends with a flourish with material from the
opening. Technically challenging work, particularly the high, quick figures
in the upper tessitura.

Range: c–c³

Duration: 5:15

McGuire, Edward (1948–) United Kingdom (Scotland)

Prelude 17 (1995)
Warwick Music, 2003
Composed for Maurice Temple, premiered by Hugh Potts in 1996 in Glasgow. This work begins quietly, unmeasured, with wide-ranging gestures that grow increasingly active. This is followed by a rhythmic Presto before a return to the opening mood to end the piece quietly. Many different colors of the horn are explored, with large dynamic contrasts, chromatic gestures, and stopped and half-stopped passages.
Range: c–b♭^{2}
Duration: 5:00

Mellnäs, Arne (1933–2002) Sweden
Mellnäs was an award-winning Swedish composer, who studied with Erland von Koch, Lars-Erik Larsson, and Karl-Birger Blomdahl as well as at the Darmstadt summer courses. *New Grove* indicates that "he was one of the first Swedes to introduce aleatory and deliberately theatrical elements into instrumental music."

Estampes, per corno solo
Edition Reimers, 1991
"For the 25th anniversary of 'Grafikgruppen' 1995." Dedicated to Sören Hermansson. Contemporary techniques abound in this work, with flutter tonguing, whispering words into the instrument, stopped writing, glissandi, and making air sounds through the horn.
Range: F–c^3
Duration: 6:00

Meriläinen, Usko (1930–2004) Finland

Grandfather Benno's Night Music (Isoisä Bennon iltasoitto) (1976)
Fazer, 1976
Composed for the National Brass Competition in Helsinki, 1976. Unmeasured, with bar lines used to indicate phrase groupings. Marked Liberamente sempre moderato, this mostly flowing, expressive work is not technically demanding, with only a few stopped notes and several wide leaps.
Range: F–a♭^{2}
Duration: 2:30

Merkù, Pavle (1927–) Slovenia, born in Italy

Metamorfosi di un canto popolare (1973)
Edicije Drustva Slovenskih Skladateljev, 1974
Theme ("Tema") and development ("Metamorfosi") of a folk song that starts very simply then becomes increasingly complex as the work unfolds, with heroic rhythmic figures, wide leaps and modal inflections.
Range: c–c^3
Duration: 4:00

Miller, J. Greg (1984–) United States

Foglissimo! for Unaccompanied Horn
Veritas Musica Publishing, 2010
A short and intense one-movement work, marked *bombastically, ala carnival.* A
    running sixteenth-note motive is played *fortissimo*, with a middle section
    that quotes the obbligato movement of Mahler's fifth symphony.
Range: f♯–g♯ (ossia to c³)
Duration: 2:45

Seven Sets on The Odyssey (2009)
Veritas Musica Publishing, 2010
Each movement depicts a scene from *The Odyssey* and is composed in a different
    mode. Includes flutter tonguing, glissandi, and multiphonics.
Range: G–d³
Duration: 10:00

Mishori, Yaacov (1937–) Israel
Mishori played first horn in the Israel Philharmonic Orchestra, was a member
of the Israel Brass Quintet, and taught at the Music Academy of the Tel Aviv
University.

Prolonged Shofar Variations for Horn Solo
Israel Brass Woodwind Publications, 1981
Dedicated to Mishori's father, a famous cantor and teacher of biblical cantilla-
    tions, on the occasion of his eightieth birthday. This piece is based on mel-
    odies from Jewish prayer services.
Range: B–b²
Duration: 3:30

Mitsuoka, I. (1946–)

Pachyderms, for Unaccompanied Horn (1976)
The Musical Evergreen, 1977
Marked *With rampage and imagination.* Written in graphic notation using only
    lines of different shapes and lengths, with rests indicated in seconds. With
    no performance notes, nearly every aspect of this work is left up to the
    performer, and the notation just provides a very rough idea about length
    and shape of phrase. This could be fun, and a good exercise in improvisa-
    tion. The only other performance instructions provided by the composer is
    the suggestion of adding "a small amount of electronic amplification with
    reverberation."
Range: left up to the performer
Duration: ca. 2:30, but varies

Moylan, William (1956–) United States
Sonata for Horn (1982)
Seesaw Music, 1983

Commissioned by Kent Leslie. This can be performed as a solo sonata or as a sonata for horn and piano. This work is in one continuous movement and may be divided into four large sections that alternate unaccompanied horn with horn and piano. There are challenging technical passages to work out, and long-range endurance is required for several sections, however the moderate range makes this work more accessible than many contemporary works for solo horn.

Range: f♯–a² (horn and piano version) or g♯–g♭² (solo horn version)

Duration: 11:00 (horn and piano version) or 5:30 (solo horn version)

Nagel, Jody (1960–) United States

Theme and Variations (1999)

JOMAR Press, 1999

For Fred Ehnes. In twelve short movements, with a Maestoso theme, ten variations (Poco meno mosso—Più mosso, Alla marcia—Presto—Ländler—Slowly—Fleeting—Carelessly—Grandioso—Slow gigue—Sharply percussive), and a finale. A good deal of variety throughout the piece. Technical challenges include wide-ranging legato passages and chromatic writing, but overall, this is an accessible work, suitable for the college-level player and above.

Range: B–a²

Duration: 9:00

Nagy, Zsolt (1957–) Hungary

Happy Blues (2000)

RM Williams, 2004

Freely written in an improvisatory style, full of jazz idioms, glissandi, shakes, and multiphonics, this fun and challenging work leaps through the different ranges of the horn. A showstopping encore piece, several prominent horn soloists delight audiences with this in their repertoire.

Range: G–c♯³

Duration: 4:17

Naigus, James (1987–) United States

Primary Ignition for Solo Horn

RM Williams, 2012

Commissioned by and written for Patrick Smith for the 2013 Southeast Horn Workshop, this was the required piece for the first round of the solo competition at the workshop. It features syncopated rhythms, changing meters, stopped writing, and a few slides from stopped to open. The two outer sections are in a fast tempo, the middle section is played freely with rubato.

Range: d–b♭²

Duration: 2:02

Naulais, Jérôme (1951–) France

Composer, arranger, trombonist. Played with Boulez' Ensemble Intercontemporain.

Miroir

International Music Diffusion, 1987

Dedicated to Jacques Deleplancque, principal horn of the Orchestre National du
    Capitole de Toulouse. The work alternates lyrical lines with flourishes of
    fast horn writing, with the horn dipping into the low range and midrange
    throughout. A challenging work requiring good long-range endurance.

Range: G–c³

Duration: 6:30

Nicholas, James (1957–) United States

Panachida, for Solo Natural Horn in E

Birdalone Music, 1989

James Nicholas wrote this work in memory of two friends who died within days
    of each other in 1987. "Panachida," also known as "Mnemósynon" in Greek,
    refers to a memorial service in the Orthodox Church. In three movements,
    with melodic writing with elements of chant, melismatic writing, and calls
    with echoes, creating a solemn character. Fairly difficult writing for the
    natural horn player, with fast hand technique and passages with closed
    high A for the final calls and echoes of the last movement. This work has
    well thought-out quarter-tone echoes in the last movement.

Range: c¹–c³ for horn in E

Duration: 5:45

Nystedt, Knut (1915–2014) Norway

Canto (1990)

Norsk musikforlag, 1990

Premiered by Frøydis Ree Wekre at the Norwegian Academy of Music, Oslo. The
    opening is marked Adagio espressivo, with wide-ranging phrases at a soft
    dynamic, becoming more animated with triplet and dotted eighth-sixteenth
    figures before a return of the opening material. The piece ends quietly in the
    low range. Modest technical demands and reasonable range make this an
    accessible work.

Range: c♯–b²

Duration: 4:30

Obst, Michael (1955–) Germany

Obst is known for his electro-acoustic works, was a founding member of Ensemble Modern (Frankfurt), and composer in residence at many European electronic
music studios.

Sechs Skizzen (2000–2002)

Breitkopf & Härtel, 2003

These six sketches present dynamic contemporary music for solo horn through
    intricate rhythmic gestures and articulations. The fifth sketch contrasts

with the others, with rubato ascending harmonics above a specified root that alternate with long tones in the low range. This challenging work is full of contemporary techniques, including glissandi, multiphonics, flutter tonguing, quick trills, and random embellishments around notes, however the overall range demands are modest.

Range: c–a²
Duration: 7:30

Olive, Vivienne (1950–) United Kingdom

Text V, Scarista Bull, für Horn (1991)
Furore Edition, 1993
Inspired by the photograph "Scarista Bull" by Scottish photographer Oscar Marzaroli which shows a bull in front of a background in the Hebrides. An energetic work, with juxtapositions in character and dynamics. One passage in the middle section goes up to high c³, however much of this work is in the middle or low range. Extended techniques include stopped horn, flutter tonguing, and multiphonics. At times these extended techniques are fairly difficult because of the low range.

Range: F♯–c³
Duration: 2:30

Olsen, Sparre (1903–1984) Norway

Twilight Tones (Skumringstone)
Norsk Musikforlag, 1979
In the written key of E♭, this is a student piece, suitable for a younger player. In ABA form, with outer sections of Andantino and a middle section in a light minuet style, it extends into the low range, and there are a few leaps to g².

Range: e♭–g²
Duration: 1:30

Orval, Francis (1944–) Belgium
Belgian horn soloist and orchestral player, premiered many new works for horn.

Libre-free-frei (1981)
McCoy's Horn Library, 1982
Written as an examination piece for Orval's students at the Royal Conservatory of Music in Liége, this explores the different colors of the horn using alternate fingerings. The preface indicates that these fingerings should be used to create "micro-intervals by utilizing the natural harmonics." The harmonic language is based on the twelve-tone system but "used without respecting the strict rules." Written in mixed meters, some sections nonmeasured. Other techniques in this work include stopped horn, glissandi, and trills.

Range: E–c³
Duration: 3:45

Triptych (1987)
Editions Marc Reift, 1994

In three movements: I. Force, II Sagesse, and III. Beauté. This work is atonal, with angular lines and sections of lyrical writing. The many tempo changes, contrasts in dynamics, large leaps, stopped writing, flutter tonguing, and quarter tones make this a challenging work.

Range: E♭–c³

Orval, Jules-Louis (1913–2015) Belgium

Jules Orval, father of hornist Francis Orval, was a cellist who studied composition and cello at the Liege Conservatory.

Alla mente: improvisation pour cor solo
Editions Marc Reift, 1994
Moderately paced unaccompanied work in contrasting sections. Many opportunities for expressive playing, with rubato sections and phrases that grow in intensity then return to the opening theme or its variation. Technical challenges include writing above the staff and several wide leaps.

Range: c–b²
Duration: 3:00

Pascal, Claude (1921–) France

Music critic, composer, and professor at the Paris Conservatory.

Sonate pour cor seul
Editions Combre, 1997
Dedicated to Michel Molinaro. In four movements. The first movement begins moderately and grows increasingly animated, with contrapuntal writing in changing meters. The second movement, marked Calme, features legato lines in a straightforward ⁴. The third movement, Presto, is in a fast ⅔ felt in one, and the final movement, marked Assez lent, brings back the motive of the opening of the first movement. An accessible work for the college-level hornist and above.

Range: d–c³
Duration: 9:40

Penderecki, Krzysztof (1933–) Poland

Capriccio per Radovan "il sogno di un cacciatore" (2012)
Schott Music, 2013
For Radovan Vlatkovic, who premiered it July 20, 2012, at the Escuela Superior de Música Reina Sofia in Santander. This is a relatively short one-movement work, marked Tempo giusto. The title translates to "The dream of a hunter." The first section is a series of short phrases of dotted rhythms and repeated notes that explore extended techniques and colors with multiphonics, stopped writing, and muted passages. Specific instructions are given, such as *breathe out into the instrument, waggle with valves, articulate "t" with the tongue*. A Piu mosso leads into the second section, which is quick and driving, with changing patterns of note groupings. Extended techniques

and wide leaps at quick tempos make this a challenging work, however the length and overall range make it a good option for a recital program.

Range: c–a^2

Duration: 4:00

Perder, Kjell (1954–) Sweden

Vocuna V "cielo oscuro" (1997)

Edition Suecia, 2001

Dedicated to Sören Hermansson, who premiered the work at the Musikmuséet Stockholm in November 1997. This work opens with extended declamatory figures on f^2 at the top of the staff, gradually moving away into other gestures that are both lyrical and acrobatic, yet continually returning to the f^2 motive. Contemporary techniques abound, including flutter tonguing, tremolos, multiphonics, bending of pitches. This is a challenging contemporary work. It requires endurance, yet there are dedicated breaks, which aren't just quick pauses but are points where the hornist is instructed to "drop" the instrument.

Range: F–c^3

Duration: 7:00–8:00

Pérez, Raúl (1969–) Spain

Los pecados capitales per trompa sola (1993)

Brotons & Mercadal, 2003

Commissioned by Francisco Rodríguez for the International Music Competition in Munich, 1993. In three movements, the first opens in a Largo tempo, with expressive wide upward leaps with dynamic contrasts. An Allegro follows, with changing meters. The second movement, "Cadenza ad libitum," begins lyrical and plaintive, then builds energy and momentum. The third movement, Moderato pastorale, is a bright and steady §, with chromatic and modal scales.

Range: c–b♭^{2}

Duration: 10:00

Persichetti, Vincent (1915–1987) United States

Parable for Solo Horn, op. 120 (1972)

Elkan-Vogel, 1973

Persichetti composed twenty-five parables for solo instruments, string quartet, brass quintet, and one for band. Based on a theme from his own *Symphony no. 7,* the *Parable for Solo Horn* has three sections, the outer sections are measured, while the middle section is unmeasured and in the style of a cadenza. Music throughout the work is derived from the melodic material of the opening theme. The middle cadenza section is chromatic and stepwise, and the final section is quite challenging technically, consisting of wide leaps and going up to high b^2. Extended techniques include stopped horn,

flutter tonguing, and glissandi. A standard in the horn repertoire, this is a
    popular choice for college recitals.
Range: A♭–b²
Duration: 6:45

Petit, Pierre (1922–2000) France

Lâtouf, thème & variations pour cor seul
Max Eschig, 1977
For Georges Barboteu. A theme with six short variations of contrasting char-
    acter. The fourth variation has the most technical challenges, with fairly
    quick legato passagework, ending with a flourish up to a high b². The fifth
    variation is entirely in the low range, and the sixth is short and sweet. This
    is a suitable piece for the early-college player.
Range: F–b²
Duration: 5:40

Petrić, Ivo (1931–) Slovenia

Hornspiele, eine Sonatine für Peter Damm (1989)
Pizzicato Verlag Helvetia, 1994; also at ivopetric.com
Premiered October 14, 1991, in Ljubljana, Slovenia by Peter Damm. This work
    moves through contrasting sections of mood with expressive musical ges-
    tures. Unmeasured but traditionally notated, with wide leaps, stopped play-
    ing, glissandi. This is a virtuoso work requiring solid technique, flexibility
    between ranges, and endurance, yet there are breaks between sections and
    opportunities for thoughtful pauses.
Range: e♭–a²
Duration: 9:00

Pflüger, Hans Georg (1944–1999) Germany

Kaleidoskop für Naturhorn (1983)
Bote & Bock, 1984
Composed for the first International Natural Horn Competition, in 1984. A vir-
    tuosic work for the natural horn, with many contemporary techniques,
    such as glissandi and multiphonics, with wide leaps and dramatic dynamic
    contrasts.
Range: c–c♯³ (for natural horn in F, key is not specified)
Duration: ca. 2:45

Pilon, Daniel (1957–) Canada

Élégie pour cor Francais
Centre de Musique Canadienne, 1977
A short lament, very straightforward and in the darker midrange of the horn.
Range: a–c²
Duration: 1:30

Plagge, Wolfgang (1960–) Norway

Monoceros (1990)

2L Electronic Scores, 2004; available from imslp.org

Written for Frøydis Ree Wekre. The composer writes in the preface that "this piece is about the legendary Unicorn, an animal everybody has heard about but nobody has ever seen. In the work it shows itself with fervor where you wouldn't expect to find it, and as soon as you think you know where it is, it gallops out of sight. . ." In an interview with Carrie Strickland, the composer describes several different motives and their connection to the myth of the unicorn: a "galloping" motive and a contrasting "lamenting" motive. Several passages are technically demanding, however the work is very accessible and idiomatic for the horn.

Range: e♭–b^2

Duration: 3:30

See also: Carrie Strickland, "A Performance Guide for Wolfgang Plagge's Music for Horn." DMA Thesis, University of Georgia, 2004.

Plog, Anthony (1947–) United States

Postcards for Solo Horn (1995)

Editions BIM, 1995

Written for Gail Williams. In four movements. The first movement, Allegro, consists of fast rolling eighth notes, with very quick interjections of a single note sung with the voice. The second movement, Allegro moderato, is in $\frac{3}{2}$ and features a syncopated motive. The third movement, marked Moderato, is composed in repeated patterns of six notes per beat, with notes that emerge to create an interesting line. The fourth movement, Allegro, is reminiscent of the first, with sung notes interjected and wider leaps in groups of two. This is challenging writing for the horn, with each movement featuring intricate motivic development.

Range: c–g^2

Duration: 5:00

Pope, Conrad (1951–) United States

Aria, Arie (1976)

Mobart Music Publications, 1984 (In collection *Five Compositions for Solo Horn*)

    I. Lirico
    II. Andantino cantabile
    III. Ansioso
    IV. Aigitato
    V. Alla misura
    VI. Brilliante
   VII. Scherzando
  VIII. Feroce
    IX. Tempo giusto

X. Sostenuto
XI. Arioso
XII. Sereno
XIII.Coda
XIV. Ansioso

In fourteen short movements, each with a different character. These can be played
as a set or individually in different combinations. There are changing meters throughout, and many extended techniques, including stopped notes,
flutter tonguing, and large leaps.

Range: F♯–c³
Duration: 10:00

Pousseur, Henri (1929–2009) Belgium

Naturel per corno solo (1981)
Servini Zuboni, 1981
Written for the 1981 International Horn Competition in Liège. This piece is to
be played entirely on the natural harmonics. The fingerings for each note
are indicated, and symbols are used (explained in the preface) to show the
slight intonation differences in the naturally occurring harmonics. This is
a challenging work full of contemporary techniques such as multiphonics,
flutter tonguing, and trills. The effect of stopped writing for harmonics in
the high range is haunting. Notated in barred groupings, with some durations of notes indicated in seconds.

Range: F–c³
Duration: 11:45

Presser, William (1916–2004) United States

William Presser taught theory, orchestration, and conducted the orchestra at the
University of Southern Mississippi. Also a violinist and a composer, he founded
Tritone Press & Tenuto Publications in 1961, a publishing firm that promotes
American composers.

Three Pieces for Horn
William Presser, 1966, also published by Faust Music, 2006
Three Pieces for Horn has a recurring legato passage throughout each movement.
The first movement is the most serious, with tempo changes throughout.
The second movement is a humorous waltz that quotes famous horn pas-
sages from Strauss, Wagner, and Rossini. The final movement is a challeng-
ing ⁴ at a fast tempo, with quick sixteenth-note passages, finishing with a
restatement of the recurring theme jumping throughout the horn's range.

Range: G–b²
Duration: 11:40

Proust, Pascal (1959–) France

Arkeos, petite suite
Editions Combre, 2010

Seven short movements, intended as a "game-exercise" to teach younger players to read modern notation and develop musical storytelling skills. These are suitable for the student in their third or fourth year of horn playing. Modern techniques include aleatoric writing, playing the highest note possible, slow vibrato, and making a breathy sound through the horn. In addition to working through the signs and symbols, the student writes a brief story based on each title, and can then "present a brief entertainment where the horn, with sounds ranging from the mysterious to brilliant, is used as an illustration to the story."
Range: b♭–f²
Duration: 4:00

Quadranti, Luigi (1941–) Switzerland

Arrampicate, solo per corno in Fa
Pizzicato Verlag Helvetia, 2000
This work begins very slowly in the low range, becoming increasingly more agitated and intense, culminating on a high c³, then returns to an Adagio reminiscent of the opening material. This work is unmeasured but written in traditional notation. Extended techniques include flutter tonguing, glissandi, stopped writing. Wide leaps and fast passages move through the different ranges, requiring flexibility, good endurance, and solid technique.
Range: F♯–c³
Duration: 7:00

Rabe, Folke (1935–) Sweden

Vuolle, for French Horn Solo (1991)
Reimers, 1991
Folke Rabe wrote this work as the cadenza for his concerto *Nature, Herd and Relatives,* which was written for Sören Hermansson. The concerto is based on four Swedish "yoiks" or, in Lappish, "vuolle." In comments on his website (folkerabe.se), the composer describes the vuolle as "one of the most individualistic among musical expressions; a highly affected singing, often practiced in solitude." *Vuolle* is in four distinct sections, with an energetic middle section. Dexterity and flexibility are required, as there are many grace notes of wide intervals. Intricate hand stopping from very fast closed notes to open notes makes this a challenging work. There are breaks between each of the four sections, and it remains in the middle-to-upper range, with only the last ten bars above the staff, going to a high c³.
Range: c♯¹–c³
Duration: 3:00

Raheb, Jeff, United States

A Quick Glance
Topazz Music, 1992
In four movements, mostly flowing, and written in a jazz style.
Range: d♯–c³

Raihala, Osmo Tapio (1964–) Finland

Soliloque 2, la tornade (2012)
Music Finland, 2013
Dedicated to Jukka Harju, who premiered it in 2012. Contrasting sections, with
   different rhythmic patterns that move the music forward yet continually re-
   turn to a gesture that rapidly accelerates and decelerates on a repeated note.
   There is some graphic notation and a few instances of glissandi, stopped
   passages, and flutter tonguing, but this work is mostly about the sound of
   the horn and its virtuosic capabilities.
Range: D–a^2
Duration: 7:30

Raphling, Sam (1910–1988) United States

Concert Studies for Unaccompanied Horn, Introduction and Workout (1956)
Edition Musicus, 1956
To David Anderson. This fun piece is in two sections, the "Introduction" is a slow
   quasi-blues style, with swung dotted eighth-sixteenths, played expressively
   with rubato. The "Workout" is in ABA form, sprinkled with syncopated
   jazz motives and hemiolas.
Range: b♭–c^3
Duration: 2:30

Concert Studies for Unaccompanied French Horn, Sonata
Edition Musicus, 1955
    I. Very moderately, lively and freely
    II. Fast-playfully
    III. Not too slow.
Straightforward, in traditional meters and rhythmic patterns, and written in
   contrasting sections. Moderately wide leaps make this a challenge for the
   younger hornist, but it would be suitable for the young college student, as a
   nice supplement to etudes.
Range: d–b^2
Duration: 5:20

Concert Studies for Unaccompanied French Horn, Variations
Edition Musicus, 1956
To Maxwell Saibel. Theme with fourteen variations. Each variation is relatively
   short, and poses a specific technical challenge or musical characteristic to
   explore. Of moderate difficulty, this is a suitable supplement to etudes for
   the intermediate player.
Range: c–b♭^{2}
Duration: 8:00

Raum, Elizabeth (1945–) Canada, born in the United States

Idiom for Solo Horn (1982)
Canadian Music Centre, 1982

Written for Philip Meyers. Based on a galloping $\frac{9}{8}$ theme, with contrasting sections of lyrical writing. Written in a contemporary tonal style.

Range: F–b♭²

Duration: 6:00

Raum, Erika (1972–) Canada

Confessions of St. Augustine

Warwick, 2000

Commissioned by Jane Aspnes for premiere on December 29, 2000, at the "Donne in Musica" concert series in Rome for the Jubilaeum A.D. 2000. Subtitled "A Tone Poem for Solo Horn in F," this work is a musical realization of the life of St. Augustine, with contrasting sections: Youth and pagan beginnings—The mystical voice of the child in the garden—St. Augustine, bishop of Hippo—The debate at the baths of Sozius. The composer indicates it is "to be played freely much as a fantasy." This is an accessible work, suitable for the college player and above.

Range: f–a♭²

Duration: 6:00

Rausch, Carlos (1924–) Argentina

Fanfarra I for Solo Horn in F (1983) (In collection *Five Compositions for Solo Horn*)

Mobart Music Publications, 1984

For David Sternbach. A rhythmically complex work with quick rhythmic gestures throughout, often on the intervals of fourths and fifths. Written in complex time signatures that alternate every measure, for example, $\frac{6}{16}+\frac{5}{32}$, $\frac{2}{8}$, $\frac{7}{32}$. Wide leaps, changing dynamics and extended techniques explore sound possibilities on the horn, such as flutter tonguing, a "smacking "kiss" sound, and tongue pops.

Range: F–c³

Duration: 4:00

Rechberger, Herman (1947–) Finland, born in Austria

The King's Hunt (1977)

Edition Modern München, 1978

Dedicated to Esa-Pekka Salonen. This is an improvisatory theater piece that uses aleatoric techniques, notated graphically, with the durations of different musical ideas notated in seconds. Full of extended techniques and theatrical moments, such as breathing on the horn then polishing it. This happens several times, the final time it is done sitting on the ground, while singing.

Range: f♯–d³

Duration: 6:00

Reinhardt, Bruno (1929–) Israel, born Romania

Music for Horn Solo
Israeli Music Publications, 1965
    I. Moderato
    II. Recitativo
    III. Tempo di marcia
In three movements, the first two in classical form. The composer calls the first
    movement a "miniature sonatina, condensed to the utmost." The second
    movement is a free recitative, unmeasured, with muted and stopped pas-
    sages, and a few trills. The third movement is a march. There are very sim-
    ilar versions of this work for trumpet and trombone.
Range: e–c^3
Duration: 5:15

Reynolds, Verne (1926–2011) United States
Verne Reynolds was a prominent horn player, teacher, and composer who taught
    and played in a number of places, most notably the Eastman School of Mu-
    sic and the Rochester Philharmonic.

Elegy for Solo French Horn
Belwin-Mills, 1986
This contemplative and expressive work was written for Douglas Hill. It does
    not delve very far into extended techniques and is unmeasured and rhyth-
    mically straightforward. It unfolds slowly, becoming more agitated, with
    several recurring motives. There are wide leaps, some within long and slow
    legato phrases, requiring good control.
Range: d♭–b♭^{2}
Duration: 7:30

48 Etudes for French Horn
G. Schirmer, 1961
A collection of etudes that present a methodical approach for mastering advanced
    technique on the horn. The first twenty-three etudes are pairs, with one fast
    etude and one slow etude; each pair is built on only one interval, from the
    minor second up to the octave. Subsequent etudes focus variously on the
    low register, high register, unmeasured playing, meter changes, multiple
    tonguing, lip trills, and hand stopping. Reynolds states in his preface that
    he hopes that several of the etudes will "contain sufficient intrinsic musical
    merit to warrant their inclusion into the solo horn literature: specifically
    Numbers 3, 6, 8, 10, 12, 16, 18, 30 and 44." James Thatcher has recorded nos.
    3, 6, 8, and 12, and the Northeastern Horn Workshop in 2005 featured per-
    formances of all of the Reynolds etudes.
Range: F–c^3
Duration: 2:00–4:00 (varies)

Richards, Scott (1951–) Switzerland, born in Scotland

Bella Gitana (2008)
Editions Marc Reift, 2008
For Zora Slokar. Short work in traditional harmonic language, reminiscent of an
    eastern European folk melody, suitable for the high school or early-college
    player.
Range: G–c³
Duration: 2:13

Robin, Greg (1976–) United States

Far Beyond the Dissonance
Potenza Music, 2012
For Travis Bennett. The preface explains that this work "continues the compos-
    er's exploration of color and distance in musical composition. With a tight-
    ly-controlled half-step motive that repeats with various color alterations,
    the work aims to represent subtle and not so subtle shifts of the familiar."
    Modern techniques used to achieve these colors include flutter tonguing,
    multiphonics, half-step glissandi, and stopped and muted passages. There
    are a few wide leaps, but the overall range is modest, and the technical de-
    mands suited to a college-level hornist.
Range: c–e²
Duration: 3:30

Robinson, Marty (1969–) United States
Marty Robinson is professor of trumpet and jazz at the University of Wisconsin
    Oshkosh.

Les Parcs de Paris (1999)
RM Williams, 2001
    I. Jardin du Luxembourg
    II. Jardin du Ranelagh
    III. Place des Vosges
    IV. Jardin des Tuileries
    V. Parc de Bagatelle
    VI. Parc du Champs de mars
    VII. Parc de Monceau
Eight miniatures conceived as "postcards from Paris," each based on a different
    park and reflecting Parisians' interactions with their green space, as well
    as the composer's own experience. Elegant, whimsical, stately, romantic,
    these are written in an expressive and contemporary harmonic language.
    Pitch bending, flutter tonguing, and stopped writing are used expressively,
    but these do not dominate the music. Wide leaps and some venturing above
    the staff, but overall, this is an accessible work, suitable for the advanced
    college player through professional.
Range: c–b²
Duration: 6:15

Roddie, Matthew (1974–) United Kingdom (Scotland)

Close-up

University of York Music Press, 2004

After an opening call that quotes Rimsky-Korsakov's *Scheherezade,* there are a variety of gestures that often move quickly through the range of the horn, with wide leaps and quick chromatic runs. Trills, glissandi, making a "kissing" sound with the mouthpiece while flicking the bell, and pointing the bell in different directions all create a kaleidoscope of sound. Proportional notation and durations measured in seconds.

Range: $D\sharp-c\sharp^3$

Duration: 11:00

Photon Clockwork

Warwick Music, 1999

Opens with three octave leaps that jump from written B to high b^2, then continues with quick groupings of notes, moving through the ranges of the horn. At one point, the soloist slowly rotates 360 degrees while playing.

Range: $F-c^3$

Duration: 3:30

Roger, Denise (1924–2005) France

Trois Pieces pour cor

D. Roger, 1978

      Comme une cadence

      Tres expressif

      Bien rythme

Written in a free contemporary harmonic language, following the traditional three-movement form of fast-slow-fast. The first movement has contrapuntal writing in changing meters, the second is flowing and expressive, and the final movement is quick, with jaunty triplets in changing meters. Appropriate for the college player.

Range: $g\sharp-b\flat^2$

Duration: 6:35

Rosenthal, Irving, United States

Irving Rosenthal played horn in orchestras in the United States, Australia, and South Africa and toured with Stan Kenton's band in the 1950s.

Partita

Western International Music, 1968

Dedicated to Wendell Hoss, this work is in four movements, Prelude—Air—Bouree—Gigue, and is based on these baroque forms. Each movement is in ABA form, and the piece features idiomatic writing for the horn, with some challenging chromatic passages. Suitable for the college player.

Range: $G-b^2$

Duration: 6:00

Rosner, Arnold (1945–2013) United States

A Plaintive Harmony, op. 85, *A Rhapsody for Unaccompanied Horn*
Phoebus Publications, 1995
To Meir Rimon. A flowing work, which alternates sections of quiet legato writing in the low range with declamatory statements. Accessible writing in traditional notation and written in a contemporary harmonic language. Requires flexibility, good endurance, and a solid command of both high and low ranges.
Range: c–c³
Duration: 11:00

Rosolino, Richard

Variations on Amazing Grace for Solo Horn
Hidalgo Music, 1993
In contrasting sections, this is an ornamented and florid realization of this traditional song.
Range: G–b²
Duration: 3:25

Rossignol, Bruno (1958–) France

Philémon, pour cor en fa (2010)
Billaudot, 2012
For Jean-Paul Quennesson. Rossignol has composed other works for horn and piano aimed at the younger hornist. In three short movements: I. Philémon—II. Beaucis—III. Lamentation sur la mort de Philémon. This accessible work contains stopped writing in different ranges, trill effects on the F horn (32nd notes), and expressive glissandi, all notated in straightforward time signatures.
Range: g–a²
Duration: 8:50

Rossini, Gioacchino (1792–1868) Italy; Baumann, Hermann (1934–) Germany

Le Rendez-vous de chasse
McCoy's Horn Library, 1983
Hermann Baumann arranged this from the famous horn quartet by Rossini and used it as an encore. The original is entitled *Grande Fanfare par Rossini* and is for four horns and orchestra. Includes stopped passages and multiphonics. Versions for both valve horn in E♭ and natural horn in E♭ are included.
Range: g–g² for horn in E♭
Duration: 2:00

Roth, Michel (1976–) Switzerland
Professor of composition and music theory and member of the Institute of Music Research at the Hochschule für Musik Basel.

Töne oder Tiere, für Naturhorn Solo (2006)
Tre Media Edition, 2007
The title (translated as *Sounds or Animals*) is derived from a quote from Peter
    Weber's *Silber und Salbader*. This work explores colors of the horn with the
    naturally occurring harmonic series. The hand moves in the bell between
    open and closed notes, there are glissandi, multiphonics, and wild con-
    trasts in dynamics.
Range: A♭–b♭² (written range for natural horn in the chosen key)
Duration: 5:00

Sain, James (1959–) United States
Sain is professor of music at the University of Florida, where he teaches acoustic
and electroacoustic music composition as well as music theory.

Syllogism No. 1 for Solo Horn (1994)
American Composers Edition, 2012; also available from jamespaulsain.com
Sain explains in his preface that this work is a "teleological extrapolation of
    two musical premises . . . though obviously symmetrically related around
    a pivotal interval of a semi-tone, are recontextualized and combined to
    form a logical musical conclusion." Written for Paul Basler, it has wide
    leaps, fast technical passages, quick dynamic changes, multiphonics, half-
    valve glissandi, glissandi up to the highest note possible, and stopped
    writing.
Range: d–c♭²
Duration: 5:00

Saint-Marcoux, Micheline Coulombe (1938–1985) Canada

Composition I pour cor (1981)
Salabert, 1985
Dedicated to Sonia Delaunay. Combines graphic and traditional notation, with
    the duration of some notes indicated in seconds. Contemporary writing
    with fast chromatic passages, repeated patterns on a single pitch, and
    contrasting dynamics. There are interesting aleatoric effects, where the
    performer chooses the order in which to play certain passages. Extended
    techniques abound, with multiphonics, flutter tonguing, trills, and slow
    glissandi effects. A challenging work that extends far into the high range
    of the horn.
Range: d–e³
Duration: ca. 5:20

Salonen, Esa-Pekka (1958–) Finland

Concert Étude for Solo Horn in F (2000)
Chester Music, 2005
Commissioned by the Lieksa Brass Week, Finland, for the Holger Fransman Me-
    morial Competition, 2000. Salonen studied horn with Holger Fransman

while a student at the Sibelius Academy, and this piece is written in his
honor. The composer writes "In this piece I treat the horn as a virtuoso instrument, capable of acrobatics as well as idiomatic melodic expression. In
a way, I wrote the piece for the great horn player I never became." This is a
virtuosic piece full of trills, thrills, and spills, with effects such as alternating
open and stopped notes, multiple tonguing, and multiphonics.

Range: F–d♭³
Duration: 6:00

Sári, József (1935–) Hungary

Novellette (1981)
Editio Musica Budapest, 1983
To John MacDonald. Consists of contrasting sections emphasizing different contemporary effects, including light staccato passages with *sfz* punctuations
that create a line in the foreground, groupings with different accents, upward scooping on patterns of notes. Unmeasured, with clearly indicated
rhythmic notation.

Range: c–b♭²
Duration: 10:21

Scelsi, Giacinto (1905–1988) Italy

Quattro pezzi per corno in fa (1956)
Salabert, 1987
In four movements. This work is an interesting study in sonority, exploring quarter tones and different timbres of closed and semi-closed tones, muted writing and vibrato. The piece is organized into measures, but no time signatures
are included, only metronome markings.

Range: A–b♭²
Duration: 12:00

Schilling, Hans-Ludwig (1927–2012) Germany

Floriani Suite, for Trumpet or Horn Solo (1996)
W.G. Haas, 1996
Written as a solo contest piece for trumpet or horn, particularly suited to the
advanced high school or college player. In five movements of different
character, utilizing traditional idioms such as fanfares, calls, and dot-
ted-eighth-sixteenth motives in a freely altered tonal harmonic language.
One movement is written with a nod to Mahler and another to Bruckner,
the piece being written on the one hundredth anniversary of his death.
Bruckner's early musical training was at St. Florian Monastery, Austria,
from which this piece takes its title.

Range: a–g²
Duration: 13:30

Schlaepfer, Jean-Claude (1961–) Switzerland

Schlaepfer studied piano and composition at the conservatory in Geneva, and later composition with Betsy Jolas in Paris. He currently teaches at the Conservatoire supérieur de musique de Genève and the Conservatoire populaire de Genève.

Instances II (1993)
Editions Marc Reift, 1993
This work was written for the 1993 Concours International d'Exécution Musicale
  de Genève. It explores different colors and effects on the horn, including
  quarter tones, flutter tonguing, blowing air through the horn, stopped
  playing, and trills. Technically challenging, with multiple tonguing in uneven groupings. Large dynamic contrasts and intricate rhythms make this
  a challenging work, suitable for the advanced player.
Range: C–c³
Duration: 5:00

Schnyder, Daniel (1961–) Switzerland

Saxophonist, flutist, and composer Daniel Schnyder has written music in a wide
  variety of styles and moves freely between classical and jazz writing.

le monde minuscule (1995)
Second Floor Music, 1995
  I. la danse du microbe (dance of the microbe)
  II. le petit Americain (the little American)
  III. l'insecte et le pachiderme (the insect and the pachyderm)
  IV. email
  V. poussières de sable sur flacons de neige (sand dust on the snowflakes)
Composed for David Jolley. The first movement illustrates a microbe dancing
  throughout the range of the horn, burrowing with sixteenths and trills in
  the midrange, then jumping into the low range, then the high range. The
  second movement ("Le petit Americain") is relaxed and swinging. In the
  third movement, an insect trills, flutter tongues, and buzzes about to annoy
  the lumbering elephant. "Email" is a postmodern take on the post horn,
  the instrument traditionally used to signal the arrival of the mail coach.
  In notes accompanying his recording of the work on the Arabesque label,
  hornist David Jolley describes the final movement as follows: "Schnyder
  seeks to suggest yet another way in which our world has grown smaller;
  where people and creeds are blown about the globe just like the sands of the
  Sahara that blow northward to colour the winter snows of France." Quite
  a challenge, with wide leaps and quick passages. The range is extensive,
  particularly getting into the bottom of the horn's low range (F and G) on
  very short notice.
Range: F–d³
Duration: 11:30

Schollum, Robert (1913–1987) Austria

Rufe für Horn (Horncalls), op. 81e (1970)
Verlag Doblinger, 1973
Thirteen movements of varying length, all are measured, with occasional stopped
notes but no extended techniques. Many of these are traditional horn "calls"
and intervals in atonal language, much of it brooding and dark sounding.
Not very taxing or difficult, these are suitable for the younger college player
delving into atonal music.
Range: c–a²
Duration: 15:00

Schroeder, Hermann (1904–1984) Germany
Schroeder was a conductor, composer, and music theorist.

Sonate für Horn solo (1971)
Edition Gerig, 1973
The first movement, Allegro changes meter between $\frac{3}{4}$, $\frac{4}{4}$, and $\frac{5}{4}$. The second move-
ment is a flowing Larghetto, and the last movement is a challenging Vivace
in $\frac{6}{8}$.
Range: c–c³
Duration: 5:30

Schultz, Mark (1957–2015) United States
Composer and co-editor of the music publishing company JOMAR Press. Earned
degrees in theory and composition from University of Nebraska Omaha and
University of Texas Austin, where he was professor of composition.

Glowing Embers for Solo Horn (1994)
JOMAR Press, 1994
Commissioned by Kristen Ruby, the title pays homage to her name—a glowing
red gemstone—and also refers to glowing embers in a fire. Marked *flar-
ing, with greatest extremes,* this work is organized around quick rhythmic gestures, often on repeated notes, and fast legato passages. There are
many extended techniques, including flutter tonguing, quickly alternating between stopped and open tones, hand glissandi, half-valve glissandi,
and "air only" gestures. There are detailed explanations of the extended
techniques.
Range: d–b♭²
Duration: 5:00

Podunk Lake for Amplified Solo Horn
JOMAR Press, 1993
To Ellen Campbell, in memory of Neill Sanders. This won an honorable men-
tion in the 1993 International Horn Society Composition Competition.
This piece also has wind chimes, struck occasionally by the hornist, using the right hand. The composer recommends that the horn and chimes
be amplified slightly. Marked *wistful, distant (free and with rubato),* with

expressive extended techniques such as "air only" sounds, vowel sounds, buzz tones, and half-valve glissandi. An extensive section of multiphonics has a singing part that goes beyond being an "effect," and is an actual melodic line. Detailed instructions for extended techniques are included. This work is suitable for the college-level player and above. There are passages that extend above the staff, but most of the challenge lies with coordinating the expressive effects.

Range: e–b^2

Duration: 9:00

Shaw, Lowell (1930–) United States

Just Desserts, Frippery Style

The Hornists' Nest, 1999

Lowell Shaw began writing horn quartets, called "Fripperies," for his students, so they could learn how to play in a swing style. Over the years, he expanded on these with "Bipperies" (two horns), "Tripperies" (three horns), and "Quipperies" (five horns). *Just desserts* is a collection of thirteen studies for solo horn written in the same style. With swinging eighth notes and jazz idioms, these are lighthearted, enjoyable to play, and can be a challenge to work out.

Range: c–a^2

Shchelokov (Schelokov), Vi͡acheslav (1904–1975)

Diptych for Unaccompanied Horn

The Musical Evergreen, 1975

In two movements. The first is in ABA form, with expressive opportunities in a minor theme and a middle section of melismatic sixteenth notes. A bit taxing, staying in the middle-to-upper range, then going into the high range at the climax of the middle section, with no real rest. The second movement is majestic, in $\frac{4}{4}$, with dotted eighth-sixteenth rhythms. This piece would work well as a supplement to etudes.

Range: a–c^3

Duration: 5:50

Sheriff, Noam (1935–) Israel

Invention for Horn (1968)

Israel Music Institute, 1969

Free and expressive contemporary work, wide intervals and melismatic writing are punctuated with contemporary gestures such as glissandi, trills, alternating open and stopped notes, and slow vibrato with the right hand in the bell. Relatively short, with judicious breaks for the hornist, all in a manageable range.

Range: A–a^2

Duration: 4:00

Silver, Sheila (1946–) United States

Dynamis (1978)

MMB Music, ca. 1990

Written for David Hoose, who premiered the work in 1979 at the American Academy in Rome. In the program notes of the CD entitled *To the Spirit Unconquered* (William Purvis, horn), Sheila Silver explains that *Dynamis* "was written in the summer of 1978 while I was living on the Greek island of Sifnos. I was constantly fascinated by the ever present sound of the wind—sometimes violent, sometimes gentle, but always dramatic. This, along with the awesome sea views, stark landscapes, and the tranquil solitude of the mountain tops, inspired *Dynamis*. The piece is a 'windscape' of warring elements; the aggressive with the lyrical, the high with the low, the fast with the slow. The natural harmonic of the 7th, which is slightly flat, is used as a timbral element throughout." This is a dramatic work with sweeping gestures that takes the horn to the far reaches of its range, with large leaps, bending of pitches, and quick virtuosic passages. There is interesting use of flutter tonguing, a "noodling" figure with the valves before notes, tremolo, quarter tones, and moving from stopped to open writing, all clearly notated, with clear explanations in the preface.

Range: $E\flat–d\flat^3$

Duration: 7:32

Sims, Ezra (1928–2015) United States

Ezra Sims is known as a composer of microtonal music.

Tune and Variations, for One or Two French Horns (1982)

Frog Peak Press, 1982

For Tracy Whisonant. The piece includes a set of preliminary exercises on the microtonal aspects of the music, bending notes as they naturally occur on the harmonic series on both the F and B♭ sides of the horn. This short work, in modified rondo form, puts familiar rhythms and phrase structure into microtonal language. It can be played as an unaccompanied work or as a duet for two horns. An interesting piece for exploring the mechanics and sounds of microtonal writing.

Range: $g–c^3$

Duration: 2:40

Sitsky, Larry (1934–) Australia

Composer, pianist, and musicologist, taught at Queensland Conservatorium, University of Queensland and the Canberra School of Music.

Mertzazil, for Solo Horn (1984)

Seesaw Music, 1987

This work is in four movements. The opening, marked Cerimonioso, is based on a fanfare motive that centers around and continually returns to d^2. The second movement, Allegretto, scherzando, is quite short and reminiscent of a sea shanty with its dotted triplet figures, with much of it in the middle to low range. The third movement, Quasi fantasia, weaves quick runs into its legato line, making this movement sound wistful and contemplative. The final movement is entirely muted, working a plain-chant motive into contrasting octaves. This is an accessible work, very well paced, with each movement allowing the performer a great deal of freedom in phrasing and expression.

Range: F–c♭²
Duration: 10:00

Slavický, Klement (1910–1999) Czech Republic

Musica per corno solo (1988)
Hofmeister, 1992
In three movements: Prologo drammatico—Intermezzo lirico—Finale di bravura. An atonal work, unmeasured, with unfolding motives that develop freely. The two outer movements are in ternary form, the middle movement is modified ternary. Extended techniques include multiphonics, trills, and stopped horn.
Range: g♭–b♭²
Duration: 14:00

Slavický, Milan (1947–2009) Czech Republic

Tre pezzi per corno solo (1996)
Editions BIM, 1996
This work was written for the 1997 Prague Spring International Music Competition and is made up of three short movements: Echo—Canto—Danza. The first movement resembles a fanfare with recurring calls based on a perfect fourth and tritone. There is a very brief, slow, and quiet section before the double- and triple-*forte* ending. The second movement, marked Tranquillo, is full of slow legato playing. The final movement is a dance with triplets. Large leaps, a few stopped notes, muted sections, glissandi, and trills are all present. The piece is unmeasured, but with traditional rhythmic notation.
Range: B♭–c³
Duration: 10:00

Sleeper, Thomas (1956–) United States

Seven Deadly Dwarfs (1987)
Uroboros Music, available from the composer at www.sleepermusic.com
The composer notes that "from my improvisatory work in the 70's with the group 'fermata' in Austin, I became very interested in distilled music gestures and extremely short structures . . . *Seven Deadly Dwarfs* are a set of 7 very short pieces for solo horn written for Margaret Smythe and premiered in Boston in 1987. Each one is based on the coupling of a deadly sin (lust, gluttony, avarice, sloth, anger, envy and pride) with one of Snow White's dwarfs. (Grumpy with Anger . . . etc)" (email exchange with the composer and Linda Dempf, November 24, 2014). In seven movements: I. Andante—

II. Vivace—III. Largo—IV.—V. Waltz—VI. Feroce—VII. Allegro. Much of this work is in the lower and middle ranges of the horn. Written in changing meters, there are a few stopped notes and trills. Requires bass trombone straight mute.

Range: F–b♭²

Duration: 7:00

Snedeker, Jeffrey (1958–) United States

Jeff Snedeker is professor of horn at Central Washington University. Horn soloist, chamber musician, orchestra musician, natural hornist, writer, composer/arranger, and contributor to the horn community with service to professional organizations and their journals.

Goodbye to a Friend, Natural Horn Solo (1997)

Birdalone Music, 1997

The composer writes that this work was "not conceived to be as emotionally intense as an elegy, [but] it has a similar progression of emotions and can certainly be interpreted in that way." It is written for natural horn pitched in E or E♭, but can also be performed on the valve horn with some notes stopped or muted. The opening is free and unmetered with plaintive calls that make expressive use of the horn's stopped colors. The middle section, in ⅜, is a gentle and rolling dotted-eighth figure that expands on the opening idea, and the final section returns to the opening calls of the beginning.

Range: written G–a♭² (for horn in E or E♭)

Duration: 4:30

Suite for Unaccompanied Horn (1995)

JOMAR Press

In four short movements that can be performed individually or as a suite: Ranier fanfare—Chorale—Waltz—Blues. In addition to being fun, these serve, according to the composer, as "musical excuses to work on certain technical problems and extended techniques such as multiple tonguing, multiphonics, whole tone scales and arpeggios, and jazz articulation." A thorough introduction explains the composer's inspiration for each movement.

Range: F–a♯²

Duration: 12:00

Two Solo Etudes for Natural Horn (1997)

Birdalone Music, 1997

These two etudes are arrangements of famous works. The first, "Tchaiked out," is based on the famous horn solo from Tchaikovsky's Symphony no. 5, written for natural horn in D. The second etude, "Habanera," is for natural horn in F, E, or E♭ and begins with the famous habanera from the opera *Carmen,* then moves into the familiar habanera of Cuban popular music. Valve horn players will be familiar with these works, so they provide a good opportunity for students to transfer familiar music to the natural horn.

Range: B♭–a² (written range for natural horn in the chosen key)

Duration: ca. 6:00

Solomons, David W. (1953–) United Kingdom

Klezhorn
Musik Fabrik, 2011
Written for Delphine Gauthier-Guiche. The composer writes that this is a "se-
    quence of melodies with the feel of a European-Jewish mix, incorporat-
    ing the typical augmented second for the hint of Eastern promise." In four
    short movements: Hora-esque—Jericho—Schlof, schlof—Rabbi O'Shaugh-
    nessy's jig. Several sections are in the low range, with quick leaps from low
    range up to the midrange.
Range: B♭–g^2
Duration: 6:30

Otto ottimo
Musik Fabrik, 2011
Written for Delphine Gauthier-Guiche. This is a theatre piece, with the soloist
    speaking, acting, playing, and using props (such as an Italian dictionary,
    a glass of liquid, and pictures of composers). All of the spoken words are
    related in sound to "octatonic," and the horn illustrates these words with
    acting and playing snippets of themes by Respighi, Wagner, and Gluck,
    "before finally returning definitively to the octatonic with a final swig of
    gin and tonico." The soloist has a choice between three different endings.
    The horn solo is not too difficult, allowing for coordination of theatrical
    elements.
Range: c–f^2
Duration: 4:00

Songer, Lewis

Le Mime
Koko Enterprises, 1982
In an easygoing $\frac{3}{4}$, this short work features a continuous eighth-note motive
    that repeatedly returns to its tonal center of C. Of medium difficulty, this
    would be a suitable study piece for increasing flexibility, range, and overall
    endurance.
Range: C–c^3
Duration: 5:00

Stacy, William Barney (1944–) United States
Stacy was horn professor at the University of Wyoming for many years.

H*O*R*N (1973)
Ludwig Music Publishing, 1974
Dedicated to William K. Kearns, Stacy's teacher at the University of Colorado. In
    four movements, each of which has a unique pitch center, rhythmic struc-
    ture, and character. Stacy provides detailed program notes and perfor-
    mance instructions. The first movement is light and quick, and a repeated

motive contrasts with various interjections of special effects, including tonguing through the horn without making a tone, sounding a note through a slide that has been removed, and playing a harmonic with a half valve. The second movement is a "klangfarbmelodie," exploring colors and special effects on a third space C. The third movement is very free, leaving choices up to the performer. The score has four columns with four motives each, creating a graph of sixteen motives to choose from. Each motive has a different rhythm and instruction, such as *tonguing out of horn, pitchless noise, sing through horn,* etc. The player then selects which motive to play from each column. The final movement of the work is slow and lyrical, and opens with calls of a perfect fifth. In contrast with the first three movements, it is simply the pure sound of the horn.

Range: c–c^3
Duration: 6:25

Stanhope, Paul (1969–) Australia

Dawn Interlude (1999)
Australian Music Center, available from reedmusic.com
Extracted from the composer's work *Songs for the Shadowland* (for soprano, winds and piano). The composer writes on the Australian Music Centre website that "this piece is in some ways a commentary on Oodgeroo's poem *Dawn Wail for the Dead* but also, in its own way, a personal gesture of sorrow for past wrongs perpetrated against Indigenous Australians. The use of descending glissandi, the use of stopped notes and a 'natural horn' quarter-tone harmonic emphasize the mournful nature of the piece."
Duration: 3:30

Stein, Leon (1910–2002) United States

Sonata for French Horn
American Composers Edition, Composers Facsimile Edition, 1969
    I. Recitative
    II. Canto
    III. Finale
The first movement is in ABA form, with heroic figures characteristic of the horn. The second movement is lyrical, with modal harmonies. The third movement is a quick $\frac{3}{4}$ rondo with a section of changing meters. Contemporary harmonic language, with perfect fourths and sequences. This work is suitable for the college player with solid technique.
Range: f–a^2
Duration: 7:30

Stephenson, James M. (1969–) United States

3 Impromptus
Stephenson Music

These can be played unaccompanied or with piano. Written for Amy Handelman. First composed as unaccompanied works, the composer later added piano. The first impromptu is energetic, in changing meters; the second, lyrical and played with rubato; and the third is similar to the first movement, in a quick tempo in changing meters.
Range: g–c³
Duration: 4:30

Steptoe, Roger (1953–) United Kingdom, resides in France

3 Dances for Solo Horn (2012)
Editions BIM, 2013
Dedicated to Bruno Schneider. In three short movements: I. Ritual—II. Sarabande—III. Gigue. The first movement, "Ritual," features motives that move throughout the ranges of the horn in continuously changing meters. "Sarabande" is lyrical, with opportunities for rubato and changing character. The third movement, "Gigue," in § is rhythmic, featuring horn call motives on open fifths. Contemporary harmonic language, dynamic contrasts, and a few stopped passages; this is an energetic and expressive work requiring good technique and endurance.
Range: c–c³
Duration: 4:00

Stockhausen, Karlheinz (1928–2007) Germany

In Freundschaft (In friendship) (1977)
Stockhausen-Verlag, 1985
Composed for Suzanne Stephens for her birthday. The composer has made versions of this piece to be played on various instruments. Stockhausen describes the structure of the piece as a main "formula" in five sections in the beginning, then the formula enters into three "layers" throughout the piece, a high melody, a low melody, and trills in the middle. Each layer should include physical movements that indicate which layer is being played, such as pointing the instrument to one side, to the other side, and in the middle. Also, "energetic fragments should be played animatedly and markedly, and the quiet fragments motionlessly." There are also specific stage instructions in the score, such as *sway back and forth very lightly* and *empty the horn by rotating it to the right (very stylised)*. Much of the work is free and full of cadenza-like passages, technically challenging, with trills and grace notes made up of wide leaps. An interesting work. Stockhausen also indicates that it should be performed by memory.
Range: B–a²
Duration: 16:42

Stout, Gordon (1952–) United States
Composer and percussionist on the faculty at Ithaca College, specializing in marimba.

Five Movements for Solo French Horn (1976)
Nichols Music, 1992
Written for and dedicated to Martin Hackleman. In five short movements, marked
  Broadly—Evenly, with precision—Agitated and excitedly—Sonorously and
  sustained—Simply and lightly. Wide-ranging and fluid, with a great deal
  of writing in bass clef.
Range: E♭–a^2
Duration: 5:00

Stroud, Richard (1982–) United Kingdom

Fragmenti (2003)
Warwick Music, 2004
In four short movements: Preambulum—Continuum—Cantus—Spectrum. The
  first movement begins slowly, and contrasts phrases on the open harmonic
  series, with phrases played with valves. The second movement is muted,
  with light and rapid groups of four notes that propel the music forward.
  The third movement is a flowing legato in mixed meters. The final movement is declamatory, with wide leaps and dynamic contrasts. Suitable for
  the college player and above.
Range: D–b♭^{2}
Duration: 4:00

Sturzenegger, Christophe (1976–) Switzerland

Râ, dieu solaire, Incantation for Horn in F
Woodbrass Music, 2005
Meaning Râ, Sun God. Written in a contemporary musical language, with chromatic gestures on recurring groups of pitches. The different sections are
  highly varied, and the use of rests and space make this work feel like a
  soliloquy for horn. A few instances of contrasting color are provided with
  multiphonics, stopped and muted notes, trills, and flutter tonguing. This is
  well paced for the soloist.
Range: A–d^3
Duration: ca. 4:30

Sturzenegger, Kurt (1949–) Switzerland
Bass trombonist with the Orchestre de la Suisse Romande and professor of counterpoint and chamber music at the Geneva Conservatory.

Cornicen, Solo Horn in F
Editions Marc Reift, 2002
The composer dedicated this work to his son Christophe Sturzenegger, professional hornist. Seven sections of contrasting melodic ideas, written in a
  contemporary style feature declamatory writing, wide intervals, and two
  sections of quick writing marked Allegro vivace and a middle section of
  Andante misterioso. The piece ends with a return to the opening declamatory material. This is a challenging work, appropriate for the college-level

hornist and above. Includes some stopped writing and playing on the harmonic series.

Range: G–b♭²
Duration: 3:30

Stutschewsky, Joachim (1891–1982) Israel, born in the Ukraine

Kol Koreh for Horn Solo
Israeli Music Publications, 1969
This work is written in a freely chromatic style. The title translates to "A voice is calling," making reference to the biblical "voice in the wilderness." The piece develops the melodic and rhythmic material of the opening bars. In three movements, with contrasting characters within each movement.

Range: a–a²
Duration: ca. 7:00

Tamusuza, Justinian (1951–) Uganda

Okukoowoola kw'ekkondeere (Horn Call) (2006)
International Opus, 2007
Developed from a longer ensemble piece written for horn, string quartet, and maracas, this unaccompanied work was premiered at the 2006 International Horn Symposium in Cape Town, South Africa by hornist Adam Lesnick. It introduces elements of traditional Kigandan music. It is based on the pentatonic scale and uses colorful extended techniques to achieve traditional sounds, such as *eggono* (where the last note of the phrase is raised a quarter tone right before the cutoff), quarter tones, harmonics (played with tuning slides removed), ostinatos, and drumming effects with the mute. This is an accessible work that adds variety to the solo-horn repertoire, suitable for advanced students and professionals alike.

Range: f–f²
Duration: 4:00
See also: Adam Lesnick, "New African Music for Horn," *The Horn Call* 37 (February 2007): 57–59.

Tautenhahn, Gunther (1938–2014) United States, born in Lithuania

The Last Farewell (1975)
Seesaw Music, 1976
Short, flowing cantabile work in $\frac{3}{4}$ that stays in the middle to low range of the horn.

Range: e–f²
Duration: 3:00

Terwilliger, Eric (1954–) United States, resides in Germany

Till Eulenspiegels lustige Streiche, fur Horn solo / frei nach Richard Strauss
C. F. Peters, 1994

A transcription of themes from Richard Strauss' tone poem *Till Eulenspiegels lustige Streiche,* Terwilliger wrote this for himself and has often used it as an encore. Contains multiphonics and has a challenging range, extending up to a high d³.
Range: B–d³
Duration: 2:30

Thompson, Bruce (1937–) United States
Of Unicorns in Curvet
Thompson Edition, 1990
In ABA form and written in a tonal harmonic language. The outer two sections feature a fanfare-like motive based on a triad. A lyrical middle section features a rising theme that builds in intensity.
Range: A–b²
Duration: 5:00

Tisné, Antoine (1932–1998) France
Tisné studied at the Paris Conservatory with Rivier, Milhaud, and Jolivet, and won the Prix de Rome in 1962. *New Grove* states that his "eclectic technique underlies a belief in lyrical and emotional expression: music must respond to human experience and the spiritual dimension in the cosmos." He often collaborated with the poet David Niemann. His works for unaccompanied horn reflect his eclectic compositional language, with large dynamic contrasts, wide-ranging phrases, and explorations of contemporary sonic effects.

A La Fenêtre
International Music Diffusion
Based on a poem by David Niemann and dedicated to André Cazalet. The text of the poem appears throughout the music.
Duration: 11:00

Monodie V pour un espace sacré
Musik Fabrik, 1998
This is among a series of works for solo instruments, and like many of Tisné's compositions, explores sacred and spiritual themes. In six contrasting sections; Prologue—Recit expressif—Animé—Clamé—Attente et appels.
Range: F–b²
Duration: 5:00

Sensation
Billaudot, 1989
After a poem of David Niemann by the same title. The text of the poem appears throughout the music. Includes quarter tones, some graphic notation, and rhythmic durations notated in seconds.
Range: c♯–b²
Duration: 14:00

Turner, Kerry (1960–) United States, resides in Luxembourg

Characters for Solo French Horn (1985)
Phoenix Music Publishers, 1995
The composer set out to write an etude that "would in a short amount of time
  cover the entire spectrum of modern French Horn playing." This was developed into a recital piece made up of "an array of extreme styles and per-
  sonalities, each representing a different aspect of the Horn's multi-person-
  alitied capabilities." Alternatives are presented for more difficult passages.
Range: C–e^3 (ossia F$\sharp$–c^3)
Duration: 5:00

Nine Pieces for Solo Horn (2005–2006)
Kerry Turner, 2006 (pieces also published individually)
Colorful pieces, each illustrating a character, location, or event. Notes in the preface of the score describe each piece in detail.
  1. Phantom shanties (Reflections on Rotterdam Harbor): A "complex tone-
     poem" with six different themes related to the history, depths, or sea
     shanties of Rotterdam Harbor.
  2. La entrada de los caballeros: Based on memories of attending a rodeo in
     San Antonio, echoing fanfares, Mariachi trumpets, and great bravura.
  3. Crossing Union Square: Written with arpeggios that are common to ev-
     ery horn player's warm-up, a musical depiction of a busy and colorful
     park in New York City.
  4. The hunt of the cheetah: A cheetah is "making its slow and concentrated
     approach on a group of springbok [who] suddenly burst into a frenzied
     sprint. The cheetah, a master of speed, explodes into pursuit."
  5. La viuda de Salamanca (The widow of Salamanca): According to the
     composer, "lamenting a lost love."
  6. Caprice: Written as an encore piece to show off both lyrical playing and
     technical virtuosity.
  7. Echoes of Glastonbury: Full of ancient spirits of Arthurian times.
  8. Twelve tone waltz: a "neurotic waltz . . . using a twelve-tone row . . . Cau-
     tion though, as this one may take a few hours' practice."
  9. The testament of Saladin: "has all the sounds one is looking for in a fan-
     tasy impression piece about 'arabic' legends . . . a sort of 'Scheherezade'
     for solo horn."
Range: G–d^3 (c–c^3 if alternative parts are chosen)
Duration: varies, pieces average 2:00

Tutino, Marco (1954–) Italy
Considered a neo-romantic composer, Tutino is known for his operas, where he
often combines traditional operatic conventions with modern elements such as
disco and film music.

The Game is Hard (1988)
Edizioni Suvini Zerboni, 1988

Traditional harmonic language reiterating a motive of repeating g^1 in common time, with some syncopated rhythms. This work is suitable for the intermediate player at the high school or early-college level.

Range: e^1–$f\sharp^2$

Duration: 2:30

Uber, David (1921–2007) United States

Solo Etudes for Horn, op. 420

Hornists' Nest, 2001

Twelve etudes in varying styles; most do not venture into the highest range of the horn. Uber notes that "some of these etudes might be considered suitable for use as unaccompanied solo recital pieces. It is suggested that two or more be performed together, arranged in contrasting tonalities, meters and tempi."

Range: c–c^3

Duration: varies

Valero Castells, Andrés (1973–) Spain

Les Trois roses du cimetiere de Zaro (1996)

International Music Diffusion, 1996

Dedicated to Daniel Bourge. This work takes its name from the final chapter of the novel *Zalacain the Adventurer* by Spanish writer Pio Baroja. In four short movements: 1. La infancia—Martín y Catalina—2. Andanzas y correrías—3. La muerte de Zalacaín—4. Las tres rosas, epitafio. It is in a contemporary harmonic language and style, with contrasting sections of dramatic, sometimes intricate writing; wide leaps; and extended techniques such as flutter tonguing and glissandi. A challenging work, it has been used for competitions

Range: F–b^2

Duration: 7:00

Van den Booren, Jo

See: Booren, Jo van den

Van Rossum, Hans

See: Rossum, Hans van

Vander Woude, Mary

Atonalism for French Horn (1975)

Fema Music Publications, 1975

In nine movements, many in ABA form, written in an atonal style with occasional unmetered sections, but no extended techniques.

Range: a–$b\flat^2$

Duration: 14:00

Varner, Tom (1957–) United States

All Mortal Flesh (1997)

Tom Varner Music, available from tomvarnermusic.com

The composer wrote this piece for David Jolley, in exchange for horn lessons. Virginia Thompson premiered the work in January 2001. It is based on the French seventeenth-century Picardy hymn "Let all mortal flesh keep silence." It is made up of a theme with ten variations, a fantasy, and final theme. In program notes in the score preface, the composer writes that he drew on the vocabulary he has developed over twenty-five years as a jazz hornist, describing it as "this legato, 16th note, highly chromatic yet melodic, sometimes repetitive, at times 12 tone and at times diatonic, 'tenor saxophone grafted to the horn yet still the horn' expressionistic vocabulary."

Range: D–c^3 (ossia F–c^3)

Duration: 12:00–13:00

Vass, George (1957–) United Kingdom

Four Capriccios for Horn Solo (1976)

Basil Ramsey, Banks Music Publications, 1980

    I. Horn call
    II. Capriccio ritmico
    III. Siciliana lamentoso
    IV. Capriccio precipitoso

This is in a series called "Cornucopia," edited by British horn player Ifor James. Each movement is slightly over one minute long and is tuneful with simple motives and melodies. Not taxing at all, suitable for the high school player.

Range: d–b♭^{2}

Duration: 4:30

Vieira, Fátima (1974–) Portugal

in.cantus (2009)

AVA Musical Editions, 2010

Vienne, Bernard de (1957–) France

See: de Vienne, Bernard

Vogel, Roger C. (1947–) United States

Roger Vogel taught composition and music theory at the University of Georgia.

Partita for Horn (1977)

Tritone Press, 1978

For David Pinkow. In five movements: Fanfare—Nocturne—Scherzo—Song—Toccata. Features changing meters and traditional forms, with a few instances of extended techniques of stopped writing and half-step downward glissandi. There are indications that passages that go far into the low range may be played an octave higher.

Range: E–c^3

Duration: 9:00

Voirpy, Alain (1955–) France

Motum II, pour cor en fa

Henry Lemoine, 1983

To André Cazalet. Marked Libre, this unmeasured work uses traditional nota-tion with a few graphic symbols. The opening and closing of this work are a sonic exploration of horn colors and sounds at different dynamics, often leaping between the ranges. The middle section is fast moving, with quick groups of chromatic gestures. The work includes flutter tonguing, quick repeated notes, and stopped writing. There are a few notes at the extreme ranges of the horn and several passages that extend above the staff, but much of the tessitura is in the middle to upper-middle range of the horn.

Range: F–e^3

Duration: 6:00–7:00

Wagemans, Peter-Jan (1952–) Netherlands

Solo for Horn (1991)

Donemus, 1995

New Grove writes that Wageman's music strives to "combine sensitivity, mobil-ity and well thought-out counterpoint with strong emotional expression." This work is in one continuous movement of contrasting sections of dif-ferent characters: Liberamente—Pesante—Impetuoso—Pesante marcato. Features lyrical writing, wide leaps, large dynamic contrasts, and angular writing. Notation is unmeasured, and extended techniques include flutter tonguing, stopped, and half-stopped tones.

Range: B–c^3

Duration: 8:00

Wehage, Paul (1963–) France, born in the United States

Wehage is a saxophonist, composer, and conductor.

Naissances d'argile

Musik Fabrik, 2012

For Delphine Gauthier-Guiche. The title refers to the 2010 book of the same name, conceived by the poet Joëalle Pagès-Pindon and the painter Marie-Pierre Thébaut. The composer notes in the preface that this work "be-gins in the lower register of the instrument, suggesting a smooth, black mass of ink. From this dark texture emerges flashes of brighter colors in the medium and high registers. After a more rapid passage, the darker motif returns to finish the piece in the low register, perhaps to suggest a return to a mass of black ink at the bottom of a page." Slow and calm

sections alternate with rhythmic gestures, developing into the middle
section, marked Allegro vivo, before returning to the calm opening motive. This short work features wide leaps, virtuosic passages, writing in
the low range, flutter tonguing, and trills. Rubato and complete freedom
for the performer offer many opportunities for expression and thoughtful
pacing.
Range: B–c³
Duration: 3:45

Weinhart, Christoph (1958–) Germany
Composer, conductor, organist, and pianist Christoph Weinhart studied composition with Berthold Hummel and electronic music with Klaus Hashagen. He is
lecturer in music at the Hochshule für Musik in Würzburg and the Bayerischen
Theaterakademie in Munich.

Notes perdues (1988)
Verlag Dohr, 2006
The score preface indicates that "Notes perdues" ("lost notes") is a term used
in the performance practice of French baroque music. The piece consists
of four variations on a theme, but the theme is not stated, as if the theme
has been lost. The first variation is five short phrases that end with a repeated note diminuendo, fading away. The second variation is based on
quick eighth notes with a syncopated figure; the third is short declamatory
phrases with fermatas, reminiscent of the diminuendos of the first section.
The fourth variation is a fast and light ⅜. Written in mixed meters, with a
few stopped notes, this would be suitable for a high school or early-college
player.
Range: c–f²
Duration: 2:50

Wellesz, Egon (1885–1974) Austria
Wellesz studied with Schoenberg and had a career as a composer, musicologist,
and teacher in Austria and in England.

Fanfares for Horn Solo, op. 78 (1957)
Rongwen Music, 1958
In two movements: "Horncall on a spring morning" and "Hornpipe." This is
straightforward writing with reasonable technical demands and range,
suitable for the intermediate horn student.
Range: f–g²
Duration: 3:45

Werner, Jean-Jacques (1935–) France

L'appel, pour cor en fa solo (1996)
Éditions Delatour, 2006

For Hervé Moinard. Below the title, Revelations 3:8 is quoted: "J'ai mis devant Toi une porte ouverte, que personne ne peut fermer." Contemporary musical language, this work alternates sections of quasi-recitative with cantabile playing, growing more agitated, then relaxing back into the cantabile style.

Range: c–a²
Duration: 4:50

Widmann, Jörg (1973–) Germany
Composer and clarinetist. From 2009–2011 Widmann was composer-in-residence for the Cleveland Orchestra's Daniel R. Lewis Young Composer Fellow Program.

Air für Horn solo (2005)
Schott, 2006
Written for Bruno Schneider, as a commission from the 54th International Competition ARD. Opens slowly with beautiful echoing horn tones, marked *easy, free, calmly, floating*. There are quarter-tone pitches, uncorrected on the harmonic series in different keys, with clear notation of the partial and which fingering is to be used. Contains abrupt changes in character, with forceful outbursts and a section of marcato, but the music continually returns to the echo motive of the opening. The composer writes in the score preface that "through this microtonal cosmos and the constant fluctuation between open and stopped notes, a natural work on the themes of proximity and distance is created."

Range: B♭–d♭³
Duration: 8:00

Wiggins, Christopher (1956–) United Kingdom

Echoes for Solo Horn, op. 113 (1990)
Emerson Horn Editions, 1994
This work begins slowly and quietly, growing increasingly piu agitato into an animated middle section, then returning to the material of the quiet opening. Wide ranging dynamics and color changes of open and stopped passages give contrast to the varying gestures. A few taxing phrases that remain above the staff, large intervals, and dramatic dynamics make this work a challenge.

Range: G–c³
Duration: 3:00

Soliloquy I, for Solo Horn, op. 94 (1990)
Emerson Horn Editions, 1990
Deliberate sections of ⁴⁄₄ interspersed with active writing and modified recurrence of the opening motive. Slow sections are contemplative with plenty of rests for effect (and for the horn player). Some stopped notes. This is a well-paced work, suitable for college level and above.

Range: e–c³
Duration: 5:30

Wigglesworth, Frank (1918–1996) United States

Sky Song for Solo Horn (1988)
American Composers Edition
Marked *leisurely,* notated in $\frac{3}{4}$, this work begins with upward-flowing lines and
    becomes more agitated with syncopated rhythms and disjunct gestures.
    There are a few stopped notes for color.
Range: A–b²
Duration: 3:30

Wilby, Philip (1949–) United Kingdom

Four Winds
Four stands are set up on stage, the performer moves to different stands through-
    out the piece and turns in different directions while playing at each stand.
    There are also instructions at several points to make a circular motion with
    the bell, "if possible." In four sections of different character: Veloce—Mis-
    terioso—Allegro nervosa—Presto eroico. Extended techniques include flut-
    ter tonguing, multiphonics, and breath sounds.
Range: f–c³
Duration: ca. 3:15

Wilder, Alec (1907–1980) United States

12 Pieces for Solo Horn (1975)
Margun Music, 1975
Although no longer available in print, and only a few libraries own the set, we
    include these because of Alec Wilder's contribution to the solo horn liter-
    ature. For the younger player, these are a good introduction to his music.
    They vary in difficulty, and several are a bit taxing, but a combination of
    two or three pieces on a recital would work well. Harmonically and rhyth-
    mically interesting, with syncopated writing and a few stopped passages,
    several pieces have lyrical writing that is characteristic of the composer's
    style. Syncopations and a few "swing" moments make this interesting with-
    out sounding corny. Very well written for the horn. These work well as horn
    etudes, and will hopefully make their way back into print again.
Range: B♭–c³
Duration: 17:50 for entire set, pieces average 1:30, shortest is 0:50, longest is 2:20

Little Detective Suite No. 1 for Solo Horn
Margun Music, 1980
In six short movements, each under half a minute, with descriptive titles: Lov-
    ingly—Strutting About—Warmly—Strictly—Not slowly, in fact, quite fast
    —Finally. Very nice tunes for the young player.
Range: a–d²
Duration: 2:24

Little Detective Suite No. 2 for Solo Horn
Margun Music, ca. 1990
Six short movements that range in length from forty seconds to over one minute. Moderately easy for the hornist, appropriate for a solid high school player. Wilder's writing is playful and idiomatic, this suite is more chromatic than the other two *Little Detective Suites.*
Range: f–g^2
Duration: 4:00

Little Detective Suite No. 3 for Solo Horn
Margun Music, 1996
Ranging in length from thirty seconds to one minute, these short character pieces are suitable for the middle school or early high school player.
Range: g–f^2
Duration: 3:30

Williams, Edgar Warren (1949–) United States
Composer, music theorist, and conductor Williams studied composition with Iain Hamilton, Wuorinen, Davidovsky, Sollberger, Babbitt, and J. K. Randall. He has taught at Princeton, UC Davis, and College of William and Mary.

Movements, for Horn Solo (1972)
Mobart Music, 1984 (In collection *Five Compositions for Solo Horn*)
Dedicated to Larry Bassman. This work consists of one movement, unmeasured and marked Freely expressive with glissandi, tremolos, stopped horn. Challenging fast passages in short bursts alternate with a recurring legato motive in the low range; many dynamic contrasts throughout. Fermatas provide breaks between sections.
Range: C♯–c^3
Duration: 6:00

Wilson, Dana (1946–) United States

Graham's Crackers, for Solo Horn (2005)
Dana Wilson, 2005
Commissioned by Adam Unsworth with funding from Temple University. "Dedicated to Adam and his son, Graham, who was being born as this piece was." In three movements, which may be performed individually or as a set. The first movement, "Ballad," is full of blues inflections, with pitch bends and half-valve effects. In the second movement, "Swing," (which is an optional movement) the performer can choose to improvise in the jazz style, and chord changes are notated. The third movement, "Samba," features the soloist whispering rhythms as well as playing, and has many color changes through quick open and stopped writing.
Range: G–d♭^{3}
Duration: 8:00 or 11:00 with optional second movement

Wilson, Ian (1964–) Ireland

She Passes . . . Passes . . . Passes by . . . (1991)
Contemporary Music Centre, 1993
A fast triplet motive unifies the quick outer sections of this work and occurs
    through different permutations and ranges, providing a bit of a challenge
    as it goes through the low range. A cantabile middle section has passages
    on natural harmonics, not obvious at first, then an increasing emphasis on
    the "out of tune" eleventh partial (a sharp-sounding f²).
Range: c♯–c³
Duration: ca. 6:00

Wilson, Thomas (1927–2001) United Kingdom (Scotland)

Chanson de geste, for solo horn (1991)
Queensgate Music, 1991
Premiered by Peter Francomb in the Merlin Theatre, Sheffield, July 1991. In four
    contrasting sections, the opening is marked Lento, quasi improvisando,
    poco lontano, and begins with a low theme that returns several times
    throughout the work. The second section, Marziale—Agitato is to be played
    brassy (like a battle), Sixteenth-note figures gather momentum, then grad-
    ually recede into the distance. A moderato section is then followed by a
    return of the opening lento motive.
Range: C–b²
Duration: 11:00

Winteregg, Steven (1952–) United States

Blue Soliloquy (1999)
Pasticcio Music, 1999 (dist.by Manduca Music)
Commissioned by the International Horn Society, and by Richard Chenoweth
    who premiered it on February 7, 1999. Composed in memory of Paul Che-
    noweth. In ABA form, with outer sections that are slow and contempla-
    tive, and a middle section of eighth notes in a fast swing style, in changing
    meters. There are a few jazz effects, judicious pitch bends and shakes. In a
    review of this work in *The Horn Call* (May 2000), Richard Chenoweth says
    it was composed as a tribute to his father, and evokes "an empty stage, after
    a concert, an empty hall, and the horn player sitting on stage playing an
    improvisatory meditative reflection."
Range: A–ab²
Duration: 5:00

Wolschina, Reinhard (1952–) Germany

Präludium für Horn-Solo (1987, rev. 2006)
Hoche, 2007
Composed for the International Horn Competition 1988 in Markneukirchen/
    Vogtland. This is marked Molto vivace and features syncopated lines that

move at an energetic pace. A few sections of cantabile writing and multiphonics marked Calmo provide brief contrast. Notated in a friendly ⁴⁄ throughout, this is an interesting and challenging contemporary work, requiring good long-range endurance.
Range: B–c³
Duration: 4:00–5:00

Woodson, Thomas C. (1954–) United States
Sonata No. 1 for Unaccompanied Horn (1997)
T. Woodson, 1997
In three movements: Intonation—Adagio—Theme and 6 Variations. Written for Karen McGale, doctoral student in horn at Arizona State University. This work was written to add to the canon of contemporary horn literature, yet provide a work that an undergraduate horn student could master and perform on a recital. The piece stays in the mid-range of the horn, making it suitable for a young college player. Harmonic language is modal and not very dissonant.
Range: c–a♭²
Duration: 12:20

Wright, Maurice (1949–) United States
Music for French Horn (1975)
Mobart Music Publishers, 1984 (In collection *Five Compositions for Solo Horn*)
For Larry Bassman. In three movements, the first, entitled "The strongest man," has alternating time signatures and fast passages that leap through different ranges of the horn. The second movement, "The search for knowledge," is a twenty-measure interlude marked cantabile. The third is entitled "The unobtrusive model" and features a dotted-triplet motive throughout with leaps between low and high ranges, notated in changing meters and proportional notation.
Range: C–g²
Duration: 8:00

Yancich, Milan (1921–2007) United States
Yancich was a hornist in the Rochester Philharmonic and taught at the Eastman School of Music.

Suite Royale for Solo Horn
Wind Music Publications, 2003
    Prelude
    Allemande
    Adagio
    Moderato—Allegro—Moderato
    Allegro

In five movements, these are in the style of the Bach unaccompanied cello suites, written for the middle range of the horn, and at an intermediate level of difficulty.
Range: g–a^2
Duration: 8:30

Yasenchak, Michael

Lamentations, for Horn Solo in F
Israel Brass Woodwind Publications, 1983
Modal harmonic language effectively expresses the sorrow of this lamentation. It begins in a slow $\frac{4}{4}$, with a middle piu mosso section in $\frac{3}{4}$ that builds poco a poco furioso to a declamatory *fortissimo* section, then returns to the quiet mood of the opening. Of medium difficulty if lower octave options are taken.
Range: A♭–d♭^{3} (ossia A♭–b♭^{2})
Duration: ca. 6:15

Zarzo Pitarch, Vicente (1938–) Spain
Horn player and teacher, recipient of the International Horn Society Punto Award.

Penta-monólogo, para trompa sola
Piles, 2002
Five pieces of different character, each with contrasting sections. The fifth "monologue" is in memory of Richard Strauss. These are extensive works, requiring good facility, flexibility, and endurance. They range from three to six pages in length, so individual movements could stand on their own in performance. They are also suitable works for study as etude material.
Range: c–c^3
Duration: varies

Zobel, Emely (1964–1996) Germany

Flodigarry, op. 2, *3 Stücke für Horn solo in F* (1994)
Furore Verlag, 1998
In memoriam Gertrude Stein. Commissioned and premiered by Urla Kahl. In three sections. This avant-garde work has multiphonics, glissandi, flutter tonguing, singing into the horn, singing into the mouthpiece, and reciting words. Coordination of these effects is challenging, such as the "clucking" notes interspersed with quick horn writing, however the moderate technical demands and freedom this piece allows makes it accessible and a good entrée into avant-garde writing. Instructions in German accompany the work.
Range: d–b^2
Duration: 8:00

Žuraj, Vito (1979–) Slovenia
Studied composition with Marko Mihevec, Lothar Voigtländer, and Wolfgang Rihm. He has been composer-in-residence with major new music ensembles and workshops in Europe.

Cadenza per corno (2002)
Drustvo slovenskih skladateljev (Society of Slovene Composers), 2010
Premiered by Radovan Vlatkovic, September 26, 2002, at the International Music
    Festival Musical September 2002, Maribdsor.
Duration: 4:30

The French Open (2010)
Drustvo slovenskih skladateljev (Society of Slovene Composers), 2010
First performed June 30, 2010, by Saar Berger, horn, International Ensemble Mod-
    ern Academy Composer's portrait.
Duration: 5:00

2

Music for Horn and Keyboard
Piano, Organ, Harpsichord

INTRODUCTION

The literature for horn and piano represents by far the largest number of works represented in this book. The genre dates back to just before the beginning of the nineteenth century and came about for many different reasons. Some pieces were written as serious chamber music, as in the case of countless sonatas and other works; many were written in the earlier style of the duo, with the horn and piano being equals, as in the Beethoven *Sonata,* op. 17. Others were conceived as salon music or show pieces, which are very much solos with accompaniment. Another large group of horn and piano music is more educational in nature, having often been written as exam pieces, such as the French repertoire for Paris Conservatory exams. Horn teachers have also written graded teaching pieces for their students of all levels. Into the twentieth century, as the valve horn came into its own as a technically capable solo instrument, composers became interested in exploring and furthering the musical and technical possibilities of the horn. Many of these pieces by composers from around the world have helped to establish the horn as a legitimate solo instrument.

Horn and piano music is a collaborative genre; it often provides one of the first experiences that the student has of truly expressing their musical personality and having an equal voice in shaping the performance with another musician. As horn players, this genre follows us through our careers, from earliest student days, through university recitals, and into the professional world in any number of settings. Music for horn and piano is the basis of most solo horn recitals. Composers from every country and from every period of music history since 1800 have contributed to the literature, giving the performer a huge variety of musical styles, many levels of difficulty, and a wide range of expression to choose from.

For the purposes of this section of the book, standard repertoire pieces by major composers have been supplied with lengthy entries and firsthand information obtained from examination of scores, recordings, or the authors' own experiences of having performed, or at least played through the pieces. Other pieces are more obscure, and in some cases music was not available for examination. In these cases, the works are cited with the composer's name, birth and death dates (if known), title, and publisher, but without comment. In the case of very obscure and rare pieces, the decision to include a piece in the list was based on whether the reader would ever be able to obtain the piece, either through purchase from a publisher or distributor, or through libraries or online resources. Many of the standard works remain readily available, while many others of those listed are no longer in print. We have made no effort to determine if individual works were available for purchase at the time of writing, since works go in and out of print regularly.

As with the other sections of this book, we have made no attempt to establish a grading system for individual works, but instead try to give some idea of the difficulties and appropriateness of each work for players of different skill levels through description in the text of the various techniques required, and the challenges that each presents. Teachers, students, and professional horn players will find this list useful in gathering ideas for recital programs and other occasions, and for simply getting to know the wide range of music that has been written for this most popular combination.

MUSIC FOR HORN AND KEYBOARD

Abbott, Alan (1926–) United Kingdom

Alla Caccia for horn in F and piano
Arcadia Music Publishers, 1962
A short single-movement work of moderate difficulty in a light, agile style marked
    Allegro ritmico. The meter throughout most of the piece is $\frac{6}{8}$. Some stopped
    horn. New notation bass clef.
Range: e♭–a♭² (ossia A♭–c³)
Duration: 2:36

Abbott, Clifford (1916–1994) New Zealand

Sonata for Horn and Piano
Australian Music Centre
A five-movement work: Prelude—Andante cantabile—Allegro—Fuoco—Con
    gravita—Coda. Technically straightforward, traditional in its notation, of
    medium difficulty, and accessible for the college-level horn player.
Range: g–a²

Absil, Jean (1893–1974) Belgium

Rhapsodie No. 6 pour Cor et Piano, op. 120
Henry Lemoine, 1964
A single-movement work with several tempo and meter changes ($\frac{6}{8}$, $\frac{9}{8}$, $\frac{3}{4}$). The piece
    requires strength throughout the range and clean, agile articulation. A
    rather difficult work with a wide dynamic range, trills, and a cadenza sec-
    tion that includes stopped horn. New notation bass clef.
Range: d–c³
Duration: 7:00

Adams, Leslie (1932–) United States

"Largo" from *Empire Sonata for Horn and Piano* (1960)
Associated Music Publishers, 1960
A single movement in ¾ meter marked Largo, sostenuto e cantabile. Of moderate
     difficulty with some stopped horn.
Range: f♯–a²
Duration: 6:45

Adler, Samuel (1928–) United States, born in Germany

Sonata for Horn and Piano (1948)
Robert King, 1951
A moderately difficult sonata in four relatively short movements, tonal and pleas-
     ant, that is very well suited to a student recital.
Range: c–b♭²
Duration: 9:30

Agababov, Arkadi (1940–) Russia

Sonata for Horn and Piano (1983)
Soviet Composers Publishers, 1988
Russian horn sonata in a rather atonal style. One continuous movement with
     frequent meter changes and a wide range. After a maestoso/moderato be-
     ginning, the tempo is allegro throughout, with the exception of a lengthy
     unaccompanied cadenza. Old notation bass clef.
Range: d♯–b²

Agrell, Jeffrey (1948–) United States

September Elegy for Natural Horn in E♭ and Piano
Written in four sections:
     I. Prologue: for improvised piano solo on a set of pitches.
     II. Chorale: the natural horn plays a written out and metered melody with
          piano accompaniment.
     III. Reflection: the pianist improvises over a held note in the horn.
     IV. Improvisation: for piano solo on a set on pitches.
Range: c–a♭ for E♭ horn

Agobet, Jean-Louis (1968–) France

Cobalt (2004)
Jobert, 2004
Duration: 5:00

Akimenko, Fedir (1876–1945) Ukraine
Akimenko was a student of Balakirev and Rimsky-Korsakoff.

Melody for Horn in F and Piano
Leeds Music, 1945

A short, lyrical piece marked Andante moderato in $\frac{4}{4}$.
Range: g♯–a^2
Nocturne pour cor en fa avec accompagnement de piano, op. 18
Belaïeff, 1903

Aladov, Nikolaï (1890–1972) Russia

Sinfonia pastoral
The Musical Evergreen, 1975
A short, lyrical Andante cantabile. Very easygoing midrange playing in a melodic
 style.
Range: g–f^2

Albert, Thomas (1949–) United States

Permutations for French Horn and Piano (1967)
Media Press, 1969
A short single movement in contemporary atonal style, of very moderate
 difficulty.
Range: a♭–f♯^{2}

Albright, William (1944–1998) United States

Romance (for Horn and Organ)
Henmar Press Inc., 1987, sole selling agent C. F. Peters
Commissioned by John Holtz and premiered at the Hartt College International
 Festival of Contemporary Organ Music, June 22, 1981. First prize, Interna-
 tional Horn Society Composition Contest, 1982. A very contemporary work
 with difficult intervals and rhythms, stopped and echo effects, and metri-
 cally free sections. A dramatic piece, with a wide range and wide dynamics.
 New notation bass clef.
Range: F–c^3
Duration: 9:00

Alexander, Josef (1907–1990) United States

Sonata for Horn and Piano
General Music Publishing, 1981
    1. Allegro con spirito
    2. Adagio sostenuto
    3. Allegro scherzoso
A three-movement sonata in contemporary style with numerous meter changes
 and requiring a good deal of technique. Techniques include some rather
 difficult stopped horn. Old notation bass clef is used in the first movement,
 and new notation in the third movement.
Range: c–b^2

Alfvén, Hugo (1872–1960) Sweden

Nocturno elegiaco, op. 5
Carl Gehrmans Musikforlag, Stockholm, 1952
For horn and organ or piano. A slow single movement with interesting flowing
    lines, mostly in the lower middle range. Dedicated to Axel Malm.
Range: e–a²

Allers, Hans-Günther (1935–) Germany

Suite for Horn und Klavier, op. 34
Edition *mf,* 1997
    I. Pastorale
    II. Fantasia
    III. Capricio
    IV. Ländler
    V. Rondino
Five movements of moderate difficulty.
Range: d¹–a²

Kleine Suite, op. 36
Edition *mf,* 1989
    1. Präludium
    2. Chaccone
    3. Scherzo ritornello
    4. Echo—Spiel
    5. Humoreske
Five very short and technically easy pieces for the young horn player.
Range: a–f²

Toccatina passionate, op. 48, no. 1 *for horn and organ* (1989)
Edition *mf,* 1991
In one movement. A mostly quiet work that explores the timbres of the horn and
    organ in a counterpoint of flowing triplets. Stopped writing in the horn
    lends color.
Range: B♭–b♭²
Duration: 7:00

Almeida, Antonio Victorino D' (1940–) Portugal

Wiener Sonate, op. 98 *for horn and piano*
AVA Musical Editions
Dedicated to horn player Antonio Costa and actor Fritz Muliar, this piece is an
    homage to the city of Vienna. Written in three movements.
Range: e♭–c³
Duration: ca. 15:00

Casamento à moda antiga (Old Fashioned Wedding), op. 86 *for horn and piano*
AVA Musical Editions
Range: f♯–b²
Duration: ca. 3:30

Altmanis, Alvils (1950–) Latvia

Prelude
Musica Baltica, 2002
A short work in several sections, with a brief cadenza. There are a few changing
    meters between $\frac{3}{4}$ and $\frac{3}{4}$.
Range: b♭–g²

Ambrosius, Hermann (1897–1983) Germany

Sonate für Waldhorn und Klavier
Hofmeister, 1995
An idiomatic romantic work in three traditional movements: Allegro non troppo
    —Andante con moto—Vivace. Good long-range endurance required, as
    there are few rests for the horn. The final movement is a ripping $\frac{6}{8}$, which is
    felt in two, with hemiola figures.
Range: b♭–c³ (ossia c–g♯²)

Ameller, André (1912–1990) France

Belle province, rimouski
Alphonse Leduc, 1973
A single movement in a slow $\frac{6}{8}$ with a simple flowing melody of very moderate
    difficulty for the horn.
Range: c♯¹–f²
Duration: 2:15

Gavotte
Pierre Noël, 1953; International, 1954
One of the short pieces in the collection entitled *Contemporary French Recital
    Pieces*.
Agile, but not too difficult.
Range: c¹–a²

Nocturne pour cor et piano
Editions Combre, 1983
A calm and expressive piece in $\frac{3}{4}$, relatively easy technically.
Range: a–g²

Three Easy Pieces
Hinrichsen, 1960
Three short pieces of very limited technique and range: Prélude—Canzone—
    Rondo.
Duration: 5:30

Texas
Billaudot, 1977
A relatively easy single-movement student piece in two sections, the first slow
    and lyrical, and the second faster and more articulate.
Range: g–d²

Virginie
Billaudot, 1977
A short elementary piece of very limited range.
Range: g–a¹ (ossia g–d²)

Coradieux
Editions Philippo & M. Combre, 1969
A short piece with a few technical and rhythmic difficulties. A part for horn in C
    is included, possibly as a transposition exercise.
Range: f–a²

Corcoricco
Editions Combre, 1983
A short, moderately easy French exam piece for F or E♭ horn.
Range: a–g² (with optional c²)

Amis, Kenneth (1970–) United States, born in Bermuda
Tuba player with the Empire Brass Quintet.

Preludes No. 1–5 (2000)
Amis Musical Circle, 2000
Five movements that are all longer than the title "Prelude" would suggest. Inter-
    esting pieces that require a good bit of technique and a solid high range
    and endurance.
Range: a♯–c³
Duration: 20:30

Amrhein, Karen (1970–) United States

Sonata
Happy Lemon, 1996
Written in two movements entitled "Missing" and "Free."
Duration 4:00

Amy, Gilbert (1936–) France
Composer and conductor, studied at the Paris Conservatory with Milhaud, Messiaen, and Loriod; studied with Boulez at the Darmstadt summer courses.

Mouvement pour cor en fa et piano (2000)
Durand, 2004
A technically demanding work centered around a driving triplet motive, full of
    contemporary techniques and colors for both the horn and piano.
Range: F♯–c³
Duration: 8:00

Ancelin, Pierre (1934–2001) France

Bercuse pour le cor de champs, pièce récréative pour cor et piano
Billaudot, 1985
Duration: 1:45

Bercuse pour le cor de villes
Billaudot, 1985
Appears in the publisher's collection of contemporary works for horn, "Panorama Cor 2."
Duration: 1:45

Andersen, Arthur Olaf (1880–1958) United States
Nocturne for Horn and Piano
Carl Fischer, 1956
A simple, short melodic piece in a Moderato tempo for the student who has gained control of the range up to the top of the staff.
Range: c^1–g^2

Anisimov, Boris Ivanovich (1907–1997) Russia
Poema for Horn and Piano
Musgiz Leningrad, 1961
A single movement in a romantic Russian style, reminiscent of the Gliere pieces op. 35, but a bit longer. Many flowing melodic lines and a few articulate technical passages, but not too difficult for a good high school horn player. Includes a short cadenza near the end of the piece and some stopped horn.
Range: c^1–$a\flat^2$

Appleford, Michael
Three Easy Pieces
Editions Marc Reift, 1999
Three short very elementary pieces.
Range: c^1–a^1

Aprahamian, Maia (1935–2011) United States
Batter My Heart, Three Person'd God, for French Horn and Organ,
Based on the Sonnet by John Donne (1982)
Unpublished manuscript, 1982, available from Barry Tuckwell Collection, University of Melbourne
Written for Barry Tuckwell and John Fenstermacher.

Archer, Violet (1913–2000) Canada
Sonata for Horn and Piano (1965)
Berandol Music Limited, 1980
    I. Andante energico
    II. Interlude
    III. Arioso
This contemporary tonal sonata was commissioned by the Canada Council and premiered in 1965. Each of the three movements is of rather moderate length, and not overly difficult technically, making it quite accessible even for the advanced student who is ready for a serious modern piece.
Range: d–g^2

Arends, Michael (1939–) Germany

Fantasie für Horn und Klavier
Keturi Musikverlag, 2005
Short work in four sections: Vivace—Adagio—Langsamer walzer—Vivace. Of medium difficulty, suitable for the intermediate student player, with flexibility required for fast slurs in vivace, and endurance for phrases to high $b\flat^2$ in the Adagio section.
Range: c^1–$b\flat^2$

Armstrong, John Barton (1923–2010) United Kingdom

A Celtic Chase (A Horn Rhapsody), op. 35 (1962)
Fand Music Press, 1962
An energetic rondo in $\frac{6}{8}$, written at a level that is accessible to the advancing high school horn player.

Arnn, John (1939–) United States

Fantasia for Horn and Piano
Fema Music Publications, 1973
A relatively short lyrical piece with a more active middle section. Straightforward technically.
Range: b–a^2
Duration: 5:08

Arrieu, Claude (1903–1990) France

Le Coeur volant
Billaudot, 1976
Though this short single movement in a Lento tempo is listed as a student piece, it requires some skill in the upper range, and the ability to play clean fast repeated notes.
Range: f^1–$b\flat^2$

Atkinson, Condit (1928–2009) United States

Moods for Horn
Schmitt Music Center, 1973
A contemplative lyrical piece with flowing melodies.
Range: e^1–g^2

Aubain, Jean (1928–) France

Sonatines pour cor et piano
Editions Choudens, 1971
Written for Lucien Thévet, this Sonatine consists of four movements:
   I. Allegro moderato
   II. Vivo

III. Canabile
IV. Presto giocoso
Quite technical and taxing, composed in a mid-twentieth-century French style.
Range: B♭–b♭²

Aubin, Tony (1907–1981) France

Si Vis Pacem. . . pour cor en fa et piano
Henry Lemoine, 1979
A single-movement work of moderate difficulty. New notation bass clef.
Range e♭–b²

Auclert, Pierre (1905–1975) France

Lied pour cor et piano
Alphonse Leduc, 1952
A short, easy lyrical piece.
Range: e–g²

Avalon, Robert (1955–2004) United States

Zeal (2003)
Southern Music, 2006
Dedicated to Thomas Bacon. Light and rhythmic, in ABA form. The opening is
    impressionistic, followed by a contemplative middle section with wide leaps
    and sustained writing, some of it muted. Requires agility, with its quick
    legato phrases and sustained notes above the staff.
Range: c–b♯²
Duration: 6:40

Badings, Henk (1907–1987) Netherlands

Canzone, per corno e organo
Donemus, 1967
Duration: 5:00

Bach, Jan (1937–) United States

NIU MIUSIC (Still Life with Castle and Lagoon) (1999)
Distributed by Cimarron Music Press, 2012
Written for hornist Debra Ann Fialek. Quite a technically challenging piece,
    written in several connected sections and described by the composer as
    a modified sonatina form. Includes a wide variety of horn techniques, in-
    cluding long lyrical passages; fast articulation; challenging, agile intervals;
    and a wide range of dynamics. Based in part on the Northern Illinois Uni-
    versity (NIU) Alma Mater.
Range: A–b²
Duration: ca. 7:00

Bachelet, Alfred (1864–1944) France

Dans la Montagne, ballade pour cor et piano (1907)
Alphonse Leduc, 1959
A rather free single-movement work in several sections in various meters and tempos. Plenty of rhythmic challenges, stopped and muted effects, and cadenza-like sections.
Range: c–c³

Bacon, Ernst (1898–1990) United States

Song after the Rain (A Little Rhapsody in the Transylvanian Mode)
Rongwen, 1959
Written for Wendell Hoss, this short, freely composed piece in a slow ⅝ is very improvisatory in character. New notation bass clef.
Range: c–a♭²
Duration: 2:20

Bakaleinikoff, Vladimir (1885–1953) United States, born in Russia
The following are two short easy pieces of very limited range and technique for the young horn player.

Canzona
Belwin, 1939
An easy song-like piece in ¾.
Range: d¹–e²

Cavatina
Belwin, 1939
Another simple student piece in ¾.
Range: e¹–e²

Baker, Ernest (1912–1992) United Kingdom

Cantilena for Horn and Piano (or Cello, Oboe, Clarinet)
Chester, 1969
Short, easy, lyrical piece in ¾, marked Tranquillamente.
Range: b–f²

Baker, Michael Conway (1937–) Canada, born in the United States

Cantilena for French Horn and Piano, op. 46 (1979)
Harmuse, 1980; Canadian Music Centre 1980; Evocation, 1998
Short, slow piece that includes stopped horn, and extremes of dynamics and range. Written for Martin Hackelman.
Duration: 5:00

Remembrances for Horn and Piano
Evocation Publishing, 2005, available from Canadian Music Centre
A short, contemplative piece.
Range: g–b♭²
Duration: 7:00

Bakki, József (1940–1981) Hungary

Sonatina per corno e piano
Editio Musica Budapest, 1975
A very contemporary piece written in modern graphic notation in events of approximate duration in seconds. The notes written in the horn part are not excessive in range, and the performers are free to interpret them as they choose in terms of tempo and duration. Both parts are printed on a single score, with no separate horn part, making it necessary to have two copies of the full score for performance.
Range: c–a^2
Duration 7:30

Baksa, Robert (1938–) United States

Horn Sonata (second version 2002)
Composers Library editions (Theodore Presser), 2003
A very playable and well-written sonata in contemporary tonal style. The three movements are marked: 1. Boldly—2. Very calm—3. Quite fast. Technically very accessible, and not overly taxing, this would be a good student recital piece.
Range: g–a^2
Duration: 14:00

Balay, Guillaume (1871–1943) France

Chanson du forestier
Evette et Schaeffer, Alphonse Leduc, 1925
An early twentieth-century French character piece. Composed in several contrasting sections. Rather technical but not overly difficult. Includes short cadenzas and trills.
Range: g–a^2

Baldwin, Daniel (1978–) United States

Appalachian Suite (2006)
Imagine Music
Written for Jeffrey Powers, this piece is composed in four programmatic movements based on the Strauss *Alpine Symphony*: Maggie Valley snowfall—Braving the storm—Oceans of starlight—At the summit.

Baratto, Paolo (1926–2008) Switzerland

Andantino Romantico (1983)
Editions BIM, 1993
A very short romantic piece for horn and organ in an Allegretto tempo dedicated to Gerhard Görmer.
Duration 1:45

Barbier, René (1890–1981) Belgium
Composer and conductor, winner of the Belgian Prix de Rome in 1920.

Sonate pour cor en fa et piano, op. 12 (1916)
CeBeDeM, 1971
In three traditional movements, shimmering and colorful harmonies in the piano underlay the often lyrical writing of the horn. Well paced, but with passages that move into the high range, requiring long-range endurance.
Range: e♭–c³
Duration: 20:00

Barboteu, Georges (1926–2006) France, born in Algeria
Médium
Editions Choudens, 1988
A moderately slow, flowing piece written in memory of François Brichard. Lyrical, but with many fast-moving notes and agile range changes. Includes flutter tongue, stopped horn, and trills.
Range: E–a♯²

Pièce pour Quintin
Editions Chouden, 1983
Dedicated to Michel Cantin, this is a very difficult single-movement contemporary piece that uses many stopped effects, trills, and wide vibrato and features an extended unaccompanied cadenza at the beginning in which the pianist holds down the pedal so that the horn notes ring in the open piano. Full of difficult notes and rhythms but allowing much freedom to the performers.

Saisons
Editions Choudens, 1983
Four pieces depicting each of the seasons, ending with a "Danse." "Automne" is written in the character of stylized hunting horn calls, finishing with an andante lyrical melody. "Hiver" is a simple Andante with flowing eighth notes. "Printemps," which begins and ends with open and stopped horn calls, is more involved technically. "Ete" is in an Andante cantabile tempo and is rhythmically free and flowing, featuring stopped and flutter tongued notes. The concluding "Danse" is truly technically difficult, covering a wide range with fast articulated notes and using many of the above mentioned effects.
Range: c♯–a²

Barnes, Arthur P. (1930–) United States
For Leah
Emerson Horn Editions, 2010
Two movements, ¾ and ⁶⁄₈, written for the senior recital of the composer's granddaughter, Leah Wolfeld. Interesting music, idiomatically written, technically of medium difficulty.
Range: g–c³ (with ossia to a²)

Barnett, Carol E. (1949–) United States

Sonata (1973)
Thompson Edition, 1984
    I. Andante
    II. Espressivo
    III. Grazioso
A three-movement sonata in contemporary tonal style. The first movement is
    written in a pleasant melodic style, the second is slow and contemplative,
    and the finale features an agile style in mixed meters.
Duration 8:30

Baron, Maurice (1899–1964) Born in France, resided in the United States

Nirvana, Meditation for Trombone (or Horn) and Piano
M. Baron, 1962
To Davis Shuman. Flowing, lyrical work in $\frac{3}{4}$, with changing tempos and oppor-
    tunities for rubato.
Range: $c–f^2$ (ossia $f–f^2$)

Barraine, Elsa (1910–1999) France

Crépuscules for Horn (or Saxophone) & Piano
Gras, 1936; Alphonse Leduc
A short, flowing, lyrical piece in French early twentieth-century style.
Range: $a–g^2$

Fanfare
Gras, 1936; Alphonse Leduc
Written for Jean Devémy. A short movement in $\frac{6}{8}$ in the style of a fanfare. Empha-
    sizes the upper range of the horn.
Range: $B–b^2$

Barrows, John R. (1913–1974) United States
These two short, simple melodic pieces by horn player John Barrows, are part of
the Hal Leonard Elementary Solo Series, and are written in a very limited range
for the beginning horn student.

Autumn Reverie
Hal Leonard, 1966

Moon Shadows
Hal Leonard, 1966

Bartoš, Jan Zdeněk (1908–1981) Czech Republic

Adagio elegiaco und Rondo
Schott, 1979
Written in two movements, the Adagio is a lyrical $\frac{4}{4}$, and the Rondo (Allegro
    molto) is in $\frac{3}{4}$ with some stopped horn. Both are of very moderate difficulty
    and range.
Range: $b–g\sharp^2$

Basler, Paul (1963–) United States

Canciones for Horn and Piano

RM Williams, 2004

Canciones was commissioned by and written for Myrna Meeroff. The work is a
    set of three lyrical, connected "songs."

Range: b–a²

Duration: 7:00

Diversions for Horn and Piano (2012)

RM Williams, 2012

Written for and dedicated to James Naigus. In four movements: Prologue (bells)—
    Waltz—Nocturne—Presto. Written in a very comfortable style, pleasant
    and interesting for both listener and player, this piece, as with much of
    Basler's music, takes advantage of the lyrical and ethereal qualities of the
    horn, but also doesn't neglect its agile and energetic side. Well written, not
    overly taxing, but not without technical challenges.

Range: e–b²

Duration: 10:16

Divertimento

RM Williams, 1998

Dedicated to Barry Benjamin. In five movements, the piece was written in Nairobi,
    Kenya, and the composer indicates that it "combines elements of American
    'classical' music, jazz, and Kenyan folk elements."

Folk Songs

RM Williams

Dedicated to various students in Basler's horn studio as well as to Michelle Steble-
    ton. The playing level ranges from simple to moderately advanced.
    Alegría (Puerto Rico)
    Funiculì, funiculà (Italy)
    Round dance (Native American—Kiowa)
    Hills of Arirang (Korea)
    Nihavend Şarki (Turkey)
    The drunken sailor (British sea shanty)
    Shenandoah (United States of America)

Folk Songs from the British Isles (2004)

Southern Music, 2006
    1. Sao Gan (Wales)
    2. Admiral Benbow (England)
    3. The minstrel boy (Ireland)
    4. The Campbells are coming (Scotland)

Duration: 11:00

Three Hymn Tune Settings, (1988–1989)

Southern Music, 1997
    1. Abide with me
    2. Amazing grace
    3. Shall we gather at the river

Written in a lyrical style, and of moderate difficulty.
Range: b–g²

Three Songs of Praise (2008)
RM Williams, 2008
Written for Charles "Skip" Snead, this piece is a "sequel" to the composer's *Three Hymn Tune Settings*.

Reflections
RM Williams
Dedicated to Manuel de Jesús Germán. In five descriptive movements, this piece can be considered the "sequel" to Basler's *Canciones for Horn and Piano* and *Lacrymosa for Two Horns and Piano*.

Serenade
RM Williams
Dedicated to Patrick Smith. Described as follows by the composer: "While the surface appears light and breezy (and it is to a certain extent), the piece contains deep spiritual and personal messages—of completion and anticipation."

Bassett, Leslie (1923–) United States

Sonata for Horn and Piano
Edwin H. Morris, 1954; Robert King, 1954
  I. Allegro moderato
  II. Andante cantabile
  III. Allegro, ma non troppo
A rather difficult work, requiring a wide range and good endurance, with some wide leaps and difficult intervals.
Range: B–b²

Bax, Arnold (1883–1953) United Kingdom

Sonata for Piano and Horn (1901)
Edition db, 2013
Dedicated to G. Allaby Aldar, Esq. This piece, written in a single movement marked Allegro molto moderato, is easygoing, light, and active for both instruments throughout.
Range: c–g²

Beck, Conrad (1901–1989) Switzerland

Intermezzo pour cor et piano (piece de concours)
Heugel, 1948
Rather short competition piece with a wide range, including trills, stopped horn in the low range, and rhythmic and articulation challenges. Old notation bass clef.
Range: F♯–c³

Beckel, James (1948–) United States

The Glass Bead Game (1997)
Hal Leonard, 1997
This is the horn and piano version by the composer.
See: Horn and ensemble

Beckler, Stanworth R. (1923–) United States

Little Sonata for Horn and Piano (1961)
Seesaw Music, 1981
From a set entitled *Seven Little Wind Sonatas,* op. 49; this piece, fifth in the set, was written for Rod Swearengin. The three movements of this short contemporary sonata are marked: March, Dirge, and Gigue. The horn writing is interesting, but not terribly difficult, with a few stopped and flutter-tongued notes.
Range: d–a♯²

Beethoven, Ludwig von (1770–1827) Germany

Sonata for Horn and Piano, op. 17 (1800)
Early Editions: Mollo, 1801; Simrock, 1801; André, 1805
Modern Editions: Breitkopf & Härtel; Peters; Schott; Carl Fisher; Schirmer; Henle; International; and others
   I. Allegro moderato
   II. Poco adagio, quasi andante
   III. Rondo, Allegro moderato
Composed in 1800 and dedicated to Josephine (Josepha) Freifrau von Braun. Written for the famous natural horn virtuoso Giovanni Punto, with whom Beethoven performed the piece in a concert on April 18, 1800, this sonata is one of the standards of the repertoire and has been published in numerous editions and recorded many times. The piece is written in the classical style of instrumental and keyboard sonatas, in which the horn and piano are equal partners. The decidedly low-horn style of writing covers a wide range, and is stylistically characteristic of low-horn writing of the period. Wide leaps, accompanying figures, trills, fast arpeggios, and pedal notes make this a challenging piece for players of all levels. Written for natural horn in F.
Range: G–g²
Duration: 12:30

Bellonci, Camillo (1781–?), Leidesdorf, Maximilian Joseph (1787–1840) Austria

Sonata pour pianoforte et cor, op. 164
Hans Pizka Edition, 1982; Robert Ostermeyer, 2011
A collaboration between a horn player, Bellonci, and pianist M. J. Leidesdorf. A substantial sonata of three movements in late classical style. A rather virtuosic and agile cor-basse piece written for natural horn in E♭.
Range: B♭–a♭² (c–b♭² for horn in E♭)

Benjamin, Thomas (1940–) United States

Horn!
Southern Music 1997
A rather free single-movement work with numerous changes of tempo, meter, and
    character. Special techniques include stopped horn, muted writing, and glis-
    sandi. Commissioned by and dedicated to Peter Landgren and the Interna-
    tional Horn Society.
Range: c♯–a²

Bennett, David D. (1892–1990) United States

Hornascope
Southern Music, 1959
Originally for horn and piano or horn and band, this is a good student piece for
    the advancing school-band horn player.
Range: g–g²
See: Horn and ensemble

Bennett, Richard Rodney (1936–2012) United Kingdom

Romances for Horn and Piano (1985)
Novello, 1990
Written for Barry Tuckwell.
Duration: 12:00

Sonata for Horn and Piano (1978)
Novello, 1990
An extremely difficult contemporary piece, written for Barry Tuckwell in 1978. A
    single-movement work in several sections played without a break. Sections
    include: Declamato—Molto vivo—Lento e lirico—Molto vivo—Lento e rit-
    mico—Con brio—Cadenza—Declamato. Features frequent difficult meter
    changes, difficult intervals and leaps, flutter tonguing, muted and stopped
    passages, and fast articulation in all ranges.
Range: A–c³
Duration: 13:00

Benson, Warren (1924–2005) United States

Soliloquy for Horn and Piano
Piedmont, 1959, distributed by Edward B. Marks Music, Hal Leonard
Very easy, short, lyrical piece for the beginner who can play to the top of the
    staff.
Range: a♭–f²

Bentzon, Niels Viggo (1919–2000) Denmark

Sonata, op. 47
Hansen, 1950

A difficult work in three movements: I. Moderato ma non troppo—II. Quasi menuetto, Allegretto—III. Rondo: Allegro ma non troppo. The horn part is quite
persistent and requires excellent endurance.
Range: F–c³
Duration: 16:00

Berg, Stephen A. (1945–) United States/Germany

Stufen für Horn und Klavier
Noetzel, 1993
A short contemporary piece intended to be an early recital piece for the young
hornist with limited range. Technically fairly easy.
Range: b♭–f²

Berghmans, José (1921–1992) France

"Les lutteurs" from *Tableaux Forains*
Alphonse Leduc, 1958
The first of seven movements, each written for a different solo instrument with
chamber orchestra or piano accompaniment, depicting scenes from a traveling circus. The title of this movement, for solo horn, means "The wres-
tlers." Moderately difficult technically, but in a fast tempo.
Range: e–a♭²

Bergonzi, Benedetto (1790–1840) Italy
Musician and wind-instrument maker, invented a type of early valve horn in
1824.

*Variationen über O mattutini albori aus der Oper La donna del lago
von Gioachino Rossini*
Doblinger, 2002
This is a free-form theme and variations. It begins with a fairly extensive Introduction in an Allegro maestoso tempo, followed by a theme and six
variations, ending with a Polacca. A challenging work, due to many fast
passages in E horn.
Range: B–a♯² (c–b² for horn in E) An F horn part is also supplied with this edition.

Bernaud, Alain (1932–) France

Scherzo pour cor et piano
Editions Max Eschig, 1975
A single movement in § with quite a number of technical and rhythmic diffi-
culties and an emphasis on the high range. Techniques include stopped
and echo horn, trills, and flutter tongue. A difficult showpiece written for
Georges Barboteu.
Range: c–c³

Bernstein, Leonard (1918–1990) United States

Elegy for Mippy I
G. Schirmer, 1950
Largo in $\frac{4}{4}$. Written in memory of the composer's brother's dog, Mippy, this short, expressive piece covers a wide range, and range of dynamics. Includes stopped horn.
Range: a$\sharp$–c^3

Berthelot, René (1903–1999) France

Frère Jacques
Alphonse Leduc, 1964
Theme and five variations on "Frère Jacques." A good recital encore of very moderate difficulty. Includes stopped horn.
Range: a–a^2

Variations brèves sur un chant scout
Alphonse Leduc, 1964
As with the previous piece, this is a theme and variations, this time on "Auld Lang Syne," and, as the title implies, the melody is used as a closing to Boy Scout jamborees and other functions around the world. Relatively easy and within a limited range.
Range: c–g^2

Bertran, Moisès (1967–) Spain

Improvisação (1993, rev. 2008)
CLIVIS Publications, 2010
A fairly short single movement written for Brazilian hornist Fernando de Morais. Composed in an improvisatory style, with a short introduction followed by the main lyrical theme which is then gradually developed. The piece stays in the extreme upper register much of the time, requiring the player to play d^3 several times.
Range: g–d^3

Beversdorf, Thomas (1924–1981) United States

Sonata (1945)
Andraud, 1949; Southern Music, 1958
    I. Scherzo
    II. Andante sostenuto
    III. Allegro moderato
Dedicated to Conrad Bohn, Wendell, Hoss, and William Valkenier, Christmas 1945.
This sonata features frequent meter changes between $\frac{3}{8}$ and $\frac{4}{4}$ in the first movement and $\frac{3}{4}$, $\frac{4}{4}$, and $\frac{6}{8}$ in the third movement. The second movement in $\frac{4}{4}$ is quite sustained. The third movement is based on the Christmas carol "Hark the Herald Angels Sing"
Range: B$\flat$–b^2
Duration: 10:22

Beydon, Jean-Olivier (1956–) France

11 mélodies originals
Billaudot, 2011
Eleven very short movements for the beginning horn player.
Range: f–d²
Duration: 7:50

Biddington, Eric (1953–) New Zealand
All of the following pieces are available from sounz.org.nz

Andante (1995)
Written for Anne Harrow. This single movement is the first of a set of which the
    following piece, *Carillon,* is the second. Intermediate difficulty.
Duration: 3:00

Carillon (1995)
Also written for Anne Harrow. This piece and *Andante* are also published together
    under the title *Two Pieces for French Horn and Piano.*
Duration: 3:00

Concetto (2006)
A single movement of intermediate difficulty written for Bernard Shapiro and
    Amy Huang. Tonal and pleasant with flowing melodic lines.

Prelude and Andante (2001)
The prelude was composed in 2001, the Andante was composed in 1995
Duration: 6:00

Prelude and Romanza (2002)
Two movements written for Henning Slott Jensen.

Bigelow, Albert

Winter Carousel
Kendor Music, 1986
A short, flowing work in ¾ for the beginner, in ABA form, in the key of D for the
    hornist.
Range: a–d²
Duration: 1:35

Bigot, Eugène (1888–1965) France

Récit, scherzo et finale
Henry Lemoine & Cie, 1956
A fairly difficult piece written in several connected sections of contrasting tem-
    pos and characters. Includes trills, stopped horn, and a wide range.
Range: f–c³

Bigot, Pierre (1932–2008) France

Prelude et habanera
Billaudot, 1976

A simple piece for the young horn player written in two sections of contrasting tempos.
Range: g–f²

Intrada
Robert Martin Editions Musicales, 1989
An easy melody in a limited range for the very young horn player.
Range: a–c²

Bishop, Jeffrey (1943–) United Kingdom

Spells and Incantations for Horn and Piano (1972)
Novello, 1972
Written in seven movements: I. Shabriri (Hebraic)—II. The cancerian kiss—III. The glorious hand-nocturne of the leaden eyes—IV. Occult invocation of Herne the Hunter—V. Psalmody of the steward of voluptuous and monstrous sins —VI. Orgiastic ode to creation—VII. Kabbalistic flight into the eye of the night. A rather contemporary piece with many contemporary techniques and sound effects. Includes stopped and muted playing, trills, glissandi, and instructions such as *hand out of bell, wild and tough,* and *like the bark of a dog.* Range is not extreme except in a single measure in which f³ and e³ are written with the instruction *like the cry of a bird.* Otherwise the range goes only to b♭². Notation is quite standard with metered measures.
Range: B♭–f³
Duration: 9:00

Bissill, Richard (1960–) United Kingdom

Valse Noire
Available from www.richardbissill.com/horns.html
Written for Nigel Black and Vladimir Ashkenazy

Fat Belly Blues
Available from www.richardbissill.com/horns.html
A version for horn and piano of the composer's work for six horns and rhythm section.

Bitsch, Marcel (1921–2011) France

Choral pour cor et piano
Alphonse Leduc, 1965
For Jean Devémy, professor at the Conservatoire National Superieur de Musique. Written as an exam piece for the Paris Conservatory, this work opens with a solemn, declamatory theme, followed by five different variations of moderate difficulty, showcasing different styles, tempos, ranges, and techniques for the horn. There are a few stopped passages, and the final variation is a fast ⅜.
Range: c–c³
Duration: 6:00

Variations sur une chanson française
Alphonse Leduc, 1954
French recital piece consisting of a simple theme and four variations in different
    characters. Asymmetrical rhythms and meters including $\frac{3}{8}$, $\frac{4}{4}$, $\frac{3}{8}$, $\frac{5}{8}$, $\frac{7}{8}$, $\frac{8}{8}$, and $\frac{9}{8}$.
    Muted and stopped sections and accompanied cadenza.
Range: d♭–c³

Blaha, Joseph L. (1951–) United States

Sonata for Horn and Piano (1984)
Joseph L. Blaha, 1984
Commissioned by Willard Zirk. This substantial and rather contemporary sonata
    is written in four movements: Soliloquies—Fantasies—Songs—Dances.
    Each title is descriptive of the character of the music. Written in a comfort-
    able range throughout, the piece is technically challenging, but well written
    and idiomatic. Includes trills, stopped, and muted horn.
Range: c♯–b²
Duration: 27:00

Blanc, Adolphe (1828–1885) France

Sonata, op. 43
Hans Pizka Edition, 1982
A very late sonata of the hand horn period in France. Dedicated to J. Mohr, pro-
    fessor of horn at the Paris Conservatory. Composed in four movements,
    the piece is idiomatically written for the natural horn, taking advantage of
    the colors of the instrument, but not overly technical.
    I. Allegro
    II. Scherzo: Presto
    III. Romanze: Andante quasi Adagio
    VI. Finale: Allegro ma non troppo
Range: c–a²
Duration: 19:00

Blanquer, Amando (1935–2005) Spain

Sonate (1983–1984)
Billaudot, 1989
Written for Vicente Zarzo, this rather long sonata has plenty of interesting mu-
    sical and technical things to do for the horn player. An active and flowing
    first movement, marked simplice, is followed by a second movement with
    several unaccompanied sections, including some stopped effects, and end-
    ing with a third movement full of agile technical passages.
Range: f♯–a♯²
Duration: 15:00

Blauth, Brenno (1931–1993) Brazil

Sonatina para trompa e piano, T. 48
Editora Novas Metas, 1978
A three-movement sonata of medium difficulty in a twentieth-century tonal style.
    Straightforward in its horn technique, and well paced.

Blažek, Zdeněk (1905–1988) Czech Republic

4 Romantic Compositions, op. 42
Editio Supraphon, 1969
Four relatively short movements in a romantic style: Andante mesto—Allegretto
    scherzando—Lento Simplice—Lento. Moderately difficult, but predomi-
    nantly midrange horn playing, and not overly technical. A few trills and
    muted passages that may have to be played stopped, as there isn't time to
    remove a mute.
Range: g–a^2

Bloch, André (1873–1960) France

En Forêt d'Île de France
Alphonse Leduc
A single-movement piece of moderate difficulty, very playable for the advancing
    high school student. Consists of an opening Allegro in $\frac{6}{8}$, an Andante also
    in $\frac{6}{8}$, a lengthy cadenza, and a closing Allegro.
Range: e–a^2

Bödecker, Louis (1845–1889) Germany

Serenade, op. 20
J. Reiter, Biedermann, 1884
A short romantic piece, published for horn or violin and piano, but very idi-
    omatic for the horn. A short, lyrical Andante, of only moderate difficulty
    for the horn, leads into an even shorter $\frac{6}{8}$ section marked Grazioso, with
    some fast articulations and scales, but all very straightforward and quite
    playable.
Range: B♭–g^2

Two Phantasiestücke, op. 35
Breitkopf & Härtel, 1894
    1. Elegie
    2. Capricio
Two late-nineteenth-century romantic, lyrical pieces of moderate range and dif-
    ficulty.
Range: e^1–g^2

Boieldieu, François-Adrien (1775–1834) France

Solo pour cor
Billaudot, 1975
A short early nineteenth-century cor-mixt natural horn piece in a flowing, lyrical style. Originally written for horn and harp or piano.
Range: g–g²

Boisseau, Jean-Thierry (1949–) France

Légende pour cor en fa et piano
Musik Fabrik, 2007
This work is divided into sections marked: Ballade—Héroïque—Récitatif—Poursuite—Choral—Rideau! Technically rather difficult, with a wide range and many agile passages. Requires a strong upper range.
Range: c–c²

Boliart, Xavier (1948–) Spain

Duet per a un estiu, tres divertiment per trompa i piano
Editorial de Musica Boileau, 2007
Composed in three relatively short movements marked: Animato—Cantabile—Deciso. The first consists of almost continuous running sixteenth notes in the midrange, based on the intervals of the opening of *Till Eulenspiegel* by Richard Strauss, the second movement is a flowing eighth-note melody in $\frac{6}{8}$, and the third is a decisive dance-like movement.
Range: g–g²

Espurnes (2007)
Editorial de Musica Boileau, 2011
Composed for hornist Francisco Rodriguez, this is a single-movement work in several sections. Mostly in the midrange, with one passage that ascends to f³. Predominantly in a fast tempo, with a couple of slower sections, and a cadenza. Includes some stopped horn.
Range: B♭–f³
Duration: 10:00

Bonnard, Giulio (1885–1972) Italy

Sonata vergiliana per corno in fa e pianoforte
Ricordi, 1937

Bonneau, Paul (1918–1995) France

Souvenir
Alphonse Leduc 1953
Written for hornist Louis Courtinat, this single-movement lyrical piece flows freely throughout the range of the horn without being overly difficult technically.
Range: e♭–a♭² (ossia e♭–b²)

Bořkovec, P. (1894–1972) Czech Republic

Intermezzo (1965)
Panton, 1969
A single movement in mid-twentieth-century avant-garde style. Rather technical
and virtuosic. Old notation bass clef.
Range: G♯–c³

Borroff, Edith (1925–) United States

Sonata for Horn and Piano
Robert King, 1970
A substantial four-movement work: I. Rhapsody—II. Scherzo—III. Sarabande—
IV. Estampie. Of moderate difficulty technically, with a few stopped pas-
sages, but very straightforward horn writing.
Range: d–a²
Duration: 14:00

Boucard, Marcel (1892–1976) France

Légende rustique, pour cor en mi♭ ou fa et piano
Editions M.-R. Braun, 1964
Prize-winning composition of the Confederation Musicale de France, 1964. A sin-
gle movement of very moderate difficulty and range.
Range: a–e♭² (b–f² for horn in E♭)

Bourrel, Yvon (1932–) France

Sonate pour cor et piano, op. 58 (1982)
Editions Delatour, 2008
A contemporary tonal piece in three movements, marked: Très modéré—Très vif
—Calme. Of moderate difficulty, but requires a fairly wide range with some
rather fast and agile changes of range, and some low stopped notes.
Range: b♭–b♭²
Duration: ca. 10:00

Bousquet, Francis (1890–1942) France

Agrotera
Éditions Musicales Ch. Gras, 1939
Written for Jean Devèmy, this single movement in French twentieth-century
style has a few technical challenges, but could be played by the advancing
high school student who has good command of the low range and agile articulation throughout the range. Includes a couple of stopped passages and
trills.
Range: e–a²

Boutry, Roger (1932–) France

Chassacor
Alphonse Leduc, 1956

A single movement with several contrasting sections in a tonal twentieth-century French style. Includes glissandi, stopped horn, uneven meters, and agile technique over a relatively wide range.

Range: B♭–b♭^{2}

Triade
Salabert, 1976
Written for Georges Barboteu. Three fairly short movements in a contemporary French style. Very technical, and rhythmically challenging; includes stopped horn and cadenza-like sections.

Range: g♯–c^3

Bowder, Jerry Lee (1928–2005) United States
Jerry Bowder was a professor at the University of Southern Maine.

Sonata for Horn and Piano
Manduca Music Publications
A substantial three-movement sonata.

Bowen, York (1884–1961) United Kingdom

Sonata in E♭ (1937)
Emerson Horn Editions, 1993
A substantial sonata in three movements with a wide range and technical demands. Includes stopped horn and trills. Old notation bass clef.

Range: G–c^2
Duration: 19:15

Two Preludes
Josef Weinberger Limited, 1997
Two very short pieces in twentieth-century style of moderate difficulty: I. Grave— II. Allegro con fuoco.

Range: E–b^2

Bowers, Timothy (1954–) United Kingdom

Sonata for Horn and Piano (2008)
Queen's Temple Publications, 2010
Commissioned by Professor James Watson for the brass faculty of the Royal Academy of Music.

Boysen, Andrew Jr. (1968–) United States

Nightsong
Emerson Horn Editions, Solid Wood Publishing
Commissioned by Virginia Thompson, this piece was the first-prize winner of the 1999 International Horn Society composition contest. Composed in three sections. The first is slow and expressive, focusing on the low range. The second is faster, accelerating to a fast pace, with loud dynamics and ascending to the upper range, with faster note values and much intensity,

followed by a return to the mood of the opening in the third section, which fades out at the end. Covers a wide range, with a lot of new notation bass clef, wide leaps, and difficult intervals.

Range: G–c³

Bozza, Eugène (1905–1991) France

Chant Lointaine
Alphonse Leduc, 1957
A single-movement work of moderate difficulty with a slow lyrical opening in §
 (Lent et soutenu) followed by a faster ¼ section (Allegro moderato). Includes
 stopped horn and trills.
Range: b♭–g♯²
Duration: 4:00

En Forêt
Alphonse Leduc, 1941
A standard of the horn recital repertoire, this piece is composed in several sections, and incorporates virtually every aspect of horn playing, as did many
 of the pieces used for examinations at the Paris Conservatory. Agile technique and articulations, lyricism, glissandi, muted and stopped horn, trills,
 and wide range and dynamics are all featured, as well as a quote of the horn
 solo used by Respighi in his orchestral work *Feste Roman*.
Range: B–c³

En Irlande
Alphonse Leduc, 1951
A relatively easy piece written in three sections: Andantino (§)—Chasse, Allegro
 giocoso maestoso (§)—Angélus, Calme moderato (¾). New notation bass
 clef. Some muted and stopped horn.
Range: A–f♯²

Sur les Cimes
Alphonse Leduc, 1960
A slightly longer and more challenging piece, which features many of the elements of Bozza's other solo-horn music, including a cadenza-like opening
 section, a melodic Andantino in §, and several other technical sections of
 different characters, much in the style of his *En Forêt*. Includes stopped
 horn, glissandi, and trills. New notation bass clef.
Range: F♯–c³
Duration: ca. 8:00

Entretiens (1974)
Editions Chouldens, 1974
Written for Georges Barboteu, this piece is a dialogue between the horn and piano. Very free and extremely technical and atonal, with stopped passages,
 flutter tongue, glissandi, and a wide range. In the cadenza, the performer is
 asked to improvise using a set of pitches. New notation bass clef.
Range: F♯–b²

Bradford-Anderson, Muriel, United Kingdom

March in Canon
Boosey and Hawkes, 1952
A short, pleasant march in $\frac{4}{4}$, requiring relatively easy technique and range.
Range: e–g²

Prelude in Canon
Boosey and Hawkes, 1973
In canon with the piano, this short piece is straightforward, but more difficult
     than the *March*, having a wider range.
Range: f♯–b²

Branscombe, Gena (1881–1977) United States, born in Canada

"Pacific Sketches" from *American Suite*
James Madison University Archives, 1956
Duration: 10:45

Braun, Yehezkel (1922–2014) Israel
Little Serenade for Horn and Piano
Israel Music Institute, 1982
A relatively easy piece in five short movements of different characters: I. Marcia—
     II. Melody I, Andante cantabile—III. Play, Vivace—IV. Melody II, Molto
     moderato e semplice—V. Marcia.
Range: a–a♭²

Sonata for Horn and Piano (1969)
Israel Music Institute, 1975
Composed in several sections of varying characters in a tonal contemporary
     style.
Range: d–b♭²

Brémond, François (1844–1925) France
Student of J. B. Mohr; eventually succeeded his teacher as professor of horn at the
Paris Conservatory.

1er Solo pour cor avec piano
Sempre piú Editions, 2012
Bremond was a proponent of the valve horn and was instrumental in establishing
     the valve horn as the type of horn taught at the conservatory in the early
     twentieth-century. This piece is a conservatory exam piece, written in three
     sections of contrasting tempos and characters.
Duration: 8:10

Brenet, Thérèse (1935–) France

Le Cor éclate et meurt, renait et se prolonge, deux pieces pour cor en fa et piano
Musik Fabrik, 2013

Bretón, Tomás (1850–1923) Spain

Pieza concertante (1913)
Unión Musical Ediciones, Cantiga e-musicales, 2013
A sight-reading piece for the horn examinations at the Madrid Conservatory in
     1913. Consists of an opening lyrical section marked Ben moderato, and a
     faster section marked Allegro marcial. Technically accessible for the high
     school or college horn player.
Range: c–a^2
Duration: 7:45

Briggs, Kendall Durelle (1959–) United States

Duo concitato (1985, rev. 1995)
Alessi Publications, 1985, 1995

Sonatine
Alessi Publications, 1996
A fairly short four-movement work in contemporary style. The first movement
     is very active with many passages of scalewise running sixteenth-notes.
     The second is a spirited Vivace with some difficult slurred passages in a
     fast tempo. The third is a short, flowing siciliano, and the fourth, marked
     Presto, is a technical sprint with fast articulations in scalewise patterns.
     Not easy, but idiomatic and reasonable in range and endurance.
Range: G–b^2

Brightmore, Victor (1902–1994) United Kingdom
Brightmore was a professional horn player and teacher in England.

Three Easy Solos
June Emerson Edition, 1990
Three short movements: Morning ride—Sad story—German folk song. Very ac-
     cessible to the young horn player with a limited range.
Range: g–d^2

Four Peaceful Pieces
June Emerson Edition, 1994
Four movements: Pastorale—Barcarolle—Lullaby—Rêverie. More advanced horn
     technique, on the level of the more advanced high school horn player. New
     notation bass clef.
Range: c–g^2

Intermezzo in A Minor
June Emerson Edition, 1986
A short Allegretto of rather easygoing technique for the student horn player.
Range: b–g^2

Sicilienne
June Emerson Edition
This is the same as the first movement, "Pastorale," of the *Four Peaceful Pieces*.
Range: c–g^2

Broadbent, Nigel (1952–) United Kingdom

Cumulus
Broadbent & Dunn, 1994
A single movement in $\frac{6}{8}$ ($\frac{3}{4}$) marked Impetuoso. Straightforward horn technique,
    but rhythmically challenging in that one instrument often plays in a triple
    feel against the duple feel of the other. One short stopped passage.
Range: c^1–a^2 (with ossia to c^3 on last note)

Brotons, Salvador (1959–) Spain

Fantasia, op. 12, Trompa i Piano
Cilvis Publicacions, 1988
See: Horn and ensemble

Broughton, Bruce (1945–) United States

Sonata for Horn and Piano (1999, rev. 2012)
Brubel Music, 2013
    1. Broad and lyrically expressive
    2. Lyrically expressive; with a sense of timelessness
    3. With a relentless drive
This challenging and musically substantial sonata was written for Dale Clev-
    enger. Difficult technically and requiring good endurance, it includes some
    complicated stopped-horn passages as well as rhythmic and metric chal-
    lenges. New notation bass clef. Recorded by David Griffin of the Chicago
    Symphony.
Range: A–c^3
Duration: 18:45

Brouquières, Jean (1923–1994) France

Pièce pour Minouche, pour cor en F ou Mi♭ et piano
Editions Robert Martin, 1983
Relatively easy Andantino $\frac{3}{4}$ and Allegretto $\frac{4}{4}$, with a limited range, easy tech-
    nique, and a short cadenza.
Range: g–f♯^{2}
Duration: 3:15

Brouwer, Margaret (1940–) United States

Sonata for Horn and Piano (1996)
Pembroke Music Co, 2000
Commissioned by the eleven hornists of the Horn Consortium Commission-
    ing Group, this substantial and technically challenging work is composed
    in two movements entitled: I. Hymn—II. Riding to higher clouds. Some
    muted and stopped horn, but straightforward in its horn technique.
Range: f–b^2
Duration: 15:00

Brown, Charles (1898–1988) France

Légende pour cor et piano
Alphonse Leduc, 1955
A piece of moderate difficulty in several short sections of different meters and
tempos. Includes muted and stopped horn.
Range: g–a²

Élégie
Editions Phillippe Fougerères, 1945
Dedicated to Jean Devémy. There is a short text under the title by Maurice Schu-
mann, French politician, writer, and World War II hero. Written in the
sounding key of E major, this relatively short piece consists of a flowing
Lento first section, followed by a faster declamatory middle section marked
Allegro moderato, which presents some fingering difficulties and agile ar-
ticulations before returning to the opening material. Aside from the key,
not overly difficult. There is also a version for horn and orchestra.
Range: g♯–a²
Duration: 8:00

Brown, Richard E. (1947–) United States

Sonatina
RM Williams, 2005
A three-movement work of moderate length, written in a style and technical level
of difficulty that makes it quite accessible to the student who has achieved
a good college level of technique and musicianship. Well written and idi-
omatic for the horn, but moderate in its demands of range and endurance.
Range: a–a²
Duration: 9:00

Brünauer, Tibor (1919–)

Habanera Appassionato for Horn and Piano (1997)
Musikverlag Bruno Uetz, 2008
Range: c♯¹–c³ (ossia c♯¹–d³)
Duration: ca. 5:00

Bruneau, Alfred (1857–1934) France

Fantasie
Editions Choudens, 1901
Written for the Concours du Conservatoire National de Musique de Paris.

Romance (1882)
J. Hamelle, 1885
Dedicated to M. Garigue. The horn and piano version was published in 1885,
and a horn and orchestra version was published in 1909. A single Andante
movement in ⅜ in a comfortable flowing, romantic style.
Range: c–g²

Bucchi, Annibale

Trois lieder
Alphonse Leduc, 1966
Written for Domenico Ceccarossi. In three relatively short and moderately difficult movements: 1. Improvviso—2. Barcarola—3. La giovine pescatrice. The first is a flowing Andantino mosso ed espress, with some stopped horn. The second, marked Andantino moderato, is also in a dancing vocal style. The third, marked Andante mosso, is a little more spirited and agile, and the most technically difficult, but still songlike.
Range: a♭–a²

Buianovskii, Vitalii (1928–1993) Russia

Tri p'esy dlia valtorny i fortepiano
Muzyka, 1982
A rather difficult and substantial three-movement work by the prominent Russian hornist and teacher that covers a very wide range and makes use of a number of horn effects and colors, including stopped horn, flutter tongue, glissando, trills, multiphonics, and several unaccompanied sections.
Range: F–d³

Bunting, Christopher (1924–2005) United Kingdom

Cortege and Toccata (1978)
Thames Publishing, 1979
Two rather short movements of medium difficulty in a twentieth-century tonal style. The melodic "Cortège," in an Andantino tempo (dedicated to the memory of Alexander Tcherepnin), is followed by the more agile and articulate toccata in ⅜, marked Allegro giocoso, which presents a few rhythmic and technical challenges. New notation bass clef.
Range: A–a²

Burdick, Richard O. (1961–) Canada, born in United States

Hornist and composer Richard Burdick has written quite a number of works for horn and piano. His eclectic compositions explore the nature of artificial scales. The following is a list of compositions that are available from www.i-ching-music.com.

Sonata No. 1 for Horn and Piano, op. 23
Sonata No. 2, op. 29
Andante "Victoria" for Horn and Organ, op. 41
Sonata for Horn and Organ, op. 42
The Hermit for Horn and Organ, op. 53
Romance for Horn (or Bassoon) and Piano, op. 55
Mocking Bird Sonata for Horn and Piano, op. 68
Chromatic Universal Rhythm, Horn & Piano Version, op. 95.2.1
Sinfonia IV for horn and piano, op. 113

Sonata for Horn and Piano in Four Movements, op. 117

"Jazz Horn Sonata" for horn and piano, op. 153

Burkhard, Willy (1900–1955) Switzerland

Romanze für Horn und Klavier
Baerenreiter, 1964
A short tonal romance in several sections of contrasting tempos and characters.
    Old notation bass clef.
Range C–b♭²
Duration: 7:10

Burkhardt, Joel G.

Little Rondo in Classical Style
Southern Music, 1987
A short, easy rondo dedicated to "Liesel." Very melodic and pleasant in a limited
    range. A good recital piece for the young horn player.
Range: b–e²

Bush, Alan (1900–1995) United Kingdom

Autumn Poem, op. 45
Schott, 1955
A single-movement melodic piece marked Con moto moderato, with a relatively
    wide range. Written in memory of Noel Mewton-Wood.
Range: f♯–c³

Trent's Broad Reaches, op. 36
Schott, 1952
Short piece in ⅝ marked *flowing but leisurely.* Moderately difficult.
Range: a♭–b♭²

Busler-Blais, Lydia (1969–) United States

Moon Lilies for Horn and Piano (2006, rev. 2007)
Westleaf Edition, 2006
A flexible, flowing contemporary tonal piece in an improvisatory style. Includes
    multiphonics, in which the horn player sings while playing.
Range: B♭–b♭²
Duration: 7:00

Buss, Howard J. (1951–) United States

Ballade
Brixton Publications, 2004
A lyrical work that requires a good bit of range, technique, and flexibility. The
    piece has a wide range of moods, from sweet and nostalgic to animated and
    aggressive, but always remains in a lyrical character.
Range: c–b♭²
Duration: 6:00

In Memorian
Brixton Publications, 2007
"A sonic tribute to the millions of soldiers who have made the ultimate sacrifice
    in times of war." Written for hornist Pamela Titus in 2005. Technically dif-
    ficult and dramatic in character. The two movements are named after the
    poems "In Flanders Fields" by John McCrae, and "In Flanders Fields (An
    Answer)" by C. B. Galbreath. Plenty of complex rhythms, stopped effects,
    trills, and other effects are used to express the theme of the piece.
Range: f♯–b♭^{2}

Busser, Henri (1872–1973) France

Cantecor, op. 77
Buffet Crampon, 1926; Alphonse Leduc, 1961
Paris Conservatory exam piece of 1926, composed in several contrasting sections
    to display various aspects of horn technique. Includes stopped and echo horn.
Range: d–c^3

La Chasses de Saint Hubert, op. 99
Alphonse Leduc, 1937, 1990
Composed in several contrasting sections, this piece is based on the "Saint Hu-
    bert Fanfare" of the French hunting horn tradition. Includes muted and
    stopped horn, trills, and glissandi.
Range: c–c^3

Pièce en ré, op. 39 (Concert Piece in D)
Alphonse Leduc, 1900, 1961; Albert J. Andraud; Wind Instrument Music Library;
    Southern Music
Written in three sections: Moderato—Andante poco lent—Allegro vivo. This
    short, tuneful work opens with a dotted motive based on horn fifths, fol-
    lowed by an impressionistic section, ending with a fast Allegro vivo in $\frac{3}{4}$.
    With brief stopped passages and trills, this is a straightforward work that
    adds to the repertoire of horn works for the high school or younger college
    player. It was written as a contest piece for the yearly competition at the
    Paris Conservatory, where Busser taught for many years.
Range: e–a^2
Duration: 4:30

Butt, James (1929–2003) United Kingdom

A Horn Suite
Hinrichsen, 1961
Three movements entitled:
    I. Hunting call
    II. Soliloquy
    III. Gigue
The music states that the piece can be performed with piano, orchestra, or un-
    accompanied. The three movements are relatively easy, the first featuring

hunting horn figures and stopped horn, the second a simple flowing melody, and the third a spirited dance in $\frac{6}{8}$.
Range: d–g²
Duration: 3:40

Butterworth, Neil (1934–) United Kingdom

Prelude and Scherzo
Chappell, 1961
Two very short and easy movements, an andante prelude in $\frac{4}{4}$ with articulate agile moving passages, and a scherzo in $\frac{6}{8}$. Appropriate for the middle school or high school horn player.
Range: a–f²

Büttner, Max (1879–1948) Germany

Improvisation für Horn und Klavier, op. 30
Carl Merseburger, 1927
Composed in five short and quite difficult movements.
Range: E–c³

Butts, Carrol M. (1924–1980) United States

Ballad for Horn
C. L. Barnhouse, 1969
Relatively easy short, lyrical piece in $\frac{4}{4}$.
Range: d–g²

Buziau & Alexis de Garaudé

Fantasie (1823)
See: Garaudé, Alexis de

Cabus, Noël Peter (1923–2000) Belgium

Alla caccia
Andel, 1989

Canto e ballo
J. Maurer, 1975
A short piece in two sections: a lyrical melody in $\frac{3}{4}$, marked Lento, and an Allegro leggiero in $\frac{6}{8}$. Relatively easy technically and could be played by the advancing middle school or high school student.
Range: c¹–g²

Cacavas, John (1930–2014) United States

Danse ancienne
Hal Leonard, 2011
A short, flowing, lyrical piece for the beginner.
Range: c¹–c²

Poem
Hal Leonard, 2011
Lyrical work for the student hornist, with sixteenth notes and triplets, that ventures into key areas beyond the home key.
Range: b–f♯²

Summer Pastiche
Hal Leonard Publishing, 2011
Short lyrical work in ABA form with a coda, in the key of G major, suitable for the beginning player.
Range: d¹–e²

Caliendo, Christopher (1960–) United States

Horn Sonata No. 1
Caliendo World Music Publishing, christophercaliendo.com
Written for, and premiered by, Richard Todd. This three-movement work is written in a jazz style, and is quite challenging, both technically and musically. The first movement is a jazz waltz, the second a slow ballad, and the third is in a fast driving bop tempo.
Duration: ca. 16:00

Callabro, Louis (1926–1991) United States

Chanterelle, op. 68
Thodore Presser, Elkan Vogel, 1983
Originally written for horn and string quartet (1978), commissioned by the Composers Conference of the East, but later adapted for horn and piano.
Duration: 8:00

Callaway, Ann (1945–) United States

Four Elements
Subito Music, 1974
A very contemporary piece in four movements entitled: Wind Fantasy—Water Portrait—Earth—Fire Music. The first movement, written in a graphic notation, is composed over a timeline divided into units, fifty-six of which equal one minute. The piece includes many effects of plucking, strumming, or hitting the piano strings; muted and stopped effects; and glissandi in the horn part. The piece has many improvisatory elements, but the composer asks the performers to follow the score as closely as possible without sacrificing spontaneity. The second, third, and fourth movements are more conventional in their metered notation for the most part, with sections of great freedom, and some difficult precise rhythms that must be played together by the two instruments. Not overly difficult for the horn in terms of range, endurance, or technique but a challenging contemporary piece for both players, musically and rhythmically.
Range: B♭–b♭²
Duration 17:15

Campanelli, Richard (1949–) United States

Duo, Nocturnus III
Dorn Publications, 1985
A very difficult contemporary work, written for Alan Taplin. The three movements
   are marked: Poco rubato—Largo molto lirico—Con moto sempre animato.
   Each movement is full of technical and rhythmic challenges. Includes stopped
   and muted sections, trills, glissandi, and new notation bass clef.
Range: c–c^3

Campolieti, Luigi (1905–1975) Italy

Andante pastoral & allegro
Ricordi, 1960
In two short sections, Calmo in $\frac{3}{4}$ and an Allegro in $\frac{6}{8}$. Moderately difficult tech-
   nically.
Range: g–c^3

Canavesio, Adrien (1913–) France

Cantehorn
Editions Transatlantique, 1973
A single-movement work with several sections of varying tempos. Moderately
   difficult, it includes a cadenza, trills, and a bit of challenging technique.
Range: F–b♭^{2}
Duration: 6:30

Canteloube, Joseph (1879–1957) France

Dance
Pierre Noël, 1953; International, 1954
One of the short pieces in the collection entitled *Contemporary French Recital
   Pieces* published by International Music. Not overly difficult, but it in-
   cludes sustained trills.
Range: G–g^2

Capdevielle, Pierre (1906–1969) France

Èlègie de duino, pour cor et piano
Alphonse Leduc 1960
A technically very difficult single-movement work in several contrasting sections, requiring strength and endurance in the upper range. Includes difficult rhythms and advanced techniques such as glissandi; trills; flutter
   tongue; and fast changes between muted, stopped, and open horn. New
   notation bass clef.
Range: G♭c^3

Carles, Marc (1933–) France

Choral, pour cor et piano
Alphonse Luduc, 1962

A moderately easy melodic piece marked Molto lento in $\frac{4}{4}$. Uses stopped horn.
Range: c–a♭²
Duration: 4:30

Carr, Gordon (1943–) United Kingdom

A Day in the Country
Broadbent & Dunn Ltd, 1994
Dedicated to "Laura." Three short movements entitled: The Happy Fox—Idyll—
    To Home! Technically fairly challenging, featuring a wide range, and agile
    articulations, as well as some stopped passages. The outer movements are
    written in a hunting horn style, while the middle movement takes advan-
    tages of the flowing and lyrical qualities of the horn.
Range: c–a²

Elegy for Lennie
Broadbent & Dunn Ltd, 2000
Written in memory of Lennie Clarke. A slow, solemn piece with a wide array of
    colors and dynamics. Not too difficult technically, but requires trills and
    stopped horn.
Range: d–a²

Soliloquy
Broadbent & Dunn Ltd, 1994
A contemplative lyrical piece, marked Lento, that requires some control at the
    top of the staff and above.
Range: b♭–c³

Carrapatoso, Eurico (1962–) Portugal

Sweet Rustica (1996)
Editions BIM, 2007
A rather difficult contemporary work in seven movements.
Duration: 17:00

Carrière, G. L. France

Air de chasse pour cor et piano
Editions Robert Martin, 1975
A short, very easy piece for the elementary player.
Range: c¹–c²

Carse, Adam (1878–1958) United Kingdom

Two Easy Pieces, Serenade and Scherzino
Stainer and Bell, 1939
Two short, easy movements for the very young horn student; a simple flowing
    melody and an easygoing scherzo with a hunting horn flavor.

Castérède, Jacques (1926–2014) France

Nocturne
Billaudot, 2007
An easygoing lyrical piece in a contemporary tonal style. A good work for the
  student who wants a pleasant, flowing, melodic piece that doesn't go above
  the staff. Also exists in a version with string orchestra.
Range: a–f$\sharp^2$
Duration: 5:00

Western
Billaudot, 1984, 1998
A short, spirited piece in $\frac{6}{8}$, in the midrange. For the student who is beginning to
  develop some facility and clean articulation.
Range: c$\flat^1$–g^2
Duration: 1:10

Catelinet, Philip Bramwell (1910–1995) United Kingdom

Caprice "Encore"
Hinrichsen, 1953
A fairly short, spirited rondo, mostly in $\frac{6}{8}$ with a $\frac{4}{4}$ andante section in the middle.
  Agile and fast. Moderately difficult, but well written for the horn. Has a bit
  of stopped horn.
Range a–c^3 (a–a^2 with ossias)

Ten Little Indians Standing in a Line
Hinrichsen, 1953

Cazden, Norman (1914–1980) United States

Sonata for Horn and Piano, op. 33
Independent Music Publishers, 1941

Cecconi-Botella, Monic (1936–) France

Automne pour cor en fa et piano
Editions Philippo, 1962
A short, lyrical piece dedicated to Jean Devémy.
Range: g–g^2
Duration: 2:00

Scherzetto pour cor et piano
Editions Philippo, 1962
A short piece in a light, fast $\frac{6}{8}$ that presents some difficult and agile passages.
Range: f–b^2
Duration: 2:00

Cellier, Alexandre (1883–1968) France

Ballade pour cor et piano
Alphonse Leduc, 1949
A moderately difficult piece with alternating melodic and technical passages. New
     notation bass clef.
Range: c–g^2

Ceremuga, Josef (1930–2005) Czech Republic

Sonatina pro lesní roh a klavír (1975)
Panton, 1975

Chaffin, Lon W. (1957–) United States

Unfolding Motives
Potenza Music, 2008, 2012
A three-movement work for horn and piano: Toccata—Canzona—Fugue.

Chailley, Jacques (1910–1999) France

Élégie
Billaudot, 1985
Dedicated to Daniel Lesur, this solemn piece consists of slow-moving melodic
     lines over a relatively simple accompaniment.
Range: c♯^{1}–g^2
Duration: 3:45

Chajes, Julius (1910–1985) United States, born in Poland

Melody for Horn and Piano
Transcontinental Music Publications, 1959
Originally for cello and piano, adapted for horn by the composer. A short, melodic
     piece in the sounding key of A minor.
Range: e–g^2

Chambers, Alex (Pseudonym for Charles O'Neill)
See: O'Neill, Charles

Chandler, Hugh, United States

Sonata in One Movement (2001)
JOMAR Press, 2001
Written for Jeffrey Powers. A substantial single-movement work, in a relatively
     fast ⁴, marked *bold, majestic,* that ends with the same melodic material in a
     slower section that becomes more peaceful and serene.
Range: c^1–a^2
Duration: ca. 10:00

Charpentier, Jacques (1933–) France

Pour Diane pour cor en fa et piano
Alphonse Leduc, 1962
A short, lyrical piece.
Range: a–b²

Charron, Jacques (1954–) France

Au Refuge blue. op.63
Andel

Caprice d'oiseau, op.58
Andel

Coraline, op. 45
J. M. Fuzeau, 1989

Cornissimo, op. 30, pour cor et piano ou orchestra
Editions Fuzeau, 1989
See: Horn and ensemble

L'Acroche coeur, op.32
Andel, 2008

Chaussier, Henri (1854–1914) France

Elegy
McCoy's Horn Library, 1982
Short piece for horn and harp or piano from the late nineteenth-century hand
    horn period in France.
Range: c–c³

Cherubini, Luigi (1760–1842) Italy, resided in France

Sonatas No. 1 and 2 (Original title: *Deux sonates ou études pour le cor*
avec accompagnements) (1804)
Sikorski, 1954; Schirmer (Tuckwell, ed.); International
Though originally written for horn with string accompaniment, these two so-
    natas, or "Concert etudes" have become a staple of the horn and piano
    literature. The first *Sonata* is a short single movement in F major which
    highlights the natural horn's lyrical qualities, and the second, with its long
    opening recitative and fast technical passages, displays the horn's flashy
    technique, as it had been developed by the French school of natural horn
    players of the early nineteenth-century. Techniques required in addition to
    fast articulations and intervals include trills and turns.
Range: f♯–a²
Duration: 8:30
See: Horn and ensemble

Chevillard, Camille (1859–1923) France

Allegro, op. 18
Alphonse Leduc, 1900
A late nineteenth-century single-movement piece in three sections, moderately
    difficult technically.
Range: g–b²

Chevreuille, Raymond (1901–1976) Belgium

Prelude, scherzando et marche, op. 92 (1968)
CeBeDeM, 1968
For Georges Caraël. A challenging work with a slow and brooding Prelude with
    wide intervals, a quick, intricate Scherzando in mixed meters, and a regal
    March with complex triplet figures.
Range: a♭–c³
Duration: 9:30

Chillemi, Salvatore (1935–) Italy

Idillio, op. 35/a
Edizioni Bèrben, 1986
An expressive, lyrical single-movement piece. Requires good endurance of the
    horn player, as there are few rests.
Range: f♯–a²

Chiti, Gian Paolo (1939–) Italy

Donizetti suite, fantasie sure des airs d'opera
Musik Fabrik
A medley of six opera arias.
Duration: ca. 12:00

Cioffari, Richard (1947–) United States

Festive Rondo (1988)
Southern Music, 1992
A short and not too difficult rondo in ⅜, commissioned by the students of Louis
    Stout in honor of his twenty-eighth year of teaching at the University of
    Michigan.
Range: g–g²

Clapisson, Louis (1808–1866) France

Fantasie et variations pour piano et cor, op. 2
Richault, nineteenth century (copy in US Library of Congress)
Theme and variations piece in F major in the nineteenth-century French hand
    horn style. Includes many fast slurred and articulated passages.
Range: g–g²

Clearfield, Andrea (1960–) United States

Songs of the Wolf (1994)
Andrea Clearfield, 1994; JOMAR Press, 1994
Written for Frøydis Ree Wekre, the two movements of this piece were inspired
    by Manfred Fischbeck's poem "Songs of the Wolf," and the story "La Loba"
    from *Women Who Run With the Wolves* by Clarissa Pinkola Estés, PhD.
    Technical and dramatic, the horn part uses stopped and half-stopped ef-
    fects, glissandi, and a wide range of dynamics.
Range: f–d³
Duration: 14:00

Clergue, Jean (1896–1969) France

Prélude, lied et rondo
Henry Lemoine, 1934
Moderately difficult piece in two sections: Moderato ¼ and Rondo vif ⅝.
Range: d–a²

Clérisse, Robert (1899–1973) France

L'Absent
Alphonse Leduc, 1957
A simple, melodic piece in ¾ for the young horn player, marked Poco andante.
Range: b♭–c²

Le Chant du sonneur
Billaudot, 1969
A short piece for the younger student horn player, in several sections of varying
    tempos, from adagio to andante, written in a twentieth-century tonal style.
    Technically very easy. Includes parts for F and E♭ horns.
Range: c¹–d♭²

Chant sans paroles pour cor et piano
Alphonse Leduc, 1952
An easy, lyrical piece.
Range: b–e²

Chanson a bercer
Buffet-Crampon
A short, lyrical piece.
Range: e♭¹–a♭²

Matines pour cor en mi♭ et piano
Alphonse Leduc, 1956
A short, easy, melodic piece.
Range: c¹–f² (for horn in E♭)

Sur la diligence
Editions Philippo, 1962
Another short, easy piece.
Range: a♭–f²

Clews, Eileen (1935–) United Kingdom

Nine Pieces for Horn and Piano
Paterson's Publications, 1988
Nine short pieces of varying tempos and styles for the young horn player, limited
   in range and endurance, but with some agile figures and rhythmic difficul-
   ties, as well as some stopped horn.
Range: f–e²

Partita for Horn and Piano
Paterson's Publications (Novello), 1984
Three relatively short movements: I. Burlesca—II. Serenata—III. Finale brilliante.
   Of moderate difficulty, but not without its technical challenges, especially
   in the agile and articulate last movement ⅝. New notation bass clef.
Range: B–a²

Coakley, Donald (1934–) United States

Four Colloquies (2004)
Eighth Note Publications, 2005
Written for Andrew Mee, this is a fairly difficult work in which each of the
   four movements is a dialogue between the horn and piano. Movements
   are marked: I. Decisively—II. Expressive and lyrical—III. With fire and
   verve—IV. Energetically. Includes a few mixed meters and muted passages.
Range: g–a²
Duration: 11:00

Cochereau, Emile

L'Antique cor
IMD Diffusion Arpeges, 1986
Short, lyrical work in ¾ in a minor key, with one passage that extends down to a
   low e. Expressive work for the young hornist.
Range: e–e²

Cochereau, Emile and **Largueze, Jacques**

Kuklos
Editions Combre, 2000
One of a series of educational pieces for young horn players in France. Simple
   technique and range but musically interesting.
Range: g–e²

L'Harmonie du cor
IMD Diffusion Arpeges, 1985
Nine very short pieces in contrasting styles and tempos with accompaniment for
   the advancing young horn student.
Range: c–e²

Coenen, Johannes Meinardus (1824–1899) Netherlands

Morgandämmerung
Edition Compusic, 1989
Short, romantic piece in the typical "salon" style of the nineteenth century.
Range: d♯^{1}–a^2

Cohen, Sol B. (1891–1988) United States

Fantasy in F major
Belwin, 1939
A single-movement student piece of moderate difficulty.
Range: a♭–g♯^{2}

Pastorale
Belwin, 1955
A short, lyrical student piece.
Range: b♭–f^2

Legend of the Hills
Belwin
Another melodic student piece.
Range: a–g^2

Coiteux, Francis (1944–) France

Songe d'un soir
Robert Martin, 1989
Dedicated to Daniel Milliere, professor at the National Conservatory in Troyes, where Coiteux also teaches. Short, lyrical work in a moderate tempo. Coiteux wrote exam pieces, and the indication "Noveau elementaire" indicates this was probably a conservatory exam piece. There are a few instances of stopped writing. Includes part for horn in E♭.
Range: f^1–f^2

Collins, Brendan, Australia

Senegal, for Horn and Piano (2003)
Australian Music Centre, Reed Music, 2007
Duration: 3:00

Collorafi, James (now known as James Nicholas) (1957–) United States

Sonata for Natural Horn and Piano (1985)
Shawnee Press, 1986
Three movements, written for Richard Seraphinoff. A dramatic piece for natural horn which takes advantage of the colors of various crooks (D, E♭, E, F, and A) and the expressive qualities of the stopped notes. Also includes a part for valve horn in F.
Range: a–g♯^{2} (for F horn)
See: Nicholas, James

Colomer, Blas María (1833–1917) Spain, worked in France

Fantasie légende pour cor chromatique en fa
Alphonse Leduc
An early twentieth-century contest piece from the Paris Conservatory in one
    movement. Rather technical with stopped horn and trills.
Range: B–a^2

Colomer, Juan J. (1966–) Spain

Visions for Horn in F and Piano (2007)
Editions BIM, 2007
A difficult contemporary work written for the 2007 Philip Jones brass competi-
    tion in France.
Duration: 15:30

Constant, Franz (1910–1996) Belgium

Couleur provençale, op. 42
Andel, 1960
A single-movement concert piece in several sections of contrasting tempos rang-
    ing from Andante to the final Vivace. Not overly technical but with an
    emphasis on the upper range that could prove taxing.
Range: a–c^3

Constantinides, Dinos (1929–) United States, born in Greece
Violinist and composer on the faculty of Louisiana State University.

Reflections VI—The Tyger
Conners Publications, 1996
Inspired by the William Blake poem *The Tyger;* portrays the personality of the
    composer's cat Tiger. The composer writes that "the piece employs a repeated
    note motive that pervades the entire work. A descending chromatic chord
    progression controls the harmonic structure of the composition and creates
    mood changes that were very much a part of every day with Tiger's life."
Range: g–g^2
Duration: 6:10

Cooke, Arnold (1906–2005) United Kingdom

Rondo in B flat
Schott, 1952
A short, spirited rondo, of moderate difficulty. A pleasant piece that contrasts
    well with heavier pieces on a recital program.
Range: c–g^2

Cooman, Carson P. (1982–) United States

Of Ice and Silver Swans, op. 246
MMB Music, 2001

Written for Hazel Davis, the piece is composed in two sections. The first consists of two ad lib passages that are to be repeated three times, and need not synchronize with the piano's ad lib passages. The second is completely metered and fast. Not easy, but very playable and well written for the horn.
Range: f♯–a♯²

Cope, David (1941–) United States
Sonata for Horn and Piano
Seesaw Music, 1976
In three movements of changing meters, the first has a variety of contrasting sections. The slower second movement has extended muted passages, and the final movement is similar to the first in its intensity and rhythmic complexity.
Range: B♭–c³
Duration: 12:00

Coppens, Claude A. (1936–) Belgium
Hornithography (1985)
CeBeDeM, 1997
For horn solo with ad lib piano accompaniment. The instructions say that the piano part is never essential.
See: Unaccompanied horn

Coriolis, Emmanuel de (1907–1977) France
Dans la forêt, pour cor et piano
Editions Musicales Transatlantique, 1971
A short, lyrical piece.
Range: c¹–g²
Duration: 2:10

Dix piécettes pour cor et piano
Éditions musicales Transatlantiques, 1972
Ten short pieces for the young horn player.

Nocturne
Alphonse Leduc, 1968
Dedicated to Lucien Thévet, this short, lyrical piece has pleasant flowing melodic lines and a simple accompaniment.
Range: a–g²
Duration: 3:35

Corret, A. (ca. early 19th cent.) France
First horn of the Grand Theater in Rouen, 1815–1862.

Solo für Horn und Klavier, op. 2 (ca. 1820)
Robert Ostermeyer, 2005
This solo for natural horn in E♭ is composed in several contrasting sections. Consists of equal proportions of operatic melodic playing, and acrobatic passagework.
Range: B♭–a² (c–b² for horn in E♭)

Fantasie für Horn und Klavier, op. 6 (ca. 1820)
Robert Ostermeyer, 2005
Written for natural horn in E and piano, this solo was dedicated to Corret's student, Mr. E. Bazile. This cor-mixt-style piece consists of a lyrical melodic
opening section that leads into a faster $\frac{3}{4}$ in sounding E minor, and finally,
a section in E major with fast but not difficult triplets to end the piece. Not
difficult and a good choice for a solo piece for the early stages of natural
horn study.
Range: b–g♯² (c¹–a² for horn in E)

Cortese, Luigi (1899–1976) Italy

Sonata per corno e pianoforte
Carisch, 1958
A relatively easy piece in two movements, Andante mosso $\frac{4}{4}$ and Allegro moder-
ato $\frac{6}{8}$.
Range: a–b²

Coscia, Silvio (1899–1977) United States

Romanza: A Romantic Song for French Horn in F and Piano
M. Baron, 1948
A short midrange piece.
Range: a–e²

Recitativo and Fugue for French Horn and Organ (or Piano)
North Easton, 1963

Cossetto, Emil (1918–2006) Italy

Aria e minuetto (1966)
Schott, 1988
Two movements: Andante—Moderato, ma pesante. Not terribly difficult techni-
cally, but both movements do tend toward the top of the staff and above,
making them difficult for range and endurance. A few stopped notes.
Range: f–b♭²

Cosma, Edgar (1925–2006) France, born in Romania

Sonatine (1954)
Editions BIM, 1988
One of the composer's earlier works, this is a very expressive contemporary tonal
piece of moderate difficulty in three movements:
1. Allegro deciso
2. Andante nostalgico
3. Ritmico
Duration: 15:00
Range: g♭–a♭²

Coulthard, Jean (1908–2000) Canada

Fantasy Sonata for Horn and Piano (1983)
Canadian Music Centre, 1988
Written for Martin Hackleman. A single-movement work in contemporary style, written in standard metered notation. Presents a good number of technical and rhythmic challenges, but is very idiomatically well written for the horn. Includes a cadenza and a few stopped notes.
Range: d♯–a² (ossia d♯–b♭²)
Duration: ca. 10:00

Couson, Laurent, France

Lune triste (Sad Moon)
IMD Diffusions Arpeges, 1999
Written for Hervé Joulan. A short but fairly difficult piece written for horn or cello that depicts, in the words of the composer, "in tribute to the night and its secrets." Requires a strong upper range.
Range: G♯–c³

Couturier, Jean-Louis (1963–) France

Lied
Editions Combre

Cox, Philip, W. L. (1883–?) United States

Horniste
The Cundy-Bettoney Co. Inc., 1940
A short school-contest piece, for high school level players.
Range: f♯–g²

Lullaby for Second Horn
Jack Spratt Music Company, 1956
Short, easy contest piece that explores the lower range in a way designed for younger players.
Range: e–g²

Craft, Jonathan (1986–) United States

Dreams, Yearning
JOMAR Press, 2008
Written for Thomas Bacon. A dreamy, ethereal piece, mostly lyrical and in a free singing style. Uses echo horn technique and mute.
Range: c–a²
Duration: 8:00

Crépin, Alain (1954–) Belgium

Voyage d'Hadrien
Robert Martin Editions Musicales, 1995

This work for the beginning player is in ABA form. The outer sections are in $\frac{4}{4}$, staying mostly within the range of a fifth, with a brief Largo in $\frac{3}{4}$ in the middle.
Range: b¹–b²

Crepy, Bernard de (1939–) France

Synopse, pour cor et piano
Editions Transatlantique, 1972
Dedicated to Georges Barboteu, this piece was written for the Paris Conservatory exams of 1972. A difficult work involving many contemporary techniques and effects, written in both graphic and traditional notations.
Range: g–b²

Criotier, Louis

Notturno romantico pour cor et piano ou harpe
Billaudot, 1979
A short piece in a lyrical style that can be played all on the overtones of the E♭ horn. It may have been composed for alphorn and piano, which is consistent with the style of the music. If this is the case, stopped-horn passages may have been added to this edition by the editor, Edmond Leloir, and the piece may have been transposed down from the common alphorn key of F.
Range: B♭–f²
Duration: 3:00

Criswell, J. Patrick, United Kingdom

Four Interludes for Horn and Piano
Galliard, 1965
Four short movements. Technically quite easy and straightforward.
Range: a–g²

Crusell, Bernhard (1775–1838) Sweden, born in Finland

Horn Concerto
Edition Marc Reift, 1999, Swedish Music Interest
The first movement of an original concerto from 1813 by Crusell which is now considered to be lost. This edition is based on a version discovered in an archive in Stockholm that was arranged for solo horn and brass ensemble in 1840. This is a horn and piano arrangement of that version. A typical classical-concerto first movement for horn in F that stays within the staff for the most part with flowing melodies as well as virtuosic scale and arpeggio passages.
Range: g–c³

Cunningham, Michael G. (1937–) United States

Horn Sonata, op. 163 (1993)
Seesaw Music Corp., 2003

I. Rubato Agitato
II. Poem to Persichetti
III. Frolic

A medium-length sonata with some technical challenges, but very accessible. The
last movement presents some articulation and agility difficulties, but all in
a comfortable range.

Range: a–c²

Horn Sonata No. 2, op. 232
Seesaw Music, 2010
A fairly short sonata in three movements, only moderately difficult and quite well
written for the horn. The first movement is a moderate ⅜, marked Simplice,
with rather flowing lines. The second is a more agile staccato alternation of
⅜ and ¾. The third is marked Nobilmente, and has a slower-moving grand
character.

Range: b–b²

Custer, Calvin (1939–1998) United States

Caprice for Horn and Piano
Kendor Music, 1992
A student piece from the "Graded Solo Series" of the publisher.

Czerny, Karl (1791–1857) Germany

Andante e Polacca, für Horn in E und Klavier
Doblinger, 1973 (Friedrich Gabler, ed.)
A longer work for natural horn in E which includes a rather operatic Andante in
⅜ with very chromatic hand horn technique and ornaments, followed by an
agile Polacca in ¾ with many technical difficulties, especially when played
on the valve horn in F. This is a major work and worth the effort.

Range: B–b² (c–c³ for horn in E)

Drei Brillante Fantasien, op. 339, nos.1, 2, and 3
Hans Pizka Edition, 1987; Cimarron Music Press
Each piece, published separately, is a free standing work. These three fairly long,
taxing pieces are written on themes from Schubert songs. The horn parts,
playable on hand horn, but most likely written for the early valve horn, are
technically difficult, with numerous virtuosic cadenzas. The piano parts
are extremely difficult and virtuosic.

Nos. 1 and 3 are for horn in F, no. 2 for horn in E.

Range: G–a² (for Horn in F)
Duration: each of the pieces has a duration of ca. 18:00

Introduction, Variations Concertantes, op. 248
Hans Pizka Edition, 1987; Edition Kunzelmann, 1999
Written for Joseph Lewy Jr. Another fairly long salon piece that is virtuosic for both
hornist and pianist. Includes an introduction and five variations and a finale
on a "tirolienne" theme. Very idiomatically written for the early valved horn.

Range: B♭–a²

Damase, Jean-Michel (1928–2013) France

Aspects, 5 pieces pour cor et piano (ou harpe)
Billaudot, 1988
Five fairly easy student pieces, technically not too difficult, but interesting to play.
Range: g–e²
15:00

Berceuse, op.19
Alphonse Leduc, 1951
A short, easy piece but very pleasant and melodic.
Range: g–e♭²

Chant de matelot
Billaudot

Pavane varièe pour cor et piano
Henry Lemoine, 1956
Another short piece of limited range but of melodic interest.
Range: a–g²

Sonate pour cor en fa et piano
Henry Lemoine, 1996
　　I. Allegro
　　II. Andante
　　III. Allegro vivo
Dedicated to Hervé Joulain, this is a lengthy and involved sonata. The horn tech-
　　nique is difficult, but accessible, and though there are rhythmic difficulties,
　　they are straightforward with no extended techniques or contemporary
　　notation. The composer has provided well-spaced rests for the horn player,
　　but the piece still requires a good bit of endurance.
Range: d–c³ (G–b² with ossias)

Danburg, Russell (1909–1994) United States
Poeme (1973)
Southern Music, 1973
Flowing, melodic single-movement piece. One section calls for cup mute.
Range: a–a²

Danner, Gregory (1958–) United States
Five Miniatures for Horn and Piano
Medici Music Press, 1988
Five short movements: Ode—Elegy—Sonnet—Hymn—Caprice. In various tem-
　　pos and moods and written at a technical level appropriate for the advanc-
　　ing middle school or high school player.
Range: g–f²

Danzi, Franz (1763–1826) Germany

Sonata in E♭, op. 28 (Sonata pour le piano-forte avec accompanement d'un cor ou violoncelle)
Breitkopf und Härtel, ca. 1800; Hofmeister, International, 1963
    I. Adagio—Allegro
    II. Larghetto
    III. Allegretto
This classical sonata is one of the earlier works for horn and piano. Written for E♭
    natural horn in a cor-basse style, it is very much a duo, with the horn often
    accompanying the piano. Not a virtuoso work, but there are some very ag-
    ile passages, and it is musically rewarding.
Range: F–f^2 (G–g^2 for E♭ horn)
Duration: 17:00

Sonata in e minor, op. 44 (Sonata pour le piano-forte avec accompanement d'un
cor ou violoncelle)
Breitkopf und Härtel, ca. 1800; Sikorski, 1957; Birdalone (facsimile of Breitkopf und
    Härtel), 1999
    I. Allegro
    II. Larghetto
    III. Allegretto
Very similar in horn and piano writing to the E♭ sonata, but in a minor key, which
    is a rarity for this period. Written for natural horn in E, the horn alternates
    between accompanying and solo lines. Contains quick articulated arpeg-
    gios and trills. There are also turns, ornaments, and grace notes, for which
    the player may want to refer to performance practice treatises of the time,
    such as the *School of Clavier Playing* by Daniel Türk.
Range: b–f♯^{2} (c–g^2 for horn in E)
Duration: 17:00

Darbellay, Jean-Luc (1946–) Switzerland

Espaces magiques pour cor natural et piano (2001)
Tre Media Musikverlag, 2007
Dedicated to Olivier Darbellay and Patrizio Mazzola, this piece is written for nat-
    ural horn and piano. Very contemporary in style with unmetered sections
    and a lot of rhythmic freedom.
Range: B♭–c^3

Dardenne, Jean (1951–) Belgium

Divertissement
Editions Choudens, 1977
A short, lyrical piece in a limited range. A short, slow introduction leads into an
    Allegretto, followed by a return to the introductory material.
Range: c^1–f^1 (ossia c^1–g^2)

Prelude et danse
Editions Choudens, 1975
A similar short piece with a slow introduction, a short dance, and return of the
    beginning theme. Of very moderate difficulty.
Range: b–g²

Quatre Pieces
Editions Choudens, 1976
Four short, easy pieces for the young horn player: Esquisse—Air tender—Au-
    tomne—Cortége. Written in a limited range and using simple note values.
Range: c¹–c²

Valse
Editions Choudens, 1975
A short waltz written in an easygoing style, all in the midrange.
Range: c¹–g²

Daucé, Edouard (1893–1967) France

Romance pour cor en fa ou cor en mi♭
Editions Philippo, 1962
Short, easy piece in a lyrical style with straightforward rhythms in mid-twenti-
    eth-century French tonal style. Some new notation bass clef. Includes parts
    for F and E♭ horn.
Range: A–d²

Dauprat, Louis Francois (1781–1868) France
Professor at the Paris Conservatory (1816–1842), solo horn of the Paris Opera,
and hand horn virtuoso. Dauprat was one of the most important teachers of the
French school, having written the *Method for Cor Alto and Cor Basse* of 1824, the
most extensive and complete hand horn method ever written. Much of his music
was written to be played by his students for exams at the Paris Conservatory. All
of Dauprat's horn and piano music was published by Zetter in Paris during his
lifetime. A few pieces have been reissued in modern editions and are available,
and some have been recorded. Francois Joseph Fétis, in his *Biographie universelle
des musicians* (1833–1844), says that "Dauprat only performed music of the very
best taste, which he composed for himself, and which was written with more care
than is found generally in the solos for wind instruments." All of the pieces listed
below were written for natural horn.

The complete list of horn and piano pieces by Dauprat, published by Zetter,
now long out of print, includes the following:
    Op. 2, *Sonata for Horn and piano*
    Op. 3, *Sonata for Horn and Harp (or Piano)*
    Op. 5, *Tableau Musical for Horn and Piano*
    Op. 7, *Duo for Horn and Piano*
    Op. 11, *Three Solos (abc) for Horn and Piano*
    Op. 12, *Two Solos (ab)* and *Duo (c) for Horn and Piano*
    Op. 16, *Three Solos (abc) for Horn and Piano*

Op. 17, *Three Solos (abc) for Horn and Piano*
Op. 20, *Three Solos (abc) for Horn and Piano*
Op. 22, *Air Eccosais for Horn and Harp (or Piano)*
Op. 23, *Theme Varie, and Bolero for Horn and Piano*
Op. 24, *Theme Varie and Rondeau for Horn and Piano*
Op. 25a, *Scene Dramatique for Horn and Piano*
Op. 25b, *Melodie for Horn and Piano*
Op. 25c, *Melodie for Two Horns and Piano*

Other available editions include:

Sonata, op. 2
Modern edition: Billaudot, 1987

Duo for Horn and Piano, op. 7
Modern edition, Billaudot, 1995

3 Solos for Horn and Piano/Orchestra, op. 11
Facsimile, Hans Pizka Edition

3 Solos for Horn and Piano, op. 16
Facsimile, Hans Pizka Edition

Scene dramatique, op. 25a (also with orchestra)
Facsimile, Hans Pizka Edition

Melodie pour le cor, op. 25b (also with orchestra)
Facsimile, Hans Pizka Edition

Dautremer, Marcel (1906–1978) France

Cortège pastoral
Editions Philippo, 1961
A very simple, melodic piece with easy rhythms and limited range for the young
     horn player.
Range: G–f^2

Thème variè
Alphonse Leduc, 1958
A simple theme and five variations of contrasting characters and tempos. More
     challenging technically than the *Cortège pastoral,* but still a good student
     piece. Includes a cadenza section and stopped horn in the low range.
Range: d–b♭^{2}

Davis, Lizzie, United Kingdom

Hornists Nest
Brass Wind Publications, 2011
Eight simple student pieces of a level to challenge the middle school or early high
     school student. Each has a short paragraph explaining some aspect of the
     music or style. Moderately challenging key signatures that go up to three
     sharps and four flats. .
Range: f–f^2

Davison, John H. (1938–1999) United States

Sonata for Horn and Piano, op. 91 (1986)
Southern Music, 1996
    I. Allegretto
    II. Adagio
    III. Vivace
A lengthy late twentieth-century tonal sonata with plenty of challenges, both
    technical and musical, for the horn player, requiring good endurance. Well
    written and idiomatic for the horn.
Range: $B\flat$–c^3

Dawes, Julian (1942–) United Kingom

Sonatina for Horn in F and Piano
SOAM Music Publishing, 2001
A three-movement sonatina: Allegro—Largo—Allegro. Written for Tony Catter-
    ick and in memory of Canon Jack Catterick. Technically straightforward
    and of a difficulty level accessible to the advancing high school student.
Range: g–g^2

Decruck, Fernande (1896–1954) France

Pastorale triste
Les Editions de Paris, 1934
A short piece in pastoral style, with both muted and stopped effects. Dedicated
    to Édouard Vuillermoz. Though musically easygoing, the piece has a wide
    range, with an emphasis on the top of the staff.
Range: d–b^2

Defaye, Jean-Michel (1932–) France

Alpha
Alphonse Leduc, 1973
Dedicated to Georges Barboteu. This fairly extended piece is composed in a late
    twentieth-century French style, and is rather technically difficult and chro-
    matic with a wide range. The first half is written very freely with no bar
    lines. New notation bass clef.
Range: A–c^3
Duration: 6:30

De Lamarter, Eric (1880–1953) United States

Ballade and poème
Witmark and Sons, 1948
The *Ballade* and *Poème* are published both together, and separately. Both were
    dedicated to Wendell Hoss and are written in a flowing, melodic style of
    moderate difficulty.
Range: f–a^2

Delerue, Georges (1925–1992) France

Poeme fantastique
Alphonse Leduc, 1952
Mid-twentieth-century French piece dedicated to Jean Devèmy, professor at the
    Paris Conservatory. Moderately difficult, with trills and stopped horn.
Range: f♯–b♭²

Delgiudice, Michel (1924–) France

Echos des bois
Alphonse Leduc, 1986
A short melodic student piece in the midrange in a moderate tempo for horn in
    F or alto saxhorn in E♭.
Range: a–e¹
Duration: 2:30

Evocation
Alphonse Leduc, 1986
Another short, melodic piece in the midrange, similar to the previous piece, for
    horn in F or alto saxhorn in E♭.
Range: a–e¹
Duration: 2:30

Appel pour cor et piano
Editions Combre, 1998
A short piece in two movements: Moderato—Allegretto. The first is composed in
    several sections of varying tempos with a hunting horn flavor. The second
    is a dance-like agile piece with crisp articulate rhythms. Fast, clean articu-
    lation is necessary for this piece.
Range: g–a²

Delmas, Marc (1885–1931) France

Claire de lune
Billaudot
A short, lyrical piece for horn and piano in a smooth flowing §. Stays mostly at the
    bottom of the staff until the end.
Range: b♭–g²

Ballade féerique (Nuits d'Esclarmonde)
Andrieu Frères, 1930; Billaudot
Written for M. Reine, professor at the Paris Conservatory. A moderately diffi-
    cult single-movement piece written mostly in a flowing style in sections of
    widely varying tempos. Some recitative-like sections and a few agile tech-
    nical passages.
Range: e–b♭²

Demessieux, Jeanne (1921–1968) France

Ballade, op. 12
Durand & Cie, 1962
Dedicated to Renè Dommange, this piece is composed in several contrasting sec-
tions with a number of passages that stay above the staff. Often fast and
agile, it includes trills and stopped horn.
Range: c–b²
Duration: 7:00

Demillac, Francis-Paul (1917–) France

Historiette
Editions Combre, 1986
A simple melody for the young horn student, with simple rhythms and a limited
range.
Range: d–f²

Denwood, Russell (1950–) United Kingdom

Songs of Provence
June Emerson Edition, 2000
Three movements based on songs from Provence: Les tres capitanis and Liseto—
Bello Viergo Courounado—La fluito and la targo. Moderately difficult horn
technique, with a few stopped notes, trills, and a glissando.
Range: g–b♭²
Duration: 9:25

De Pastel, Karen (1949–) United States, working in Austria
American born organist, composer, and professor.

Trilogie für Horn und Klavier, op. 33 (1989)
Doblinger, 1989; Wiener Waldhorn Verein
Duration: 16:00

Depelsenaire, Jean-Marie (1914–1986) France

Nocturne pour cor en fa et piano
Henry Lemione & Cie, 1958
A short piece, melodic at times with some fast agile passages. Includes stopped
horn and several contrasting tempo changes.
Range: g–a²

Les Ors et les gris l'automne
Billaudot, 1978
A short, fairly easy student piece in a slow, flowing tempo.
Range: b♭–e²

Désenclos, Albert (1912–1971) France

Cantilène et divertissiments
Alphonse Leduc, 1950
A rather complex first section in $\frac{3}{2}$ with many accidentals and complicated in-
tervals. The second section is faster and technically challenging with a ca-
denza, trills, and glissandi. Old notation bass clef.
Range: e–c³

Prèambule complainte et finale
Dedicated to Jean Devèmy and his "numerous disciples," this is a difficult piece
that was the examination piece for the Paris Conservatory in 1969. All
three sections are full of technical challenges and all of the effects that
were standard in French exam pieces, including cadenzas, trills, stopped
horn, glissandi, difficult intervals, and a wide range. New notation bass
clef.
Range: G–c³
Durand & Cie, 1969

Desportes, Yvonne (1907–1993) France

Improvisation
Alphonse Leduc, 1953
This French contest piece was dedicated to Jean Devèmy, professor at the Paris
Conservatory. Very technical and free in improvisatory style, with difficult
rhythms, trills, and stopped horn.
Range: c♯–c³
Duration: 6:30

Ballade Normande
Alphonse Leduc, 1943
Dedicated to Jean Devèmy, this straightforward piece is written in two relatively
short sections: a flowing slow section and an Allegro of moderate difficulty.
Includes stopped horn and trills.
Range: g–c³
Duration: 4:40

Sicilienne et allegro
Alphonse Leduc, 1960
A rather short piece of only moderate difficulty in mid-twentieth-century French
tonal style. The two sections, a slow and flowing sicilienne, and a fast and
articulate allegro include stopped horn and trills.
Range: e–a²
Duration: 5:30

de Roo, Paul (1957–)
See: Roo, Paul de

Devémy, Alain

J'ai 9 mois fe vor
IMD Diffusion Arpeges, 1990
Piece in $\frac{4}{4}$ that stays within the C major scale for the soloist. In ABA form. A suitable work for the beginning hornist.
Range: g–c³

Devogel, Jacques (1926–1995) France

Le Cor sage
Editions Combre, 1994
For horn in E♭ or F. A short, regal work in $\frac{4}{4}$ that features a dotted eighth-sixteenth motive with the occasional octave leap. Suitable for the young player.
Range: d¹–f²
Duration: 2:25

De Wolf, J. E. (1908–?) Netherlands

Sonatine in oude stijl
J. Maurer, 1960
A short two-movement sonatine that consists of a menuetto and a rondo, written in a very simple eighteenth-century style and a limited range.
Range: c¹–d²

Triptiek
J. Maurer, 1976

Dickson, John (1963–) United States

Laughlin Park Suite
JOMAR Press, 2012
    1. Vals de Armando
    2. Lacrima
    3. Toccata
Written for Charles Gavin. The first movement is named for Armando "Chick" Corea.
With a Spanish flavor, the second, "Lacrima," has a singing improvised feel, and the third, "Toccata," is agile and technical in a lighthearted jazzy style.
Range: G–c³
Duration: 12:00

Di Domenico, Olivio

Variationi
Alphonse Leduc, 1959
A piece of moderate difficulty, consisting of a simple theme and variations, not written in the usual form of numbered variations, but as a through-composed piece. Not difficult, but with a few agile passages and challenging rhythms.
Range: f –a² (f – g² with ossia)
Duration: 7:00

Diercks, John (1927–) United States

Fantasy
Theodore Presser—Tritone Press, 1962
A flowing, lyrical piece with a wide range. Simple melodically, but could present
    endurance challenges.

Dietrich, Albert (1829–1908) Germany
Composer and conductor, studied composition with Schumann, and was a col-
league of both Brahms and Schumann.
Einleitung und Romanze, Konzertstück für Horn (oder Violoncello)
und Klavier, op. 27
Edition Ebenos, 2005
This piece, first published in 1872, is a romantic work in $\frac{6}{8}$, with flowing expres-
    sive writing for the horn. Technical demands and range for the hornist are
    moderate, with an emphasis instead on lyrical expression and maintaining
    a beautiful singing line in a range of dynamics.
Range: g–a♭²
Duration: 8:30

Di Lorenzo, Anthony (1967–) United States

Phoenix Sonata (2012)
Art of Sound Music, 2012
    I. Allegro moderato
    II. Andante
    III. Allegro moderato
A modern tonal sonata written for William VerMeulen. All three movements are
    composed in the style of Hollywood film music with a touch of Brahms.
    In 2014, *Phoenix* was reworked into a concerto with full orchestra and also
    premiered by William VerMeulen.
Range: d–b²
Duration: 15:00
See: Horn and ensemble

Dishinger, R. C. (1941–) United States

Happy Scherzo
Medici Music Press, 2004
"Written while watching my son swimming." An active scherzo in $\frac{4}{4}$ with no rests.
    Not difficult, but persistent in its repeated eighth-note articulations.
Range: a–f²
Duration: 3:03

Dixon, Michael Hugh (1961–) Australia, born in New Zealand

Padma
Wirripang, 2003
Duration: 6:00

Dolorko, Ratko (1959–) Germany

Augenblick, für Horn und Klavier
Zeitklang, 1987
A rather short single movement in contemporary harmonic language, marked
  rubato. Technically easy in the horn part, but a bit sustained at the top of
  the staff in places. At one point the pianist is instructed to strum the notes
  of the sustained chords on the piano with the finger nails.
Range: c#^{1}–a^2

Donato, Anthony (1909–1990) United States

Sonata for Horn and Piano
Remick, 1950
    I. Briskly, with abandon
    II. Very slowly
    III. Boldly
A straightforward energetic piece in mid-twentieth-century tonal style. Many
  syncopated rhythms and a bit taxing in places.
Range: d#–a^2

Douane, Jules

En foret d'Olonne
Henry Lemoine, 1958
Short piece of very moderate difficulty in several short sections. Includes some
  stopped horn.
Range: e^1–f#^{2}

Dans Les Alpes
Editions Philippo, 1961
Dedicated to Claude Guise, this short piece in pastoral style is straightforward
  and of only moderate difficulty technically.

Dournel, Roger

En Badinant
Billaudot, 1986
A short elementary piece in limited range with easy rhythms.
Range: c^1–d^2 (c^1–f^2 with ossia)
Duration: 1:57

Downes, Andrew (1950–) United Kingdom

Sonata for Horn and Piano, op. 68
Lynwood Music, 1998
    I. Andante molto e espressivo
    II. Allegro moderato
    III. Andante leggiero

A three-movement work commissioned by Roland Horvath of the Vienna Philharmonic. A fairy difficult work, technically and rhythmically, that requires
a wide range and good endurance.
Range: A♭–b²
Duration: 25:00

Draeseke, Felix (1835–1913) Germany

Adagio & Romanze, op. 31/32
Hans Pizka Edition, Amadeus Verlag, 2011
Two romantic movements, originally published in the 1880s. The Adagio ma non
troppo is quite technically difficult, with fast flowing notes in a slow tempo
over a wide range. The Romanze is a lyrical Andante tranquillo that is also
challenging in its range and fluidity.
Range: c–b♭²

Dragstra, Willem (1956–) Netherlands

Aria con recitativo e capriccio
Rieks Sodenkamp, 1987

Dreyfus, George (1928–) Australia, born in Germany

Tender Mercies, for Horn with Piano (1982)
Australian Music Centre, Allans Publishing
Originally composed as film music and adapted for horn and piano by the composer.
Duration: 4:00

Duclos, Renè (1899–1964) France

Sur la Montagne
Alphonse Leduc, 1961
A rather technical piece written for Jean Devèmy, with challenging intervals;
accidentals; and fast, agile articulations. Includes stopped horn and new
notation bass clef.
Range: A♭–c³

Dubois, Pierre Max (1930–1995) France

A Bras le cor
Billaudot, 1984, 1998
Four very simple pieces for the young beginner. Simple rhythms in quarter, half,
and whole notes.
Range: c¹–a¹

Cornouaille
Editions Le Rideau, 1969
Musically easy piece in a flowing style that requires some control in the upper range.
Range: d¹–b²

Dans l'Ouest
Billaudot, 1982
Two short pieces of medium difficulty for the more advanced student who is be-
    ginning to develop the upper range. The movements are titled "Totem" and
    "Les poneys sauvages."
Range: a–a²

Les Bien Embouches
Billaudot, 1984
Six pieces for the beginning horn player. Simple melodies in easy note values in
    a limited range.
Range: g–d²
Duration 7:00

Poursuite
Editions Le Rideau, 1971
A fast, articulate piece marked Vivo that includes flutter tonguing.
Range: d¹–b²

Romance sans paroles
Alphonse Leduc, 1958
A simple melodic line in the horn part, accompanied by a rather complex piano
    part. Stays in the upper range throughout.
Range: c¹–b²
Duration: ca. 4:00

Dubois, Theodore (1837–1924) France

Cavatine
Heugel & Cie, 1910; Southern Music
A short, flowing Andantino written for Arthur Delgrange of the Paris Opera.
    Early twentieth-century romantic tonal style.
Range: f–a²

Duck, Leonard (1916–2002) United Kingdom

Images
Phyllosopus Publications (Spartan Press), 1999
Composed in three short movements: Legend—Oration—Outgrowth.

Dukas, Paul (1865–1935) France

Villanelle for Horn and Piano (1903)
Durand, 1906 (first edition); International,1963
This popular recital piece was composed in 1903 as an examination piece at the
    Paris Conservatory. During this period, the natural-horn class was discon-
    tinued and the valve horn was established as the official instrument that
    would be taught. In this piece, Dukas requires the player to have skill on
    both. The single-movement work consists of two sections. The first page,
    in a moderately slow lyrical §, was originally meant to be played on the

natural horn, while the second section, marked Très vif, is to be played using valves. A brief hand horn section occurs again before the final fast section that ends the piece. As with most exam pieces, it requires a variety of techniques in addition to hand horn technique, including stopped and echo horn, trills, triple tonguing, mute, and agility throughout the range. Originally written for horn and orchestra, but most often played with piano. The original orchestration is lost, but several orchestrations have been done in recent years.

Range: c–c³
Duration: 6:14

Dunhill, Thomas Frederick (1877–1946) United Kingdom

Cornucopia, op. 95
Hawkes and Sons, 1941
A sheaf of miniatures for horn and piano, written for Frank Probyn. Six short
    movements of moderate difficulty, and of contrasting characters in a tonal
    twentieth-century style. Rhythmically easy with some agile articulate pas-
    sages.
Range: c–a♭²

Dupuis, Albert (1877–1967) Belgium

Variations sur un thème populaire
Alphonse Leduc, 1926
Five variations on a traditional theme. Medium difficulty with a few stopped pas-
    sages. Some agile passages, but all within the staff.
Range: d¹–g²

Durkó, Zsolt (1934–1997) Hungary

Symbols, for Horn and Piano (1968–69)
Editio Musica Budapest, 1969
A contemporary work, delineated into ten sections with a recurring "motto." In-
    tricate writing in both parts, requiring coordination between performers.
    Includes extreme dynamics, half-muted passages, changing meters and
    tempos, and glissandi. Bass clef is old notation.
Range: B♭–b♭²

Duvernoy, Frédéric (1765–1838) France

French hand horn soloist, solo horn of the Paris Opera, and professor at the Paris Conservatory in the early nineteenth century. Duvernoy wrote many pieces for horn in the cor-mixt style that was popular in France at the time, featuring agile and technical playing in the midrange of the horn.

1st, 2nd, 3rd and 4th Divertissement
Robert Ostermeyer, 2011 (nos. 1, 2, 3); Editions Fortin-Armiane (no. 4), 2007
Four salon pieces, each published separately, composed in contrasting sections in
    the French cor-mixt style of the early nineteenth century. Many fast notes,

but relatively easy, and not very taxing. All four were originally written for natural horn in F, and are user-friendly pieces for a natural horn or valve horn recital.

Range: g–g^2 or a♭^{2} in all four pieces

Fantasie für Horn und Klavier
Robert Ostermeyer, 1999
Written in the cor-mixt style of natural horn writing of the early nineteenth century, this piece features fast scale passages, trills, and ornaments in the French handhorn style of the period. As usual with Duvernoy's music, it is written for natural horn in F, with key signatures of G minor and G major.
Range: g–g^2
Robert Ostermeyer, 1999

Fantaisies, nos. 2–8
Robert Ostermeyer, 2011
These pieces, also published individually, are all similar in character and horn technique to the previous *Fantasie* and *Divertissiments.* All are cor-mixt pieces for natural horn in F. Mostly midrange (c–g^2) and composed in several sections of varying characters. Not terribly difficult, but with many passages of fast articulated notes.

6ème fantasie, réveil de J. J. Rousseau
Hans Pizka edition, 1980
A facsimile of the original printing of no. 6 of the previous set of Fantasies.

Serenade Nr. 2 and *Serenade Nr. 3*
Robert Ostermeyer, 2012

Dvořáček, Jiří (1928–2000) Czech Republic

Due per duo, Due rondi per corno e piano, 1970
Český Hudební Fond Praha, 1972
Two pieces in contemporary style, each consisting of contrasting sections. Moderately difficult technically, but rather long and taxing. Includes flutter tongue and trills.
Range: A–c^3

Dvorak, Robert James (1919–) United States

Prelude for Horn and Piano (1937)
Alliance Publications, Inc, 2009
Short, melodic piece marked Andante espressivo. Includes a short cadenza.
Range: f–a♭^{2}
Duration: 4:24

East, Harold (1947–) United Kingdom, born in Canada

Four Occasional Pieces for Horn and Piano
Ricordi, 2000

Dedicated to Martin Shillito, these four short pieces of rather moderate difficulty and contrasting characters are marked:

1. Slow and languorous
2. Resolute and rhythmic
3. Not too fast with a strong lilt
4. Lively

Range: g–g^2 (with one ossia passage to a^2)

Sonatina for Horn and Piano
Ricordi, 1987
Written for Frank Lloyd, this three-movement piece covers a wide range and presents a number of difficulties, including quick changes of range, difficult intervals, and stopped horn. The notation changes often between bass and treble clef.
Range: b–c^3

Echevarria, Victorino (1898–1965) Spain

Intermezzo
Alphonse Leduc, 1958
A single movement that incorporates technical and lyrical elements in a French mid-twentieth-century style. Fairly difficult, technically.
Range: g–b^2
Duration: 8:00

Edelson, Edward (1932–) United States

The Final Hour
C & E Enterprises, 1992
A very simple, lyrical piece for the young player.
Range: d^1–d^2

Eder, Helmut (1916–2005) Austria

Vier Fantasiestücke, op. 103 (1993)
Doblinger, 1995
Four short contemporary pieces, rather difficult technically, with a few rhythmic difficulties, stopped horn, and mute. New notation bass clef.
Range: G–c^3
Duration: ca. 16:00

Sonatine, op. 34, no. 6
Doblinger, 1996
Written in three movements: 1. Adagio—2. Allegro leggiero—3. Allegro moderato. A rather short work in the post-Webern school of serial-composition technique.
Range: a–a^2
Duration: 6:30

Edstrom, Brent (1964–) United States

Sonata
TrumCor Music, 2004
Composed in three movements: Allegro moderato—Andante cantabile—Scherzo. Written in a contemporary tonal style that presents the horn player with some technical challenges, but idiomatically written.
Range: f–a² (ossia f–c³)

Eechaute, Prosper van (1904–1964) Belgium

Nachtpoëma (poéme nocturne)
Editions Metropolis, 1963
A flowing piece, marked Andante non troppo lento, that features several scale-wise flourishes and a wide range. Old notation bass clef. Also available for horn and orchestra.
Range: c♯–b♭² (with ossia d³)
See: Horn and ensemble

Effinger, Cecil (1914–1990) United States

Rondino
G. Schirmer, 1970
A short, agile piece in ¾ of moderate difficulty.
Range: e–g²

Egea, J. Vincent (1961–) Spain

Sonata
IMD Diffusions Arpeges, 1998
    I. Allegro marcato
    II. Lento
    III. Allegro marcato
This piece, premiered by Javier Bonet in 1997, is very contemporary in its horn writing, presenting both players with many complex rhythms, difficult articulation patterns, a wide range, and challenging contemporary techniques, including multiphonics and stopped horn. The piece includes a glossary of the contemporary notation and effects used. The second movement, which has a long unmeasured section, includes multiphonics with an alternate version that can simply be played as single notes, stopped. The last movement is filled with difficult intervals and fast articulation, and features an extended cadenza.
Range: G–d³ (with ossias to c³)

Ehle, Robert C., United States

Sonata for Horn in F and Piano, op. 79C (1984)
JOMAR Press
A fairly short sonata in three movements: I. Cordoba—II. Ronda—III. Sevilla.

The first movement consists of half notes and slow triplets over a single line of
   flowing sextuplets in the piano. The second movement is a slow, decisive
   melody in $\frac{4}{4}$. The third is faster, and more agile, again over a flowing sextuplet accompaniment.
Range: d–c³
Duration: 8:00

Eichborn, Hermann Ludwig (1847–1918) Germany

Sonata, op. 7
Breitkopf and Härtel, 1899, available on www.imslp.org
   I. Allegro assai
   II. Andante
   III. Vivace
A relatively short three-movement sonata in mid-nineteenth-century romantic style
   dedicated to hornist Georg Wieland. Moderately difficult horn technique.
Range: b♭–a²

Erste Suite für Waldhorn (oder Violine) mit Klavierbegleitung, op. 12
Breitkopf and Härtel, 1893
Three short movements in mid-nineteenth-century romantic style: Romanza—
   Gavotte—Allegro non troppo. Straightforward horn writing, though a bit
   taxing, due to the small number of rests. A few agile passages and wide
   intervals in the Gavotte. Out of print, but available in U.S. libraries.
Range: c–g² (with ossia a²)

Einem, Gottfried von (1918–1996) Austria

Jeux d'amour, Drei Capricen für Horn und Klavier, op. 99 (1993)
Doblinger, 1995
Three short movements of varying tempos with a wide range, but with an em-
   phasis on the low range. Of moderate difficulty technically. Contemporary
   tonal style.
Range: G–b♭²
Duration: ca. 9:00

Eisner, Carl (1802–1874) Germany

2 Pièces de Salons, op. 16 (ca. 1860)
Robert Ostermeyer, 2000
The first of these salon pieces, "Le Repos," covers a wide range in an operatic
   style, while the second is of a more flowing melodic nature. Some orna-
   ments and trills, but not overly difficult. Written for the valve horn.
Range: G–b♭²

Album für Horn und Pianoforte
Robert Ostermeyer, 2002
Contains several short pieces by Eisner that were collected together from a man-
   uscript in the Dresden Library, all previously unpublished: Capriccio for
   valve horn—L'anniversaire (The birthday)—Der Blinde (The blind man)—
   Two etudes with piano.

Epstein, David (1930–2002) United States

Petit March and fantasia
Belwin, 1963
Two short pieces with a few technical challenges. Includes muted and stopped horn as well as glissandi.
Range: f–b♭²

Escaich, Thierry (1965–) France

Ground V pour cor en fa et orgue
Billaudot, 2012.
Duration: 10:00

Eschmann, Johann Carl (1826–1882) Germany

"Im Herbst" Fantasiestucke, op. 6
Breitkopf & Härtel, 1852; Amadeus Verlag, 1999
Six movements, in mid-nineteenth-century style. Includes spoken poetry.
Range e–a²

Ewazen, Eric (1954–) United Sates

Sonata
Southern Music, 1998
A major work in contemporary tonal style in four movements, written for Scott Brubaker and premiered by Brubaker with the composer at the piano in 1992 at the Weill Recital Hall in New York City. A very strenuous and technical horn part.
Range: B–d³ (with ossia B–c³)

Faith, Richard (1926–) United States

Movements for Horn and Piano (1965)
Shawnee Press, 1968
Published in two volumes. The first volume contains movements one through three, and the second volume has movements four and five. Five simple melodic movements, each portraying a specific mood.
Range: g–b²

Fasce, Albert (1930–) France

Corail
Editions Combre, 1987
A short piece for the student hornist consisting of a lyrical Andante opening followed by an Allegretto with not too difficult articulated sixteenth-note passages, ending with a return to the material of the opening section.
Range: b–g²

Faust, Randall E. (1947–) United States

Celebration for Horn and Organ (1977)
Randall Faust, 1977
A short, festive movement, marked Maestoso con brio, written in the style of a
    fanfare.
Range: d♭–g²
Duration: 2:10

Declamation—Fantasy Variations for Horn and Harpsichord
Randall E. Faust, 2004
As the title suggests, this is a declamatory piece, some of which is to be played on
    the natural horn in F using hand stopping. Written for Lars and Sebastian
    Bausch.
Range: c–a♭²

Epitaph
Randall E. Faust, 2012
Commissioned by Douglas Campbell in memory of Ellen Campbell. A fairly dif-
    ficult work with a wide range and a wide range of expression.
Range: B–b²

Fantasy (2001)
Randall E. Faust, 2006
For horn and organ. Written for Ashley Leland, this is a fantasy on the hymn
    "Vom Himmel Hoch." Includes trills and pitch bending through hand
    stopping.
Range: c–b♭²

Festive Processional
Randall E. Faust, 2001
A short processional for horn and organ of rather moderate difficulty.
Range: d¹–g²

Meditation (1983)
Randall E. Faust, 1983, 2005
For horn and organ. A short, meditative piece, but quite active in its intervals and
    range changes. Composed as a preface to Faust's other piece for horn and
    organ, *Celebration* of 1977. Written for Jim Kellock
Range: e♭–a♭²

Three English Folk Songs
Randall E. Faust, 2006
Written for Andrew Pelletier. These three folk song settings are entitled: I. Henry
    Martin—II. The Water is wide—III. Gently, Johnny. The horn part is only
    moderately difficult.
Range: g–c³

Rondo for Horn and Piano (1997)
Randall E. Faust, 1997

Composed in honor of Roger Collins, hornist with the Camerata Woodwind
    Quintet. This piece quotes the Reicha E♭ quintet op. 88, no. 2.
Range: b♭–b♭²

Sesquicentennial Prelude (2004)
Randall E. Faust, 2004
For horn and organ. A set of variations on the hymn "Standing on the Promises
    of God."
Range: g–a²

Feld, Jindrick (Jindřich) (1925–2007) Czech Republic

Pièce de concert (1966)
Alphonse Leduc, 1966
A brisk concert piece in mid-twentieth-century French style. The first section in
    $^{12}_8$–$^4_4$ is followed by a meno mosso section in $^3_4$ followed by more $^{12}_8$–$^4_4$ to the
    end. Much emphasis on the upper range of the horn and repeated staccato
    notes. Also arranged for horn and chamber orchestra.
Range: F♯–c³
Duration: 6:00

Fennelly, Brian (1937–) United States

Coralita (Corollary I) for Horn and Piano (1986)
American Composers Alliance, 1987
A single-movement work, first performed by David Jolley.
Duration: 7:00

Ferrari, Giorgio (1925–2010) Italy

Sonata
G. Zanibon, 1973
    I. Allegro Moderato
    II. Adagio
    III. Vivace
A three-movement work in twentieth-century tonal style. Fairly difficult but
    straightforward in its horn technique.
Range: e–b²

Fine, Elaine (1959–) United States

Sonata for Horn and Piano
Seesaw Music, 2003
A contemporary tonal sonata in three movements: Allegro—Canzona—Fugato.
    Requires substantial horn technique, but is reasonable for the player with
    a solid high range.
Range: g–c³

Finke, Fidelio (1891–1968) Germany

Sonata (1946)
Breitkopf & Härtel
    I. Largo
    II. Intermezzo
    III. Introduktion und Scherzo-Finale
Dedicated to Joseph Keilberth. A very serious first movement which is quite
    sustained and slow, followed by a lightly moving second movement, and
    a spirited finale.
Range: G–c³

Finko, David (1936–) United States, born in Russia

Reminiscence of Childhood
Theodore Presser, 1986
Rather contemporary single-movement piece with a wide range. Some stopped
    horn and glissandi, and a few rhythmic difficulties.
Range: d–b²
Duration: 5:00

Fisher, Charles W.

Entries
RM Williams, 2008
Four technically rather difficult movements: Entry 1—Entry 2—Entry 3—Entry
    4. Written for John Jacobson. The first, second, and fourth movements are
    very fast and technical, the third movement is slower but still full of tech-
    nical challenges, difficult intervals, and articulations.
Range: e–c²

Exits
RM Williams, 2008
Written for Gail Williams, these four fairly short movements are prefaced with
    this comment: "These pieces are for those horn players who need a little
    bit more to end their performances!" In their varying tempos, each has
    many technical challenges, and each would make an exciting end to a re-
    cital program.
Range: B♭–c³

Rhapsody Fantasia
RM Williams, 2008
A fairly long single movement that stays in the same character and moderato
    tempo throughout, while going through several changes of key.
Range: B♭–b♭²

Sonate
RM Williams, 2008

This sonata of fairly substantial length is in the three movements marked: Moderato—Rubato—Allegro. The piece features some rather technical passages
and covers a wide range. Written mostly in short melodic gestures rather
than long lines.
Range: d–c³

Flem, Paul
See: Le Flem, Paul

Font, Luis (?–1911) Spain
Professor of horn in Madrid in the late nineteenth century.
4th Solo de concert
IMD Diffusion Arpeges, 1997
His fourth solo is written in several sections of contrasting tempos and styles,
and features some very agile horn technique, highly ornamented flowing
melodies, fast articulations, and trills, all in a late nineteenth-century style
reminiscent of the French exam pieces. A difficult work.
Range: e–b♭²

Forsyth, Malcolm (1936–2011) Canada, born in South Africa
Dreams, Drones, and Drolleries (1981)
Canadian Music Centre
This piece, commissioned by the Canadian Music Centre for horn player Margaret Bunkall, is in three movements. The first features articulated repeated
notes, stopped and muted effects, and double-tongued tremolos. The second is more dramatic and covers a wide range with glissando flourishes
and a quasi-recitative section. The third movement has an energetic and
agile jazzy feel.
Range: B♭–c³
Duration: 13:00

Fossa, Matthew, United States
Concertpiece
Written for Scott Bacon, this piece is a short single movement, not overly technical, but challenging in its range and agile intervals. Due to the demands
of range and endurance in the second half of the piece, the composer has
supplied an alternate version of the same music in a more limited range
from measure sixty-one to the end.
Range: g–c³ (ossia c–a♭²)

Fournier, Henri (Pseudonym for Charles O'Neill)
See: O'Neill, Charles

Fox, Adrienne (1941–) United Kingdom

Two Chrome Vignettes for Horn and Piano
June Emerson Edition, 2007
Adrienne Fox began playing the horn at age sixty after a long career as a music
     educator in England, and these pieces were dedicated to her horn teacher
     Paul Kampen in appreciation for his teaching and encouragement. These
     two very simple movements are in an easy range for the beginner. The first
     is marked Andante, and the second is marked "Boisterously."
Range: g–c¹

Frackenpohl, Arthur (1924–) United States

Largo and Allegro
G. Schirmer collection *Solos for the Horn Player,* 1962 (Mason Jones, ed.)
Two short movements: a flowing Largo, and an easy going but agile Allegro. Mod-
     erately difficult, this piece is a good choice for the advancing high school stu-
     dent. A version for horn and strings is available from G. Schirmer on rental.
Range: f–b♭² (with low range ossia, B♭–b♭²)
See: Horn and ensemble

Three Diversions for Horn and Piano
Arthur Frackenpohl, 1994
     1. Tango
     2. Blues Opus 1.125
     3. M.P. Rag (Danke, R. Str.)
Written for Roy Schaberg, the titles are descriptive of the character of each move-
     ment, and the horn part is very playable technically but requires a good feel
     for the three styles. The first two movements have sections with optional
     chord changes notated so that the performer could improvise instead of
     playing the printed part. The last movement is a rag based on the horn solo
     from the opening of *Till Eulenspiegel,* by Richard Strauss.
Range: g–c²
Duration: 8:50

Francaix, Jean (1912–1997) France

Canon en octave
Pierre Noël, 1953; International, 1954; Billaudot
A popular short recital piece of about one-minute duration and a favorite recital
     piece of Philip Farkas. Rhythmically straightforward, but fast and agile.
Range: b–f♯²

Divertimento
Éditions musicales transatlantiques, 1959
     I. Introduzione
     II. Aria di cantabile
     III. Canzonetta

An energetic and somewhat difficult work with a bit of a jazz flavor. The first and last movements feature a lot of staccato articulation and fast technique. The second movement is a lyrical song in the midrange. Includes stopped horn and flutter tongue. New notation bass clef.
Range: c–c#^{3}
Duration: 7:00

Frangkiser, Carl (1894–1967) United States

Melodie Importune, Solo for Horn in F
Boosey & Hawkes, 1946
Short, easy piece with a limited range.
Range: f^1–f^2

Franz, Oscar (1843–1886) Germany

Adagio, op. 1
Leipzig, 1873
Short, romantic late nineteenth-century piece. Rather sustained with an emphasis on the top of the staff.
Range: A♭–b♭^{2}

Lied ohne Worte, op. 2
McCoy, 1981; Dorm 40 Music
A short, lyrical late nineteenth-century piece of moderate difficulty.
Range: c–e^2

Adagio, op. 1; *Lied Ohne Worte,* op. 2; *Ländler,* op. 5
Hans Pizka Edition, 1990 (published as a set)

Frehse, Albin (1878–1973) Germany

Andante
Hofmeister
A short single-movement lyrical work in sounding G♭major.
Range: a♭–g♭^{2}
Duration: 4:00

Serenade
Hofmeister
Short piece of medium difficulty with a waltz feel.
Range: a–g^2
Duration: 3:00

Studienkonzert
Hofmeister, 1954
A virtuoso three-movement work specifically for the low-horn player. Quite technical and agile in the low range.
Range: F–g^2
Duration: 20:00

Fricker, Peter Racine (1920–1990) United Kingdom

Sonata for Horn and Piano, op. 24
Schott, 1956
A substantial mid-twentieth-century piece in two movements, each of which is
   divided into several contrasting sections. Straightforward technically, with
   no unusual techniques or overly complex rhythms. Accessible to the advanced college-level horn player.
Range: c♯–b♭²

Fries, Albin (1955–) Germany

Horn Sonata "Herbst," op.20 (2008)
Available online at www.imslp.org
A tonal twenty-first-century sonata in three movements: Allegro maestoso—
   Langsam—Lebhaft. A very dramatic work in which the horn's noble char-
   acter is emphasized. Not too difficult technically, but rather taxing, due to
   an emphasis on the upper range and full dynamics.
Range: e♯–b²
Duration: 12:00

Frith, John (1947–) United Kingdom

Sonata
June Emerson Edition, 2007
Written for Adrien Uren, this substantial three-movement sonata requires agile
   technique and good endurance. Movements are marked: Quasi scherzando
   ($\frac{3}{8}$)—Andante con moto e tranquillo ($\frac{2}{2}$)—Vivo ($\frac{2}{4}$). Includes a few trills, some
   fast wide leaps, and fast articulations.
Range: d–c²
Duration: ca. 10:00

Gabaye, Pierre (1930–2000) France

Sérénade de printemps
Alphonse Leduc, 1959
An easygoing piece marked Allegretto. Technically quite easy.
Range: g–a²

Gabelles, Gustave Ferdinand Elie (1883–1969) France

Image
Philippo et M. Combre, 1961
A short, flowing lyrical piece of moderate difficulty written for Jean Devémy.
Range: c♯–g²

Concertino for Horn and Piano
Southern Music Company, 1988

An examination piece from 1905 for the conservatory of Lille, in France. Written in a single movement of several sections, it contains all of the elements of a good exam piece, cadenzas, lyrical and technical sections, stopped horn, and trills.

Range: g–g²

Fantasie

Andrieu Freres, 1938; Alfred Music; Billaudot

Single-movement solo piece in early twentieth-century French style. Fairly difficult and technical, with stopped horn, trills, and a lengthy section to be played using hand horn technique.

Range: g–g²

Gagnebin, Henri (1886–1977) France

Aubade

Alphonse Leduc, 1960

Written for Edmond Leloir. A single movement divided into several sections of different tempos. A few challenges technically, but not overly difficult. Includes stopped horn, trills, and old notation bass clef.

Range: G–b♭²

Duration: 7:40

Gallay, Jacques François (1795–1864) France

Hand horn virtuoso and professor at the Paris Conservatory, 1842–1864.

Gallay wrote at least fourteen solos for horn and piano to be used as examination pieces at the conservatory. All were written for the natural horn, using the highly developed hand technique of the period. The general scheme of these includes a slow, lyrical opening; fast technical sections with scales and arpeggios; trills; cadenzas; and modulations into different keys. All of these features are meant to demonstrate every aspect of horn playing needed for music of the period. He also wrote shorter pieces that range from arrangements of Schubert songs to fantasies on themes from operas. A few are available in modern editions.

2nd Solo, op. 7

Hans Pizka Edition, 1996

A shorter exam piece in two sections, starting with an Adagio non troppo in a vocal style followed by an Amoroso poco andante that gets fairly technical by the end. The entire piece centers around the keys of C and F major, comfortable tonalities for the natural horn in F.

Range: d♯¹–a♭²

3rd Solo, op. 9

Hans Pizka Edition, 1980

An exam piece written in two sections, a 𝄢 Andante sostenuto, and an Andante mosso, with plenty of technique to test the conservatory student's agility and hand-horn skills.

Range: c¹–g² (b♭² with ossia)

4th Solo, op. 11
Hans Pizka Edition
An exam piece written in two sections, an Adagio sostenuto and a Polacca. Includes a variety of natural horn techniques, including trills, cadenzas, and
a good bit of nonstop technical playing in the Polacca. Almost all within
the limits of the staff for F horn.
Range: e^1–a^2

Premier nocturno concertant, op. 36
Hans Pizka Edition, 1983
A more extended lyrical piece in F minor, which puts the hand horn in F in its
written key of C minor, resulting in many veiled colors of half-stopped
notes. Some quite technical passages, and a bit taxing, all together,
Range: c^1–c^3

9th Solo, op. 39
Hans Pizka Edition
An interesting exam piece in two sections, including an operatic Adagio introduction, and an Allegro moderato flowing melodic section, with an Allegro
risoluto ending. Not as technical as the previous solos, but more melodic
throughout. One section modulates into E major putting the F horn into written B major, with predominantly stopped colors for an overall muted effect.
Range: c^1–ab^2

10th Solo, op. 45
Hans Pizka Edition
A more extended exam piece, and more high horn oriented. A rather chromatic
Largo introduction leads into a fairly long, flowing Allegro risoluto section
in two flats for the F horn. The Allegro finale is quite persistent, though not
overly technical, making the entire piece rather taxing.
Range: b–a^2

11th Solo, op. 52
Hornseth Music, 1979
This exam piece focuses on intense minor-key melodies. Written in several short
sections alternating major and minor, the major sections also rarely let up
on their musical intensity.
Range: g–a^2

12th Solo, op. 55
Hans Pizka Edition
An exam piece for low horn, and, unlike the previous exam pieces, written for horn
in E♭. The Adagio introduction in E♭ minor gives the horn an opportunity to
express ominous dark colors with the stopped notes on natural horn. A cor-
basse-style cadenza leads into a major key fast section followed by a slightly
slower section in G minor, again with dark colors and low stopped notes,
ending with an agile major-key finale. Full of the typical low horn playing
techniques of the French school of the time.
Range: B♭–g^2 (ossia to f^2) (c–a^2 [ossia to g^2] for horn in E♭)

Fantasie sur la romance "Ma Normandie," op. 34
Robert Ostermeyer, 2006
A theme and variations piece for F horn
Range: c^1–a^2

Fantasie sur l'elisire d'amore, op. 46
Hans Pizka Edition
A fairly long fantasy piece written for horn or cornet in F. A Larghetto operatic
    introduction leads into an Andantino theme with a technical variation. Af-
    ter an Adagio section ending with a cadenza, the piece ends with a spirited
    Allegro finale.
Range: e^1–c^3

Souvenirs, melodie pour cor et piano, op. 56
Hans Pizka Edition, 1983
A shorter, flowing, melodic piece in E major. Includes some fluid sixteenth-note
    passages that need to be played in a smooth vocal style.
Range: $d\sharp^1$–b^2 (e^1–c^3 for horn in E)

Les Echos, op. 59 (1855)
Hans Pizka Edition, 1983
Originally published as *Trois Petite Fantasies.*
    1. Le cor des Alpes
    2. Les Combats du coeur
    3. Je pence à toi
Only the first two are included in this reprint. These are fairly easy lyrical pieces
    in C and B♭ major, written for horn in F.
Range: $d\sharp^1$–g^2

Romance on themes from Bellini's Bianca e Fernando
Carl Fischer, 1976
A short, lyrical piece in A minor. Lots of interesting colors when played on hand
    horn. A very good choice for the new natural horn player.
Range: $d\sharp^1$–g^2

Gallon, Noël (1891–1966) France

Andante et presto
Henry Lemoine, 1957
Dedicated to Jean Devémy, this was the Paris Conservatory competition piece for
    1957. Written in a single movement of several sections, it contains many of
    the elements of a good exam piece, lyrical and technical sections, stopped
    horn, and trills.
Range: $f\sharp$–b^2

Gantchoula, Philippe (1956–) France

Danse de l'ours
Editions Combre, 1998

Chant d'automne
Editions Combre, 2003
An elementary piece of limited range and technique for the beginner.
Range: g–d²

Garaudé, Alexis de & **Buziau** (1779–1852) France

Fantaisie & variations sur l'air de la Molinara "Nel cor piu non mi sento" (1823)
Robert Ostermeyer
A collaboration between French composer Alexis de Garaudé and a horn player
    named Buziau, about whom no information is available. The piece, written
    for natural horn in F, is a theme and variations on a French song. Though
    written in a nineteenth-century cor-mixt style, and therefore of limited
    range, the piece is quite technical. Requires agility and the ability to do lip
    trills. The piano part is also rather virtuosic.
Range: g–g²

Garfield, Bernard (1924–) United States

Soliloquy
Editions Musicus, 1954
Originally composed for bassoon, the piece was transcribed by the composer for
    horn. A short, contemplative piece of very moderate difficulty.
Range: e–f♯²

Garland, Chris, United Kingdom

La Bise (Breeze on the Lake)
Edition db, 2010
A musically straightforward piece in ¾ that is relatively simple for the horn, but
    requires a bit of upper range and a few stopped notes.
Range: g–a² (c–a² with ossia)

Memorial Sonata
Edition db
The preface states "Memorial Sonata evokes different ways of remembering the life
    of someone very close to you." Written in six movements of varying lengths
    and moods: 1. Cri du cor (for unaccompanied horn)—2. Obituary—3. Pian-
    gevole (for piano solo)—4. Elegy—5. Corale—6. Celebration. Straightforward
    traditional horn writing that is very expressive, and covers a wide range.
Range: d–b♭²

Garlick, Antony (1927–2000) United States

Suite for Horn and Piano
Seesaw Music, 1981
Six short movements entitled: Habanera—Basse dance—Gavotte—Allemande—
    Ungaresca—Langaus. Written in various styles and characters. Fairly easy
    midrange horn playing throughout.
Range: e–e²

Gartenlaub, Odette (1922–2014) France

Pour le Cor
Editions Rideau Rouge, 1968
A Paris Conservatory exam piece for 1968, dedicated to Jean Devémy. Quite difficult, with an opening unmeasured section, stopped horn, trills, glissandi, cadenza, and some rather technical passages.
Range: c–c^3
Duration: 7:00

Gastinel, Gérard (1949–) France

Cor a cor III
Editions Fuzeau, 1989
Three short movements in contemporary style with frequent meter changes, and, in a few sections, note lengths indicated in seconds. Includes a key to some of the graphic notation. Not difficult technically for the horn.
Range: g–e^2

Gates, Crawford M. (1921–) United States

Sonata for Horn and Piano, op. 48 (1974)
Pacific Publications, 1991, Potenza Music
    1. Prologue and toccata
    2. Romanza
    3. Rondo and epilogue
A demanding and substantial work in a contemporary style written in standard notation. Commissioned in 1974 by the School of Music at Ball State University in Indiana for the International Horn Workshop, and premiered by Barry Tuckwell. Some muting and stopped horn.
Range: G–d^3
Duration: 24:30

Geert, Octaaf A. Van (1949–) Belgium

Collage for Horn and Piano (2007)
CeBeDeM, 2007
This work consists of short sections of differing styles and moods: Feel free—Mini-Ragtime—Dreaming. . .under a starry sky. . .and 29 degrees centigrade. . .—Enjoy life—Finale: Memories. These are broken up by a recurring declamatory "signal" of four bars. Rhythmic, often jagged, lines in a contemporary style, mostly in the midrange of the horn.
Range: g–d^2
Duration: 5:18

Genzmer, Harald (1909–2007) Germany

Sonatine
Littolf/Peters, 1969

Relatively easy, but interesting, four movement sonatina, straightforward technically and rhythmically. Could be a very effective student-recital piece.
Range: g–a♭²

Ghidoni, Armando (1959–) Italy

Évocation en swing
Alphonse Leduc, 2001
A simple piece in a limited range for the young player.
Range: g–c²

Mississipi souvenir
Alphonse Leduc, 2000
Also a simple piece for the young player.
Range: g–e♭²

Ballade et jeux
Alphonse Leduc, 1966
An elementary piece.

Poésie et gaîté
Alphonse Leduc, 1999
Described as an elementary piece, this work actually presents a few technical challenges for the young horn student. An Adagio opening section with a two-octave range leads into a relatively agile fast section. Includes a cadenza, some stopped horn, and fast articulations.
Range: d–f²
Duration: 5:15

Gibbs, Christopher (1938–) United Kingdom

Meditation for Horn and Piano
Phyllosopus Publications (Spartan Press), 1999

Gillam, Russell

Rondino
Kendor Music Co., 1972
Dedicated to Glen E. Morgan. A straightforward rondo of moderate difficulty for the advancing student.
Range: a–f²
Duration: 2:00

Gillespie, Don (1942–) United States

Sonata da chiesa
Seesaw Music, 1991
In four movements: Andante—Risoluto—Lento—Allegro brioso. Written in a contemporary tonal style. A moderately difficult work with some agile passages, but idiomatically written for the horn.
Range: f–a²
Duration 12:40

Gillet, Bruno (1936–) France

Avanti
Billaudot, 1990
A fairly difficult contemporary piece for horn and piano with technical challenges for the horn player including difficult atonal intervals, fast articulations, and difficult rhythmic patterns. Effects include muted and stopped
notes, and flutter tongue. Challenging for both players in terms of ensemble and rhythmic precision. New notation bass clef.
Range: B♭–b²
Duration: 5:00

Gillingham, David R. (1947–) United States

A Baker's Dozen
C. Alan Publications, 2002
Described by the composer as "A set of thirteen miniature pieces in various
styles and moods. . . The movements vary in mood from 'tongue in cheek'
(i.e. 'Hornpipe') to solemn seriousness (i.e. 'Elegy'). . . . Challenging for
both the horn, (on a virtuoso level) and the pianist, yet friendly to the
listener."
Range: a–c³

Gipps, Ruth (1921–1999) United Kingdom

Sonatina for Horn and Piano, op. 56
Sam Fox Publishing Company, 1961
Short three-movement work of medium difficulty and range.
Range: g–g²
Duration: 8:00

Girard, Anthony (1959–) France, born in United States

L'Homme et son ombre
Editions Combre, 1997
A contemporary piece in which the piano improvises a constant accompaniment
using a given set of notes, under the written out melodic horn part. The
piece is very free and flowing, without bar lines, and with many fermatas. The horn part is only of moderate difficulty and mostly of a lyrical
character.
Range: B♭–b♭²
Duration: 8:00

Glazunov, Alexander (1865–1936) Russia

Rêverie, op. 24, *for Horn and Piano*
Cundy-Bettony; Leeds Music, 1945; M. P. Blelaieff, 1979
A short, lyrical piece often played on student recitals. The style is very romantic,
like that of the short horn and piano pieces of Gliere. A good piece for the

high school or early-college horn player. Includes stopped horn and old no-
tation bass clef.
Range: A♭–a♭^{2}
Duration: 3:30

Gliere, Rheinhold (1875–1956) Russia

Romance, op. 35, no. 6

Valse Triste, op. 35, no. 7

Nocturne, op. 35, no. 10

Intermezzo, op. 35, no. 11
International, 1982 (Joseph Anderer, ed.)
These four short pieces in a romantic early twentieth-century Russian style are
    from the composer's set of eleven pieces, op. 35 for various instruments and
    piano. Numbers 10 and 11 are originally for horn and piano, while numbers
    6 and 7 were originally scored for clarinet and piano and were adapted for
    horn at an unknown date. All four of these popular recital pieces are inter-
    esting and melodic, and of medium difficulty.
Range: e–a^2

Godel, Didier (1945–) Switzerland

Rondo
Editions Marc Reift, 1994
A single movement of substantial length marked Andante non troppo. Quite ag-
    ile and articulate. Stopped horn and old notation bass clef.
Range: c–g^2

Godfrey, Philip (1964–) United Kingdom

Three Impromptus for Horn
Brass Wind Publications, 2009
Three short movements: Prelude—Romance—Gigue. Of medium difficulty for
    the advancing high school horn student who has good command to the top
    of the staff.
Range: b♭–g^2
Duration: 9:00

Gotkovsky, Ida (1933–) France

Concerto pour cor et piano (1984)
Billaudot, 1984
See: Horn and ensemble

Gottwald, Heinrich (1821–1876) Germany

Fantasie heroique, op. 25
Cundy-Bettony (distributed by Carl Fischer)

Single movement mid-nineteenth-century work of a single march-like heroic character throughout. Fairly easy going and accessible to the good high school hornist.
Range: g–g²

Gough, Christopher (1991–) United Kingdom

Pour une Perte (For a Loss)
Edition db, 2011
A short piece marked Andante con rubato. Covers a wide range and provides plenty of opportunities for flexibility of tempo. Contains a few stopped notes.
Range: c♯–b♭²

Gould, Janetta (1926–) United Kingdom

Suite
St. Annes Music, 1958
Five movements written for Ifor James entitled: Pastoral—Hornpipe—Sarabande—Gavotte—Finale: Rondo. These rather short dance movements cover a very wide range, in a variety of tempos and moods, from the Sarabande's largo tempo and low range, to the fast agile finale that explores the horn's extreme upper range. New notation bass clef.
Range: F–d³
Duration: 9:30

The Highland Horn (1994)
St. Annes Music, 1978
Traditional Scottish melodies arranged for horn and piano.
Duration: 14:00

Gounod, Charles (1818–1893) France

Six Melodies for Horn and Piano
McCoy's Horn Library, 1982 (Daniel Bourgue, ed.)
Billaudot (in 3 volumes)
These six short, melodic pieces were dedicated to Marcel August Raoux, instrument maker and hornist in the Royal Italian Theater in Paris. Written for the early two-valve horn using a combination of hand stopping and valve technique made popular by J. J. Meifred.
Range: c–g²

Gousset, Bruno (1958–) France

Destination cor, op. 77
Billaudot, 2006
Eight pieces in various tempos and moods for the intermediate to advancing student. Well crafted with many technical and rhythmic challenges, such as asymmetrical meters for the student, but at a level that makes them accessible. New notation bass clef and a few stopped notes.
Range: d–f♯²
Total duration: 20:00

Graap, Lothar (1933–) Germany

Sonatine
Hofmeister, 1971
A short three-movement work of moderate difficulty in a straightforward twentieth-century tonal style. Movements are marked: Mäßig bewegt, energisch—Ruhig-verträumt—Lebhaft-fast Ganze.
Range: f♯–b²

Graham, Peter (1958–) United Kingdom

Episode
Rosehill Music Publishing Co., 1992
Written for horn in E♭ or F, this single movement in B♭ minor is very agile with many fast scalewise passages, especially if the performer adheres to the printed metronome markings. Includes two short cadenzas. Would be a very flashy encore piece for a recital program.
Range: b♭–b♭²

Grahl, Kurt (1947–) Germany

Elegie und kleine Fuge, über den Namen Dietrich Bonhoeffer (2005)
Dohr, 2006
For horn and organ.

Grant, James (1954–) United States

Why/Because, for Horn and Piano
Potenza Music Publishing, 2013
Two lyrical "songs without words." As described by the composer, "Why is introspective and tender, suggesting a kind of gentle longing and questioning, while Because is extraverted and assertive, confident and secure and has all the answers."
Range: b♭–a♭²

Graves, Richard (1926–2002) United Kingdom

Romance and Requiem
June Emerson Edition
Two easy pieces, a Romance that focuses on the octave up to F at the top of the staff, and a Lento Requiem that stays in the bottom half of the staff.
Range: b♭–f²

Graziani, Yitzhak (1924–2003) Israel, born in Bulgaria

Variations on Haydn's Theme
Israel Brass Woodwind Productions, 1978
Several variations on the theme from Haydn's "Surprise Symphony." Some technical difficulties and wide intervals.
Range: G–a²
See: Horn and ensemble

Green, Anthony (1946–)

A Yeats Fantasietta, Double, and Theme
Anthony Green, 2003
A short single-movement piece in contemporary style. Challenging in terms of range changes and going in and out of bass clef (new notation) a number of times.
Range: d–c³
Duration: 5:00

Gregson, Edward (1945–) United Kingdom and Ridgeon, John (1944–) United Kingdom

Nine Miniatures for Horn
Brass Wind Publications, 1980
Nine short elementary pieces with a limited range for the beginner.
Range: g–e♭²

Grenfell, Maria (1969–) New Zealand

Prelude, Fugue, and Foxtrot
Sounz (Centre for New Zealand Music), 1997
Three relatively short movements commissioned by Ed Allen. The slow, expressive Prelude, which focuses on the horn's lower and middle range, is followed by a more active and technical Fugue in $\frac{6}{8}$, and a Foxtrot, with an agile swing feel, both of which take advantage of a wider range.
Range: d–c²
Duration: 4:00

Grgin, Ante (1945–) Serbia

Sonata
Editions Marc Reift
Dedicated to Professor Milan Radić.

Gropp, Helmut (1899–1972) Germany

Sonate in a minor, op. 5
Breitkopf & Härtel, 1922
Long out of print early twentieth-century piece in two substantial movements. Old notation bass clef. Very long and dense in texture. Copy in the US Library of Congress.
Range: E–b♭²

Gubaidulina, Sofia (1931–) Russia, resides in Germany

Two Pieces for Horn and Piano (1979)
Sikorski, 1988, 1991
This student work by prominent contemporary composer Gubaidulina is suitable for the pre-college player and features two very short movements: "Far

away," and "The hunt." Interesting music for the younger player, with back-and-forth between horn and piano providing an opportunity for learning how to work on ensemble playing in a chamber setting.

Range: g–d²
Duration: 2:00

Gugel, Heinrich (1743–1802) Germany

Nocturne et pastorale
Edition Kunzelmann, 1995
A lyrical work written for either horn or basett horn in F and piano. Of rather moderate difficulty, ascending only once to the high c³ of the natural horn in F.

Range: c¹–c³

Guilbert, Robert (Unknown–1952) France

Puzzle
Alphonse Leduc, 1947
Dedicated to Jean Devémy, this piece was written as a Paris Conservatory competition piece. Composed in a single movement of several sections, it contains all of the elements of an exam piece, lyrical and technical sections, stopped horn, trills, glissandi, and rhythmic difficulties.

Range: G–c³

Guillonneau, Christian (1958–) France

De Frère Jacques à cadet Rousselle
Editions Combre

Guillou, René (1903–1958) France

Mon Nom est Rolande
Lucien de Lacour, 1948; Billaudot
Dedicated to Jean Devémy, this piece was composed as the exam piece at the Paris Conservatory in 1948. As with all French competition pieces, it has a little of everything, a flowing, lyrical opening section followed by short sections that present technical and articulation challenges, a bit of stopped horn, and a lip trill. Not overly difficult, but requires a wide range and some strength and agility.

Range: A–c³

Gwilt, David (1932–) United Kingdom

Sonatina
Bayley & Ferguson, 1965; G. Schirmer
A three-movement work in twentieth-century tonal style. Challenging, but idiomatic for the horn, and not excessively difficult.

Range: g–b♭²

Haas, Joseph (1879–1960) Germany

Sonata, op. 29 (1910)
Schott
Dedicated to Professor August Schmid-Linder. A three-movement work: Allegro
   maestoso—Larghetto e tranquillo—Allegro vivace e con spirito. In a twen-
   tieth-century tonal style. Straightforward technically and mostly written
   in a very comfortable range, but with few rests.
Range: c–a²
Duration: 19:00

Haddad, Don (1935–) United States

Allegro giocoso
Shawnee Press, 1968
A good recital piece for the moderately advanced horn student. One short, rela-
   tively easy movement, but musically interesting.
Range: b♭–g²

Sonata for Horn and Piano
Shawnee Press, 1966
A three-movement work: I. Allegro moderato—II. Largo—III. Allegro Moderato.
   Written predominantly in the Lydian mode and of moderate difficulty. New
   notation bass clef. Includes stopped horn.
Range: F–g²

Sonata No. 2 for Horn and Piano
Wingert-Jones Music, 1998
A single-movement work in several sections of varying tempos. Of moderate dif-
   ficulty, tonally straightforward, and rhythmically interesting. New nota-
   tion bass clef. Includes stopped effects.
Range: e–g²

Adagio and Allegro for Horn
Templeton Publishing, 1969
Two movements for horn and piano or symphonic band. Well written idiomat-
   ically for the horn with plenty of rests and moderately difficult technique,
   but requires an agile high range.
Range: b♭–b♭²
Duration: 7:00

Four Sketches (1975)
Seesaw Music, 1975
Four short pieces of moderate range and technique, though rhythmically and
   musically interesting.
Range: d–a²

Encore
Wingert-Jones Music, 1999
A short, fast articulate piece of moderate difficulty that includes stopped-to-open
   effects.
Range: c–a² (ossia ending to c³)

Air and Dance
Wingert-Jones Music Inc., 1993
A short piece in two sections: "Rainbow" (Adagio) and "Hope" (Allegretto). Technically appropriate for the advancing middle school or high school player. The Adagio features flowing melodies, and the Allegretto is crisp and light.
Range: a–f²

Hailstork, Adolphus C. (1941–) United States

Sonata for Horn and Piano
Manuscript copy, 1966, at Indiana University Music Library
Four-movement sonata written for hornist Sharon Moe. Movements include:
  I. Andante
  II. Vivace assai
  III. Soliloquy (mostly for horn alone)
  IV. Finale.
Requires some stopped horn.
Range: c–c³

Hakim, Naji (1955–) France, born in Lebanon
Suite Rhapsodique for Horn and Organ
United Music Publishers, 2002
Six movements, based on songs from various regions in France: Noel—Offrande—Incantation—Air—Alleluia—Mariale.
Range: d–b♭²

Hamilton, Iain (1922–2000) United Kingdom

Aria
Schott, 1952
A short, slow expressive piece that includes stopped horn.

Sonata Notturna (1965)
Schott, 1968
A very difficult contemporary work, both rhythmically and technically; written for Barry Tuckwell and Margaret Kitchin. Composed in several sections of varying tempos and characters. New notation bass clef.
Range: A♭–b²

Hanke, Roland

Romanze
Hofmeister
Dedicated to Herman Neuling, this piece is an easygoing expressive Romance that covers a fairly wide range, with an emphasis on the low.
Range: d–a²

Hanmer, Ronald (1917–1994) United Kingdom

Suite for Horn
June Emerson Edition, 1976
A not very difficult four-movement work, good for the young player. Straightforward melodic lines and easy range.
Range: b¹–e²

Hardy, Mabel (1875–1971) United Kingdom

Moody Horn
Imperial, 1974
Duration: 3:00

Harmon, John (1935–) United States

Sacred Hills
Nichols Music Co., 1996
Written for Bill Scharnberg. This piece depicts the "reverence and joy Native Americans have for the land on which they live." The horn begins with a recitative played into the open piano with pedal depressed, and then moves into a quick ¾ tempo.
Range: a–g♯²

Harris, Floyd O. (1913–2007) United States

A Short Suite for French Horn
Ludwig Music Publishing, 1954
Four short pieces for the advancing young horn player entitled: A garden of memories—An idyll—A twilight reverie—The hunter's call.
Range: c¹–f²

Harris, Paul (1956–) United Kingdom

Five Bagatelles
Associated Board of the Royal Schools of Music, 1992
Five movements: Fanfare—Cavatina—Slapstick—Meditation—Toccata. Written in various tempos and styles in the middle register for the young horn player.
Range: b♭–d♭¹

Hartley, Walter S. (1927–) United States

Meditation (1979)
Theodore Presser—Tritone Press, 1980
A short, slow piece in singing style. Fairly easy technically but expressive.
Range: a–g²

Sonorities II (1975)
Theodore Presser-Tenuto Press, 1976
Written for Calvin Smith, with special thanks to Frank Lloyd. A very dramatic contemporary piece filled with tone clusters and other effects such as

multiphonics, mute, glissandi, and wide dynamic range. New notation bass clef.

Range: F–b^2

Duration: 5:00

Hartzell, Eugene (1932–2000) Austria, born in United States

Sonata for Horn and Piano (1981)

Doblinger, 1987

    I. Molto lento—Allegro moderato

    II. Molto lento—Allegro scherzando

Written in contemporary tonal style with a rather busy and, at times, thick accompaniment. Rhythmically challenging with some difficult technical passages but not excessive in range or endurance.

Range: B♭–b♭^{2}

Harvey, Wallace (Pseudonym for Charles O'Neill)

See: O'Neill, Charles

Haselbach, Josef (1936–2002) Switzerland

Paraphrases for Horn and Piano

Hug & Co., 1985; Editions Marc Reift, 1985

A required piece for the Zurich International Competition, 1985. A rather difficult contemporary piece in three movements. Features unmetered sections with free rhythm and contemporary notation. Many stopped-horn effects, fast articulations, and lots of notes.

Range: B♭–c^3

Duration: 15:42

Haugland, A. Oscar (1922–2013) United States

Suite of Two Pieces

Belwin, 1948

Two short pieces, Lento and Allegro. Dedicated to Max Pottag. Some stopped horn and difficult tonalities, including F♯ major for the horn, as well as some light articulated passages in the Allegro.

Range: f–g♯^{2}

Hauser, Eric (1891–1964) United States

Twilight Thoughts

At the Fair

Soldier Song

Woodland Memories

Carl Fischer, 1935

Four short, very simple pieces for the beginning horn player.

Range: b♭^{1}–e^2

Hauser, Ernst, Germany

Andante appassionato, op. 34

Carl Giessel Verlag, 1900

A short, expressive piece with a wide range and a full range of dynamics. Dedicated to Ernst Ketz, solo horn of the Städtisches Orchestra of Cologne. Long out of print. Copy in US Library of Congress.

Hayes, Joseph (1919–2011) United States

Recitative and Air

Cor Publishing Co., 1960

Two short pieces, a dramatic and rhythmically free Recitative and an Air, both of which take advantage of the horn's full range of expression.

Range: d–g^2

He, Jianjun (1958–) China

Sonata (2004)

RM Williams, 2006

In three movements, in a fast-slow-fast form, this is a substantial sonata for horn and piano that synthesizes Chinese musical elements with contemporary Western music. Lots of interesting rhythms, articulations, and intervals. The third movement features a very fast tempo, and an unaccompanied larghetto section with very free rhythms. Includes some stopped-to-open effects, and a wild and energetic ending with glissandi.

Range: f♯–c^3

Head, Michael (1900–1976) United Kingdom

Scherzo

Boosey & Hawkes, 1974

Written for Ian Smith. A short, lively piece that explores the horn's agility in the low range. New notation bass clef.

Range: F–g^2

Heiden, Bernhard (1910–2000) United States, born in Germany

Professor of composition at Indiana University. Studied under Paul Hindemith and was highly influenced by his music.

Sonata for Horn and Piano (1939)

Associated Music Publishers Inc., 1955

    I. Moderato

    II. Tempo di menuetto

    III. Rondo allegretto

A standard recital piece written mostly in the mid-to-upper range, this piece of moderate difficulty features highly chromatic melodies, tonal ambiguity, and mixed meters in a mid-twentieth-century style. The second movement uses rhythmic displacement to create asymmetrical phrasing.

Range: b♭–b^2

Duration: 13:15

Hekster, Walter (1937–2012) Netherlands

Eclogue for French horn and Piano (1989)
Donemus, 1991
A very contemporary piece in complex modern notation. Both the hornist and
  the pianist must play from the full score. Many contemporary effects such
  as varying degrees of hand stopping, glissandi, flutter tonguing, complex
  rhythmic patterns, and a very wide range.
Range: D–c³

Helmschrott, Robert Maximilian (1938–) Germany

Sonata da chiesa XI (1993, rev. 1997)
Boosey and Hawkes, Bote & Bock, 1998
The two movements of this sonata for horn and organ are entitled I. Accentus and
  II. Concentus. The first movement is solemn and slow with some free ca-
  denza-like sections without notated values on the notes. The second move-
  ment is entirely metered, and has some long sustained lines that require
  good endurance. Includes lots of stopping effects.
Range: F–c³
Duration: 18:30

Herberigs, Robert (1886–1974) Belgium

Cyrano De Bergerac
CeBeDeM, 1961
See: Horn and ensemble

Hérold, Ferdinand (1791–1833) France

Duo pour piano et cor (1810)
Birdalone Music, 1999
A classical French sonata from the early years of the nineteenth-century, consisting of an Adagio introduction and a rondo Allegretto in ⅜. The horn
  writing is consistent with the cor-basse style of the period in France, only
  ascending above the staff briefly in the introduction.
Range: B♭–b♭² (c–c³ for E♭ horn)

Hess, Willy (1906–1997) Switzerland

Fünf Tonstücke, für Horn und Klavier, op. 100 (1978/79)
Kunzelmann, 1981
Five pieces in very traditional tonality and style with the titles: 1. Im Menuett-
  Ton—2. Fanfaren—3. Sarabande—4. Marsch—5. Notturno. The form and
  style is drawn from the baroque and classical periods, and the piece is well
  written for the horn. Not overly difficult, but challenging enough in terms
  of range and agility.
Range: d–c³

Sonata, op. 83
Edition Breitkopf, 1980

I. Allegro energico, ma non troppo
II. Lento, quasi andante
III. Scherzando, non troppo vivaci (theme and variations)

This three-movement sonata is written in a very traditional tonal style but presents a number of technical difficulties for the horn while still being idiomatically written for the instrument and providing ample rests. The very short twenty-eight-measure second movement leads into the theme and variations third movement, which is technically quite agile. A good upper range is required. Old notation bass clef.
Range: c–c³

Hessenberg, Kurt (1908–1994) Germany

Nocturne et Rondo, op. 71, no. 4
Alphonse Leduc, 1964; Schott, 2009
Two straightforward movements of moderate difficulty. The Rondo is very fast, agile, and articulate.
Range: g–a²

Higdon, Jennifer (1962–) United States

"Fanfare" from *Ceremonies*
Lawdon Press, 2001
From a collection of seven movements for brass and organ by the Pulitzer-Prize-winning composer. The movements can be played in any combination, or played separately. This is the third movement, "Fanfare," which the composer writes "plays upon the horn's variations of color."

Hilfiger, John Jay (1948–) United States

Variations on a Spiritual Song
Wehr's Music House, 2003
The composer writes that this work is based on a well known spiritual, "Were You There When They Crucified My Lord." In ¾ with three short variations. Syncopated rhythms, dotted eighth-sixteenth fanfares, sixteenth-note runs, and a variation in four flats make this work suitable for the advancing young horn player.
Range: f–f²

Hill, Douglas (1946–) United States

Haiku Readings for Horn and Piano (1988)
Available from www.reallygoodmusic.com
A seven-movement work, based on haiku by Robert Spiess. The players are asked to read each poem aloud and print out each poem for the audience to read. Descriptive sound effects are included.

Six (Recycled) Melodies for Horn and Piano (2012)
Available from www.reallygoodmusic.com

A selection of six of the composer's favorite, contrasting melodies from six previous original compositions. presented with piano to be enjoyed by intermediate to advanced players. It includes a ballad, a beguine, an aria/recitative, a jazz waltz, a love song, and a country dance.

Song Suite in Jazz Style for Horn and Piano (1993)
PP Music, Manduca Music Pub.
A set of five original songs published as lead sheets for improvising and as a fully composed twenty-two minute set of recital pieces. It includes "Easy going" (jazz waltz), "Quiet tears" (ballad/latin), "Dream scene" (mystical, new-age-like song in $\frac{5}{4}$), "All alone" (a romantic love song), and "Blackened blues" (a Count Basie-like romp.)

Hilliard, Quincy C. (1954–) United States
"Encore" from *Concerto for Young Artist(s) and Band*
Carl Fischer, 2000
Commissioned by the 1999 New Music Festival of Sandusky, Ohio, this movement is part of a larger work entitled *Concerto for Young Artist(s) and Band*. A very simple piece in sounding E♭ major for the young horn player. The form is ABA with a short cadenza.
Range: b♭–f^2

Hindemith, Paul (1895–1963) Germany and United States
German-born composer, conductor, violinist, violist, and music educator. Hindemith emigrated to the United States in 1940 and taught primarily at Yale University, where he trained and influenced a large number of American composers. He returned to Europe to live and teach in Switzerland in the 1950s.

Sonate für Horn und Klavier (1939)
Schott, 1940
    I. Mässig bewegt
    II. Ruhig bewegt
    III. Lebhaft
A standard recital piece, this sonata is very straightforward in its horn writing, never requiring extremes of high or low playing, though it does cover a wide dynamic range. It is very well written for both the horn and piano and satisfying musically to play. It is a very dynamic work requiring a strong horn tone, and a driving musical energy. The horn and piano work together with complex rhythms and trading of melodic material. No unusual techniques are used in the piece, but the endurance and wide intervals can be challenging. An excellent recital piece that is approachable by the talented high school student while still being musically and technically substantial enough for the college-level and professional horn player.
Range: e♭–a^2
Duration: 17:00

Sonata for Alto Horn and Piano (1943)
Schott, 1956
> I. Ruhig bewegt
> II. Lebhaft
> III. Sehr Langsam
> IV. Lebhaft

Written for the alto horn, but most often played on the French horn, this sonata
is similar stylistically, and in its idiomatic writing, to Hindemith's *Horn
Sonata.* The horn part is notated in E♭ for the alto horn, requiring the hornist to transpose, sometimes in written keys with a number of accidentals.
As with the *Horn Sonata* the writing is straightforward, but endurance,
dynamics, and intervals are difficult. There is more use of the upper range
of the instrument than in the *Horn Sonata,* and the end of the fourth movement can be quite taxing when played with a full sound. The piano part, as
with most Hindemith sonatas, is quite difficult. Hindemith also included
a poem entitled "Das Posthorn" (in German or English), which is to be
recited as a dialog between the hornist and pianist between the third and
fourth movements. This poem is the basis of the piece.
Range: g♯–b♭^{2} (a♯–c^3 for E♭ alto horn)
Duration: 10:00

Hlobil, Emil (1901–1987) Czech Republic

Andante pastorale
Bärenreiter, Hudebnímatice, 1947
A short, lyrical piece of moderate difficulty, with some stopped horn.
Range: g–g^2

Sonata pro lesní roh a klavír, op. 21
Panton, 1967
An extended sonata in three movements.
Range: B♭–b♭^{2}

Arie a rondo pro lesní roh a klavír, op. 37
Panton, 1981
A piece of medium length, consisting of an aria in a largehtto tempo in a flowing
style, followed by a Rondo marked Allegro giocoso with some fast articu-
lated passages. Not overly difficult, but agile and interesting.
Range: g–b♭^{2}

Hlouschek, Theodor (1923–2010) Germany

Quattro intonazioni, per corno e (grande) organo
F. Hofmeister, 1995

Hoddinott, Alun (1929–) United Kingdom

Sonata, op. 78, no.2
Oxford University Press, 1972

Written for Barry Tuckwell. A three-movement work: 1. Moderato, quasi allegretto
—2. Adagio—3. Presto. Of moderate difficulty technically and rhythmically,
though it does venture above the staff several times, and could present some
endurance challenges for the younger player.
Range: c^1–c^3
Duration: 11:00

Høeberg, Georg (1872–1950) Denmark

Andante for Horn and Organ
Willhelm Hansen, 1942
A short, lyrical piece for horn and organ in a romantic twentieth-century style,
dedicated to Hans Sørensen. Straightforward and relatively easy horn part.
Range: $g\sharp$–$g\flat^2$

Hofmann, Wolfgang (1922–2003) Germany

Sonatine für Horn und Klavier oder Orgel (1993)
Florian Noetzel, 1993
This piece is divided into three sections:
Allegro Moderato
Adagio
Kadenz—Allegro—Kadenz—Allegro
The horn part is straightforward and of moderate difficulty.
Range: g–a^2
Duration: 8:00

Holcombe, Bill (1924–2010) United States

Azure (Blues for French Horn) (2001)
Musicians Publications, 2001
A piece of moderate difficulty in a jazz style. Includes a cadenza.
Range: e–$c\sharp^2$ (with ossia to $b\flat^2$)

Sonata for French Horn (2001)
Musicians Publications, 2008
    I. Allegro Moderato
    II. Slowly
    III. Moderato
Three rather technical movements in a contemporary tonal style. The first movement is a mixture of fast articulated repeated notes, and scalewise slurred
sixteenth notes. The second is more flowing in character, while the third
movement is almost nonstop eighth-note rhythmic patterns in $\S$. Some rather difficult writing requiring clean technique and endurance.
Range: F–c^2

Holliday, Kent (1940–) United States

Sonata for Horn and Piano
Dorn Publications, Needham Pub, 2002

Triptych
Seesaw Music, 1982
In three movements: Premonition—Idyll—Tarantella. The Tarantella is the most extensive of the three. This is a well-paced work for the horn soloist, straightforward with a few technical runs.
Range: b–a♯²

Holmes, Paul (1923–) United States

Serenade
Shawnee Press, 1962
Short, lyrical piece in the Dorian mode marked andante. One muted section.
Range: f♯–a²
Duration 4:00

Holstein, Jean-Paul (1939–) France

Les Yeux dores de l'aurore
Editions Musicales Transatlantic, 1978
A lyrical piece that requires great flexibility with wide range changes and a solid sense of rhythm, since the parts are quite independent. Includes some stopped effects.
Range: g–b♭²

Horvit, Michael (1932–) United States

Circus Suite
Southern Music, 1990
Five movements of moderate difficulty that depict scenes from the circus. Good difficulty level for a student recital. Commissioned and recorded by Thomas Bacon.
Range: f–b♭²

Chaconne and Burlesque
Southern Music, 1993
Written for Thomas Bacon, this piece of rather moderate difficulty begins with an easy melodic line over the recurring chaconne bass line, followed by a fast and energetic Burlesque that is agile, but technically not too difficult.
Range: a–g²

Hoss, Wendell (1892–1980) United States

Etude for Horn and Piano
A Moll Dur Publishing House, 1978
A short, spirited technical etude with piano. Includes fast slurred passages and trills.
Range: c¹–a²

Houdy, Pierrick (1929–) France

Lamento pour cor et piano
Alphonse Leduc, 1955
Short, melodic piece in mid-twentieth-century French style.
Range: a–a♭²

Howarth, Frank (1905–1994) United Kingdom, worked in Canada

Canzona for Horn and Organ
Canadian Music Centre, 1968

Hughes, Mark (1934–1972) United States

Sonata for Horn and Piano
Theodore Presser—Tritone Press, 1966
A three-movement work with a wide range and some technically difficult passages,
    mixed meters, and rhythmic difficulties. Movements include:
    I. Allegro
    II. Adagio
    III. Fugue and Cadenza
Range: c–a²
Duration: ca. 16:00

Hulin, Eric (1961–) France

Songe d'une journee d'hiver
Alphonse Leduc, 1998
A short, lyrical work by the solo horn of the opera of Limoges and Limousin.
    Features several wide leaps that show the horn's expressive capabilities.
Range: c¹–g²

Hummel, Bertold (1925–2002) Germany

Sonatine, op.75a (1981)
Schott, 1982
Straightforward twentieth-century tonal sonata in three movements: I. Maes-
    toso—II. Ballade—III. Finale: Presto. Very moderate range and technical
    difficulty. Some stopped horn and muted passages.
Range: g–a²
Schott, 1982

Hurrell, Clarence Elmer (1912–1975) United States

The Horn of Heimdall
Rubank, 1968
A rather easy piece of limited range based on the Teutonic legend of Heimdall,
    gatekeeper of Asgard. For the young student.
Range: a–c²

Hutcheson, Jere (1938–) United States

Wonder Music V
Seesaw Music, 1976
A complex and involved contemporary piece using graphic notation and many
contemporary effects, such as plucking and hitting piano strings with the
hand, combined trill and double tongue on the horn, stopped and muted
effects, glissandi. Many grace notes, difficult intervals, and fast articulated
passages add to the challenge.
Range: c♯–c³ and also highest and lowest notes possible.

Hutschenruyter, Wouter (1859–1943) Netherlands

Romanze, op. 12
Edition Compusic, 1989
Slow, romantic piece for horn in E♭ marked Adagio molto espressivo—ma non
tanto.
Range: c–c³ (for horn in E♭)

d'Indy, Vincent (1851–1931) France

Andante
Billaudot, 1976
A short piece from the latest period of hand horn playing in France. Lyrical and
pleasant. Also available with string orchestra accompaniment.
Range: c–g²
Duration: 2:10

Isoz, Etienne (1905–1986) Switzerland, born in Hungary

Trois Bagatelles pour cor en fa et orgue
Edition *mf*, 1992; Christoph Dohr, 2002

Jacobs, Mark Eliot (1960–) United States

Amor-Schall (version 2)
A traditionally tonal, lyrical single movement. The title translates as "Cupid's
horn."
Range: a–a²
Duration: ca. 6:00

Jacobson, Harvey, United States

Sonata in One Movement for Horn and Piano
Hornseth Music Co., 1978
A short, spirited piece of moderate difficulty.
Range: c♯¹–a²

Jacques, Michael (1944–) United Kingdom

Four Bagatelles
Stainer & Bell, 1988
Four short and rather easy pieces, entitled: Fanfare—Cantilena—Burlesque—Hymn.
Range: g–f²

Jadin, Louis-Emmanuel (1768–1853) France

3 Fantasien für Horn und Pianoforte (ca. 1810)
Robert Ostermeyer, 2002
Three very typical nineteenth-century salon pieces for horn. Each piece consists
of several sections of varying tempos and styles, and includes lyrical and
rather technical sections. The horn writing is very much in the French cor-
mixt style of the period, very seldom going above or below the staff. Nice
agile pieces to play on the natural horn.
Range: g–b²

Quatre Airs pour harpe (piano) et cor
Hans Pizka Edition, 2002
Four short pieces written originally for natural horn and harp or piano in the
French cor-mixt style of the early nineteenth century:
1. Maestoso—Pastorale non troppo lento
2. Andante
3. Andante ma non troppo
4. Allegretto
Range: g–g²

James, Ifor (1931–2004) United Kingdom

Chiostro della donna
Editions Marc Reift, 1999
A short, relatively simple piece for the young horn player, but using some con-
temporary music elements, such as playing into the open piano with the
pedal down, some very simple graphic notation, and free cadenza sections.
Includes parts for F and E♭ horn.
Range: g–g²

Day Dreams
Editions Marc Reift, 1998
A simple, lyrical piece for the young horn player who is able to play up to the top
of the staff. Includes parts for F and E♭ horn.
Range: c¹–e²

4 Pieces for Horn & Piano
Editions Marc Reift, 2001
Nocturne—Waltz—Eine kleine Sonatine—Lahr Suite. Easygoing works with a
manageable range for the beginning student.
Range: b♭–e♭²

Merrygoround
Editions Marc Reift, 1998
This piece is written for the more advanced student who has developed some facil-
ity and range. Depicting a merry-go-round, the piece is in constant motion
with few rests.
Range: a–c^2

St. Hubert's Day
Editions Marc Reift, 2006
Composed in several short contrasting sections, this piece is flashy without being
overly difficult. Includes one short muted section.
Range: c^1–a♭^{2}

Repetition Waltz
Editions Marc Reift, 1998
Very simple beginner's piece of limited range.

Rondo Capriccio
Editions Marc Reift, 1998
A moderately difficult, spirited single movement in $\frac{6}{8}$, written for Gail Williams.

Scandinavian Wedding Waltz
Basil Ramsey, 1983
A simple waltz for the young horn player. Includes a few measures to be played
stopped.
Range: e^1–e^2

Similarities
Editions Marc Reift, 2000
A fast-moving technical piece made up of articulated sixteenth-note patterns.

Trinity Rag
Editions Marc Reift, 1998
In ragtime style, this short piece is very simple musically, but too high for the
beginning horn player.
Range: g–a^2

Little Suites No. 1–5
Editions Marc Reift, 1999–2000
Five short suites of very moderate difficulty. Each published separately.

Janssens, Robert (1939–) Belgium

Prelude et danse
J. Maurer, 1969
In this rather short piece, a recitative-like opening, marked Andante quasi ad lib,
is followed by an Allegro ma non troppo dance. Contains a few quick range
changes and intervals, but altogether very straightforward and technically
accessible for the high school or university horn student.
Range: a–g^2 (with ossia e–g^2)

Jemain, Joseph (1864–1954) France

Romance, op. 29
Evette et Schaffer, 1925
A short, straightforward piece in lyrical style.
Range: c–g²

Johns, Terence, United Kingdom

Holland Park
Broadbent & Dunn Ltd., 1994
A relatively simple, lyrical single movement marked Tempo rubato focusing on
the midrange to the top of the staff.
Range: e¹–f♯²

One Day
Broadbent & Dunn Ltd., 1993
A single movement, marked Reflective and Rubato.
Range: c¹–a♭²

Jollet, Jean-Clément (1954–) France

Petit Suite sur 5 ou 6 notes
Billaudot, 1988
Three very easy tunes for the beginner that, as the title suggests, are composed
using five or six notes.
Range: c¹–a¹ (with ossia to c²)

Jones, Donald R.

Allegro for Horn
Pro Art Publications, 1963
Spirited, short piece marked Allegro non troppo, with a wide range.
Range: c–c³

Jones, Robert A.

Etude for F Horn and Piano Solo
Trowel Music Publishers, 1990
A very slow and very short piece with a wide range of dynamics.
Range: f –g²

Jones, Wendal (1932–2013) United States

Three Fantasies for Horn and Piano
Associated Music Publishers, 1969
Written for James Miller. Three fairly short pieces of different characters with
some moderately difficult technical challenges. Uses mute, stopped horn,
glissandi, and flutter tongue.
Range: e–b♭²
Duration: ca. 7:00

Jongen, Joseph (1873–1953) Belgium

Lied pour cor et piano, 1899
CeBeDeM, 1960
A short, expressive lyrical piece.
Range: B–a♭²
Duration: ca. 4:00

Jordahl, Robert (1926–2008) United States

Introduction & Allegro
Seesaw Music, 1977
The introduction, marked *smoothly,* is lyrical, followed by a crisp Allegro organized around a dotted eighth-sixteenth figure that moves through changing meters of ⅝, ⅜, ⅝, and ⅞.
Range: b♭–b♭² (with ossia e♭–b♭²)

Joubert, Claude-Henry (1948–) France

Ballade de l'enfant juif
Robert Martin Editions Musicales, 1992
A student piece of moderate difficulty, written using six themes and honoring the
eighteenth-century musician and poet, Gautier de Coinci.
Range: a–g²

Chanson de Guiguemar
Editions Combre, 1982
A work for the beginning student, written in ¾ in the written key of C major.
Range: a–e²
Duration: 2:00

Kaefer, John F. (1976–) United States

Dialogues for Horn (1997)
International Horn Society Manuscript Press, 1997
A five-movement work with the titles:
    1. Reflective
    2. Light and fast
    3. With menace
    4. Constrained
    5. Vicious
Premiered at the Western U.S. Horn Symposium, 2002, by hornist Bruce Atwell
and pianist Jeffrey Meyer.

Kalabis, Viktor (1923–2006) Czech Republic

Variationen, op. 31
Schott, 1971
A single-movement theme and variations of very moderate difficulty.
Range: f♯–g²

Kalkbrenner, Friedrich (1785–1849) Germany

Nocturne
Hans Pizka Edition
A virtuoso piece for the piano with a relatively easygoing horn part, written for
natural horn and dedicated to J. F. Gallay.

Kalliwoda, Johann Wenzel (1801–1866) Germany (Bohemian), born in Prague

Introduction et rondeau, op. 51
Musica Rara, KaWe, 1972; Kunzelmann
Piano version of a piece originally written for horn and orchestra. Early nineteenth-century style of virtuosic horn writing with dramatic leaps and cadenzas in the introduction and an agile, spirited rondo. The original, of
which the KaWe edition is a facsimile, has two alternate lines in numerous
passages for natural horn and valve horn.
Range: $c-c^3$

Kaminski, Heinrich (1886–1946) Germany

Ballade für Waldhorn und Klavier
Bärenreiter
An unusual contemporary-sounding piece in all likelihood written for E♭ natural
horn with very complex rhythms.
Range: c^1-c^3 (for horn in E♭)

Kampe, Gordon (1976–) Germany

Pickman's Model (2010)
Edition Juliane Klein, 2011
Duration: 11:00

Kantušer, Božidar (1921–1999) Slovenia

Évocations pour piano et cor
Editions Musicales Transatlantiques, 1971
Three short, contemporary atonal pieces, mostly in the low range. Includes muted
and stopped horn, some nonmeasured sections, and new notation bass
clef.
Range: $E-g^2$

Kaplin, David (1923–) Canada

Soliloquy and Serenade
Belwin, 1956
Two short, easy student pieces, published individually. For the very young horn
student.
Range: c^1-d^2

Karaev, Kara (1918–1982) Russia

Music for Horn and Piano
The Musical Evergreen, 1975
A pleasant Adagio in §, with flowing melodies and a few stopped notes at the end.
Range: f♯–g²

Kastel, Fabrice (1966–) France

Tango
IMD Diffusion Arpeges, 1994
Short, lyrical work with long sustained melodies over a syncopated piano line.
    Suitable for the beginning player.
Range: f♯–d²

Tchatch' à Chat
IMD Diffusion Arpeges. 1994
Short work featuring a brief eighth-note gesture that alternates with the piano.
    Suitable for the beginning player.
Range: c¹–c²

Kauder, Hugo (1888–1972) Austria and United States, born in Czech Republic
Three sonatas of similar character that have no bar lines throughout.
Range: Generally c¹–a², with an emphasis on the middle range

Sonata, No. 1
Written for William Valkenier.
Southern Music, 1977

Sonata, No. 2
Southern Music, 1975

Sonata, No. 3
Southern Music, 1974

Two Little Suites
Seesaw Music, 1987
As with the sonatas, there are no bar lines in these short suites. The first consists
    of sections entitled: Prelude—Melody and dance—Melody with variations.
    The second suite has three sections: Prelude—Melody with variations—
    Fugue. Fairly challenging technically in places, but traditional in their
    technical demands for the horn.
Range: f–c³

Kazandzhiev, Vasil (1934–) Bulgaria

Sonata
KaWe, 1972; Hans Pizka Edition
A substantial three-movement work, quite demanding for both players, but
    straightforward and traditional in its writing for the horn. The first move-
    ment, in a moderate tempo, covers a wide range and includes stopped pas-

sages. The second, in a faster tempo, is very articulate, and, like the first, it covers a wide range, although it dwells on the low register. The third, marked Tranquillo molto, is mostly flowing in nature, with a few technical passages, and ends softly and gently in stopped horn. Old notation bass clef.

Range: G–c³

Keim, Aaron, United States

Nocturne for Horn and Piano
Pelican Music, 2003
A short lyrical piece that mixes the style of the nocturnes of Chopin and Field with the harmonic language of jazz.
Duration: 3:30

Keldermans, Raymond (1911–1984) Belgium

Pastoraal, voor hoorn F en piano
Muziekuitgeverij Scherzando, ca. 1970s

Kelley, Daniel, United States

Three Concert Works
Last Resort Music Pub., 2004
Three pieces, entitled: A tempered hero—Lea DeLinkley's theme and variations —Running to safety.

Kelly, Bryan (1934–) United Kingdom

Dance Preludes for Horn and Piano
Spartan Press, 2012
A suite of six short dance movements in contemporary tonal style: 1. Entrada— 2. Polka—3. Sarabande—4. Mazurka—5. Elegy—6. Burlesca.

Kennaway, Lamont, United Kingdom

Autumn Moods
New Wind Music
A short, easy student piece. For the young horn student who can play to the top of the staff.
Range: d¹–g²

Kern, Frida (1891–1988) Austria

Scherzo for Horn and Piano, op. 43
Thomi-Berg, 1979
A short, energetic scherzo that includes both technical passages of scales and intervals, and flowing lyrical lines. Difficult in its agility, but very idiomatically written.
Duration: 7:00

Kershaw, Richard (1946–) United Kingdom

Night Ride
Broadbent & Dunn, 2002
Dedicated to Jacqueline O'Dell. A short rondo in ⅜, not terribly difficult, but agile, with crisp dotted rhythms. Begins with a slow introduction marked Lento misterioso that leads quickly into the main fast section marked Allegro ritmico.
Range: g–g²

Kersters, Willem (1929–1998) Belgium
Award-winning composer who also served as professor of composition at the Antwerp Conservatory.

Sonatine
De Haske Muziekuitgave BV (Denis Wick solo collection), ca. 1990s
In three movements: Synopsis—Largo—Allegro risoluto. The first movement is for unaccompanied horn, opening with declamatory statements that are echoed with stopped horn. The second movement is a dialogue for horn and piano, with the piano playing sustained octaves in the bass and a single line in the right hand.
Range: d–c³

Ketting, Otto (1935–2012) Netherlands

Autumn for Horn and Piano
Domenus, 1980
A short, sustained work with a rhythmic pattern that ties over bar lines throughout the piece. Not technically difficult but requires good rhythm and counting in the asymmetrical rhythms and mixed-meter sections. Begins and ends with long stopped sections over a single line of moving eighth notes. Only the texturally more dense middle section of the piece is played open.
Range: c♯¹–b♭²
Duration: 6:45

Kilar, Wojciech (1932–2013) Poland

Sonate
Polskie Wydawn, Muzyczne, 1959
A substantial work for both horn and piano. Written in two movements entitled: Allegro and Recitativo e arioso. Straightforward horn writing, but persistent, with few rests.
Range: f–c²

Kimmell, Jack Normain (1932–) United States

Dyad for Horn and Piano (1995)
Manduca Music Publications, 1995
Duration: 7:00

Kinney, Gordon J. (1905–1981) United States

Fantasy for Horn and Piano

A relatively short three-movement work of medium difficulty, appropriate for student recitals. The first is in an energetic fanfare style, the second is a lyrical, flowing, melodic piece, and the last movement is spirited and happy with mixed meters.

Duration: ca. 8:00

Kirchner, Volker David (1942–) Germany

Lamento d'Orfeo (1986)

Schott, 1986

Commissioned by the Concert Artists Guild of New York for Marie-Luise Neu-necker, winner of the 1986 Concert Artists Guild competition. A very con-temporary single-movement work full of stopped effects and playing the horn near the piano strings with the pedal depressed to produce sympa-thetic vibrations. Not overly taxing for the horn player, but it has some rhythmic and interval challenges. New notation bass clef.

Range: G–a^2

Tre poemi

Schott, 1990

Also written for Marie-Luise Neunecker in the same style as the previous piece, these three short movements, marked: Lamento—Danza—La gondola fu-nebre, are packed with rhythmic difficulties, fast articulations, and stopped effects. Very intense dramatic music. New notation bass clef.

Range: G–a^2

Duration: ca.14:00

Klauss, Noah (1901–1977) United States

Andantino, French Horn Solo with Piano

Mills Music, 1961

Short piece with some rhythmic challenges and stopped horn.

Range: g–a^2

Cabalétta (Song for a Little Horse)

Pro Art Publications, 1963

A fairly easy short piece marked moderato. Dedicated to Meredith Germer.

Range: b♭–e^2

Klebe, Giselher (1925–2009) Germany

Veränderung der Sonate für Klavierop. 27/2, von Ludwig van Beethoven in Sonate für Horn und Klavier (1985–1986)

Bärenreiter, 1986

    I. Adagio sostenuto

    II. Allegretto (trio)

    III. Allegro agitato

On themes from the *Piano Sonata Op. 27/2* by Ludwig van Beethoven. A rather
extensive contemporary three-movement sonata, not overly difficult technically, but persistent and requiring good endurance. Includes stopped
passage and old notation bass clef notation.
Range: e♭–c³

Kling, Henri (1842–1918) Switzerland, born in France

Sonate en la mineur
Editions Marc Reift, 1999
> 1. Allegro moderato
> 2. Adagio cantabile
> 3. Allegretto scherzando

A rather long and difficult late nineteenth-century romantic sonata in three
movements. Kling was a horn player and professor, and wrote very idiomatically for the instrument, but the piece is, nonetheless very technical and
persistent. Most of the playing is within the staff, but with very little rest,
and requires flexibility and good articulation for agile intervals and long
passages of constant sixteenth notes.
Range: B–g²
Duration: ca. 20:00

3 Fantasies sur des airs d'opéras de Mozart, Auber, & Donizetti
Casterjon Musi Editions, 2008
Three late nineteenth-century-salon-style fantasies composed using themes from
the operas *Don Giovanni, La Favorite,* and *La muette de Portici.* These
tuneful pieces are of medium difficulty technically for the horn, and quite
accessible as student recital pieces.
Range: c–a²

Knight, Judyth

A Candle on a Cake and *A Candle in a Church*
Stainer & Bell, 1986
Two short pieces of limited range for the young horn player.
Range: a–e²

Knight, Morris (1933–2013) United States

The Chivalric Sonata
Woodsum Music Ltd., 1989
A programmatic sonata in four movements: The joust—The grail—The fair damsel
—The hunt.
Range: a–e²

Koch, Frederick (1923–2005) United States

Sound Pictures
Southern Music, 1991

Two movements entitled "Blues Macabre," and "Playful." Technically not too difficult, but with much stopped horn and new notation bass clef. Very much
a low horn piece.
Range: A–e²

Two Movements for Horn and Piano
Seesaw Music, 1972

Kocsár, Miklós (1933–) Hungary

Repliche No. 2 'per corno e zimbalo Ungherese (o piano)'
McCoy's Horn Library, Editio Musica Budapest, 1979
A contemporary piece without bar lines and rhythmically very free with lots
of discretion left to the performers. Written for horn and the traditional
Hungarian cembalo, but may also be played with piano. Challenging notes,
intervals, and stopped effects in the horn part. Written for Ferenc Tarjáni.
Range: f♯–b²

Koechlin, Charles (1867–1950) France

Sonata, op. 70
Editions Max Eschig, 1970
  I. Moderato, très simlement et avec souplesse
 II. Andante, très tranquille, presque adagio
III. Allegro moderato, assez animé cependant
Published after the composer's death. The first two movements are of a lyrical
flowing nature with a very active accompaniment. The third movement is
quick and spirited. Some stopped-horn and muted passages.
Range: e–b²
Duration: 12:50

Sonata for Bassoon or Horn, op.71
Billaudot, 1990
  I. Andante con moto—Allegretto schrezando
 II. Nocturne—Andante quasi adagio
III. Final—Allegro
A three-movement work originally written by the composer for bassoon or horn,
centering mostly on the low range up to the top of the staff. Very technical
and agile, especially below the staff. Written in a mid-twentieth-century
contemporary style with difficult rhythms and meters.
Range: b♭–c♯³ (to g♯² when optional ossias are played)
Duration: 10:00

15 Pieces for Horn and Piano, op. 182 (1942)
Billaudot, 1984 (published in three volumes)
Fifteen short pieces of various tempos:
  1. Dans le Foret romantic
  2. Allegro (for horn quartet)
  3. Andante presque adagio

4. Allegro vivo
5. Adagio
6. Allegro
7. Andante
8. Nocturne (for horn quartet)
9. Adagio
10. Andante
11. Allegro vivo
12. Adagio
13. Allegro
14. Andante con moto
15. Presque adagio

Interspersed between the horn and piano pieces are two movements for horn quartet, playable on natural horns in D. The pieces range in duration from one minute to five minutes. An emphasis on the upper range of the horn makes these pieces difficult for endurance.

Range: F–c³ (with ossia passages to e♭³)

Koetsier, Jan (1911–2006) Netherlands

Choralfantasie, Gib Dich Zufrieden Und Sei Stille
Editions Marc Reift, 1997
A solemn and dramatic work for horn and organ with a horn part of moderate difficulty.
Range: c–g²

Romanza, op. 59/2
Donemus, Editions Marc Reift, 1991
A pleasant, flowing piece, with some fast repeated articulations and a wide range, but only moderately difficult.
Range: A♭–a♭²

Scherzo brillante, für Horn und Klavier, op. 96 (1983)
Donemus, 1984; Editions Marc Reift, 1993
A lively scherzo, written for Marie-Luise Neunecker, consisting of scherzo, trio, and scherzo da capo. Not overly difficult, but technically challenging with fast articulations and some stopped horn.
Range: f–c³
Duration: 4:00

Sonatina, op. 59/1
Donemus, 1972, 1986; Editions Marc Reift, 1993
Three short movements in a contemporary tonal style. Good student recital piece. Challenging and interesting but very idiomatically written and playable.
Range: c–c³

Variationen für tiefes Horn und Klavier, op. 59/3
Specifically written for low horn, these variations offer a full range of low horn playing, including slow lyrical, fast flowing, and fast agile articulated passages, as well as stopped horn and flutter tongue.

Kofroň, Jaroslav (1921–1966) Czech Republic

Sonatina
Panton, 1974
A relatively short three-movement work with agile technique and flowing me-
     lodic lines. This piece requires the hornist to be just as agile and articulate
     in the lower range as in the middle and upper ranges.
Range: d–c³

10 Little Compositions for Horn and Piano
Edition Supraphon, 1962
Ten very short character pieces of moderate difficulty for the advancing young
     horn student.
Range: b–a²

Kogan, Lev (1927–2007) Israel

Hassidic Tunes (Nigunim) for Horn and Piano
Israel Brass Woodwind Publications, 1979
Four movements based on Hassidic melodies, not technically difficult, but with
     an emphasis on the upper range and very little rest.
Range: G–c³

Hassidic Suite (Chabad)
Israel Brass Woodwind Publications, 1979
Similar to the previous piece, four movements based on Hassidic melodies.
Range: B–c³

Prayer (Tfila)
Israel Brass Woodwind Publications, 1979, String parts from OR-TAV Music www
     .ortav.com
A slow, expressive piece with short cadenzas throughout. Written in a comfort-
     able range. Also available with string accompaniment.
Range: d–f²
Duration: 4:43

Kohler, Siegfried (1927–1984) Germany

Sonate für Horn und Klavier, "Rotterdam 14.5.1940," op. 32 (1966)
VEB Deutscher Verlag für Musik Leipzig, 1970
A very serious work in three movements: 1. Prolog—2. Klage—3. Verwandlung.
     It commemorates the bombing of the city center of Rotterdam by the Ger-
     mans on May 14, 1940. First performed and recorded by Peter Damm.

Kohn, Karl (1926–) United States, born in Austria

Encounters II, Horn and Piano (1967)
Carl Fischer, 1972
A contemporary piece in which some sections are without bar lines, often using ar-
     rows to indicate how the horn and piano parts are to be aligned. Measured
     sections are in traditional notation. Because of the complex rhythms and dif-

ficulty of lining up very intricate patterns in the two parts, both players must play from a full score. Plenty of very difficult rhythms to learn, agile intervals, and range changes, but not excessive in its demands in terms of range and endurance. Includes stopped passages, flutter tongue, and glissandi. A soft stopped e♭ below middle c¹ at the end of the piece may require a stopping mute.
Range: c–c²

Variations (1971)
Carl Fischer, 1972
Similar in its horn writing to the previous piece, but measured throughout, and generally not quite as complex in its ensemble difficulties. As with *Encounters II*, not excessive in range, but quite persistent, with few rests. Requires the horn player to play into the piano with the pedal depressed to sound sympathetic tones. Also requires fast articulation, agility in intervals, and good hand stopping.
Range: c–c²
Duration: 10:15

Kopke, Paul (1918–2000) United States

La Chasse
Rubank, 1964
A simple, spirited piece for the young horn player.
Range: b–f²

Körling, August (1842–1919) Sweden

Pastorale for Horn and Organ (1899)
Wessmans Musikförlag, 1988
A short and only moderately difficult lyrical piece in a flowing late nineteenth-century romantic style.
Range: c–a²
Duration: 4:00

Korn, Peter (1922–1998) Germany

Sonate, op. 18
Benjamin, Simrock, 1959
A rather extended and taxing work in three long movements: Allegro Tranquillo ma bene mosso—Andante con moto—Rondo a la Gigue. Some stopped horn, and a quite difficult piano part.
Range: B–b²

Kreisler, Alexander von (1893–1969) United States, born in Russia

Sonatina
Southern Music, 1968
A light three-movement work of very moderate difficulty. Well suited to a younger student
Range: b–f²

Krenek, Ernst (1900–1991) Austria and United States

Opus 239, für Horn und Orgel (1988)
Universal Edition, 1989
A serious and dramatic piece for horn and organ. Technically challenging for the
    horn.
Range: d–b♭²
Duration: 4:40

Krol, Bernhard (1920–2013) Germany

Ballade für Horn und Klavier
A. Bohm und Sohn, 1985
A short mostly lyrical piece in an ABA form, with a middle section that is more
    rhythmic in nature.
Range: c¹–g²

Drei Stücke für Horn (in F) und Klavier, op. 72
Bote and Bock, 1979
Three fairly short movements written for Rainer Ruß, with the titles: Impromptu—
    Canto mest—Geschwindmarsch. These well-written pieces cover a wide
    range of tempos and moods in a twentieth-century tonal style. The horn
    part is only of moderate difficulty and in a comfortable range for the student
    horn player. Includes a couple of stopped passages.
Range: d–a²

Missa muta, fünf Miniaturen für Horn und Orgel, op. 55
Bote & Bock, 1973
    I. Miserere (unmeasured)
    II. Gratias agimus—Andante tranquillo
    III. Suscipe—Allegro comodo
    IV. In mei memoriam—Allegro assai/Allegro molto
    V. Ite—Grave marciale
Five short movements of a solemn character, with several cadenza-like sections
    and melismatic passages over a sustained pedal in the organ. Very dra-
    matic, with some rather difficult horn technique, a bit of stopped horn, and
    old notation bass clef.
Range: B♭–c²

Sonata, op.1
Pro Musica Verlag, Leipzig
A fairly short sonata in two movements, written for Helmut Kranz. Consisting
    of a ¾ Allegro con brio and a Theme with four variations, and ending with
    a cadenza. Technically challenging, the piece covers a wide range and is
    rather active.
Range: g–b²

Sospiri—3 Moments musicaux
Wolfgang G. Haas Musikverlag, 2002
Three short movements: I. Andante con moto—II. Tranquillo molto—III. Adagio
    dolente. Written in a gentle melodic style. Not too difficult for the horn, and

as with all of Krol's music for horn, very idiomatic writing, taking advantage of the best qualities of the instrument. Includes one stopped passage.
Range: g–g²

Kronke, Emil (1865–1939) Germany

Two Hunting Pieces, op. 59, no. 1
Southern Music, 1989
Two pieces, one in D major, and one in F major, in hunting horn style. Not too long, but active and persistent.
Range: c¹–c³

Krufft, Nicolaus von (1779–1818) Austria

Sonata in E major for horn and piano (Sonata pour le pianoforte avec accompaniment de cor)
Breitkopf & Härtel, 1812 (first edition), 1836; Birdalone Music (Facsimile of the 1836 Breitkopf & Härtel, V. Roth, ed.) 1997; Billaudot (E. Leloir, ed., edition in F major, with composer's name spelled "Cruft")
   I. Allegro moderato
   II. Andante espressivo
   III. Rondo alla polacca
This beautiful sonata in E major is classical in style and oriented toward a lyrical high-horn style of writing. The virtuoso piano part is of the level found in the sonatas by Beethoven and Ferdinand Ries. The second movement is very romantic in character, with Chopin-like figures and ornaments. The polacca requires fast articulated scales, trills, and arpeggios. Very well written for the natural horn in E, but presents a few fingering difficulties on the modern valve horn. On either horn, a worthwhile recital piece and a great addition to the repertoire.
Range: f♯–b² (g–c³ for horn in E)
Duration: 20:50

Variations sur la cavatine de l'opéra "Der Augenarzt"
Robert Ostermeyer, 2001
Based on a theme from the opera, *Der Augenartzt* ("The Optometrist") by Adalbert Gyrowetz, the piece consists of an adagio sostenuto introduction, a theme in F major, and seven very typical nineteenth-century variations, written for natural horn in F in a cor-mixt style with an emphasis on midrange technical playing.
Range: c–a²

Krug, Arnold (1849–1904) Germany

Romanze
Ortel, 1901
Romantic late nineteenth-century piece in one movement.
Range: b♭–g²

Krug-Waldsee, Josef (1858–1915) Germany

Romance, op. 7
Bosworth and Co.
A short, relatively easy nineteenth-century romantic piece in F major.
Range: b–g²

Kryukov, Vladimir (1902–1960) Russia

Italian Rhapsody, op. 65
International Music Company, 1960
An expressive character piece, quite playable and well written. Composed in contrasting sections linked together.
Range: g–b♭²

Küffner, Joseph (1776–1856) Germany

Divertissement, op.227, *für Horn und Klavier*
Robert Ostermeyer, 2007
Dedicated to Gustav Wappers, this fairly short piece is written in four contrasting sections, and was most likely meant to be played on natural horn in F. Not too difficult technically, but requires some agility and light articulation. Includes just a couple of trills and ornaments.
Range: c–a²

Kuhlau, Fredrich (1786–1832) Germany

Andante e polacca
Eulenburg, 1977
Written for natural horn in F, this piece features an operatic but simple Andante in F minor, and a light articulate polacca with plenty of arpeggios and fast scale passages. A good example of the chromatic style of solo hand horn playing of the time.
Range: c–c³

Kvandal, Johan (1919–1999) Norway

Introduction and Allegro for Horn and Piano, op. 30
Norsk Musikforlag, 1971
Composed in two sections: Andante maestoso, ⁴₄—Allegro, ⁶₈. Modern notation bass clef. A difficult, but straightforward work. Contains glissandi. Written for hornist Ingegärd Øien.
Range: c–b♭²

Labor, Josef (1842–1924) Czech Republic

Thema und Variationen, op. 10
Amadeus Verlag, 1995; G. Schirmer (collection *Solos for the Horn Player*), 1962 (Mason Jones, ed.)

A straightforward theme and variations, probably intended originally for natural horn in E♭. After a dramatic opening Andante, the theme is followed by four variations of varying characters. Of moderate difficulty, and accessible to the advancing high school student.

Range: f–b♭²

Lachner, Franz (1803–1890) Germany

Fantasie in f moll für Horn und Klavier (1825)
Edition Kunzelmann, 1983
Theme and five variations for natural horn in F. Wide leaps and fast articulated scales, all in an easy key, but with very few rests.

Range: c–a²

Variatione über ein Schweizer Volkslied
Schott, 1985
Introduction, theme, and five variations for natural horn in F and piano. The theme and variations one through four are in F minor, and the introduction and variation five are in F major. Mostly midrange technical playing with some wide leaps and fast articulations. Includes trills, ornaments, and new notation bass clef.

Range: B–c²

Lachner, Ignaz (1807–1895) Germany

Notturno für Horn und Klavier, op. 37
Hans Pizka Edition, 1999
A typical nineteenth-century-salon piece, consisting of an operatic recitative opening, and an Andante arioso. Wide leaps and vocal lines with a very wide range and plenty of turns, trills, and other ornaments. Most likely for early valve horn.

Range: c–c³
Duration: 7:26

Lacour, Guy (1932–2013) France

Juste au Cor
Billaudot, 1997
A relatively easy piece in a limited range, but not beginner level. Easy, but musically interesting.

Range: e♭–f²
Duration: 3:55

Lamy, Fernand (1881–1966) France

Cantabile et scherzo
Alphonse Leduc, 1949
Dedicated to Jean Devèmy, this piece in French twentieth-century style contains a vast array of technical difficulties, like many of the Paris Conservatory exam pieces. Fairly lengthy, but separated into several sections of varying

tempos and moods. Covers a wide range, and includes muted and stopped passages, trills, glissandi, and a cadenza. Technically fairly difficult, but approachable by the advanced student.
Range: c–c^2

Lancen, Serge (1922–2005) France

Mississipi
Lido Mélodies, 1970
A short, melodic piece in the lower middle range for the young horn player.
Range: f–e^2
Duration: 2:30

Si J'etais. . . . (If I were. . . .)
Lido Melodies, 1981
Three short pieces in the styles of Lulli, Monteverdi, and Bach. Written in an easy range for the young horn player.
Range: a–e^2
Duration: 6:15

Lane, Richard (1933–2004) United States

Theme and Variations (1991)
Editions BIM, 2006
Written for David Wetherill and dedicated to Adeline Tomasone. Variations on "Sweet Adeline." Not terribly difficult for the horn, but interesting and fun. A note from the composer says: "Toujour avec une expression grave" ("always with a serious expression").
Duration: 5:00

Lansky, Paul (1944–) United States

Pieces of Advice (2007)
Carl Fischer, 2007
    I. Be mysterious
    II. Be proud
    III. Be patient
    IV. Be annoying
Four movements written for Bill Purvis and Mihae Lee. Interesting and active music, with intricate and difficult rhythms, and some challenging horn technique.
Range: c–c^2

Largueze, Jacques
See: Cochereau, Emile

Lauber, Anne (1943–) Canada, born in Switzerland

Mouvement
Canadian Music Center, 1980
Duration: 10:00

Lawrence, Peter (1954–) United Kingdom

Six Modern Pieces
Brass Wind Publications, 1980
Six short and relatively easy pieces of contrasting characters for the young horn
    player.
Range: b♭–d²

In Concert
Brass Wind Publications, 1988
Seven student pieces, more difficult than *Six Modern Pieces,* with a wider range
    and more developed technique suitable for the high school horn player.
    One of the movements, entitled "Interlude for horn in F," is to be played
    unaccompanied on the natural harmonics of the F horn, with a note from
    the composer that the f² will be sharp when played open.
Range: g–a♭²

Leclaire, Dennis (1950–) United States

Three Fairy Tales, op. 42 (1989)
Southern Music, 1993
Settings of the fairy tales "Rumpelstiltskin," "Thumbelina," and "Wee Willie
    Winkie" for horn and piano. Written for Thomas Bacon. Technically of
    moderate difficulty, but covers a wide range, and has some agile passages.
    New notation bass clef.
Range: G♯–b♭²
Duration: 7:05

LeClerc, Michel (1914–1995) Belgium

Five Piecettes
Maurer Muziekuitgeverij, 1970
Five short pieces written for Francis Orval: 1. Kicsi—2. Bateau Fleuri—3. Spleen
    —4. Le Tortillard—5. Travesti. All well within the range and technique of
    the high school horn player.
Range: a–a♭²

Ledbury, Oliver (1963–) United Kingdom

Cornucopia
Brass Wind Publications, 1988
Six short movements: Fanfare—Pastorale—Folk dance—Cantilena—Bagatelle—
    Ragtime. Of medium difficulty, these movements of varying characters are
    also in various keys, up to five flats for F horn. Some challenging rhythms
    for the younger horn player.
Range: g–g²

Lefebvre, Charles (1843–1917) France

Romance, op. 30
G. Schirmer (collection *Solos for the Horn Player*), 1962 (Mason Jones, ed.)

A lyrical piece in one medium-length movement that appears to have been written for natural horn in F.

Range: c^1–a^2

Le Flem, Paul (1881–1984) France

Pièce
Editions Max Eschig, 1952
Written for Jean Devémy, this very typical mid-twentieth-century French single-movement solo is divided into several sections of contrasting tempos and characters. Includes trills and stopped horn, and a good number of agile technical difficulties.

Range: $d\sharp$–c^3

Leidesdorf, Maximilian Joseph (1787–1840) Austria

Fantasie für Klavier und Horn (oder Flöte), über Themen aus der Oper
"Il Pirata" von Bellini
Robert Ostermeyer, 2005
A fantasie piece on themes from the opera *Il Pirata* by Bellini for natural horn in F and piano. Not terribly difficult, but a substantial piece of music requiring some agility with wide intervals and articulation. Mostly cor-mixt style playing in the staff.

Range c–c^3

Sonata pour pianoforte et cor, op. 164
See: Bellonci, Camillo, *Sonata pour pianoforte et cor,* op. 164

Leloir, Edmond (1912–2003) Belgium

Aubade
Billaudot, 1977
A very simple piece for the young horn player. Marked Andante and in a slow $\frac{6}{8}$.

Range: g–d^2
Duration: 2:10

Lemaire, Félix (1926–)

Nocturne
Alphonse Leduc, 1973
A very simple, lyrical piece.

Range: a–g^2 (with ossia a–$e\flat^2$)

Lemeland, Aubert (1932–) France

Cor lointain, op. 90
Billaudot, 1980
A relatively short single movement in French twentieth-century style. Mostly slow and melodic with a few interesting rhythmic passages, a cadenza, and a few stopped notes. Dedicated to Pierre-Yves Courtis.

Range: b–$a\flat^2$
Duration: 4:30

Lenom, Clément (1865–1957) Belgium

Mélodie
Rubank Inc., 1961
A straightforward melody in a moderate tempo for the advancing student. Includes a short cadenza, a turn, and a trill.
Range: b–g²

Leroux, Xavier (1863–1919) France

Sonata
Alphonse Leduc, 1897; International, 1963 (James Chambers, ed.)
Late nineteenth-century French conservatory piece written in a single movement with several contrasting sections. Though the technique looks very valve-horn-like, this piece is listed as having been played in the natural horn final-exam competition at the Paris Conservatory in 1897.
Range: g–a²

Leroy, Camille (1949–) France

Plagiola pour cor et piano
Editions Combre, 1998

"Le Loiret" Valse facile pour cor et piano
Editions Combre, 1998

Lersy, Roger (1920–) France

Préface en noir et jaune pour cor et piano
Editions Combre, 2000
A contemporary piece, dedicated to Hervé Moinard, composed in a single movement divided into several contrasting sections. The horn part presents a few challenges in technique and range, but is altogether quite accessible to the college student or talented high school horn player. Straightforward in its rhythms and intervals.
Range: c–b²

Lesaffre, Charles (1949–) France

Tanguetude
Billaudot, 1982
An elemenarary piece composed for the Prix de Composition de la Confédération Musicale de France, 1982.
Duration: 2:10

Le Siege, Annette (1945–) United States

Airs and Dances (1980)
Seesaw, 1980
Written for Fred Bergstone, this piece in late twentieth century style is composed in a single movement of varying meters and characters. Idiomatically well

written for the horn, and technically not overly difficult, but it does present
some rhythmic challenges and some agile intervals, as well as some stopped
passages.
Range: e–a²
Duration: 10:00

Levy, Frank (1930–) United States

Suite
Cor Publishing, 1961
Eight fairly simple, short movements of moderate difficulty.
Range: d–g♯²

Lewy, Joseph Rudolf (1802–1881) Germany, born in France

Divertissement, op. 13
Hans Pizka Edition, 1997
Based on themes of Franz Schubert, this fairly long piece, written for the early
valve horn, is straightforward and melodic, with a bit of technical difficulty
at the end.
Range: B♭–a²
Duration: 1:26

Grand Duo für Pianoforte und Horn, op. 6
Robert Ostermeyer, 2009
The first publication date of 1829 makes this one of the earliest pieces written spe-
cifically for valve horn. An opening Allegro with agile midrange technique
and many turns and ornaments is followed by a theme and five variations.
The piece ends with a § Rondo with fast scalewise passages.
Range: b–a♭²

*Morceau de salon, nach Motiven aus "I Puritani" von Bellini, für Horn und
Klavier,* op.12
Robert Ostermeyer, 2008
Lewy was a pioneer of the early valve horn, and his early approach to the use of
the valve is evident in this piece. An introduction, written in F horn, leads
into an Adagio in G♭ horn transposition. When the piece returns to F horn,
fingerings are specified by the composer for three stopped sections. This
straightforward salon piece includes several turns and ornaments.
Range: c–a²

Divertissement, op. 11, *sur motifs de l'opera "Les Huguenots" de Meyerbeer*
Hans Pizka Edition, 1998
A fairly difficult salon piece of the early nineteenth century, written for the early
valve horn. Includes recitative-like sections in a very operatic style, caden-
zas, and agile technical playing over a wide range.
Range: F–b²
Duration: 13:42

Lézé, Jean-François (1971–) France

Sonhos (dreams) (2005)
Editions BIM, 2007
A short piece of intermediate difficulty in a tonal contemporary style.
Duration: 5:00

Lhotka, Fran (1883–1962) Croatia, born in Czech Republic

Uspomena
Udruženje Kompozitora Hrvatske, 1968
A single-movement piece in lyrical style with a wide range.
Range: A–b♭²

Link, Joachim-Dietrich (1925–2001) Germany

Sonata
Breitkopf, 1977
    I. Allegro Giusto
    II. Interludium
    III. Variationen über eine altdeutsche Jagdweise
Written for Egon Wirth. A fairly long sonata in three movements. Very traditional horn writing in a twentieth-century tonal style with some technically difficult passages and requiring some endurance and strength in the
upper range. The last movement is a theme and variations on an old German hunting song, "Es blus ein Jäger wohl in sein Horn" ("A hunter blew
his horn") Includes a few trills and a couple of glissandi.
Range: F♯–c³

Lischka, Rainer (1942–) Germany

A Jazzy Joke
Hofmeister, 1994
An agile piece in jazz and blues style written for Peter Damm. Difficult rhythms,
intervals, and trills. Published with Lischka's unaccompanied piece *Steps
and Leaps.*
Range: g–c³

Litaize, Gaston (1909–1991) France

Triptyque, pour cor et orgue
Schott, 1994
A fairly difficult contemporary piece for horn and organ.

Llàcer Plà, Francisco (1918–2002) Spain

Relantando Imàgenes, op. 58 (1992)
International Music Diffusion, 1996
Written for Javier Bonet, this is composed in a very contemporary style and no-
tation. The five movements feature a multitude of difficulties and special
effects including hand stopping, glissandi, trills, and mute.
Range: f–c²

Lloyd Webber, William (1914–1982) United Kingdom
Composer, organist, and father of Andrew Lloyd Webber. He was director of the London College of Music.

Summer Pastures, Friesian Elegy for Horn and Piano
Ascherberg, Hopwood & Crew, 1960
"For Andrew." Short lyrical, flowing piece in ⁶⁄₄.
Range: c–g²

Longinotti, Paolo (1913–1963) Switzerland

Melodie romantique
Billaudot, 1980
Dedicated to Edmond Leloir. A short piece, consisting of a pleasant, flowing melody in ⁶⁄₈, marked Andante libero.
Range: b♭–a♭²

Longstaff, Edward (1965–) United Kingdom

Mattheson's Rhetoric (2001)
Maecenas Music, 2002

Lonque, Armand (1908–1979) Belgium

Oktobernacht voor hoorn en klavier, op. 48
Editions Maurer, 1958
A single movement marked Maestoso with a flowing, lyrical melody. Of moderate difficulty, good for the high school-level horn student.
Range: g–f²

Loos, Armin (1904–1971) Germany

Three Pieces for Horn and Piano (1963)
Association for the Promotion of New Music, Mobart Publications, 1978
Three movements in contemporary atonal style: I. Allegro impetoso—II. Lento, deciso—III. Con moto. Includes trill and stopped horn. New notation bass clef. Not without its technical difficulties, but idiomatic and playable for the horn.
Range: d–b²

Lorenz, Carl Daniel (1816–1866) Germany

Abendgesang, op. 10 and *Der Abschied. Fantasie,* op. 11
Hans Pizka Edition

Andantino with Variations
Hans Pizka Edition
Published with Lorenz's *Notturno Adagio,* these two pieces are written in a nineteenth-century salon style. This work consists of a short introduction, theme, and four variations of different characters. Rather technical, with lots of articulated notes, mostly scalewise, and in a limited range.
Range: c¹–g²

Notturno Adagio
Hans Pizka Edition
Published with the composer's *Andantino with Variations,* this piece is in a song-
   like style to be played muted throughout. Technically straightforward, and
   all in the staff.
Range: c^1–a♭^{2}

Elegie, op. 24
Hans Pizka Edition, 1997
A straightforward lyrical piece that requires agility and clean articulation from
   the horn player, but mostly features the horn's vocal qualities.
Range: f♯–g^2
Duration: 5:58

Fantasie, op. 13 *(Fantasie über Themas aus der Oper "Die Puritaner")*
Southern Music, 1987
Nineteenth-century fantasie piece on themes from Bellini's opera, "I Puritani."
   Relatively long with a bit of virtuosic technique, but in a comfortable range
Range: b–a^2

Fantasie melodique, op. 21 and *Thüringer Gebirgs Klänge, Fantasie,* op. 22
Hans Pizka Edition
Two separate pieces published together.
The *Fantasie melodique,* op. 21 is a single movement in melodic vocal style with
   some challenges in smooth agile playing, including some fast chromatic
   passages and quick movement through the range.
Range: e–g^2
The *Fantasie,* op. 22 is also written in a single movement, but in a ¾ Ländler feel.
   Entitled *Thüringer Gebirgs Klänge* ("Thuringen Mountain sounds"), it is more
   technical than the previous piece and based on alphorn motives and intervals.
Range: c^1–g^2

Frühlings Fantasie, op. 25
Hans Pizka Edition
A fairly short salon piece of rather moderate difficulty in a single tempo, Andante
   con moto. Written in a flowing, melodic style with some fast lines in vocal
   style and several trills.
Range: f–g^2

Melancholie, op. 16, no. 1 and *Elegie,* op. 20
Hans Pizka Edition
The *Melancholie* is a lyrical piece of medium difficulty in F major. The *Elegie* is
   a bit more technical and in a lyrical style with faster note values and more
   agility.
Range: g–g^2 (d–g^2 with ossia)

Romance, Sehnsucht des Entfernten nach seiner Heimat
Hans Pizka Edition
A short, flowing melodic piece that stays predominantly in the staff.
Range: b–g♯^{2}
Duration: 4:43

Rondo Original, op. 12, and *Fantasie on Themes from "Lucrezia Borgia,"*
by G. Donizetti
Hans Pizka Edition
A straightforward fantasie piece using themes from the opera *Lucrezia Borgia.*
   Composed in three sections with ample rest in between, including an
   opening Moderato in a melodic style, an Adagio with florid subdivisions in
   32nd notes, and ending with a more technical moderato section. Not terribly taxing, but technical and articulate. An early piece for valve horn in F.
Range: c¹–g² (a² with ossia)

Lotzenhiser, George W. (1923–) United States

Autumn Dream
Belwin, 1956
A short, simple piece for the beginning horn player.
Range: b–c²

Louël, Jean (1914–2005) Belgium

Ritmico ed arioso (1980)
CeBeDeM, 1987
Written for the National Music Competition Pro Civitate, this is an intricate con-
   temporary work in two short movements. It opens with a free quasi-cadenza,
   with horn and piano answering each other. Quick runs throughout require
   dexterity, agility, and solid multiple tonguing.
Range: d♭–b♭²
Duration: 5:00

Louvier, Alain (1945–) France

Hydre à cinq têtes, pour cor (ou trombone, ou saxophone alto, ou clarinet en sib,
ou bassoon) et piano
Alphonse Leduc, 1976

Lovelock, William (1899–1986) United Kingdom, worked in Australia

Rhapsody for Horn and Pianoforte
Australian Music Centre
A single-movement work composed in two sections, a flowing ¾, followed by a
   faster and more agile and articulate ⅝.
Range: B–b♭²

Lowe, Laurence (1956–) United States

Intermezzo
RM Williams, 2012
A fairly short, very expressive, flowing song dedicated to the memory of the com-
   poser's father.
Range: b♭–a²

Sonata No. 1 (2003)
RM Williams, 2004
A three-movement work described by the composer as "being in the post avant
    garde new romantic style that I hear so often as I play for motion pictures
    and television." The composer describes the first movement as a "loose
    sonata form" and comments that the range is rather high, conforming to
    modern expectations of the instrument. The second movement, which fea-
    tures lyrical range changes and some wide leaps, is an elegy to the com-
    poser's brother. The third movement is a loose rondo form that is agile and
    technically challenging. The composer comments in the preface "Take it
    fast!" The three movements are challenging for the horn in both range and
    technique, covering more than three octaves.
Range: A–c³

Lu, Wayne (1970–) United States

Cor de Force (2010)
Veritas Musica Publishing, 2010
Written for hornist J. Greg Miller. A short, agile piece that is rather technical and
    energetic. Includes a short cadenza.
Range: c–c³

Legacy
Cormont Music, 2008
Dedicated to Kendall Betts, this short, but fairly challenging piece features varied
    tempos and characters, a short cadenza, and four additional offstage horn
    parts that play with the solo horn in the last twelve measures.
Range: B–a² (off stage quartet G–d²)

Perigee Ballad
Veritas Musica Publishing, 2012
Written for Carrie Vertin. A challenging single-movement lyrical work that moves
    freely through the range.
Range: f♯–b²

Sonata for horn and Piano (1991–2003)
Veritas Musica Publishing, 2009
    I. Rush
    II. Intermezzo
    III. Exclamation
A three-movement work originally written for the composer's senior recital at the
    University of Illinois, and revised in 2003. The two outer movements are en-
    ergetic and articulate, with a middle movement in a gentle, flowing adagio
    tempo.
Range: f–b²

Summer Song
Veritas Musica Publishing, 2011
Dedicated to Jenny Stadtlander Lu. A single movement with alternating slow and
    fast sections.
Range: g–b²

Xi
In Chinese, "Xi" can mean "air," "energy," or "personal aura," and this piece de-
    picts all of these concepts. This short piece includes slow free sections that
    alternate with fast articulate ones, as well as a cadenza.
Range: g–d³

Zenith
Veritas Musica Publishing, 2012
A short piece consisting of flowing melodic lines alternating with fast staccato
    sections.
Range: g–c³

Luigini, Alexandre (1850–1906) France

Romance, op. 48
Billaudot
A relatively short late nineteenth-century romantic piece, probably meant for nat-
    ural horn.
Range: c–g²

Lundberg, Staffan (1952–) Sweden

Pastorale for Horn and Organ (1978)
Libitum Musik, 1981; Spaeth/Schmid
A short piece for horn and organ in a lyrical style. Musically straightforward but
    requires a bit of upper-range playing.
Range: c–b²

Lutyens, Elisabeth (1906–1983) United Kingdom

Three Duos, Op. 34, No. 1
Schott, 1956; Billaudot, 1975
Range: c–g²

Madsen, Trygve (1940–) Norway

Sonate Hommage à Franz Schubert for Horn og Klavier, op. 24
Musikk-Huset, 1979
Written for Frøydis Ree Wekre. Three relatively short movements: I. Allegro—
    II. Quasi menuetto—III. Moderato e poco rubato. Well written and well
    paced for the horn, with an emphasis on the upper register.
Range: b♭–b♭²

Maganini, Quinto (1897–1974) United States

Peaceful Land (Canzone Pastorale)
Editions Musicus, 1946
A short, lyrical Andantino in $\frac{3}{4}$, mostly in the staff. Appropriate for the high school
    horn player.
Range: a–a^2

Maggio, Robert, United States

Divide (1999)
Theodore Presser, 2003
Written for Daniel Grabois. In three movements: I. Low—II. High—III. Divide.
    The first movement, consisting largely of quintal harmonies, uses only the
    bottom half of the range of the piano, and the horn part is rather active, but
    not too difficult technically. The second movement uses the top half of the
    piano's range, and the horn part is quite sustained and higher, but not ex-
    cessively so. In the third movement, the piano plays a rhythmic pattern on
    two notes, f^1 and e♭^{1} for the first half of the movement before becoming full
    and sonorous to the end, with the horn sustained in the midrange. Some
    stopped and half-stopped writing, and directing the horn into the piano to
    create sympathetic vibrations.
Range: a–a♭^{2}
Duration: 12:00

Mai, Peter (1935–2014) Germany

Miniaturen
Hofmeister, 1974
Ten very short, simple pieces for the beginning horn player in a variety of tempos
    and time signatures. The pieces gain in difficulty from the first to the last,
    with the last two being a bit more demanding technically.
Range: g–e♭^{2}

Makarov, Evgenii Petrovich (1912–1985) Russia

Romance, op. 11, no. 1
VAAP), 1950
A Russian romantic piece in a lyrical, melodic style throughout. If the optional
    ending is taken, the piece ends on a stopped high b♭^{2}, much like the second
    movement of the Gliere horn concerto, which was written a few years after
    this piece.
Range: f–g^2 (with optional b♭^{2} at the end)
Duration: 6:00

Mallié, Loïc (1947–) France

Papyrus pour cor et piano
J.M. Fuzeau, 1989

A piece in contemporary style consisting of an opening introduction in an improvisatory feel, followed by a very articulate section in a fast $\frac{7}{16}$. After a brief section in the unusual meter of $\frac{6}{8} + \frac{1}{16}$, another cadenza section for both instruments leads into a return of the material of the previous fast section. Difficult horn technique, range, and meters make for plenty of challenges for the horn player.

Range: g–d³

Maltby, R. (1914–1991) United States

Blues Essay
Hal Leonard, Piedmont Music, 1969 (also exists with band accompaniment)
A short single movement for trombone or horn in a slow jazz style. The composer notes that the piece is to be played in strict notation but with a blues feeling. Technically fairly easy.

Range: b–g²
Duration: 3:15

Marc, Edmond (1939–) France

Gethsemani, méditation pour cor chromatique en fa et piano (1946)
Lucien De Lacour, Costallat, 1946
Meditative single movement in mid-twentieth-century French style. Flowing and lyrical.

Range: A–c³

Marechal, Henri (1842–1924) France

Fantasie pour cor
Belwin
French conservatory piece from the latter part of the nineteenth century written in a single movement with several contrasting sections. This piece is listed as having been played in the final-exam competition at the Paris Conservatory in 1899. Includes trills and stopped horn.

Range: c–a²

Mari, Pierrette (1929–) France

Cor-dialité pour cor et piano
Editions Combre, 1996
A study piece that is fairly straightforward musically and rhythmically but requires a wide range. Written in a single movement in sections of varying tempos. Includes stopped sections.

Range: c–c♭³

Marks, Günther (1897–1978) Germany

Jesu, meine Freude, Choralpartita für Horn und Orgel
Hänssler-Verlag, 1970; Carus Verlag

Six short movements dedicated to Kurt Janetzky based on the chorale *Jesu, meine Freude*. Of moderate difficulty for the horn. The composer states that the piece was conceived for horn, but could be played by any other melodic instrument.
Range: g–a²
Duration: 7:00

Marques, Telmo (1963–) Portugal

Waxed Floor for horn and piano (2010)
AVA Musical Editions, 2011
Range: c–c³

Martelli, Henri (1895–1980) France

Waltz
Pierre Noël, 1953; International, 1954
One of the short pieces in the collection entitled *Contemporary French Recital Pieces*. Not difficult technically.
Range: e–g♯²

Maslanka, David (1943–) United States

Sonata for Horn and Piano (1996, rev. 1999)
David Maslanka, 1996
Commissioned by William Scharnberg, with assistance from the International Horn Society. A contemporary three-movement sonata with a number of technical and rhythmic challenges. Described by the composer as follows: "The first movement begins in a mountain meadow and opens into a very passionate dream. The second movement is a quiet and serenely beautiful canoe trip across a mountain lake, while the third is a fast and furious race." Requires a strong upper range and endurance, especially in the third movement.
Range: F♯–c³
Duration: 20:00

Mason, John

Tenuto for French horn in F with Piano
The Composers Press, Inc., 1957
A short, easy piece that is rather sustained.
Range: a♭¹–g²

Massenet, Jules (1842–1912) France

Andante for Horn and Piano
Billaudot, 1977
A slow, dramatic piece in late nineteenth-century style in ¹²⁄₈. The piece features a wide range of dynamics, while remaining relatively easy in terms of endurance.
Range: c¹–a♭²
Duration: 5:00

Maugüé, J. L. M.

Motifs forestiers

Lucien De Lacour, Costallat, 1944

Paris Conservatory contest piece of 1944, dedicated to Jean Devémy. An extended
piece in several sections, which includes the typical array of technical difficulties, range, and tempos necessary for an exam piece. Technically challenging, with trills, cadenzas, and some stopped horn. New notation bass
clef.

Range: G–a²

Maurat, Edmond (1881–1972) France

Petites Inventions, op.21, no. 2

Editions Max Eschig, 1966

Five short pieces with the titles: Aubade—Cor de nuit—Angoisse—Sorcellerie—
Songe. One of a series of pieces called "Petite Inventions pour instruments
de bouche et piano." This set is very idiomatically written for the horn,
using stopped and muted effects, and a full range, all in a French twentieth-century style of horn writing. The pieces vary in character from gently
lyrical to articulate and agile. A bit challenging technically, but not too
taxing.

Range: c–a♭²

Duration: 17:35

Mayer, Jacques

Fantasie for Horn oder Bassethorn und Klavier

Edition Kunzelmann, 1997

This piece, which can be played by either horn or bassetthorn, is written in a
romantic salon style, filled with recitatives and flowing melodic sections
featuring trills, turns, and other ornaments, as well as some very technical
scale passages.

Range: c–c³

Mazellier, Jules (1879–1959) France

Rhapsodie Montagnarde

Éditions Salabert, 1933

Paris Conservatory exam piece from 1933. Dedicated to Professor Reine. Features
a full array of technical difficulties and muted and stopped effects.

Range: B♭–b♭²

McCabe, John (1939–2015) United Kingdom

The Castle of Arianrhod: the Goddess Trilogy I

Floraison: the Goddess Trilogy II

Shapeshifter: the Goddess Trilogy III

Novello, 1978 (set of three pieces); also published individually by Novello

These three pieces, written for Ifor James, may be performed separately or together as a single piece. They are very contemporary and atonal in style, with many dramatic effects, wide dynamic range, complex rhythms, stopped horn, and unmetered sections. The horn parts stay mostly in the staff, with very few exceptions, but present many difficulties, both technical and rhythmic.

Range: a–a²
Total duration: 28:00

McKay, George Frederick (1899–1970) United States

Three Pastoral Scenes
G. Schirmer, 1953
Three very simple pieces for the beginning horn player.
Range: c¹–e²

McTee, Cindy (1953–) United States

Circle Music IV
Rondure Music Publishing, 1988
Duration: 8:00

Images
Rondure Music Publishing, 1987
Duration: 10:20

Meijering, Chiel (1954–) Netherlands

The Run-around, for Horn and Piano
Donemus, 1990
A short piece that begins with the horn and piano trading off fast articulated triplets that gradually come together, with the horn alternating open and stopped notes. After a middle section in which the horn plays a more melodic line over an active accompaniment, the piece concludes with the return of the triplet figures, again, alternating open and stopped, and ending in short figures in the piano separated by silences. Includes stopped and muted passages.
Range: a–b²
Duration: 7:30

Mengal, Jean-Baptiste (1792–1878) Belgium

Valse, op. 20
Robert Ostermeyer, 2006
Based on themes from the 1816 opera *Charles de France* by Adrien Boieldieu and dedicated to M. Dauverné. A midrange French cor-mixt piece for natural horn in F. An Andante poco adagio introduction in $\frac{4}{4}$ leads into an easygoing, flowing $\frac{3}{8}$ Valse.
Range: e¹–a²

Souvenir de boieldieu, op.17, for horn and piano
Robert Ostermeyer, 2007
Also based on themes from the opera *Charles de France* by Adrien Boieldieu.

Mengal, Martin Joseph (1784–1851) Belgium

Solo pour cor
Billaudot, 1976
A single movement for natural horn in F in the French cor-alto style of the early
    nineteenth-century. Quite technical, with trills, ornaments, and fast artic-
    ulated passages. Also exists in a version with orchestra.
Range: e^1–c^3

2 Fantaisies für Horn und Klavier
Robert Ostermeyer, 2007
Two midrange French cor-mixt pieces for natural horn in mid-nineteenth-century
    French style, composed in short contrasting sections. Many fast articulate
    passages and ornaments, mostly in the octave from g^1 to g^2 of the F horn,
    the most agile octave for fast hand horn technique.
Range: c–g^2

Méreaux, Max (1946–) France

Eglogue
Zurfluh, 2004

Impromptu
Editions Combre, 2008
Dedicated to Gérard Jacque, this piece is a single movement of moderate diffi-
    culty, written for the advancing student. It covers a fairly wide range and
    includes stopped horn, trills, and a cadenza, as well as some fast articulated
    sixteenth-note passages.
Range: c–a^2

Talisman
Editions Combre, 1993

Mersson, Boris (1921–2013) Switzerland, born in Germany

Molnaresca—Kleine Suite in drei Sätze für Horn und Klavier, op. 53 (1994)
H. & B. Schneider AG, 1998
Three short movements of medium difficulty entitled: Parade—Idylle—Cupidon.
    Dedicated to hornist Jozsef Molnar. Contemporary tonal style with some
    mixed meters and rhythmic difficulties. Some stopped horn.
Range: $e\flat$–a^2
Duration: 10:00

Meseguer Llopis, Juan Bautista (1959–) Spain

Santium para trompa y piano, (2011)
Musicvall, 2011

A three-movement work dedicated to hornist Santiago Abel Muñoz. The first movement, marked Moderato, is in a classical tonal style, the second, Adagio espressivo, is more impressionistic, and the third, introduced by a cadenza, has an ostinato accompaniment. Medium difficulty.
Duration: 9:00

Meulemans, Arthur (1884–1966) Belgium

Prelude
Schott, Frères, Brussels, 1976
Straightforward, short horn and piano piece in lyrical style. One stopped passage.
Range: g–a♭²

Meunier, Gérard (1928–) France

Jolicor
Editions Combre, 1983

Meunier, Jean-René

Jeux de classe
Alphonse Leduc, 1968
A French conservatory competition piece, unusual, in that the first half of the piece is a dramatic unaccompanied cadenza. Horn and piano begin playing together about midway through the piece. Moderately difficult in technique and rhythms. Includes stopped horn, glissandi, and trills.
Range: c–b²
Duration: 6:30

Meyer, Jean

Cordelinette
Henry Lemoine, 1964
A short, easy, melodic piece written for horn or trombone in a moderato tempo.
Range: f♯–d²

Meyer-Selb, Horst (1933–2004) Germany

Sechs Episoden—nach einem Thema von Ludwig van Beethoven
Hofmeister, 1994
A theme by Beethoven with six interesting variations, or "episodes," in contemporary tonal style. Fairly difficult technically, with a wide range and stopped horn.
Range: c♯–c³

Michel, Paul-Baudouin (1930–) Belgium

Paysage (1980)
CeBeDeM, Brussels, 1984

A contemporary piece, difficult for both instruments, that features unusual meters, some graphic notation, glissandi, and stopped effects.
Range: F#–c³
Duration: 9:00

Mignion, Rene (1907–1981) France
Chant de la foret
Billaudot, 1977

Mihalovici, Marcel (1898–1985) France, born in Romania
Épisode
Alphonse Leduc, 1959
Dedicated to K. H. Ruppel, this single-movement work in twentieth-century
French style is written in three sections of contrasting tempos. Not overly
difficult in range or technique. Includes muted and stopped horn.
Range: g#–g#²
Duration: 6:30

Variantes, op.96
Huegel & Cie, 1970
Written for Georges Barboteu. This is a difficult late twentieth-century work, written in a single movement. Metered throughout and in standard notation,
but featuring many complex rhythms together with, and in opposition to,
the piano. Includes stopped horn, flutter tongue, mute, and many fast articulations and difficult intervals.
Range: c #–c³
Duration: 10:15

Milde, Friedrich (1918–) Germany
3 Miniaturen für Horn und Klavier
Wolfgang G. Haas-Musikverlag Köln, 2000
Three short contrasting pieces written for his eleven-year-old daughter Carla.
The horn technique in these pieces might be more appropriate to the high
school horn player. Interesting musically, not terribly difficult, but not beginner music.
Range: f#–e²

Miller, Brett, United States
Adagio
Potenza Music, 2008
Blue
Horn Dog Publishing, 2001
Andante
Horn Dog Publishing, 2007

Hunting Songs for Low Horn
Brass Arts Unlimited, 2013
Commissioned by Denise Tryon. A short piece in three sections written almost
    exclusively in new notation bass clef. The titles of the three sections are "The
    crow," "The owl," and "The falcon."
Range: F–c²

Miller, J. Greg (1984–) United States

Cloak and Dagger Games (2010)
Veritas Musica Publishing, 2010
Written in several sections, ranging from a very free opening section to an ag-
    ile Molto vivace. Fairly difficult, especially at the printed tempos. Includes
    several trills.
Range: d–b²

Mindlin, Adolfo (1922–) Argentina

Elégie
Alphonse Leduc, 1988
An easygoing student piece in a melodic style and Andante sostenuto tempo. Easy
    intervals and range for the young horn player.
Range: b–e²
Duration: 3:15

Rêve au bord de l'eau
Alphonse Leduc, 1988
A very easy, short student piece in a single movement that stays in the staff and
    presents only very moderate challenges in rhythm and intervals for the very
    young horn player.
Range: g♯–e²
Duration: 2:30

Souvenir d'Espangne
Alphonse Leduc, 1988
A relatively easy student piece for the young horn player who has good control
    and articulation from written g below middle c¹ to the top of the staff. Writ-
    ten as a scherzo in a spirited tempo with straightforward, but agile, articu-
    lated passages, mostly scalewise and in closer intervals.
Range: g–f♯²
Duration: 3:15

Miroshnikov, Oleg (1925–) Russia

Rondo
Gos. muzykal'noe izd-vo, 1962
An extended rondo in § with a wide range and agile technique. Some stopped
    passages.
Range: g–b²

Mohr, Jean-Baptiste (1823–1891) France
Mohr was a student of Gallay, and his successor as professor of natural horn at the Paris Conservatory from 1864 until 1891.

3ème solo de cor, op. 8
Sempre Piu, 2012
A typical conservatory-exam piece for natural horn in F, mainly written within the staff. Musically and technically similar to the music of Gallay. This is one of at least ten solos for horn and piano that Mohr composed.
Range: c^1–a^2
Duration: 5:40

Molina, Antonio (1894–1980) Philippines

Interlude
Southern Music, 1990
Short, relatively easy piece with a limited range.
Range: f–f^2

Molyneux, Garth E. (1958–) United States

Sonata (1995)
JOMAR Press
A substantial three-movement sonata: I. Andantino—II. Adagio—III. Malagueña, vivace. Mostly written in the staff, but persistent with few rests. Straightforward horn technique with a few technical challenges.
Range: g–$a\sharp^2$
Duration: 20:00

Monjo, Didac (1949–) Spain

A Day in the Country for Horn and Piano
Hans Pizka Edition, 1986
Seven short movements in a Spanish style. Straightforward musically, but very active and agile technically for the horn.
Range: b–b^2

Friendship Suite for Horn and Piano
Hans Pizka Edition, 1986
Twelve short movements in a contemporary pop style.

Montbrun, Raymond Gallois (1918–1994) France

Ballade
Alphonse Leduc, 1950
Relatively easy, lyrical piece with a limited range.
Range: f–g^2

Morawetz, Oskar (1917–2007) Canada, born in Czech Republic

Sonata for Horn and Piano
Aeneas Music, 1982; Canadian Music Centre
A four movement work: Adagio—Allegro—Adagio—Allegro.
Commissioned by Eugene Rittich and the CBC and premiered in 1980, this is
    a rather large scale and fairly difficult sonata. Lots of meter changes and
    rhythmic challenges, as well as lots of notes and agile intervals for the horn.
Range: d–b♭²
Duration: 20:00

Morel, François (1926–) Canada

Phases (2008)
Éditions Doberman-Yppan, 2009
Written in five sections. The composer indicates the "compositional material
    consists of a 'mirror mode' for the horn part and likewise a different mode
    for the piano part, both modes containing harmonic elements and multiple
    melodic motives." The fourth section is a cadenza for the horn. Contains
    flutter tonguing, stopped writing, trills, and multiple tonguing.
Range: d–c³

Moscheles, Ignaz (1794–1870) Born in Czech Republic, worked in Austria,
United Kingdom, Germany

Thême Varié, Feuillet d'album de Rossini, op. 138b
Edition Eulenburg, 1977
Based on a theme of Rossini, this piece is written for natural horn in E, and con-
    sists of three variations with lots of interplay between the horn and piano.
    Very virtuosic piano part, and very agile horn part.
Range: B–b² (c–c³ for horn in E)

Duo, op. 63, *Introduction & Rondeau Ecossais* (1821)
Music Rara, 1974
Written for hand horn virtuoso Giovanni Puzzi, this piece begins with a slow
    introduction followed by a rondo based on an old Scottish theme. The horn
    part is written in the cor-mixt style of the early nineteenth-century, limited
    in range, but rather agile and technical.
Range: g–g²

Moss, Piotr (1949–) Poland

Themes varies, cinq pièces pour cor et piano
Editions Max Eschig, 1994
Five short movements in contemporary style that use a number of effects, in-
    cluding flutter tongue, trills, stopped, and muted horn. Difficult rhythmi-
    cally, but written in a comfortable range that doesn't present endurance
    difficulties.
Range: g–f²
Duration: 11:00

Mourey, Colette (1954–) France

Chant de la terre
Editions Marc Reift
A lyrical piece marked Andantino molto cantabile.

Bonheurs d'eté (grand duo concertant)
Editions Marc Reift
Also in a lyrical style, and marked Andantino molto cantabile.

Moylan, William (1956–) United States

Sonata for Horn (1982)
Seesaw Music, 1983
Commissioned by Kent Leslie. This can be performed as a solo sonata or as a
    sonata for horn and piano. This work is in one continuous movement and
    may be divided into four large sections that alternate unaccompanied horn
    with horn and piano. There are challenging technical passages to work out,
    and long-range endurance is required for several sections, however the
    moderate range makes this work more accessible than many contemporary
    works for solo horn.
Range: f$\sharp$–a^2 (horn and piano version) or g$\sharp$–g$^{\flat2}$ (solo horn version)
Duration: 11:00 (horn and piano version) or 5:30 (solo horn version)

Moyse, Louis (1912–2007) France

Ten Pieces for Horn and Piano, op. 37, no. 4
G. Schirmer, 1991
Ten short pieces of limited range and difficulty: Days gone by—Roaming—Can-
    tilena—To idle away—In torment—Bravura march—Memories. . .—Lei-
    surely—In the forest—Sunrise on the mountains
Range: f–a$^{\flat2}$

Muelbe, William (1888–1966) United States

Concert Miniature, Based on a Study of Oscar Franz
Boosey & Hawkes, 1948
As the title implies, the melodic material of this piece comes from a study from
    the Oscar Franz *Method for Horn.* An agile piece, with a wide range. Old
    notation bass clef.
Range: F$\sharp$–c^3

Elegy for Horn and Piano
Boosey & Hawkes, 1948
A second piece based on a study from the Oscar Franz *Method for Horn.* Very
    slow, but very florid with lots of fast scale passages and a wide range, with
    just a couple of stopped notes. Unlike the previous piece, this one uses new
    notation bass clef.
Range: A–a^2

Rondino
Boosey & Hawkes, 1948
Yet another piece based on a study from Oscar Franz. Fast and agile, but not ex-
     cessively difficult, with a couple of trills.
Range: g–b²

Mueller, Bernhard Edward (1842–?) Germany
Mueller wrote a series of short pieces, all published by Zimmermann, Leipzig,
1905–1910. All of these pieces, now long out of print, are single-page compositions
of very moderate difficulty, with a range that lies almost exclusively within the
staff for F horn.

Am Abend. Lied ohne Worte, op. 71

Andante Religioso, op. 74

Erinnerung an Carl Maria von Weber, Fantasie, op. 66

Fantasiestück, op. 70

Gebet (Prayer), op. 65a
Also published by Marvin McCoy editions, 1989, arranged for horn and organ.

Nocturno, op. 73

Melancholie, op. 68

Recitativ und Gebet aus der Oper "Der Freischütz" von Weber, op. 75

Romanze in B dur, op. 69, no. 2

Ständchen, op. 67

Wiegenlied, op. 69, no. 1

Mueller, Otto (1870–1960) United States, born in Germany
Lyrical Romance
For horn and piano or orchestra.
See: Horn and ensemble

La Chasse
For horn and piano or orchestra.
See: Horn and ensemble

Mulder, Herman (1894–1989) Netherlands
Sonate, op. 43, no. 4
Donemus, 1950
In three movements: Allegro risoluto—Adagio—Allegro con spirito. A freely tonal
     rhythmic work in traditional forms, well paced for the horn player.
Range: f–g²

Müller, Christian Gottlieb (1800–1863) Germany
3 Notturni für Horn und Klavier
Pfefferkorn Musikverlag, 2008

Three pieces in a mid-nineteenth-century romantic style, with tempo markings
of Allegro agitato—Allegro quasi andantino—Allegretto. They are very
idiomatically written for the natural horn in F. The pieces range in style
from a spirited, flowing Allegro in the first piece to an agile $\frac{6}{8}$ with lots of
arpeggiated and scale passages in the second, and finally a technical and
articulate $\frac{2}{4}$ in the third.

Range: c–b♭²

Muneta, Jesús María (1939–) Spain

Concierto para trompa y piano, op. 113/2
Piles, 1998

Murgier, Jacques (1912–1986) France

Étude concert no. 1
Billaudot, 1978

Musgrave, Thea (1928–) United Kingdom

Music for Horn and Piano
Chester, 1967
Written for Barry Tuckwell and Margaret Kitchin and premiered at the Zagreb
Festival of Contemporary Music in 1967. A very technical piece with much
rhythmic freedom. Musically very contemporary with difficult rhythms,
quick range changes, and stopped and muted effects.

Range: B–c³
Duration: 9:00

Nagel, Jody (1960–) United States

As You Like It (1980, rev. 1986 and 1999)
JOMAR Press
A fairly short single movement with pleasant, flowing melodies that ends quietly
in stopped horn.

Range: g–g²
Duration: ca. 6:00

Nagy, Zsolt (1957–) Hungary

Music for Dénes
RM Williams, 2012
Dedicated to the composer's student Szilágyi Dénes. A short, spirited piece with
agile sixteenth-note passages and interesting rhythms in a relatively narrow range.

Range: b♭–f²

Naigus, James (1987–) United States

Episodes
RM Williams, 2012

Seven short movements written for Paul Basler.

1. New Beginnings
2. Child's Play
3. Amour
4. Drive
5. Reflection
6. Joy
7. Resolve

Moderately difficult and accessible to the advancing student horn player, with a good mix of moods and tempos.

Range: g♭–a²

Songs of Sorrow

In three movements that can be played separately or as a single piece: Chanson— Valse—Elegy. The first piece, in a very slow tempo, features some complex rhythms, but altogether the horn technique required is moderate. Lots of melodic, flowing lines in all three pieces.

Range: g–a♭²

Näther, Gisbert (1948–) Germany

Divertimento für Horn und Klavier (1987)
Musik und Buchverlag Werner Feja, 1990
A three-movement student work, limited in range for the young horn player, but interesting rhythmically and musically.

Range: b♭–c²

Ballade für Horn und Orgel
F. Hofmeister, 2001

Schlaf Wohl, du Himmelsknabe, du, Fantasie für Horn in F und Orgel.
F. Hofmeister, 1997

Naulais, Jèrôme (1951–) France

Cor accords
Editions Combre, 2000
A rather extended through-composed piece in contemporary tonal style, with several sections of varying tempos and characters. Includes cadenza and recitative sections, trills, and flutter tongue.

Range: A–b♭²

. . . Au Fond des bois
Robert Martin Editions Musicales, 1995
A simple student piece in four sections of different tempos. Very limited range and technique.

Range: f–c²

Nedellec, Patrick (1946–) France

12 Pièces
Billaudot, 1992
Twelve short movements of rather limited range and technique, written espe-
    cially for the young horn player.
Range: g–f²
Total duration: 13:45

Nelhybel, Vaclav (1919–1996) United States, born in Czech Republic

Scherzo Concertante
General Music, 1966
A short, spirited piece in a fast ¼. Rhythmically interesting but not overly difficult.
    Mostly written in the staff. A very effective recital piece.
Range: a–b♭²
Duration: 3:00

Neubert, Günter (1936–) Germany

Sonate für Horn und Klavier (1964)
Edition Peters, Collection Litolff, Leipzig, 1969
This mid-twentieth-century sonata in three movements was dedicated to hornist
    Peter Damm. Technically only of moderate difficulty, it does stay in the
    upper range more than might be comfortable for many players. The third
    movement, in an agile ⅜, is particularly indicative of Peter Damm's ability
    to play lightly and easily above the staff.
Range: g–c³

Neukomm, Sigismund von (1778–1858) Austria

Marche réligieuse pour cor et orgue (1822)

Andante pour cor et orgue expressif (1843)
London Gabrieli Edition, 2000 (Christopher Larkin, ed.)
Two nineteenth-century pieces for horn and organ, very idiomatically written for
    the natural horn of the period in France, where Neukomm spent much of his
    career. The march, in C major, is relatively simple in its horn technique, and
    solemn in its character. The Andante, in F major, is more developed in its
    use of chromatic hand stopping, and is more vocal in its musical character.
Range: c–c³

Neuling, Hermann (1897–1967) Germany

Bagatelle
Pro Musica, 1956
One of the most important pieces written specifically for the low-horn player,
    often played on recitals and even more often used as an orchestral audition
    piece for low horn in orchestras around the world. Very agile writing in

the low range of the horn, the piece covers all aspects of low-horn playing.
Musically simple and lighthearted.
Range: G–a♭²

Konzert Cadenz, für tiefes Horn und Klavier
Pro Musica, 1954
Marked "Frei nach H. Kling," this concert cadenza with piano accompaniment
is a free arrangement with many alterations of Etude No. 31 from Kling's
40 Characteristic Etudes for French Horn. Stylistically and technically very
much like the *Bagatelle.*
Range: F–a²

Nicholas, James (1957–) United States
The following sonatas for natural horn and piano were written by cellist and
composer James Nicholas in a contemporary tonal style. Very well written, with
a good understanding of the possibilities and colors of the natural horn.

Sonata No. 2 "Exile" for Natural Horn in E♭ and Piano (1993)
Birdalone Music, 1997
Range: d¹–g² (e¹–a² for horn in E♭)

Sonata No. 3 "Searching" for Natural Horn in F and Piano (1997)
Birdalone Music, 1997
Written for Paul Austin.
Range: f♯–a²

Sonata No. 4 "The Ranks of the Fiery Spirit" for Natural Horn in E♭ and piano (1999)
Birdalone Music, 1999
Written for Richard Seraphinoff.
Range: B♭–g♭² (c–a♭² for horn in E♭)

See: Collorafi, James

Nielsen, Carl (1865–1931) Denmark

Canto serioso (1913)
Skanndinavisk, Copenhagen, 1944
A short piece originally written for the low horn as an orchestra audition piece. It
exploits the low range of the horn with singing melodies, fast articulation,
and light arpeggios through the range. A pleasant little recital piece.
Range: G–f♯²

Nisle, Jean, Germany
Likely the same person as Johann Martin Friedrich Nisle.

Six Duos Brillants, op. 51
Hans Pizka Edition, 1981; Southern Music, 1993
Six short movements in mid-nineteenth-century style for horn in F, probably for
natural horn.
Range: g–b♭²
Duration: 4:00–5:00 for each of the six pieces

Nisle, Johann Martin Friedrich (1780–1861) Germany

Fantasia für Horn und Klavier
Robert Ostermeyer, 1999
Written in five sections of varying tempos, this fantasy piece appears to be playable on natural horn. Composed in a mid-nineteenth-century salon style, there are plenty of agile notes to play and one trill.
Range: g–c^3

Niverd, Lucien (1879–1967) France

Six Petites Pièces de style
Éditions musicales Andrieu frères, 1939; Billaudot
For piano and horn (or bassoon, tuba, trombone, saxophone, bugle, cornet, or bass saxhorn). Pieces are titled: Chant melancolique—Complainte—Historiette dramatique—Hymne—Romance sentimentale—Scherzetto.

Noble, Harold (1903–1998) United Kingdom

Arietta (In Classical Style)
British & Continental Music Agencies Ltd., 1975
Simple, lyrical piece with a range that stays strictly in the staff.
Range: d^1–g^2
Duration: 4:00

Norden, Hugo (1909–1986) United States

Passacaglia in F Major
J. & W. Chester, 1959
Written for Francis Finlay. Composed with an eight-measure passacaglia accompaniment throughout, played alternately by the horn and the piano, with variations. The horn part is agile, but moderate in its difficulties.
Range: a♭–b♭^{2}

Nowlin, Ryan (1978–) United States

Forbidden
McGinty Music, 2006

Elegy
McGinty Music, 2004
Written in memory of hornist and professor Herbert A. Spencer.

Nyquist, Morine (1909–?) United States

Golden Summer for Solo French Horn
Belwin, 1952
Easy student piece with limited range and technical difficulty.
Range: d^1–e^2

Mazurka in A Minor
Belwin, 1952
A slightly more interesting easy student piece, also of limited range and technical
difficulty.
Range: d^1–e^2

Melody for Horn
Belwin, 1952
Very similar in character to the composer's *Golden Summer* in range, technical
difficulty, and musical content.
Range: c^1–c^2

Oestreich, Carl (1800–1840) Germany

Andante
Wiener Waldhorn Verein, 1992 (Kristin Thelander, ed.)
A short, pleasant, easygoing, lyrical piece with a limited range from the early
nineteenth century for natural horn in E♭.
Range: f–e♭^{2} (g–f^2 for Horn in E♭)

Oldberg, Arne (1874–1962) United States

Serenade
Horn and piano version of the composer's *Le Son du Cor* for horn and orchestra.
See: Horn and ensemble

Olson, Judith (1940–) United States

Four Fables for Horn and Piano(1961)
Hornseth Music Co., 1978
Four short movements of varying characters and tempos. Third movement is
muted throughout.
Range: g–c^3

O'Neill, Charles (1882–1964) Canada

Menuetto for Horn and Piano (Written under the name of Wallace Harvey)
Waterloo Music Co., 1954
A technically simple minuet for the young horn player.
Range: a–g^2

Cavatina for Horn in F and Piano (Written under the name of Alex Chambers)
Waterloo Music Co., 1954
A slightly more technically challenging, melodic piece, but still for the young horn
player.
Range: c^1–f^2

Onofrio, Marshall, United States

Romanza Antico e Moderno, for Horn and Piano
Margun Music, 1995

Opitz, Erich (1912–2001) Austria

Sonatine für Horn und Klavier
Musikverlag Fritz Schulz, 1979
A two-movement sonatina intended to be a study and recital piece for the advancing horn student. Easygoing technique and range.
Range: f–e²

Orr, Robin (1909–2006) United Kingdom

Serenade
Schott, 1952
A rather easy, slow piece with a few dramatic moments. Technically quite easy.
Range: c–f♯²

Orval, Francis (1944–) Belgium

Champaign (1983)
Editions Marc Reift, 1994
Written for hornist Nico De Marchi, this is a flashy showpiece in the style of twentieth-century French compositions for solo horn. Very technical, with some unusual contemporary notation features, rhythmic freedom, and stopped effects.
Range: A–c³

Osborne, Chester, G. (1915–1987) United States

Aisling
Pro Art Publications, 1977
Pronounced "Ash-ling," the title means "fantasy" in Gaelic. An easy lyrical piece based on a Gaelic folk tune, written for Richard Rosolino. Includes one stopped passage.
Range: f–e♭²

Osbourne, Roy

Serenade
Boosey & Hawkes, 1935
A flowing, lyrical piece in several sections, including a Valse brilliante and two cadenzas. Medium difficulty, and all in an easy-going limited range.
Range: b–f²

Ostransky, Leroy (1918–1993) United States

Ballade
Rubank, 1964
An easy piece, good for the elementary school or middle school horn player.
Range: b–e²

Ott, Joseph (1929–1990) United States

Serenade
Claude Benny Press, 1985

Painter, Paul (1908–?)

Sylvan Colors
Carl Fisher, 1937
Not overly difficult, this short, rather energetic solo piece can also be played with
    orchestra.
Range: b♭–b♭²

Pakhmutova, Aleksandra (1929–) Russia

Nocturne
Moskva: Gos. muzykajl'noe izd-vo, 1958

Panos, Alexander (1980–) United States

Lithium
Brassworks 4, 2006
Intense and driving, in a fast two with occasionally changing meters and quick
    chromatic runs.
Range: A♭–c³ (ossia A♭–g²)

Pantaleon, Arturo (1965–) Germany, born in Mexico

Romanza "Recuerdos" (*Erinnerungen*, op. 18b)
Stark, 2009

Parsons, Alan (1931–) United Kingdom

Sonata for Horn and Piano
Anglian Edition, 1990
Written for Clare Hutchings. In its opening and ending, this three-movement
    piece in modern style uses the open notes of the F horn played over the
    piano sound board to excite sympathetic vibrations. The remainder of the
    piece is played with standard fingerings and intonation. Some technically
    difficult writing, but very playable. Stopped and muted horn are used, as
    well as glissandi.
Range: F♯–c³

Pärt, Arvo (1935–) Estonia

Spiegel im Spiegel
Universal Edition, 1978, 2004
A minimalist piece written by the composer in versions for a number of different
    instruments. Slow and sustained, the horn part consists solely of a single
    page of dotted whole notes at ♩=80 in a slow-moving meditative progression.
Range: a–b♭²

Pascal, Andrè (1932–2001) France

Fantasie élégiaque
Editions Phillippo
Written for hornist Lucien Thévet, this piece is energetic, precise, and rhythmically interesting. In one movement of medium difficulty.
Range: a–b²

Pascal, Claude (1921–) France

Equinoxe pour cor et piano
Editions Combre, 2004
Written for Michel Coquart and Yoshiko Otsu, this is a rather difficult contemporary piece, with a wide range, difficult intervals and leaps, and technical passages with a lot of notes. Includes some stopped passages, and new notation bass clef. An interesting piece musically for player and audience.
Range: c♯–b²

Sonate
Durand & Cie, 1963
Written in several sections that are linked together, this piece in mid-twentieth-century French style presents a few technical difficulties, but is quite playable by the skillful college-level horn student. Includes some fast tonguing, stopped passages, and a wide range.
Range: d–c³
Duration: 7:15

Passani, Emile (1905–1974) France

Vesperal
Pierre Noël, 1953; International, 1954
One of the short pieces in the collection entitled *Contemporary French Recital Pieces* published by International Music Co. Not difficult, includes muted and stopped horn effects.
Range: f♯–g♯²

Sarabande et Bourrée
Alphonse Leduc, 1969
Two relatively short movements for horn or cello. The Sarabande in ¾ in an andante tempo is mostly scalewise and flowing. The Bourrée, in ⅜, is faster and more agile, with some rather technical passages covering a wide range. Includes a trill and flutter tongue.
Range: c♯–a♯²

Pauset, Brice (1965–) France

Theorie der Tränen: Gesang
Henry Lemoine, 2007
Duration: 9:00

Paviour, Paul (1931–) Australia, born in United Kingdom

The Havisham Canticle and Litanies, Two Pieces for Horn and Piano (1975)
The Australian Music Centre, Keys Press, 2000
Duration: 10:00

Peçi, Aleksandër (1951–) Albania

Variacione mbi një temë, për korno dhe piano
Aelfior Editions, 2008
A simple theme and six variations, all of moderate difficulty with straightfor-
    ward rhythms and technique. A few trills and a couple of glissandi, but
    traditional in its horn writing. Also exists in a version for horn and or-
    chestra.
Range: b–c³

Pehrson, Joseph (1950–) United States

Romance
Seesaw Music Corp., 1986
Dedicated to Linda Pehrson. Three movements in a contemporary style that cen-
    ter more on the horn's low range, touching only briefly on notes at the top
    of the staff.
Range: A–a♭²
Duration: ca. 9:00

Pelinka, Werner (1952–) Austria

Epitaph für Franz Schmidt, op.10a *(für Horn und Klavier)*
W.W.V.   Wien, 1988

Pellegrini, Ernesto (1932–) United States

Mahleriana (1994)
JOMAR Press
A single-movement work dedicated to Fred Ehnes, written in four connected
    sections: I. Grave e sostenendo al più possible—II. Tempo di valzer, ma
    molto rubato—III. Andante comodo—IV. Allegro moderato. The short
    introductory first section is followed by a flowing waltz with a few stopped
    effects. The third section is in the style of an accompanied recitative or ca-
    denza using material from Gustav Mahler's ninth symphony, followed by
    the finale, which ends with a march-like melody based on the first move-
    ment of the third symphony. Quotes from "Nun seh' ich wohl warum so
    dunkle Flammen," from the composer's song cycle *Kindertotenlieder* are
    used in the short interludes of the four sections. Some muted and stopped
    horn.
Range: b♭–c³
Duration: 18:00

Pelz, William

Ballad
Belwin, 1956
A simple beginner's piece that goes a little higher than may be comfortable for
   many beginners.
Range: a–f²

Lady in Blue
Belwin, 1956
A similar piece to the composer's *Ballad*.
Range: c¹–f²

Pernoo, Jacques (1921–2003) France

Fantaisie Brève
Alphonse Leduc, 1952
Written for Jean Dévemy, this rather easy, short French twentieth-century piece
   is mostly lyrical in character with an agile fast ending.
Range: f–g²

Peron-Cano, Carlos (1976–) Spain

Sonatina para trompa y piano (2003)
Kemel, 2009

Perrin, Jean (1920–1989) Switzerland

Sonate, op. 7 (1953)
Editions BIM, 1992
A moderately difficult, but musically straightforward twentieth-century piece.
Duration: 17:00

Perrini, Nicholas J. (1932–) United States

Legend
Southern Music, 1962
A short piece, marked Andante, of moderate difficulty and tonally straightforward.
Range: c¹–a²

Pessard, Emile (1843–1917) France

In the Forest, op. 130
Albert J. Andraud, 1941; Southern Music
A fairly difficult contest piece with short sections of varying tempos and charac-
   ters. Uses echo-horn effect.
Range: c–a²
Duration: 5:30

Pièce mélodique, en ut, pour cor à pistons avec accompagnement de Piano, op. 39
Alphonse Leduc

Peterson, Christian, W. (1964–) Germany

Divertimento für Horn und Klavier
Pfefferkorn, 2012
A four-movement modern tonal work of a difficulty level appropriate for the advancing student. The first movement consists of variations on two themes, the second movement is in a slow song-like character, the third is a humorous waltz, and the last is a rondo in a ragtime style.

Peterson, Hal

Sonatina for Horn and Piano
Blixt Publications, 1973
A single-movement work in sections of contrasting characters. Other than rhythmic and metric complexities, the horn technique required is of moderate difficulty. It includes a section for each instrument in which the performer is asked to improvise on a series of notes. Includes stopped horn.
Range: g–a^2

Petit, Pierre (1922–2000) France

Flakallaos
Editions Max Eschig, 1980
Late twentieth-century-style piece written for Georges Barboteu. The texture is transparent and there are some rhythmic difficulties, as well as challenging horn technique over a wide range. A few stopped notes.
Range: ab–bb^2

Petrić, Ivo (1931–) Slovenia

Lyrisms for Horn and Piano (Lirizmi za rog in klavir) (1969)
Hans Gerig, 1975
    I. Tempo moderato
    II. Tempo agitato
    III. Tempo largo
A contemporary piece in three movements written in graphic notation without bar lines or definite note values. The composer gives very specific performance instructions in the preface about durations of notes and the interpretation of the notation and other effects, such as playing on the strings of the piano with felt or wooden sticks. Aside from the atonality and interpretation of the contemporary style, the horn part is not technically difficult. Includes stopped and muted effects.
Range: a–a^2
Duration: 8:00

Sonata No. 1 (Sonata za rog in klavir) (1960)
Hans Gerig, 1977
A three movement work: Preludio—Variazioni—Postludio.

Not an overly difficult work technically, but substantial and idiomatic horn writing in a twentieth-century tonal style.
Range: b–g^2
Duration: 13:00

Sonata No. 2 (1990)
Pizzicato, Edizioni Musicali, 1992
Also not overly difficult, this substantial one-movement sonata is written in a flowing contemporary style.
Range: e–g^2
Duration: 8:00

Pflüger, Hans Georg (1944–1999) Germany

Impeto (1986)
Bote & Bock, 1988
Written for Hermann Baumann, this thickly textured and dramatic piece is difficult for both instruments and includes multiphonics, stopped effects, echo horn, glissandi, flutter tongue, and hand-out-of-the-bell playing. Though composed originally for horn, the composer has adapted the piece for trombone as well. The pedal C in measure fifty-nine of the horn part may be notated in the wrong octave. The piano part notates the low C in measure fifty-nine an octave higher.
Range: C–b^2 (more likely E–b^2).

Concerto für Horn und Orgel (1983)
Bote & Bock, 1984
A contemporary piece for horn and organ which is a horn and keyboard version of the composer's *Concerto for Horn and Orchestra* written in 1983 for Hermann Baumann. Written in two movements: Maestoso (quasi cadenza)—Grave. A rather difficult contemporary work technically and tonally. Includes multiphonics, stopped effects, echo horn, glissandi, flutter tongue, and several unmeasured sections. The second movement is based on the composer's 1975 piece *Klangfiguren über "Es ist das Heil uns kommen her,"* also for horn and organ.
Range: F–c^3 (and highest note possible)
Duration: 15:00
See: Horn and ensemble

Klangfiguren über "Es ist das Heil uns kommen her," op. 17 (1975)
Bote & Bock, 1979; Boosey & Hawkes, 1998
A very contemporary piece for horn and organ written for Hermann Baumann that consists mostly of sustained chords and clusters in the organ, over which the horn adds interjections using stopped effects, flutter tongue, glissandi, and many different colors and dynamics over a wide range.
Range: B–b^2

Phillips, Craig (1961–) United States

Serenade for Horn and Organ
Oxford University Press, 2004
A meditative piece for horn and organ.
Range: g–f♯²
Duration: 5:45

Piacquadio, Peter (1945–) United States

Pavana e rondo
Shawnee Press, 1982
Composed for Julie Landsman and dedicated to Carmine Caruso. A lyrical and
    melodic piece in contemporary tonal style, composed in several sections of
    varying tempos. Covers a wide range, with an emphasis on the upper range.
Range: G–d³
Duration: 7:30
See: Horn and ensemble

Piantoni, Louis (1885–1958) Switzerland

Air de chasse
Alphonse Leduc, 1954
A short, easygoing fast piece of limited range with mixed meters.
Range: g–f♯²
Duration: 4:40

Pichaureau, Claude (1940–) France

Cornotests
Alphonse Leduc, 2001

Pilss, Karl (1902 –1980) Austria

Tre pezzi in forma di sonata
Doblinger, 1969
    I. Sinfonia
    II. Intermezzo
    III. Rondo alla caccia
Three pieces that are published separately, but can be played as a single work.
    Challenging both technically and tonally. All three are of substantial
    length, not overly difficult, but fairly long.
Range: B♭–b♭²

Pinkham, Daniel (1923–2006) United States

The Salutation of Gabriel, for Horn & Organ (2000)
ECS Pub, 2001
A contemporary work for horn and organ.
Duration: 7:08

Pitfield, Thomas (1903–1999) United Kingdom

A Folkish Tune
British and Continental Music Agencies, 1975
A very short, simple, flowing tune for horn and piano.
Range: g–g²

Plagge, Wolfgang (1960–) Norway

A Litany for the 21st Century, Sonata for Horn and Piano, op. 39
Musikk-Husets Forlag A/S, Oslo, 1993
    1. Lamento over a divided world—Allegro lamentoso
    2. Libra nos, domine—lento
Written for Frøydis Ree Wekre, this dramatic work is very challenging technically
    and presents some difficult loud dynamics in the upper range, as well as
    some stopped horn.
Range: c♯–c♯³
Duration: 12:51

Horn Sonata II, op. 67 (1992)
2L Electronic Scores, 2003, available on www.imslp.org
    I. Tranquillo; Allegro moderato
    II. Con eleganza (Time Collision)
    III. Determinato
Also a technically difficult piece with a rather persistent horn part with few rests.
Range: d–b² (d– d³ with ossia)

Horn Sonata no. 3, op. 88
Musikk-Husets Forlag A/S, Oslo, 2000
    I. Tranquillo
    II. Siciliano
    III. Determinato
A difficult and substantial three-movement work with many dramatic, flowing,
    melodic lines in both slow and fast note values. Requires a strong upper
    range and good endurance for loud passages above the staff, as well as agil-
    ity to navigate difficult, flowing, fast passages with tricky wide intervals.
Range: d–b²

Horn Sonata IV, op. 115 (2002)
2L Electronic Scores, 2005, available on www.imslp.org
    I. Veni Creator—Allego molto
    II. Summi Triumphum Regis (Nedaros book of sequences; 11th century)—
    Molto liberamente
This piece makes use of two medieval song sequences, "Veni Creator Spiritus"
    and "Summi Triumphum Regis." Less technically intense than the previ-
    ous sonatas, but still quite challenging.
Range: f–b²
Duration: 12:00

Horn Sonata V (. .lux et umbra. .), op. 164 (2009–10)
Available from the composer.

Planel, Robert (1908–1994) France

Caprice
Alphonse Leduc, 1958
Dedicated to Prof. Jean Devèmy. This single-movement piece in twentieth-century French tonal style has several tempo changes and sections of contrasting characters. Features a wide range and some flashy passages, but not overly technical. Some stopped passages and trills.
Range: c–c^3

Légend
Alphonse Leduc, 1966
Written for Jean Devèmy, this is a very typical mid-twentieth-century French solo piece, through-composed, with contrasting sections, cadenzas, and an array of rhythmic and technical difficulties. Trills, muted and stopped horn, and some metric difficulties make this piece challenging.
Range: g–c^3

Plog, Anthony (1947–) United States

Nocturne
Editions BIM, 1991
Written for Gail Williams, this short nocturne covers a wide range. Mostly connected and lyrical, there are also a few technical articulate passages. Also exists in a version with string orchestra.
Range: A–b^2
See: Horn and ensemble

Three Miniatures
Editions BIM, 1997
Written for Frank Lloyd, these three short pieces are rather technical and active, while not too excessive in range. Fun for performer and audience.
Range: g–a^2
Duration: 8:00

Ployhar, James D. (1926–2007) United States

Intrepido
Belwin, 1971
A short student piece of moderate difficulty. Begins with a fanfare motive and moves into a lyrical melodic section.
Range: f♯^{1}–g^2

Ponjee, Ted (1953–) Netherlands

Autumn Themes (1988)
Donemus, 1989

An adaptation of the composer's *Third Themes* for bass clarinet and marimba/
   vibraphone.
Duration: ca. 7:00

Poole, Reid (1919–2006) United States

Song of a City
Belwin, 1965
A short piece of very moderate difficulty for the young student.
Range: d¹–e²

Poot, Marcel (1901–1988) Belgium

Légende
Alphonse Leduc, 1958
A single-movement work of medium difficulty in French twentieth-century style.
Range: a–a²

Sarabande
Alphonse Leduc, 1953
A very easy single movement in a slow triple meter.
Range: b–e²

Porter, Quincy (1897–1966) United States

Sonata for Horn and Piano
Robert King, Gamble Hinged Music Co., 1948
      I. Lento—Allegro moderato
      II. Largo
      III. Allegro molto
Written for William Valkenier and commissioned by the National Association
   of Schools of Music in 1946, this three-movement sonata was intended to
   be a recital piece for advancing horn students. Nonetheless, it presents
   some substantial technical difficulties and the challenge of a wide range.
   The second movement is unmetered without barlines. The third movement, especially, could be taxing for the younger player. Interesting, tonally and rhythmically.
Range: c–c³
Duration: 14:41

Poser, Hans (1917–1970) Germany

Sonata, op. 8
Sikorski, 1955
A three-movement sonata with tempo markings of: "Ruhig fließend"—"Larghetto
   fließend"—"Etwas schnell, rhytmisch bewegt."
Range: d–g²
Duration: ca. 17:00

Potter, Cipriani (1792–1871) United Kingdom

Sonata di bravura, op. 13

Facsimile by Hans Pizka Edition, 1987

An unusual sonata for horn and piano from the early nineteenth century. Written
for natural horn virtuoso Giovanni Puzzi for natural horn in E♭. It exploits
all of the resources of that instrument in the form of a theme and four variations followed by a finale in $\frac{3}{4}$. Quite technical, but in a very limited range
for the most part. At one point, a note appears in the score stating that
"The composer, who wrote this sonata for the famous hornist, Mr. Puzzi,
understands that this passage, with its unusual modulations, is very difficult on the horn, and suggests that those who find it too difficult may make
a cut to the next section."

Range: B♭–g² (c–a² for E♭ horn)

Poulenc, Francis (1899–1963) France

Elegie (1957)

Chester, 1958

Written in memory of Dennis Brain. Composed in several contrasting sections
of varying characters. Dramatic articulations, dynamics, and wide range
make this a very intense, expressive piece. Extended techniques include
glissandi. Old notation bass clef. Of medium difficulty technically.

Range: d–a²

Duration: 9:00

Presle, Jacques de la (1888–1969) France

Le Rêve du Jeune Faon

Alphonse Leduc, 1949

Dedicated to Jean Devémy. A French piece of medium length that consists of a
slow, flowing, melodic section followed by a faster section and ending in
the original tempo. Moderately difficult.

Range: A–a²

Scherzetto

Editions Costallat, 1935

A short, rhythmic piece of rather moderate difficulty in $\frac{6}{8}$.

Range: c–g²

Presser, William (1916–2004) United States

Sonatina

Theodore Presser—Tritone Press, 1979

Written for Marvin Howe. An agile, active piece with a full range in three movements. The piece requires extremes of high and low range, but is quite idiomatic and playable.

Range: G–c³

Elegy and Caprice

Theodore Presser—Tritone Press, 1997

Written for Randall Faust. In memory of Marvin C. Howe, the piece consists of a slow, flowing Elegy, and fast agile Caprice. Stopped horn and flutter tongue are used, as well as new notation bass clef.
Range: G–b²

Fantasy on "The Mouldering Vine" (1963)
Theodore Presser—Tritone Press
A relatively short piece based on a nineteenth-century hymn tune. Mostly lyrical but there are a few technical passages throughout the range.
Range: A–b²

Proch, Heinrich (1809–1878) Austria

Der tolle Musikant, op. 91
Hans Pizka Edition, 1983
A setting of a melodramatic poem by Ludwig Löwe. In this romantic piece for horn and piano, the horn player recites the poem, in German, between the sections where the horn and piano play together. In only one short section at the very end does the spoken voice part take place when the horn is playing, and presumably the pianist could recite the words at this point. Dedicated to hornist Richard Lewy.
Range: g–g²

Lied ohne Worte, op. 163
Hans Pizka Edition, 1995
Written for Viennese horn-player Richard Lewy. A moderately short lyrical piece for the early valve horn, of which Lewy was a pioneer. Fairly agile in its changes of range in spite of the andante tempo marking. Requires a fluid singing technique.
Range: a–b♭²
Duration: 3:50

Procter-Gregg, Humphrey (1895–1980) United Kingdom

Duettino for Horn and Piano
Editions db, 2005
A short, lyrical piece marked Andante con moto, reminiscent of the music of Frederick Delius.
Range: a♭–a♭²

Horn Sonata (1975)
Editions db, 2005
Written for Robert Ashworth, this is a substantial work in a romantic style, composed in three movements: I. Andante mosso—II. Poco lento—III. Allegro. Covers a wide range, but there is quite an emphasis on the middle and lower end of the horn's range. The first movement is smooth and flowing, the second is described by the composer as nostalgic, and the last movement is more lighthearted in a fugal style.
Range: A♭–b²

Prosperi, Carlo (1921–1990) Italy

Segnali per corno e pianoforte (1977)
Edizioni Suvini Zerboni—Milano, 1980
A rather long four-movement work written for Italian hornist Domenico Cec-
    carossi. Very contemporary style, and complex metrically, in that the bar
    lines in the horn and piano parts are independent of each other very often.
    Difficult intervals and leaps, and an emphasis on the low range, with much
    use of stopped, echo, and muted horn—all favorite effects in the music and
    etudes that Ceccarossi wrote for himself.
Range: E–b^2

Proust, Pascal (1959–) France
Horn player and composer Pascal Proust has written many short pieces for young
    horn players of all levels, as well as more substantial music for horn. Proust
    was professor of horn at Conservatoire d'Orléans and currently professor
    of chamber music at CRR de Paris. Among his many works, the list below
    is a good representation.

Avenue Mozart
Editions Combre, 1999
A very simple beginner's piece.
Range: a–a^1

Cap Horn
Editions Combre, 1993
Written in several connected and contrasting sections, this piece features lots of
    agile fast notes and articulations and wide intervals.
Range: c–c♯^{3}

Gamins d'Paris
Billaudot, 2002
A short piece for the young player. In three sections, and includes a short cadenza.
Range: a–f^2
Duration: ca. 3:00

La grande école, huit pièces faciles
Billaudot, 1987
Eight very short movements, averaging about one minute each, for the young horn
    player of limited range and technique. The titles are those of the subjects
    taught in French schools: Mathématiques—Géographie—Récitation—His-
    toire de France—Lecture—Récréation—Musique—Gymnastique.
Range: g–d^2
Duration: ca. 8:00

Les caprices de Pierrot, pour cor en fa et piano
Editions Combre, 2003
A very simple piece for the beginning horn player in one short movement.
Range: g–b^1

Pimperl, pour cor et piano
Billaudot, 2008
Pimperl was the name of the Mozart family dog. An easy work for beginners in
$\frac{2}{4}$ with a few legato sections. In C major with a few accidentals, and an op-
portunity for a short cadenza.
Range: g–b^1
Duration: 2:00

Prélude et escapade
Billaudot, 2012
A short Andante and an Allegretto written for the very young horn student with
a limited range. Includes a brief cadenza.
Range: g–c^2 (with ossia g–f^2)
Duration: 3:15

Première sonatine pour cor et piano
Billaudot, 2000
In three short movements, this work presents interesting challenges for the intermediate student. The first movement is in $\frac{6}{8}$, with a variety of passages that
alternate declamatory "intense" writing with legato phrases, and a stopped
passage concluding the movement. The second movement is an Andante
espressivo with a middle section of moving sixteenth notes marked cantabile. The final movement is in $\frac{2}{4}$ with syncopated figures and a brief cadenza.
Range: e–a^2 (with ossia e–g^2)
Duration: 6:30

Scènes paysannes
Robert Martin Editions Musicales, 1994
A simple piece for the beginner with a limited range.
Range: b–c^2

Sur un Theme classique
Billaudot, 1996
A relatively short piece in several short sections of varying tempos. Pleasant and
tuneful, with a short cadenza. A very accessible young-student piece with a
bit of agility and technique.
Range: d–f♯^{2}
Duration: 4:15

Une Incroyable Histoire
Editions Combre, 2007
This short work, translated as "An Incredible Story," introduces contemporary
notation and techniques to the advanced-beginning or intermediate student hornist, including unmeasured writing, dynamic contrasts, trills,
notes on the harmonic series, and notation using beamed groups to indicate variations in speed.
Range: a–d^2
Duration: 4:00

Variations studieuses
Editions Combre
A student work at the intermediate level.
Range: F♯–g²

Voiles
Billaudot, 1993
A very elementary piece for the beginner with limited range and technique.
Range: a–b¹

Puentes, José A. Pérez (1951–) Cuba

Sonata I para corno en fa y piano
Editora Musical de Cuba, 1978
A sonata of only medium difficulty, through-composed in several contrasting
    sections. Some stopped horn and glissandi. Old notation bass clef.
Range: c–a²

Pugno, Stéphane-Raoul (1852–1914) France

Solo
Alphonse Leduc, 1958 (rev. by L.Thévet)
A single-movement work in late nineteenth-century style. Straightforward but
    with some technical difficulties. A solo by Pugno is listed as having been
    performed on one of the last hand horn exams at the Paris Conservatory in
    1900, and the idiomatic horn writing of this piece suggests that this could
    be the piece mentioned.
Range: c–g²

Puzzi, Giovanni (1792–1876) Italy
Italian horn virtuoso who lived and worked in London.

Theme varie
Facsimile by Hans Pizka Edition
A theme and seven very straightforward variations for natural horn in E♭. Lots of
    notes and articulate scale passages.
Range: e¹–f² (f♯¹–g² for horn in E♭)

Pyncou, Samuel, France

Berceuse et petite gavotte
Alphonse Leduc, 1963
Two short, easy pieces for the young hornist. Notated in F horn with an alter-
    nate part for B♭ horn ("Berceuse") and G horn ("Gavotte"), presumably for
    transposition practice.
Range: d¹–g²
Duration: 2:50

Chanson et danse paysanne
Alphonse Leduc, 1963

A melodic song in $\frac{6}{8}$ and a lively dance in $\frac{6}{8}$, both technically very easy. Alternate
   parts for horn in A (Chanson) and horn in C (Danse paysanne), presum-
   ably for transposition practice.
Range: c^1–f^2
Duration: 4:00

Rêverie Syncopee
Alphonse Leduc, 1963
A slow, flowing, contemplative reverie and a fast syncopated Allegro. Also very easy.
   Alternate parts for E♭ horn ("Rêverie") and A♭ horn ("Danse"), presumably
   for transposition practice.
Range: c^1–g^2
Duration: 3:40

Raff, Joachim (1822–1882) Germany

Two Romances, op. 182 (1873)
Siegel, Leipzig, 1880; Hornseth Music Co., 1978; Amadeus, 2004
Two short pieces, no. 1 is in F major and no. 2 is in B♭ major. Both are in a roman-
   tic style with rather limited range, but somewhat tiring due to the absence
   of rests.
Range: c^1–g^2
See: Horn and ensemble, no. 1 is available for horn and orchestra

Ramovš, Primož (1921–1999) Slovenia

Zvočna slika
Ljubljana, 1962
A short mid-twentieth-century style piece in a slow tempo with a number of ef-
   fects, including stopped horn, flutter tongue, and trills. Quite dramatic, with
   a rather dense piano part.
Range: $g\sharp$–$b\flat^2$

Ramsey, H. F.

A Celtic Lament
Carl Fischer, 1967
A short, lyrical piece with a Celtic flavor. One stopped passage.
Range: $b\flat$–g^2
Duration: 2:30

Randall, Anthony (1937–) United Kingdom

Concert Suite for Horn and Piano (2007)
Editions db
A substantial three-movement work: 1. Capriccio—2. Notturno—3. Introduction
   and Rondo. Technically challenging with a number of effects, including
   stopped-to-open glissandi, muted and stopped passages, and trills. Requires
   a solid high range.
Range: e–b^2
Duration: ca. 18:00

Lullaby
Broadbent & Dunn Ltd., 1993
A short, simple, vocal-style piece for the advancing student.
Range: e^1–g^2

March
Broadbent & Dunn Ltd., 1993
A march for the slightly more advanced young horn player, who is ready to go to
  the top of the staff with some control of articulation and to play in the more
  difficult key of sounding D major.
Range: a–$f\sharp^2$

Marching Tune
Broadbent & Dunn Ltd., 1993
A simple march for the beginner, encompassing a single octave.
Range: d^1–d^2

Nocturne
Broadbent & Dunn Ltd., 1993
Written for Ifor James, this piece is slow, solemn, and expressive in a short single
  movement, alternating between a slow $\frac{3}{4}$ and a faster $\frac{9}{8}$. Some stopped pas-
  sages add to the mood of the piece.
Range: g–f^2

Scherzo
Broadbent & Dunn Ltd., 1993
A much more ambitious piece technically, for the advancing student. Agile and
  articulate, requiring some control in the upper range.
Range: c–c^3

Swings and Roundabouts
Broadbent & Dunn Ltd., 1993
A very simple piece for the beginning horn player, encompassing the range of a
  sixth.
Range: c^1–a^1

Waltz
Broadbent & Dunn Ltd., 1993
A flowing waltz, not very difficult, for the young horn player.
Range: c^1–f^2

Raphling, Sam (1910–1988) United States

Sonata for French Horn and Piano
Ricordi, 1961
A three-movement sonata of moderate difficulty, good for the advanced high
  school student recital. Straightforward tonally and rhythmically, and easy
  going in terms of range.
Range: e–a^2
See: Horn and ensemble

Rasmussen, Alfred

Mood and Nocturne (Stimmung und Nocturne), op. 11, nos. 1 and 2
Wilhelm Hansen, also available on www.imslp.org
Two rather short, slow, lyrical pieces of medium difficulty in a romantic style.
Range: c♯–a²

Rateau, Johanne Michel (1938–) France

Fiction pour cor et piano
Editions Max Eschig, 1974
A single-movement mid-twentieth-century-style French piece with unusual time
   signatures and a number of technical and rhythmic difficulties. Demand-
   ing for both players.
Range: A–c♯³
Duration: 5:00

Raum, Elizabeth (1945–) Canada, born in United States

Romance for French Horn (1992)
Cherry Classics, 2012
Commissioned by the Concours de Musique du Canada with the help of the Can-
   ada Council. A pleasant, lyrical piece and a good choice for the advanced
   high school or college-level student recital.
Range: g–a²
Duration: 5:00

Fantasy for French Horn (1985)
Canadian Music Centre, 1989
A fairly short piece marked Allegro agitato that features the middle and low range
   of the horn. Medium difficulty.
Range: B♭–g²

Raxach, Enrique (1932–) Netherlands, born in Spain

The Hunting in Winter
Donemus, Amsterdam, 1980
Commissioned by the Dutch government for Johan Donker Kaat and Jan Slot-
   houwer. A rather long single movement with a thick, complex piano part,
   and complex rhythms for both players. Includes stopped, muted, and wa-wa
   muted sections, as well as glissandi and wide intervals over a full range.
Range: c–c³
Duration: 14:00

Raymond, Lewis

Design
Western International Music, 1966
A lyrical and dramatic, piece of moderate difficulty, with a wide dynamic range.
Range: b–a²

Read, Gardner (1913–2005) United States

De Profundis, op. 71
Leeds Music, 1948; Robert King
Written for horn and organ, this piece in the unusual meter of $\frac{3}{4}$ consists of long
gently flowing lines in slow quarter notes throughout. The sustained notes
and directions for various organ stops and colors suggest that it was defi-
nitely intended to be played on the organ, rather than piano.

Poem, op. 31
Carl Fisher, 1937
Written for James Stagliano, this piece is a gentle, lyrical Andante in easy, chang-
ing meters.
Range: e♭¹–a♭²
Duration: 3:40

Reeder, Haydn (1944–) Australia

Movement through Obstacles
Australian Music Centre, 2004
A very complex contemporary piece that includes multiphonics, complex rhythms,
and muted and stopped effects. Not overly difficult in terms of horn tech-
nique, but challenging musically.
Range: E–e♭³ (or highest note possible)

Reeman, John (1946–) United Kingdom

A Little Light Horn
Piper Publications, 1992
Dedicated to "Erik," this piece consists of four short, easy movements, two fast
and two slow.
Range: b♭¹–e♭²

Reger, Max (1873–1916) Germany

Scherzino for Horn and Strings (1899)
Musica Rara, 1976 arranged for horn and piano by J. Madden. Orchestra parts
for hire.
Short piece in $\frac{6}{8}$, would be a good encore for a recital. Not taxing, ends quietly. ABA
form, B section is brief.
Range: c¹–g²
Duration: 2:30

Reicha, Anton (1770–1836) Worked in Germany, Austria, and France;
born in Czech Republic
Born in Prague, Reicha spent many years in Paris, where he became familiar with
French hand horn technique.

Solo for Horn and Piano
London Gabrieli Edition, 1992; Doblinger, 1988; Hans Pizka Edition, 1985

This piece, written around 1820 for natural horn in E, is typical of the cor-mixt style of the French school of the early nineteenth century. In three sections: Adagio ($\frac{3}{4}$)—Andante ($\frac{3}{4}$)—Allegretto ($\frac{6}{8}$). Contains many ornaments and agile passage work.
Range: a$\sharp^1$–b^2 (b^1–c^3 for Horn in E)

Reichel, Bernard (1901–1992) Switzerland

Sonata da chiesa
Billaudot, 1972
For horn and piano or organ. Four relatively short movements of moderate difficulty, marked: Maestoso—Moderato—Allegro—Moderato.
Range: f$\sharp$–g^2

Reinecke, Carl (1824–1910) Germany

Notturno fur Horn und Klavier, op. 112
Schott, 1985 (Hermann Baumann, ed.)
Marked Andante ma non troppo lento, this single movement in E♭ major is of moderate difficulty in a romantic style.
Range: B♭–a♭^{2}

Reinhart, Hugo (1958–)

Adagio et rondo
Billaudot, 2003
Duration: 6:30

Reissiger, Carl Gottlieb (1798–1859) Germany

Solo per il corno
Henry Litolff's Verlag/C. F. Peters, 1980
Dedicated to Joseph Rudolph Lewy Jr., this is a true nineteenth-century salon piece. A dramatic, operatic opening section with ornaments, trills, and a wide range leads into a flowing major section with a cadenza that ends the piece, using material from the opening. Also available for horn and orchestra.
Range: G–c^3
See: Horn and ensemble

Elegie, suive d'un rondo agreeable, op. 153
Facsimile edition from Hans Pizka Edition, 1981
Virtually identical to the *Solo* described above, also dedicated to Joseph Rudolph Lewy. With the addition of a second movement in the form of a rondo in $\frac{6}{8}$, also quite virtuosic.
Range: F–c^3

Reiter, Albert (1905–1970) Austria

Sonatine für Horn und Klavier (1961)
Doblinger, 1962

Short piece in two movements, divided into sections of contrasting tempos. Emphasis on the upper range makes for short-term endurance difficulties in this dramatic work.
Range: g♯–c³

René, Charles (1863–1935) France

Strophes (la fiancée)
Rubank, 1939
A short, flowing, melodic movement marked Andante con moto.
Range: b–g♭²

Reuter, Hermann (1900–1985) Germany

Chant du soir
Alphonse Leduc, 1969
Inspired by a melody by J. A. P. Schulz. A very slow, gentle piece, about half of which is muted. Simple slow-moving lines of quarter and half notes.
Range: b♭¹–d♭²
Duration: 5:00

Thème varié
Alphonse Leduc, 1957
An andante theme with four variations that stays rather high in the range for such a simple piece. Otherwise not overly difficult.
Range: e♭¹–b♭²

Reuter, Willi Albrecht (1906–) Germany

Canto appassionato (1958)
Edition Peters, 1973
An extended and very dramatic single movement, quite difficult technically and rhythmically, but not excessive in its use of the upper range.
Range: f–c³

Reynolds, Verne (1926–2011) United States

Fantasy—Etudes for Horn and Piano
Prairie Dawg Press, 2009

Partita
Southern Music, 1964
    I. Malinconia
    II. Caccia
    III. Aria
    IV. Alla marcia
Written for Norman Schweikert, this piece has become a standard of the recital repertoire. Though idiomatic for the horn and not excessive in range, it is a difficult piece with challenging intervals, rhythms, and agile technique, but well worth the effort.
Range: c–a♭²

Sonata
Southern Music, 1971
    I. Moderately
    II. Slow
    III. Fast
Commissioned by the National Association of College Wind Instructors, this
    piece is also idiomatically well written for the horn in a contemporary style,
    with similar challenges to the *Partita*. Rhythmically and tonally complex
    and interesting.
Range: c–b♭²

Sonata Concertare for Horn and Piano (2001)
Prairie Dawg Press, 2009
    1. Dialogue
    2. Fragments
    3. Lament
    4. Caccia
This four-movement sonata is the composer's last work for horn and piano. A
    rather sparse piece in its sound textures, the first movement is completely
    unmetered and free. The second consists of short, melodic fragments
    passed back and forth between the horn and piano. The third is a slow
    lament with wide intervals and range changes, and the fourth is a spirited,
    technically agile movement with fast articulations, also fairly transparent
    in its texture.
Range: A–b²
Duration: ca. 18:00

Rheinberger, Josef Gabriel (1839–1901) Germany, born in Liechtenstein

Sonata, op. 178 (1894)
Kistner, Leipzig, 1894; Schott, 1967; Mainz, Carus-Verlag, 2008
    I. Con moto
    II. Quasi adagio
    III. Con fuco
Dedicated to hornist Bruno Hoyer, the successor to Franz Strauss as solo horn
    of the Munich Hoforchester and teacher at the Munich Academy of Mu-
    sic. A major work in the standard repertoire, this sonata is composed in a
    mid-nineteenth-century romantic style. Well written for the horn and very
    expressive, especially in the second movement. The horn writing is remi-
    niscent of Brahms and Carl Reinecke.
Range: F–b♭²

Richards, Paul (1969–) United States

Rush Hour
IHS Online Music Library, 2000
Written for Paul Basler, this piece consists of three connected sections: 5 o'clock
    drive—Getting nowhere—Open road.

Richardson, Mark (1962–) United States

A Garden Path
Brass Arts Unlimited, 2013
A relatively short piece in a very contemporary style and tonality.
Range: g–a²
Duration: 5:30

Richmond, Jeffrey W. (1981–) United States
Sonata No. 1 for Horn and Piano
Prairie Dawg Press, 2009
A three-movement sonata in a contemporary style in the standard fast-slow-fast
    form. Of moderate difficulty technically, venturing both above and below the
    staff only occasionally, with some agile fast passages in the last movement.
Range: B–b²

Richter, Frederico (1932–) Brazil

Noturno lírico, para trompa e piano
Goldberg Edições Musicais, 1997

Richter, Hans (1843–1916) Austria-Hungary

Romanze für Horn und Klavier, op. 37 (*"Sehnsucht des Entfernten nach seiner
Heimat"*)
Hans Pizka Edition, 1996
An original composition for horn by the famous nineteenth-century conductor
    who premiered many works by Wagner, Brahms, and Bruckner.

Ridgeon, John
See: Gregson, Edward

Ridout, Alan (1934–1996) United Kingdom

Six Diversions for Horn
The Associated Board of the Royal Schools of Music, 1991
Six short contrasting sketches, written very simply both musically and technically
    for the young horn player.
Range: b–f²

Ries, Ferdinand (1784–1838) Germany

Sonata in F, op. 34
Böhme, early 19th century; Richault; Schott, 1969
    I. Larghetto—Allegro molto
    II. Andante
    III. Rondo allegro
A major work, written for natural horn in F and piano, similar in character to the
    Beethoven horn sonata. Very much an equal duo for the two instruments,

with difficult passages for both. The horn part has many octave leaps and broken chords.

Range: B–g^2

Duration: ca. 20:00

Introduction et Rondo, op. 113, no.2

Musica Rara, 1973 (Georg Meerwein, ed.); Breitkopf & Härtel, 2000

A salon piece written for natural horn in E♭ consisting of an introduction in ⅜ that covers a wide range in operatic style, followed by a rondo in ⅝, with many technical challenges and acrobatic passages.

Range: B♭–a^2 (c–b^2 for horn in E♭)

Rindt, Markus (1967–) Germany

Impressions in Jazz, op. 32

Friedrich Hofmeister, 1996

Dedicated to Peter Damm, this piece consists of three movements entitled:

1. Harlequin
2. Once upon a time . . .
3. Rapids

All three movements have a jazz flavor, rhythmically driving in the first, ballad-like in the second, and agile in the third. A focus on the top of the staff and above makes this piece a bit taxing, but fun. Includes glissandi and trills.

Range: g♯–d♭^{3}

Ristori, Emile (1893–1977) Switzerland

Solo de cor avec accompagnement de piano

Editions Helca, 1951

Rodriguez, Robert Xavier (1946–) United States

Gambits, Six Chess Pieces for Horn and Piano

G. Schirmer, 2002

Six short pieces using contemporary compositional techniques, written for Andrew Riehm. Each movement depicts themes from the game of chess. Includes many open-to-stopped effects, glissandi, complex rhythms, and some contemporary notation.

Range: A–a^2 (with ossia to b♯^{2})

Duration: 12:00

Roe, Betty (1930–) United Kingdom

Introduction and Allegretto

Thames Publishing, 1977

Written for "Lesley," this piece starts with a short adagio introduction, and moves into a straightforward, not too technical Allegretto in a contemporary tonal style.

Range: d–b♭^{2}

Conversation Piece
Thames Publishing, 1999
Written for Daniel Beer, this is a rather simple single movement for the young
    horn player, with the melodic lines moving in straightforward quarter and
    eighth notes in a comfortable middle range.
Range: g–g² (a–f² with ossias)

Rollin, Robert (1947–) United States

Sonata Pastorale (1985)
Seesaw Music, 2009
This is a horn and piano transcription of the composer's *Concerto Pastorale* for
    horn and orchestra.
See: Horn and ensemble

Rom, Uri (1969–) Israel

Rondo Es Dur für Naturhorn
Christoph Dohr, 2002
See: Horn and ensemble

Röntgen, Julius (1855–1932) Germany

Variations and Finale
Edition Compusic, 1989
Dedicated to hornist Louis Savart, the theme is based on an old German folk
    song about Saint Nepomuk of Prague. The theme is followed by thirteen
    straightforward variations and a finale in ⅜. Not difficult technically.
Range: c–g²

Roo, Paul de (1957–) Netherlands

Notturno for Horn and Piano (1986)
Donemus, 1986
A single movement in a slow tempo, with the horn muted throughout. The horn
    and the piano both play a line that consists of short figures, often one or
    two notes, separated by rests, so that there is often more silence than sound.
    A middle section provides brief contrast with a sustained line. Challenges
    include moving through ranges with accuracy and a sustained high b² in a
    very slow tempo.
Range: F♯–b²
Duration: 15:00

Triptiek, voor hoorn en piano
J. Maurer, 1976

Rooth, Laszlo (1919–) Israel, born in Romania

Quiet Monday for Horn and Piano
Israel Brass Woodwind Publications, 1980

Short piece in lyrical style, but somewhat difficult in its wide intervals and range changes.
Range: c♯–b²

Roper, Harrison (1932–) United States
Concertino for Horn and Piano
A Touch of Brass, 1987
A three-movement concertino, dedicated to Nathan Bell, and composed specifically to be accessible both musically and technically to the advancing high school student. The movements are marked: I. Moderato—II. Andante—III. Allegro. Straightforward in its technical demands for the horn, it includes several easier alternative passages to avoid technical difficulties and notes above the staff. Stylistically similar to the writing of Franz Strauss. Also exists in a version for horn and band.
Range: a–a² (a–g² with ossias)
See: Horn and ensemble

Rosner, Arnold (1945–2013) United States
Sonata for Horn and Piano No.1 in C minor, op. 71
Phoebus Publications, 1994
This three-movement sonata is dedicated to Marc Spetalnik. The movements are marked: 1. Passacaglia, lento—2. Allegro—3. Andante sostenuto. A serious and substantial work with a wide range and wide dynamics. The last movement features some difficult asymmetrical meter changes.
Range: d–c²

Ross, Walter (1936–) United States
Canzonetta for Horn and Piano (1993)
Nichols Music Co, 1993
Consists of a lyrical introduction and a ⁶⁄₈ Allegro festivo.
Range: a–g²
Duration: 5:30

Rossari, Gustavo (1827–1881) Italy
Fantasia sopra vari pensieri di Bellini
Hans Pizka Edition, 1990
A fantasy piece on themes from the Bellini opera *Il Puritani*, consisting of an operatic introduction followed by sections of varying tempos culminating in a highly virtuosic ⁶⁄₈ Allegretto that ends in a flash of scales and arpeggios. Quite playable on the natural horn in E♭.
Range: f–b♭² (g–c³ for horn in E♭)

Poliuto di Donizetti, fantasia
Hans Pizka Edition, 1991
A fantasy on themes from the Donizetti opera *Poliuto*. Begins with a Larghetto section in a florid operatic style moving agilely through a wide range, followed

by a simple melodic Moderato section, and ending with a virtuosic Allegro full of fast notes. Though playable on natural horn in E♭, several low diatonic passages suggest that a valve horn may have been intended originally.
Range: f–b♭² (g–c³ for horn in E♭)

Fantasia sopra alcuni motivi dell'opera i due foscari di G. Verdi
Hans Pizka Edition, 1990
A fantasy piece on themes from the Verdi opera *I Due Foscari*. A very agile piece for horn in E♭, most likely intended for natural horn. Written in several short sections of varying tempos, predominantly fast and virtuosic.
Range: B♭–b♭² (c–c³ for horn in E♭)

Rossignol, Bruno (1958–) France

Carillon
Alphonse Leduc, 1984
An elementary piece with a bell-like, accented melody.
Range: a–c²
Duration: 1:10

Pavane en deux tons
Alphonse Leduc, 1984
An elementary piece with a slow, flowing melody in quarter and half notes.
Range: a–c²
Duration: 1:35

Jean Paul's March (1997)
Billaudot, 2000
A short march in ⁴ in a limited range for the young horn player. Includes glissandi.
Range: a–d♯²

Rossini, Gioachino (1792–1868) Italy

Introduction, Andante, and Allegro
Editions Choudens, 1970 (E. Leloir, ed.)
For natural horn in F. Written for J. F. Gallay, solo horn of the Italian Theater in Paris, and professor at the Paris Conservatory. The first section is based on the extended horn solo from Rossini's overture to *The Turk in Italy*. An Andante section in D minor follows, and the final section is an Allegro in F major with agile scale passages. Not a difficult piece, but very flashy and effective musically. A good recital piece for a talented high school or university student, and quite playable on natural horn.
Range: c–a²

Prelude, Theme, and Variations (1857)
Fondatione Rossini (in F, D. Ceccarossi, ed.); International (in F, edited and abridged by J. Egger); Billaudot (in E, E. Lelior, ed.); Schirmer (in F, Tuckwell, ed.); Paxman, 1981 (in E, Merewether, ed.)
Written for hornist Eugène-Léon Vivier, this piece comes from the collection entitled "Sins of My Old Age." An operatic prelude filled with lyrical lines and fast notes leads to a theme reminiscent of music from a comic opera

and variations that include technical and recitative-like sections. Originally in the key of E major, but more often played in F. A very technical and acrobatic salon piece for natural horn, and a standard of the repertoire.

Range: f♯–b² (g–c³ for horn in E) (g–c³ for horn in F in the the F major versions)
Duration: 10:30

Rossum, Frederik van (1939–) Belgium
Pianist and award-winning composer.

Intrada, op. 76, per corno in fa e pianoforte (2005)
CeBeDeM, 2005
This work features mixed meters, wide leaps, and dynamic contrasts. The first section builds momentum, culminating in a glissando to a high c³. After a brief pause, the second section begins quietly, continuing the dialogue between horn and piano with a variety of gestures.
Range: e♭–c³
Duration: 7:00

Rossum, Hans van (1958–)Netherlands
Playtime
De Haske Muziekuitgave, 1990
Commissioned by horn player Oldrich Milek in 1983. A light work in ⁴, with legato and flowing solo-horn lines and a cheerful piano accompaniment. For the advanced beginner, in the key of C major with several chromatic passages. Includes parts for both F and E♭ horn.
Range: g–g²

Rougeron, Philippe (1928–) France
La conque d'or
Editions Combre, 1990
A short, flowing work in ³ for the young player. In written C major for the horn with only a few accidentals. Ventures into the range below middle c¹.
Range: g–e²
Duration: 2:00

Petit prélude
Billaudot, 1975
A relatively easy, lyrical piece of medium length with pleasant flowing melodies. Uses new notation bass clef to go briefly into the low range.
Range: c–f♯²

Rueff, Jeanine (1922–1999) France
Cantilène pour cor et piano
Alphonse Leduc, 1963
A short, simple, slow piece of limited range for the young horn player.
Range: g–g²

Ruijters, René (1955–) Netherlands

Prelude and Finale
Andel, 2008

Rummel, Christian (1787–1849) Germany

Fantasie
Hans Pizka Edition, 1981; Kunzelmann, 1993
A highly florid and extended fantasy piece in mid-nineteenth-century salon style
    with operatic recitative sections, ornaments, trills, and fast scale passages.
    This difficult cor-alto piece was written for J. F. Gallay, implying that it was
    meant for natural horn, for which it is quite idiomatically written.
Range: g–c^3

Nocturne pour cor à pistons ou cor de bassette et piano
Schott und Söhne, Mainz (first edition); Edition Kunzelmann, 1998
An Andantino that can be played either by horn or basset horn. Very idiomatic
    for the early valved horn with a lavish salon-style piano part. Rummel was
    a pianist and clarinetist.
Range: c–g^2

Ruesink, Linda (1964–) United States

Solace
Alliance Publications, 1996
A short student piece of medium difficulty.
Duration: 1:48

Rychlík, Jan (1916–1964) Czech Republic

Sonatina Školní
Editio Supraphon, 1964
A good student piece in three short movements. Straightforward but interesting,
    with some stopped passages.
Range: c–g^2

Ryelandt, Joseph (1870–1965) Belgium

Sonate, op. 18 (1897)
CeBeDeM, Brussels, 1957
    I. Lento—Andante religioso
    II. Allegro
The first movement is very flowing and lyrical. The second movement is similar
    in character, but in an allegro tempo. Both movements are for horn in E.
    Some stopped horn.
Range: B–g♯^{2} (c–a^2 for Horn in E)
Duration: 12:00

Sabatini, Guglielmo (ca. 1902–1967) United States

Elegia, for Solo Horn and Strings
Camara Music, 1960
For horn and piano or orchestra.
See: Horn and ensemble

Sachse, Hans Wolfgang (1899–1982) Germany
German composer and conductor, studied at Leipzig Conservatory.

Sonate, op. 71 (1962)
Peters, 1963; Collection Litolff
In three movements. The first, Allegro energico, carries the most weight. The
    second movement is an Andante sostenuto, and the third is an Allegretto
    scherzando, mainly in ⅜ but with changing meters. Interesting counter-
    point between horn and piano, where the piano is a true partner. Written
    for hornist Peter Damm and pianist Gunther Hauer.
Range: a–a♯²

Sack, Theodor (1910–1989) Switzerland

Sonate (1956)
Amadeus Verlag, 1975
    I. Allegro deciso
    II. Lento
    III. Allegro
A medium-length sonata, but a substantial piece of music. The first movement
    is powerful and dynamic, with accented figures and flowing lines in an
    allegro tempo. The second movement alternates between a lento quasi-rec-
    itative feel and an allegro scherzando tempo and includes some muted sec-
    tions. The third movement is a short, spirited Allegro in mixed meters. Not
    overly difficult horn technique, but plenty to practice, both musically and
    technically. Tends to stay high in the range.
Range: a♭–b²

Saglietti, Corrado Maria (1957–) Italy

Suite for Horn and Piano
Editions BIM, 1993
Composed in three movements: 1. Tango—2. Canzone—3. Speedy. Also exists in
    a version for horn and string quartet, and in a versions for alto trombone
    and piano, or alto trombone and strings. Described by the composer as
    "A cocktail of passion, nostalgia, and virtuosity that captures and amuses
    both the performers and the audience." Quite a difficult piece, including
    trills, muted sections, and a few other sound effects, such as air through
    mouthpiece or striking the bell of the horn.
Range: d¹–c³
Duration: 12:00

Virtuoso
Hans Pizka Edition, 1989
First-prize winner in the International Horn Society composition contest, 1989.
Duration: 2:19

Saint-Saëns, Camille (1835–1921) France
Andante pour cor et orgue
London Gabrieli Brass Edition, 1992 (Christopher Larkin, ed.)
This Andante for horn and organ, from early in the composer's career, was prob-
    ably written around 1854 while Saint-Saëns was organist at the church of
    Saint-Méry. It is written in an early valve-horn style which may have in-
    cluded a combination of valve and hand stopping taught by Joseph Mei-
    fred in the first decades of the development of the valved horn in France.
    Saint-Saëns would undoubtedly have known Meifred at the Paris Con-
    servatory, and it is likely that the piece was written for him or one of his
    students. It is written in a cor-basse style, very lyrical, with passages in
    the low range that would only be playable on the valve horn and chromat-
    icism that would suggest Meifred's combination valve and hand stopping
    technique.
Range: A♭–g²

Concertpiece (Morceau de concert), op. 94
Durand & Cie, 1891; International, 1956
    I. Allegro moderato
    II. Adagio
    III. Allegro non troppo
A romantic work written for hornist Henri Chaussier, to be played on a late
    nineteenth-century type of omnitonic valve horn. Originally written for
    horn and orchestra and in a horn and piano version, it includes a theme
    and variation first movement, a lyrical second movement that uses the low
    range and stopped horn, and a technical third movement with trills and
    wide range changes. A standard of the repertoire and a good advanced-stu-
    dent piece.
Range: B♭–c³
Duration: 9:00
See: Horn and ensemble

Romance in F, op. 36
Durand & Cie, 1874; International; G. Schirmer collection *Solos for the Horn
    Player,* 1962 (Mason Jones, ed.)
A good piece for the young horn player. This easy, lyrical romance, marked Mod-
    erato and in ¾, was originally written for natural horn, and is a good first
    solo piece for that instrument as well. There is also an orchestra accompa-
    niment.
Range: b–f♯²
Duration: 3:50
See: Horn and ensemble

Romance in E, op. 67
J. Hamelle, 1885
This Romance, an Adagio in ⅜, is more substantial musically and more difficult
    technically than the *Romance,* op. 36. The E-horn transposition is an added
    difficulty. Originally written for natural horn in E. Also playable with or-
    chestra accompaniment.
Range: B–b² (c–c³ for horn in E)
Duration: 7:00

Salminen, Susan (1957–) United States

Piempi or "Poor Mr. Parshley," op. 26
Emerson Horn Editions, 1994
An expressive little piece in three sections, a fast ⅝, a slow expressive section, and
    a fast ¾.
Range: e♭¹–f²
Duration: 3:30

Salonen, Esa-Pekka (1958–) Finland

Hornmusic No. 1 (1976)
Seesaw, 1977
A fairly difficult single-movement piece in three sections. A fast opening sec-
    tion with changing meters presents some metric challenges. This leads
    into a middle recitative with a lengthy cadenza, followed by a closing sec-
    tion in the character of the opening. Many difficult notes and a couple of
    glissandi.
Range: G–c²

Sampson, David (1951–) United States

Sonata Forty (1991)
Editions BIM, 1999
A rather technical contemporary work commissioned by Scott Brubaker and the
    International Horn Society. In four movements:
    1. Crisis
    2. Shadows
    3. Sentiments
    4. Resolve
Duration: 14:10

Samuel-Rousseau, Marcel (1882–1955) France

Romance
Alphonse Leduc
A short, early twentieth-century lyrical piece of moderate difficulty with a bit of
    stopped horn.
Range: a–a²

Sancan, Pierre (1916–2008) France

Ballade
Durand & Cie, 1982
Paris Conservatory competition piece from 1982. Written for Georges Barboteu, this single-movement work in mid-twentieth-century French style is rather technical and taxing. Includes flutter tonguing, difficult rhythms, and fast technique.
Range: d♭–c²

Sanders, Bernard Wayne (1957–) United States, works in Germany

Rhapsodie Nr. 2 für Horn und Orgel (1999)
Christoph Dohr, 2000
As the title implies, this is a very freely composed piece. In three sections. It is meant to be played either as a concert piece, or for a church service.

Sanders, Robert Levine (1906–1974) United States

Sonata (1958)
Robert King, 1963
    I. Allegro cantabile
    II. Tempo di valse Scherzando
    III. Lento—VivaceA substantial, well-written sonata for the horn. Tonal and musically interesting, with plenty of challenges for the horn player without being overly difficult.
Range: c–c²
Duration: 11:00

Santamaria, Gaëtan (1957–) France

Pastorale
International Music Diffusion, 1997
A short work in written E♭ major for the horn, marked Modéré and with a very moderate range for the soloist. This mostly lyrical piece has moving triplets, some syncopated rhythms, and changing meters.
Range: g–c²

Santoro, Claudio (1919–1989) Brazil

Duo para trompa (horn) e piano (1982)
Edition Savart, 1982

Sarcich, Paul (1951–) New Zealand

Sonata Circolare for Horn and Piano
Australian Music Centre, Warwick Music
Written in three movements: Fanfare, Capriccio—Notturno, Romanza—Riffs, Toccata.
Duration: 13:40

Sargon, Simon A. (1938–) United States

The Weeping Shofar (1998)
S. Sargon, 1998
Through the use of many contemporary effects, the horn depicts the sound of the
    shofar and the human voice in this piece that was inspired by memories of
    the Holocaust. Dedicated to two of the composer's friends who survived
    the war.
Range: G–b^2

Vermeer Portraits (2002)
S. Sargon, 2002
Six movements inspired by paintings of Jan Vermeer.
    1. Christ in the house of Mary and Martha
    2. Allegory of faith
    3. The guitar player
    4. Woman with a balance
    5. The astronomer
    6. The soldier and the laughing girl
Technically and musically challenging, the piece depicts the feelings evoked by
    each of the six paintings.
Range: A–c^3

Scarmolin, Anthony Louis (1890–1969) United States, born in Italy

Romanza and Allegro
Pro-Art, 1942
A student piece, consisting of an Andante in $\frac{6}{8}$, followed by a straightforward
    Allegro in $\frac{4}{4}$. Mostly lyrical, with excursions into a few different key areas
    beyond C major.
Range: g–e^2

Schaefer, August. H.

Spring in the Forest, Concertino
Fillmore Bros., 1948
Dedicated to Erwin Bellstedt, horn soloist. In three connected sections: Allegretto
    —Andantino /—Allegretto. Straightforward melodies with traditional har-
    monies, light music. Part for E♭ mellophone included.
Range: c–f^2

Scherbachev, Vladimir (1887–1952) Russia

Pavane for Horn and Piano
Musical Evergreen, 1975

Scheurer, Rolf (1918–2006) United States

Elegie for French Horn Solo with Piano
Belwin, 1939

Lyrical student piece for the beginning-intermediate player, venturing into three flats.
Range: c¹–f²

Schibler, Armin (1920–1986) Switzerland

Prologue, invocation et danse, op. 47
Ahn & Simrock, 1956
Written as the set piece for the 1956 Geneva International Music Competition, this piece exists in versions for horn and piano and horn and orchestra. In three sections, the piece includes a number of difficulties and different musical characters suited to a competition piece. Includes stopped horn and old notation bass clef. A slow, expressive Lento leads into a quasi-cadenza section. The piece ends with an agile and articulate final section with many meter changes.
Range: c♯–b♭²
Duration: 7:00

Schickele, Peter (1935–) United States

What Did You Do Today at Jeffey's House? Three Pieces for French Horn and Piano (1988)
Elkan-Vogel, 1992
In three sections, entitled: First we had a parade—After lunch Jeffey's mom made us take a nap—Then we did a carnival with a haunted house and dancing bears. Written for Tom Bacon. Requires some agility for first-movement sixteenth notes, ability to swing the eighth notes in the last movement. A fun piece.
Range: d–c³
Duration: 5:00

Schiltz [full name unknown, possibly Jean Baptist Schiltz or H. Schiltz] (dates unknown, worked in Paris from approximately 1830 through some time after 1850)

Fantasie für Horn und Klavier über Motive aus der Oper "Du Brasseur de Preston"
Robert Ostermeyer, 2006
Based on the opera *Le Brasseur de Preston* by Adolphe Adam, this light work is in several sections of different characters that show the horn's lyrical and technical abilities. Trills, ornaments, and flexible tempos offer many opportunities for expression.
Range: c¹–a²

Schjelderup-Ebbe, Dag (1926–2013) Norway

Humoreske für Horn in f und Klavier (1975)
Henry Litolff's Verlag, Peters, 1977
A short, dissonant scherzo, not very difficult for the horn. Could work as a good introduction to contemporary music for a younger student.
Range: d♭–f♯²

Schlemm, Gustav Adolf (1902–1986) Germany

Variationen über ein romantisches Thema
Stuttgart Das Bläserschiff Dortmund München Grosch, 1955
Folk-song theme with four variations.
Range: b♭–f²
Duration: 6:00

Schmalz, Peter (1947–) United States

Processional and Recessional for Horn and Organ
Phoebus Publications, 1988
Two fairly short movements composed in the style that the title implies. Of me-
    dium difficulty and very well written for the horn.
Range: a–a²

Scherzo
Phoebus Publications, 1988
A short, spirited scherzo with a straightforward, simple horn part, quite limited
    in range and technique.
Range: a–f²

Subterranea (1985)
Phoebus Publications, 1988
In three movements: I. Cleric—II. Hydra—III. Elve. This piece is technically
    simple and the range is very limited. In the first movement, the horn
    plays a simple Gregorian chant melody over a more complex, but tonal,
    accompaniment. The second movement is a dramatic, but simple horn line
    over a repetitive eighth-note accompaniment marked "menacingly." The
    third movement is in a fast ⅝, and the eighth notes are grouped 2+2+2+3
    throughout.
Range: a–e²

Schmid, Heinrich Kasper (1874–1953) Germany

Im Tiefsten Walde, op. 34, no. 4
Schott's Söhne; Southern Music; Kalmus, Belwin; Associated Music Publishers
A short, lyrical piece with an ethereal quality, flowing lines, and wide range of
    dynamics.
Range: a–a²

Schmidt, William (1926–2009) United States

Sonata for Horn & Piano
Avant Music, 1978; Western International Music
A three-movement work written for Calvin Smith. In the first movement, the horn
    makes declamatory statements in large intervals. The second movement is
    a lyrical Largo, with a few changing meters, and includes a piu mosso sec-
    tion with expressive grace notes and turns, followed by a return to the largo
    tempo primo. The final movement is a theme with four different variations.

This piece requires agility, flexibility, and endurance. Recorded by Calvin Smith on *Brass Tacks* on vinyl LP.

Range: f♯–g^2

Duration: 19:00

Schmitt, Florent (1870–1958) France

Lied et scherzo, op. 54

Durand & Cie, 1912

Dedicated to Paul Dukas. This piece exists in two versions, one for double-wind quintet with solo horn part, and another for horn and piano. A difficult work rhythmically with challenging articulations, range, and trills. Includes muted and stopped sections.

Range: B–b♭^{2}

Schnyder, Daniel (1961–) United States, born in Switzerland

Sonata

Editions Marc Reift, 1997

    I. Blues

    II. An American ballad

    III. Below surface

A very jazz-oriented piece, originally written for trombone and piano and adapted by the composer for horn. Lots of technical passages in unison with the piano. The first movement features a cadenza with accompaniment and quite a number of glissandi, stopped and muted effects, and flutter tongue. The second movement is a slow jazzy ballad, all muted. The third movement is fast with difficult meter changes and some virtuoso low-horn playing.

Range: F–b♭^{2}

Duration: ca. 12:00

Schonthal, Ruth (1924–2006) United States, born in Germany

Music for Horn and Piano (Horn and Orchestra) (1978)

Furore Verlag, 1997

This is the horn and piano version of the piece, which was arranged for horn and chamber orchestra in 1979.

See: Horn and ensemble

Schorr, Eva (1927–) Germany

Sonata, Nach Drei Portraits Von Sebastian Schorr, für Horn und Klavier (2004)

Edition Gamma, 2012

Duration: 12:00

Schouwman, Hans (1902–1967) Netherlands

Legenden No. 1 en 2, voor hoorn en piano, op. 35 (1944)

Donemus, 1949

Written in 1944, these two serious pieces are rather difficult in technique and cover a wide range but are idiomatically written for the horn. New notation bass clef.

Range: A–b♭²

Duration 10:00 total

Schreiter, Heinz (1915–2006) Germany

Sonatine, op. 12

Bote & Bock, 1954

Written for Dennis Brain. Featuring contrapuntal writing, the piano is an equal partner in this work. Two outer sections of lively, driven writing are broken up by a middle section of relaxed andantino grazioso marked poco rubato. Challenges for the hornist include a few technically demanding runs and continually shifting meters.

Schudel, Thomas (1937–) Canada, born in United States

Etchings for Horn and Piano

Southern Music, 1988

Easy three-movement work of very limited range. Dedicated to Hilary and Gary Borton.

Range: d¹–e²

Schuller, Gunther (1925–2015) United States

Nocturne

Mills Music, 1946; Margun Music, 1985

A short, dramatic, atonal piece with a wide range and a wide range of dynamics. This piece is also the second movement of the composer's horn concerto (1943–44).

Range: G–c³

Sonata for Horn and Piano (1988)

Margun Music, 1989

  I. Andante, with innermost expression
  II. Allegro energico
  III. Adagio mesto
  IV. Allegro giocoso

Commissioned by the International Horn Society in celebration of its twentieth anniversary. The first and third movements are lyrical and contemplative, the third features an extended cadenza for horn with enharmonics. The second movement is jaunty, developing a regal dotted eighth-sixteenth motive and triplet figures. The final movement is full of energy, an intricate dialogue with the piano that includes jazz rhythms. This challenging contemporary work pushes technical limits, requiring good endurance and command of the extreme ranges of the horn. Extended techniques are used judiciously and effectively, and include stopped writing, rips, and delicate trills.

Range: D–d³

Duration: 19:35

Trois hommages, for horn(s) and piano
Margun Music, 1979
Three fairly short movements of moderate difficulty written in homage to Frederick
    Delius, Maurice Ravel, and Darius Milhaud. All three are in slow or moderate
    tempos and a lyrical style. The third movement is for two horns and piano.
Range: e¹–b♭² (second horn part for No. 3 is b–e²)

Schultz, Mark (1957–2015) United States

I and My Annabel Lee (1998)
JOMAR Press, 1994
A short piece with gentle, flowing melodies in the midrange of the horn, marked
    with great tenderness.
Range: d♯²–f²

Over your Shoulder, Don't Smile (1994)
JOMAR Press, 1994
Written for Ellen Campbell in memory of Neil Sanders. A fairly difficult single
    movement in a contemporary style, requiring open-to-stopped effects, use
    of a plunger, glissandi, and rips.
Range: g–d♭³
Duration: 6:00

T. Rex
JOMAR Press, 1990, rev. 1999
Written for Thomas Bacon. In two movements: 1. Little feet—2. Big feet/fast feet.
    The short first movement, marked *seamless, without emphasizing the pulse,*
    is slow and sustained in the upper range of the horn. The second, marked
    seething, reptilian, is faster, using many contemporary effects, including rips
    to indeterminate pitches, half-valve glissandi, stopped horn, and air sounds.
Range: e–c♯³
Duration: 5:00

Schumann, Robert (1810–1856) Germany

Adagio and Allegro, op. 70 (1849)
Breitkopf & Härtel, 1887; Litolff, Peters; Schirmer; J.R. Lafleur; Southern Music;
    International; Kalmus; Durand; Henle; and others
One of the first pieces written by a major composer for the three-valve horn in
    F and one of the best known and most often performed pieces for horn
    and piano. The piece is in A♭ major and is divided into two sections. The
    Adagio, in ⁴⁄₄, uses an unusually wide range and requires excellent control
    of slurs and lyrical playing. The spirited Allegro, in ⁶⁄₈, gives the hornist very
    few rests and requires agility, endurance, and strength in the upper range.
    Quite difficult. The piece also exists in an arrangement for horn and or-
    chestra by Ernst Ansermet recorded in 1973 by Hermann Baumann with
    the Munich Philharmonic Orchestra.
Range: A–c³
Duration: 8:22

Schuncke, Gottfried (1777–1861) Germany

Exercice für Horn mit Begleitung des Pianofortes
Robert Ostermeyer, 2001
Württemberg court orchestra horn player Gottfried Schuncke intended this
    piece to be used as exercises for horn with piano accompaniment. It con-
    sists of a theme and eight highly virtuosic variations for the early valve
    horn crooked in E. This very simple (musically) composition is made up
    almost solely of difficult scale and arpeggio patterns.
Range: B–b³ (c–c³ for horn in E)

Schuncke, Ludwig (1810–1834) Germany
Son of Gottfried Schuncke, and a well known pianist of his time.

Grand Duo
Carus, Stuttgart, 2000; Robert Ostermeyer, 2000 (under the title *Duo Concertant*)
This is a true duo for horn and piano in the tradition of the sonatas of Beethoven,
    Ries, Danzi, and Krufft, with substantial material and musical equality for
    both instruments. In two movements, an Allegro with an introduction,
    and a Rondo in ⅜. Typical of the period (ca. 1830) compositionally and not
    terribly difficult in the horn part technically, though there are some agile
    leaps in the rondo. The piece is written in a way that suggests it was written
    for the natural horn, and could be played that way, but could also have been
    intended for the early valve horn. Even though the Carus and Ostermeyer
    editions have different titles, they are the same piece.
Range: c–g²

Schwartz, George W. (1918–2010) United States

International Folk Song Suite
Southern Music, 1973
Six short pieces based on folk songs from various countries: 1. In the Town
    (France)—2. Carol of the Bagpipes (Sicily)—3. The Wassail Song (England)
    —4. Sumer Is Icumen In (England)—5. Lovely Moon (Germany)—6. Valen-
    cianita (Venezuela). All are written in an easy range and technically simple
    for the young horn player.
Range: g–c¹

Scriabin, Aleksandr Nikolayevich (1872–1915) Russia

Romance
Billaudot, 1977; Universal Edition, Leeds Music Company, 1954
Written for hornist Louis Savart in the mid-1890s, this piece is rather simple and
    melodic, harmonically unlike Scriabin's usual innovative writing. Good
    student recital piece.
Range: b–e²
Duration: 2:00

Segers, Jan (1929–) Belgium

Essay, for Horn and Piano
Scherzando, 1990s
Written for Andre van Driessche, this contemporary piece is based on a twelve-tone row. Originally written for horn and symphonic band. A rather technical atonal piece with requirements of extreme high range that encompasses a wide range of emotions.
Range: c–e♭³ (c–b² with ossia)
See: Horn and ensemble

Seigle, Fernand

Legend pour cor
Buffet Crampon, 1927
Very typical French solo piece of the early twentieth century, in several sections and including trills and echo horn effects. Written for Edouard Vuillermoz.
Range: b–a²

Selmer-Collery, Jules (1902–1988) France

Pièce concertante
Alphonse Leduc, 1954
Concours du Conservatoire National de Musique. Written for Jean Devèmy, professor at the Paris Conservatory. The horn takes the lead throughout this work, which has many opportunities to play in a bravura style. The piano is truly accompaniment, as the piece works its way through different styles, tempos, and cadenzas.
Range: b–b²

Semini, Carlo Florindo (1914–2004) Switzerland

Invenzioni per corno e pianoforte
Edizioni Curci, 1971
A lively, wide-ranging piece that utilizes the full range of the horn, moving quickly between sections, with technical passages, large leaps, stopped and muted timbres.
Range: c–c³
Duration: 6:40

Servais, Thèo

Cantilène sicilienne pour cor et piano (ou orchestre)
Maurer, 1971
See: Horn and ensemble

Premier solo pour cor avec accompagnement de piano
Brogneauz, 1951
Straightforward piece with traditional harmonies and rhythms. In four sections:
    Allegro—Andantino—Andante con moto—Allegretto—Rondo Allegro.
Range: g–f♯²

Deuxième solo pour cor en fa avec accompagnement de piano
Éditions du Zephyr, 1972

Ma Normandie, air et variations brillantes (Thème de Frédéric Berat)
Schott, 1973

Šesták, Zdeněk (1925–) Czech Republic

Concertino (instruktivní)
Supraphon, 1968
    I. Moderato quasi melancolico
    II. Poco allegro
Two short movements for the advanced-beginner to intermediate student, with
    fingerings for each note included. The first movement is in ¼ with a few
    changing meters. The second movement is in ⅜ with a middle section
    marked Molto cantabile.
Range: c–e²

Concertino No. 2 (1979)
Panton, 1975
    I. Poco moderato elegiaco
    II. Allegro giusto
Much more of a concert piece than his "instructive" *Concertino*, the first move-
    ment is quite somber, with long legato lines in the horn. The second move-
    ment features a rhythmic motive in a march-like character, with a middle
    section of cantabile. Moderate technical demands, suitable for the early
    college player and above.
Range: F–g²
Duration: 6:43

Shepherd, Willard I.

Nocturne and Rondolette
Southern Music, 1962
An easygoing piece of moderate difficulty written in several sections of varying
    tempos.
Range: g¹–a♭²

Sibbing, Robert (1929–) United States

Concert Piece for Horn and Piano
Theodore Presser—Tritone Press, 1979
A single movement in ⅜ and in a moderately fast tempo. Straightforward but not
    at all easy, due to fast and agile range changes and a good deal of playing
    above the staff as well as very little rest. New notation bass clef.
Range: c–c³

Sichel, John A., United States

Loon Songs
Puna Music Company, 1999

Three songs: Dawn song—Flight—Hymn to the moon. The first is slow and lyrical and not technically difficult or taxing. The second is more agile in a fast
tempo but stays, as does the first movement, in a rather narrow range. The
"Hymn" is again a slow contemplative melody. Playable by the advancing
high school horn player. A few stopped passages.
Range: g–a²

Sieber, Georges Julien (1775–1847) France

2. Nocturne für Horn (oder Violone, Flöte, Oboe) und Klavier (ca. 1812)
Robert Ostermeyer, 2009
One of four nocturnes for horn and piano written by the Paris music publisher,
who was the son of a German horn player who moved to Paris in the 1750s.
Composed in three sections, an Allegro, a Romance, and a Rondo, it is mu-
sically simple, but charming and idiomatic in the natural-horn cor-mixt
style of the time in France. Dedicated to Madame Lafitte.
Range: c¹–g²

Siebert, Friedrich (1906–1987) Germany

Scherzetto
Edition Kunzelmann
Originally for horn and strings but later arranged for horn and wind octet and
for horn and piano. A short, light work in ABA form, in a vivace tempo in
¾, felt in one. Mostly diatonic writing, with a few chromatic passages, this
work is suitable for the intermediate player.
Range: c¹–g²
Duration: 3:30
See: Horn and ensemble

Simaku, Thomas (1958–) United Kingdom, born in Albania

Six Albanian Folk-Songs
June Emerson Edition
Six short songs: The Radiant bride—The white dress—Wedding song—Song of the
forest—Two flowers over the Mountain—The blossoming rose. All based on
Albanian Folk songs. Flowing,melodious, and easygoing technically.
Range: d¹–f²
Duration: ca. 6:00

Simon, Robert

Humeurs
Alphonse Leduc, 1986
An elementary piece for the young horn player.
Duration: 2:50

Simrock, Heinrich (1760–?) Germany, worked in France

Thema mit 6 Variationen für Horn & Harfe oder Klavier oder Gitarre
Robert Ostermeyer, 2009
A very straightforward theme and six variations for natural horn in F and harp, or piano, or guitar. The accompaniment for guitar is written on a separate line in the piano part and is a simplified version of the harp or piano part. Not too difficult for the horn, but does stay predominantly at the top of the staff in a very limited range.
Range: g^1–a^2

Sinigaglia, Leone (1868–1944) Italy

Zwei Stücke, für Horn und Pianoforte, op. 28
Breitkopf & Härtel, 1905; Marvin M. McCoy, 1979
Two short pieces, a pleasant lyrical "Lied," and a spirited "Humoresque." Available from McCoy's Horn Library in the collection *Frøydis' Favorite Prunes.* Medium difficulty.
Range: c^1–a^2

Romanze, op. 3
G.Ricordi, 1902
A flowing romance marked Andante mosso. Also exists in a version for horn and string quartet.
Range: g–a^2

Siqueira, José (1907–1985) Brazil

Drei Etüden für Horn und Klavier
Leipzig Veb Deutscher Verlag für Musik, 1969

Sisask, Urmas (1960–) Estonia

Symbiotische Sinfonie, "Kalt und Heiss" (1997)
Edition 49, 1997

Skolnik, Walter (1934–) United States

Sonatina for Horn and Piano (1975)
Theodore Presser—Tritone Press
A short three-movement work of very moderate difficulty and range. Good for the younger student who is ready for a serious recital piece.
Range: b–$f\sharp^2$

Slavický, Klement (1910–1999) Czech Republic

Capricci (1967)
Supraphon (Bärenreiter), 1969
A substantial three-movement work in contemporary style.

   I. Capriccio drammatico
  II. Capriccio lirico
 III. Capriccio burlesco
Rhythmically complex and technical. Muted and stopped effects, trills, and mixed
    meters.
Range: f–b^2
Duration: 13:00

Smallman, Jeff (1965–) Canada

Il trittico barocco
Lighthouse Music Publications, 2006
Three movements in baroque style: Toccata—Air—Gigue.
Duration: 6:45

Smith, Leonard B. (1915–2002) United States

Enigma
Belwin, 1970
Very short, easy piece covering a small range. This piece consists of four-bar
    phrases of slurred quarter notes and eighth notes, suitable for the beginner
    student. To Bob and Marilyn Hoe. Includes parts for both F and E♭ horn.
Range: d^1–c^2

Indigo
Belwin, 1970

Mountain Shadows
Belwin, 1970
Suitable for the beginning horn student. Andante moderato, slurred half and
    quarter notes, and in the key of C. To Otto and Dorothy Stein, includes
    parts for both F and E♭ horn.
Range: c^1–a^2

Nobility
Belwin, 1963

Smolanoff, Michael (1942–2013) United States

Essay, op. 19
Piedmont Music Company, 1969
Written for Joel Winter. A not too difficult, short, lyrical piece for horn and organ
    that takes advantage of the expressive qualities of the horn. Also exists in a
    version for horn and string orchestra.
Range: b–b♭^{2}
Duration: 4:00
See: Horn and ensemble

Solomon, Edward S., United States
Several interesting student pieces for the beginner through high school student.

Dramatic Interlude
Southern Music, 1993
A very short student piece, suitable for the beginner who has worked their way to
     the top of the staff. Marked *Gently,* with flowing phrases of dotted quarter-
     eighth note rhythms.
Range: f¹–g²

Night Song
Southern Music, 1989
Moderately easy student piece in a flowing $\frac{3}{4}$ Andante in G minor.
Range: d¹–g²

November Nocturne
Southern Music, 1987
Short, sustained student piece in $\frac{4}{4}$ in ABA form. Easy, but with a range going to
     g². Appealing harmonies, reminiscent of a popular ballad.
Range: c¹–g²

Sonatina
Southern Music, 1985
Student piece with three short movements of rather moderate difficulty: Danza—
     Andante Cantabile—Capriccio buffo. The last movement has a few stopped
     notes.
Range: c♯¹–g²

Waltz Theme
Southern Music, 1981
A very easy midrange student piece.
Range d¹–e♭²

Solomons, David W. (1953–) United Kingdom

Petticoat Lane for Horn and Piano
Musik Fabrik, 2002
An easygoing tune, written in $\frac{4}{4}$, but the eighths are divided 3+3+2 throughout.
Range: g–c²

Soproni, József (1930–) Hungary

Sonata for Horn and Piano (1976)
Editio Musica, 1978
A modern work with contemporary compositional techniques and notation,
     written with many rhythmically free sections without meter. The horn part
     is written in a comfortable range, but is challenging rhythmically with dif-
     ficult intervals. For Ferenc Tarjáni.
Range: c–b♭²

Souffriau, Arsène (1926–) Belgium
Conductor and prolific composer.

Ballade pour cor et piano, op. 15
Editions Musicales Brogneaux, 1949

Alternating sections of $\frac{6}{8}$ and $\frac{3}{4}$, this work is full of chromatic horn writing and contemporary harmonies within the traditional $\frac{6}{8}$ that characterizes so much horn music. There are glissandi, muted passages, flutter tonguing, and triple tonguing. Dedicated to Adhémar Pluvinage.

Range: b–c³
Duration: 4:45

Spindler, Fritz (1817–1905) Germany

Sonata, op. 347
Siegel, 1884, available at www.imslp.org
    I. Bewegt
    II. Sehr Langsam
    III. Lebhaft
A relatively short three-movement sonata in mid-nineteenth-century romantic style dedicated to Oscar Franz. Moderately difficult horn technique.

Range: G–g²

Spontini, Gaspare (1774–1851) Italy

Divertimento for Horn and Piano or Harp
Billaudot, 1981
An Andante and Allegretto in late classical style. The accompaniment looks more suited to the harp than piano. The horn part is very much in the French cor-mixt syle for natural horn of the early nineteenth-century made popular by Frederic Duvernoy, with fast passage-work and arpeggiated accompaniments to the melodic lines in the piano. Lots of ornaments and trills.

Range: g–g²
Duration: 6:00

Stache, Heinrich

Romance pour cor mi♭ (ou cor en fa ou saxophone alto et piano)
Brogneaux, 1952
Part included for horn and also alto saxophone. The dedication reads, "Cordialement á Mr. Robert Rombaux, professeur au Conservatoire de Charleroi." Short lyrical piece in ABA form with traditional harmonies and staying in the midrange of the horn.

Range: c¹–f²

Stanton, Harry (1945–) United States

Gazebo Waltz
Shawnee Press, 2003
Advanced-beginner to intermediate work for the young hornist, this is a theme and variations in $\frac{3}{4}$ with a short cadenza.

Range: g–e²
Duration: 4:30

Stefanelli, Matthieu (1985–) France

Bal des lueurs nocturnes
Billaudot, 2012
A short single-movement contemporary piece dedicated to Philippe L'Orsa. Very free, but not difficult technically. Contains a few extended techniques, such as multiphonics, stopped effects, playing into the resonating piano, and accelerando notated with expanding note beams.
Range: g–b^2

Steiner, Gitta (1932–1990) United States

Duo for French Horn and Piano (1970)
Seesaw, 1971
An aleatoric piece, with many instances of improvisatory playing and interplay between the horn and piano. Includes a completely aleatoric section at the end of the work where performers choose which "events" they would like to play. Full of contemporary effects, including muted horn, trills, flutter tonguing, brass mute (stopped), large sudden contrasts in dynamics—all clearly notated with useful instructions.
Range: c–c♯^{3}

Stekke, Léon (1904–1970) Belgium

Poème sylvèstre, op. 21
Brogneaux, 1943
For horn and orchestra or horn and piano.
See: Horn and ensemble

Stephenson, James M. (1969–) United States

Sonata for Horn and Piano
Stephenson Music, 2012
Commissioned by a consortium of prominent American horn players and teachers, this contemporary sonata is written in three movements: I. Passionato —II. Passacaglia: Adagio—III. Allegro energico. A rhythmically and tonally challenging piece, with a technically difficult, but idiomatically well-written, horn part.
Range: d–c^3

3 Impromptus for Solo French Horn
For unaccompanied horn, or with piano.
See: Unaccompanied horn

Steup, Hendrik C. (1778–1827) Netherlands
Steup was a music publisher, pianist, and composer from Amsterdam.

Sonate No. 11 in E♭ for Horn and Piano (1820)
Edition Compusic, ca. 1989 (Louise Schepel, ed.)

The first movement is an Allegro brilliante, and freely quotes the Beethoven *Horn Sonata*. The second movement, "Les adieux" is a lyrical §, and the final movement is a traditional § rondo with quick figures.

Range: f–b♭²

Stevens, Halsey (1908–1989) United States

Sonata for Horn and Piano
Robert King Music, 1955
    I. Allegro moderato
    II. Poco adagio
    III. Allegro
Dedicated to George Hyde. Composed in mid-twentieth-century tonal style, this piece covers a wide range and requires fairly difficult technique. Not overly taxing, but many large intervals.

Range: A–c³

Four Short Pieces for Horn (or Clarinet) and Piano (1958)
Camara Music Publishers, 1960
    I. Andante con moto
    II. Allegro
    III. Andante con moto
    IV. Allegro non troppo
For "Kit." Easygoing writing for the horn, with interesting interplay with the piano and some mixed meters. Appealing mid-twentieth-century American music, suitable for the high school player and beyond.

Range: a–b♭²
Duration: 7:00

Stevenson, Ronald (1928–) United Kingdom (Scotland)

Bergstimmung (Mountain Mood) (1986)
The Ronald Stevenson Society, 1998
"Written for Darryl Poulsen and Kenneth Weir to play in memory of Alban Berg."
A single-movement piece written in a flowing, ethereal style, which depicts the various moods of the mountain—peaceful, majestic, and stormy. It begins and ends with the horn player playing unaccompanied into the open piano with the pedal depressed to create a sympathetic vibration.

Range: B♭–d♭³
Duration: 10:00

Stewart, Don (1935–) United States

First Sonata for Horn and Piano, op. 19
Trillenium Music, 1987
Duration: 12:00

Stirling, Ian (1919–2002) United States

Three Horn Miniatures
Editions Marc Reift, 2001
Three very short works for the intermediate student with a solid high range: 1. Horn-core—2. Sarah Hodges—3. Improvisation. Includes part for horn in F and horn in E♭.
Range: c–c³

Stokes, Harvey J. (1957–) United States

Sonata
Seesaw Music, 2004
    I. Allegro
    II. Lento
    III. Allegretto
Written for Marlene Ford. This is an extended and substantial work for the horn. The first movement is quite lyrical, and quite persistent, modulating through a number of keys. The second movement uses stopped-to-open effects and features many slowly flowing lines through the horn's range. The third movement is an agile mix of ⅝, ⅞, ¹²⁄₈, and other meters, that is quite technical. Not unreasonably difficult, but it will need to be carefully practiced.
Range: f♯–a²
Duration: 21:00

Story, Brian S. (1955–) United States

Morceau de Repére
Cimarron Music Press, 2008
Written for the composer's son Matthew upon his high school graduation. An active and technically quite difficult single-movement work.
Duration: ca. 6:00

Strauss, Franz (1822–1905) Germany

Empfindungen am Meere, Romanze (Seaside Impressions), op. 12
Edition Compusic, Southern Music, 1988
A lyrical Andante con moto, in ⅜, that emphasizes the singing qualities of the horn. Could be taxing, as there is little rest after the return of the opening thematic material.
Range: a♭–b♭²
Duration: 4:20

Fantasie über den Sehnsuchtswaltzer von Schubert, op. 2
Belwin, 1940 (Max Pottag, ed.)
In this theme and variations, each of the three variations is full of sixteenth-note passages on traditional diatonic scales. This could be a fun supplement to etudes of this period and style.
Range: G–b²
Duration: 10:46

Fantasie über Motive aus G. Donizettis "Lucia di Lammermoor"
Hans Pizka Edition, 2007
A nineteenth-century operatic-style introduction in a larghetto tempo ending
with a short cadenza leads into the main theme, which is followed by a
rather technically agile variation, a second variation in minor, and a third
in a faster tempo to end the piece. The music states: "Revised and arranged
for piano accompaniment by Hans Pizka," implying that the accompaniment may have originally been some other instrumental ensemble.
Range: b–a²

Originalfantasie, op. 6
Hans Pizka Edition, 1979
A fairly long piece written in four connected sections, consisting of an operatic
introduction in F minor, followed by an F major section in ¾, another minor
section in ⅜, and an F major ending with some fast sixteenth-note passages.
Only of moderate difficulty technically, and stays mostly in the staff.
Range: f♯–a♭²
Duration: ca. 8:00

Nocturno, op. 7
Universal Edition 1900; Master Music Publications, Inc.; International
This very popular student-recital piece is a standard of the repertoire. Features a
wide range and a very operatic romantic style.
Range: A♭–a♭²
Duration: 5:00

Theme and Variations, op. 13
Zimmermann, 1957
This work is actually a theme and variations situated within a horn sonata, with
an Adagio introduction, then the theme and two variations serving as the
first movement. A second movement, Andante cantabile, is followed by a
lively and extensive ⅜ rondo that incorporates ideas of the theme. Full of
charming moments for the horn, lyrical, yet full of bravura.
Range: b♭–b♭²
Duration: 10:25

Lied ohne Worte
Hans Pizka Edition
Duration: 2:15

Les Adieux (Romance for horn and piano)
Robert King, 1972 (rev. by Harold Meek)
Short romantic piece that challenges the player with difficult keys and a wide
range of dynamics.
Range: b♭–g²
Duration: 9:00

Strauss, Johann Jr. (1825–1899) Austria

Dolce pianti
McCoy's Horn Library, 1983 (Hermann Baumann, ed.)

Edited by Hermann Baumann, this charming piece may or may not be an original horn and piano version by the "Waltz King" himself. The original song
for voice is lost, but a version exists for cello and piano. It is, however, a very
well-written and pleasant piece of moderate difficulty, appropriate for the
young hornist.
Range: a¹–g²

Strauss, Richard (1864–1949) Germany

Andante for Horn and Piano, op. posth.
Boosey & Hawkes, 1973
Written for the occasion of the composer's parents' twenty-fifth wedding anni-
versary. A short, expressive piece of medium difficulty in flowing, romantic
style. This is a standard in the horn solo repertoire—a beautiful work that
exploits the horn's ability to sing long, lyrical phrases.
Range: g–g♯²
Duration: 3:42

Introduktion, Thema und Variationen, (AV 52) (1878)
Schott, 1995
An early work for horn in E♭ and piano, written by Strauss for his father, Franz
Strauss, when the composer was fourteen years old. Consisting of an intro-
duction, theme, and five variations with some challenging horn technique.
The piece was not published during the composer's life, but has recently
been published by Schott.
Range: e♭–b♭² (f –c³ for horn in E♭)
Duration: 10:00

Stringer, John (1967–) United Kingdom

Getting Even (1999)
University of York Music Press, 2004
Duration: 6:00

Sturzenegger, Christophe (1976–) Switzerland

The Two Léa's Songs for Horn and Piano, op. 3
Woodbrass-music, 2008
Two songs in a lyrical style, the first cantabile and flowing, the second faster, but
still very song-like, with a short interlude for the piano between. Both are
full of energy and in a romantic style.
Range: e♭–b²
Duration: 11:00

2 Légendes (pour Luka) pour cor et piano, op.7
Woodbrass-music
The first of these two *Légendes* is a lyrical, romantic piece in a slower, flowing
tempo. The second, also in a singing style, is faster and more active.
Range: b♭–b♭²
Duration: 11:00

Sturzenegger, Kurt (1949–) Switzerland

Ballade for Horn and Piano
Editions Marc Reift, 1991
A dramatic work in a serious, declamatory twentieth-century style that covers a
    wide range.

Süssmayr, Franz Xaver [also **Süßmayr**] (1766–1803) Austria

Allegro, Sonatensatz für Horn und Klavier
Hoffmeister, 1997
Reconstruction and completion by Dutch hornist Herman Jeurissen of an unfin-
    ished manuscript in the British Library. A single movement of a sonata for
    natural horn in E♭ and piano, written in classical high-horn style. This is
    one of the earliest available pieces written specifically for horn and piano.
Range: f–c³ (g–d³ for horn in E♭)

Suttner, Josef (1881–1974) Germany, born in Czech Republic

Erinnerung für Waldhorn und Klavier
Musikverlag Grosch, 1955
A single movement written in several sections. Begins with a flowing Andante
    followed by a Vivo-Scherzando with agile articulations and ornaments. The
    Andante returns and the piece ends with a muted section, closing gently in
    the lowest range of the horn. Requires a wide range and some flexibility with
    range changes.
Range: G–b♭²

Swan, John D. (1937–) Canada

Sonata for Horn
Trombacor Music Services, 1983
A medium-length three-movement sonata.
Range: a♭¹–b♭²

Sweete, Don, Canada

Sonatina (1990)
Eighth Note Publications, 1997
A three-movement sonata written for Derek Conrod. Quite difficult technically,
    requiring a good upper range and agility with wide intervals and articulate
    scale passages. A largo second movement with a faster, flowing middle sec-
    tion is followed by the energetic last movement, which has some asymmet-
    rical and mixed meters in a fast tempo.
Range: c–b²

Sydeman, William Jay (1928–) United States

Duo for Horn and Piano (1970)
Okra Music, 1971

A contemporary work, bordering on avant-garde as horn and piano exchange short phrases and gestures. Includes theatrical elements, such as instructions for the pianist to *exhort horn on by verbal exclamations . . . erotic—approaching orgasmic.* Score indicates various directions depending on gender of performers. Contemporary techniques for horn include stopped or muted horn, glissandi, half valve, blowing through the horn, trills. Contemporary techniques for pianist include scraping a dime or a pencil over strings or using fingernails on strings.
Range: d–c³

Sylvan, Sixten (1914–2001) Sweden

Largo för horn och orgel, op. 10, no. 1 (1981)
Svensk musik, 1989
Written for hornist Ib Lanzky-Otto. A slow, meditative piece for horn and organ.
Range: c¹–b♭²
Duration: 5:37

Sonat för horn och piano, op. 7 (1963)
Swedish Music Information Center
A three-movement sonata in a mid-twentieth-century style with a fast, spirited first movement, an expressive andante second movement with an articulate faster middle section, and an agile § last movement. Moderately difficult for the horn, but quite playable for the university horn student.
Range: d–a²

Szabo, Csaba (1936–2003) Hungary

Sonatina for Horn
Cellissimo, 2011

Székely, Erik (1927–) Switzerland

Rhodoraies (1975)
Editions Henn, 1976
Written for the Geneva International Music Competition, 1976, this piece includes a variety of contemporary horn techniques but is composed very idiomatically for the horn and written in standard notation, metered throughout. Consists of several sections of varying tempos, but predominantly this piece features slower, lyrical playing. Includes stopped-to-open effects, glissandi, muted passages, and two sections to be played on the open uncorrected overtones of the F horn.
Range: F–c³
Duration: 9:30

Székely, Endre (1912–1989) Hungary
Székely was active in Hungarian musical life as a composer, conductor, and music critic.

Sonata per corno e pianoforte (1979)
Editio Musica Budapest, 1982

This complex work in two movements is full of intricate play between the horn
and piano, requiring careful coordination. There are sections of aleatoric
writing and proportional notation. Extended techniques for the horn include stopped writing, flutter tongue, and trills. Bass clef is old notation.
Range: A–c♯³

Tautenhahn, Gunther (1938–2014) United States, born in Lithuania
Duo for French Horn & Piano (1972)
Seesaw Music, 1973
A short work with quickly changing moods, moving from Misterioso to Con
spirito. Horn techniques include stopped writing, trills. Its moderate range
makes this an approachable modern work. Longer lyrical gestures allow
exploration of different colors on the horn.
Range: d–g²
Duration: 3:00

Tcherepnin, Nicholas (also Tschérépnine, Nicholai) (1873–1945) Russia
Enchantment
Boosey & Hawkes, 1936
Short, lyrical piece in ⅜, with rather sustained lines that stay near the top of the
staff most of the time. Begins with three stopped notes, and then remains
open to the end.
Range: c♯–a²

Mélodie d'amour
Boosey & Hawkes, 1936
Expressive, lyrical work in ¾ that stays in the mid-to-low range of the horn. Good
flexibility is required to negotiate some of the upward gestures from low to
high.
Range: G–f²

Esquisse. op. 45 no. 2
Hans Pizka Edition, 1994
A short, tuneful piece, of moderate difficulty, but with an extremely wide range and
contrasts of dynamics for the horn, which makes the piece quite dramatic in
its expressiveness and colors. Some stopped horn, old notation bass clef.
Range: G–c³

Thieriot, Ferdinand (1838–1919) Germany
Friend and contemporary of Brahms, studied composition with Marxsen and
Rheinberger.
Sonate Es-dur für Horn und Klavier (1915)
Amadeus Verlag, 2004
    I. Allegro non troppo
    II. Andante tranquillo
    III. Allegro con brio

This sonata typifies later romantic style and harmonic language.
Range: e♭–b♭²

Thistle, Robert (1945–) Germany, born in United States

Bagatelle
W.G. Hass-Musikverlag Köln, 2008

Romantische Suite
W.G. Hass-Musikverlag Köln, 1995
In three movements that are thematically related: I. Appassionata—II. Notturno
—III. Scherzo finale. Traditional harmonies and forms, an accessible work
written by a horn player and composer.
Range: c–g²

Miniaturen für Horn und Klavier
W.G. Hass-Musikverlag Köln, 2008

Thomas, Edmond John (1959–)

Invictus
K.C. Henslee Pub., 1999

Thompson, Bruce A. (1937–) United States

Venatic Chronicle for Horn and Piano
Thompson Edition, 1986
Written for David Thompson, the three movements of this piece are entitled:
Pronouncement and assemblage—Cadences of a darkened wood—Dawn
foray. In a contemporary tonal style, the horn part is well written, but very
challenging, with fast technical passages, intervals, open and stopped effects, glissandi, and other contemporary horn effects. The first and third
movements have unaccompanied cadenza sections.
Range: F–d³

Thurner, Friedrich Eugen (1785–1827) Germany

Grande Sonate E-Dur für Horn and Klavier, op. 29 (ca. 1818)
Robert Ostermeyer, 2011
 I. Allegro
 II. Largo molto
 III. Rondo: Allegro moderato
A sonata written in the tradition of the Beethoven horn sonata, in a classical
style with the horn and piano as equal partners taking turns accompany-
ing each other. Essentially a low-horn piece for natural horn in E, with a
couple of alternate high-horn passages. Another similarity to the Beetho-
ven sonata is the second movement, which is only thirty-eight measures
long.
Range: F♯–a♭² for horn in E (with alternate high-horn passages to d³)

Tillotson, Natalie, United States
Studied with Otto Leuning at Columbia.

Fantasy for Horn and Piano (1959)
Chamber Music Library, 1962
A short work in one movement and ABA form that begins mysteriously with
the piano in open octaves and the horn playing legato lines with increasing intensity before moving into an Allegro, then returning to the opening
mysterious material.
Range: b–a²

Tisné, Antoine (1932–1998) France

Lied pour cor et piano, op. 32, no. 3
Alphonse Leduc, 1967
For Isabelle Laennec. A lyrical piece in 𝄴 scored for the midrange of the horn.
Begins slowly, in *pianissimo*, then increases in volume and momentum in
the middle section.
Range: g–e²

Tomasi, Henri (1901–1971) France

Chante corse pour cor en fa et piano
Alpnonse Leduc, 1932
In this lyrical Andantino the phrasing allows the horn player ample rest. Sections
of rubato and tempo changes allow for expressive moments. This same
piece is also available for other instruments.
Range: g–a²

"Danse profane, no. 2" from *Cinq danses profanes et sacrées* (1959)
Alphonse Leduc, 1960
Short and jaunty Scherzando that moves quickly through changing meters and
different ranges of the horn. From a five-movement work, each movement
originally for a solo instrument with piano or orchestra.
Range: f–b²
Duration: 3:00

Tosi, Daniel (1953–) France

Siegfried's Song
IMD Diffusions Arpeges, 1996
Three very contemporary movements, dedicated to Eric Sombret, with the titles;
Crazy dragon—L'extase de Brünhilde—Le triomphe de Zorro (Hagen). In-
cludes graphic notation, flutter tongue, trills, lots of grace notes, and diffi-
cult intervals. Contemporary in its rhythmic challenges and technique, but
within a comfortable range.
Range: g–a♭²

Toulon, Jacques (1933–) and Vernier, Jacqueline

Olibrius
IMD Diffusion Arpéges, 1988
For André Cazalet. A tonal work in several contrasting sections with regular
  phrase structure. A free rubato opening is followed by a dolce section in $\frac{3}{4}$,
  then a quick $\frac{2}{4}$ rounds out this work. Some stopped and muted passages. A
  very approachable work, suitable for the high school or early college player.

Turner, Kerry (1960–) United States
Composer, horn player, and founding member of the American Horn Quartet.

Sonata
Music Press Distributors, 1992
A fairly difficult work in three movements:
   I. Allegro
   II. Andante
   III. Allegro non troppo
Written in a contemporary tonal style. Includes trills and glissandi.
Range: f♯–b♭²

'Twas a Dark & Stormy Night. . .Fantasy for Horn and Organ (or Piano)
Phoenix Music Publications, 1993
A rather freely composed piece in which the composer starts with a simple motive and lets his imagination run freely with it. Technically difficult and
  agile, the piece begins with a cadenza that gradually becomes more of an
  accompanied recitative, leading into the main material of the piece, which
  is followed by short sections that play with the motive in different ways.
  Includes stopped horn, glissandi, and a wide range.
Range: B–c♯³

Turok, Paul (1929–2012) United States

Sonata for F Horn and Piano, op. 36 (1973)
The Brass Press, 1973 (available from Editions BIM)
Commissioned by Dennis Behm. A contemporary work, through-composed
  with pauses, contains aleatoric elements and freely coordinated sections
  where piano and horn play freely then coordinate their parts through cues.
  Intricate horn writing with stopped, brassy passages, quarter tones, much
  ad lib writing.
Range: b–a♭²
Duration: 10:00

Uber, David (1921–2007) United States

Capriccio for Horn and Piano, op. 163
TAP Music sales, 1992
Range: d–a²
Duration: 6:20

Four Sketches
Edition Musicus, 1965
> I. The Mountain and the river
> II. Ghost train
> III. The valley
> VI. The hunt

Four pieces of varied characters that present some technical challenges for the horn, but in a comfortable range.
Range: g–g²

Sonatina, op. 181
Southern Music, 1985
A version for horn and piano of the composer's *Sonatina for Trombone and Piano.* Three short movements that center on the low and middle register of the horn. Rather technical and active.
Range: c–g²

Summer Nocturne
Southern Music, 1983
Written for horn, trombone, or tuba, this single-movement work lies almost exclusively in the staff, but is rather active technically.
Range: g–g²

Mosaic, op. 100
Shawnee Press, 1986
Written for Jane Richter. This piece presents more substantial challenges for the horn player than the previous two and features a long cadenza in the middle that, according to the composer's note, can be omitted. Requires light, agile articulations, but written mostly in the staff with no wide leaps.
Range: c¹–b♭²

A Simple Song
Manducca Music Publications
A romantic, lyrical piece for the intermediate horn student.

Thou Holiest of Rivers, for Horn and Piano (2004)
Imagine Music, 2009
Written for Jeffrey Powers. In two parts, this work features flowing writing for the horn and piano. The preface states that the work is based on and encompasses all of the holy rivers of the Bible and that the composer uses "elements from gospel, blues and hymn-like traditional harmonies."
Range: b♭–b♭² (ossia b♭–a²)
Duration: 10:00

Vacek, Milos (1928–2012) Czech Republic

Evenings at Pekluva (1976)
Panton, 1978
A suite of three contemporary tonal-sounding movements. "Through a rowan-berry valley—elegia," is an Andante moderato in ¾. "Story of the long-bow,"

is a quick scherzo in $\frac{6}{8}$ with grace notes and a bit of flutter tonguing. "Fare-well under the aged linden tree—a romanza," is a Lento lirico in $\frac{4}{4}$.
Moderately difficult technically, but quite agile.
Range: e–c³

Valenti, Michael (1942–) United States

On Russian Hill
Kendor Music Co., 1993
A student piece from the "Graded Solo Series" of the publisher.
Duration: 2:40

Vallée, Georges Robert (1897–1976) France

Fantaisie-impromptu
IMD Diffusion Arpéges, 2001
Dedicated to Pierre Del Vescovo. This piece, in the unusual modern horn key of sounding E major, consists mostly of flowing lines with a few technical passages.
Range: a–a²
Duration: 4:00

Vallier, Jacques (1922–) France

Sonatine pour cor et piano, op. 55
Editions Max Eschig, 1964
For Jean Devémy, Professor at the Paris Conservatory. In three short movements, light and lyrical. The first movement is an Allegretto in three, the second is an Andante in $\frac{6}{8}$, the third is a spirited Allegro. The second and third movements have multiple sections of changing tempos and character.
Range: g–a²

Van Eechaute, Prosper
See: Eechaute, Prosper van

VanderCook, Hale Ascher (1864–1949) United States

Altair for Horn in E♭ and Piano
Rubank, 1952
A student work in several short sections.
Range: b♭–e²

Lyra for E♭ Horn and Piano
Rubank, 1952
A student work with a small range.
Range: c¹–d²

Vega for E♭ Horn and Piano
Rubank, 1952
Student work in several short sections in $\frac{4}{4}$ and $\frac{2}{4}$, including sixteenth-note passages.

Vasks, Peteris (1946–) Latvia

Musique du soir, pour cor en fa et orgue ou piano (1988)
Alphonse Leduc, 1993

Vernier, Jacqueline
See: Toulon, Jacques

Verrall, John (1908–2001) United States

Eusebius Remembered, Fantasy Sonata for Horn and Piano
American Composers Alliance, 1976
Dedicated to Christopher Leuba, this is a fairly short three-movement sonata in
a late twentieth-century tonal style. A slightly different version of this piece
was done by the composer with the title *Rhapsody for Solo Horn and Strings*
(1979).
Range: g–b^2
Duration: 8:00
See: Horn and ensemble

Evocation to Eos (1983)
American Composers Alliance
Duration: 8:00

Serena (1984)
American Composers Alliance
Duration: 3:00

Sonata for Horn and Piano (1941)
American Composers Alliance, 1977
In three movements. the first is a Pastorale-allegro, the second is a relatively brief
Nocturne-andante, which is followed by a spirited § Vivace. Only moder-
ately difficult, with a few technical passages. Suitable for the student hornist.
Range: g–a^2
Duration: 15:00

Three Fantasy Legends (1990)
American Composers Alliance
Written in three movements: 1. The Mysterious stranger—2. Quiet night singer—
3. The prodigal returns.
Duration: 10:00

Viana, Andersen (1962–) Brazil

Fantasieta, for F Horn and Piano (1984)
Brazilian Music Enterprises, 1996
This piece was the first-prize winner in the 1984 National Composition Compe-
tition of Rio de Janeiro.

Vidal, Paul (1863–1931) France

Pièce de concert pour cor en fa et piano
Alphonse Leduc, 1961; Buffet Crampon, 1924
This was a Paris Conservatory competition piece for 1924. Dedicated to Fernand
    Reine, professor at the Paris Conservatory. Of moderate difficulty, this
    work has declamatory passages, opportunities for bravura playing, canta-
    bile writing, and a final section that shows off technical dexterity. Flexibil-
    ity and endurance required.
Range: f–b♭²

Vignery, Jane [Vignery, Jeanne Emilie Virginie] (1913–1974) Belgium

Sonate pour cor et piano, op. 7
Brogneaux, 1948
Written for Maurice Van Bocxstaele, professor of horn at the Conservatoire Royal
    de Gand. Opens with a fanfare, which is followed by a dotted eighth-six-
    teenth rhythm that carries throughout the first movement, alternating with
    a lyrical theme in three. A bit taxing, since the penultimate measures are
    a held high a². The second movement is a Lento ma non troppo; the third
    movement is an Allegro. Full of changing character, this is an interesting
    work typical of early twentieth-century style.
Range: a–b♭²
Duration: 19:07

Vinter, Gilbert (1909–1969) United Kingdom

Hunter's Moon
Boosey & Hawkes, 1942
A relatively short, humorous character piece of moderate difficulty in three sec-
    tions. A ⅜ theme of hunting horn character, including stopped-to-open ef-
    fects and glissandi, contrasts with a lyrical middle section. A favorite re-
    cital piece of Philip Farkas.
Range: G–b²

Viozzi, Giulio (1912–1984) Italy

Sonata per corno e pianoforte (1971)
Pizzicato Verlag Helvetia, 1998
Traditional forms and rhythms, in three movements. Reminiscent of Hindemith
    in its intense harmonic language and the counterpoint between horn and
    piano.
Range: A♭–b²

Vojaček, Hynek (1825–1916) Czech Republic

Pezzo di concerto, sonata in Es
Hans Pizka Edition, 1988

A three-movement sonata that appears to be written for natural horn in E♭. Composed in a nineteenth-century romantic style, the piece is idiomatically written for the natural horn using hand stopping and would not present too many difficulties for the experienced natural horn player. Mostly written in the staff but does venture both above and below at times. All three movements feature some technical playing of moderate difficulty with the Finale being particularly light and agile.
Range: B♭–b♭² (c–c³ for horn in E♭)

Vollrath, Carl (1931–) United States

Concert Piece for Horn and Piano (1961)
Independent Music
Composed in three connected sections: Somber—Fast—Somber.
Duration: 8:51

Vuataz, Roger (1898–1988) Switzerland

Thrène, chant funèbre, op.58, no. 7
Edition Henn-Chapuis
A solemn piece in an andante tempo that begins in the low range, quietly, then gradually works its way above the staff and into higher dynamics and musical intensity, and then gradually progresses toward the end while getting softer and lower. Not technically difficult, but requires a wide range, and range of dynamics.
Range: B–b♭²

Wall, Robert, United States

Adagio
Brodt Music Co., 1982
A short, lyrical piece in ¾.
Range: a♭–a♭²

Wallach, Joelle (1946–) United States

In a Dark Time (the Eye Begins to See), Three Meditations for Horn and Piano or Chamber Orchestra
See: Horn and ensemble

Warren, David

Meditation
Ludwig Music Publ. Co., 1959
Straightforward, flowing piece in common time, with longer phrases than most pieces for the younger player. Appropriate for the junior high or high school hornist.
Range: c¹–f²

Warren, Norman (1934–) United Kingdom

Elegy
June Emerson Edition
A short movement of easygoing horn technique, but with a rather wide range for its level of difficulty.
Range: B–g²

Washburn, Robert (1928–2013) United States

Hornography
Thompson Edition, 1994
Written for Roy Schaberg and the Crane Horn Ensemble at Potsdam, State University of New York. A novelty piece that incorporates themes from well-known orchestral and solo pieces for horn in the famework of a 𝄴 rondo.
Range: g–a²

Wasielewski, W.J. von (1822–1896) Germany

Notturno
Oliver Ditson Company, 1891
A lyrical piece in 𝄴, in ABA form. The first section is an Andante quasi allegretto with flowing accompaniment in the piano. The middle section, Allegro molto, is in a bravura style, *fortissimo* with dramatic flair typical of a late nineteenth-century work. Also available for violin, cello, viola, and clarinet.
Range: g–a²

Weber, Alain (1930–) France

Improvisation
Alphonse Leduc, 1958
This short piece features repetitive clusters of sounds in the piano, with the horn adding an often simple lyrical line over interesting harmonies.
Range: b♭–c³
Duration: 1:40

Preludio
Alphonse Leduc
Written for horn and harp or piano, composed in a free contemporary style with each measure marked with the number of seconds of its duration. Within each measure, the performers have total rhythmic freedom. Intended for the young horn player as an introduction to contemporary notation and style.
Range: c¹–d²
Duration: ca. 2:55

Weigel, Eugene (1910–1998) United States

Maine Sketches, for Horn and Piano (1952)
Fema Music Publications, Interlochen Press, 1958

"For Marvin Howe." In five movements: Maliseet—Rock—Penobscot—The moving tides—Sea Call. Changing meters, slow, sustained playing, flowing lines. Evokes scenes of Maine.

Range: A–a♭²

Weiner, Stanley (1925–1991) Belgium, born United States

Bremen Suite für Horn und Organ, WeinWV 162
Wolfgang G. Haas
    1. Allegretto
    2. Adagio
    3. Allegro vivace
Range: A–b²
Duration:13:57

Fantasie für Horn und Orgel, WeinWV 160
Wolfgang G.Haas, 1994

Weinhart, Christoph (1958–) Germany

Sonate für Horn und Klavier (1987)
Christoph Dohr, 2010
    I. Maestoso
    II. Elegie
    III. Variationen
A substantial three-movement sonata in which all three movements are based on the same musical material, featuring the intervals of a tritone and minor second. The last movement is a theme and variations with the theme being stated at the end of the movement. The horn part is difficult, but idiomatically written and provides plenty of rests.
Range: c♯–c³

Weinzweig, John (1913–2006) Canada

Divertimento for Horn and Piano (1993)
Canadian Music Centre, 1993
This is an arrangement for horn and piano by the composer of his *Divertimento no. 7 for Horn and String Orchestra* (1979).
See: Horn and ensemble

Werner, Jacob (1938–2006) Germany

Suscipe Verbum, für Horn in F und Orgel (1996) nach einem Responsorium des "Maulbronn-Lichtentahler Antiphonale"
Edition Gravis, 1997
    I. Andante con moto
    II. Molto calmo, quasi recitativo
    III. Allegro vivo

Written for Joachim Bänisch, horn, and Erika Budday, organ. This is a lengthy
  piece written in a contemporary style, but metered throughout, and in standard notation. There are many short unaccompanied passages for the horn,
  and the piece includes trills, glissandi, stopped effects, muted passages, and
  a good number of rhythmic and interval difficulties.
Range: g–c³
Duration: 22:00

Werner, Jean-Jacques (1935–) France

3 Inventions (1961)
M.R. Braun, 1966 (Billaudot)
Three short pieces in varying tempos and moods in a mid-twentieth-century
  French style entitled:
    I. Rythmé, recitativo
    II. Intense, adagio
    III. Robuste, allegro aperto
A good short piece for a student recital. The horn part is substantial and interest-
  ing, but not overly difficult technically.
Range: c–g²
Duration: 7:00

Pastorale pour cor en fa et piano
M.R. Braun, 1961 (Billaudot)
Dedicated to Robert Meyer. A slow, quiet work in ¾.
Range: c¹–f♯²

Wessel, Mark (1894–1973) United States

Lento Fantasia e funebre
Carl Fischer, 1941

Wessman, Harri (1949–) Finland

Topics, käyrätorvelle ja pianolle (for horn and piano) (1993)
Modus Musiikki Oy, 1996
A rather contemporary work written for the Second Scandinavian Horn Competition in 1994. The piece combines four different musical styles; French
  overture, jazz waltz, chorale, and Latin rhythms, brought together by similar motives and a softly dissonant harmony throughout.
Range: c–c³

Viisi käyrätorvikappaletta Jenni Kuroselle (Five horn pieces
for Jenni Kuronen) (1993)
Edition Love, 1994
Duration: 7:00

Whear, Paul W. (1925–) United States

Pastorale Lament for Horn and Piano
Ludwig Music Publishing Co., 1971
This brief, lyrical piece was the first-prize winner of the 1956 Youngstown Symphony Contest.
Range: c¹–a²

Whettam, Graham (1927–2007) United Kingdom

Duo declamando
Theodore Presser Co., 1993
Written for Ifor James and Rodney Smith in 1972. This dramatic and technically difficult work begins with a long unaccompanied section that becomes an accompanied recitative, and then a true duo, ending with the return of the unaccompanied theme.
Range: a♯–c³
Duration: 10:00

White, John (1931–) United States

Time and the Water (1996)
RM Williams
Dedicated to Paul Basler, the composer describes this as a "musical apotheosis of the long poem *Timmen og Vatnid* ('Time and the Water') by Steinn Steinarr, the father of modern Icelandic poetry." A highly expressive piece written in several sections, mostly in slower tempos, that feature a full range and wide range of dynamics and expression.
Range: c♯–d♭³
Duration: ca. 13:00

Wiggins, Christopher D. (1956–) United Kingdom

Caprice, op. 98a
Emerson Horn Editions, 1992; Solid Wood Publishing
A spirited, short piece, agile and technically challenging, with some tricky passages at the top of the staff and above.
Range: B–b²

Four Easy Sketches for Horn and Piano
Phoenix Music Publications, 1995

Pieces of Eight. op. 157
Emerson Horn Editions, 2009; Solid Wood Publishing
Eight short pieces in various styles and characters. Movements include: Preludium—Berceuse—Gavotte—Valse—Lullaby—Czárdás—Carol—Reflections. Not overly difficult, but with some technical challenges, and an emphasis on the upper end of the range.
Range: g–c³

Reverie, op.98B
Emerson Horn Editions, 1991; Solid Wood Publishing
A short Andante with flowing lines and some dramatic dynamics.
Range: d¹–g²

Sonata, op.98 (1991)
Emerson Horn Editions, 1991; Solid Wood Publishing
A substantial three-movement piece with straightforward, but sometimes challenging horn technique. A rhythmically driving first movement is followed by an expressive, but powerful Andante, ending with an agile and technical finale. The movements are marked:
  I. Poco allegro
  II. Andante
  III. Allegro non troppo
Range: G–c³

Three Pieces for Horn and Piano (1991)
Emerson Horn Editions, 1991; Solid Wood Publishing
Though the title page says three, this piece actually has four short and relatively easy pieces, which are marked:
  1. Fanfare
  2. Branle
  3. March
  4. Lament
Range: c¹–g²

Three Pieces for Natural Horn and Piano, op. 88 (1989)
Emerson Horn Editions, 1989; Solid Wood Publishing
Three movements written for natural horn in F and E♭. Contemporary style with fairly frequent stopped notes. Bass clef notation is ambiguous, implying that the E♭ horn plays C (pedal C) in the second movement. Throughout the rest of the piece, bass clef appears to be modern notation.
Range: B♭¹–c³ (C–d³ for horn in E♭)

Wilby, Philip (1949–) United Kingdom

Fantasie Concertant (2003)
Winwood Music, 2004
  1. Don Quixote's Dream
  2. Burlesque
  3. Soliloquy
  4. Valse Caprice
  5. Finale
Referred to by the composer as a concerto, this piece, written for Lesley Howie, was originally written with an accompaniment of a solo quintet of two cornets, euphonium, trombone, tuba, and brass band. "Like the 18th century Serenade form there are five movements arranged symmetrically around the slow movement—Soliloquy—which separates the movements entitled Burlesque (two) and Valse Caprice (four) respectively. The first and last

movements share common material of a more symphonic nature, and the concerto ends with a brisk fugato." Rather technical, with a lot of notes, in the style of British brass band writing.

Range: G–b♭²

Wilcher, Phillip (1958–) Australia

Two Nocturnes (2007)
Australian Music Centre, Keys Press, 2007

Wilder, Alec (1907–1980) United States
A composer of both American popular songs and serious instrumental solo and chamber music, Wilder wrote much of his horn music for John Barrows, who performed and recorded it. All three sonatas and the suite are rather difficult works, requiring good range and endurance, with some wide leaps, difficult intervals, and technical difficulties. The characters of the various movements range from very agile and technical, to lyrical and flowing, and they are often in a style that suggests popular song or jazz idioms.

Sonata No. 1
CFG Pub. Co., 1964; Margun Music, 1990
  1. Allegro
  2. Andante
  3. Allegro giocoso
Range: d–c³

Sonata No. 2
CFG Pub. Co., 1964
  1. Allegro ritmico
  2. Andante espressivo
  3. Scherzo fantastico
  4. Allegro ostinato
Range: c–c³

Sonata No. 3
Margun Music, 1976
  1. Moderately fast
  2. Slowly
  3. With a solid beat and a jazzy feeling
  4. Tempo di valse—Joyously
Written for Tait and John Barrows.
Range: d–b♭²
Duration: 15:00

Suite for Horn and Piano
Margun Music, 1964
In five movements: Danse quixotic—Slow and sweet—Song—Epilogue—Suitable for dancing. Nice melodies that show Wilder's gifts for lyrical writing, along with jazz rhythms and fun effects like glissandi and upward sweeps

and pitch bends. Moderately difficult, suitable for the college-level hornist, this is a good introduction to Alec Wilder's works for horn.
Range: d–c³
Duration: 11:00

Four Easy Pieces
Associated Music Publishers, 1980
Written for Lorraine Bouras, these four easygoing movements are marked: Slowly and tenderly—Waltz-like—Spirited—Andante.
Range: g–d²

Five Love Songs
Israel Brass Woodwind Publications
See: Horn and ensemble

John Barrows
Israel Brass Woodwind Publications
See: Horn and ensemble

Wildgans, Friedrich (1913–1965) Austria

Sonatine, op. 5
Doblinger, 1962
A rather taxing piece in three short movements that remains in the upper register a good deal of the time. Written for hornist Franz Koch.
Range: g♭–c³

Willmore, Alan (1935–1993) Australia

Fantasie for Horn and Organ (1976)
Oliver Brockway Music, 1984
A short single-movement piece in several contrasting sections. Quite lyrical, and not terribly difficult technically, but tends to stay rather high in the range.
Range: b♭–a♯² (to c³ with ossia)
Duration: 4:00

Wilson, Dana (1946–) United States

Deep Remembering, for Horn and Piano
Dana Wilson, 1995
    I. Prologue / Where there was silence
    II. . . . Stepped into fire / Epilogue.
Commissioned by and dedicated to Gail Williams and Mary Ann Covert, who premiered the work in Hamamatsu, Japan. The composer's preface states that the piece "is perhaps an attempt to conjure the expanse of human experience, while not pretending to capture it. The work draws upon musical relationships that are not rooted in any single cultural tradition but synthesized from many—Indian scales, African pitch bending, European chords, and so forth. What may seem on first hearing to be 'contemporary' techniques are, ironically, also the most ancient, dating back centuries,

even millennia, in other cultures." This is a challenging work, contemplative, haunting, punctuated with sections of great rhythmic vitality.
Range: F–c^3
Duration: 15:00

Musings (An Ode to the Greek Muses)
Written as a tribute to each of the nine muses, each of these relatively short movements depicts the character of each muse.

1. Calliope—muse of eloquence and epic poetry
2. Polyhymnia—muse of sacred song
3. Thalia—muse of comedy
4. Melpomene—muse of tragedy
5. Euterpe—muse of lyric poetry
6. Erato—muse of erotic love
7. Clio—muse of history
8. Urania—muse of astronomy
9. Terpsichore—muse of whirling dance

Rather difficult technically, with agile passages of fast notes and articulations, wide intervals, a wide range, and a number of extended techniques, including glissandi, stopped effects, flutter tongue, open harmonics, and specific fingerings to obtain intonation and color effects. The piece covers a wide variety of colors, styles, and moods, making it challenging and satisfying for both performers and listeners.
Range: G–c^3

Winkler, Peter (1943–) United States

Returning to the Root (2000)
IHS Online Music Library, 2004
Commissioned by Paul Basler and premiered in 2004.
Duration: 11:00

Winter, James H. (1919–2006) United States

Sonata for Horn and Piano
Available through www.hornlessons.org

I. Andante con licenza—allegro non troppo
II. Un poco lento
III. Vivo

A three-movement sonata in twentieth-century tonal style by horn player and professor James Winter, consisting of much dialogue between the horn and piano, with lyrical melodic lines contrasting with technically agile sections and a wide range of emotions, most notably in the second movement. The last movement, which is reminiscent of Shostakovich stylistically, uses the B-A-C-H motive (B♭-A-C-B♮) in various permutations in an energetic finale. Recorded by Andrew McAfee.
Range: B♭–b♭^{2}
Duration: ca. 17:00

Winteregg, Steven (1952–) United States

Three Moods (1979)

Pasticcio Music, distributed by Manduca Music

Dedicated to Richard Chenoweth. In three movements: Dramatic—Lyrical—
Playful. The first movement consists of counterpoint between horn and
piano, with the piano keeping a steady, accompaniment, while the horn
and piano play back and forth with each other. The second movement is
relatively short and expressive, and the third movement is very fast, alternating between $\frac{2}{8}$ and $\frac{3}{8}$. Recorded by Richard Chenoweth.

Duration: 8:09

Wirth, Adam (ca. 1846–1879) Germany

Fantasie, op. 3

Hans Pizka Edition

A mid-nineteenth-century romantic piece beginning with a lyrical section in D
minor, followed by a march-like faster middle section in F major, and ending with a return of the opening material.

Range: $e^1–a^2$

Duration: 4:36

Wittell, Chester (1893–1988) United States

Suite for Horn and Piano

McCoy's Horn Library, 1986

    1. Prelude

    2. Scherzo

    3. Dirge

    4. Air varié

A fairly difficult work in four movements written in a romantic twentieth-century
tonal style.

Range: $e–a^2$

Wolber, Gary (1968–) United States

Night Music for John

Day Something Publishing, 2004

Wolff, Christian (1934–) United States

Duet II (1961)

Peters Edition, 1961

Written in graphic notation with very few actual notated pitches on staves; horn
and piano parts are printed on a single sheet and organized in six sections that may be played in any order and may have any duration and any
number of repetitions. Sections are begun arbitrarily by one player, and
the other must immediately decide which section is being played and join
in. When finished, another section is begun. There are three pages of text

explaining the notation and how to perform the piece, ending with "End when neither performer wants to go on."
Range: left to the performers
Duration: left to the performers

Woodman, James (1957–) United States

Chamber Sonata II for Horn and Organ (1995)
International Horn Society Manuscript Press, 1996

Woolfenden, Guy (1937–) United Kingdom

Horn Dances
Brass Wind Publications, 1998
Six short dances for the student horn player: War dance—Moonlight dance—Spanish dance—Shore dance—Lotus waltz—Sword dance. Not necessarily easy, but idiomatically written and interesting for the advancing high school student. Each piece has a paragraph of performance suggestions and description of the musical character.
Range: f♯–g²

Wuensch, Gerhard (1925–1980) Canada, born in Austria

Lento and Vivace for Horn and Piano, op. 16
Western International Music Inc., 1966
A dramatic Lento and a lively Vivace, rather easy going technically for the horn, but agile and articulate. Some stopped horn and glissandi.
Range: f–g²

Xanthoulis, Nikos (1962–) Greece

Fantasia di Cesare
Edition Orpheus, 2011

Young, Scott (1970–) United States

Boggart Rondo alla Twelve-Tone
RM Williams
A fast and agile rondo mostly in ⅜, but with frequent meter changes, hemiolas, and other rhythmic challenges.
Range: e–b²

Dance of the Chupacabras (2005)
RM Williams, 2008
Dedicated to Hermann Baumann, this piece is based on the mythical creatures called the Chupacabras (Spanish for "goat suckers"). A lighthearted, agile piece written in four short sections: Declamation—Arrival of the chupacabras—Courting of the chupacabras—Fight and final cry.
Range: B–b²

Zádor, Eugene (1894–1977) United States, born in Hungary

Lullaby
Music Graphics Press, 1980
"For Master Thomas Tuckwell." A short lullaby, with legato writing that moves
through the low and midranges of the horn.

Zapff, Oskar (1862–1920) Germany

Barcarole für Horn und Klavier, op. 4
André Offenbach, 1895
A short, romantic, lyrical piece in $\frac{3}{4}$. Lies in the midrange for horn, except for a
series of triplet runs from low c.
Range: c–e^2

Zbinden, Julien-François (1917–) Switzerland

Episodes, op. 95
Editions BIM
This piece exists in two versions, one with piano and one with orchestra.
See: Horn and ensemble

Zdechlik, John P. (1937–) United States

Balade
Neil A. Kjos Music Company, 2007
Dedicated to Lee Dummer. A lyrical work in common time, suitable for the
younger student hornist. Several different sections of varying tempos, al-
ways returning to the initial lyrical theme.
Range: e–f^2

Zehm, Fredrich (1923–2007) Germany

Ballade (1981)
Schott, 1983
Written for Michael Höltzel. This piece is organized in several sections: Molto moderato—Vivo—Andante—Allegro—Molto moderato—Vivo. Though called
a ballade, it is quite technical and agile, with difficult intervals and leaps,
stopped passages, fast articulation, and glissandi.
Range: d–c^3

Zeller, Georg

Charakterstück
Hanz Pizka Edition, 2004
A lively, short piece marked Presto that is written very much in hunting horn
style and is intended to be played on natural horn in D with virtually no
stopped notes. Includes trills, glissandi, and agile articulated passages.
Range: G–c^3 for horn in D

Zenger, Max (1837–1911) Germany

Sonata, op. 90
Hans Pizka Edition, 1987
> I. Allegro, ma non troppo
> II. Notturno
> III. Allegro vivace

A musically straightforward mid-nineteenth-century romantic sonata that re-
    quires a good command of the entire range of the horn, with a special em-
    phasis on the low range, and requiring some endurance, since the piece
    has relatively few rests. Due to its length, this could be the centerpiece to a
    recital program, around which other smaller works could be programmed.
Range: G–c^3

Zeuner, Charles (1795–1857) United States, born in Germany

Variations pour le cor, for Horn and Orchestra
Birdalone Music, 1997 (Horn and piano reduction)
Included here because the horn and piano version is the only performing version
    currently available of this piece.
See: Horn and ensemble

Zinn, William (1924–) United States

Romance
Theodore Presser Company, 1981

Ziring, Vladimir (1880–1968)

Four Short Pieces, (1960)
Cor Publications, 1958
Four moderately difficult little pieces.
Range: a–b♭^{2}
Duration: 7:00

Zucker, Laurel (1955–) United States

Elegy for Horn and Piano
Seesaw Music, 1988
A fairly short lyrical piece in an andante tempo, written in a contemporary tonal
    style. Only moderately difficult technically.
Range: g–g^2
Duration: 6:00

3

Music for Horn and Ensemble
Orchestra, String Orchestra, Band, Wind Ensemble, or Other Instrumental Group

INTRODUCTION

In instrumental music, the term *concerto* has come to mean a work with two or more contrasting performing forces. As the horn became recognized as a solo instrument during the baroque period, the earliest solo concertos were written for horn and strings with the horn playing in the clarino style, with florid and virtuosic writing using the upper partials of the horn. During the classical period, performers such as Giovanni Punto and Ignaz Leutgeb exploited the full range of technical possibilities of hand horn technique, inspiring composers such as Mozart and Rosetti to write the excellent works that solidified the horn's place as a solo instrument. With the development of the valve horn, composers became interested in exploring and furthering the musical and technical possibilities of the horn concerto even further. This has come to include solo works for horn and the contrasting forces of orchestra, string orchestra, band, wind ensemble, and brass band, and in contemporary music, the wide variety of instrument combinations that make up the modern ensemble.

There are many chamber pieces, such as the Mozart *Quintet for Horn and Strings*, K.407, with soloistic parts for the horn, but for the purposes of this book, we are including works only if the composer conceived the work as featuring the horn as a solo voice, with contrasting performing forces. This leaves room for gray areas and interpretation of what exactly *is* a concerto piece or solo for the horn, and the authors made their best judgments, depending on the work. From Mozart's friendship with Ignaz Leutgeb to Barry Tuckwell's association with Thea Musgrave, composers have worked with horn players and written for individual soloists' capabilities and preferences. For this reason, we have included information on dedications and premieres, when known.

Marshalling orchestral forces for horn and ensemble performance is no small task. Many interesting concertos are premiered and ultimately do not become part of the standard repertoire, for many reasons. The expense and effort of producing a performance can be prohibitive, or the piece, having been written for a specific virtuoso, may be too difficult to be accessible to the majority of horn players. It is the piano reduction that brings many of these works to listeners and horn players. In some cases, a work may have been scored for horn and ensemble, but is so firmly established in the repertoire as a piece for horn and piano, we have only listed it with a cross reference to the chapter on horn and keyboard.

As with the other sections of this book, we have made no attempt to establish a grading system for individual works, but instead try to give some idea of the difficulties and appropriateness of each piece for players of different skill levels through description in the text of the various techniques required and the challenges that each work presents.

MUSIC FOR HORN AND ENSEMBLE

Abel, Karl Friedrich (1723–1787) Germany

Concerto a cornu principale con piu stromenti accompagnanti
Friedrich Hofmeister, 2014, piano reduction, orchestra score (Mathias Pflaum, ed.)
For horn in E♭. Hofmeister attributes the piece to Abel, but there is an edition of
   this work published by Hans Pizka Edition in which the composer is not
   identified (anonymous). Based on a set of manuscript parts preserved in the
   Badische Landesbibliothek, Karlsruhe (Mus. Hs. 1057). In two brief movements; both are in $\frac{3}{4}$ and both offer opportunities for short cadenzas. The
   first movement is slow and lyrical with singing passages in the high register. The second movement is an Allegro felt in one, with triplet passages
   for the horn. This is a challenging work, with high entrances and the horn
   staying in a high tessitura.
Range: f^1–c^3 (g^1–d^3 for horn in E♭)
Duration: 7:30

Concerto per il cornu di caccia con piu stromenti
Friedrich Hofmeister, 2014, piano reduction, orchestra score (Mathias Pflaum, ed.)
For horn in E♭. Based on a set of manuscript parts preserved in the Badische
   Landesbibliothek, Karlsruhe (Mus. Hs. 1058). In two movements, the first
   is in $\frac{3}{4}$ and marked Andante un poco, and the second is in an Allegro mod-
   erato in $\frac{2}{4}$. This is a virtuosic work, with many florid passages of sixteenth
   notes and arpeggios in the clarino range of the E♭ horn, ascending as high
   as g^3.
Range: d^1–f^3 (e^1–g^3 for horn in E♭)
Duration: 9:00

Actor, Lee (1952–) United States

Concerto for Horn and Orchestra (or horn and band)
Polygames, 2007, piano reduction; Polygames, 2008, full score (orchestra); Polygames, 2009, full score (band)

1. Allegro moderato
2. Adagio
3. Allegro vivo

This work was the winner of the 2007 International Horn Society Composition Contest and premiered by the Silicon Valley Symphony, May 19, 2007, by Christophe Gillet, horn. Also in an arrangement for horn and band, which premiered March 23, 2009, by Bernhard Scully, horn, with University of South Dakota Symphonic Band. The first movement follows an ABA form, opening with a horn-call motive over an undulating string line, developing the opening motives of fourths and fifths. A lyrical second theme, marked Tranquillo, leads into a dramatic cadenza. The second movement has the horn playing long lines over lush and changing harmonies in the strings, building in intensity, then returning to its quiet opening. The third movement features a lyrical horn line, driven by an eighth-and-two-sixteenths motive in the orchestra, which is then taken up by the horn, with a return of the first-movement theme. Idiomatic writing for the horn, this is well paced, with the horn effectively balanced with the ensemble.

Range: d–c♭²
Duration: 13:30

Adler, Samuel (1928–) United States, born in Germany

Concerto for Horn and Orchestra (2002)
Theodore Presser, 2006, piano reduction
Written for William VerMeulen who premiered the work with the Houston Symphony on February 8, 2003. In three movements, opening with a declamatory introduction that leads into a quick ¾ marked "fast and energetic," full of contrapuntal writing of legato sixteenth notes, moving all over the ranges of the horn. The second movement is slow, in changing meters, and marked "quite freely," with an expressive call the composer says is "reminiscent of *shofar* calls used in High Holyday services in a synagogue" (Charles Gavin, "The Concerto for Horn and Orchestra by Samuel Adler: New Directions for the Future with an Eye to the Past," *The Horn Call* 34 [May 2004]: 93.) The second movement concludes with quiet stopped passages. The third movement, marked "fast and very rhythmic," alternates between ⅝ and ⅜ and is similar to the first movement, with legato lines, sometimes angular, at a fast tempo. Virtuosic and exciting writing for the horn.

Range: B–c³
Duration: 20:00

Agobet, Jean-Louis (1968–) France

Award-winning composer and professor of music composition at the Conservatory of Bordeaux.

Concerto Scorrevole (2006)
Peer Music Classical, 2006, orchestra score only

Premiered by Eric Sombret, horn, Orchestre Lyrique de Région Avignon-Provence, June 28, 2007. In one continuous movement of contrasting sections, with changing meters. Lyrical gestures, declamatory writing, and includes a brief cadenza. Sections of atmospheric writing, such as the horn playing quick downward legato figures at a very quiet dynamic, achieved using a practice mute.

Range: G–d^3

Duration: 20:00

Agthe, Friedrich Wilhelm (1794–1830) Germany

Agthe was cantor and music director of the Kreuzschule in Dresden.

Grand concerto per corno principale

Hans Pizka Edition, 1979, piano reduction and orchestra score

For horn in F. This work is in three traditional movements: Allegro moderato—Adagio—Rondo moderato. The first movement opens with a regal double-dotted theme, and has many sixteenth-note runs that extend into the high range of the horn. The second movement is quite active, and the third movement is a light rondo with virtuosic triplet figures that showcase the horn's technical facility.

Range: g–c^3

Duration: 19:00

Allers, Hans-Günther (1935–) Germany

Konzert für Horn, Streicher und Pauken, op. 20 (1980)

Möseler Verlag, 1982, orchestra score only

For horn, string orchestra, and timpani. Dedicated to Jan Schroeder. The first movement is an Adagio sostenuto, alla marcia, espressivo, with the horn alone in a declamatory twelve-bar passage that sets up the first movement. The second movement, marked Allegro non troppo, is in $\frac{3}{8}$, $\frac{5}{8}$, and $\frac{2}{8}$, with the horn in counterpoint with the strings throughout. There is an extensive cadenza that features dialogue between the horn and timpani. This is a very approachable contemporary work that does not make extensive technical demands on the soloist, but rather emphasizes intimate timbres and the counterpoint of horn with the ensemble.

Range: G–c^3

Duration: 16:00

Amram, David (1930–) United States

Horn player, composer, conductor, and jazz hornist; his works are infused with elements of jazz and world music.

Concerto for Horn and Orchestra (or Horn and Wind Symphony) (1965)

C. F. Peters, 1971, piano reduction

Originally written for wind band, this work features intervals of fourths and fifths that are associated with horn calls. The writing for horn is lyrical, in traditional notation, and with free and expressive horn lines. The first movement, "Prologue," is full of intimate writing, with the solo horn accompanied by harp and crotales. The second movement, marked Allegro, contains challenging writing for the horn and jazz inflections. An extended cadenza includes a recapitulation of the opening material from the "Prologue," then continues to explore a few extended techniques for the horn, such as glissandi, multiphonics, and more jazz inflections. This is a technically demanding and interesting work for the horn.

Range: B♭–c³
Duration: 12:00

Andersson, B. Tommy (1964–) Sweden

Concerto for Horn and Orchestra (1985/1993)
Edition Norsk Musikforlag A/S, piano reduction
    1. Misterioso, a piacere—Allegro energico
    2. Lento
    3. Vivace
To Henrik Nilsson. Premiered April 17, 1994, Johan Ahlin, horn, Lulea Symphony
    Orchestra, the composer conducting. This is based on the composer's *Sonata for Horn and Piano* (1985). Recorded by Sören Hermansson.
Duration: 18:00

Anonymous

Concerto a cornu principale (Karlsruhe no. 1057)
Hans Pizka Edition, 1983, piano reduction, orchestra score
The Hofmeister edition of this work has been attributed to Karl Friedrich Abel.
See: Abel, Karl Friedrich, *Concerto a cornu principale con piu stromenti
    accompagnanti*

Concerto a corno con piu stromenti accompagnanti (Karlsruhe no. 1058)
Hans Pizka Edition, 1987, piano reduction, orchestra score
The Hofmeister edition of this work has been attributed to Karl Friedrich Abel.
See: Abel, Karl Friedrich, *Concerto per il cornu di caccia con piu stromenti*

Anonymous

Concerto de Schwerin
Billaudot, 1974, piano reduction, orchestra score

Concerto a 5 ex dis, corno, due violin, viola e basso
Robert Ostermeyer, 1999, piano reduction, orchestra score
The *Concerto de Schwerin* and the *Concerto a 5 ex Dis* are different editions of
    the same piece. A low-horn concerto in two contrasting sections: Adagio
    —Allegro. It is similar in style to the baroque concertos of the Lund manuscripts, the eighteenth-century collection of horn music in the Universitetsbiblioteket in Lund, Sweden. Writing extends into the high range with
    hand stopping in the lower register as well.
Range: B♭–c³ (c–d³ for horn in E♭)
Duration: 4:30

Anonymous (Anton Joseph Hampel?)

Concerto ex D-Dur

Robert Ostermeyer, 2005, piano reduction, orchestra score

An early concerto for low horn, written for natural horn in D, which consists
  almost exclusively of acrobatic low-horn passage-work. This piece is no. 13
  in the Lund manuscript (Katalog Wenster Literature I/1–13 in the Universitetsbiblioteket in Lund, Sweden). Anton Josef Hampel is a likely candidate
  for the composer of this piece, since his high-horn colleague in the Dresden court orchestra, Knechtel, composed two of the other concertos in the
  Lund manuscript, and Hampel is credited with developing and teaching
  the art of hand stopping, which appears to be necessary in the playing of
  this piece. Contains many wide leaps to low notes and fast arpeggiated and
  scale passages. The second movement has a two-octave diatonic scale from
  g^2 down to g, which is unusual for this period.

Range: A–f♯^{2} (c–a^2 for horn in D)

Aristakesian, Emin Aspetovich (1936–1998) Armenia

Kont͡sert dli͡a valtorny s orkestrom (Concerto for horn and orchestra)

Sov. Kompozitor, 1989, piano reduction

    I. Moderato, recitando e rubato

    II. Andante assai

Published in an anthology of five horn concertos by Soviet composers, entitled
  *Kontserty dlia mednykh dukhovykh instrumentov s orkestrom, kontserty
  dlia valtornyvolume 4,* (Concertos for Brass Instruments and Orchestra,
  Vol. 4, Concertos for French Horn) which includes concertos by Aristakesian, Kolodub (for two horns), Raukhverger, Sat'yan [Satian], and Trubin.
  This two-movement work opens with an extended recitative for horn alone,
  followed by an expressive Andante that builds in momentum to agitated
  and quick writing in changing meters, before a return to the cantabile writing of the Andante. The second movement is expressive, with legato lines in
  the horn over slowly changing harmonies, and a coda that brings back the
  recitative from the opening of the concerto.

Range: B–a^2

Duration: 12:00

Arnold, Malcolm (1921–2006) United Kingdom

Burlesque (1944)

Novello, 2004, orchestra score only

The manuscript for this concerto movement for horn and small orchestra was recently discovered among Arnold's sketches. Written before the composer's
  first horn concerto, the title *Burlesque* was given by the publisher. A quick
  romp through diatonic arpeggios with triplets and sixteenth figures, in ¾
  and ⅜, with a brief contrasting middle section marked meno mosso. Idiomatic and light writing for the horn that moves mostly through the middle

and low ranges. Ends quietly, with a quick muted passage up to high c³, as if heading off into the distance with a final farewell.
Range: E–c³ (ossia c♯–c³)
Duration: 6:00

Concerto No. 1 for Horn and Orchestra, op. 11 (1945)
A. Lengnick, 1992, piano reduction
    I. Allegro commodo
    II. Andante con moto
    III. Allegro con brio
Written for Charles Gregory, who played the first performance in December 1946 with the London Philharmonic. In three movements. The opening evokes a pastoral mood, and starts with a horn call that answers back and forth with the orchestral winds in short declamations. The middle section develops sixteenth-note runs and triplets, before a return of the opening pastoral motive. The contrasting second movement is serious, and the longest and most intense of the three movements, with the horn and orchestra contemplating weighty musical ideas and images. The final movement returns to more traditional horn writing in a quick ⅜. Idiomatic writing, wonderfully orchestrated, and fun to play. Challenging writing for the horn (although the d³ is arrived at by glissando, if that makes a high d³ any easier!).
Range: E–d³ (ossia c–d³)
Duration: 22:30

Horn Concerto No. 2, op. 58 (1956)
Novello, 2008, piano reduction (reprint); Paterson's Publications, 1988; the second movement is also published separately by A. Lengnick, 1947
Written for Dennis Brain. For horn and strings, the piano reductions of the complete concerto also include a part for tenor horn in E♭. In three movements. The first is marked Con energico and is in 4/4, with lyrical writing that alternates with fast technical passages, staying in the upper range of the horn. The second movement, Andante grazioso, is in 3/4 with lilting lines that are broken up by sixteenth-note declamations. In the middle section, shimmering strings provide an atmospheric accompaniment while the horn floats above in a haunting line that hovers around a major third, until the spell is broken by the return of the sixteenth-note declamation. The final movement is marked Vivace, with chromatic sixteenth-note scales and more lyrical writing with inflections of blues harmony. This work is full of challenging legato technical passages and requires endurance. The writing stays in the upper-middle and high range of the horn, with trills and grace notes requiring finesse and flexibility.
Range: c¹–c♯³
Duration: 20:35

Arutiunian, Aleksandr Grigori (1920–2012) Armenia

Horn Concerto (1962)

International, 1973, piano reduction by the composer

Arutiunian's trumpet concerto is widely known, while this work for horn is, curiously, much less familiar. In two contrasting movements. The first is marked Largo and in ¾, and the second is an Allegretto that moves quickly along in a very fast ⅝, with a brief cadenza. This work is enjoyable to play, suitable for the college-level player, requiring good endurance and facility.

Range: A♭–b♭²

Duration: 10:00

Aschenbrenner, Johannes (1903–1964) Germany

Konzert für Horn und Orchester (1956/57)

Sikorski, orchestra score only

In three movements: Moderato—Adagio molto—Moderato (alla marcia). Angular writing for the horn in counterpoint with the orchestra, with cadenzas in the first and second movements. The second movement is sparsely orchestrated at times and moves forward in slow quarter notes, in dialogue with different instruments. The third movement march features dotted eighth-sixteenth figures and changing meters. Long-range endurance required with the occasional held notes above the staff. A serious work in contemporary harmonic language.

Range: e–c³

Duration: 23:00

Atterberg, Kurt (1887–1974) Sweden

Atterberg was a composer, conductor, and music critic who championed the music of Swedish composers.

Konzert für Horn und Orchester, op. 28 (1926)

Breitkopf & Härtel, 1928, piano reduction

This work begins with bravura calls, giving way to a lyrical second theme. Features sustained loud playing and a cadenza-like introduction, which returns at the recapitulation. There is contrast in the second movement, with a lyric melody against string pizzicati. Interesting use of the piano in the orchestra texture, and the percussion in the last movement plays a large role. The final movement is a characteristic horn ⅝ with echoes of Wagner's "Siegfried" call. Challenges in this work include endurance, sustaining long lines, keeping the intensity throughout, and fast passage-work in final movement.

Range: e–c³

Duration: 21:00

Aubin, Francine (1938–) France

Concerto pour cor et orchestre à cordes

Alphonse Leduc, 1998, piano reduction

For André Cazalet. In three movements. The first is an Allegro ma non troppo, mostly in $\frac{3}{4}$ and written in a traditional sonata form, with lyrical writing and sixteenth-note gestures throughout. The second movement is an Adagietto in minor, quite challenging due to range extending above the staff. The final movement is an energetic $\frac{6}{8}$ marked Molto vivace. The harmonic language is tonal with chromatic inflections.

Range: e–d♭³ (ossia e–c³)
Duration: 20:00

Ayres, Richard (1965–) United Kingdom

No. 36, (NONcerto for Horn) for Horn and Large Ensemble (2002)
Schott, 2006, orchestra score only
Each movement contains theatrical elements. The first movement, entitled "Valentine Trageshian dreams . . . of the Swiss girl," calls for raised podia on either side of the stage, behind the ensemble. The horn soloist plays a call from the podium on one side of the stage, then runs to the opposite side of the stage to play the echo of the call. The orchestra and horn calls become increasingly agitated and complex, until the horn is ending the calls on a high e♭³. Difficult staging (running then playing) and very effective scoring. The second movement, entitled " . . . of Jan Snaegl and the pearly gates," has the horn soloist situated behind a closed door, with the door opening each time the soloist plays. The orchestra is frenzied at times, then melts suddenly into shimmering harmonies, with harp glissandi. The third movement is a series of eleven very short scenes, and the music takes the listener through a narrative while brief descriptions of each section are projected behind the stage or on story boards. Avant-garde and theatrical. Challenging horn writing, extensive range, very high notes in the first movement.

Range: E♭–e♭³
Duration: 25:00

Bach, Jan (1937–) United States

Horn Concerto (1983)
ECS Publishing, 1983, orchestra score only
    I. Fantasia
    II. Elegy e scherzo
    III. Rondo
Written for the Orchestra of Illinois and Jonathan Boen, principal horn, who first performed the concerto with the orchestra in June, 1983. Dedicated to the memory of Hal Cyril Skopin. The first-movement Fantasia has elements of jazz reminiscent of Gershwin, with syncopations and lush orchestration, as well as a waltz section, all with challenging technical passages for the horn soloist. The second movement is more somber, and features cantabile writing for the horn with many moving parts, making it sound more active than a typical slow movement. There is a middle section of $\frac{6}{8}$, then a return to the cantabile. According to program notes on Boen's CD, Bach had in

mind a bel-canto aria for this movement, a nod to Boen's position as principal horn of Lyric Opera of Chicago. The third movement begins with theatrical moments, with the horn preparing to play then being interrupted by various instruments. At the end of the movement, a rhythm section starts a jam session, led by percussion, then, one by one, the horns from the orchestra join the soloist at the front of the stage for a final jam. This is challenging writing for the horn, with a few extended techniques, such as quarter tones, trills, a multiphonic chord, stopped notes, and glissandi. This is a large-scale work, very involved, with lush and romantic orchestration.

Duration: 35:00
Range: F–b^2

Kammerkonzert (1955–1957)
Cimarron, 2014, piano reduction
For horn and string orchestra. In three movements: Tocatta—Idyll—Rondo. The opening movement is in a fast two, marked "Vigorously," with the horn in dialogue with strings and a contrasting legato second theme. The brief second movement, marked "Very slowly and reflectively," presents a single lyrical line in the horn. The third movement brings back the spirit of the first movement, with counterpoint between soloist and strings in a quick four, finishing with a brief cadenza in the horn. This is a well-paced work for the horn soloist, and a solid addition to the repertoire for horn and strings that is suitable for the college-level player and above. The composer explains that this piece was made up of "short bits and pieces from other works which I wanted to put into a performable form. The third movement, Rondo, was an independent movement which I wrote for horn and piano as a high school senior and performed in a chamber music recital, then later arranged the piano part for the DeKalb summer park band I played with, and then for string orchestra. The middle movement was originally from my 1957 sonata for clarinet and piano which I had decided to remove from that work before its first performance. The first movement, Toccata, also dated from that period and was originally a single movement for horn and string orchestra. The German title of the resulting three-movement work was an adolescent affectation I used then, attempting to give the work a bona fide standing when linked with my famous German surname." (email correspondence with the composer, September 25, 2014)

Range: F–b^2
Duration: 10:30

Bach, P. D. Q. (1742–1807)

P. D. Q. Bach is the fictional composer invented by musical satirist Peter Schickele.

Concerto for Horn and Hardart, S. 27 (1965)
Theodore Presser, full score only
    I. Allegro con brillo
    II. Tema con variazione
    III. Menuetto con panna e zucchero

Horn & Hardart was a chain of food automats in New York and Philadelphia, where food and drink were served by coin-operated vending machines. Parody and satire abound in this work, with three movements spoofing on classical form and style using snippets of familiar tunes and conventions. Very straightforward horn part, with difficulty being the coordination of the "hardart," represented by sound effects from percussion instruments.
Range: e–g♭²
Duration: 15:44

Backofen, Johann Georg Heinrich (1768–1839) Germany
Backofen was a composer, clarinetist, bassett horn player, flutist, and harpist.

Concerto in F
Hans Pizka Edition, 1979, piano reduction; Hans Pizka Edition,1980, full score
This work is listed in Herman Haug's *Bibliography and Discography* as being originally published by Breitkopf & Härtel in 1823. It was written for early valve horn, which can be seen right away, as the opening phrase for the horn includes notes in the low range that would not have been practical (or possible) on the natural horn. In three movements, fast-slow-fast, and typical of the classical style, this work has several cadenza passages for the horn virtuoso. Technical demands include challenging sixteenth-note passages and agile horn writing that moves through the ranges, typical of cor-basse-style playing.
Range: c–a²
Duration: 19:00

Bainbridge, Simon (1952–) United Kingdom

Landscape and Memory (1995)
Novello & Co., 1995, full score only
Commissioned by the London Sinfonietta. Premiered Nov. 5, 1995, Michael Thompson, horn, with the London Sinfonietta conducted by Markus Stenz. The title is taken from the book of the same title by historian Simon Schama. The composer states in his program notes that "I have rediscovered the idea that first came to fruition in *Path to Othona,* written in 1982. In both compositions the listener is invited to hear the work, not necessarily as a 'right to left' musical continuity of thematic and temporary development, but rather as an exploration in 'frozen time' of a complex multi-layered musical landscape, where both background and foreground detail are perceived from endlessly changing perspectives. The listener is in effect walking through and around the musical 'objects'" The horn begins with a minor-seventh call that is repeated, and returns throughout the piece, while being modified and built upon as the work progresses. The soloist is surrounded by three snare drums, and there are also off-stage echo horns at the back of the auditorium.
Range: B♭–f♯
Duration: 16:00

Path to Othona (1982, chamber orchestra arrangement 1987)
United Music Publishers, 1987, orchestra score only
This self-contained work, part of Bainbridge's *Three Pieces for Chamber Ensembles,* was originally scored for small chamber ensemble with a four-channel sound system projecting multi-layered alto flute music. The composer arranged it for horn and chamber orchestra. This is an ethereal work, with a wind instrument paired up with a violin and each duo seated spatially on the stage. A group of strings is seated at the back of the stage and plays sustained chords throughout the piece. The work opens with an extensive alto flute solo, and gradually the various groups of players lay a foundation of sound until the horn enters, seemingly from nowhere, repeating a sustained note. The horn line becomes more complex as various sounds are explored over time. Control is required for the very soft dynamics, yet this is an approachable work for the horn and does not push the instrument's technical limits but instead emphasizes color and atmosphere.
Range: e–g^2
Duration: 8:00

Ball, Christopher (1936–) United Kingdom
Conductor, clarinetist, recorder player, and self-taught composer Christopher Ball is known for his concertos and his works for clarinet.

Concerto for Horn & Orchestra
Emerson Horn Editions, 2009, piano reduction by Russell Denwood
In three movements. This work is full of harmonies and orchestration in the English folk-song tradition. The horn writing is lush and tuneful, with the focus on the melodies and rich sound of the horn, rather than the horn's technical prowess.
Range: d–c^3
Duration: 22:00

Balmages, Brian (1975–) United States
Pele, for Horn and Wind Ensemble (2003)
Canzonique Music, 2004, wind-ensemble score only
Brian Balmages has written extensively for wind ensemble, orchestra, and brass ensemble. Commissioned by Jerry Peel, who premiered the work with the University of Miami Wind Ensemble. The composer describes in the score preface that this work was inspired by Pele, the Hawaiian goddess of fire (or volcano goddess) "who was passionate, volatile, and capricious." It depicts her wide range of emotions, her "loneliness, anger, fury, and passion." The piece begins with a flowing motive in the horn that becomes increasingly active, leading into an Allegro agitato with declamatory figures and calls. Marcato groups of six, marked Con furore, are followed by a lively section of § before returning to the quiet and flowing material of the opening. This is an expressive work that is very well paced for the horn soloist.
Range: g–c^3
Duration: 10:00

Banks, Don (1923–1980) Australia

Concerto for Horn and Orchestra (1965)
Schott, 1968, orchestra score only
    I. Lento
   II. Adagio
  III. A tempo; drammatico
  IV. Tenero
   V. Misurato
  VI. Con spirito
 VII. Tranquillo
VIII. A tempo
Dedicated to Barry Tuckwell, who played its premiere with the London Sym-
    phony Orchestra conducted by Colin Davis, February 27, 1966. In eight
    sections that are all connected to each other, this is an atmospheric work
    that sets the horn against a backdrop of neo-romantic orchestral colors,
    with bursts of dramatic writing. Many horn passages are marked *liber-
    amente,* allowing freedom within the changing meters. Effects include
    stopped writing; trills; and alternating open, half-stopped, and stopped
    notes.
Range: F–b^2
Duration: 17:30

Barbier, René (1890–1981) Belgium

Concerto pour cor et orchestre, op. 106 (1963)
CeBeDeM, 1964, piano reduction
This work was composed for the competition of the Royal Conservatory of Liège,
    at the request of horn player Adhémar Pluvinage. In three movements. This
    is a very traditional work, with romantic orchestration that is full of color.
    The first movement, Allegro, opens with an orchestral tutti, with the horn
    entering with a quick rhythmic figure that continually moves up and down
    the horn's range, and is developed throughout the movement. The second
    theme is a lyrical Plus calme that grows increasingly intense, until we are
    back into the opening material. The movement rounds out with an agitato
    section. The second movement is sparsely orchestrated, with the horn given
    ample opportunity for lyrical passages alone, in alternation with the wind
    choir. This movement is very free sounding. The third movement is a spir-
    ited Allegro molto, with the horn charging through in the traditional $\frac{6}{8}$-$\frac{9}{8}$
    idiom.
Range: c–c^3
Duration: 16:00

Barboteu, Georges (1926–2006) France, born in Algeria

Limites Concerto
Edition Choudens, full score only, available through Music Sales Classical
Barboteu performed this work on November 10, 1971 with the Orchestre de Paris
    at the Théâtre des Champs Elysées.

Barnett, Carol (1949–) United States

Concerto for Horn and Orchestra (1984)
Thompson Edition, 1993, piano reduction
For Charles McDonald. First performed in its horn-and-piano version by hornist
    Charles McDonald at the University of Minnesota, 1985, then premiered
    with orchestra by hornist Krista Smith and the Women's Philharmonic
    in San Francisco in 1993. In three movements: La chasse—Nocturne—La
    course d'auto (The auto race). Features mixed meters in a contemporary
    harmonic language; the final movement incorporates jazz rhythms and
    quotes the Dixieland tune "Here Comes Charlie."
Range: b–b^2
Duration: 20:00

Basler, Paul (1963–) United States
Composer; performer; teacher; on the faculty at the University of Florida, College
of Fine Arts where he teaches horn and composition.

Symphonic Dances for Horn and Wind Ensemble (1997)
Paul Basler, 1997, wind ensemble score only
Four contrasting movements full of energy and rhythmic vitality, with contrast-
    ing writing that is either easygoing and flowing or with a lyrical character
    that is more intense. Overall tessitura is in the midrange, and the piece is
    well paced and idiomatic for the horn, making this an accessible work for
    the advanced high school hornist and above.
Range: g–b^2 (to g–a^2 if ossia taken for final note)
Duration: 13:15

Baumgartner, Jean Paul (1932–2012) France
Baumgartner studied at the Paris Conservatory with Messiaen, Milhaud, and
Aubin.

Poème: pour cor solo et orchestre de chambre (1985)
Edition Choudens, 1985, piano reduction
For Georges Barboteu. Opens with free, unmeasured phrases in the horn, fol-
    lowed by sections of different characters, from expressive writing to declam-
    atory statements, all in a contemporary harmonic language. Old notation
    bass clef.
Range: A♭–c^3
Duration: 9:10

Bayliss, Colin (1948–) United Kingdom
Director of Da Capo Music, self-taught composer, studied history and librarianship.

Conversation Concerto No. 2 for Horn and String Orchestra
Da Capo Music, 1995, full score only
The composer has written "conversation" concertos for other instruments, and
    explains that these are "intended partly for good amateurs who would

normally not be attracted to some overly difficult modern pieces but want the challenge of today's music." In three movements; this is a satirical piece, with the horn playing music characteristic of string writing, and the strings playing characteristically horn music. Combines twelve-tone melodies with tonal writing, and horn and strings quote famous pieces from each other's repertoire.

Range: d–b^2 (ossia e–b^2)
Duration: 23:00

Beckel, James (1948–) United States
Award-winning composer whose works have been performed by many symphony orchestras in the U.S., he is also principal trombone with the Indianapolis Symphony.

The Glass Bead Game, for horn and chamber orchestra (or horn and band, or horn and percussion, piano and harp) (1997)
Hal Leonard, 1997, piano reduction
    1. The Call and Awakening
    2. Father Jacobus
    3. Master Ludi: Coronation and Death
The Glass Bead Game was nominated for a Pulitzer Prize. It was commissioned
    by and dedicated to Kent Leslie, who premiered it with the Indianapolis
    Chamber Orchestra on November 10, 1997. It was originally written for
    horn and chamber orchestra, with versions for horn and piano; horn and
    band; and a chamber version for horn with percussion, piano, and harp
    (which Kent Leslie has recorded). The work is loosely based on the Herman
    Hesse novel of the same name. This dramatic work is full of contrasting
    character, with motives based on fifths developed from the opening calls.
    Written in a contemporary tonal style, with the two tonal centers (E♭ and
    A) musically depicting Hesse's philosophy of the conflict between man and
    his environment. Changing meters, and some wide leaps, but suitable for
    the advanced college player and above.

Range: f–c^3
Duration: 18:00

Becker, John J. (1886–1961) United States
American composer, known as one of the "American Five," along with Cowell, Ruggles, Riegger, and Ives; their music is distinctly modern, American, and consciously breaks with European tradition.

Concerto for Horn in F (1933)
New Music Orchestra Series, 1936, full score only
Written for William Muelbe of the Minneapolis Symphony Orchestra, and first
    performed by Weldon Wilbur on a radio broadcast in the 1950s (New York
    Public Library Sound Recording Archives). Through-composed, it flows
    from an opening recitative in the horn to contrasting sections with de-
    scriptive titles. "A Poem" features atmospheric figures in the strings. "A

Satire," marked *mockingly,* features a very fast triple-tongued gesture over
legato trumpets. After a brief Allegro there is "A Song" followed by "A Choral," where the horn plays a simple line expressively on its own, joined by
the strings playing a fugue. There is interesting interplay between the horn
and orchestra, with expressive writing for the horn. Overall, this is an accessible contemporary work.

Range: f♯–b^2
Duration: 15:00

Belloli, Agostino (1778–1839) Italy

Concerto di corno di caccia
Robert Ostermeyer, 2006, piano reduction and orchestra score
Based on a manuscript from the library of the Milan Conservatory (Conserva-
torio di musica Giuseppe Verdi, Milano), this is a light work in two movements. The first movement, Allegro non troppo, begins in minor, with dramatic writing in an operatic style that embellishes lyrical passages with
triplet and sixteenth-note flourishes. The second movement, Andantino
mosso, is a theme with variations. This work is mostly in the middle and
low ranges of the horn, with wide intervals and arpeggiated passages that
extend into the low range of the horn, requiring good flexibility.

Range: c–g^2
Duration: 8:11

Belloli, Luigi (1770–1817) Italy

Concerto f moll für Horn und Orchester (1807)
Robert Ostermeyer, 2006, piano reduction and orchestra score
In three continuous sections: Largo—Allegro agitato—Allegro: Theme and Variations. This is a flashy showpiece for the horn, moderately difficult and requiring good endurance. There are extended lip trills, technical sixteenth-note
passages in the theme and variations, and an eighth-sixteenth scalar figure
that repeats with the changing harmonies.

Range: c–c^3
Duration: 14:30

Concerto per corno di caccia, denominato "il trionfo dell' innocenza" (1808)
Robert Ostermeyer, 2006, piano reduction and orchestra score
This work showcases the horn's technical prowess, with wide leaps and traditional arpeggiated figures characteristic of cor-basse writing. The second
movement, Andantino, is extensive, featuring a theme with variations that
leads to a cadenza, followed by a final Allegro vivace with acrobatic leaps
at lightning speed.

Range: B–d^3
Duration: 14:00

Gran concerto per corno di caccia (1816)
Robert Ostermeyer, 2006, piano reduction and orchestra score

In three movements, with contrasting sections within the first and third movements. This work is a showpiece, extreme in its range and technical acrobatics. The first movement features a horn recitative, followed by an
Allegro in $\frac{4}{4}$ with agile sixteenth-note passages and arpeggios. The flowing second movement in $\frac{6}{8}$ does not extend above the staff, offering a break
for the hornist. The third movement, marked Tempo di marcia, alternates
sections of a dotted eighth-sixteenth motive with acrobatic writing for the
hornist. A challenging work, with alternate phrases provided for the passages that go up to the high g^3 and for the sixteenth-note runs in the last
movement.
Range: G–g^3 (ossia G–d^3)
Duration: 16:30

Bennett, David (1892–1990) United States
Hornascope for Horn and Band
Southern Music, 1959, piano reduction
Short work in ABA form; the outer sections are in a march character in $\frac{2}{4}$, with
diatonic eighth- and sixteenth-note figures in the solo line, and a contrast-
ing middle section of lento. Technical demands and range make this a suit-
able work for the younger intermediate student.
Range: f–g^2
Duration: 4:15

Bennett, Richard Rodney (1936–2012) United Kingdom
A highly versatile composer, Bennett wrote concert music, jazz songs, and music
for film and television.

Actaeon (Metamorphosis I), for Horn and Orchestra (1976–77)
Novello, 1980, orchestra score only
Actaeon was composed at the request of Barry Tuckwell, who premiered it with
the BBC Symphony Orchestra, Royal Albert Hall, August 12, 1977. Based
on one of the legends from Ovid's *Metamorphoses,* the work tells the story
of Actaeon, a famous huntsman, who is turned into a stag by the goddess
Artemis as a punishment—so the hunter then becomes the hunted. This
atmospheric work begins and ends with an Adagio, and is followed by
three continuous sections: Allegro ritmico—Pastorale—Presto. Contemporary writing, with gestures that range from jagged and chromatic to
lyrical and expressive. There is an extensive cadenza for the horn soloist.
Range: e–c^3
Duration: 20:00

Berghmans, José (1921–1992) France
"Les Lutteurs" from Tableaux forains
See: Horn and keyboard

Berkeley, Michael (1948–) United Kingdom

Concerto for Horn and String Orchestra
Oxford University Press, 1984, rev. 1994, orchestra score
Commissioned by the Cheltenham Festival, premiered by Michael Thompson,
horn, with the Polish Chamber Orchestra, conducted by Jerzy Maksyniuk,
July 17, 1984. The first movement opens with a brief introduction of quiet
horn calls in fifths in a duet with solo viola, marked "Free and dreamy—as
though improvised." This is followed by driving rhythmic writing marked
"Malizioso," with contrasting sections of different characters, such as the
horn playing over muted strings or playing freely over aleatoric improvised
figures. The second movement is marked "Con malincolia, adagio," and
is slow and introspective. It also opens with the solo horn and viola, and
develops the quiet horn calls in fifths from the first movement, leading to
the horn playing motives from *The Last Post,* the British memorial trumpet
call, while the strings play a chorale quoting Bach's *St. Matthew Passion.*
Challenging and intense horn writing, with wide leaps, fairly difficult agile
passages, and phrases that extend into the high range.
Range: F–c^3
Duration: 16:00

Bertini, Gary (1927–2005) Israel, born in Russia
Bertini was a well-known Israeli conductor and composer.

Horn Concerto (1952, rev. 1965)
Israeli Music Publications, 1965, reduction for horn and piano by Frank Pelleg.
This work for horn and strings was written for Simha Arom. In three movements:
Allegro energico—Molto calmo ma espressivo—Allegro molto. The first
movement opens with quick and declamatory writing in $\frac{5}{4}$, with a more
relaxed middle cantabile section of $\frac{3}{4}$. The second movement is slow and lyr-
ical and carries the most weight, being the longest movement of the piece.
The last movement is lively, with changing meters of $\frac{5}{8}$ and $\frac{6}{8}$, and is rather
fun to play. Challenging work due to fast tempos, this is contemporary
writing that rests on traditional forms and harmony.
Range: d–b♭^{2}
Duration: 16:00

Bertolozzi, Joseph (1959–) United States

The Contemplation of Bravery (2000)
Blue Wings Press, 2000, full score, for horn and concert wind band; also ar-
ranged by the composer for horn and orchestra
Commissioned for the bicentennial of the United States Military Academy at
West Point, premiered March 18, 2001 USMA Concert Band, Sargeant.
Harry F. Ditzel, horn soloist. In one movement and written in a traditional
harmonic language. This is a meditative work, with broad, sweeping lines
that take full advantage of the heroic and majestic sound of the horn. Re-

quires good long-range endurance for sustained writing that extends above the staff.

Range: e–c³

Duration: 10:00

Bertouille, Gérard (1898–1981) Belgium

Concerto for Horn and Strings, Piano, Timpani (1975)

CeBeDeM, 1976, orchestra score

The CeBeDeM website states that the composer's works are written in a traditional style, in a "flexible and varied language. Well acquainted with the modern extentions [sic] of the consonant idea, his music without being classically tonal has never reached absolute atonality." (www.cebedem.be/en /composers/b/41-bertouille-gerard). In two movements. The first is marked Poco lento and features lyrical expressive writing in a dolce character and in changing meters. The second movement, Allegro, is angular and resolute in character, also with contrasting sections marked dolce. Triplet figures at a fast tempo are challenging, but overall this is a well-paced work for the horn. The tessitura is mostly within the staff, and there are judicious breaks. Piano and timpani add interesting dimension to the string orchestra scoring.

Range: f–a²

Duration: 12:30

Bestor, Charles (1924–) United States

Award-winning composer Charles Bestor studied with Paul Hindemith, Vincent Persichetti, Peter Mennin, and Vladimir Ussachevsky. He has been on the faculty at several colleges and universities, and is professor of composition emeritus and director of the electronic and computer music studios at University of Massachusetts Amherst.

Concerto for French Horn and Orchestra (2006)

Tamar Music, 2005, orchestra score only

Written for Laura Klock, who premiered and recorded the concerto. As a former horn player himself, Bestor wrote this work "to return to his long lost musical youth by writing a piece in which the horn is the center of the universe" (recording liner notes, Albany Records, 1255). The first movement opens with an extended dialogue between horn and timpani, with the orchestra increasingly entering into the conversation as the movement progresses. The second movement is lyrical, featuring wide intervals in the horn line over a lush and romantic orchestration. The final movement is a relatively short and fast Furioso with colorful syncopated figures that drive the movement. Challenging leaps in the horn line require flexibility, but overall, this is a well-paced contemporary work.

Range: e–b♭²

Duration: 12:00

Biddington, Eric (1953–) New Zealand

Peace for Hanna (Adagio for French Horn and Strings)
Eric Biddington, 2006, orchestra score only
A short, slow work that moves forward in expressive eighth-note rhythms, written in tonal harmonic language.
Range: b–c³
Duration: 6:00

Bjelinski, Bruno (1909–1992) Croatia
Bjelinski was a composer and professor of counterpoint and fugue at the Zagreb Academy of Music.

Concertino for Horn, Strings, Celesta and Percussion (1966)
Musikverlag Hans Gerig, 1969, piano reduction
Premiered March 16, 1967. *New Grove* calls Bjelinski's music "neo-classical . . . notable for its lively rhythms, strong melodic appeal and sharply etched harmonic structure." The first movement, Allegro, is in a declamatory style, built around a perfect-fourth motive. The second features flowing lines for the horn in an andante tempo, and the final movement is a lively Allegro con spirito in changing meters.
Range: d–a²
Duration: 10:21

Black, Daniel (1979–) United States

Concertino for Horn and Orchestra (2003)
Available from the composer, for horn and piano, or orchestra score, www
.danielblackconductor.com
Dedicated to Lin and Bernie Foulk. The version for horn and orchestra was premiered in April 2008 in St. Petersburg, Russia. It was a finalist in the Fifth International Prokofiev Composition Contest. In two movements. The first is a pastorale, opening quietly in the winds with a legato figure that is taken up by the horn then building momentum to a loud and sustained Maestoso. The second movement, Waltz, is a bit haunting, bordering on sardonic. The range and technical demands are manageable, with a few challenging entrances on high a² in the first movement, but overall this is an accessible work, appropriate for the college-level player and above.
Range: d–a²
Duration: 10:00

Blanquer, Amando (1935–2005) Spain
Blanquer studied horn, piano, and composition in Valencia, then studied in Paris from 1958–1962. He won a Prix de Rome in 1962, eventually returning to Valencia to compose, teach, and write books on counterpoint and analysis.

Concerto pour cor et orchestre (1976)
Billaudot, 1983, piano reduction

In memory of Miguel Falomir. In three movements. The first movement is a fairly quick § that takes the opening motive through contrapuntal passages, with occasional wide leaps that are reminiscent of horn calls. Agitated piu mosso sections punctuate this movement. The second movement is marked Cantabile, opening with a slow melody that grows increasingly ornamented and free in the middle section before returning to an echo of the opening phrase. The final movement is in ¾ and marked Alla marcia, with eighth-sixteenth note contrapuntal writing. This is the most chromatic movement, with wide leaps, some fast grace notes, and occasional trills for effect.
Range: a–a♯²
Duration: 12:00

Blume, Hermann (1891–1967) Germany

Konzert für Horn und Orchester
Philipp Grosch Musikverlag, 1930, piano reduction
In three movements: Allegro moderato—Andante—Allegro scherzando. With contrasting sections within each movement and written in traditional harmonic language and in the style of a late nineteenth-century concerto.
Range: B♭–b♭²
Duration: 16:00

Blumer, Theodor (1881–1964) Germany

Blumer is known for his wind chamber music, which is receiving more attention of late with an increase in recordings of his works.

Serenade für Horn und Streichorchester, op. 93
Simrock, orchestra score only
This serenade is full of romantic writing, long lines for horn, and traditional horn gestures, such as light and playful writing in §. In one continuous movement, with quickly changing moods, from *lebhaft* to *ruhig*.
Range: e–b♭²
Duration: 15:00

Boerma, Scott (1964–) United States

Composer, arranger, and conductor; on the faculty at Western Michigan University, where he is director of bands and conducts the University Symphonic Band and Western Winds. He studied composition with William Bolcom, Ramon Zupko, and Anthony Iannaccone.

Isle of Sky for Horn and Band
Madison Music Works, full score
Premiered at St. Cuthbert's Church in Edinburgh, Scotland, Katy Ambrose, horn soloist with the Andover (Michigan) High School Band. Listed as Grade 4 on the composer's website.
Duration: 6:05

Zirk for Horn and Band (2007)
Madison Music Works, full score
Listed as Grade 5 on the composer's website.
Duration: 8:45

Bonneau, Paul
See: Devevey, Pierre and Paul Bonneau, *Poeme for horn and orchestra*

Børresen, Hakon (1876–1954) Denmark
Serenade, for Horn, Strings, and Timpani (1943)
Edition Dania, 1943, piano reduction; Edition·S-music-sound-art, piano reduction and orchestra score (www.edition-s.dk)
In three sections, in ABA form, and written in a late romantic style. The outer
   sections are marked Allegro, with a main theme that is both lyrical and
   heroic. The slow and expressive middle section opens with a simple theme,
   followed by contrasting sections of light and active figures, tranquillo writing, and a long declamatory phrase that builds to *fortissimo* before ending quietly. This piece is not as technically demanding as Richard Strauss'
   first horn concerto, but is very similar in style, suitable for the early college
   player and above.
Range: g–a^2
Duration: 17:14

Böttcher, Eberhard (1934–) Sweden and Norway, born in Germany
Konzert für Horn und Streichorchester (1982)
Ries & Erler, 1986, orchestra score only
   I. Fantasia
   II. Notturno
   III. Burlesca
Written in twelve-tone (dodecaphonic) language. The work opens with expressive
   writing in the strings, and the horn enters with a cadenza followed by a
   disjunct and loping theme that unfolds with a rubato feel, with contrasting
   sections that are driving and rhythmic. The second movement, "Notturno"
   is marked sostenuto, with atmospheric writing and a middle section of piu
   mosso. The final movement is rhythmic, with colorful trills, some flutter
   tonguing, and stopped writing. Challenging horn writing, with fast chromatic gestures and wide-ranging lines, in a high tessitura.
Range: g♯–c^3
Duration: 16:27

Bowen, York (1884–1961) United Kingdom
Concerto, op. 150, for Horn and Strings (1955)
Emerson Horn Editions, 1956, piano reduction
To Dennis Brain, who premiered the work in 1956. In three movements. The first
   opens with a fanfare in the horn, giving way to interesting, flowing lines

between horn and strings, with echoing stopped effects in the slow section. The second movement is brief and atmospheric, and the third movement is a light §. Lushly orchestrated and written in romantic harmonic language in a distinctive voice. Bowen was a horn player and the writing is idiomatic and well paced. A suitable work for the advanced college player and above.

Range: F–d♭³
Duration: 18:00

Bozay, Attila (1939–1999) Hungary
Bozay studied composition with Ferenc Farkas and taught composition at the Ferenc Liszt Academy of Music in Budapest.

Concertino for Horn and String Orchestra, op. 36 (1988–1989)
Editio Musica Budapest, orchestra score
    I. Moderato, energico
    II. Andantino sostenuto [larghetto]
    III. Allegretto vivace
In three movements. The first presents contrasting gestures that can quickly change character, concluding with a cadenza. The second is lyrical and delicate. The third is energetic, with quick sixteenth-note runs trading back and forth with the strings.

Range: F♯–b♭²
Duration: 13:00

Bracegirdle, Lee (1952–) United States, works in Australia
Composer, conductor, and hornist, Bracegirdle has played in several orchestras and was former assistant principal horn with the Sydney Symphony.

Threnos for Solo Horn, Winds, and Percussion (2007)
C. F. Peters, 2007, wind band score; C.F. Peters, 2009, piano reduction
True to its title, this somber lament has lyrical and slow outer sections marked Lento, with a contrasting middle section of piu mosso that increases in intensity, before a return of the character of the melancholy opening. The composer writes in the recording's liner notes that "although the main melodic figure of the soloist and the thematic material of the accompaniment are based on dodecaphonic rows, the work's tonal structure and developed material are not." (CD, American Wind Symphony Orchestra, William Purvis, horn soloist).

Range: e–a♯²
Duration: 8:00

Braun, Yehezkiel (1922–2014) Israel

Concerto for Horn and String Orchestra (1978)
IMI Israel Music Institute, 1978, orchestra score
In three continuous sections that roughly follow ABA form. A brief introductory Tranquillo introduces a plaintive theme in the horn. This is followed by

an Allegro with the horn in counterpoint with the strings. The slow and expressive second section features the horn over muted strings, leading into a brief cadenza. A third section is a spirited Allegretto in $\frac{6}{8}$, featuring the horn at its most virtuosic before returning to the opening tranquillo material.

Range: f–c³
Duration: 14:00

Bree, Johannes Bernadus van (1801–1857) Netherlands

Szene für Horn und Orchester (1840)
Bärenreiter, orchestra score only
Written for hornist Nicolaas Josef Potdevin, in memory of Potdevin's son, also
    named Nicolaas, and also a horn player, who died at age twenty-one. He-
    roic and lyrical, written in a romantic style, this was recorded by Ab Koster.
Duration: 11:00

Bresgen, Cesar (1913–1988) Austria, born in Germany
Award-winning composer, influenced by Hindemith, Orff, Stravinsky, and Bartok.

Concerto for Horn and Orchestra (1963)
Musikverlag Hans Gerig, 1967, orchestra score only
This horn concerto is in three movements. The first movement, marked Alle-
    gro, alternates between $\frac{2}{2}$, $\frac{3}{2}$, and $\frac{4}{2}$, with contrapuntal writing followed by a
    lyrical second theme and a challenging cadenza ascending to db³. The sec-
    ond movement, marked Sostenuto is full of rhythmic shifts and alternat-
    ing time signatures, beginning with a subdued statement that grows more
    agitated with marcato and *fortissimo* writing. The final movement, marked
    Molto allegro, is in changing meters, with fast triplets and arpeggiated
    runs requiring agility. Although there is a high db³ in the first-movement
    cadenza, this is an accessible work, similar in style to Hindemith's writing
    for the horn.
Range: f–db³
Duration: 16:00

Broadstock, Brenton (1952–) Australia

Nearer and Farther, for Horn and String Orchestra (or String Quintet) (1991, rev. 1993)
G. Schirmer, 1993, orchestra/quintet score; Australian Music Centre, horn and
    piano version
Commissioned by the Australian Music Centre. The title comes from a poem by
    Walt Whitman, part of which is included in the preface. The work begins
    fast and furious, with the horn darting in and out of the texture in quick
    sixteenth-note figures amidst the changing texture of strings playing piz-
    zicato and arco. This is followed by abruptly contrasting sections that al-

ternate between fast (vivo) writing and slow sections (intensivo, cantabile). A fast and agile technique is needed for this work, but there are several sections that stay in the low range, which helps with the pacing for the hornist.

Range: c–g²

Duration: 8:00

Brotons, Salvador (1959–) Spain

Horn Concerto "Ab Origine" for Horn and Orchestra, op. 114 (2009)

Brotons & Mercadal Edicions Musicals, 2010, piano reduction

Brotons wrote this work for hornist Javier Bonet. Written for conch shell, alphorn, natural horn, and valve horn; or the entire piece may be played on the valve horn. In three movements: I. Ab origine—II. Ciaccona, Cadenza —III. Giga. The composer indicates in the score preface that *"Ab origine (From the origins) evokes the first instruments (the sea snail, the alpine horn and the natural horn) and highlights the expressive possibilities of the instrument in its simplest and purest conception, playing with the natural sounds."* The first movement begins with the sound of calls on a conch shell pitched in the key of A, then a similar motive follows on the alphorn in the key of E♭. Changing to the natural horn in E♭, an easygoing and jaunty theme emerges and builds in intensity before the soloist moves to the valve horn. The movement concludes with the horn returning to its origins, moving back through the instruments of natural horn, alphorn, and finally the conch shell. The second movement begins tranquillo and features long lyrical lines for the horn, with a cadenza featuring the natural horn. The final movement, Giga, in ⁶⁄₈, is bright and spirited. Written in a contemporary tonal language.

See also: Salvador Brotons and Javier Bonet, "Concerto for Horn and Orchestra: Ab Origine," *The Horn Call* 40 (May 2010): 47–48.

Range: B♭–d³ (written b♭² for conch shell or horn in A)

Duration: 31:00

Fantasía para trompa y cuerdas, op. 12 (1976, rev. 1988)

Clivis Publicacions, 1988, version for horn and piano; 2005 version for horn and strings

In two sections. This work opens slowly; the first section is marked Adagio lugubre, with muted horn, somber and lyrical character. This is followed by energetic fast writing with the horn in counterpoint with strings, marked Allegro marcato, building momentum to an Allegro vivace in ³⁄₄ that is felt in one. The string ensemble is rich and full, with tinges of Shostakovich. Interesting and challenging writing for the horn, with wide leaps and quick passages, and venturing above the staff; suitable for the advanced college player and above.

Range: f♯–b²

Duration: 8:16

Broughton, Bruce (1945–) United States
Broughton is an Oscar-nominated Hollywood film composer, winner of many awards for his film and television scores.

English Music for Horn and Strings (1995)
Lengnick, 1997, piano reduction by Adam Gorb
Premiered November 1995 by Michael Thompson, horn, with the Beaconsfield Music Society, who commissioned the work. In two movements. The first-movement pastorale moves along at an energetic clip through changing meters and syncopated figures. The second movement is a relaxed "Air varie" that begins with a folk-song melody that goes through many permutations, recalling familiar tunes. Good long-range endurance needed for passages that stay up in the high range, and quick figures with multiple tonguing require facility. Includes some stopped horn writing.
Range: c–c^3
Duration: 15:00

Brown, Charles (1898–1988) France

Élégie für Horn und Orchester
Éditions Philippe Fougères, 1945, also published in a horn and piano version.
See: Horn and keyboard

Brumby, Colin (1933–) Australia

Concerto for Horn and Strings (1971)
Australian Music Center, full score only
Dedicated to Alex Grieve. Premiered April 2, 1975, by Stanley Fry, horn, and the Queensland Symphony Orchestra. Includes a declamatory first movement with horn in counterpoint with strings. The second movement, Largo, features a cantabile horn line over muted string pizzicati, and the third movement is quick and light, alternating between $\frac{2}{4}$ and $\frac{6}{8}$.
Range: B–c^3
Duration: 15:00

Bruneau, Alfred (1857–1934) France

Romance pour cor et orchestra (1882)
J. Hamelle, 1909, horn and orchestra version
See: Horn and keyboard

Brusselmans, Michel (1886–1960) Belgium and France
Brusselmans was known for his programmatic orchestral music written in a neo-romantic style.

Légende du Gapeau
Salabert, 1931, piano reduction
This straightforward work, originally for horn and orchestra, opens with a brief introduction of lyrical writing, marked Andante con moto, ma cantabile,

followed by a declamatory $^{12}_8$ before a return to the opening material. Of medium difficulty, technically accessible, and lying well on the horn.

Range: b♭–b♭²
Duration: 5:00

Rapsodie pour cor et orchestre (1938)
CeBeDeM, 1938, orchestra score
A mostly flowing work in contemporary tonal language in two parts, each with a cadenza. The first part is in a Moderato tempo, beginning quietly with a lyrical melody over arpeggios in the harp, with contrasting sections of poco piu animando. The second part is marked Scherzando and is in $^6_8$, with a slower, fugue-like middle section, with imitative writing throughout the orchestra, which the horn eventually joins. The piece ends quietly, with a return of the opening mood. Moderately difficult for the horn, with enough breaks for the soloist throughout to make it a well-paced work.

Range: f♭–b♭²
Duration: 12:00

Burdick, Richard O. (1961–) Canada, born in United States
Hornist and composer Richard Burdick has written quite a number of works for horn. His eclectic compositions explore the nature of artificial scales. He has written several concertos, which are available in full score and parts from www .i-ching-music.com.

Concerto No. 1 for Horn, op. 56a, for String Orchestra and Percussion (1990)

Concerto No. 1 for Horn op. 56b, for Band (1990)

Concerto No. 2, op. 74 (1992 rev. 2014)

Busser, Henri (1872–1973) France

Pièce en ré: pour cor en fa et orchestra, op. 39
Alphonse Leduc, 1961, piano reduction
A Paris Conservatory contest piece.
See: Horn and keyboard

Butt, James (1929–2003) United Kingdom

Horn Suite
The music indicates that this work can be performed with piano, orchestra, or unaccompanied.
See: Horn and keyboard

Butterworth, Arthur (1923–2014) United Kingdom

Romanza for Horn and Strings (1954)
Hinrichsen, 1960, horn and piano; also available with five string parts (double bass ad lib)
Originally for horn and string quartet or horn and string orchestra, later arranged for horn and piano. Flowing work in different sections that ebb

and flow, this work is somber, written in a contemporary tonal harmonic language. Beginning in a slow character, marked Lento cantabile, with a middle section of piu mosso, then returning to the opening material. It ends with a coda marked Molto adagio e quasi misterioso. Requires good endurance for maintaining long lines with intensity, and for phrases with high points above the staff.

Range: e–b♭²
Duration: 8:30

Carter, Elliott (1908–2012) United States

Horn Concerto (2006)
Hendon Music, Boosey & Hawkes, 2007, orchestra score
An important addition to the canon of works for horn by one of America's most well-regarded composers. Carter wrote this concerto at the age of ninety-eight. It was commissioned by the Boston Symphony Orchestra and premiered on November 15, 2007, by Jamie Sommerville, principal horn of the Boston Symphony Orchestra. The work is in seven continuous sections, and the horn plays throughout. The orchestration is full of blocks of sound and interjections that offset the horn colors and allow the timbral changes in the horn to project. The horn writing is lyrical, with passages floating up in the high tessitura of the horn. These alternate with quick angular passages and manic gestures. Not a concerto in a bravura character, but an understated work that explores horn timbres against the colors of the orchestra.

Range: G–c³
Duration: 11:00

Casablancas, Benet (1956–) Spain

". . . der graue Wald sich unter ihm schüttelte," Chamber Concert Nr. 2
for Horn solo and Ensemble (2011)
Unión Musical Ediciones, 2011, full score
Commissioned and premiered on May 21, 2011, by Cantus Ensemble Croatia for its tenth anniversary, Radovan Vlatkovic, horn soloist. The ensemble instrumentation is flute, oboe, clarinet, bassoon, trumpet, trombone, percussion, 2 violins, viola, cello, and bass. The title is a reference to Georg Büchner's novella *Lenz,* a "text that is at the same time beautiful and distressing, something which determines the tone and colour of this work" (musicsalesclassical.com/composer/work/4155/47603). In four movements: I. Cantus—II. Notturno—III. Scherzo—IV. Epilogo. Estatico. This work features long horn lines that weave in and out of the texture, with percussive punctuations from the ensemble. The third movement has contrasting sections of different characters: scherzando, a jaunty giocoso section, and maestoso writing. The final epilogue and chorale bring back the long lines and character of the first movement. Challenging horn writing in a contemporary rhythmic style, with changing meters and expressive gestures.

Range: G–c³
Duration: 16:00

Castérède, Jacques (1926–2014) France

Nocturne for Horn and Strings
See: Horn and keyboard

Chabrier, Emmanuel (1841–1894) France

Larghetto pour cor et orchestre (1875)
Salabert, 1913, horn and piano version; Billaudot, 1975, orchestra score ("reconsti-
    tution, orchestration et arrangement par Edmond Leloir"); Kalmus, 1989,
    conductor's score
Premiered in Paris in 1878 at the Société des Compositeurs. A recitative-like
    opening is followed by lyrical writing marked Andante molto sostenuto
    that becomes more agitated before returning to the material of opening.
    This is now a standard work in the horn repertoire; the horn and piano
    version is often played and has been recorded by several hornists. It exem-
    plifies nineteenth-century lyrical writing for the horn.
Range: c–a²
Duration: 10:00

Charpentier, Jacques (1933–) France
Composer, organist, and arts administrator, Charpentier studied composition at
the Paris Conservatory. He also studied Hindu music in Bombay and Calcutta,
which *New Grove* says "had a profound effect on his music."

Concert no. 8, pour cor en fa et cordes (1976)
Alphonse Leduc, 1979, orchestra score only
In one continuous movement of contrasting characters, the piece opens with the
    horn slowly rising out of its low range, continuing with expressive legato
    phrases that often rise and fall throughout the range of the horn. A lively
    Vivace leads into an extensive cadenza for the horn, and the piece con-
    cludes with a section of aleatoric writing. A challenging contemporary
    work requiring flexibility and good endurance.
Range: G–c³
Duration: 15:00

Charron, Jacques (1954–) France

Cornissimo, op. 30, *pour cor et piano ou orchestra*
Editions J. M. Fuzeau, 1989, piano reduction
Dedicated to Gilles Rambach, horn professor at Toulouse Conservatoire. Com-
    posed in contrasting sections of expressive and energetic writing, with wide
    leaps, quick technical passages, and some stopped writing. Several passages
    stay up in the higher tessitura, requiring good endurance. This is a chal-
    lenging work, suitable for the college student and above.
Range: F–d³
Duration: 5:00

Chasalow, Eric (1955–) United States

Horn Concerto (2008–09)
Suspicious Motives Music, 2009, orchestra score, available from the composer
Written for Bruno Schneider who first performed the concerto at the 2012 South-
    west Regional Horn Workshop on January 14, 2012, and again on January
    27, 2012, with the Boston Modern Orchestra Project. In four movements:
    Confident and insistent—Meditative, a long expanding breath—Distant—
    Moving by angle and accent. In a contemporary harmonic language, this
    work mixes together elements of a traditional horn concerto in unexpected
    ways. After an extended tutti, the horn enters, but instead of the expected
    big horn moment to match the orchestra, the soloist plays different motives
    on one pitch, delaying the big moment until the end of the movement. The
    second movement expands on the preceding material, ending with a short
    cadenza. Another (unexpected) slow movement ensues, with lyrical muted
    horn over muted strings followed by an energetic fourth movement that
    finally returns to the "one note" idea of the opening. Changing colors in
    horn and orchestra, stopped writing, dynamic contrasts, atmospheric un-
    derpinnings, and energetic writing are some of the characteristics of this
    work.
Range: b–d♭³
Duration: 15:00

Chemberdzhi, Yekaterina [Chemberdgi, Ekaterina] (1960–) Russia

Horn Concerto (1992)
Boosey & Hawkes, orchestra score only
For horn and chamber orchestra.
Duration: 19:00

Cherubini, Luigi (1760–1842) Italy, resided in France

Konzert F-Dur für Horn und kleines Orchester (1833)
Doblinger, 1996 (Jirí Stefan, ed.), piano reduction
Four short movements that showcase the horn's virtuosity: Adagio—Andante—
    Theme con variazioni—Polacca. Of medium difficulty in range and techni-
    cal demands, it lies well on the horn, making it an accessible work requir-
    ing flexibility and a sense of flair.
Range: c–g²
Duration: 9:30

Sonatas No. 1 and 2 (1804) Original title: *Deux sonates ou études pour
le cor avec accompagnements*
Sikorski, 1954, solo horn and string parts
Originally written for four-part string accompaniment, either quartet or string
    orchestra.
See: Horn and keyboard

Cheslock, Louis (1898–1981) United States
Cheslock was on the faculty at Baltimore's Peabody Conservatory for many years.

Concerto for French Horn and orchestra (1936)
Manuscript score and parts at the Fleisher Collection, Free Library of Philadelphia
In three movements. The first movement is in a moderately fast $\frac{2}{4}$, with the horn
    entering on a cadenza-like passage after the orchestral tutti, then devel-
    oping a *dolce* theme based on a syncopated gesture. The movement ends
    with a cadenza, finishing with a flourish on a high c^3 held for three bars.
    The second movement is slow and lyrical. The third movement, in $\frac{6}{8}$, begins
    slowly and builds to a scherzando tempo. The cadenza includes multipho-
    nics. This work requires good long-range endurance and fluid technique
    for fast passage-work.
Range: c–c^3
Duration: 20:00

Cheung, Anthony (1982–) United States
Award-winning composer whose works have been commissioned and performed
by major orchestras and contemporary ensembles, Anthony Cheung is on the
faculty at the University of Chicago.

Fog Mobiles, for solo horn and orchestra (2010)
Orchestra score available from the composer, www.acheungmusic.com
There are two versions of *Fog Mobiles,* one is for an orchestra of thirty-two musi-
    cians, and the other is for an orchestra of fifty-eight musicians. Originally
    commissioned—and premiered on November, 26, 2011—by the Frankfurt
    Radio Symphony Orchestra, with Saar Berger, soloist, who also premiered
    the chamber orchestra version with the Orchestra of the League of Com-
    posers in New York on June 4, 2012. *The New York Times,* writes that the
    piece "evokes San Francisco, where [Cheung] grew up, with its unending,
    varied symphony of foghorns, waves and wind." (Zachary Woolfe, "Some
    new sounds end a season," *New York Times,* June 5, 2012)
Duration: 12:00

Chevreuille, Raymond (1901–1976) Belgium

Concerto, op. 43 (1949)
CeBeDeM, 1954, orchestra score only
For Georges Caraël. Contrasting movements notated with changing meters, writ-
    ten in contemporary tonal language: Exposition—Interméde—Variation 1
    —Interméde—Variation 2. The two "Interméde" have pastoral characters,
    pairing the solo horn with clarinet and flutes, respectively. Challenging
    writing for the horn, with a tessitura that extends above the staff.
Range: e–c^3
Duration: 24:00

Chiapparelli, D. [Domenico Saverio?]

Concert per a trompa i orquestra
Tritó, 2013, orchestra score only
    I. Allegro
    II. Andante
    III. Allegro
First published in 1780 by Berault, also listed in Breitkopf and Sieber publisher's
    catalogs in the 1780s. Based on a recently discovered eighteenth-century
    score in the Library of the Royal Conservatory of Music in Madrid, edited
    by Elies Moncholí. Three traditional movements: Allegro—Andante—Al-
    legro. Written in the classical style for horn in E♭.
Range: b♭–d³ (c¹–e³ for horn in E♭)
Duration: 10:00
See also: Javier Bonet, "A Lost Horn Concerto is Found after 233 Years: An In-
    terview with Elies Moncholí Cerveró," *The Horn Call* 44 (October 2013):
    52–53.

Cilensek, Johann (1913–1998) Germany
Cilensek studied organ and composition at the conservatory in Leipzig and was
active as a composer and in the musical life of East Germany, serving as professor of composition and also as director of the Conservatory Franz Liszt in
Weimar.

Konzertstück für Horn und Orchester (1982)
Edition Peters, 1986, orchestra score only
This is a challenging contemporary work: colorful, atmospheric, featuring the
    horn against a backdrop of orchestral effects, such as harp glissandi, blocks
    of sound colors from strings and brass, pizzicati, and multitudes of percus-
    sion. In one movement of contrasting sections, the horn interjects various
    gestures into the conversation, often in soliloquy, or with sparse accompa-
    niment. The piece has an unmeasured feel to it, with sections of aleatoric
    writing, like a spontaneous conversation.
Range: E–c³
Duration: 20:00

Cliff, Tony, United Kingdom

Night Breezes, for Horn and String Orchestra
Tony Cliff Music, 2006, piano reduction and orchestra score
In three movements. The writing for all three movements is flowing, and the
    harmonic language has a laid-back, popular feel to it, with jazz inflections.
Duration: 12:00

Cohen, Fred (1958–) United States
Conductor and composer, Fred Cohen is currently professor of music and director of the School of Music and Dance at San José State University.

Great Scott! for Horn and Wind Ensemble (2004)
Seesaw Music, 2004, wind ensemble score only
Commissioned by Mary Ann Craig, director of bands at Montclair State University for the MSU Wind Ensemble, and dedicated to Jeffrey Scott.

Collorafi, James (now known as James Nicholas) (1957–) United States
Concerto for Natural Horn and Small Orchestra, A Romantic Horn Concerto (1984)
Shawnee, 1986, piano reduction, includes part for valve horn in F and natural horn in E♭
James Collorafi wrote this piece for natural horn player and instrument-maker Richard Seraphinoff, who also edited the valve horn part. The preface indicates the piece is "the outcome of a friendly wager the composer and hornist made prior to entering a competition in Boston. Mr. Seraphinoff won the competition. The music herein represents Mr. Collorafi's promise to write a concerto for his friend." The piano reduction includes parts for both the valve horn and the natural horn, and Mr. Seraphinoff indicates in the preface that "the hand-stopping and mute indications in the valve horn part are not necessarily meant to simulate the natural horn, but rather to produce the colors which the composer had in mind." In three movements. The writing is romantic, with lush harmonies and melodic lines for the horn. Difficult natural-horn playing, but worth the effort.
Range: f–b♭^{2} (g–c^3 for horn in E♭)
Duration: 27:30

Constant, Marius (1925–2004) France, born in Romania
Award-winning composer and conductor, studied with Aubin, Messiaen, Boulanger, and Honegger; founded several new music ensembles in Paris, and was a professor at the Paris Conservatory.
Choruses and Interludes for French Horn and Orchestra (1987)
Editions Salabert, 1988, piano reduction and orchestra score
 Chorus I. Disco feel
 Interlude II. Molto lento
 Chorus II. Very slow and lazy
 Interlude II. Vivace
 Chorus III. Slow
This work uses many colorful effects on the horn, including quarter tones, rips, breathy sounds, trills, and glissandi. Scored for orchestra and jazz quartet (keyboard, bass, drums, and tenor saxophone). A challenging work, good command of high range is needed, and a feel for different styles (disco, rubato blues style, swing).
Range: d♭–d♭^{3}
Duration: 15:00

Cooman, Carson P. (1982–) United States

Enchanted Pathways, Concerto for Horn and Ensemble (2002)
Lauren Keiser Music Publishing, ensemble score and parts
The small ensemble consists of flute, clarinet, percussion, piano, violin, and violoncello. Dedicated to Hazel Dean Davis, who premiered it with the Harvard Group for New Music. The composer explains in the preface that "the image behind the work sees the horn as an adventurer on a search through a whole series of 'enchanted pathways'—traveling through the ensemble and musical material." In one continuous movement of contrasting sections plus a coda. Opens with a quasi-cadenza and includes sections of chorale-like writing; fast, frenzied sections; and a slow section marked "distant recollections," before the quick coda. Notation is in common time, which helps with ensemble coordination. While several sections stay in the mid-range of the horn, there is challenging writing above the staff at the end of the piece, requiring good endurance.
Range: g♯–b²
Duration: ca. 12:00

Corrette, Michel (1707–1795) France

Concerto "La Choisy" für Horn solo, zwei Oboen, Fagott, Streicher und Basso continuo
Heinrichshofen, C.F. Peters, 1967, piano reduction and ensemble full score (both edited by Edmond Leloir)
The original version of this piece is no. 14 from Corrette's series of "Concertos comiques." Originally for horn in C basso, musette, two violins, and continuo. The first movement, in ⁶⁄₈, is based on hunting horn motives. In the second movement, Adagio, the horn is tacet. The third movement is, measure for measure, identical to the first movement, but this time in ²⁄₄, with light-sixteenth note figures in the baroque style. The original setting has been recorded by Claude Maury. The Leloir arrangement consists of four-part strings with added oboes and bassoon.
Range: d¹–g²
Duration: 7:00

Cosma, Edgar (1925–2006) France, born in Romania

Concerto pour cor et orchestre (1991)
Editions BIM, 1991, piano reduction
    I. Voix dans la Nuit (Preciso, Calmo)
    II. Spirales (Giusto)
    III. Le Poète nous parle . . . (Andante, con eloquenza)
    IV. Péripéties (Con impeto ma preciso)
Composed for the International Festival of Music, Toulon, 1992, and dedicated to Daniel Bourge. In four movements, notated in changing meters and tempos, with a few instances of graphic notation. Valve glissandi, trills,

multiple-tonguing effects, flutter tonguing, quarter tones, all add color
to the contemporary gestures that make up this challenging work. The
piano reduction includes performance instructions and explanations of
symbols. Alternative phrases or notes are provided for several difficult
passages.
Range: G♯–c♯³ (ossia G♯–b²)
Duration: 16:23

Cronin, Stephen (1960–) Australia
Stephen Cronin is on the faculty at the Queensland Conservatorium, Griffith
University.

Concerto for Horn and Orchestra (1983)
Australian Music Center, 1999, orchestra score only
Driving and intensely lyrical at times. In three movements that follow the tradi-
tional fast-slow-fast form. The horn part is accessible and well paced, with
an emphasis on expressive motives and the interplay between solo and
ensemble.
Range: f♯–c³
Duration: 15:00

Cruft, Adrian (1921–1987) United Kingdom
Cruft studied composition with Gordon Jacob and Edmund Rubbra and was a
double bassist in several orchestras in London.

Elegy for Horn and Strings (1967)
Joad Press, 1977, piano reduction
This work was written in memory of Dennis Brain, ten years after his death.
Solemn writing, in ABA form, with outer sections that develop an angular
half-step motive, and a middle section of poco meno mosso.
Range: A–b²
Duration: 7:30

Crusell, Bernhard, (1775–1838) Sweden, born in Finland

Horn Concerto
The original concerto has been lost, but there is a horn and piano arrangement
based on a version that was written for solo horn and brass ensemble.
See: Horn and keyboard

Damase, Jean-Michel (1928–2013) France

Concerto pour cor et orchestra (1995)
Henry Lemoine, 1995, piano reduction
First performed by Michel Garçin-Marrou and the Orchestre National Bordeaux
Aquitaine in July 1995. In four movements. The first is marked Moder-
ato and opens with a heroic double-dotted motive, continuing through
changing meters and jaunty, irregular phrasing, with quick, wide-ranging

phrases. The second movement, Allegro scherzando, trades figures between horn and various voices of the orchestra. The third movement, Andante, is richly orchestrated, romantic, and shows off the horn's legato capabilities, particularly over wide intervals. The final movement is a challenging Allegro vivace.

Range: g–a^2

Duration: 16:30

Rhapsodie pour cor et orchestra (1987)

Henry Lemoine, 1997, piano reduction

Commissioned by Barry Humphries and written for Barry Tuckwell, who premiered the work on April 16, 1986 at Royal Festival Hall, with the London Symphony Orchestra. In one movement, with a variety of colors and moods expressed by the horn. Heroic writing and lyrical lines that melt into dotted figures, all moving seamlessly over the lush orchestration. Recorded by Ben Jacks, horn, with the Orchestra Victoria, Barry Tuckwell conducting.

Range: f♯–c♯^{3}

Duration: 14:30

Danzi, Franz (1763–1826) Germany

Konzert in F für tiefes Horn und Orchestra (P 240)

Hainholz Verlag, 1998, piano reduction and orchestra score (Peter Damm, ed.)

    I. Allegro vivace

    II. Adagio non troppo

    III. Allegretto

Three movements in the classical style. The last movement is a theme and variations on Gluck's opera *Le Rencontre Imprévue*, which Mozart also used for his variations for piano *Unser dummer Pöbel meint* (K. 455). Features agile writing spanning the range of the horn, wide leaps, and a passage that features descending notes in the pedal range of the horn.

Range: G–a^2

Duration: 17:00

Concerto in E Major (P 239)

Deutscher Verlag für Musik, 1970 (in E, Peter Damm, ed.); International, 1986 (in E♭, David Byrne, ed.); Heinrichshofen, 1968 (in E♭ E. Leloir, ed.); all editions are piano reductions

    I. Allegro

    II. Romance

    III. Rondeau, Allegro

Originally written for horn in E. Based on a manuscript from the Fürst Thurn und Taxis Schloss Museum, Regensburg. Elegant writing in the classical style. The second movement in particular has long and pleasant melodic lines, with a contrasting section in minor. This is a challenging concerto that lies in the middle and upper tessitura of horn. The writing is very similar in character to Rosetti's concertos C48 and C40. Cadenzas are written out in the editions listed here, and the Peter Damm edition includes "Eingang" cadenzas, which are brief improvised passages leading into the rondo theme each time it appears. The piece is played more often in E♭, the key of the International edition.

Range: f♯¹–c♯³ (ossia f♯¹–b²) (edition in E)
Duration: 16:04

Darbellay, Jean-Luc (1946–) Switzerland
Clarinetist, composer, conductor, and founder of Ludus Ensemble. Many of his compositions for horn were written for and premiered by his son, Olivier Darbellay.

Concerto Discreto, (horn solo, bassetthorn, violine, viola, violoncello) (2004–05)
Tre Media, 2007, full score
Written for a small chamber ensemble, but included here since it was conceived as
    a concerto for horn. This is a short, subtle work in a slow tempo that allows
    for each instrument to explore the colors of sound that evolve throughout
    the piece. Aside from some stopped writing, the horn part is straightfor-
    ward, with the emphasis on the exploration of color. Premiered February 14,
    2005, Arithmeum in Bonn, Olivier Darbellay, horn, with the Orion Ensemble.
Range: c–g²
Duration: 5:00

Espaces, für Horn und Streicher (1995)
Tre Media, full score
An orchestration of Darbellay's unaccompanied piece of the same title. Can be
    performed unaccompanied, with string quintet, or with string orchestra.
Duration: 6:00
See: Unaccompanied horn

Incanto, für Horn und Orchester (1994/95)
Tre Media, full score
Duration: 14:00

Mana, für Horn und Orchester (2008)
Tre Media, full score
Premiered by Olivier Darbellay, horn, with the Bieler Symphony Orchestra, Feb-
    ruary 18, 2009.
Duration: 19:00

Mégalithe, "Lutèce," pour cor solo et ensemble (2007/08)
Tre Media, 2008, full score
For solo horn and flute, oboe, clarinet (bass clarinet), bassoon (contra bassoon),
    horn, trumpet, tenor trombone, percussion (one player), piano, and string
    quintet. Premiered June 26, 2007, Olivier Darbellay, horn with the Ludus
    Ensemble, Bern. A musical realization of megaliths—the great stone struc-
    tures of the past—with the full sonority of the horn and a wide range of
    musical expressions. In one movement, with upward gestures that continu-
    ally return to a prolonged written c², bold dynamics, trills, stopped writing,
    and a cadenza.
Range: c–c³
Duration: 20:00

Dauprat, Louis François (1781–1868) France

Dauprat was professor at the Paris Conservatory 1816–1842, solo horn of the Paris Opera, and a hand horn virtuoso. He wrote many works for horn, including six works for horn and orchestra, and an orchestration of his *Trois Melodies pour le cor*, op. 25, which was originally written for horn and piano, the third part of which is for two horns and piano. Several of his concertos were revised later in his career to accommodate both cor-alto and cor-basse styles of playing. There are many passages in Dauprat's works that are very technical, indicating the advanced hand horn technique that horn players of the time possessed.

Concerto No. 1, op. 1

Robert Ostermeyer, 2005, piano reduction and orchestra score; Hans Pizka Edition, 1979, piano reduction and full score
> I. Allegro spiritoso
> II. Adagio religioso
> III. Rondo: Allegro

For horn in F. Composed for and dedicated to Jean-Joseph Kenn, who was Dauprat's teacher and the principal cor basse at the Paris Opera. The concerto was originally written for cor basse, then revised in 1860 to include a part for cor alto, so it has been referred to and published in the past as the *Concerto for Cor Alto or Cor Basse*. The Ostermeyer edition is based on the original cor-basse version, and the Pizka full score that was consulted includes alternate passages where the two parts differ. In three movements, with several opportunities for cadenzas in the first and third movements.

Range: c^1–c^3

Duration: 15:00

Concerto No. 2 for Cor Basse, op. 9

Robert Ostermeyer, 2005, piano reduction and orchestra score; McCoy's Horn Library, 1987, piano reduction (Daniel Bourgue, ed.)
> I. Allegro fieramente
> II. Poco adagio
> III. Rondeau: Allegro

For horn in F. Written for cor basse. Composed for and dedicated to Mr. Le Comte Nabert de la Ferté-Meun. In three movements in the classical style. The first is in $\frac{4}{4}$, with an emphasis on challenging passages that would be typical technical writing for the cor-basse player. The second movement is in $\frac{3}{4}$, with a middle section of minor, followed by an orchestral interlude in $\frac{4}{4}$ that leads into the last movement.

Range: c–$b\flat^2$

Duration: 14:30

Concerto No. 3 for Cor Basse or Cor Alto en Mi, op. 18

Robert Ostermeyer, 2005 (includes solo parts for both cor alto and cor basse), piano reduction and orchestra score
> I. Allegro maestoso e risoluto
> II. Andante capriccio
> III. Allegro

Originally for horn in E. The dedication on the title page reads: "Hommage d'Amitié et de Reconnaissance" ("In Friendship and Recognition"). Dauprat wrote two different versions of the solo part, one for cor alto and one for cor basse. The two parts are similar, with the cor basse occasionally playing low acrobatic passages, and the cor alto playing a more singing high line, with several passages at the top of the staff and above. Composed in three movements. The first is in $\frac{4}{4}$, sonata form, followed by a slow second movement, with a lilting character in $\frac{6}{8}$, and a third-movement rondo in $\frac{2}{4}$. The solo-horn part is in the unusual written key of g minor, which provides interesting tonal colors and expressive possibilities on the natural horn. For the valve-horn player, this is also a challenging work, due to the fast passages in E horn transposition.

Range: cor basse in F: f–a²; cor alto in F: b–b² (cor basse in E: f♯–b♭²; cor alto in E: c¹–c³)

Duration: 17:30

Concerto No. 4 in F, op. 19
Robert Ostermeyer, 2005, piano reduction and orchestra score
    I. Allegro moderato
    II. Adagio non troppo
    III. Rondo: Allegro
Hommage à la mémoire de Punto (dedicated to the memory of Giovanni Punto). After a lengthy orchestral tutti, the horn soloist's opening motive sets up the spirit of this work, with diatonic runs up to the written high c³ of the F horn and back down to low c, followed by a contrasting theme marked dolce. The slow second movement is simple in its lyricism and refreshingly unadorned. The last-movement rondo is light and fun, a fitting tribute to Giovanni Punto.

Range: c–c³
Duration: 19:00

Concerto No. 5, op. 21, *for Cor Basse*
Robert Ostermeyer, 2005 (includes solo parts for both cor alto and cor basse), piano reduction and orchestra score
    I. Allegro risoluto
    II. Introduction, Poco adagio
    III. Rondo-Bolero: Allegro moderato
For horn in E. Dedicated to M. Corret, first horn of the Grand Théâtre de Rouen. Originally written for cor basse, the cor-alto part was added later. Following three-movement form. The second movement is thirty-four bars, marked "Introduction," and moves directly into the "Rondo-Bolero."

Range: cor basse in F: F♯–g²; cor alto in F: a♯–d♯³ (cor basse in E: G–a♭²; cor alto in E: b–e³)

Duration: 14:30

Concertino par cor mixte (1825)
Robert Ostermeyer, 2005, piano reduction and orchestra score

I. Allegro moderato
II. Andantino
III. Rondo-Bolero: Allegro moderato

For horn in E. Dedicated to Signore Barone di Quintella, this work was recently
    found in the Biblioteque Nationale, Paris. In his other concertos, Dauprat
    emphasized differences between high and low horn. This work has a smaller
    range, with virtuosic writing in the midrange.
Range: b–a² (c¹–b♭² for horn in E)
Duration: 12:30

Dávid, Gyula (1913–1977) Hungary

Dávid studied composition with Kodály and was a violist and conductor, as well
as professor of wind chamber music at the Liszt academy and professor of chamber music at the Budapest Conservatory. *New Grove* states that due to his background as an orchestral violist, his music is "clearly composed and professionally
crafted."

Concerto per corno e orchestra (1971)
Editio Musica, 1976, piano reduction
Dedicated to Ferenc Tarjáni, the concerto is composed in three traditional move-
    ments, often dark and brooding, with inflections of folk music. The first
    movement, Allegro assai, is in a fast ⅔ with syncopations and eighth-note
    figures that move the horn line along, leading into a cadenza. The second
    movement, marked Andante molto tranquillo, begins very slowly and is
    contemplative, then builds to a *fortissimo* against an oscillating figure in
    the orchestra. The third movement is the most playful and sardonic, with
    an active duple meter in dialogue with the orchestra. A challenging work
    for horn in terms of range and endurance, including a high c³ held for four
    bars at the end of the piece.
Range: e–c³
Duration: 12:30

Davies, Peter Maxwell (1934–) United Kingdom

Horn Concerto
Chester Music, 2000, orchestra score, (horn and piano version for rehearsal pur-
    poses only)
Written for and premiered by Richard Watkins and the Royal Philharmonic Or-
    chestra. In an article by Rick Kimberley in *The Independent* (April 28, 2000),
    Davies explains that he "wanted to create music to exploit Richard's partic-
    ular lyrical qualities: above all his singing and the extraordinary 'presence'
    of each note he plays: that's why I've composed a concerto which 'breathes'
    in one, long connected argument, right through to the final cadenza and
    coda. The solo writing is extremely virtuoso, not least in exploring the
    horn's full range, from deepest bass range to the most exposed high sos-
    tenuto. It presents challenges of embouchure and of sheer stamina which I
    should think are fairly unprecedented." An introduction is followed by an

Allegro moderato, leading directly into a very slow Largo, with a penulti-mate recitative section, marked *con fantasia, liberamente*. The final Allegro acts as a coda, ending the piece with a run up to a high c³ trill, then a *sffz* held g¹ to a *ppp*. The work has a run up to high e♭³ but an alternate ver-sion with repeated high c³ is provided—still a challenge! Contains trills, tremolandos.

Range: F♯–e♭³ (ossia to c³)
Duration: 23:00

De Angelis, Ugalberto (1932–1982) Italy

Concerto per corno in fa e orchestra (1956–1957)
Casa Musicale Sonzogno, 1965, piano reduction
Contemporary work presenting a kaleidoscope of changing moods and meters. The opening is marked Largo misterioso and the horn enters over quiet strings and harp, which gives way to an Allegro vivo, heard first in the orchestra, then briefly taken up by the horn before a cadenza. The move-ment concludes in the largo tempo. The second movement alternates fast-slow-fast sections, and is full of changing meters. The final movement is an Adagio, marked *elegiaco e soleme*. It begins with stopped horn alone, soon joined by the basses and cellos.

Range: c–b♭²
Duration: 20:45

DeBaar, Mathieu (1895–1954) Belgium

DeBaar was a violinist, an active orchestra and chamber musician, and taught at the conservatory in Verviers.

Concerto pour cor et piano (ou orchestre)
J. Maurer, 1965, piano reduction
In three traditional movements in a romantic style, this work incorporates many traditional characteristics of the horn concerto: heroic writing, lyr-ical playing, and a finale in § that is fun to play. Good endurance and fa-cility are required. This work would be suitable for the advanced college hornist.

Range: F–c³
Duration: 18:30

De Frumerie, Gunnar

See Frumerie, Gunnar de

De Jong, Marinus

See Jong, Marinus de

Delerue, Georges (1925–1992) France

Student of Milhaud and Büsser at the Paris Conservatory and winner of the Prix de Rome in 1949, Delerue is best known for his film scores for French, British, and

American cinema. He wrote music for over 350 films, including films by François Truffaut, Jean-Luc Godard, Bernardo Bertolucci, Oliver Stone, and Mike Nichols. His orchestral works include operas, a ballet, concertos, and chamber music.

Concerto pour cor et orchestre à cordes (1980)
Billaudot, 1980, piano reduction
The horn concerto was written for Daniel Bourge for the Concours International du Festival de Musique de Toulon. In three movements. The first is the most angular writing for the horn, with leaps throughout, and fast gestures in groups of six. The second movement is marked Poco lento, with a plaintive motive growing out of a single repeated note that is echoed throughout the movement. The third movement is in ¾, an Allegro with jaunty writing for the horn and a quasi-cadenza.
Range: G–c³
Duration: 16:00

Demar, Johann Sebastian (1763–1832) France, born in Germany

Concerto D-Dur, für Horn und Orchester
Robert Ostermeyer, 2007, piano reduction and orchestra score
    I. Allegro maestoso
    II. Romance con dolcezza
    III. Rondo: Allegro
The outer movements are for horn in D, while the second movement is for horn in F. Written in classical concerto form, with arpeggiated triplet runs in the first movement and a traditional final-movement rondo in ⁶⁄₈. Moderate range makes this a good student piece. Demar was influenced by the cor-mixte style of Duvernoy, and is known to have visited Paris.
Range: e–e² (g–g² for horn in D)

Dennison, Sam (1926–2005) United States

Sam Dennison was a composer, writer, and curator of the Fleisher Collection of Orchestral Music at the Free Library of Philadelphia.

Adagio for Solo Horn & Chamber Orchestra (1977–1978)
Kalmus, 1983, orchestra score only
First performed in Philadelphia, May 21, 1978, by the Orchestra Society of Philadelphia, Andrzej Jurkiewicz conducting, Morris Goldman, horn soloist; later performed at the Pennsylvania Music Educators Festival by the Eastern State Regional Orchestra. A flowing work with colorful contemporary harmonic language. The horn part is very well paced, with many breaks for the hornist.
Range: f♯–a♭²
Duration: 6:00

Derungs, Gion Antoni (1935–2012) Switzerland

Konzert für Horn und Streichorchester in einem Satz, op. 107 (1985)
Pizzicato Verlag Helvetia, 2000, orchestra score, parts

The published edition is for horn and strings (two violins, viola, cello, and bass) and can be performed with string orchestra or string quintet. The work was premiered in 1989, with the orchestra of the Glarner Musikkollegium, directed by Rudolf Aschmann, Jakob Hefti, horn soloist. In five sections: Moderato—Piu vivo—Lento—Vivo—Quasi allegro—Vivo. This work is full of contrapuntal writing, with legato passages that often sweep upwards from the midrange to the upper midrange and high range of the horn. Being in one continuous movement makes this a difficult work due to endurance challenges, however there are several well-placed breaks.
Range: f♯–b²
Duration: 14:00

Devevey, Pierre and Paul Bonneau

Poeme, pièce pour cor solo et orchestre (ou piano)
Chappell, 1966, piano reduction
Flowing piece in ABA form, with an active middle section that ventures into chromaticism, suitable for the intermediate hornist.
Range: e–b♭²
Duration: 3:28

Devienne, François (1759–1803) France

Flutist, bassoonist, composer, and teacher; known for his flute method.

Horn Concerto in C Major (1785)
KaWe, 1974, piano reduction (Leloir, ed.)
Written for horn in F in the sounding key of C, as was common with French works for horn of this period. Consists of simple melodies embellished with turns and trills. In three continuous sections, it begins with an extensive Allegro in the orchestra, with the horn entering fifty-seven bars later with an Adagio that embellishes a simple tune, followed by a return of the Allegro. Moderately technical, with triplets and sixteenth notes in friendly and familiar patterns. The second section is in § and marked Andantino; the final section is an Allegretto moderato alla polacca.
Range: d¹–b²
Duration: 10:30

Devienne, François, and Duvernoy, Frédéric Nicolas

Horn Concerto in F
The title page of Duvernoy's *Concerto no. 5* lists both Devienne and Duvernoy as composers.
See: Duvernoy, *Concerto No. 5*

Dietrich, Albert (1829–1908) Germany

Einleitung und Romanze, Konzertstück für Horn (oder Violoncello) mit Begleitung des Orchesters, op. 27
Edition Ebenos, 2005 (for horn and piano)
See: Horn and keyboard

Di Lorenzo, Anthony (1967–) United States

Phoenix Horn Concerto (2012)
Art of Sound Music, 2012 (piano version is *Phoenix Sonata*)
> I. Allegro moderato
> II. Andante
> III. Allegro moderato

Originally written for William VerMeulen as a sonata for horn and piano, this
was reworked by the composer into a concerto for horn and full orchestra,
also premiered by VerMeulen in 2014. Modern and tonal, written in the
style of Hollywood film music with a touch of Brahms. The horn part is
virtuosic but very well written for the instrument, showing off its best qualities, both technical and expressive.
Range: d–b²
Duration: 15:00
See: Horn and keyboard

Dillon, Lawrence (1959–) United States

Revenant: Concerto for Horn and Orchestra (2004)
American Composers Alliance, piano reduction
Commissioned and premiered by David Jolley and the Carolina Chamber Symphony on February 25, 2005 at the North Carolina School for the Arts. It
won second prize in the 2005 International Horn Society Composition
Contest. In three movements: Resonance—Revenant—Revelry. A "revenant" is a person who returns from the dead. The composer's preface explains that he was addressing issues surrounding the death of his father,
but was surprised to realize that "the person returning from the dead was
actually me," and the piece is about "losing one's way, and stumbling back
into a renewed awareness and appreciation of life . . . The first movement is
a dirge . . . the second movement is a simple song form, with the return of
the opening melody floating off into the distance. The third movement . . .
is an exuberant dance: short, fast and life-affirming." Contemporary tonal
harmonic language, multiple tonguing, sustained high notes, but overall,
the horn writing is well paced for the soloist.
Range: c–b²
Duration: 18:00

Dimmler, Franz Anton (1753–1827) Germany
Dimmler was a horn player in the Mannheim orchestra and later in his career
was a double-bass player after the orchestra moved to Munich.

Concerto in Es (mi♭) per corno
Hans Pizka, 1983, piano reduction and full score
This classical concerto is in the typical three-movement form: Allegro—Adagio
—Rondeaux. The first movement has several technical passages that stay
up in the high range. The second-movement Adagio is brief, and the last
movement is a spirited rondo in ¾.
Range: f¹–c³ (g¹–d³ for horn in E♭)

Domažlický, František (1913–1997) Czech Republic

Koncert pro lesní roh a orchestr (1971)
Editio Supraphon, 1974, piano reduction
  I. Allegro non troppo, un poco marciale
  II. Andante religioso
  III. Allegro vivace

The first movement is relatively short, with contrapuntal motives, dissonant at times, and angular writing for the horn. The second movement begins with a lyrical melody that grows increasingly active. The final movement, in changing meters, develops a syncopated theme. Moderately difficult, with some chromatic writing. Lower-octave options are given for high b♭²s at the end of the first and third movements.
Range: A–b♭²
Duration: 16:00

Domnich, Heinrich (1767–1844) France, born in Germany
Domnich came from a family of horn players, was born in Germany, and moved to Paris in 1783 to study with Giovanni Punto. He remained in Paris, played with the Paris Opera, and taught at the Paris Conservatory. He wrote the first method book for horn, *Méthode de premier et de second cor,* as well as chamber music, three horn concertos, and a concerto for two horns and orchestra.

Concerto No. 1 for the First Horn (ca. 1800)
Solitárius Press, 2013, piano reduction (Evan Chancellor, ed.)
In three movements: Allegro moderato—Romanza—Rondo. This work is for cor alto, emphasizing the horn's high range and lyrical capabilities. Good endurance is required, as many passages venture above the staff.
Range: g–c³
Duration: 10:43

Concerto No. 2 for the Second Horn (ca. 1805–1810)
Solitárius Press, 2013, piano reduction (Evan Chancellor, ed.)
In three movements: Maestoso—Romance, Andantino—Rondeau. Emphasizes the agility characteristic of cor-basse writing. Flexibility and negotiating wide leaps are necessary technical skills required of the horn soloist for this work.
Range: c–g²
Duration: 11:37

Doren, Theo Van (1898–1974) Belgium

Concerto voor hoorn in fa en klavier: pour cor en fa et piano
Editions Metropolis, 1958, piano reduction
In three short movements played without pause, quite straightforward writing for the horn, with regular phrases in traditional rhythmic patterns and harmonic language.
Range: c–a²
Duration: 11:00

Driessler, Johannes (1921–1998) Germany
Driessler was a composer, organist, and teacher, best known for his choral music. He wrote several instrumental concertos in the early 1950s.

Concerto for Horn and String Orchestra, op. 16 (1950)
Bärenreiter, 1951, orchestra score
This work is in traditional harmonic language and form. The first movement, marked Allegro non troppo, is in $\frac{3}{4}$, with shifting rhythmic patterns. Passages alternate between stopped and open writing for the horn and contain large leaps. The second movement, marked Molto adagio, is in $\frac{3}{2}$, and explores the horn's midrange, with legato passages on and around middle c, requiring flexibility in moving between the high and low ranges. The final movement, in $\frac{3}{2}$, is an Allegro vivace con brio, which does not let up in intensity.
Range: d–b♭²
Duration: 18:00

Dubois, Pierre Max (1930–1995) France
Dubois was trained and later taught at the Paris Conservatory. Winner of the Prix de Rome in 1955, he was a prolific composer of instrumental music, and in particular is known for his music for winds.

Concerto pour cor et orchestre (1957)
Alphonse Leduc, 1957, piano reduction
This is an engaging work in three movements. The first movement is propelled along with a continuous sixteenth-note motive. The second movement is a lyrical Andante molto in $\frac{4}{4}$, and the third movement, marked Allegro vivo, is in $\frac{6}{8}$. This work is witty and fun to play. With traditional major-minor tonality, phrasing, and rhythm, the technical requirements are kept at a reasonable level. The challenge in this work is the endurance required. Careful pacing from the hornist will be important, particularly in the last movement, with a cadenza that builds up to an exciting high c³.
Range: e–c³
Duration: 15:00

Dubois, Theodore (1837–1924) France

Cavatine pour cor avec de petit orchestra
See: Horn and keyboard

Dukas, Paul (1865–1935) France

Villanelle
See: Horn and keyboard

Durkó, Zsolt (1934–1977) Hungary

Iconography No. 2 for Horn Solo and Chamber Ensemble (1971)
Editio Musica Budapest, 1971, full score only

Dedicated to and written for Marek Kopelent. For solo horn and flute, oboe, clarinet, violin, viola, cello, and percussion. In nine movements that vary in length, this is an atmospheric work, written in contemporary harmonic language. Expressive and colorful writing in legato, often in wide intervals over the active and colorful ensemble. There are also fast chromatic gestures and scherzando-like writing. Challenging writing, but there are intervals of rest for the horn soloist.

Range: f–b^2
Duration: 10:20

Duvernoy, Frédéric Nicolas (1765–1838) France
Horn virtuoso, one of the first members of a truly French school of horn players and teachers. He played in the Comédie-Italienne, Opéra-Comique, before becoming solo horn of the Paris Opera. Duvernoy taught at the Paris Conservatory from its founding in 1795 until 1815. He composed twelve concertos for horn and orchestra and many other chamber and solo works. In contrast to other horn virtuosi in France, such as Domnich and, later, Dauprat (and apparently much to their consternation), Duvernoy was a proponent of cor-mixte writing, in which the horn was played almost exclusively on the F crook, and in the written range of g below middle c to g^2 at the top of the staff, removing the higher notes of the cor-alto range, as well as the lowest notes of the cor-basse range. Within this range he specialized in agile technique and fast notes. This smaller range can be seen in each of his concertos, and all concertos are pitched in F. Duration for each is between twelve and fifteen minutes.

Concerto no. 1 (1795)
Robert Ostermeyer, 2008, piano reduction and orchestra score
   I. Allegro
   II. Adagio
   III. Rondeu
Range: g–g^2

Concerto No. 2 (1796)
Robert Ostermeyer, 2008, piano reduction and orchestra score
In three continuous sections: Adagio—Andante—Allegro. Written for horn in F, in the keys of C minor, G major, and C major.
Range: f♯–a♭^{2}

Concerto No. 3
Robert Ostermeyer, 2008, piano reduction and orchestra score
In three continuous sections: Allegro—Andante—Rondo: Allegro. The end of the first section has a recitative section, with opportunities for short cadenzas.
Range: g–g^2

Concerto No. 4 (ca. 1800)
Robert Ostermeyer, 2008, piano reduction and orchestra score
In three contiguous sections: Allegro—Adagio—Polanaise.
Range: g–g^2

Concerto No. 5 in F Major for Horn and Orchestra (ca.1788)
KaWe, 1965, piano reduction (Leloir, ed.); Robert Ostermeyer, 2008, piano reduction and orchestra score
   I. Allegro
   II. Andantino, Pastorale
   III. Rondeau: Allegretto
Duvernoy wrote this with his colleague, the flutist and bassoonist François Devienne. There is an extensive tutti introduction, similar to Devienne's horn concerto. Some cor-basse moments of fast notes, and much of the passage-work centers around the bottom of the staff, in the octave between g and g^1, but idiomatically written.
Range: $g–g^2$
Duration: 15:00

Concerto No. 6
Robert Ostermeyer, 2008, piano reduction and orchestra score
   I. Allegro
   II. Andantino
   III. Polonaise: Allegro
Range: $g–g^2$

Concerto No. 7 (1805)
Robert Ostermeyer, 2008, piano reduction and orchestra score
   I. Allegro moderato
   II. Larghetto
   III. Rondo: Allegretto
Range: $c–a\flat^2$
Duration: 12:00

Concerto No. 8 (1805)
Robert Ostermeyer, 2008, piano reduction and orchestra score
   I. Allegro
   II. Cantabile
   III. Rondo: Allegretto
Duration: 14:00
Range: $f\sharp–a\flat^2$

Concerto No. 9 (1812)
Robert Ostermeyer, 2008, piano reduction and orchestra score
   I. Allegro maestoso
   II. Cantabile
   III. Allegretto
Range: $c–a\flat^2$

Concerto No. 10
Robert Ostermeyer, 2008, piano reduction and orchestra score
   I. Allegro
   II. Larghetto
   III. Allegro
Range: $f\sharp–a\flat^2$

Concerto No. 11
Robert Ostermeyer, 2009, piano reduction and orchestra score
    I. Allegro moderato
    II. Siciliano
    III. Allegretto
Range: f–a♭²

Concerto No. 12
Robert Ostermeyer, 2009, piano reduction and orchestra score
    I. Allegro
    II. Larghetto
    III. Allegretto
Range: f♯–a♭²

Dvarionas, Balys (1904–1972) Lithuania
Composer, conductor, and pianist, taught at the Kanas Conservatory, composed the Lithuanian national anthem.

Concerto for Horn and Orchestra (Kontśert dlíā valtorny s orkestrom) (1963)
Muzyka, 1966, piano reduction
In four movements and full of variety and character. The first movement is bold, marked Allegro risoluto, the second is a biting Allegretto marciale with contrasting sections of cantabile writing, the third movement is marked Tempo di sarabanda in ³⁄₂, and the fourth movement is a very light and fast Allegro molto. Only moderately technical, with a tessitura mostly in the staff.
Range: g–a²
Duration: 15:00

Edwards, Ross (1943–) Australia
New Grove says that Ross Edwards is in possession of "one of the most convincing voices in Australian music in the decades either side of the millennium, and its development is ongoing, especially in the growing body of solo concertos."

Aria and Transcendental Dance, for Solo Horn and String Orchestra (1990)
Universal, 1990, orchestra score only
Written for Hector McDonald, horn, and the Rantos Collegium. The aria opens with an extensive passage for horn alone, which the composer describes as a "dramatic horn monologue whose thematic substance is ideally suited to development along symphonic lines." The strings enter, the music builds to a climax, and there is resolution "with protracted Mahlerian cadential gestures." The dance features the horn over "drone-based" strings, leading to a "full-blooded episode which silences the horn. There is no final resolution, however, and the work ends abruptly and mysteriously like a chorus of cicadas." (www.rossedwards.com) This is a challenging work for horn, written in contemporary language with mixed meters and intricate rhythmic gestures.
Range: A–b²
Duration: 12:00

Eechaute, Prosper van (1904–1964) Belgium

Poème nocturne: pour cor et orchestre ou piano (1938)
Editions Metropolis, 1963, piano reduction
Highly romantic one-movement work, marked Andante non troppo lento, with
    expressive, dramatic writing for the horn. The orchestration is rich and full,
    with colorful wind writing. Premiered by Maurice van Bocxstaele, horn,
    November 17, 1962, with the composer conducting.
Range: A–d^3 (ossia to high b♭^{2})
Duration: 8:45

Eisma, Will (1929–) Netherlands, born in Indonesia
Throughout his career, Eisma has experimented with different composition techniques such as serial music, graphic notation, and electronic music.

Vanbridge Concerto for Horn and Orchestra (1970, rev. 1986)
Donemus, orchestra score
Commissioned by the NOS (Nederlands Omroep Stichting), written for Jan Ver-
    bruggen.
Duration: 16:00

Eisner, Carl (1802–1874) Germany
Eisner was a horn virtuoso who also held court orchestra positions in St. Petersburg and Dresden.

Scene und Arie, für Horn und Orchester, op. 10
Robert Ostermeyer, 2009, piano reduction and orchestra score
Written for the valve horn, this work is dedicated to Carl Schunke. Made up of
    several sections in $\frac{4}{4}$ and played without break, it opens with an extensive
    recitative for the horn, followed by andante and allegretto sections. This is
    a showpiece for the horn soloist, with straightforward melodic writing and
    technical passages of sixteenth notes and several brief cadenzas to show-
    case the horn's technical abilities.
Range: e–b^2
Duration: 8:30

Eklund, Hans (1927–1999) Sweden
Concerto for horn and chamber orchestra (1979)
Carl Gehrmans Musikförlag, 1980, piano reduction and orchestra score
    I. Adagio ma non troppo
    II. Allegro giocoso
For solo horn, strings and timpani. Premiered April 5, 1979, Albert Linder, horn,
    with the Gothenburg Symphony Orchestra, Charles Dutoit conducting.
    Written in contemporary tonal language, the first movement opens with
    a dramatic motive in the strings, with wide intervals of dotted eighth-six-
    teenths, answered by a declamatory statement in the horn. This is followed
    by a cantabile melody, slow and plaintive. The driving second movement is

based on the wide intervallic gestures of the first movement opening, with an extensive cadenza for the horn. Moderately technical, with wide leaps in the second movement, many in a high tessitura.
Range: c♯–c³
Duration: 12:00

Eler, André-Frédéric (1764–1821) France

Concerto Nr. I für Horn und Orchester
Robert Ostermeyer, 2008, piano reduction and orchestra score
For horn in F. Originally published in 1796, this is the first of two concertos by Eler; the second is unpublished. Written in the cor-mixte style, the range does not extend far above the staff. In three traditional movements, the writing for horn is light and pleasant. The technical demands are manageable, with many tutti breaks for the hornist and sixteenth and triplet figures in diatonic patterns. The second movement is a nice melody that becomes more heavily ornamented as it progresses. Pleasing music in the French style.
Range: B–a²
Duration: 20:00

Eversole, James (1929–) United States

Athedra V: Dances of Life, for Horn and String Orchestra (1994)
James Eversole, 1994, piano reduction
In three movements. The first, "Dance of passion," is rhythmic, in a 3+3+2 pattern. The second movement, "Dance of love," is flowing and lyrical over rich romantic harmonies. The third movement, "Dance of joy," also highly rhythmic, is based on the composer's recollections of his youth in Kentucky, incorporating its rhythms and its open fourths and fifths.
Range: b♭–c³
Duration: 13:30

Ewazen, Eric (1954–) United States

Concerto for Horn and String Orchestra (2002)
Theodore Presser, 2011, piano reduction
Written for Gregory Hustis, principal horn of the Dallas Symphony, who also recorded the work. In three traditional movements. Ewazen explains in the liner notes of the recording that the piece is "filled with sonorities that I heard growing up. My background is Polish/Ukrainian, and I always heard the music of Eastern Europe as a youngster. My father used to do traditional Ukrainian dancing. I enjoyed the exciting rhythms and the modal harmonic world of that music, and I have incorporated that sound into this concerto." The horn opens the first movement with a declamatory line over driving eighth notes and continues its dialogue with the strings throughout, with singing wide leaps, fast eighth- and sixteenth-note figures. The second movement is lyrical, in ¾, with the horn singing in the more mellow

midrange. There is a contrasting middle section that becomes more active with sixteenth notes before returning to the main theme. The third movement, in $\frac{4}{4}$, is full of syncopated rhythms in counterpoint with the strings. Requires long-range endurance and solid technique, but well paced for the horn soloist.

Range: d–c³
Duration: 21:44

Faust, Randall (1947–) United States

Concerto for Horn and Wind Ensemble (1987)
Faust Music, 1987, full score; piano reductions published separately for each movement
    I. Prelude-Nocturne
    II. Scherzo
    III. Cadenza and fanfare
    IV. Rondo
Premiered at the 1987 International Horn Society Workshop, Thomas Bacon, horn soloist with the Provo Wind Consort. Each movement is for a different hornist. The first movement is for Marvin Howe and is scored for horn and percussion and features legato lines in the horn and stopped writing. The second movement is dedicated to Thomas Bacon, and is a riff on a semitone pattern that Thomas Bacon would warm up on. The third movement is dedicated to Paul Anderson and borrows features from Gallay's unmeasured preludes. The fourth movement is dedicated to Ignaz Leutgeb, for whom Mozart wrote his horn concertos, and it is full of humor and lighthearted playing in rondo form.

Range: G–c³
Duration: 14:00

Festive Processional for Horn and Band (2001, 2013)
Faust Music, 2013, horn and wind ensemble, horn and organ
Originally scored for horn and organ, later arranged for horn and wind ensemble in the key of concert B♭. The composer indicates it is grade III for band.

Range: c¹–f²
Duration: 3:00

Feld, Jindrick (Jindřich) (1925–2007) Czech Republic

Pièce de concert, pour cor en fa et piano ou orchestre (1966)
Duration: 6:00
See: Horn and keyboard

Fesca, Friedrich Ernst (1789–1826) Germany

Andante und Rondo für Horn und Orchester, op. 39 (1825)
Robert Ostermeyer, 2001, piano reduction and orchestra score

Dedicated to Carl Schunke. The Ostermeyer edition is based on a Simrock edition from 1826. The lyrical Andante is in $^6_8$, in minor, with echo effects at the end of the piece. The Rondo is marked Allegretto in $^2_4$, full of virtuosic sixteenth-note and triplet-eighth runs.
Range: c–c³
Duration: 18:30

Fick, Peter Joachim (?–1743) Germany
Little is known about Fick, who worked as an organist, composer, and copyist at the Court of Schwerin.

Concerto a 5 ex Dis-Dur, für corno da chasse, due violin, viola con bassus
Robert Ostermeyer, 1999, 2004, piano reduction and orchestra score
This concerto in E♭ major is in three movements. The first is an Allegro moderato, the second a brief Larghetto, the third an Allegro ma non troppo in $^6_8$. It is written in the baroque *concertato* style, with the horn playing many florid passages above the staff.
Range: f¹–c³ (g¹–d³ for horn in E♭)
Duration: 12:00

Filas, Juraj (1955–) Czech Republic, born Slovak Republic
Composer, pianist, singer. Filas is professor of composition at the Prague Conservatory.

Concerto for Horn and Wind Orchestra (2004)
Editions BIM, 2004, wind band score; study score with solo part
The concerto is dedicated to Musikgesellschaft Belalp-Naters. Through-composed in two sections, with smaller sections within that alternate in character and tempo, this piece features traditional idioms, such as horn calls on open fifths, heroic figures, legato writing, and syncopated lines that give it a romantic character in a contemporary tonal language.
Range: e♭–c³
Duration: 15:00

Firsova, Elena (1950–) United Kingdom, born in Russia

Chamber Concerto No. 4 for Horn and 13 Performers, op. 37 (1987)
Sikorski, 1993, full score only
One of many chamber concertos that Firsova has written featuring solo instruments, it was premiered March 18, 1989, at Queen Elizabeth Hall, London, with Michael Thompson, horn and the London Sinfonietta conducted by Oliver Knussen. This work is in one continuous movement and is intimate like a chamber work but has the drama and intensity of a horn concerto, with flowing writing, virtuosic passages, and a cadenza.
Range: B–c³
Duration: 12:00

Flosman, Oldrich (1925–1998) Czech Republic

Koncert pro lesní roh a orchestr (1970)
Panton, 1972, piano reduction (rev. by Miloš Petr)
  I. Grave—Allegro
  II. Adagio
  III. Vivace
Premiered March 4, 1971, Miloš Petr, horn with the Plzeň-Radio-Orchestra. Expressive and brooding, in three traditional movements, and reminiscent of Shostakovich. The middle movement is accompanied by the steady beat of a lone snare drum (piano reduction includes snare drum).
Range: A♭–b²
Duration: 18:00

Flothuis, Marius (1914–2001) Netherlands
Musicologist and composer; worked with the Concertgebouw Orchestra as assistant to the music director and later became professor of musicology at Utrecht University.

Concerto pour cor principal et petit orchestra, op. 24 (1945)
Donemus, 1950, piano reduction
The first movement opens with a declamatory statement in the horn, followed by angular writing in a fast three, interspersed with sections of longer legato lines. The second movement is a somber Grave et très soutenu, requiring endurance to maintain an intense *forte* through most of the movement. The final movement alternates between ¾ and ⅛ and is not technically difficult, but the lighting fast tempo adds to the challenge.
Range: a–b²
Duration: 16:00

Förster, Christoph (1693–1745) Germany

Concerto in E♭ for Horn and String Orchestra
Hofmeister, 1956, piano reduction (Janetzky, ed.); Schirmer, 1977, piano reduction, includes E♭ and F parts (Tuckwell, ed.); Robert Ostermeyer, 2013, piano reduction and full score
In three movements: Con descrezione—Adagio—Allegro. This is concerto I/5 from the eighteenth-century-manuscript collection of horn music, Katalog Wenster Literature I/1–17b in the Universitetsbiblioteket in Lund, Sweden. The Hofmeister edition is based on another set of parts in the Sächsischen Landesbibliotek in Dresden. Written in the clarino style of the high baroque, this piece is typical of the florid solo-horn writing of the period, including fast sixteenth notes, trills, and other characteristic ornaments throughout. The Hofmeister edition is a clean edition without ornaments. The Schirmer edition contains ornaments, added by Barry Tuckwell.
Range: b♭–c³
Duration: 12:20

Concerto No. 2 in E♭ for Horn and Strings
Hans Pizka Edition, 1981, piano reduction, orchestra score with five parts; Mc-
    Coy's Horn Library, 1981, piano reduction (Scharnberg, ed.)
This is concerto I/12 from the eighteenth-century-manuscript collection of horn
    music, Katalog Wenster Literature I/1–17b in the Universitetsbiblioteket in
    Lund, Sweden. In three movements: Allegro—Adagio—Allegro assai. This
    piece exemplifies florid baroque writing, with a lyrical second movement.
    Similar to many baroque works in its demanding tessitura.
Range: f¹–d³
Duration: 9:30

Fox, Frederick (1931–2011) United States
Fred Fox studied composition with Bernhard Heiden and Ross Lee Finney, and
was on the composition faculty at Indiana University for many years.

Essay for French Horn and Wind Ensemble (1962)
University Microfilms, 1967, wind ensemble score
Written under the auspices of the Music Educators National Conference's Con-
    temporary Music Project for Creativity in Music Education Composers in
    Public Schools program, this work was first performed in 1963 by the Uni-
    versity of Minnesota Concert Band. It opens with a somber theme for the
    horn accompanied by two flutes, then develops freely, heading into more
    declamatory writing for the horn soloist before returning to the opening
    theme. The preface indicates the level of difficulty is for advanced high
    school band. Appropriate for college ensemble as well, with a few mixed
    meters, syncopated rhythms, and chromatic writing for the winds. The
    horn writing is well paced, with one section of double tonguing, making
    this suitable for the high school or early college player.
Range: a–a♭²
Duration: 8:00–9:00

Frackenpohl, Arthur (1924–) United States
Frackenpohl studied at Eastman; McGill; Tanglewood, with Darius Milhaud;
and at Founatainbleau, with Nadia Boulanger. He taught composition and piano
at the Crane School of Music, State University of New York Potsdam, for over
thirty-five years.

Largo and Allegro for Horn and String Orchestra (or Horn and String Quartet)
(1962)
Piano reduction in G. Schirmer collection *Solos for the Horn Player,* 1962 (Mason
    Jones, ed.)
This work features flowing counterpoint between the horn and strings. The Largo
    is somber and lyrical, with expressive wide leaps in the solo horn. The Alle-
    gro features syncopated rhythms that move the piece forward. Of medium
    difficulty.
Range: f–b♭² (ossia f–c³)
Duration: 6:00

Francaix, Jean (1912–1997) France

Divertimento for Horn and Strings
Édition Musicales Transatlantiques, 1959, version for horn and strings available
    on rental
See: Horn and keyboard

Francis, Alun (1943–) United Kingdom (Wales)

Serenata for Horn and Strings (1962)
J. Weinberger, 1972, orchestra score only
    I. Andante, sempre rubato
   II. Allegro giocoso, sempre marcato
In two movements. The first is expressive, with a short cadenza. The second is in
    ABA form, with outer sections of a driving motive in $\frac{3}{4}$, occasional changing
    meters and a slow middle section that is a passacaglia. Written in contem-
    porary tonal/modal language. There are a few technical motives to negoti-
    ate in the second movement and some passages above the staff, but, over-
    all, the tessitura and pacing make this a suitable work for the college-level
    player and above.
Range: d–b^2
Duration: 15:00

Frehse, Albin (1878–1973) Germany
Frehse was solo horn of the Gewandhausorchester Leipzig and taught at the
Staatlichen Hochschule für Musik Leipzig; he is also known for his editions of
Kopprasch etudes, Reicha trios, orchestral-studies books, and his own trios and
duos for horns.

Konzert für Waldhorn mit Klavier oder Orchesterbegleitung
Hofmeister, 1952, piano reduction
Frehse wrote this concerto for his friend and colleague, Wilhelm Krüger, solo
    horn with the Gewandhausorchester Leipzig. Typical nineteenth-centu-
    ry-style writing, in three movements. This is a work that showcases the
    horn soloist, with the orchestra (or piano) playing a simple accompani-
    ment. Pleasing, traditional, and not too difficult.
Range: g–b♭^{2}
Duration: 16:00

Fridl [Friedl, Friedel], Carl, Germany
Carl Fridl is listed in the Electoral Bavarian Court Calendar as late as 1802 as
court trumpeter, and there were several other court trumpeters and timpanists
in the family Fridl.

Concerto ex dis per corno principale
Hans Pizka Edition, 1979, piano reduction and orchestra score
This edition is based on an autograph manuscript in Hans Pizka's personal col-
    lection. In three movements, written in the classical style: Allegro mae-

stoso—Amoroso andante—Rondo: Allegretto. Challenging cor-alto writing, limited to one-and-a-half octaves with many runs up into the high register. The middle movement is identical to the second movement of the Anton Teyber first concerto. It is possible that Carl Fridl may have been the copyist only. If this is the case, the concerto would be attributed as Anonymous.

Range: f^1–c^3 (g^1–d^3 for horn in E♭)
Duration: 12:30

Friedman, Stanley (1951–) United States
Stanley Friedman is a trumpeter and award winning composer.

Jerusalem Fugue, for Solo Horn & Strings (1996)
Editions BIM, 1996, piano reduction and orchestra score
For horn and string quartet or string orchestra, with optional basses. Commissioned by James Cox and the International Horn Society, Meir Rimon Commissioning Assistance Fund. Dedicated to "Jim and Eva." In one continuous movement of contrasting sections. Quite free, with many opportunities for rubato and expressive playing. Muted passages, with a horn-call motive that returns and is developed throughout the piece.

Range: e–c^3
Duration: 15:00

Frumerie, Gunnar de (1908–1987) Sweden

Konsert för valthorn och orkester, op. 70 (1971–72)
C. Gehrmans Musikförlag, 1974, piano reduction
Written for Ib Lanzky-Otto. In two movements. The first is lyrical and dramatic, with colorful pastoral moments that contrast with driving motives that move the piece forward with intensity. The second movement, marked Andante sostenuto, begins with an extensive solo for horn alone, with horn-call motives and echo effects of stopped writing. The winds join in for an Allegretto in ⁶⁄₈. Features romantic and big writing for horn, mostly traditional in its harmonic language with colorful orchestration. Good endurance required, particularly for several passages that begin above the staff and remain there.

Range: B–c^3
Duration: 20:00

Fuchs, Kenneth (1956–) United States

Canticle to the Sun, Concerto for Horn and Orchestra (2005)
Piedmont Music, 2007, piano reduction
Dedicated to Timothy Jones. Premiered by Richard Todd and the Hartford Symphony Orchestra, April 29, 2008. Inspired by the Protesant hymn, "All Creatures of Our God and King." The composer's preface explains that the soloist plays the role of celebrant, "leading the players of the orchestra in

a vibrant affirmation of beautiful melody, color, and texture." In one continuous movement. The horn rises out of a sparkling opening string texture, "weaving a lyrical strand of melody based upon the hymn tune." The work is full of contrasting sections—Energico, Scherzando, Nobilmente, Maestoso, Fugato—interspersed with two cadenzas for the horn. The final section, Fugato, is followed by a coda, with a return of the opening melody.

Range: e–c³
Duration: 20:00

Fuchs [Fux], Peter (1753–1851) Austria

Konzert in E-Dur für Horn in E and Orchester
Hans Pizka Edition, 1988, piano reduction and full score (revised and arranged by Edmond Leloir)
    Allegro
    Romance, Adagio
    Rondo, Allegretto
Although this piece is billed as a concerto in E in the title, the piano reduction is in E♭. This could mean that the piece was originally in E, and was arranged in E♭ for this edition. The three movements follow the form and style of a classical concerto, however the outstanding feature is the extreme range for the horn, extending up to written high g³.

Range: f¹–f³ with ossia d¹–f³ (g¹–g³ with ossia e¹–g³ for horn in E♭)
Duration: 14:00

Fujikura, Dai (1977–) United Kingdom, born in Japan

wave embraced (2006)
Ricordi, full score
For solo horn and ensemble of flute, oboe, bass clarinet, bassoon, trumpet, trombone, two percussion, piano, two violins, viola, cello, and double bass. Commissioned by BIT20 Ensemble, who premiered the work with Saar Berger, horn soloist, December 5, 2009. The ensemble is organized in two groups on stage with the horn soloist in the center. The composer writes that he "imagined two different ensembles containing two different kinds of liquid, which make up a pond. The solo horn excites this liquid and sounds grow out of it, and sometimes absorb back in to it . . . the right hand side group is reacting to the 'open' notes of the solo horn. Their reaction is espressivo and romantic in character. The left hand side group is reacting to the 'stopped' notes played by the solo horn . . . their musical material is plucking, harsh and hard." (www.daifujikura.com/un/lw_wave_embraced .html) The horn writing has wide leaps in continuously changing tempos and meters, wide dynamic contrasts, "same note" trills, flutter tonguing, and stopped writing.

Range: g–a♯³
Duration: 13:43

Fürst, Paul Walter (1926–2013) Austria
Violist and composer. Was a member of the Munich Philharmonic and the Vienna Philharmonic.

Rannoch-Concerto, op. 59
Doblinger, 1984, piano reduction
In one continuous movement of contrasting sections. The first section is energetic, with motives that shift between ⅜ and ¾. A slow second section features the horn playing expressive gestures against the orchestra texture, and an extensive cadenza. This is followed by a ⅜ reminiscent of traditional hunting horn character. A slow section of expressive writing is followed by an energetic finale in two. This is a challenging work for the horn soloist, suitable for the advanced college student and above, requiring solid technique and good endurance. There are a few extended techniques such as trills, flutter tonguing, stopped writing, glissandi.
Range: B♭–c³
Duration: 20:00

Gabler, Egon (1876–1959) Germany

Konzert für Waldhorn
Louis Oertel, 1904, piano reduction (available on imslp.org)
    I. Allegro moderato
    II. Adagio
    III. Allegro molto
Dedicated to Emil Wipperich, first horn in the K.K. Hofoperntheaters in Wien. Late romantic concerto in traditional three-movement form and harmonic style. The writing stays mostly in the staff, but this is an extended work, and the relatively long stretches of melodic material for the soloist require good long-range endurance.
Range: c–b♭²
Duration: ca. 22:00

Gallay, Jacques François (1795–1864) France
Renowned hornist, composer, and professor at the Paris Conservatory, Gallay wrote chamber and solo works for horn as well as studies and a method book.

Concerto for horn and orchestra, op. 18 (1818)
KaWe 1969, piano reduction (Leloir, ed.); Breitkopf & Härtel, parts are on imslp.org
Gallay wrote two concertos for horn, this is the only one published in a modern edition, and is sometimes referred to as *Concerto No. 1.* This is written for horn in F and in three movements: Allegro risoluto—Adagio ma non tanto—Rondo. There are opportunities for brief cadenzas in the second and third movements. By the time of this composition, the hand horn was viewed as a fully chromatic instrument. Like all of Gallay's music, this work pushes the boundaries of hand horn technique. Written in a style similar to the etudes, with straightforward lyrical melodies and diatonic

scalar and arpeggiated passages with chromatic inflections. The tessitura often hovers at the top of the staff, requiring good endurance.

Range: c¹–b²
Duration: 13:30

Gedike [Goedicke], Aleksandr Fyodorovich (1877–1957) Russia

New Grove calls Gedike the "guardian of strict classical traditions in Russian music."

Concerto, op. 40, for horn and piano
International, 1967, piano reduction (James Chambers, ed.)
This is unabashedly romantic writing for the horn, harking back to Russian romantic style and to Richard Strauss. The first movement is in $\frac{4}{4}$, with lyrical writing that gives way to triplet motives and finishes with an extensive cadenza. The second movement, marked Adagio, is in $\frac{3}{4}$, with few breaks for the horn soloist, and several stopped passages. The third movement is a rondo in $\frac{6}{8}$. Agile writing requiring good endurance, suitable for the upper-level undergraduate player and above.

Range: d♭–c³
Duration: 18:00

Gehra, August (Heinrich?) (1715–1785) Germany

Concerto ex D-Dur für cornu concertato, 2 Violinen, Viola & Basso
Robert Ostermeyer, 1999, piano reduction and orchestra score
This work is known as no. 17b of the horn concerto manuscripts located at Lund University Library, in the Ms. Kat. Wenster Litt. I/1–17b. Written for horn in D, it is in three movements characteristic of the classical style: Allegro molto—Affetuoso—Allegro un poco presto. Wide leaps between low and high octaves, triplet figures, and arpeggio runs signify a typical cor-basse concerto. The first movement has several passages that extend diatonically from g below written middle c down to low C, showing off the soloist's command of these "factitious" low notes on the natural horn, which are particularly challenging.

Range: A–f♯² (c–a² for horn in D)
Duration: 17:00

Genzmer, Harald (1909–2007) Germany
Genzmer studied composition with Paul Hindemith, and taught composition at the Hochschule für Musik in Freiburg im Breisgau and later in Munich.

Notturno for Horn and Strings
Henry Litolff's Verlag / C.F. Peters, 1971, piano reduction
A short work in ABA form, opening with a flowing Andante tranquillo in $\frac{3}{4}$, with an expressive horn line over moving sixteenth notes in the strings. The contrasting middle section is marked Vivace and is organized around a triplet motive. The expressive lines of the opening melody return, this time with the strings playing pizzicato, reaching a quiet conclusion. The moder-

ate range, diatonic language, and modest technical requirements make this suitable for the intermediate hornist.

Range: c¹–a²
Duration: 4:15

George, Thom Ritter (1942–) United States
George was a composer and arranger for the United States Navy Band in Washington, D.C., and is currently professor of music at Idaho State University.

Concerto Grosso No. 5, CN 168, for French horn and string orchestra (1963)
Luck's Music Library, 1972, piano reduction
This piece was written while George was a student at Eastman. In three short
    movements. The first is in $\frac{4}{4}$, marked cantabile with long legato lines and a
    faster middle section of syncopated rhythms. The second movement is an
    Adagio in $\frac{3}{4}$, and the final movement is in $\frac{6}{8}$, with a return of the first-move-
    ment theme. Well paced and of medium difficulty; quick tonguing is re-
    quired in the final $\frac{6}{8}$. First performance March 16, 1964, Eastman School of
    Music, Herbert Spencer, horn, Byron Hanson, Piano.
Range: c–c³
Duration: 9:00

Horn Concerto (2006–2007)
Available from the composer
        I. Fanfares: Allegro moderato,
        II. Oh, waillie! waillie! Lamentoso
        III. Rondo: Allegro giocoso
Premiered by Alexander Ritter George and the Idaho State Civic Symphony on
    April 18, 2007. In three movements and written in a tonal style.
Range: g–b♭²
See also: Alexander Ritter George, "Concerto for Horn by Thom Ritter George,"
    The Horn Call 39 (February 2009): 41–43.

Gerster, Ottmar (1897–1969) Germany
Gerster, a violinist and violist, attended the Hoch Conservatory in Frankfurt
where he studied with Bernhard Sekles. He played in the Frankfurt Symphony
then held several teaching posts during his career.

Konzert für Horn und Orchester (1958)
Edition Peters, 1962, piano reduction by Gunther Hauer
This work is in three traditional movements, reminiscent of Hindemith, with
    motives based on fourths and fifths, dotted rhythms, and contrapuntal
    writing. The first movement is in $\frac{3}{4}$, with a cadenza; the second movement
    is a lyrical notturno in a very slow tempo, requiring control in phrasing.
    The third movement is in $\frac{6}{8}$ and develops a motive based on fourths and
    fifths. This is a very accessible work, very well paced, and suitable for the
    college-level player.
Range: f–c³
Duration: 15:00

Gillingham, David (1947–) United States

Concerto for Horn and Symphonic Band (2007)
C. Alan Publications, 2008, piano reduction and full score
  1. Fanfares
  2. Supplication
  3. Dance Refrains
Commissioned and premiered by the Gower Community Band of St. John's, New-
  foundland, Edsel Bonnell, director, Bruce Bonnell, horn. In three movements. The first develops a fast and agile fanfare motive, with contrasting
  lyrical writing that is interrupted by the horn fanfares. The second movement is based on a lovely hymn tune by Edsel Bonnell, and begins with a
  simple lyrical line in the horn, followed by a section of obbligato sixteenth
  notes as the horn takes on a supporting role under solo lines in the band,
  before a triumphant return of the opening melody. The final movement,
  marked *with fire & spirit* in §, is the most virtuosic for both the soloist and
  the ensemble, with a frenzied, dance-like character and writing that moves
  all over the ranges of the horn. Themes from the first and second movement
  return, followed by a cadenza. This is a challenging work for the advanced
  player, requiring agility, good endurance, flexibility, and solid high range.
Range: c♯–c³
Duration: 20:00

Gillmann, Kurt (1889–1974) Germany
Harpist and composer Kurt Gillmann was born in Berlin, played in the Hannover
Opera Orchestra, and was professor of harp at the West Berlin Musikhochschule.

Konzert für Waldhorn und Orchester, op. 45
H.L. Grahl, 1950, piano reduction
In three movements. The opening movement, marked Moderato con moto, is full
  of changing tempos, with short sections of agitato that relax into expressive
  tranquillo writing. Momentum builds to the end of the movement through
  triplet figures. The second movement is marked Andante, and the third
  movement is a spirited rondo in ¾ that borrows from the traditional syncopated rhythms of the polacca.
Range: b♭–b²
Duration: 22:00

Gipps, Ruth (1921–1999) United Kingdom
Ruth Gipps, composer, conductor, pianist, and oboist, studied composition with
Gordon Jacob, R. O. Morris, and Vaughan Williams. She is known for her sym-
phonic music and chamber works.

Horn Concerto (1968)
Tickerage Press, 1991, piano reduction
    I. Con Moto—Tranquillo—Cadenza
   II. Scherzo: Allegretto
  III. Finale: Allegro ritmico—giocoso

Dedicated to the composer's son, hornist Lance Baker, who first performed the
piece with the London Repertoire Orchestra, November 15, 1969, with the
composer conducting. This is an engaging work, full of challenging horn
writing. In three movements. The piece alternates between horn in F and
horn in E. This is romantic horn writing, with lyrical melodic gestures that
show off the horn's ability to sing. The first movement cadenza is not flashy,
but is an expressive dialogue between horn and orchestra. The second movement is a scherzo in $\frac{6}{8}$, with a contrasting section of slow, atmospheric music, carried by the orchestra, and the finale is energetic, intricately crafted.
A challenging concerto with triple tonguing in the first movement, agile
writing in the final movement, and lyrical sections that extend above the
staff.
Range: F–d^3
Duration: 18:00

Glière, Reinhold Moritsevich (1875–1956) Russia

Concerto in B♭ Major, op. 91 (1950)
International Music, 1958, piano reduction (Valery Polekh, ed., with his cadenza)
Dedicated to Valery Polekh, Russian horn virtuoso, who premiered it May 10,
1951, with the Leningrad Radio Symphony Orchestra. In the traditional
form of three movements: Allegro—Andante—Moderato. Featuring very
technical playing and beautiful long phrases and melodies written in a heroic style, this is one of the standards of the solo horn literature. Glière
remained firmly in the Russian romantic tradition, using the traditional
harmonic language of his predecessors of the nineteenth century. This is
a challenging work requiring good long-range endurance and solid technique. Widely performed and recorded.
Range: A–b♭^{2}
Duration: 24:00

Godfrey, Daniel (1949–) United States

Shindig, for Solo Horn and Wind Ensemble (2000, rev. 2001)
Pembroke Music, 2009, wind ensemble score only
Commissioned by the Big Ten Band Directors Association, dedicated to H. Robert Reynolds. The composer writes in the preface: "I think of this piece as
something akin to a big barn dance, with the soloist playing the braggart,
the blow-hard (forgive the pun), continually sounding off, cutting in, and
demanding center stage." This work features interplay between soloist and
ensemble, based on the minor-third opening in the horn, with touches
of Philip Glass. Horn techniques in this energetic work include shakes,
stopped writing, and glissandi. Recorded by William Scharnberg and the
North Texas Wind Symphony.
Range: f–c^3
Duration: 11:24

Goedicke, Alexander
See: Gedike, Aleksandr Fyodorovich

Goldhammer, Siegmund (1932–) Germany
Concertino für Horn und Orchester
Hofmeister, 1996, piano reduction
In three movements: Moderato con animoso—Andante con dolendo—Allegro.
    Declamatory writing in tonal language that features the dialogue between
    horn and orchestra.
Range: c^1–c^3
Duration: 15:30

Gordon, Christopher (1956–) Australia
Award-winning composer Christopher Gordon writes concert music and music
for film.

Lightfall for horn and orchestra (2009)
Australian Music Centre, 2010, orchestra score only; also available at horncon
    certo.net
Dedicated to hornist Robert Johnson, who first performed it September 9, 2009,
    with the Sydney Symphony. The piece was a finalist as Orchestral Work
    of the Year in the Australian Art Music Awards 2011. In two movements.
    The first features the horn playing expressive legato figures over sparse or-
    chestration of wind chords, piano, low strings, and timpani, followed by a
    triplet figure that gathers momentum, building until the horn solo is play-
    ing together with the tutti material. A dramatic cutoff ends the movement.
    The second movement, marked "Slow and free," begins unmeasured, with
    divisi strings in aleatoric sections. This is followed by light, bright, atmo-
    spheric writing, with the horn darting above sixteenth-note figures in the
    piano and gestures in the strings. Light and colorfully orchestrated, this
    movement makes interesting use of orchestra horns, echoing or doubling
    the soloist. The horn writing is not terribly technical, with more emphasis
    on lyrical lines and shapes, but there are some agile figures, plus phrases
    that extend above the staff, requiring good long-range endurance.
Range: B–c^3
Duration: 26:00

Gotkovsky, Ida (1933–) France
Concerto pour cor et piano (1984)
Billaudot, 1984, piano reduction
Dedicated to Georges Barboteau, professor at the Paris Conservatory. This was
    an exam piece at the conservatory. In one movement. This dark, atonal
    work uses the horn well, with a theme that develops out of the opening
    motive, then returns to it. The middle section is fast, with changing meters.
    Overall, the writing is free and fluid, with cadenza sections that frame the
    middle section. This is a technically demanding work, with wide leaps, vir-

tuosic writing, and passages that often go above the staff, requiring good endurance. Interesting sonorities, well organized.

Range: F–c³
Duration: 6:30

Grant, Parks (1910–1988) United States
Grant studied with Howard Hanson and Harold Gleason at Eastman and was on the faculty at Temple University then at the University of Mississippi.

Concerto for French Horn and Orchestra (1940)
American Composers Alliance, 1979, full score; Manuscript score and parts are in the Fleisher Collection, Free Library of Philadelphia
   1. Largo—Allegro molto
   2. Molto adagio
   3. Finale: Vivace.
Dedicated to hornist Harold Meek, who first performed it in Rochester, New York, April 10, 1941, with the Rochester Civic Orchestra, Howard Hanson conducting, in a performance broadcast over the Blue Network. Opens with a low passage, using the naturally occurring notes on the harmonic series. A driving first motive is followed by a second motive that is more lyrical. Includes stopped writing and trills. The slow second movement ends with "alla recitativo" for the horn. The third movement, in ⅜, moves through different modes and tonal centers, gaining momentum until a return of the opening low passage from the first movement, ending with a quick coda.

Range: G–d³
Duration: 18:00

Graun, either **Johann Gottlieb** (1702/3–1771) or **Carl Heinrich** (1703/4–1750) Germany
Both of the Graun brothers were students in Dresden and were later employed by Crown Prince Friedrich of Prussia, who became King Friedrich II.

Concerto in D Major for Horn and String Orchestra
Birdalone Music, 1995, piano reduction and full score; Robert Ostermeyer, 1999, piano reduction and full score
This work is no. 16 of Lund University Library Ms. Kat. Wenster Litt. I/1–17b and presumed to be by one of the Graun brothers. This concerto for natural horn in D exhibits florid writing for the horn, yet most of it is in the upper midrange, making it one of the more accessible works from the baroque era. The first movement opens with an appoggiatura figure that sets the tone for the ornaments and flourishes throughout, requiring flexibility and an elegant approach. The brief, slow movement is lovely in its simplicity, and wide open for ornamentation of the type that can be found in Johann Quantz's book *On Playing the Flute* of 1752. The final movement is an Allegro full of grace notes and quick figures that show off the horn's agility.

Range: e¹–a² (g¹–c³ for horn in D)
Duration: 9:03

Graziani, Yitzhak (1924–2003) Israel, born in Bulgaria

Variations on Haydns Theme (Varyatsyot `al nose shel Haydn)
Israel Brass Woodwind Publications, 1978, piano reduction
Short, clever, and virtuosic sounding, this accessible work is a playful take on
the theme and variations form. It includes a hunting horn variation in ⁶⁄₈,
an Andante with wide leaps, a boogie-woogie variation, and a variation
with hemiolas à la *West Side Story* followed by a brief cadenza—all in
good fun.
Range: c–b²
Duration: 4:45

Gregorc, Jurij (1916–1985) Slovenia
Violinist and composer, taught at the Pedagogical Academy in Maribor.

Koncert za rog in godala (Concerto for French Horn and Strings) 1966
Edicije Drustva Slovenskih Skladateljev, 1975, piano reduction
    I. Allegro giusto
    II. Andante
    III. Presto
In three movements that follow traditional concerto form and infused with
brooding and somber modal inflections. The first movement is a quick ²⁄₄,
with the horn developing threads of the robust opening theme. The second
movement, in ⁵⁄₄, opens with slowly changing harmonies that set up a horn
melody that is reminiscent of a folk song. The final movement, in ⁶⁄₈, is the
most challenging for the horn, with quick chromatic passages.
Range: c♯–b♭²
Duration: 24:00

Gregson, Edward (1945–) United Kingdom

Concerto for Horn and Brass Band (or horn and orchestra) (1971)
Chester Music, 1994, horn and piano reduction, horn part in E♭ also available
Written for Ifor James, commissioned by the British Federation of Brass Bands.
Movements include: Allegro non troppo—Andante cantabile—Allegro
brioso. The first movement is in sonata form, developing the opening figure of ascending fourths, with a few challenging runs for horn. The second movement begins with a lyrical horn melody, followed by free cadenza
sections. The last movement is a rondo that moves between ⁶⁄₈ and ⁹⁄₈, with a
lyrical middle section in ²⁄₄. The brass band scoring is effective, particularly
the first-movement duet between trumpet and horn, and the brass scoring
of the second movement. Recorded by Ifor James with Besses o' the Barn
on the Chandos label. It is surprising that this work is not played very often,
since it is very accessible writing for the horn, of medium difficulty, with
some triple tonguing and flutter tonguing.
Range: G–b²
Duration: 18:00

Guérinel, Lucien (1930–) France

Petite Musique de jour (2001)
Jobert, 2003, full score only
Commissioned by Eric Sombret for the sixth Festival de Cor d'Avignon in Pays
    Vaucluse. Premiered in Avignon June 28, 2002, at the Opera d'Avignon
    by Antoine Dreyfuss, solo horn, and Opera Orchestra Region Avignon-
    Provence. In memory of Raphaël Sommer. A contemporary work in one
    movement, with changing meters, notated by note groupings within bar
    lines. Trills, stopped writing, flutter tonguing, and glissandi add to the un-
    expected and continuously changing gestures of this intricate work.
Range: G♯–b²
Duration: 15:00

Haag, Hanno (1939–2005) Germany

Scherzo für Horn und kleines sinfonisches Orchester, op. 33, op. 33A, and op. 33B
Schott, piano reduction
Op. 33 is for horn and small orchestra, op. 33A is for horn and strings, op. 33B is
    for horn and piano.
Duration: 5:35

Habe, Tomaž (1947–) Slovenia
Habe is particularly known for his choral and vocal music, and he incorporates
Slovenian melodic elements and style into his works.

Folk Tune and Scherzo (Narodna in Scherzo), for horn and orchestra (1983)
Edicije DSS, 2005, piano reduction
Premiered June 10, 1986, by the Simfonicni orkester Domzale-Kamnik, Jože
    Falout, horn, with the composer conducting. In two sections: Tranquil-
    lo-pastorale—Scherzo-giocoso. This is an accessible work, with only mod-
    est demands in range, endurance, and technical facility.
Range: a♯–a²
Duration: 9:00

Concerto for Horn and Strings (Koncert za rog in godala) (2000)
Society of Slovene Composers, available from www.dss.si
Duration: 26:00

Haddad, Don (1935–) United States

Adagio and Allegro for Horn and Band
Shawnee Press, 1969, piano reduction
In two contrasting movements. The Adagio is lyrical, in ⁴⁄₄; the Allegro is full of
    energy, with changing meters and a declamatory horn theme that returns
    throughout the movement. Suitable for the intermediate hornist with a
    good command of the high range to b♭².
Range: b♭–b♭²
Duration: 7:00

Hagen, Daron (1961–) United States
Hagen's works have been performed throughout the world, and he has won numerous awards, including a Guggenheim Fellowship and the 2014 American Academy of Arts and Letters award.

Concerto for Horn with Winds and Strings (1993)
Burning Sled Music, 1993, full score only
This concerto was commissioned by Sören Hermansson, who premiered it with
the Wisconsin Chamber Orchestra, November 1, 1996. For solo horn and instrumental ensemble of flute, oboe, clarinet (doubling soprano saxophone), bassoon, violins, violas, and violoncellos (can be a single player on the string parts). In five movements: 1. Nightfall—2. Serenade—3. Midnight— 4. Aubade—5. Daybreak. The composer writes in the score preface that the piece "follows the soloist protagonist wrestling with night thoughts from dawn to dusk." The movements are of contrasting characters and moods: lyrical, introspective, and at times melancholy, including a jazz-waltz with soprano saxophone. The final movement is the most virtuosic for the horn, in changing meters with heraldic fanfares, culminating in a cadenza.
Range: B–c$\sharp^3$
Duration: 17:00

Hallnäs, Eyvind (1937–) Sweden
Organist and prolific composer who has written for orchestra, solo instrument, ensemble, choir, and voice.

Concerto for Horn (2001)
Swedish Music Information Center, orchestra score only
Two very short movements written in a tonal harmonic language. The first is
marked Allegro, and develops a characteristic hunting theme in $\frac{6}{8}$, and the second is an Allegretto con spirito, in $\frac{4}{4}$ and in contrasting minor. The first movement is quite fast, and there are a few high entrances at the top of the staff, but overall moderate range and technical demands make this suitable for the high school player and above.
Range: d^1–g$\sharp^2$
Duration: 6:00

Hamilton, David (1955–) New Zealand

The Ripe Breath of Autumn, for solo horn and small chamber orchestra (1982/1985)
Waiteata Press, 1991, orchestra score only
Although not a programmatic work, the title is taken from the text of a poem by
Walt Whitman. In the composer's words, this is a "dark brooding work, and might be best described as a rhapsody. . . .The work possesses a sense of ebb and flow in the orchestra part, interrupted only by a cadenza for the horn player and a solo viola. The work finally settles on D as its tonal centre and ends quietly." The range is reasonable, but good endurance is required for long sustained lines that move over slowly changing harmonies.
Range: e–b^2
Duration: 11:56

Hamilton, Iain (1922–2000) United Kingdom

Voyage for Horn and Chamber Orchestra (1970)
Theodore Presser, 1974, orchestra score only
Commissioned by the London Sinfonietta for Barry Tuckwell. In nine continuous sections, played without break: Solo I—Interlude I—Cadenza I—Interlude II—Nocturne—Interlude III—Cadenza II—Interlude IV—Solo
II. This work is atmospheric, with quick intricate horn gestures and long
lyrical lines against a sparse, varied texture in the orchestra. Extended
techniques include multiphonics, flutter tonguing, trills, singing through
the horn, and improvisatory phrases. Extended sections stay at the top of
the staff for the horn, although there are sections where the horn does not
play.
Range: E–d³
Duration: 18:00

Hampel, Anton Joseph (ca. 1710–1771) Germany

Concerto ex D-Dur
Robert Ostermeyer has raised the possibility that this concerto, no. 13 from the
Lund University Library Ms. Kat. Wenster Litt. I/1–17b (also known as the
Lund Manuscript), may have been composed by Hampel.
See: Anonymous (Anton Joseph Hampel?), *Concerto ex D-Dur*

Hannay, Roger (1930–2006) United States
Hannay studied composition with Howard Hansen and Lukas Foss, and was professor of composition at the University of North Carolina, where he also directed
the New Music Ensemble and Electronic Music Studio.

Pastorale for Horn in F and String orchestra (1982/2001)
Media Press, 2002, piano reduction
In one movement that builds in momentum then returns to its quiet lento opening. Modest demands on range and endurance make this an accessible work
for the intermediate player. The publisher's website states that this work
"describes a dawn to dusk day as experienced at Olana, the Persian-styled
home of the American painter Frederick Church . . . high on a hill over-
looking the Hudson River Valley." (www.mediapressinc.com)
Range: B–g²
Duration: 7:30

Hasquenoph, Pierre (1922–1982) France

Concertino pour cor et orchestre à cordes
Eschig, 1964, piano reduction
Written as a contest piece for the Paris Conservatory. In three movements: Al-
legro—Andantino—Allegro vivo. The first movement is bold, in $\frac{4}{4}$, featur-
ing syncopated figures that increase in their intensity, volume, and range.
There are a few stopped passages. The second movement is lyrical, with a

contrasting section of declamatory triplets and sixteenth notes. The final movement leaps throughout the ranges at a fast pace and in changing meters, concluding with a cadenza. The first and third movements have several phrases that extend and stay above the staff, requiring good endurance.

Range: e♭–c³
Duration: 10:00

Hauff, Wilhelm Gottlieb (1755–1807)

Concerto en mi♭ majeur pour cor et orchestra
Billaudot, 1975, piano reduction ("reconstitution, revision et arrangement, Edmund Leloir")
For horn in E♭. In three movements that follow traditional form. This concerto exhibits fast sixteenth-note passage-work in the first movement, and some challenging leaps at a very fast tempo in the final § movement.

Range: f–b♭² (g–c³ for horn in E♭)
Duration: 13:30

Haugland, Oscar (1922–2013) United States
Haugland attended Eastman, where he received degrees in horn and composition, and taught theory and composition at Northern Illinois University.

Concertino for Horn
Cole Publishing Company, 1971, piano reduction
Originally for horn and string orchestra. This work is dedicated to Fred Bradley. In three movements: Allegro—Andantino—Allegro moderato. The first movement is in a declamatory character, with contrapuntal writing in changing meters. The second movement features expressive legato figures that build to a *fortissimo*, and the third movement is quick and energetic, moving between § and ⅜. This is a well-placed work for the hornist, with many breaks, suitable for the early college player. With the exception of a passage in the first movement that hovers around a high a², it is mostly in the treble clef staff.

Range: f♯–a²
Duration: 12:00

Havlik, (1956–) Czech Republic
Jiří Havlik, hornist with the Czech Philharmonic, is also a composer and conductor.

Concerto for Horn and Strings (1976)
A-Tempo Verlag, (www.belohlavek.com), piano reduction and orchestra score
In three movements: Allegro libero—Molto lento, Calmo—Vivo. The first movement is heroic and bold, in changing meters, with tangy dissonances. A lyrical second movement opens with impressionistic harmonies and with short quasi-recitatives in the horn. The third movement is fast and full of impish energy, in changing meters with a short section of cantabile writ-

ing. The horn and piano version was recorded by the composer, and hornist Steven Gross recorded the version with string orchestra, with the composer conducting.

Range: G–c^3

Duration: 16:46

Haydn, Franz Josef (1732–1809) Austria

Concerto No. 1 in D, Hob. VIId:3 (1762)

International, 1974 (Cerminaro, ed.); Boosey & Hawkes, 1954 (includes part for horn in F); Henle, 1991 (Ohmiya and Gerlach, ed.); Breitkopf & Härtel, 1986 (Mandyczewski, ed.)—all piano reductions

Written for natural horn in D. Composed when Haydn first moved to Eisenstadt to work for Prince Esterhazy. Haydn had accomplished wind players at Esterhazy and often featured them in his symphonies at the time. It is speculated that the piece was probably written for Carl Franz or Josef Leutgeb. This three-movement classical concerto exploits both high range and low range, particularly the soaring high melody of the second movement. The orchestration is for strings and two oboes, and this can also be played very effectively as a recital piece with string quartet.

Range: A–b^2 (c–d^3 for horn in D)

Duration: 16:30

Concerto No. 2 in D, Hob. VIId:4

International, 1974 (Cerminaro, ed.); Boosey & Hawkes, 1952 (includes part for horn in F); Breitkopf & Härtel, 2003 (Mandyczewski, ed.)—all piano reductions

Written for natural horn in D. Scholars have long debated whether this work was actually written by Franz Josef Haydn, or whether it was written by his brother Michael Haydn. It is included here, since, as John Jay Hilfiger argues, "although there is not documentary evidence to prove that Joseph Haydn composed this concerto, neither has documentary evidence been presented to prove that it was written by another composer." The first movement, marked Allegro moderato, is stately, centered on a regal dotted figure. The expressive second-movement Adagio, in minor, is equal in breadth to the outer movements, being weighty and somber in character. The finale is a sprightly rondo in three, with wide leaps interspersed among the running triplet figures.

Range: A–f♯^{2} (c–a^2 for horn in D)

Duration: 15:30

See also: John Jay Hilfiger, "Who composed Haydn's 'second horn concerto?'" *The Horn Call Annual* 5 (1993): 1–6.

Haydn, Michael (1737–1806) Austria

Concertino for Horn and Orchestra

Universal, 1969; Schirmer, 1977 (Tuckwell, ed.), piano reductions

Based on the recently discovered manuscript in the composer's hand in the Bavarian State Library in Munich, this concertino from the early classical period is believed to be part of a larger work. The preface of the Universal edition states that Michael Haydn often wrote symphonies, serenades, and other works that included movements featuring an instrumental soloist, and that these movements were often played by themselves and copied and circulated. This is a likely explanation for the unusual arrangement of movements in the piece. Written for natural horn in D, it is in three movements. The first is a Larghetto, the second is an Allegro non troppo in $\frac{4}{4}$, and the third movement is a Menuet. The Schirmer edition has cadenzas and added ornamentations that are written directly into the part, with the ornamentation written out in the third-movement menuet (that is, repeats are written out with ornamentation the second time through). A few challenging sixteenth-note passages with leaps, characteristic of cor-basse writing. The first movement Larghetto is particularly charming, and the entire work requires a good deal of agility with wide intervals but is altogether quite accessible.

Range: e–a^2 (g–c^3 for horn in D)
Duration: 17:00

Hedges, Anthony (1931–) United Kingdom
A prolific composer in many genres, perhaps best known for his British "light" music.

Concertino for Horn and String Orchestra, op. 105
Westfield Music, 1987, piano reduction
This work is in three movements: Allegro moderato—Lento—Allegro. The first
    movement develops a dotted eighth-sixteenth motive, centered around
    fourths and fifths; the second features a rising legato motive; and the third
    is quick and jaunty, alternating meters between $\frac{6}{8}$ and $\frac{4}{4}$. Contrapuntal, an-
    gular writing. Not technically difficult, but tessitura extends into the high
    range, such as repeated high b♭^{2}s in the slow movement that crescendo to
    fortissimo.
Range: d–c^3
Duration: 16:00

Heiden, Bernhard (1910–2000) United States, born in Germany
Heiden studied with Hindemith in Berlin and taught composition and theory at
Indiana University for many years.

Concerto for Horn and Orchestra (1969)
Associated Music Publishers, 1972, piano reduction
This work was commissioned by the University of Wisconsin School of Music
    and dedicated to John Barrows, who premiered it February 21, 1970, with
    the University of Wisconsin Symphony Orchestra, under the direction of
    Professor Otto-Werner Mueller. It is in two extended movements made up
    of two sections each, giving it an overall form of four sections: I. Prelude-
    Recitative and Aria—II. Theme and Variations-Finale. Harmonic language
    is very reminiscent of Hindemith, based on intervallic relationships and

shifting tonal centers. The second-section recitative provides ample opportunity for expression. Of medium difficulty, with legato passages throughout the range of the horn that require some flexibility. This work is sensibly paced, without being unduly taxing.
Range: d–c♭²
Duration: 14:00

Heider, Werner (1930–) Germany

Schöne Aussichten für Horn und Streichorchester, nach Gedichten von Hans Magnus Enzensberger (1991)
Edition Moeck, 1994, orchestra score only
In five movements: Aufbruchstimmung—Litanei vom Es—Zungenwerk—Valse triste et sentimentale—Zusammenfassung. Written in a contemporary style expressed through intricate and quickly changing rhythmic gestures. Some graphic notation for groups of barred notes that indicate tempo changes. Includes flutter tonguing, quick repeated tones, trills, glissandi, stopped and half-stopped writing. The first movement opens and closes with a horn monologue, played with rubato.
Range: G–c³
Duration: 16:00

Henkemans, Hans (1913–1995) Netherlands
Henkemans was an active concert pianist and composer, taught composition and instrumentation at the Groningen Conservatory and the Amsterdam Muziekly-ceum, and later in his life enjoyed a career in psychiatry.

Concerto per corno ed orchestra (1981)
Donemus, 1981, piano reduction
In one continuous movement of contrasting sections, with sweeping legato lines in the horn that move quickly through the ranges and fluid writing that connects the different moods expressed in this contemporary work. Challenging writing for the hornist, requiring flexibility, command of the high range, and good endurance.
Range: B♯–c³
Duration: 11:00

Herberigs, Robert (1886–1974) Belgium
Cyrano de Bergerac (1912)
CeBeDeM, 1961, piano reduction
  1. Allegro
  2. Andante
  3. Allegro con fuoco
Written for Charles Heylbroek, professor of horn at Ghent College of Music, who premiered the work in 1912. Belgian hornist Maurice van Bocxstaele continued to perform this work, ensuring its popularity in Belgium. In three continuous movements, this is a symphonic poem for horn. The first move-

ment, in $\frac{6}{8}$, is full of heroic writing, with alternating duple and triple figures. The lush yet delicate middle movement gives way to trumpet fanfares that announce the final movement, a jaunty Allegro in $\frac{2}{4}$ full of character and swagger. Romantic, heroic, lyrical, and Straussian, this work requires good long-range endurance and a bravura style.

Range: b♭–b♭²
Duration: 18:44

Herchet, Jörg (1943–) Germany

Komposition für Horn und Orchester (1980)
Breitkopf & Härtel, orchestra score only
Dedicated to Peter Damm, who premiered the work with the Staatskapelle Dresden, October 1983, Herbert Blomstedt conducting. In one continuous movement. Contemporary harmonic language, with chord clusters in the strings and winds and dialogues between the solo horn and these different orchestral clusters. Very intricate divisi string scoring, resulting in an often chaotic-sounding backdrop for the solo-horn line. Challenging and virtuosic writing for the soloist.

Range: F–c³
Duration: 26:00

Hermann, Ralph (1914–1994) United States

Pianist, conductor, and composer, Hermann studied composition at Juilliard with Vittorio Gianinni, was an orchestra director during World War II, and played clarinet with the NBC Symphony and the Paul Whiteman Orchestra. He is known for his works for concert band but he also composed chamber and symphonic music.

Concerto for Horn (for band or orchestra)
Educational Music Service, 1958, piano reduction
This concerto is in three movements: Allegretto—Andante moderato—Allegro. It is written in tonal harmonic language and straightforward rhythms. The first and second movements are mostly flowing, and the third features a horn cadenza followed by an energetic Allegro in $\frac{2}{4}$. Moderate range and technical requirements make this a suitable piece for the advanced high school or college player.

Range: a–c♯³ (ossia to a²)
Duration: 13:00

Hersch, Michael (1971–) United States

Currently head of the composition department at the Peabody Institute, Johns Hopkins University, Michael Hersch has garnered top composition prizes for his work, and his music is played by major orchestras, ensembles, and soloists throughout the world.

A Sheltered Corner, for horn and orchestra (2011)
Michael Nathaniel Hersch, 2014, orchestra score

This work was commissioned for the fiftieth anniversary of the Eastern Music
    Festival, where it was premiered by Jamie Hersch, horn soloist, Gerard
    Schwarz conducting. Composed in nine dramatic movements that convey
    a wide and complex range of expression, colors and textures.
Range: F–c³
Duration: 30:00

Hess, Willy (1906–1997) Switzerland
Musicologist, composer, music critic, bassoonist, and a noted Beethoven scholar.

Konzert für Horn und Orchester, op. 65
Edition Eulenberg, Educational series, 1969, piano reduction
This concerto is in three movements: Allegro—Andante quasi adagio—Rondo
    vivace. Straightforward melodies in traditional harmonic language and
    style, with a few sections of changing character within each movement.
Range: B♭–c³
Duration: 22:00

Hétu, Jacques (1938–2010) Canada

Sérénade héroïque, op. 62, pour cor et orchestra (1998)
Éditions Doberman-Yppan, 2001, piano reduction
The preface defines Hétu's style as "neo-classical form and neo-romantic expres-
    sion in a musical language of 20th century techniques." Dedicated to John
    Zirbel, who premiered it with the Montreal Symphony in 2001. In three
    movements. The first movement, "Ouverture," begins Adagio with three
    descending horn calls introducing the work. This is followed by an Allegro
    in ¾ that builds to *fff* triplet figures above the staff. The second movement,
    "Lied," is lyrical and expressive. The third movement, "Carnaval," is in ⁶⁄₈
    and joyful with tinges of madcap fun and a brief section of Adagio that
    brings back material of earlier movements.
Range: d♯–c³
Duration: 13:15

Hidas, Frigyes (1928–2007) Hungary
A prolific composer, conductor of the National Theatre, and pianist with the Hungarian Radio Orchestra.

Concerto per corno (1968)
Editio Musica Budapest, 1968, piano reduction
The concerto opens with introductory horn flourishes. Fast and jazzy motives in
    ⁷⁄₄ follow, a secondary lyrical theme is introduced, and both are developed,
    leading to a quasi-cadenza. The second movement is a lyrical Larghetto,
    with slow and soaring horn lines and a middle section in minor mode.
    The third movement is a rollicking ⁶⁄₈, with contrasting sections of laid-back
    syncopated writing. Tuneful and light, with a jazz/pop feel and a bit of Ger-
    shwin around the edges. Fun to play.
Range: d–b²
Duration: 20:00

Concerto for Horn No. 2 (1989)
Editio Musica Budapest, orchestra score only
    I. Moderato
    II. Andante
    III. Allegro leggiero
Written for Imre Magyari.
Duration: 18:00

Hill, Alfred (1869–1960) born in Australia, resided in Australia and New Zealand
Composer and conductor, educated in Leipzig, and played violin in Gewandhaus Orchestra Leipzig for several years.

Serenade for Horn and Strings
Stiles Music, 2007, full score
    1. Allegro
    2. Adagio
    3. Landler
    4. Finale
This is adapted from Hill's *Sonata for Horn and Piano,* which has been lost. No
    piano reduction is available. The same music was adapted by Hill to create
    Septet for Wind Instruments (flute, oboe, two clarinets, bassoon, and horn),
    where the horn part is the same as the *Serenade.*
Duration: 21:00

Concerto for Horn and Orchestra
Stiles Music, 2007, orchestra score
    1. Allegro maestoso
    2. Adagio—Allegro molto
    3. Finale
Dedicated to Alan Mann.
Duration: 19:00

Hilliard, Quincy C. (1954–) United States
"Encore" from *Concerto for Young Artist(s) and Band*
See: Horn and keyboard

Hindemith, Paul (1895–1963) Germany and United States
Horn Concerto (1949)
Schott, 1950, piano reduction
    I. Moderately fast
    II. Very fast
    III. Very slow—Moderately fast—Fast—Lively—Very slow
Hindemith wrote this work for Dennis Brain as a tribute after he conducted
    a Mozart concerto with Brain as the soloist. It was premiered in Baden-
    Baden by Dennis Brain with the Southwest German Radio Orchestra, the

composer conducting, on June 8, 1950. In three movements. The first is in a declamatory style with fugue-like interplay between different sections of the orchestra and the solo horn. The second movement is in a quick $\frac{2}{4}$, with the orchestra interjecting on the offbeats of the horn's repeated notes. When the horn returns with the opening theme, their roles switch, with the horn on the offbeats and the orchestra on the downbeats. There are a few intricate fingering challenges for the horn in this movement. The final movement is the most involved of the three, beginning with a very slow declamatory theme in the horn. A second idea in $\frac{6}{8}$ follows, leading into a cadenza-like section for the horn over tremolo strings. There is a declamation (printed text), which is not spoken, but represents the ideas that Hindemith was expressing through the music. The second idea returns, then back to the first statement to close the concerto. This is a very accessible work for the horn player, well paced without extensive demands on range. The second movement is playful, and the characteristic counterpoint between horn and orchestra (piano) makes this a rewarding work to play. This is a standard solo in the horn repertoire.

Range: $a\sharp-a^2$
Duration: 15:00

Hoddinott, Alun (1929–2008) United Kingdom (Wales)

Concerto for horn and orchestra, op. 65
Oxford University Press, 1972, orchestra score only
Commissioned by the Llandaff Festival, premiered by Ifor James and the Royal Philharmonic Orchestra, June 3, 1969. In three movements. The first movement, "Romanza," is an Andante in $\frac{3}{4}$, with long lines in the horn solo that gradually build, increasing in intensity, dynamic, and range. The second movement is a very fast "Scherzo," and the third movement, "Cadenza," is more like an unaccompanied work, unmeasured, with changing tempos and dynamics and technically demanding gestures for the horn. This leads directly into a brief Adagio of eight measures of sustained chords in the solo horn and orchestra.

Range: $a-c\sharp^3$
Duration: 14:00

Aubade and Scherzo for Horn and Orchestra, op. 42 (1965)
Oxford University Press, 1967, orchestra score only
Commissioned by the BBC Wales, premiered October 24, 1965, James Kiack horn, with the BBC Welsh Orchestra. Dedicated to Jon Manchip White. The Aubade is brief, opening with a wide ranging eighth-note statement in the horn over muted strings. The Scherzo, marked Presto and in $\frac{6}{8}$, is centered around a declamatory hemiola figure in the horn, with a middle section of expressive legato writing at a relaxed tempo before a return to the Presto material. There are a few instances of flutter tonguing at a quick tempo.

Range: c^1-c^3
Duration: 8:00

Hoffmann, Georg Melchior (1685–1715) [or Hoffmann, Johann Georg (1700–1780)]

Concerto a 7 ex Dis, für Horn, 2 Oboen, 2 Violinen, Viola und Bass
Robert Ostermeyer, 1999, piano reduction and orchestra score
The editor indicates that the composer could be one of the two Hoffmanns listed above. This work is scored for two oboes, strings, and horn solo. In four movements. The first movement is a brief Adagio with strings only. The second movement, Allegro ma non presto, is full of technical passages of sextuplet and sixteenth-note figures typical of baroque horn writing. The horn is tacet in the third-movement Adagio, which features two oboes and strings. The fourth movement is a menuet and trio, with the horn tacet in the trio. Based on a set of parts in the Sächsische Landesbibliothek in Dresden, this piece also appears without a composer's name as no. 2 in the Lund manuscript (Katalog Wenster Literature I/1–17b in the Universitetsbiblioteket in Lund, Sweden).
Range: d^1–b^2 (e^1–c^3 for horn in E♭)
Duration: 6:30

Hoffmeister, Franz Anton (1754–1812) Austria
Hoffmeister was a music publisher and composer.

Concerto E-Dur für Horn und Orchester
Robert Ostermeyer, 2004, piano reduction and orchestra score
In three movements: Allegro—Romance: Poco adagio—Rondo. This work features wide leaps and characteristic cor-basse arpeggiated figures, as well as elegant lyrical lines typical of classical writing for the horn.
Range: $F\sharp$–$g\sharp^2$ (G–a^2 with for horn in E)
Duration: 15:00

Concerto D-Dur für Horn und Orchester
Robert Ostermeyer, 2010, piano reduction and orchestra score
In three movements: Allegro—Andante—Rondo. The slow middle movement is relatively short. This work features writing in both cor-alto and cor-basse styles. There are large leaps—many are at the speed of half notes—and a passage in the first movement that ventures into the pedal range of the horn. Combine this with lyrical phrases in the middle and higher tessitura, and you have a piece that is perfect for the well-rounded horn virtuoso. Several challenging entrances on high b^2 in the second movement.
Range: E–$c\sharp^3$ ossia E–b^2 (G–e^3 ossia G–d^3 for horn in D)
Duration: 9:30

Holler, Georg Augustin (1744–1814) Germany
Holler was a composer and member of the guild of town musicians in Munich.

Avertissement in D
Edition Walhall, 2002, full score, parts available
Scored for horn and two violins, viola, and violone (basso). The editor indicates that this piece can be performed with a small chamber ensemble or string

orchestra. In three movements in the traditional classical style: Allegro—
Adagio—Rondo: Allegretto. The writing is simple and straightforward.
Range: g–c³ (e–a² for horn in D)
Duration: 12:30

Holloway, Robin (1943–) United Kingdom
Adagio and Rondo, op. 43b (1979–1980)
Boosey & Hawkes, full score
Premiered July 31, 1987, Northern Sinfonia, Richard Hickox conductor, Barry
Tuckwell, horn soloist. Paired with *Sonata,* op. 43a, to form the complete
Horn Concerto, op. 43.
Range: B–c³
Duration: 21:00

Horn Concerto, op. 43 (1979–1980)
Boosey & Hawkes, 1982, full score
    I. Sonata
    II. Adagio
    III. Rondo
The horn concerto was originally conceived as two separate works, the *Sonata,*
Op. 43a, and the *Adagio and Rondo,* Op. 43b. Barry Tuckwell gave the
premiere of the entire work on June 16, 1988, Northern Sinfonia, Richard
Hickox conducting, thus bringing the two separate works together. Barry
Tuckwell also recorded it on the NMC label. The form of the concerto is
neo-classical, with a first movement in sonata form and a slow, lyrical sec-
ond movement with an extensive cadenza that leads into a bright rondo fi-
nale. The orchestration is lush and romantic, with winds—bassoons, oboe,
English horn—exchanging passages back and forth between horn solo.
Range: B–c³
Duration: 35:00

Sonata, op. 43a (1979–1980)
Boosey & Hawkes, full score
Paired with *Adagio and Rondo,* op. 43b, to form the complete *Horn Concerto,*
    op. 43.
Range: g♯–c³
Duration: 15:00

Hoshina, Hiroshi (1936–) Japan
Hoshina is known for his music for wind band, and he has also written operas
and orchestral and choral music.
Miko Dance for Horn in F and Orchestra (2006)
Editions BIM, 2007, piano reduction and orchestra score
Written for the tenth anniversary of the Hoshina Academy Chamber Orchestra Ensemble Harmonia, who first performed the work February 3, 2007,
at Daiichi Seimel Hall Tokyo, Satoshi Sugimoto horn soloist. The preface
states that the work is "inspired by the slow and gentle movements of the

traditional dance of a Miko (maiden integrated into the religious ritual of the Japanese Shinto-Shrine). . . . The solo horn inserts 'cadential' phrases within the context of a formal musical structure in which the sound and expression resources of today's instruments are beautifully exploited on a richly colored orchestral accompaniment." The work begins freely, with the horn playing a cadenza-like introduction. This leads into an Allegro ritimico, with a flowing statement in the horn that moves between $\frac{3}{4}$ and $\frac{7}{8}$. At several points, the horn breaks this flowing line with cadenza-like interjections. Of medium difficulty; an accessible work that is well paced for the hornist.

Range: b♭–c³
Duration: 15:00

Hosokawa, Toshio (1955–) Japan

Horn Concerto: Moment of Blossoming (2010)
Schott, 2010, orchestra score only
Commissioned by Berliner Philharmoniker, Barbican Centre London and Concertgebouw Amsterdam, dedicated to Stefan Dohr, who premiered the work February 10, 2011, with the Berlin Philharmonic, Simon Rattle conducting. The composer writes that "this is one of the works on the theme of 'flower' and it describes the moment of blossoming. The blossoming of a flower symbolizes the awakening of a human being to the Self. The horn represents a human being, while the orchestra can be taken as nature and the universe that enclose him. Within his relationship with nature, he discovers his true self." (www.schott-music.com/shop/9/show,2777107.html) The piece begins very simply and quietly with a long sustained sounding E♭ moving throughout the orchestra. The sounds gradually change and grow, with themes passed from horn to different groups of the orchestra. In the end, we return to sounds of wind and bells, returning to the opening. This is an evocative piece with interesting moods and effects, such as off-stage brass, wind players imitating the sound of wind, and Japanese wind bells. The horn part is not very difficult, particularly for a contemporary work, but requires good control and endurance for long sustained lines that grow out of the texture of the orchestra.

Range: B♭–b²
Duration: 17:00

Hovhaness, Alan (1911–2000) United States

Artik Concerto for Horn and String Orchestra, op 78 (1949)
Edition Peters, 1968, solo-horn part with five string parts
To Carlo and Aghvani Uomini. In eight movements: Alleluia—Ballata—Laude—Canzona: To a mountain range—Processional—Canon—Aria—Intonazione. This is an effective work. It can be performed with string orchestra and also works well with string quintet. Each movement is like a chant, or a meditation, with its own character. The horn is called upon to play as

soloist, then to blend in at times with the violas. With such subtle and often repetitive writing, the horn has little rest, and must also keep the momentum going for each movement. There are fast sixteenth-note passages in the "Canon" and the final "Intonazione," but this is not a flashy work, rather the emphasis is on the sound of the horn in combination with the strings.
Range: a–a²
Duration: 18:00

Huggler, John (1921–1993) United States
Huggler studied composition at Eastman. He was a two time Guggenheim Award recipient and composer in residence for the Boston Symphony. He taught on the faculty at University of Massachusetts Boston for many years.

Concerto for Horn and Orchestra, op. 17 (1957)
Edition Peters, orchestra score only
Duration: 11:00

Hummel, Bertold (1925–2002) Germany
Hummel studied composition with Harald Genzmer and taught composition at the Bavarian State Conservatory of Music.

Musik für Horn in F und Orchester, op. 96a (1993)
Simrock (Boosey & Hawkes), 1993, piano reduction
The composer's website describes this work as having "the character of an instrumental ballade with rhapsodic elements, in which the soloist takes, so to speak, the role of the narrator. This work in one movement is subdivided into seven sections of contrasting dynamic and rhythmical structure." (www.bertoldhummel.de)
Duration: 18:00

Humphries, John (ca. 1707–ca. 1740) United Kingdom

Concerto in D Major for Horn or Trumpet
Oxford University Press, 1978, piano reduction and full score (Richard Platt ed.); Pelican Music, 2005, piano reduction by John Humphries
This is no. 12 of Humphries' *Concertos* op. 2, (the others are for strings), first published ca. 1740 by Benjamin Cooke. In three short movements. A technically easy piece for baroque natural horn in D. The Pelican Music edition is based on the original parts in Oxford's Bodleian Library (2009 email exchange with John Humphries, who coincidentally shares his name with the composer).
Range: a–f♯² (c¹–a² for horn in D)
Duration: 3:45

Hutschenruyter, Wouter Sr. (1796–1878) Netherlands
Horn player, composer, and conductor. Active in Rotterdam and Utrecht, studied composition with Johann Nepomuk Hummel. He was director of the conservatory in Rotterdam.

Concerto in E♭ for horn and orchestra, op. 2
Compusic, 1988, piano reduction (rev. by Herman Jeurissen)
    I. Allegro maestoso
    II. Adagio
    III. Polacca
In traditional three-movement form and harmonic language of the nineteenth
    century. This work has pleasant and flowing melodies and challenging
    technical passages that venture into the high range with virtuosic arpeg-
    gios and scales.
Range: B♭–b♭² (c–c³ for horn in E♭)
Duration: 17:00

Concerto for Horn and Orchestra (1872)
Donemus, 2003, orchestra score only (John Smit, ed.)
A one-movement work that shows both the lyrical and virtuosic sides of the horn,
    with a pleasing lyrical melody and sixteenth-note runs in scalar and arpeg-
    giated patterns. Of medium difficulty, suitable for the early college-level
    player and above.
Range: c–a²
Duration: 10:30

Hutschenruyter, Wouter Jr. (1859–1943) Netherlands
Son of Willem Jacob Hutschenruyter, grandson of Wouter Hutschenruyter Sr.
The composer was assistant conductor of Concertgebouw Orchestra, then led the
Utrecht Symphony, and later became director of Rotterdam Music School.

Nocturne, op. 13 (ca. 1890–92)
Jos. Aibl Verlag, 1898, copy of score and manuscript parts located in the Fleisher
    Collection, Free Library of Philadelphia
This is a short one-movement work in $\frac{6}{8}$ and $\frac{12}{8}$ with flowing horn lines. Of me-
    dium difficulty.
Range: b♭–g²
Duration: 10:00

Hybler, Martin (1977–) Czech Republic

Concertino for French Horn and Strings, op. 13 (1999)
Triga Verlag, 2005, orchestra score only
Premiered in Prague in 2000, Ondřej Vrabec, horn soloist with the Berg Orches-
    tra, conducted by Peter Vrábel. One-movement work in contrasting sec-
    tions full of variety and color. Long horn lines over active strings, heroic
    and romantic horn writing, with contrasting character that can be forceful,
    declamatory, and intense. Other times it is sardonic and biting. Harmonic
    language and gestures reminiscent of Shostakovich.
Range: A–b♭²
Duration: 16:00

d'Indy, Vincent (1851–1931) France
Andante
See: Horn and keyboard

Jacob, Gordon (1895–1984) United Kingdom
Composer, writer, and teacher, Jacob studied with Stanford, Howells, Boult, and
Vaughan Williams at the Royal College of Music, where he also taught for many
years.
Concerto for Horn and Strings (1951)
Galaxy Music, 1951, piano reduction
Composed for Dennis Brain, this engaging work is very well written for the horn,
    resulting in its popularity and assuring its place in the standard horn rep-
    ertoire. Written in traditional forms and tonal harmonic language, with
    flowing and colorful orchestration. In three movements. The Allegro mod-
    erato opens with a fanfare motive, followed by cantabile writing, with an
    extended cadenza. The second movement is slow and lyrical, in $\frac{3}{4}$. The final
    movement, the most technically challenging of the three, is in a lively $\frac{2}{4}$ and
    marked Allegro con spirito, quasi presto, reminiscent of the opening of the
    first-movement motive. Multiple tonguing, agile technique, and a strong
    high range are needed for this challenging and rewarding work.
Range: c–c³
Duration: 16:00

Jalbert, Pierre (1967–) United States
Jalbert is professor of composition and theory at Rice University's Shepherd School
of Music in Houston and he has won numerous awards for his compositions.

Concerto for Horn and Orchestra
Pierre Jalbert Music, orchestra score only
Commissioned and premiered by William VerMeulen and the Rice University
    Shepherd School Symphony Orchestra, on November 6, 2004. In three
    movements and written in a contemporary tonal/modal style, full of shim-
    mering orchestral colors and extensive percussion for the orchestra. After
    a brief misterioso introduction, with the horn starting quietly over strings,
    the horn bursts into a syncopated motive that drives the first movement,
    with very fast sixteenth-note figures, culminating in a cadenza. The sec-
    ond movement, "Mystical, suspended," features the horn in dialogue with
    different solo winds against a backdrop of slowly changing colors in the
    strings. Bells and Gregorian-chant-like motives evoke the mystical. The
    horn is featured in the middle to low ranges, then works its way up to a
    dramatic gesture with high d³s in *fortissimo*. The final movement, "Fast,
    energetic, precise" is intense and driving, with the horn in quick runs and
    leaps. This work is challenging in many respects, requiring solid range, en-
    durance, and technical facility.
Range: G–d³
Duration: 20:00

See also: Robert Johnson, "Behind the Scenes: Making History with Pierre Jalbert's New Horn Concerto," *The Horn Call* 35 (May 2005): 92–94.

Janssens, Robert (1939–) Belgium

Concerto no. 2 pour cor et orchestra (1977)
Editions J. Maurer, 1977, piano reduction
For Francis Orval, written for the Concours International de Saint-Hubert, Belgium, 1977. In three continuous movements: Allegro moderato—Lento—
Allegro. This is a showpiece for the horn, opening with virtuosic motives
in the horn that are developed throughout the first movement against a
forceful tutti orchestra. The second movement is lyrical and at times pastoral in character, with the horn line paired with individual instruments
such as flute, oboe, and harp, and trading off with the full tutti strings. An
exciting introduction in the percussion leads into a bright and energetic
final movement that moves between $\frac{6}{8}$ and $\frac{9}{8}$, with hemiolas and rhythmic
shifts. Harmonic language is based in traditional tonality, with many contemporary surprises. This is technically challenging horn writing, with
quick wide leaps but well paced overall. Recorded by Francis Orval, with
Janssen's *Concerto no. 1,* which is not published.
Range: B♭–c³
Duration: 10:14

Jevtic, Ivan (1947–) Serbia and France

Concerto for Horn and Orchestra (1993)
Editions BIM, 1993, piano reduction
First performed in Paris, in 2002. This work is organized into three sections that
are played without break: Andante tranquillo—Scherzo rustico—Allegro
ma non troppo. Written in a contemporary tonal language, with inflections of folk music. The piece opens with horn alone, as if in a soliloquy,
and there is a quasi-cadenza, muted, at the end of the second movement.
An expressive work with a balance of characters that are both lyrical and
rhythmic, it uses the entire horn range.
Range: A–d♭³
Duration: 16:00

Danse d'Été for Horn and String Orchestra (1994)
Editions BIM, 1994, piano reduction
For Pdeja and Petar Ivanovic. In three fairly short movements. The first is driving
and dramatic, with syncopations and changing meters. The second move-
ment begins slowly, with a soaring line from low to high. There is a mid-
dle section of freely sounding horn-call motives before the dolce ending.
The third movement is the most technically challenging, with octave leaps
and hemiola figures in a driving Allegro molto. The harmonic language,
with its eastern European inflections, is reminiscent of composers such as
Shostakovich.
Range: c–e♭³
Duration: 10:00

Jirko, Ivan (1926–1978) Czech Republic
Jirko was a composer, critic, and psychiatrist. He was professor at the Academy of Performing Arts in Prague and worked with the Opera National Theatre.

Divertimento für Waldhorn und Orchester (1965)
Bärenreiter, orchestra score only
Duration: 13:00

Jones, Samuel (1935–) United States
Composer in residence with the Seattle Symphony, former conductor of the Rochester Philharmonic, and founding dean of the Shepherd Music School at Rice University, where he also taught composition for many years.

Concerto for Horn and Orchestra (2008)
Campanile Music Press, 2008, orchestra score only
Written for John Cerminaro, who premiered it with the Seattle Symphony on
    February 14, 2008. In three movements and written in a tonal harmonic
    language. The first movement begins boldly, giving way to wide-ranging
    legato horn lines. A colorful bird-call motive, meant to represent the wood
    thrush, is introduced and is developed even further in the cadenza, with
    the horn playing echoing passages. The second movement begins and
    ends with a lyrical aria, with a contrasting canon in the middle section.
    The third movement "portrays the struggle and exhilaration of ascend-
    ing a large mountain," and features "chorales . . . exulting horn calls," and
    "echoes as they come from neighboring peaks." (email exchange with the
    composer and Linda Dempf, August 16, 2015) The movement ends quietly,
    alternating the chorale motive with quotations from the spiritual "There is
    a Balm in Gilead."
Range: c♯–c³
Duration: 25:00

Jong, Marinus de (1891–1984) Belgium, born in the Netherlands

Concerto pour cor en fa et orchestre, op. 145 (1966)
CeBeDeM, 1970, piano reduction
    1. Allegro risoluto
    2. Andante tranquillo e espressivo
    3. Allegro giocoso
Neo-romantic work in traditional forms. The first movement is in sonata form,
    with a heroic dotted eighth-sixteenth first theme and a lyrical second
    theme, with a brief cadenza. The second movement is lyrical, with a mid-
    dle section of triplets in a heroic style, and a return of the opening theme
    restated with chromatic ornamentation. The third movement is in rondo
    form, with a straightforward, bright tune in major that moves through
    different transformations. Not overly technical writing for the soloist, but
    requires long-range endurance.
Range: G–c³
Duration: 16:00

Kaipainen, Jouni (1956–) Finland

Concerto for Horn and Orchestra, op. 61 (2001)
Wilhelm Hansen, 2007, orchestra score only
Commissioned by the Oulu Philharmonic and written for Esa Tapani, who pre-
    miered the work in 2001. The first movement is the most intricate, with a
    jaunty angular figure that moves throughout the range of the horn then
    gives way to a second idea of longer lines in $\frac{3}{4}$. There is an extensive cadenza.
    The second movement opens with the horn playing a long melody over an
    ostinato figure in the orchestra. Several passages slip into a neo-romantic
    harmonic language before returning to the ostinato figure. A brief inter-
    lude in $\frac{6}{8}$ follows, sounding a bit like a distressed waltz, before the return
    of the main theme. The movement ends with a surprising and beautiful
    slide into a final F major chord. The last movement is quite demanding
    for the horn, with long lines that rise above the staff, punctuated with a
    sixteenth-note figure that alternates open and stopped notes. This is a sig-
    nificant recent addition to the horn repertoire, modern, accessible, and col-
    orfully orchestrated. Very demanding for the horn soloist. Recorded by Esa
    Tapani, Finnish Radio Symphony Orchestra, on the Ondine label.
Range: E–d³
Duration: 24:00–25:00

Kalliwoda, Johann Wenzel (1801–1866) Germany, born in Prague

Introduction and Rondo, op. 51 for horn and orchestra (1834)
KaWe, 1972; Musica Rara, 1978; Kunzelmann, 1980—all piano reductions
Kalliwoda wrote two separate horn parts for this piece, one for natural horn and
    one for valve horn. The Musica Rara edition is for valve horn, while the
    KaWe presents in facsimile, both the natural-horn and valve-horn versions,
    which vary substantially. The first section, Allegro moderato, is free, with
    changing tempos and characters, sometimes lyrical, other times declama-
    tory and dramatic. The second section rondo is an Allegretto grazioso in
    $\frac{2}{4}$, with typical nineteenth-century chromaticism and harmonic language,
    fully utilizing the recently invented valve horn. Quite technical and stren-
    uous, with the horn playing many long continuous sections right up to the
    brilliant sustained high c³ at the end.
Range: c–c³
Duration: 9:11

Karadimchev, Boris (1933–2014) Bulgaria
On the faculty at the National Academy for Theater and Film Arts in Sofia,
Karadimchev is best known for his compositions for film, popular music, and
music for children.

Concerto for Horn and Orchestra (1961)
Edition Ka We, 1972, piano reduction
Maestoso pesante, allegro non troppo
Andante con moto
Allegro moderato

In three movements and in contemporary tonal language, suitable for the college
    player.
Range: G♯–b♭²
Duration: 16:00

Kauder, Hugo (1888–1972) Austria and United States, born in Czech Republic
Kauder was a violinist, composer, and teacher who emigrated to the United States
in 1938.

Concerto for Horn and String Orchestra (1930)
Seesaw Music Corp., 1974, full score
This work is dedicated to hornist Willem Valkenier, who played in the Wiener
    Tonkuenstler Orchester with Kauder. In traditional harmonic language
    with mixed meters that are notated without bar lines, this piece would
    work well as a chamber work with a small string ensemble. It begins with
    a sostenuto introduction, followed by an Allegro, and ends with the soste-
    nuto material of the opening.
Range: A–c³
Duration: 12:00

Kaun, Bernhard (1899–1980) United States, born in Germany
Kaun was educated in Germany, then worked as a composer and orchestrator for
Hollywood films until 1941, after which he turned to composing concert music.

Sinfonia Concertante for Solo Horn and Orchestra (1940)
Jupiter Music Publications, 1940, piano reduction
Dedicated to Wendell Hoss. In four movements: Moderato—Lento—Allegro con
    moto e capriccioso—Allegro. This flowing piece has changing meters and
    tempos within each movement, with many opportunities for rubato and
    expressive playing. Long-range endurance required.
Range: f–b♭²
Duration: 23:30

Kayser, Leif (1919–2001) Denmark
Concerto, per corno (fa) e orchestra d'archi (1941–1951)
Copy of manuscript of the horn and piano arrangement, piano part only, at the
    University of Louisville Music Library.
In three movements: Andante—Andante—Allegro energico. The first movement
    opens with a hymn-like motive in the horn alone, joined by the strings for
    a dialogue that becomes increasingly complex as it moves away from the
    opening tonality. The second movement features luxurious writing in the
    strings, with the horn responding with ideas that are often disjunct and
    more chromatic. The final movement is rhythmic, developing syncopated
    figures and an energetic dotted eighth-sixteenth motive. Contemporary
    tonal language in a romantic style, at times reminiscent of Shostakovich.
    Recorded by Albert Linder.
Range: a–c³
Duration: 23:53

Kelemen, Milko (1924–) Croatia
Leading Croatian composer and conductor whose works have been performed internationally.

Concerto for Horn and Strings (2001/2002)
Sikorski, 2002, orchestra score only
Commissioned by Festival Strings Lucerne. Dedicated to Radovan Vlatkovic, Achim Fiedler, and the Festival Strings Lucerne, premiered January 18, 2003. In one continuous movement, the horn moves in and out of the string ensemble with long held notes and gestures that punctuate the texture. Sound explorations for the horn abound, with glissandi, quarter tones, flutter tonguing, and improvisatory figures. Endurance and control required. Includes explanation of notation.
Range: F♯–c♯³
Duration: 20:00

Kellner, Johann Andreas (1724–1785) Germany

Concerto D-Dur für Horn (corno da caccia) 2 Flöten, 2 Violinen, Viola und Bass (1781)
Robert Ostermeyer, 2003, piano reduction and orchestra score
Due to its extreme range, which consistently stays well above the staff, Ostermeyer speculates that this concerto was written for corno da caccia (baroque horn in D). The Ostermeyer edition includes parts for both corno di caccia in D (original), and a part for modern valve corno da caccia or trumpet in B♭, due to the high tessitura. In three movements. Written in the florid baroque style.
Range: e¹–e³ (g¹–g³ for horn in D)
Duration: 13:00

Kern, Frida (1891–1988) Austria

Scherzo, op. 43
See: Horn and keyboard

Ketting, Otto (1935–2012) Netherlands
Ketting was a trumpeter with Resedentie Orkest-The Hague Philharmonic before turning full time to composition.

Cheops, for Horn and Orchestra (1995)
Donemus, 1997, orchestra score only
Commissioned by the International Competition for Wind Instruments Foundation. The piece opens with the strings and solo horn presenting layers of sound in slowly changing combinations. The brass (trumpets and trombones, there are no orchestra horns) interrupt with a triplet motive, answering back and forth with the solo horn. These two ideas are developed throughout the piece in different combinations and textures, at times becoming increasingly agitated with clashing dissonance. There is an ex-

tended cadenza, once again interrupted by the brass, and the piece ends quietly on a stopped horn note. The solo horn plays different roles: as an equal partner with the orchestra, exploring different sound combinations and layers; or as a voice at the forefront of the texture, leading the orchestra into new territory. Moderately difficult in the triplet sections, there is some stopped writing, but no other extended techniques. Long-range endurance is required, as there are few breaks for the horn soloist.

Range: e♭–b♭²
Duration: 15:00

Keulen, Geert van (1943–) Netherlands
In addition to his work as a composer, van Keulen was bass clarinetist with the Royal Concertgebouw Orchestra and the Netherlands Wind Ensemble and taught at the Amsterdam Conservatory.

Horn Concerto (2001)
Donemus, 2001, orchestra score only
Premiered by Jacob Slagter and the Royal Concertgebouw Orchestra, September 20, 2001. The opening movement features a recurring horn motive that slowly descends against dramatic shifting blocks of sound in the orchestra. The second movement, Vivace, is in $\frac{6}{8}$, and features changing rhythmic figures and hemiolas between horn and orchestra, giving the movement a wonderfully unsettled feel. The third opens with quiet strings and trombone, leading into an expressive cadenza for the hornist. Contrasting sections ensue, with dramatic climaxes of sound and force in both horn and orchestra. Long lines and phrases, plus a few high entrances make this a challenging work for the hornist, and the second movement requires dexterity for negotiating quick runs in a vivace tempo.

Range: G–d³
Duration: 17:00

Kiel, Clemens August (1813–1871) Germany

Concerto for Horn, op. 23
McCoy's Horn Library, 1986, piano reduction (Linda Lovstad, ed.); Hans Pizka Edition, 2004, piano reduction and orchestra score
The first movement begins with an intense Allegro appassionato, and the opening theme is modified throughout the movement, with the tutti material of the opening unifying the sections. The second movement is marked Larghetto con moto and is in a lyrical $\frac{6}{8}$, with harmonic language and style reminiscent of the second movement of Franz Strauss' op. 8 concerto. The third-movement rondo is an Allegretto in $\frac{2}{4}$, with impishly relentless sixteenths, sixteenth triplets, and wide leaps at fast tempos that move over the range of the horn, requiring great dexterity. Written for August Cordes, hornist with the Court Orchestra of Detmold.

Range: c–e♭³
Duration:14:30

Kirchner, Volker David (1942–) Germany

Konzert für Horn und Orchester (1996)
Schott, 1996, orchestra score
      I. . . . schwebende Erinnerung
      II. Intermezzo
      III. Pastorale.

Dedicated to Marie Luise Neunecker who played the premiere on July 11, 1997, at the Schleswig-Holstein Musik Festival. In addition to its normal position in front of the orchestra, the solo horn plays from a position within the orchestra in front of the percussion with the sound reflecting off the tam-tam. The orchestra horns also play from different positions in the hall and offstage. The first movement is the longest of the three, with the horn playing different expressive motives. The second movement, "Intermezzo," is brief, featuring winds trading off continuous sixteenth-note passages in changing meters, with the solo horn joining in. The final movement, "Pastorale," returns to the lento misterioso character of the opening movement. This piece is thoughtful, pensive, soloistic, and expressive. The publisher's website states that the concerto fully explores the horn's "tonal and technical possibilities. Kirchner has never been interested in pushing the boundaries of possibilities of the horn's sound, preferring to revert to the mysticism of the Romantic era, the horn being considered its natural musical voice." (www.schott-music.com/shop/products/show,158597,,f.html)
Range: F–b^2
Duration: 18:00

Klein, Richard Rudolf (1921–2011) Germany

Signale und Sentiments, Concerto für Horn und Streichorchester
Ries & Erler, 1992, piano reduction and orchestra score
This work consists of six contrasting sections that flow together, each developing a different motive. Written in tonal harmonic language, with fast agile sections, and repetitive gestures that move the piece forward, particularly in the final Vivace in $\frac{3}{8}$. The horn part is well paced with appropriate breaks for the soloist, suitable for the advanced high school or early college player.
Range: c–b^2
Duration: 13:00

Kling, Henri (1842–1918) Switzerland, born in France

Solo hornist with the Geneva opera and Concerts Classiques, as well as professor at the Geneva Conservatory, Henri Kling is known to hornists for his etudes and for his arrangements of the Mozart horn concertos. He was also a prolific arranger and composer and wrote method books for horn and other instruments.

Concerto Brillante
Southern Music, 1987, piano reduction (Thomas Bacon, ed.)
This work is in three movements, and each exhibits the technical aspects reminiscent of the Kling etudes, with pleasing melodic material throughout.

The final movement is a tour de force of technical horn writing, in $\frac{6}{8}$ with triplet figures that require good triple-tonguing skills.
Range: g–a²
Duration: 17:30

Knechtel, Johann George (1715–1766) Germany (Bohemia)
Knechtel was the high-horn player for the Dresden Court Orchestra from 1734–1756. Both of these concertos exhibit the high florid writing that Knechtel was playing in works by Heinichen, Fasch, and other Dresden composers.

Concerto ex D per corno et archi (Concerto in D for horn and strings)
Hans Pizka Edition, 1981, piano reduction and orchestra score
No. 10 of Lund University Library Ms. Kat. Wenster Litt. I/10, this manuscript
    was inscribed "Concerto ex D dur del Sigr: Knechtel." In three short move-
    ments: Allegro—Adagio—Allegro. This work goes into the extreme high
    range of the baroque natural horn and stays there a good deal of the time,
    with intricate writing full of high trills, ornaments, and acrobatic feats.
Range: a¹–e³ (c²–g³ for horn in D)
Duration: 8:00

Concerto ex Dis per corno et archi (Concerto in E♭ for Horn and Strings)
Hans Pizka Edition, 1982, piano reduction and orchestra score
No. 11 of Lund University Library Ms. Kat. Wenster Litt. I/11. It is generally agreed
    that this piece was written by Knechtel, since it follows and is similar in
    style to no. 10 in the Lund MSS catalog. Composed in three movements:
    Allegro—Adagio—Tempo de menuet. Similar to Knechtel's Concerto in D,
    this is also a very difficult work due to the extreme high range.
Range: f¹–f³ (g¹–g³ for horn in E♭)
Duration: 8:15

Knudson, Elizabeth (1981–) Canada

Mosaic (2010)
Horn and piano version available from International Horn Society Online Music
    Sales; orchestra parts available from the Canadian Music Centre.
For Oliver de Clercq, who premiered the work with the West Coast Symphony
    Orchestra, in Vancouver, British Columbia, on June 11, 2010. The composer
    writes in the preface that the piece was "inspired by the idea of creating a
    dreamscape, with the solo horn as the central character: the one experi-
    encing the dream." In five contrasting movements played without break,
    portraying various aspects of the sleep/dream world. Atmospheric, ener-
    getic, sometimes hypnotic. The fourth movement is an extensive cadenza.
    Technically this work is not too difficult, however there are some challeng-
    ing passages that extend into the high range, and long-range endurance is
    required due to the length of the work.
Range: c–d³
Duration: 26:00

Knussen, Oliver (1954–) United Kingdom

Horn Concerto, op. 28 (1994)

Faber Music, 2002, piano reduction by Lionel Friend; study score also available

Commissioned by Suntory Limited for the Suntory International Program for
Music Composition in 1994. The first performance was given by Barry
Tuckwell, horn, with the Tokyo Metropolitan Symphony Orchestra, conducted by Oliver Knussen, October 7, 1994. In three continuous sections:
Intrada—Fantastico—Envoi. Scored for large orchestra and reminiscent of
a romantic concerto, this work is mostly lyrical and at times atmospheric
and haunting, with the horn floating above the orchestra, carrying the melodic material. The primary set of notes organizing the piece is a musical
spelling of Barry Tuckwell's name. Rhythmic complexities, with changing
meters and irregular phrasing, give the work a free and expansive character, exploring the full range of the horn's abilities for expression, dynamics, and timbre. This is a challenging work, due to the range, endurance
required, and quick changes in dynamics, often in the upper range of the
horn. Only a few instances of extended techniques, including flutter tonguing, trills, and a few stopped notes.

Range: E–c³

Duration: 13:00

Kocsár, Miklós (1933–) Hungary

Concerto in memoriam ZH: per corno e orchestra da camera (1983)

Editio Musica Budapest, 1986, orchestra score only

For Ferenc Tarjáni, who played the premiere October 3, 1983, with the Szeged
Chamber Orchestra. Written in memory of the film director Zoltán Hus-
zárik. Scored for solo horn, harp, strings, and percussion. In contrasting
sections of different characters, this work is lyrical and pointillistic, with
colorful effects of stopped writing, and many expressive rubato lines. There
are instances of aleatoric writing in all of the parts, with the soloist and
ensemble voices coming together at pre-defined moments. There is an extensive monologue for the horn before the penultimate rhythmic section,
followed by a quiet ending. Challenging chromatic figures, but this work
emphasizes color and musical line, rather than technical agility of the
soloist.

Range: g♯–b²

Duration: 15:00

Koechlin, Charles (1867–1950) France

Poëme pour cor et orchestra (1918–1925)

Manuscript score and parts are in the Fleisher Collection, Free Library of Philadelphia

1. Moderato, très simplement et avec souplesse
2. Andante, très calme, presque adagio
3. Final, assez animé

Originally composed as *Sonata for Horn and Piano*, op. 70 (1918–25). It was transcribed for orchestra in 1927, with the first performance of this orchestration taking place in Paris on March 24, 1927, with the Concerts Straram Orchestra, Walther Straram, conductor, Edouard Vuillermoz, soloist. Flowing, lyrical writing for the horn. Includes stopped horn. The spirited final movement is in $\frac{12}{8}$.

Range: e–c³
Duration: 15:00
See: Horn and keyboard

Koetsier, Jan (1911–2006) Netherlands

Concertino for Horn and String Orchestra, op. 74 (1977)
Editions BIM, 1992, piano reduction and orchestra score
    I. Allegro molto
    II. Intermezzo
    III. Rondo in modo di perpetuum mobile
Premiered by Hermann Baumann and the Netherlands Chamber Orchestra in 1979. In three movements. The first movement is in three, with lyrical horn melodies that soar over the strings. The second movement is charming, similar to the first but with a darker twist to it. The third-movement is virtuosic while showing the horn's playful side. This is light music, tuneful, with moments reminiscent of Strauss or Mahler. There are a few alternating stopped-to-open effects.

Range: d–c³
Duration: 13:00

Kogan, Lev (1927–2007) Israel, born in Russia

Hassidic Rhapsody for Horn and String Orchestra (1979)
Israel Brass Woodwind Publications, 2005, orchestra score only
Dedicated to Meir Rimon, who premiered this piece in 1979 with the Israel Philharmonic Orchestra, David Amos conducting. An expressive work in contrasting sections based on Hassidic scales and inflections of folk music, with plenty of opportunity for quasi-cadenzas in the horn.

Range: d♯–b²
Duration: 9:30

Tfila (Prayer)
Israel Brass Woodwinds Publications; String parts available on rental from OR-TAV Music
See: Horn and keyboard

Komarovskiĭ, Anatoliĭ Sergeevich (1909–1955) Russia

Concerto for Horn and Orchestra (Kontsert dli͡a valtorny s orkestrom)
Gos. muzykal'noe izd-vo, 1954, piano reduction
Written in a romantic style, with long legato lines in the first movement that lead into a cadenza. The slow second movement is a pleasant melodic tune in

five flats for the horn, marked Andante and in $\frac{3}{4}$ with some stopped-horn effects at the end. The final movement is rhythmic and energetic and brings back the theme from the first movement. A moderately difficult work, requiring good long-range endurance.

Range: e♭–b♭²

Duration: 18:00

Korn, Peter Jona (1922–1998) United States, born in Germany

Concertino for Horn and Strings, op. 15 (1952)

Boosey & Hawkes, 1959, piano reduction

To Joseph Eger, who played the first performance at the Ojai Festival in California in 1953. In three continuous movements. The opening movement is a flowing Allegretto in $\frac{6}{8}$, much of it in the low range, hovering around written middle c before it makes its way into the high range toward the end of the movement. The second movement, marked Adagio, opens with a legato horn line based on fourths, becoming more active, with sections of rubato and a recitative-like passage accompanied by strings. The final movement is a Rondino con spirito, in changing character, with a reworking of thematic material previously heard. The piece ends with a final cadenza in the horn. This is a well-paced solo for the hornist, requiring agile technique, and it is suitable for the advanced college player and above. Old notation bass clef.

Range: c–b² (ossia c–c³)

Duration: 15:13

Kostov, Georgi (1941–) Bulgaria

Kostov is a professor at the State Academy of Music in Sofia, and served as minister of culture of Bulgaria.

Concerto pour cor et orchestra (Kontsert Za Valdkhorna i Orkestur)

Nauka i Izkustvo, 1971, piano reduction

In three movements. The first features rhythmic motives with contrasting sections of declamatory writing at a slow tempo. The middle movement is slow and sustained. The final movement develops a driving sixteenth-eighth note motive through changing meters.

Range: f–b²

Duration: ca: 18:30

Kraft, Leo (1922–2014) United States

Kraft studied compositions with Karol Rathaus, Randall Thompson, and Nadia Boulanger. He has authored many texts for music theory, and was on the faculty at Queens College for many years.

L'Unicorno, for Solo Horn and String Orchestra (2003)

Seesaw, 2003, orchestra score only

This work is dedicated to David Jolley and Max Lifchitz. In one continuous movement with many contrasting sections. Agitated writing and shifting harmonies in the string orchestra are the underpinning for a colorful, often scherzando-like horn solo. Muted sections and expressive writing for the horn abound. There is a brief duet with the horn and a solo violin trading lines back and forth, then it is the bass player's turn for a solo, played over an extended low B♭ in the solo-horn line.

Range: B♭–c³
Duration: 10:12

Kraft, William (1923–) United States

Veils and Variations for Horn and Orchestra (1988)
New Music West, 1988, orchestra score only
This work was the first-prize winner of the 1990 Kennedy Center Friedheim Award for composition of best new American work in orchestral music. Commissioned by Jeff von der Schmidt, hornist, who played the premiere on January 27, 1989, with the Berkeley Symphony Orchestra. The recording's liner notes (Albany Records) describe the "veils" of the title as "layers of sonorities that combine to form a constantly changing succession of aural textures." The "Variations" grew out of Kraft's unaccompanied work for horn, *Evening Voluntaries,* with a "pastoral, far-off character" followed by a series of variations that flow into each other. Challenging writing for horn, with wide leaps, technical passages of multiple tonguing, and alternating open and stopped writing.

Range: E♭–c³
Duration: 27:30

Krek, Uroš (1922–2008) Slovenia
Krek is considered one of the foremost Slovenian composers.

Concerto for French Horn and Strings (1960)
Drustvo Slovenskih Skladateljev, 1972, piano reduction
This work opens with the horn, alone, playing an expressive legato passage, then the strings enter with an agitated syncopated figure under the horn legato, followed by a jaunty section of ⅜. An extended recitative for the horn concludes the first movement. Beautiful and jarring modal harmonies fill the slow second movement, with the horn playing sustained legato passages, *forte* and declamatory over the strings. The third movement is an energetic Vivo, with syncopated figures between horn and strings.

Range: a–b²
Duration: 17:00

Kricka, Jaroslav (1882–1969) Czech Republic
Kricka taught at the Prague Conservatory and wrote a large number of operas, including children's operas.

Concertino in F, op. 102 (1951)
Artia, 1962, piano reduction
The concertino is also arranged for horn and string quartet. Dedicated "to the Czech virtuoso of the horn, Prof. Emanuelu Kauckému," who premiered

it with string quartet in 1952. In three movements. This work is in the tradition of romantic horn writing, with lyrical lines, tonal harmonies, and idiomatic writing for the horn. Includes changes of tempi and key areas within overarching three-movement form. The second movement is based on a straightforward tune, with easygoing phrases in the midrange of the horn. The last movement, in $\frac{6}{8}$, is fun to play, with wide slurred leaps, hemiolas, and a bit of double tonguing, all within shifting characters and moods.
Range: F–b♭^{2}
Duration: 22:00

Krivitsky, David [Krivitskii, David Isaakovich] (1937–2010) Russia, born in Ukraine

Konzert für Horn und Orchester (1989)
Editions Marc Reift, 1995, piano reduction
Originally for horn and string orchestra. In two movements: Andante espressivo—Moderato pastorale. There are many sections marked *senza metro* and *ad lib* where the soloist can play freely, giving the piece an improvisatory feel. The second movement is a theme with six different variations, many of which are like recitatives. Includes colorful effects such as trills, glissandi, and flutter tonguing.
Range: g♯–b^2
Duration: 20:00

Krol, Bernhard (1920–2013) Germany

Concerto barocco für Horn und Orchester, op. 86 (1984)
Bote & Bock, 1986, piano reduction
Krol's *Laudatio* for unaccompanied horn is a standard piece in the horn repertoire, yet his many other works may not be familiar to horn players in the United States. *Concerto barocco* was first performed on October 17, 1984, by Johannes Ritzkowsky and Christoph Stepp conducting the Städtische Orchester Remscheid. Krol often uses connections with traditional musical forms of the past as a basis for his works, and in this case, he chose the baroque concerto. In three movements: Allegro giusto—Adagio—Allegro ma non troppo. Within each movement, there are changes of character and tempo. This is an accessible work for the horn. Although the length requires good long-range endurance, there are judicious rests throughout.
Range: e–c^3
Duration: 23:00

Corno-Concerto, Study in Jazz, op. 29, for horn and orchestra
(or horn and jazz orchestra, op. 29a) (1958)
N. Simrock, 1959, piano reduction
The version for jazz orchestra is scored for solo horn with piano, percussion, bass, and strings. Composed in three movements. The first, entitled "Cool," moves at a quick tempo. It takes an ABA form, with the outer sections of swing eighth-note patterns, and a cantabile middle section. The second movement,

"Sweet," is lyrical, with legato gestures that move throughout the range of the horn. The final movement, "Hot," develops several themes, including a straight sixteenth-note declamatory statement and a moving eighth-note motive. A lyrical lento section slows things down, then the opening motive returns, leading to a "quasi boogie" section, followed by a coda.

Range: a♭²–b²
Duration: 14:00

Figaro-Metamorphosen: Voi, che sapete, op. 61
Bote & Bock, 1977, piano reduction
Originally for horn and strings, this piece is based on Cherubino's aria "Voi, che sapete," from *Le Nozze de Figaro*. Played without breaks, it is made up of many sections of changing mood and style and organized into three larger sections. A brief opening cadenza-like section marked Libre is followed by an Andante di canzona where we hear three bars of Cherubino's "Voi, che sapete." A Tempo di menuetto, with cadenza, is then followed by a final presto section. This is an intricate work, with many challenges for the horn player. Premiered May 24, 1977, in Schwetzingen, Johannes Ritzkowsky, horn soloist, Württembergisches Kammerorchester conducted by Jörg Faerber.

Range: F–c³
Duration: 19:00

Innsbrucker Konzert, für Solo-Horn und 25 Blasinstrumente, op. 141 (1997)
Edition mf, wind-band score
For horn and wind band, written for the First Tyrolian Horn Society, sponsored by the Municipality of Innsbruck, the preface indicates that this is based on Heinrich Isaac's *Innsbruck muss ich lassen*, and the second theme is the intonation of the Gregorian chant *Te deum laudamus*. "The Innsbruck concerto is dedicated to the people of Tyrol and is at the same time a kind of *Innsbruck Te Deum* to this beautiful town."

Range: B–b²

Kryukov [Kriukov], Vladimir (1902–1960) Russia

Italian Rhapsody
Also exists under the title *Ital'ianskaia rapsodiia dlia valtorny s orkestrom*, Soch. 65.
See: Horn and keyboard

Kudelski, Carl Matthias (1805–1877) Germany

French Horn Concertino
Sansone, 1941, piano reduction
This short work is in three sections, an Allegro maestoso, a very brief Adagio, and a rondo, marked Allegretto, in ⅜. Very traditional writing for the horn in late nineteenth-century light-classical-music style.

Range: f–b♭² (or to c³ in the Sansone edition cadenza)
Duration: 9:00

Kurka, Robert (1921–1957) United States

Ballad for French Horn and Strings, op. 36
Weintraub Music, 1961, piano reduction
To Joseph Eger. Expressive work in ABA form, written in contemporary tonal language. The entire range of the horn is utilized, with wide legato leaps that
   span nearly two octaves and melodic writing in the low range. There is a
   thirteen-bar phrase of repeated high Bs and Cs, marked *pianissimo,* at an
   adagio tempo, with an option to play an octave lower. This phrase returns at
   the end of the piece in *fortissimo,* a bit shorter, but without the lower-octave
   option.
Range: B–c^3
Duration: 6:30

Kurz, Siegfried (1930–) Germany
Kurz studied trumpet, conducting, and composition at the Dresden Hochschule
before becoming music director at the Dresden Staatstheater and later conductor
of the Dresden Staatsoper.

Konzert für Horn und Orchester (1973)
Deutscher Verlag für Musik, 1973, piano reduction
The concerto opens with a declamatory statement in the horn based on the in-
   terval of a fourth and develops throughout the movement with-eighth
   note motives in a contrapuntal style. The second movement is lyrical and
   marked Andante, with sections of free recitative for the horn. The third
   movement, Allegro, is full of syncopations and triplet runs, driving with
   energy to the final cadenza for the horn. This work was premiered by Peter
   Damm, horn soloist, with the Staatskapelle Dresden, December 20, 1973,
   Herbert Blomstedt conducting.
Range: e♭–c^3
Duration: 25:00

Laburda, Jirí (1931–) Czech Republic

Burlesca für Horn und Orchester (1961, 1970)
Ries & Erler, 1970, orchestra score only
Light and energetic work in $\frac{2}{4}$ and $\frac{3}{8}$ marked Allegro con fuoco. Tonal harmonic
   language, with agile eighth- and sixteenth-note figures that stay mostly in
   the staff. Becomes increasingly chromatic as things progress, then returns
   to the opening motive. Suitable for the advanced high school or college-
   level player.
Range: f–c^3
Duration: 7:00

Laman, Wim (1946–) Netherlands
Laman has worked as a composer and teacher and has written works for many
contemporary ensembles.

Confronti, per corno solo e tre gruppi strumentali (1982)
Donemus, 1982, orchestra score only

This concerto was premiered by Vicente Zarzo at the Royal Conservatory of The
   Hague. Instrumentalists are organized on stage in three groups. There is an
   obbligato part for "horn folkloristico" that includes four different types of
   alphorn. This part could also be played by trombone with a mute. The horn
   line is centered around a group of pitches and continually returns to this
   group with different gestures. Sound explorations include flutter tonguing
   and quarter-tone vibrato. The emphasis is on sound and the shifts between
   the horn and the different groups of instrumentalists.

Range: B♭–g²
Duration: 14:15

Láng, István (1933–) Hungary

Concerto bucolico
Editio Musica Budapest, 1973, piano reduction
To Ferenc Tarjáni. In five movements, some of them quite short, this atonal work
   explores the colors, ranges, and extended techniques of the horn, with
   wide leaps, flutter tonguing, stopped writing, alternating stopped and open
   pitches, and quarter tones.

Range: d–c♯³
Duration: 11:00

Larsson, Lars-Erik (1908–1986) Sweden

Concertino for Horn and String Orchestra, op. 45 (1955)
Carl Gehrmans Musikförlag, 1957, piano reduction
>   I. Allegro moderato
>   II. Lento cantabile
> III. Allegro vivace

Larsson wrote a series of twelve concertinos, proceeding methodically in score
   order, starting with no. 1 for flute, through winds, brass, and strings, finishing with no. 12 for piano. This is neo-classical, traditional in form, yet in
   contemporary tonal language. The first movement is in ¾, marked Allegro
   moderato, the second movement is marked Lento cantabile, and the third
   is in a jaunty ⁶⁄₈ that incorporates the heroic theme from the first movement
   and cantabile material from the second movement. This is an engaging,
   very accessible work, suitable for the upper-level college player.

Range: c–b♭²
Duration: 13:00

Lazarof, Henri (1932–2013) United States, born in Bulgaria

Fantasia for Horn and Orchestra (1994)
Merion Music, Theodore Presser, 1995, orchestra score only, study score available
Commissioned by the Seattle Symphony, who premiered it with John Cerminaro, horn, May 19, 1997. In one movement. Ethereal and atmospheric, the
   piece begins with the horn playing *quasi una improvisation* over harp and
   percussion, soon joined by the four orchestra horns. The horn writing is
   challenging throughout this work, with wide leaps and technical passages

that move through the ranges of the horn quickly, over dramatic and colorful orchestral writing. Recorded by John Cerminaro with the Seattle Symphony.

Range: G–b²

Duration: 18:00

Leclerc, Michel (1914–1995) Belgium

Leclerc was a violinist and composer and taught at the conservatory in Liege.

Concerto pour cor et orchestra

J. Maurer, 1959, piano reduction

Dedicated to Adhémar Pluvinage. In three movements. The first is quick, organized around an eighth-note motive that moves through changing meters, alternating with cantabile sections, and ending with a brief cadenza. The second movement is relaxed, marked Andante in $\frac{4}{4}$. The final movement is an energetic Allegro. Good endurance required, as several passages remain in the higher tessitura of the horn.

Range: g♭–c♯³

Duration: 12:00

Ledger, James (1966–) Australia

Horn Concerto (2004, rev. 2009)

Australian Music Centre, orchestra score

    I. Prelude

    II. Postlude

Written for Darryl Poulsen, who first performed this with the University of Western Australia Orchestra, May 6, 2006. The Prelude opens slowly and quietly, with aleatoric writing indicated in seconds, creating an atmospheric effect. The Postlude is rhythmic, in changing meters and with agile writing in the horn, large legato leaps, and several quick chromatic gestures. Well paced, this is accessible for the advanced college hornist and above.

Range: f–a²

Duration: 12:00

Lees, Benjamin (1924–2010) United States

Concerto for French Horn and Orchestra (1991)

Boosey & Hawkes, 1992, piano reduction

Commissioned by the Pittsburgh Symphony Orchestra, premiered in May 1992, by William Caballero. In three movements: Boldly—Calmly—Lively. The first movement is driving and intense with a lyrical middle section and an extensive cadenza. The second movement opens with the horn alone, calmly cycling through horn-fifth motives, building up to rapid-fire slurred sixteenth-note patterns and triplet leaps, and moving into a demanding section that remains at the top of the staff. The final movement opens with the horn in a $\frac{6}{8}$ rondo, which quickly evolves into a jaunty alternation of meter in a triplet feel, punctuated with $\frac{7}{8}$, $\frac{5}{8}$, and occasional hemiolas, keep-

ing the listener and musicians on the edges of their chairs. Recorded by William Caballero, horn, with the Pittsburgh Symphony Orchestra, 1996.
Range: a♭–b²
Duration: 25:00

LeFanu, Nicola (1947–) United Kingdom

Amores, 5 Songs without Words for Horn and Strings (2003)
Maecenas Music, 2007, full score only
   1. Very serene
   2. Presto
   3. Sonorous
   4. Cadenza, quick
   5. Spacious
Premiered by Richard Watkins and the Goldberg Ensemble, February 6, 2004. Five lyrical movements. The composer's preface explains that in the first and last movements, the "strings create a spacious resonance in which the horn can sing." The second movement is in ABA form, with driving outer sections of very fast passages, and a contrasting middle section marked *Wayward, questing*. The third movement is developed from a love song from the composer's chamber piece *Mira clar tenebras;* the fourth movement is an extensive cadenza for the horn, followed by the final movement, with horn singing over the strings.
Range: F–c³
Duration: 20:00

Lepschies, Karl

Rondo für Horn und Orchester
R. Erdmann, 1967, piano reduction
A light classical piece, with a pleasing tune in ⅜, felt in one, and with a few opportunities for virtuosic flourishes for the horn soloist.
Range: a–b²
Duration: 5:45

Leschetizky, Theodor Hermann (1896–1948) Austria

Scherzo for Horn and Orchestra
Universal Edition, orchestra score only
Duration: 10:00

Leutwiler, Toni (1923–2009) Switzerland
Leutwiler was a violinist, composer, and arranger who worked primarily with radio orchestras throughout Europe, composing and arranging light music for broadcast.

Concertino für Horn und Orchester
Otto Heinrich Noetzel Verlag, 1960, orchestra score only

This is a short energetic piece in ABA form. The two fast outer movements are in one, with a brief Andante in between. Only moderately technical, although the tempo is quick. There are judicious opportunities for rest for the soloist, including the possibility of orchestra horns doubling the end of the Andante, if needed. There are a few stopped and muted passages.

Range: b–a♯²
Duration: 4:05

Levitin, Yury Abramovich (1912–1993) Russia

Concerto for Horn and Orchestra, op. 51

Gos. muzykal'noe izd-vo, 1963, piano reduction

The first movement, marked Allegro, is intense, written in three, but felt in one, and in a minor key that sets up the somber tone of the concerto. The second movement begins with dissonant chords in the accompaniment; the horn enters on a long f², then takes up the melody over the same dissonant chords of the opening. There is a declamatory *fortissimo* in the middle section, then a return to the quiet mood of the opening. The third movement begins with a rubato Andante, come recitativo, followed by energetic and rhythmic writing, marked Vivo.

Range: B♭–b♭²
Duration: 16:30

Lewis, Anthony (1915–1983) United Kingdom

Concerto for Horn and String Orchestra (1956)

Lengnick, 1959, piano reduction

This work is dedicated to Dennis Brain, who premiered it on April 29, 1956, in a concert at the Victoria and Albert Museum with the Boyd Neel Orchestra, Brian Priestman conducting. The first movement, marked Allegro un poco sostenuto, ebbs and flows between sections of ⅝, ⅜, ¹⁰⁄₈, and ⅝, with Animato and Energico sections. The second movement is an expressive Recitative and Aria, and the third movement is an Allegro con spirito, with changing meters throughout.

Range: g–a²
Duration: 18:40

Lewy, Richard (1827–1883) Austria

Concertino für Horn in fa

Hans Pizka Edition, 1979, piano reduction and orchestra score

The piece opens with a brief cadenza for the horn, then presents straightforward melodies in contrasting sections: Andante sostenuto—Allegro—Andantino—Rondino allegretto. Pleasant nineteenth-century music with modest technical demands, the last section is variations on a theme. The solo horn stays mostly in the staff, making this a suitable work for the intermediate student horn player and above.

Range: b–a²
Duration: 10:00

Lieberson, Peter (1946–2011) United States

Horn Concerto

Associated Music Publishers, 1999, orchestra score only

Commissioned by the Orpheus Chamber Orchestra and dedicated to the memory of Serge and Natalie Koussevitzky. Premiered on February 27, 1999, by William Purvis, who also recorded the work. In two connected parts, this work moves from graceful lyric passages, to dancing rhythmic figures and jaunty exclamations, swinging back into ethereal passages, then morphing into jazzy bits. The orchestration features colorful wind writing, lush playing, and occasional interplay between the one orchestra horn and the horn soloist. This work is a sparkling addition to the horn repertoire. Quite challenging technically, with wide leaps, quickly changing meters, fast agile writing. Good stamina is needed.

Range: $B-c^3$

Duration: 18:00

Ligeti, György (1923–2006) Austria, born in Hungary

Hamburg Concerto, for solo horn and chamber orchestra (with two basset horns and four obligato natural horns) (1998–2002)

Schott, 2004, orchestra score only

Written for Marie Louise Neunecker, who premiered the work with the Asko Ensemble in Hamburg (first six movements, January 20, 2001) and Utrecht (complete work, September 30, 2002). This concerto features very effective scoring for four natural horns in the orchestra, which provides a contrasting timbre that is softer and less edgy than the solo horn. The natural horns play non-tempered natural harmonics, are played in different keys, and therefore have different fundamentals, resulting in clashing combinations of overtones. The solo horn plays a valve horn for the first and fourth movements, and a natural horn in F for the other movements. In seven short movements, each with a different character:

1. Praeludium: features tone clusters of all the horns playing in different keys and the solo horn blending with the rest of the horns.
2. Signale, Tanz, Choral: begins as a call and response between the horns that evolves into all of the horns playing runs up and down the range of the horn simultaneously then finishing with an extended chorale.
3. Aria, Aksak, Hoketus: has the solo horn against a backdrop of pizzicato strings and bongo.
4. Solo, Intermezzo, Mixtur, Kanon: features the horn alone in an extended solo passage then followed by an extensive tutti in the orchestra.
5. Spectra: has similar material that was played by all of the horns in the Praeludium, this time with the orchestra taking the exploration of timbre even further, ending in an eerie unison D♭.
6. Capriccio: has very soloistic writing for the horn, with challenging technical passages, ornaments, and extreme high notes, all in counterpoint with the orchestra horns.

7. Hymnus: the solo horn has finished its work, and the last movement is like a Greek chorus, commenting on all that has happened during this work and providing the final commentary with progressions of chord clusters.

This is an intense work and a significant addition to the horn repertoire by one of the most well-regarded composers of our time. Marie Louise Neunecker recorded the concerto for *The Ligeti Project IV,* on Teldec.

Range: E–e♭³
Duration: 15:00
See also: Virginia Thompson, "A Long-Awaited Horn Concerto from György Ligeti," *The Horn Call* 31 (May 2001): 32–34.

Lindberg, Magnus (1958–) Finland

Campana in Aria (1998)
Boosey & Hawkes, 1998, orchestra score only
For horn and chamber orchestra, written for Esa-Pekka Salonen on the occasion of his fortieth birthday, commissioned by the Matinee op de vrije Zaterdag, Nederland 3, Dutch public broadcasting corporation. The title means "bells in the air." The horn begins dramatically with a soaring passage in the high range, and continues its virtuosic display of the high range throughout the piece, with quick figures that rise and fall, connecting to the next soaring passage. The orchestra provides a beautiful and often romantic backdrop, with interjections that answer the horn, or are in unison with the horn, such as the startling combination of piccolo/solo horn doubling. Orchestration includes extensive percussion, and the two orchestra horns are placed on the left and right sides of the orchestra. This intense work culminates in a return of the opening horn theme. An exciting contemporary work by one of the major composers of our time, with demanding writing for the horn. Requires excellent high range and endurance. Recorded by Esa Tepani, horn, with the Finnish Radio Symphony Orchestra.

Range: F–c³
Duration: 11:00

Lindorff-Larsen, Eilert (1902–1983) Denmark

Poème, corno solo et orchestre de chambre
Wilhelm Hansen, 1967, orchestra score only
Dedicated to Jens Warny. This short, flowing work is in ¾ and in ABA form, with a middle section of contrasting piu mosso. Reminiscent of a folk song, it places few technical demands on the hornist and is in a modest range.

Range: b♭–f♯²
Duration: 6:00

Lindpaintner, Peter Joseph von (1791–1856) Germany

Lindpaintner was a composer and conductor, and held the post of kapellmeister at Stuttgart for most of his career. He wrote many works for the stage as well as instrumental music, including concertante music for wind quintet and orchestra.

Concertino in E, op. 43

Hans Pizka Edition, 1983, piano reduction and full score

In two movements. A lyrical Adagio is followed by an Allegretto movement in $\frac{3}{4}$. The key of E makes this work a challenge, as the last section has 32nd note passages at a fast tempo. Harmonic language and structure are typical of early nineteenth-century writing, and this piece showcases the horn's agility and technical abilities.

Range: B–b^2 (c–c^3 for horn in E)

Duration: 12:00

Lipkin, Malcolm (1932–) United Kingdom

Pastorale for Horn and Strings (1963, rev. 1979)

Malcolm Lipkin, 1963, 1979, full score, also arranged for horn and string quintet

Written for David Cripps, who, as a young student, performed it with the Newbury String Players. A straightforward work, marked Andante con moto and in $\frac{3}{4}$, written in flowing eighth notes.

Range: g–g^2

Duration: 5:00

Lockwood, Normand (1906–2002) United States

Lockwood studied with Ottorino Respighi and Nadia Boulanger and was a winner of the American Prix de Rome in 1929. His career in the U.S. included a Guggenheim Fellowship and teaching posts at Oberlin, Yale, Columbia, and eventually the University of Denver.

Panegyric for Solo Horn and String Orchestra

Solid Wood Music, 1998, orchestra score only

This work is dedicated to Donald Sutherland (1915–1978), and was premiered February 1, 1981, John Keene, horn soloist with the Arapahoe Chamber Orchestra conducted by Carl Topilow. In four sections, played without break, featuring declamatory, angular writing for the horn. A lyrical section in $\frac{3}{4}$ is followed by an Allegro moderato with the horn playing long phrases over the strings. After a brief return of the opening material, the piece ends quietly. There are rips up to high b^2 and an extended phrase that features the horn playing alone in the low range, but overall this work is well paced for the soloist, with technical demands of moderate difficulty.

Range: c♯–b^2

Duration: 12:30

Loevendie, Theo (1930–) Netherlands

Loevendie established himself in the music profession as a jazz musician, then turned to composition later to become a leading Dutch composer of contemporary music.

Orbits, for Horn Solo, 4 horns obligato & orchestra, (1972–76)

Donemus, 1976, orchestra score only

For Pieter Gouderjaan. The solo horn is positioned centrally in front of the orchestra, and the obbligato horns are on the sides at a distance. The piece opens with static string chords that grow increasingly busy, with the horn soaring above, unfolding different motives that are both angular and lyrical. Orchestra texture is at times a mass of frenzied energy, with interesting colors, such as the English horn repeatedly cutting through the layers of sound with a repeated minor seventh. The obbligato horns begin as part of the orchestra texture, then grow increasingly present, answering the horn soloist in canon. Following an extensive cadenza for the horn solo, the obbligato horns join the soloist at the front of the stage, and the horns become a quintet, united in their wall of sound. The piece ends with a dramatic finish, as the horns exit the stage while playing, leaving the orchestra to conclude the piece quietly. Challenging horn writing that uses the colors of glissandi, flutter tonguing, pitch bends, shakes, stopped writing, and dynamic contrasts for dramatic effect.

Range: c–c^3
Duration: 18:00

London, Edwin (1929–2013) United States
Prolific and award-winning composer and conductor, London founded the Cleveland Chamber Symphony and taught at Smith College, University of Illinois and Cleveland State University.

Be-bop Dreams for Horn and Chamber Ensemble
Edition Peters, 1990, full score only
This work is scored for vibraphone/suspended cymbal, piano, harp, 2 violins, viola, violoncello, and double bass; it may also be performed with multiple strings. A short work in changing meters with expressive jazz elements such as vibrato, trills, and dips. Proportional notation.

Range: e♭–c^3
Duration: ca. 5:00

Lorentzen, Bent (1935–) Denmark
Hunting Concerto for Horn Solo, Gun Shot, Oboe and Strings (1996)
Wilhelm Hansen, 2003; piano reduction
Commissioned by the "Slotsgruppen" (a group of musicians from Copenhagen symphony orchestras) first performed at the royal castle of Charlottenlund, horn soloist Preben Iwan, 1996.
Opens and closes with "gunshots" (gun with blank cartridges), the two outer movements feature the horn in changing variations of hunting calls and signals, trading off with the oboe, over a repetitive string pattern that subtly shifts and changes. The second movement evokes nature and pastoral scenes, with the horn expressing its hunting origins with notes on the harmonic series and bending of pitches. Throughout this work, the composer deconstructs elements of the horn's hunting tradition, then pulls them all back together for a joyful, mysterious, intense ride.

Range: e♭–c^3
Duration: 14:00

Lortzing, (Gustav) Albert (1801–1851) Germany
Lortzing is most known for his operas, particularly in Germany.

Konzertstück für Horn und Orchester (1831)
Berliner Musik-Edition, 1984, piano reduction
For horn in E. There is an opening introduction with arpeggiated figures, followed
      by a theme and variations. This is a virtuosic work for the horn, with agile
      arpeggios and scalar passages. Transposition to E and large leaps make this
      work suitable for an intermediate player and above.
Range: B–d³ (or b² is given as an option for high d³) (c–e♭³ for horn in E)
Duration: 13:12

Louël, Jean (1914–2005) Belgium
Composer, conductor and pianist. *New Grove* describes his music as "a polytonal
style of great complexity and rhythmic variety, giving an impression of ceaseless
movement."

Concerto, Horn and Orchestra (1983)
CeBeDeM, 1983, orchestra score only
Dedicated to Andre Van Driessche. In four movements with contrasting sections
      within each movement. Challenging contemporary horn writing, with
      wide leaps, angular writing, extended techniques such as flutter tonguing,
      glissandi, and a generally high tessitura for the horn.
Range: G♯–c♯³
Duration: 25:00

Luigini, Alexandre (1850–1906)

Romance, op. 48
See: Horn and keyboard

Lundquist, Torbjörn (1920–2000) Sweden

Sea-room, for horn, strings, and piano (1978–1989)
Svensk Musik, 1989, piano reduction
For Thomas Kjelldén. In one continuous movement of contrasting sections and
      written in a contemporary tonal style. The horn begins alone in an extended
      monologue, joined by string chords that lead into contrapuntal writing that
      drives this piece forward in contrasting sections: Appasionato, Grazioso
      ma semplice, Largamente, and a cadenza followed by a Presto-prestissimo.
      The overall technical demands are reasonable, but the wide range and occa-
      sional high tessitura make this a challenging work.
Range: A–d³
Duration: 14:00

Lutyens, Elisabeth (1906–1983) United Kingdom

Chamber Concerto No. 4, for Horn and Chamber Orchestra, op. 8, no. 4 (1946–1947)
Mills Music, 1962, orchestra score only

To Dennis Brain, who premiered the work June 12, 1948, at the International Society for Contemporary Music Holland Festival, with the Residentie Orchestra of The Hague. In two continuous sections: Penseroso—Allegro. This small scale work uses contemporary harmonic language and is in traditional rhythms and forms. The horn begins with a *fortissimo* in a declamatory style, then moves into material that is contemplative and flowing. The second section is in $\frac{3}{4}$ and organized around a regal eighth-sixteenth motive, with double-dotted calls in the horn. Overall, this is not a virtuosic work for the soloist, but there are several challenging passages above the staff.

Range: G–c³
Duration: 12:00

Lyon, David (1938–) United Kingdom

Concerto for Horn and Strings (1978/1997)
Available from the composer, piano reduction and orchestra score
    I. Allegro con spirito
    II. Lento elegiac
    III. Allegro impetuoso
Commissioned by the Milton Keynes Festival (UK), and premiered in 1977 by Peter Clack with the Milton Keynes City Orchestra. Revised for the 1998 Naxos recording with Michael Thompson, horn, with the Royal Ballet Sinfonia, conducted by David Lloyd-Jones. In three movements. The first is full of light and energetic counterpoint with the strings, with contrasting sections of legato figures that sing in the upper ranges of the horn, and a brief cadenza. The second movement is more somber, featuring expressive lyrical lines in the horn. The third movement is fast and fun, with a driving eighth-two-sixteenth motive. A challenging work, with many passages in the upper-middle to high range.

Range: c–c³
Duration: 15:00

Machala, Kazimierz (1948–) Poland, worked in the United States

Concerto for Horn, Winds and Percussion (2002)
Capo Taso Music, 2007, wind band score only
Machala is professor emeritus at the University of Illinois and presently professor of horn at the Frederic Chopin University of Music in Warsaw. This work was premiered September 29, 2002, by the University of Illinois Wind Symphony, James Keene conducting, Kazimierz Machala, horn soloist. The first movement is an energetic and driving Allegro moderato with a cadenza, the horn in dialogue with timpani, then joined by percussion and winds. The second movement is a lyrical Larghetto, and the third movement is in $\frac{6}{8}$, marked Vivo, with a lyrical section in $\frac{3}{4}$. This work is full of energy, changing meters, and idiomatic writing for the hornist. The work is scored for twenty-four players. The wind section of a symphony orchestra (plus double bass and harp), could perform this work.

Range: c–b♭²
Duration: 20:00

Madsen, Trygve (1940–) Norway

Concertino for Horn Solo & Symphonic Band, op. 128

Musikk-Husets Forlag, 2003, piano reduction by the composer

> I. Intrada
> II. Cavatina
> III. Rondo

For Frøydis Ree Wekre. The outer movements alternate sections of declamatory themes that grow into lyrical sections, and the second movement is
in a flowing three. This spirited work requires flexibility and ability to get
around the horn but is well paced for the soloist. Like the composer's *Invitation to a Voyage,* the moderate range makes this an accessible work.

Range: e♭–g²
Duration: 13:15

Invitation to a Voyage for Horn and Symphonic Band, op. 93

Musikk-Husets Forlag, 1997, piano reduction by the composer

To Frøydis Ree Wekre. An homage to Richard Strauss, this work liberally borrows and reworks horn themes from Strauss to create a completely new
and modern piece. Great fun and technically challenging with fast runs
in ⅜, much like Strauss' second concerto and *Til Eulenspiegel.* The range,
extending to g², makes this piece quite accessible.

Range: a–g²
Duration: 8:00

Konsert for horn (F) og orkester, op. 45

Musikk-Husets Forlag, 1986, piano reduction by the composer

Commissioned by the French Ministry of Culture, dedicated to Frøydis Ree
Wekre who premiered the work in Dijon in 1984. This concerto has many
playful moments, with the horn scampering through its range with many
twists and turns. It is also lyrical and introspective, with beautiful melodies in the strings and a distinctive English-horn solo opening the slow
movement. Thematic material is carried across the three movements. In a
romantic style reminiscent of Richard Strauss, this is a fun and rewarding
work for the soloist as well as the listener.

Range: f–b²
Duration: 17:00

Maltby, Richard, United States

Blues Essay, for Solo Trombone (or Horn in F) and Band
See: Horn and keyboard

Maniet, René, Belgium

Concertino pour cor et piano ou orchestra (1960)

J. Maurer, 1960, piano reduction

A short work for horn and strings in three sections, this is a serious work to be
played with intensity and drive. Challenging passages in the third section
that move around the horn require dexterity and flexibility.

Range: g–c^3
Duration: 7:30

Pièce pour cor en fa et piano ou orchestre a cordes (1952)
Editions Maurer, 1957, piano reduction
René Maniet has written several works for brass; this work is dedicated to Jean
    Faulx, professor of horn at the Royal Conservatory, Belgium. A short, light
    piece in three sections, starting with an Allegro in $\frac{3}{4}$ then a middle Andante
    section followed by a quick Allegro vivo in $\frac{6}{8}$. This piece lies well on the
    horn, is fun to play, and is a charming short work.
Range: g–b^2
Duration: 4:00

Manzo, Silvio

Concerto per corno in Fa e pianoforte a forma di sonata
G. Zanibon, 1967, piano reduction
In three short movements: Allegro—Andante amoroso—Presto. Featuring tradi-
    tional harmonic language and rhythms, this may have been written as an
    educational or contest piece, suitable for student use.
Range: g–c^3
Duration: 10:00

Martin, Ernst, Germany

Konzert für Waldhorn und Orchester (ca. 1887)
Edition Ebenos, 2010, piano reduction
First published in 1887 and dedicated to hornist Gustav Bauer. In three continu-
    ous movements. The first, marked Allegro moderato, is in a conventional $\frac{4}{4}$
    with lyrical passages and quick sixteenth-note runs. The slow movement,
    Adagio, decorates a melodic line with ornaments throughout, and the final
    movement is light and energetic. Plenty of showy technical writing for the
    horn soloist makes this a challenging work.
Range: c–c^3
Duration: 16:00

Martland, Steve (1959–2013) United Kingdom
Martland has been described as a vibrant, unconventional force in British music
who crossed boundaries while rejecting academic dogma.

Orc, for horn and small orchestra (1984)
Schott, 1986, orchestra score
Orc premiered January 14, 1985, at The Hague Conservatory, Stefan Blonk, horn,
    ASKO Orchestra. It is dedicated "to Michael Tippett in admiration on the
    occasion of his 80th birthday." In describing this work on the publisher's
    website, Steve Martland writes that "the traditional concerto form is al-
    luded to, both in the relationship of the solo instrument to the 'tutti' and
    with regard to overall structure—fast and slow musics. However, the solo

horn plays 'within' the ensemble and the traditional three-movement layout is disrupted in favour of a continuous montage structure. . . . Orc appears as a character in Blake's prophetic poem America where he epitomizes the spirit of revolt, proclaiming Man's liberty" (www.schott-music./shop/9/show,154035.html) The orchestra sets up rhythmic background with unison chords. The horn grows out of this texture with short lyrical phrases, then gives up its role in the forefront, and becomes a layer in the orchestral texture, playing a series of long notes that begin *fortepiano*, and end explosively on a higher note, in alternation with other voices in the orchestra.

Range: $c-c^3$
Duration: 20:00

Mason, Benedict (1955–) United Kingdom

Ohne Missbrauch der Aufmerksamkeit, for actor, horn, and orchestra (1993)
Chester, orchestra score only
This work is for actor, solo horn, and orchestra, and was commissioned by the Hessischer Rundfunk and first performed on May 7, 1993, by the Radio-Sinfonie-Orchester Frankfurt; Ingo Metzmacher conducting; Udo Samel, actor; and Stefan Dohr, horn soloist. This work is in Mason's series of "Music for Concert Halls," which focus on the spatial aspects of the music and emphasize the relationship between sound and the architectural space. In *Ohne Missbrauch der Aufmerksamkeit* ("Without Misusing Attention") the composer spreads the ensemble out over the entire concert building, with musicians on the sides and the back of the hall, in the foyer, and on stage; the orchestra horns migrate from the foyer to the stage during the piece. The horn soloist has theatrical moments, such as repeatedly bringing the horn up to play, then freezing before leaving the stage, only to run back on stage to begin in earnest. The horn writing has a few challenging passages that go into the low range, but the emphasis of this work is on both sight and sound. Noted in the score: "There is nothing intentionally humorous in this piece."

Range: $F-a^2$
Duration: 18:00

Matalon, Martin (1958–) Argentina

Trame VII (2005)
Billaudot, full score only
For solo horn and instrumental ensemble of flute, clarinet, oboe, bassoon, trumpet, trombone, tuba, 2 percussionists, piano, 2 violins, viola, cello, and bass. Premiered November 6, 2005, Christie Chapman, horn solo with Musikfabrik (Cologne), Martyn Brabbins, director.
Matalon has written a series of "Trames," a cycle of concertante works he began in 1997.
Duration: 21:00

Mathias, William (1934–1992) United Kingdom (Wales)
New Grove describes Mathias as "one of the most significant Welsh composers of the twentieth century."

Horn Concerto, op. 93 (1984)
Oxford University Press, 1987, piano reduction
Written for Hugh Potts, hornist with the Northern Sinfonia, who played the premiere conducted by Richard Hickox. Scored for horn, strings, and timpani, this work is in four movements. The first movement, "Prelude," is marked Allegro moderato, is in $\frac{3}{4}$, and develops a quick motive based on a tritone, which alternates with lyrical writing. The second movement, "Scherzo," is a short, playful romp. The third movement, "Nocturne," is given the most weight of all the movements, featuring beautiful writing between horn and strings, at times atmospheric. The final movement is a Cappricio, quick, to the point, similar to the other quick movements of this concerto in its playful, sardonic writing. Recorded by David Pyatt, horn, on *William Mathias Vocal and Orchestral Music,* on the Metronome label.
Range: g–c³
Duration: 19:00

Matthews, Colin (1946–) United Kingdom

Horn Concerto (2001)
Faber Music, 2006, orchestra score only
This work was premiered by Richard Watkins and the Philharmonia Orchestra in April 2001. It begins with offstage orchestra horns, with the horn soloist answering, also from offstage, then moving onstage with the conductor and to different parts of the stage throughout the work. Composed in one continuous movement, this is an intense piece full of atmospheric writing for both soloist and orchestra. This engaging and dramatic work is full of idioms of traditional horn writing, with offstage horns, horn quartets, and the lyrical lines of horn soloist floating over the lush orchestration. There are glissandi and phrases written on the natural harmonic series.
Range: d♯–c³
Duration: 23:00

Matthus, Siegfried (1934–) Germany
Internationally renowned composer Matthus has composed in almost every genre but is perhaps best known for his operas.

Konzert für Horn und Orchester (1994)
Deutscher Verlag für Musik, 1994, orchestra score only
This concerto was written for Peter Damm, who premiered the work in Dresden, June 9, 1995. It uses contemporary harmonic language, yet remains rooted in the romantic horn tradition. This three-movement work features the horn in colorful and ever changing combinations with the orchestral instruments. The first movement opens with a declamatory statement that

continues in a fast three, settling into a slower $\frac{4}{4}$ with sweeping legato lines in the horn. There is a dialogue between the flute and horn, followed by a brief horn cadenza. The second movement, Presto, has quick runs and glissandi in the horn, with a slower section of three-part multiphonics, followed by an extensive cadenza that is joined by the principal cello. We are ushered into the third movement with a quick brass fanfare and the horn is syncopated and agitated throughout.

Range: F–c^3
Duration: 22:00

Matys, Karl (1835–1908) Germany

Matys wrote four *Konzertstück* for horn and orchestra. This is quintessential late nineteenth-century horn writing with romantic harmonic language, dramatic, with a light touch. Of medium difficulty, the pieces are in ABA format, and all have pleasing, tuneful melodies and opportunities for short cadenzas. These are quite fun to play.

Konzertstück No. 1, op. 12
Muzyka, 1988, horn and piano version published with Concerto No. 2; also available on imslp.org
In three movements: Allegro moderato—Andante—Allegro moderato
Range: c–c^3
Duration: 13:30

Konzertstück No. 2, op. 24
Muzyka, 1988, horn and piano version published with Concerto no. 1; also available on imslp.org
In three movements: Allegro ma non troppo—Andante con moto—Allegro ma non troppo. Cadenzas in all three sections.
Range: G–a^2
Duration: 12:10

Konzertstück No. 3, op. 39
Southern Music, 1940, 2005; Schott, 1880s edition available on imslp.org (horn and piano editions)
In three movements: Allegro—Andante—Allegro.
Range: B♭–a^2
Duration: 11:35

Konzertstück No. 4, op. 44
Schott, 1880s edition available on imslp.org (horn and piano edition)
In three movements: Allegro ma non troppo—Andante—Allegro ma non troppo.
Range: e♭–b♭^{2}
Duration: 11:00

McCabe, John (1939–2015) United Kingdom

Horn Concerto (Rainforest IV) (2005/6)
Novello, 2006, orchestra score only

"To David Pyatt, the nonpareil, and to the memory of Ifor James, another nonpareil." Commissioned by the BBC for the National Orchestra of Wales,
who premiered the work February 16, 2007, with David Pyatt, horn soloist.
The composer writes that the work was inspired by two elements: West
Coast jazz horn in the 1950s and 1960s, and the contemplation of the rain
forest. "It is the contrast between this, in the slow movements, and the
urban world represented by the other influence, that governs the different
characters of the movements." (www.musicsalesclassical.com/composer
/work1023/14716) In continuous sections, played without break: Adagio—
Moderato, poco pesante—Lento—Allegro—Adagio. The outer Adagio
sections serve as an introduction and epilogue; the three inner sections
make up a traditional fast-slow-fast form. Horn calls over steady rhythms
reminiscent of the rain forest are passed back and forth, with the marimba
adding continuous color. A jazzy and brassy section follows, leading into
a lyrical Lento with haunting lines that begin up in the high reaches of the
horn, and then descend. A furious and agitated Allegro pulls out all the
stops before a final Adagio and a return to the rain forest.

Range: B–b^2
Duration: 24:00

McKinley, William Thomas (1938–2015) United States

Huntington Horn Concerto (1989)
MMC, 1989, orchestra score only
    I. Saturday matinee
    II. Broadway blues
    III. Curtain call

Jazz pianist and composer McKinley dedicated this work to Jay Wadenpfuhl,
who premiered it with John Williams and the Boston Pops on May 25, 1989.
The title is a pun on the "hunting horn," and also the street name of the hall
where the piece was premiered. An homage to musical theater, this work
depicts a Saturday on Broadway, from the afternoon matinee, to the end of
the evening show. In traditional-three movement form, the first movement
is dramatic, marked Presto e vivace, in a fast one, with a brief cadenza. The
second movement, marked Moderato sensuale, is based on a bluesy triplet
motive. An energetic last movement with a cadenza finishes the piece with
a flourish. This is a challenging work, written in the style of American musical theatre. There are several ossia, where the orchestra horns can take
the solo line.

Range: G–d^3 (ossia c–d^3)
Duration: 18:30

McQuade Dewhirst, Michelle (1973–) United States

McQuade Dewhirst, currently on the faculty at University of Wisconsin Green
Bay, received degrees in composition from the University of Chicago after gradu-
ating with a degree in horn from Ithaca College. Her works have been performed
by the St. Paul Chamber Orchestra, Pacifica String Quartet, eighth blackbird,
and the New York Miniaturist Ensemble.

Chiasmus, Chamber Concerto for Horn (2002)

JOMAR Press, ensemble score

The ensemble scoring for this work is flutes, clarinets, violin, cello, percussion, and piano. The word "chiasmus" refers to a verbal construction based on the principal of reversal, where a shift in word order results in a different meaning. The composer gives the example of the famous John F. Kennedy quote "ask not what your country can do for you; ask what you can do for your country." In two contrasting movements. The first begins with a cadenza for the horn, at first repeating tones, then gradually moving into larger intervals and more angular patterns, building in momentum as the movement progresses. The second movement, marked "Cool and calculating," is energetic, punctuated with forceful gestures in the ensemble. Challenging horn writing, with colorful contemporary techniques such as glissandi, grace notes, alternating open and stopped writing, multiphonics, half-valved tones, oscillations, and "color trills" created with alternate fingerings.

Range: A–d♭³

Duration: 25:00

Meier, Jost (1939–) Switzerland

Composer and conductor, Meier studied composition with Rolf Looser and Frank Martin, and teaches at the conservatories in Basel and Zürich.

Concerto pour cor et orchestre (2002)

Editions BIM, 2008, piano reduction, study score with solo part, orchestra score

This work was commissioned by and dedicated to Bruno Schneider. In three movements: Andante sostenuto—Andante—Moderato. This is a very effective atonal work, with improvisatory sections, stopped writing, glissandi, and other dramatic flourishes. Difficult for the horn, but well paced and inventive. The composer indicates that the first movement, which is as long as the second and third movements combined, could be performed separately as a fantasy for horn and orchestra. Similarly, the second and third movements could also be performed as an Andante and Allegro.

Range: F–c³

Duration: 24:38

Mengal, Martin-Joseph (1784–1851) Belgium

From a family of horn players, Mengal attended the Paris Conservatory, studied horn with Duvernoy and composition with Reicha, played in the orchestra at the Odéon and Opéra-Comique, and had several operas produced in Paris before returning to Belgium to conduct and eventually direct the new conservatory in Ghent.

Concerto, op. 20

Hans Pizka Edition, 1987 (reconstituted, revised, and arranged by Edmond Leloir), piano reduction

In three movements: Allegro moderato—Adagio—Allegro non troppo. The outer movements are bright and energetic, with sixteenth-note runs in sounding

F major. The second movement begins in the darker parallel minor key then modulates back to F major before the traditional rondo. This is an accessible work on both valve horn and natural horn.

Range: c–c³

Duration: ca. 12:00

Solo pour cor

See: Horn and keyboard

Mengelberg, Karel (1902–1984) Netherlands

Mengelberg was a conductor and composer active throughout Europe who eventually settled in Amsterdam in 1938. Nephew of conductor Willem Mengelberg, father of jazz pianist Misha Mengelberg.

Concerto per corno ed orchestra (1950)

Donemus, 1951; piano reduction by Peter van Zanken

For Piet Schÿf. This horn concerto won the City of Amsterdam Prize. In three movements. The first opens with a cadenza based on a motive of a fifth, then moves into an Allegro moderato, in $\frac{6}{8}$, and ends with a cadenza with abbreviated themes from the opening motive. The orchestra (or piano) comes back in with a quick interjection as the horn ends on a held high c³. The lyrical second movement continues the motive based on a perfect fifth, allowing the horn many expressive moments. The final movement starts with a quick theme in $\frac{6}{8}$, with changing meters and alternating rhythmic patterns that will keep the players and listeners on their toes. A final cadenza has glissandi, arpeggiated figures, flutter tonguing, and grace note figures. A challenging work in many respects, yet the writing is idiomatic for the horn and well paced.

Range: e–c³

Duration: 17:00

Mercadante, Saverio (1795–1870) Italy

Conductor and prolific composer of instrumental, chamber, and sacred music, but perhaps best known for his operas.

Variazioni per corno ed orchestra

Edizioni Curci, 1981 (arranged by E. Leloir); Kendor Music, 2005 (arranged by L. William Kuyper)—both piano reductions

A lyrical theme with variations, full of arpeggios and embellishments that show off the virtuosity of the horn. The tessitura stays mostly in the staff, making this a suitable work for the college-level player. The theme in the Kendor (Kuyper) edition is eight bars shorter than the theme in the Curci (Leloir) edition.

Range: c¹–a²

Duration: 8:40

Concerto per corno e orchestra da camera

Edizioni Curci, 1972, piano reduction and revision by Edmund Leloir

I. Larghetto alla Siciliano

II. Polacca: Allegro brilliante

A pleasant work in two movements, the first is a flowing $\frac{6}{8}$ in minor, the second is cheerful and light, with diatonic sixteenth-note figures in accessible keys. Suitable for the college-level player.

Range: e^1-a^2

Duration: 6:40

Meulemans, Arthur (1884–1966) Belgium

Meulemans was a composer and the conductor of the Belgian Radio Symphony; he is best known for his works for orchestra.

Concerto voor hoorn en piano (1939–1940)

CeBeDeM, 1962, piano reduction

1. Allegro
2. Andante
3. Allegro giocoso

Written for Maurice van Bocxstaele. The work opens with a triplet horn-call theme that develops throughout the first movement, culminating in an extensive cadenza for the horn. The second movement is dreamy in its harmonic language and orchestration, featuring the English horn, and is reminiscent of Debussy. The third-movement rondo in $\frac{3}{4}$ requires the most bravura playing of the three movements, with dotted eighth-sixteenth motives, and quick chromatic sixteenth-note passages, leading into a cadenza. Colorful writing for the horn soloist, with muted and stopped passages throughout.

Range: $a-c^3$

Duration: 15:20

2e concerto, pour cor et piano (1961)

CeBeDeM, 1962, piano reduction

This three-movement concerto is in a neo-romantic style, with elements of heroic horn concertos of the past. Harmonies are impressionistic and at times dissonant, but this work is firmly grounded in traditional harmonic language and form. The second movement is marked Recitativo con moto e adagio, with busy ornamental figures over slowly changing harmonies. The energetic final movement is in $\frac{3}{4}$ with a contrasting section of meno mosso in $\frac{5}{4}$, followed by a cadenza, then a return of the opening theme.

Range: $a-a^2$

Duration: 16:00

Milde, Friedrich (1918–) Germany

In addition to composing, Milde was an oboist in the Stuttgart Radio Symphony and taught oboe and wind chamber music at the Musikhochschule Stuttgart.

Concertino für Horn und Orchester (1999)

Haas-Musikverlag, 2000, piano reduction

Allegro

Larghetto (Romanza)

Allegro scherzando

This work is in tonal harmonic language and form, characteristic of late nineteenth-century style. In three movements. The first is made up of contrasting sections and leads directly into the second movement, Larghetto, in $\frac{6}{8}$. The third movement is also in $\frac{6}{8}$, with a slower middle section in an andante tempo. There are a few slurred octaves to g^2, and the writing in the last movement is agile, but the modest range makes it accessible for a high school or early college player with good technique.

Range: d–g^2

Duration: 10:00

Miletić, Miroslav (1925–) Croatia

Violist and composer, member of the Zagreb Philharmonic and the Zagreb Pro Arte String Quartet.

Koncert za rog i gudače (Concerto for Horn &Strings) (1980)

Drustvo Skladatelja Hrvatske, 1981, piano reduction

In four movements. The first begins in an andante sostenuto tempo, with a slow lyrical motive, accelerating into an Allegro with syncopated figures and changing meters. The second-movement Scherzo is in $\frac{6}{8}$ and $\frac{9}{8}$, the third movement is an Andante that increases in momentum, before relaxing back into the original tempo. The final movement is very fast, and alternates duple and triple meters. The piece has glissandi, flutter tonguing (quite challenging on a pedal E), and sections that stay on top of and above the staff, however there are judicious breaks for the soloist.

Range: E–c^3

Duration: 14:00

Molter, Johann Melchior (1696–1765) Germany

Concerto in D Major for Corno da Caccia

Editions BIM, 1991, piano reduction and orchestra score; Hans Pizka Edition, 1980, piano reduction and orchestra score

For horn (corno da caccia) and strings, this work is listed as being written when Molter was in Karlsruhe, between 1742 and 1765. It exhibits characteristics of baroque horn writing, with florid lines that stays in the high register. In three movements. The first is an elegant Allegro moderato, with appoggiatura figures, triplet figures, and trills. The second movement is an expressive Andante, and the third movement is an Allegro molto in three, in a simple binary AABB form.

Range: c♯–$c♯^3$ (e^1–e^3 for horn in D)

Duration: 9:00

Montico, Mario (1885–1959) Italy

Due pezzi per corno e orchestra da camera

Carisch, 1940, piano reduction

I. Caccia
II. Elegia

In two brief movements. The first is in 𝄴 in a jaunty hunting style, with fast passages
of repeated notes and perfect fourths. The second is an Adagio in minor, beginning with a melody in the midrange that becomes increasingly agitated
with moving triplet figures before returning to a calm *pianissimo* ending.

Range: c–f♯²
Duration: 7:00

Moret, Norbert (1921–1998) Switzerland

Concerto pour cor (1994–1995)
Billaudot, orchestra score only
   I. Le soir au fond des bois
   II. Romance
   III. Burlesque

Premiered December 3, 1996, Chamber Orchestra Lausanne, with Bruno Schneider, horn soloist, who also recorded the work.

Duration: 21:00

Morgan, David Sydney (1932–) Australia

Composer, conductor, and music educator, Morgan played English horn with
the Sydney Symphony. He studied composition with Alex Burnard and Matyas
Seiber in London.

Horn Concerto No.1, "Spring" (1957, rev. 1999)
Australian Music Center, orchestra score only
   1. Allegretto giocoso
   2. Andante
   3. Allegretto grazioso

For Chrisetta McLeod, in three traditional movements and written in a contemporary tonal language. Agile writing for the horn, particularly in the last
movement.

Range: c–c³
Duration: 12:00

Moulaert, Raymond (1875–1962) Belgium

Composer, pianist, and professor of harmony and counterpoint at the Brussels
Conservatory, known for his songs.

Eroica, pour cor et piano (ou orchestra) (1946)
Brogneaux, 1940, piano reduction

This piece was written for Jean-Baptiste Faulx, professeur at the Royal Conservatory Brussels. A short one-movement work with several contrasting
sections in traditional harmonic language. The opening features the horn
alone in rising open fourths and fifths. Not very demanding technically,
and well paced for the horn soloist.

Range: g♯–c³ (ossia g♯–g²)
Duration: 7:00

Mozart, Leopold (1719–1787) Austria

Concerto in D for Horn and String Orchestra
KaWe, 1965, piano reduction and orchestra score (Leloir, ed.); G. Schirmer, 1977, piano reduction, includes parts for horn in D and F (Tuckwell, ed.)
In four movements; Allegro Moderato—Menuet—Andante—Allegro. Originally a chamber piece entitled *Sinfonia da Camera* for horn, violin, 2 violas and continuo, the piece has been arranged for solo horn and string orchestra renamed as a concerto, in which form it has entered the standard literature. The early-classical style of clarino horn writing exploits the extreme upper range of the natural horn in D, with very agile figures with trills, ornaments, and other passage work in dialogue with the violins. The KaWe edition omits the Menuet to make the piece a three-movement concerto.
Range: a^1–d^3 (c^2–f^3 for horn in D)
Duration: 11:00
See also: Leopold Mozart, *Sinfonia da Camera*, in *Denkmaler der Tonkünst in Bayern, Ausgewählte Werke von Leopold Mozart*, Volume 9, Band 2, Breitkopf & Härtel 1908.

Sinfonia pastorale für corno pastoriccio (Alp- oder Hirtenhorn, Jagdhorn, Wald- oder Ventilhorn) und Streicher
Eulenburg, 1979 (Kurt Janetzky, ed.), orchestra score
In three movements: Allegro moderato—Andante—Presto. Though not exactly a concerto, the corno "pastoriccio" is featured, and soloistic enough that it warrants inclusion in the repertoire. It could be a worthy (even amusing) addition to a program and could work with a small string group. Written for a special occasion, there are quick arpeggiated horn calls throughout. The second movement is stately, with only strings. The third movement, Presto, features more horn arpeggios, this time in $\frac{3}{8}$, and a horn line that foreshadows Beethoven's pastoral symphony.
Range: a^1–a^2 (g^1–g^2 for horn in G)
Duration: 12:21

Mozart, Wolfgang Amadeus (1756–1791) Austria

Mozart's solo-horn works, all most likely written for the hornist Ignaz Leutgeb, are among the best known and most beautiful pieces in the entire repertoire. They range from moderate to very difficult technically and challenge players of all levels in terms of musicality and interpretation. All were written for natural horn.

For convenience, we will use the numbering established by the 1881 Breitkopf & Härtel edition of Mozart's works, which identifies the concertos as nos. 1–4 and is most familiar and in use today. It does not reflect the actual chronological order of composition.

Among the many editions of the concertos are:
Johann André, (first publication) 1800–1802 (K. 417, K. 447, K.495)
Robert Forberg, 1879, ed. Carl Reineke (K. 417, K. 447, K.495)
Breitkopf & Härtel, 1881, ed. Henri Kling (K. 412, K. 417, K. 447, K.495)
Schirmer; Bärenreiter; Henle; McCoy's Horn Library; International

A detailed discussion of the different editions is beyond the scope of this book, however the Henle and Bärenreiter are the two urtext editions that are minimally edited. All editions listed are available as piano reductions.

Concerto No. 1 in D, K. 412+514 (=KV 386b)
Breitkopf & Härtel, 1881, K. 412 /514 (Henri Kling, ed.); Barenreiter, 1991, K. 412/ 514 (Franz Giegling, ed.); Schirmer, 1960, K. 412/514
Allegro K. 412 first movement by Mozart (1791)
Rondo K. 514 second movement version by Franz Süssmayr (1792)
Rondo K. 412 second movement by Mozart (not fully orchestrated) (1791)
(K. 386b refers to K. 412 and 514, the combination that most players know as *Concerto No. 1*)
Henle Verlag, 2001 (Henrik Wiese, ed.) urtext edition (contains Süssmayr and Mozart rondos)
Mozart began work on this concerto in the last year of his life, completing the first movement, and leaving only a draft of the rondo. What has commonly become known as *Concerto No. 1 in D,* K. 412 was published for the 1881 Breitkopf & Härtel edition, and consists of the first movement, K. 412, plus a second movement, Rondo, known separately as K. 514 that was written by Franz Süssmayr, using material from Mozart's unfinished rondo. The Bärenreiter *Neue Ausgabe sämtlicher Werke* identifies *Concerto No. 1* as K. 412+514 (=KV 386b). The concerto in this combination of movements (Mozart/Süssmayr) has a limited range, making it suitable for younger students, though the key of D major does present fingering difficulties. The original rondo extends one octave lower. The main technical challenges include fast articulated sixteenth-note passages and trills.
Originally horn in D
Range with Mozart rondo: e–f♯² (g–a² for horn in D)
Range with Süssmayr rondo: e¹–f♯² (g¹–a² for horn in D)
Duration: 9:00
Other editions of the *Concerto No. 1* include the *Concerto for horn and orchestra in D major,* KV 412 (386b), and the *Rondo D-dur für Horn und Orchester,* KV 412 (386b), listed below.

Concerto for Horn and Orchestra in D Major, KV 412 (386b)
Breitkopf & Härtel, 2013 (ed. Robert D. Levin)
It has been determined that Mozart wrote K. 412 in 1791. It appears that he struck out measures and made alterations from his original sketches of the piece to make it more playable for Ignaz Leutgeb, whose skills were declining due to his age. Robert Levin's edition restores these measures and alterations. The version of the first movement with the measures that Mozart had struck out and altered became the familiar Breitkopf 1881 edition. In the second-movement rondo, this edition presents a completion of Mozart's earliest sketch. The full score and its preface are very useful in understanding the evolution of this piece.
Range: e–f♯² (g–a² for horn in D)

Rondo D-dur für Horn und Orchester, KV 412 (386b)
Edition Kunzelmann, 1988, (Franz Beyer, ed.); Breitkopf & Härtel, 1980 (Karl Marguerre, ed.)
These editions present the rondo only, completed from Mozart's autograph sketches.

Concerto No. 2 in E♭, K. 417 (1783)
  I. Allegro
  II. Andante
  III. Rondo: Allegro
The earliest of the complete concertos, K. 417 is often used as an audition piece for orchestral and school auditions. The wider range, as well as articulated scale passages that must be played cleanly, make this concerto more challenging. As in all of Mozart's horn music, there is a variety of demands on the soloist, from fast scales and trills to lyrical melodies, an elegant second movement in the dominant key of B♭ major, and the typical agile hunting-horn character rondo.
Originally horn in E♭.
Range: f–b♭^{2} (g–c^3 for horn in E♭)
Duration: 13:47

Concerto No. 3 in E♭, K. 447
  I. Allegro
  II. Romance: Larghetto
  III. Rondo: Allegro
This concerto, the latest of the complete concertos, has a more limited range, making it more accessible to younger players whose upper range may not be fully developed. Unlike K. 412 and K. 417, it has a first-movement cadenza. The second movement is in the subdominant key of A♭ major. Techniques required include trills, fast articulated sixteenths, and hunting-horn-like figures in the third movement. Though it does not ascend to c^3 on the E♭ horn, making it more accessible for the player, it is in fact more musically substantial than the earlier two E♭ concertos, and requires a more highly developed hand-stopping technique when played on the natural horn. As an aside, Michael Haydn composed a *Romance in A♭* for horn and string quartet, which is a more extended piece using the themes of the second movement of this concerto.
Originally horn in E♭.
Range: f–g^2 (g–a^2 for horn in E♭)
Duration: 15:46

Concerto No. 4 in E ♭, K.495 (1786)
  I. Allegro maestoso
  II. Andante cantabile
  III. Allegro vivace
Also a popular audition piece for professional and school auditions, this concerto requires a full range and similar technical demands to *Concerto No. 2*. The first movement includes a cadenza. The second movement is in the dominant key of B♭ major. The third movement is a very spirited hunting-character piece with the possibility of a short rondo lead-in or "eingang" cadenza.

Originally horn in E♭.
Range: f–b♭² (g–c³ for horn in E♭)
Duration: 16:20

Concert Rondo in E♭, K. 371 (1781)
Barenreiter, 1987 (Giegling, ed.); Kunzelmann, 1993 (Beyer, ed.)
This rondo is often associated with (and published with) the unfinished concerto
  K. 370b. In ¾, it includes trills and fast passage work, as well as a cadenza.
  Most modern editions now include the recently discovered fragment of
  sixty measures.
Range: B♭–f² (c–g² for horn in E♭)
Duration: 6:30

Concerto Fragment in E♭, K. 370b
Hans Pizka Edition, 1980, reconstruction by Herman Jeurissen; Breitkopf & Härtel,
  2003, reconstruction by Robert D. Levin (includes Concert Rondo, K. 371);
  Birdalone Music, 1997, reconstruction by James Nicholas (includes Concert Rondo, K. 371); Sikorski, 1983 reconstruction by Herman Jeurissen (in-
  cludes Concerto fragment in E, K. 494a)
This is the earliest of Mozart's horn concertos, a first movement that is nearly
  complete. It has been completed by several editors. Though simpler musically than the three E♭ concertos, it is very similar in its technical demands.
  This is a welcome addition to the familiar Mozart concertos. It is included
  in the Barenreiter critical edition of Mozart's *Neue Ausgabe sämtlicher
  Werke*
Originally horn in E flat
Range: f–g² (g–a² for horn in E♭)

Concerto Fragment in E major, K. 494a
Hans Pizka Edition, 1980, reconstruction by Herman Jeurissen; Birdalone Music,
  1997, reconstruction by James Nicholas; Bärenreiter, 1999 (Dominic Nunns,
  ed.); Sikorski, 1983 reconstruction by Herman Jeurissen (includes Concerto
  fragment in E♭ K. 370b)
This is a concerto first movement, reconstructed from a surviving fragment consisting of a long opening tutti of sixty-five measures and a short solo section
  of twenty-six measures. In the other reconstructions (K. 371 and K. 370b),
  all—or nearly all—of the measures are accounted for. But in this case, the
  editors have had to compose a movement with very little idea of what Mozart may have intended. This has been completed by Hermann Jeurissen
  (Pizka), James Nicholas (Birdalone), and Dominic Nunns (Bärenreiter)
  among others. The reconstructions are all rather difficult for the soloist,
  due to the fingerings in the key of sounding E major, and the fact that the
  length of the opening tutti suggests a longer, more demanding movement
  than those of the other concertos. This and the E♭ reconstruction make fine
  recital and concert pieces that present some refreshing new Mozart horn
  music, especially to an audience, such as a horn workshop, who may be
  very familiar with the standard concertos.
Originally horn in E
Range: f♯–b³ (g–c³ for horn in E)

Mueller, Otto (1870–1960) United States, born in Germany

La Chasse
Camara Music Publishers, 1960, piano reduction
A short work in $\frac{6}{8}$ with a lyrical and expressive middle section, written in a tonal
  harmonic language.
Range: c^1–c^3
Duration: 5:00

Lyrical Romance for Solo Horn and Orchestra
Camara Music Publishers, 1960, piano reduction
Dedicated to William Sabatini, this tonal work, marked Andante con Espressi-
  one, features expressive flowing eighth-note and triplet figures.
Range: e–a^2
Duration: 4:00

Müller-Siemens, Detlev (1957–) Germany
Müller-Siemens studied with Ligeti and teaches in Basel and Vienna.

Konzert für Horn und Orchester (1988/89)
Schott, 1989, orchestra score only
This concerto was premiered January 9, 1990, with the Bochumer Symphoniker,
  Knut Hasselmann, horn soloist. This is an intricate contemporary work, in
  one movement with changing meters and tempos. It exploits the different
  colors of stopped, open, and half-stopped tones, often with quick intricate
  figures in the horn line that quickly move through these three colors.
Range: F–b^2
Duration: 20:00

Murail, Tristan (1947–) France
Murail was professor of computer music at the Paris Conservatoire, professor of
composition at IRCAM (Institut de Recherche et de Coordination Acoustique/
Musique) in Paris, and was on the faculty at Columbia University in the United
States for many years.

Mémoire/érosion: pour cor et ensemble instrumental (1975–76)
Éditions Musicales Transatlantiques, 1976, full score only
This work is for solo horn and ensemble of flute, oboe, clarinet, bassoon, 2 violins,
  viola, violoncello, and double bass. The horn sets out introducing soloistic
  gestures that are imitated by the other instruments. This becomes increasingly more complex as a solo line develops and instruments move further
  away from their imitations of the horn line. This piece is one of the first
  works Murail wrote that came to be known as spectral music, which, according to *New Grove,* is music that "uses the acoustic properties of sound
  itself (or sound spectra) as the basis of its compositional material." This
  work is an acoustic imitation of an electronic sound loop. Extended techniques abound, with flutter tonguing, stopped writing, quarter tones.
Range: F–c^3
Duration: 14:00

Musgrave, Thea (1928–) United States, born United Kingdom (Scotland)

Horn Concerto (1971)
Chester, 1974, orchestra score only
Commissioned by Mario di Bonaventura for the Dartmouth Congregation of Arts Festival, Dartmouth College, New Hampshire. This is dedicated to Barry Tuckwell who first performed it with the Scottish National Orchestra. This dramatic and expressive work has the orchestra brass acting as a concertante groups against the rest of the orchestra and interacting with the soloist. The soloist and the orchestra horns move to different locations in the hall—offstage, front, back, and on either side. Three extra horns may be used for larger halls, appearing on an upper balcony. Trumpets also move to the side of the stage during the piece. The concerto begins with the solo horn emerging out of the texture, staying in the low range and building on short themes until it has a full soloistic statement, followed by the back-and-forth between soloist and orchestra, and exchanging calls with the offstage horns. Contrasting sections ensue, including a Cappriccioso that creates a new backdrop for the horn with murmurs throughout the orchestra. Eventually, we hear the solo horn in counterpoint with the horns that are out in the hall. The overall effect is atmospheric, with the different groups interacting with the horn as it moves in and out of the texture. Notation is in traditional bar lines and rhythms interspersed with sections of aleatoric figures for both horn and orchestra. The solo writing is challenging with high and sustained passages, complex rhythmic figures that often require the freedom and approach of a cadenza. Extended techniques include flutter tonguing, glissandi, half-valve glissandi, quarter tones, and alternating stopped and open tones.
Range: F–c^3
Duration: 21:00

Nagel, Jody (1960–) United States
Jody Nagel is professor of theory and composition at Ball State University in Indiana.

As You Like It (also known as *"Rosalind's Theme"*)
JOMAR Press
There are four versions of this work:
1. Original version for horn and piano (1979)
2. Solo horn and strings (2011)
3. Solo horn, woodwind ensemble, harp, and one percussionist (2010)
4. Solo horn, large wind ensemble, harp, five percussionists, contrabass (2010) (Can be performed with companion piece *Touchstone's Obsession,* see below.)

A gentle and flowing work with sweet harmonies. The moderate range and few technical demands make this an accessible contemporary work for the high school student through professional player.
Range: g–g^2
Duration: 6:00

Touchstone's Obsession (2004, arranged 2010)

JOMAR Press, 2010, wind ensemble score only

Scored for solo horn, large wind ensemble, harp, five percussionists, and contrabass. Commissioned by the Ball State University Wind Ensemble, arranged for hornist Gene Berger. In one movement. The "Touchstone" in the title refers to the clown in Shakespeare's *As You Like It*. Exciting and energetic, this piece is organized around a driving rhythmic figure in $\frac{9}{8}$ grouped as 2+3+4. Fairly difficult for the horn, with angular leaps and forays above the staff, suitable for the college-level player. This is a companion piece to *As You Like It, "Rosalind's Theme,"* and the two can be performed together or separately.

Range: f♯–b♭²

Duration: 6:00

As You Like It (2010)

JOMAR Press, scored for solo horn, large wind ensemble, harp, five percussionists, and contrabass

1. Rosalind's theme
2. Touchstone's obsession

The two movements together are known under the title *As You Like It*. See above for descriptions of each movement.

Range: Range: f♯–b♭²

Duration: 12:00

Namavar, Reza (1980–) Netherlands

De Metalen Radiovlinder: Concerto for Horn and Small Ensemble

Muziek Zentrum Nederland, 2011, full score only

This exuberant work is scored for solo horn, two violins, viola, violoncello, contrabass, clarinet, and bassoon. Premiered in Amsterdam by the Ensemble Caméléon with Ron Schaaper, horn. Continuous dotted figures drive the horn line, and different layers of sound move at different times to carry the harmonic motion forward, slipping away from tonality, then moving back into it. The horn has different roles throughout the piece. It acts against the ensemble, it leads the ensemble in imitative lines, or it works together with the ensemble to form blocks of sound. Extended techniques include horn multiphonics and breathing through the instrument. Challenging horn writing that moves through the ranges quickly. Endurance required, particularly for repeated figures on notes above the staff that occur toward the end of the piece.

Range: A♯–c♯³

Duration: ca. 10:00

Nelson, Paul (1929–2008) United States

Idyll, for Horn and Strings (1961)

A Moll Dur Publishing House, 1977, full score (horn and piano version is the *Sonata*)

This is the composer's arrangement of the slow movement of his *Horn Sonata*. Marked Adagio, a legato phrase with a double-dotted figure is developed throughout this expressive work, growing in intensity to a *fortissimo agitato* passage of open fifths, up to high b², before returning to the quiet mood of the opening.
Range: G–b² (ossia c–b²)
Duration: 5:30

Neruda, Johann Baptist Georg (1711–1776) Germany, born in Bohemia
Violinist, cellist, and composer, Neruda played in the court orchestra of Count Rutowski in Dresden and composed nearly one hundred works, mostly trio sonatas, symphonies, and concertos.

Concerto in E♭ Major for Horn, Strings, and Continuo
Musikverlag David McNaughton, 1992 (Max Sommerhalder, ed.); Editions BIM, 1990, (Edward Tarr, ed.); Musica Rara, 1975, 2000, (for trumpet and piano, David Hickman, ed.); Billaudot, 1974 (Edmond Leloir, ed.)—all editions are piano reductions
Although now a standard in the trumpet repertoire, this work was originally composed for horn in E♭. The Leloir edition is an arrangement in the key of C, which brings the piece down a minor third from its original. The Editions BIM version includes two solo parts, one for B♭ trumpet, and the other for E♭ horn, however the solo-horn part is an octave lower than intended, making it more accessible to the modern horn player, but the high florid writing that the composer intended is lost. The David McNaughton Edition puts the solo-horn part in the original octave. The piece was written for a high-horn specialist of the time, and remains in the clarino range of the E♭ horn (c² and above) exclusively, ascending as high as g³ several times in florid passages of sixteenth notes and arpeggios. This range, extreme for horn players, explains why the piece is so often played by trumpet players.
Range: b♭¹–f³ (c²–g³ for horn in E♭)
Duration: 14:30

Nicholas, James (1957–) United States
Cellist and composer James Nicholas has written several works (sometimes under pseudonyms) for horn and piano, horn and orchestra, or horn in chamber settings. His music ranges from fun and whimsical to serious and dark.

Concerto in E♭ for Horn and Orchestra, "Son of Horn Concerto"
Birdalone Music, 1992, orchestra score only
    I. Allegro
    II. Romanza: Larghetto
    III. Rondo: Allegro
Using the harmonic language of the late eighteenth century as well as a good understanding of the style and the technique of the natural horn, the composer has written a piece that could easily pass as a long-lost cousin of a concerto by Mozart. The piece is as idiomatic and playable on the natural

horn as anything by Mozart and it is a fun addition to a recital program, with or without valves.
Range: f–b♭² (g–c³ for horn in E♭)
Duration: 15:46
See: Collorafi, James

Norden, Hugo (1909–1986) United States
Passacaglia for Horn and Strings
J. & W. Chester, 1959, piano reduction
Written for Francis Finlay. Composed with an eight-measure passacaglia accompaniment throughout, played alternately by the horn and the strings with variations. The horn part is agile, but moderate in its difficulties.
Range: a♭–b♭²
Duration: 7:00
See: Horn and keyboard

Northcott, Bayan (1940–) United Kingdom
Music critic, composer, and head of the recording company NMC.

Concerto for Horn and Ensemble, op. 8 (1990/1998)
Stainer and Bell, 1999, full score only
Commissioned by the Amphion Foundation for Speculum Musicae and dedicated "To Helen and Elliott Carter with Love." Scored for solo horn and flute, oboe, clarinet, bassoon, percussion, piano, violin, viola, violoncello, and bass. Includes a seating chart, with the note that "the treatment of the woodwind and string families in this work is often antiphonal. On no account should the strings be seated in front of the woodwinds." This work is in three sections, with only a pause between each section. The writing is very intricate, with changing meters and tempos and complex interplay between horn soloist and choirs of winds, strings, and percussion.
Range: E–c♯³
Duration: 20:00

Nystedt, Knut (1915–2014) Norway
Concerto for Horn and Orchestra, op. 114 (1987)
Norsk Musikforlag, 1990, piano reduction
Dedicated to Frøydis Ree Wekre. In three movements. The first movement, marked Allegro, is in changing meters and organized around the interplay of a moving eighth-note theme between horn and orchestra. The second movement, Adagietto, has slow, controlled phrases for the horn, with tension resolving in beautiful harmonies at the end of the movement. The third movement, Allegro vivace, moves in sixteenth- and eighth-note motives. This work is rambunctious, lyrical, inventive, and fresh; it takes unexpected turns in its melodic and harmonic language.
Range: A–c³
Duration: 17:00

Oldberg, Arne (1874–1962) United States
Oldberg was professor of composition and piano at Northwestern University from 1899 to 1941.

Le Son du cor
Southern Music, 1987, horn and piano version (also known as *Serenade for Horn)*
Dedicated to Helen Kotas, who premiered the work on November 28, 1953, with
    the Tri-City Symphony. In three movements, with heroic writing for the
    horn and a lyrical second movement that showcases the horn's expressive
    capabilities. There are a few challenging passages in the second movement
    that stay above the staff and require endurance, but, overall, this is a very
    accessible work. Suitable for the college player; writing is in a traditional
    harmonic language and form.
Range: f–b♭²
Duration: 16:00
See: Horn and keyboard

Olsen, Sparre (1903–1984) Norway
Olsen studied with Fartein Valen and while in Berlin he studied with Max Butt-ing and attended lectures by Hindemith and Schoenberg.

Concertino for Horn and Strings, op. 63
Edition Lyche, 1978, piano reduction
This work is dedicated to Frøydis Ree Wekre, who recorded it with the Oslo
    Philharmonic. In one movement, marked Andante moderato. Written in
    contemporary musical language, it develops several motives in contrasting
    sections, with lyrical and flowing lines that are at times angular.
Range: d–g²
Duration: 9:32

Ortleb, Willy

Burleske für Waldhorn und Orchester
Peer Music Classical, orchestra score only
In ¾ with a continuous eighth-note motive throughout, it begins in a fast tempo,
    with slower sections of lyrical writing that jump back into the quick
    tempo—or become even faster. There is a brief cadenza.
Range: f♯–c³
Duration: 9:00

Passani, Emile (1905–1974) France

Concerto pour cor avec accompagnement d'orchestre a cordes
Musicales Transatlantiques, 1965, piano reduction
    I. Allegro risoluto
    II. Adagio
    III. Allegro molto
In three movements, the first is in a fast but flowing ⅜ and develops a dotted-eighth
    motive and a contrasting legato theme. The second movement is lyrical, in

$\frac{3}{2}$, with upward-moving horn lines that extend above the staff, at soft dynamics. The third movement is a very fast $\frac{2}{4}$, featuring wide-ranging eighth-note figures. All three movements require flexibility and agility, and there are a few trills and stopped effects.

Range: c♯–c³
Duration: 22:00

Patterson, Paul (1947–) United Kingdom
Patterson studied composition with Richard Stoker, Elisabeth Lutyens, and Richard Rodney Bennett. He currently teaches composition at the Royal Academy of Music, London.

Horn Concerto (1971)
Josef Weinberger, 1974, piano reduction
For horn and string orchestra. Commissioned by the 1971 Nottingham Festival, dedicated to Ifor James who premiered the piece with the English Chamber Orchestra conducted by George Malcolm, July 21, 1971. The first movement, marked Quasi recitative, begins with a fanfare-like motive, followed by an Allegro con furia that develops material from the opening. The second movement, Adagio molto, alternates moving sections of triplet figures with longer lyrical lines. The last movement, Guerriero presto, develops declamatory sixteenth-note motives that alternate with legato passages, leading to a final cadenza. This is an energetic and challenging work that features the horn's heroic nature.

Range: c♯–d³
Duration: 20:00

Pauer, Jiří (1919–2007) Czech Republic

Koncert pro lesní roh a orchestr (Concerto for Horn and Orchestra) (1957)
Státní nakladatelství krásné literatury, hudby a umení, 1959, piano reduction
Pauer recognized the lack of solo music for wind instruments and wrote many works for the great Czech soloists that he knew. The horn concerto was premiered at the Second Review of New Compositions by Prague Composers in 1957, with Miroslav Štefek, horn soloist, and the Czech Philharmonic. In three movements. The first movement, Allegro patetico, is intense and dramatic, the second movement is a lyrical and introspective Andante, and the final movement, Allegro giocoso, is a spirited $\frac{6}{8}$. This is romantic horn writing that is colorfully orchestrated, reminiscent of Shostakovich or Prokofiev.

Range: g–b²
Duration: 20:00

Pauwels, Jean Englebert (1768–1804) Belgium
Pauwels was a violinist, conductor, and composer, well regarded by his peers during his brief life.

Premier Concerto, for Horn and Orchestra (ca. 1794)
Donemus, 2003, orchestra score

In three movements typical of the classical style: Allegro moderato—Adagio—
    Polacca allegretto. For horn in E, this is a well-paced work, elegant, with a
    nice balance between lyrical and technical writing; a solid addition to the
    classical repertoire.
Range: f♯–b² (g–c³ for horn in E)
Duration: 19:00

Peçi, Aleksandër (1951–) Albania

Variacione për korno e orkestë
See: Horn and keyboard, Peçi, Aleksandër: *Variacione mbi një temë: për korno
    dhe piano*

Pehrson, Joseph (1950–) United States
Composer and pianist, co-director of the Composers Concordance in New York.

Concertino for Horn & Eight Instruments (1987, rev. 1992)
Seesaw Music, 1988, 1992, full score only
Dedicated to Francis Orval, who premiered the work with instrumentalists at
    the University of Delaware, with the composer conducting. In one con-
    tinuous movement, with several contrasting motives that develop organ-
    ically. Things begin "Slowly, mysteriously," with a free-sounding clarinet
    line over terraced chords in the strings. The horn enters with legato group-
    ings of notes in downward patterns, followed by a contrasting declama-
    tory sixteenth-dotted-eighth gesture. Different motives combine and re-
    combine throughout the piece, with fluttering wind sounds and rhythmic
    ostinato figures that move between the solo horn and ensemble. Disparate
    lines gather energy and momentum as they become more in sync, leading
    to a horn cadenza. This is followed by a driving "Diabolus dance," set up
    first with string pizzicatos that are joined by the horn, followed by a finale
    that brings back motives from the opening. With agile legato figures in
    the horn, and modest demands in high range, this is an interesting and
    accessible contemporary work that a college-level ensemble could manage.
    Passages extend into the low range of the horn, with two phrases that end
    on pedal tones. Flexibility is needed for negotiating legato lines between
    middle and lower ranges.
Range: D–f♯²
Duration: 12:00

Penderecki, Krzysztof (1933–) Poland
New Grove states that Penderecki "has produced a substantial body of work
which challenges many assumptions about the nature and purpose of contemporary music."

Concerto for Horn and Orchestra: "Winterreise" (2007/2008, rev. 2009)
Schott, orchestra score only
The concerto is dedicated to the Philharmonic Society of Bremen and Radovan
    Vlatkovic, who premiered the work on May 5, 2008, with the composer

conducting. An important recent addition to the horn repertoire, this is Penderecki's first concerto for a brass instrument. "Winterreise" refers to the many winter impressions that Penderecki gathered while he was travelling, and the piece is organized into many different sections and moods. It begins mysteriously, with the solo-horn line emerging out of the three orchestra horns that are offstage. With little dissonance, this is romantic horn writing echoing Strauss or Mahler, with soaring lyrical passages and writing that is heroic, triumphant, and sardonic, often in quickly changing moods, all very well written for the horn. Challenging in endurance but well worth the effort. There are several cadenza-like passages for the horn (*senza misura*), multiphonics, stopped writing, changing meters, and quickly changing moods to negotiate.

Range: F–a²
Duration: 17:30

Peskin, Vladimir (1906–1988) Russia
Peskin is known for his works for trumpet.

Concerto for French Horn and Piano (Kontšert dlīa valtorny [F] i fortepiano)
Kompozitor, 2007, piano reduction
This work, originally for horn and orchestra, is in a neo-romantic style, dramatic, and at times tragic sounding. It is in contrasting sections played without break and includes a cadenza. Modest technical demands for the horn soloist.

Range: e–c♭²
Duration: 14:00

Petrić, Ivo (1931–) Slovenia

Concerto for Horn and Orchestra
Available on composer's website, www.ivopetric.com, orchestra score only
In one continuous movement of contrasting characters that grow out of the opening motive. Colorful orchestration, such as biting muted brass that sets the tone for an Allegretto scherzando, an atmospheric cadenza with interjections of percussion, celesta, and harp. Many forays above the staff and agile legato sixteenth-note passages make this a challenging work, but there are judicious rests for the soloist throughout.

Range: b♭–b♭²
Duration: 15:32

Pflüger, Hans Georg (1944–1999) Germany

Concerto für Horn und Orchester (1983)
Bote & Bok, 1984, piano reduction is *Concerto für Horn und Orgel*
Written as a commission from the Stuttgart Philharmonic, premiered July 12, 1983, Hermann Baumann, horn soloist. In two movements. The first opens with a cadenza, introducing a descending half-step theme in the low range. Contrasting tempos present different moods and effects that juxtapose strings in close, clashing pitch groups with the open sound of the horn.

Techniques for horn include alternating stopped and open timbres, echo tones, flutter tonguing, glissandi, and multiphonics. The second movement has more of the colors of the orchestra coming through, with shimmering strings melting into the Adagio sostenuto that has horn and violin in a beautiful duet in contrast to the preceding music, and eerily effective. This is a challenging work for the horn soloist, written in contemporary harmonic language.
Range: F–c³
Duration: 15:00
See: Horn and keyboard

Phan, P. Q. (1963–) United States, born in Vietnam
P. Q. Phan is on the composition faculty at Indiana University Bloomington.

Concertino for Horn and Mixed Ensemble (2011)
Available from the composer at pqphan.com, full score
Scored for solo French horn, flute, clarinet, bassoon, violin, viola, cello, and harp. Commissioned by Emilie Sargent, with assistance from the Toledo Symphony. The strings set up an ostinato figure that is heard throughout the piece, later taken up by the harp and then the winds. The horn emerges from this texture, playing long lines that alternate with the winds. Finally coming into its own as the solo voice, it takes the lead with increasingly active and bold gestures. This is an atmospheric work, with colorful dissonances that coalesce at moments that sound highly romantic, reminiscent of Richard Strauss. Good endurance is needed for sustaining long lines, often at a full dynamic, and for climactic passages that head up into the high range.
Range: f–c³
Duration: 15:00

Piacquadio, Peter (1945–) United States

Pavana e rondo
Shawnee Press, 1982, piano reduction is by the composer
Scored for solo horn, flute, oboe/English horn, clarinet/bass clarinet, bassoon, first violin, second violin, viola, and cello. Written for Julie Landsman and dedicated to Carmine Caruso. In two contrasting sections. The first half of this work is slow and flowing, with changing tempos, rubato, and a section of apassionato. The second half is a relaxed §. A challenging work due to its range—held high d³s at the end—it is in traditional rhythms and contemporary tonal language.
Range: G–d³
Duration: 7:30

Pilss, Karl (1902–1979) Austria
Pilss was a composer, conductor, pianist, and also a painter.

Concerto for Horn and Orchestra (1969)
Robert King Music, 1974, piano reduction

In three movements: Allegro non tanto—Molto tranquillo—Allegro con spirito. This concerto is written using traditional harmonic language and form. The first movement opens with declamatory heroic writing, with a middle section of appassionato. The second movement, in ABA form, has outer lyrical sections with a middle section in an allegro tempo. The third movement is a spirited § with contrasting character and mood. This is an accessible work of medium difficulty, appropriate for the college-level player.
Range: B–a²
Duration: 17:15

Pintscher, Matthias (1971–) Germany

Celestial Object II, for Solo Horn and Ensemble. (Part two from *Sonic Eclipse*)
Bärenreiter, 2009, orchestra score only
From the composer's work *Sonic Eclipse,* a three-part cycle that can be played together or separately. The first part is with solo trumpet, the second is with solo horn, and the third brings the two soloists together. The Bärenreiter website explains that the horn in *Celestial Object II* "plays in long, melodious lines. The repertoire of techniques used ranges from the smallest dynamics, through various performing techniques such as flutter tonguing, stopped, toneless blowing, to large expressive arches." (www.baerenreiter .com/en/program/20th21st-century-music/contemporary-music/matthias -pintscher/works/ensemble/occultation/)
Duration: 12:00

Plog, Anthony (1947–) United States

Nocturne for Horn and Strings (1987–88)
Editions BIM, 1991, piano reduction
For Gail Williams. Premiered on November 4, 1989, with the Illinois Chamber Symphony. This work begins with the horn alone, playing a wide-ranging lyrical passage, soon joined by the strings. This meditative opening grows into an Allegro, described in the score preface as "vigorous and brilliant," incorporating material of the opening before returning to the quiet mood established in the beginning. Lyrical and expressive writing for the horn.
Range: A–b♭³
Duration: 7:00
See: Horn and keyboard

Poelman, Alex (1981–) Netherlands

Jeanne d'Arc for Horn and Band (2006)
Molenaar, 2007, band score only
First performed in 2006 by the ensemble Wilhelmina Glanerbrug, René Pagen, horn soloist. In the score, Jeanne is represented by the solo-horn player, with romantic scoring in tonal harmonic language. The horn writing is full of heroic passages in the high range, depicting the events of the life of Joan of Arc in ten movements: France 1414—Jeanne—The garden—Voice of

god—To battle—Hit by an arrow—Return to the field—Jeanne captured—
Execution—Saint Jeanne. Sustained writing for the horn at full volume,
often in a high tessitura.

Range: E–c³

Duration: 18:30

Pokorny, Franz Xaver (1729–1794) Bohemia
Pokorny was a violinist and composer at the Court of Oettingen-Wallerstein,
then later was employed by the court orchestra of Thurn and Taxis at Regensburg.

Horn Concerto in E, for horn and strings (1755)
Artaria Editions, 2006, full score (Allan Badley, ed.); Hans Pizka Edition, 1979,
    piano reduction and orchestra score
Both the Pizka and Artaria editions are taken from a manuscript at Thurn und
    Taxis Hofbibliothek (Pokorny 160). The horn part says "Corno 2do, Prin-
    cipale in E♯." There is speculation that Pokorny wrote this work for his
    daughter, Beata Pokorny, who was a horn player. This piece is full of light-
    ning-fast leaps and arpeggios throughout the range. Not much in the way
    of thematic material, this piece is for showing off the second horn soloist's
    acrobatic moves. Being pitched in E on the natural horn makes for tricky
    negotiating on the valve horn due to the 2–3 valve combinations. It is dif-
    ficult to imagine the first movement played in the allegro tempo that is
    marked, but several sources have attested to the excellent virtuoso hornists
    that Pokorny was writing for.

Range: d♯–g♯² (e–a² for horn in E)

Duration: 12:35

Horn Concerto in D
Hans Pizka Edition, 1989, orchestra score
This work is identified as Pokorny 161, scored for strings and timpani, and is a
    high-horn concerto.

Duration: 16:00

Powers, Anthony (1953–) United Kingdom
Powers is professor of composition at Cardiff University.

Concerto for Horn and Orchestra (1989)
Oxford University Press, 1991, orchestra score only
    I. Madrigals of Love and War
    II. Winter Journeys
The concerto was commissioned by the Royal Liverpool Philharmonic, who pre-
    miered it with Michael Thompson, horn soloist. The orchestra is orga-
    nized in three groups on stage, with a "concertino" group in the middle,
    made up of solo horn, percussion, tuba, harp, and celesta. In two parts.
    Program notes on the publisher's website describe the first part having
    the horn soloist "in conflict with the orchestra and only able to 'sing' with
    other individuals or small groups, with short phrases for the horn, lyri-
    cal lines, and dramatic moments." The second part is lyrical in character,

described as "a slow process of regaining lost ground and re-building a rapport. The soloist leads the orchestra from desolation towards a new and serene prospect and an exuberant close." (ukcatalogue.oup.com/product /music/composers/powers/9780193665835.do) Challenging writing for the hornist, with intricate rhythmic gestures, long sustained lines, and several phrases that stay above the staff.

Range: B–c^3

Duration: 24:00

Punto, Giovanni [Stich, Johann Wenzel (Jan Václav)] (1746–1803)

Germany (Bohemia)

The most famous horn virtuoso of the eighteenth century, born Jan Václav Stich in Zehušice, Central Bohemia (now Czech Republic), he studied horn with Anton Josef Hampel and other teachers in Dresden. After his period of study, he returned to serve in the orchestra of Count Joseph Johann von Thun for four years, then escaped his servitude, assuming the name Giovanni Punto. Punto traveled extensively as a horn virtuoso, specializing in cor basse (as many horn virtuosi of the time did), and perfected and expanded the use of hand stopping. Punto's compositions, several of which have been attributed to other composers, include sixteen horn concertos, of which nos. 9, 12, 13, 15, and 16 are lost. The fourth concerto is incomplete, missing the solo-horn part and some of the orchestra parts.

See also: James Earl Miller, "The life and works of Jan Václav Stich (Giovanni Punto) a check-list of eighteenth-century horn concertos and players: an edition for study and performance of the Concerto no. VI in E-flat by Giovanni Punto." (PhD. thesis, State University of Iowa, 1962).

Concerto No. 1 in E

Robert Ostermeyer, 2011, piano reduction and orchestra score

This edition is based on the first printing of the concerto by the publisher Sieber in Paris, 1777. Ostermeyer argues that this concerto is indeed by Punto. It has also been argued by Sterling E. Murray that it was written by Antonio Rosetti, and Murray lists it as the *Horn Concerto in E Major, C51/ Kaun: III:42*, in his catalog, *The Music of Antonio Rosetti (Anton Rösler) ca. 1750–1792: A Thematic Catalog*. It is similar in style and character to Rosetti's other horn concertos, particularly in being more chromatic than other concertos of the time. To complicate matters further, this piece was at one point attributed to Karl Stamitz, as his *Concerto in E♭*, with the slow movement transposed. One possibility is that the concerto was written for or commissioned by Punto, who then took it to Paris and published it under his own name, a common practice at the time.

See: Rosetti: *Horn Concerto in E major C51*.

Concerto No. 2 in E Major

Robert Ostermeyer, 2007, piano reduction and orchestra score

This edition is based on a publication by Sieber in Paris from 1779. The first movement, Allegro, showcases horn technique, with the melody and architecture playing a secondary role. There is an extended section of triplets that go up to written high b². The second movement is a Romance in $\frac{2}{4}$ that begins in major then ventures into the minor, with two opportunities for cadential moments for the hornist. The third movement is a typical Rondo allegretto, in a hunting style in $\frac{6}{8}$.

Range: f♯–b² (g–c³ for horn in E)
Duration: 16:20

Concerto a cor principal no. 3
Hans Pizka Edition, 1987, piano reduction and orchestra score
This concerto follows the typical three-movement classical form. The first movement is in sonata form, with challenging runs that move through the range
of the horn, requiring good technique. The second movement, marked
Adagio, is in $\frac{3}{4}$ and in ABA form, with opportunity for ornamentation. The
third-movement rondo is a lively $\frac{3}{4}$, requiring a light touch. This concerto
is in the key of F, and therefore sits well on the valve horn. There are many
technical passages, but the key and range make this an approachable concerto for the student hornist.

Range: c–b²
Duration: 17:00

Concerto no. 5 in Fa maggiore
Robert Ostermeyer, 2011, piano reduction and orchestra score; Hans Pizka Edition, 1985, piano reduction
If recordings are any indication, this is the most popular of the Punto concertos. The opening tutti sets the stylish tone of the first movement, which is
full of quick runs and elegant phrases. The second movement is a beautiful
Adagio in minor. The third movement is a Rondeau en chasse, which can
be completely raucous but charming nonetheless.

Range: G–a♭²
Duration: 16:48

6. Concerto per corno da caccia in E♭
Hans Pizka Edition, 1980, piano reduction and orchestra score
A sprightly first movement in sonata form with cadenza, a beautiful slow movement in minor, and an elegant rondo. This is a very accessible work, requiring flexibility and good technique, particularly for the quick passages of
the last movement.

Range: f–g³ (g–a³ for horn in E♭)
Duration: 16:16

Hornkonzert Nr. 7 in F
Willy Müller, Süddeutscher Musikverlag (distributed by C.F. Peters), 1961, piano
reduction (Adam Gottron, ed.)
This is the only published edition of Punto's seventh concerto and is based on a
manuscript in the Bibliothèque Nationale in Paris. The first movement is
in the traditional sonata form with challenging florid triplet-eighth passages leading into the cadenza. The second movement is scored for horn
and strings and is one of the nicer slow movements of Punto's concertos,

with an interesting foray into minor. The third movement is from Punto's fifth concerto because the editor thought this was a much better rondo, and in his preface explains that "such an exchange on account of efficacy was familiar to musicians of the time."

Range: g–a² (ascends to c³ in the editor's cadenza)
Duration: 14:58

Concerto No. 8 in E♭
Hans Pizka Edition, 1990s, piano reduction (Edmond Leloir, ed.)
This concerto is different from other Punto concertos, with a first movement in ¾. It also combines cor-alto and cor-basse characteristics with a range that extends to a written c³ for horn in E♭, and extends into the low range that is typically seen in cor-basse writing.

Range: B♭–b♭² (c–c³ for horn in E♭)
Duration: 12:30

Concerto No. 10
Hans Pizka Edition, 1984, piano reduction and orchestra score
In F major, an Allegro maestoso first movement opens with a majestic tutti with dotted eighth-sixteenth figures that contrast with a lyrical second theme. The second movement, Lento in ¾, is in ABA form with ample opportunity for ornamentation. The final movement is a ⁶⁄₈ rondo with challenging technical passages that cover the ranges of the horn.

Range: g–a²
Duration: 16:54

Concerto No. 11 in E
Robert Ostermeyer, 2013, piano reduction and orchestra score; Medici Music Press, 1983, piano reduction with horn part transposed to F
The Imbault edition, on which the Ostermeyer edition is based, can be found on imslp.org. A relatively brief opening tutti introduces the first theme of the first movement, with the horn introducing the second theme. There is a brief cadenza finishing the movement. The second-movement Adagio is in ABA form. The final movement is entitled "Minuetto: Cantabile con variationi," and is a theme plus four variations that show off the soloist's technical prowess. The same theme and variations appears as the last piece in the Hampel/Punto method book *Seule et vraie méthode pour apprendre facilement les élémens des premier et second cors.*

Range: b–g♯² (c–a² for horn in E)
Duration: 14:30

Concerto No. 14 in Fa
Hans Pizka Edition, 1996, piano reduction and orchestra score
Very active first movement that showcases technique, featuring wide slurs and fast runs. The second movement, Adagio, is in minor, with some challenging wide legato leaps, the third movement is an easy-going Rondo in ⁶⁄₈ marked Allegretto.

Range: G–b♭²
Duration: 18:00

Puts, Kevin (1972–) United States

Pulitzer-prize-winning composer, Kevin Puts' works have been performed throughout the world. He is on the composition faculty at the Peabody Conservatory Johns Hopkins University.

Nā Pali Coast for French Horn and Orchestra (2008)

Aperto Press, 2008, orchestra score only

This piece was commissioned by the Mobile Symphony, who gave its premiere on January 17, 2009, Jeffrey Leenhouts, horn soloist. *Nā pali* means "the cliffs" in Hawaiian, and refers to the coastline that extends along the northwest of Kauai. The composer describes in the program note in the score how the piece juxtaposes two different perspectives of viewing the cliffs: one is from a boat, where the cliffs are "sad and bleak, dark caves of craggy stone imperiled by the raging elements"; and the other is by air, where the cliffs are "magical and scenic, green towers of stone majestically rising from sandy beaches and waves crashing safely below." The piece opens with a somber, contemplative horn line that trades back and forth with the strings. An active middle section of horn in triplet figures against the orchestra builds into a cadenza of repeated figures that answer various instrument groups, until the horn is left to its own majestic devices, playing on its own before resuming the opening theme. Lush, effective, and atmospheric, with long horn lines and only moderate technical demands placed on the soloist.

Range: d–b²

Duration: 9:00

Quantz, Johann Joachim (1697–1773) Germany

Quantz worked in Dresden as an oboist, violinist, flutist, and trumpeter. In 1741 he became court composer to Frederick the Great in Berlin and Potsdam. Quantz is perhaps best known for his major treatise *On Playing the Flute,* and for his compositions for flute, many written for Frederick the Great.

Concerto in E♭ Major for Horn and String Orchestra, QV 5: Anh.13, E♭ major

Birdalone Music, 1995, piano reduction and orchestra score; Edition Kunzelmann, 1986, piano reduction

This is concerto No. 3 of Lund University Library Ms. Kat. Wenster Litt. I/1–17b. The first movement is a sprightly $\frac{4}{4}$, with sections that cycle through sixteenth-note passages, requiring agility and quick fingers. The second movement is a brief interlude of Adagio cantabile in $\frac{3}{4}$, and the final movement is in three, with flashy triplet figures in the upper midrange.

Range: d¹–b♭² (e¹–c³ for horn in E♭)

Duration: 7:13

Concerto ex dis dur

Robert Ostermeyer, 1999, piano reduction, orchestra score

This is concerto No. 9 of Lund University Library Ms. Kat. Wenster Litt. I/1–17b. For horn in E♭. The original title indicated it was for corno concertato, oboe, 2 violins, and basso, and it contains a rather soloistic oboe part. In three traditional movements. The middle movement is a siciliano in minor, and the final movement has several high entrances to jump in on. This piece is typical high-horn baroque writing, yet very accessible for the modern player, since it is in the familiar key of E♭.

Range: b♭–c³ (c¹–d³ for horn in E♭)

Duration: 9:36

Rabe, Folke (1935–) Sweden

Nature, Herd, and Relatives (Naturen, flocken och släkten) (1991)

Reimers, 1991, orchestra score only

For horn and string orchestra. Written for Sören Hermansson, based on four different *yoiks*, which are traditional chants of the indigenous Sami people. Contrasting sections of different yoiks are realized in contemporary musical language and repeat in regular patterns, creating an effect that is at times hypnotic. The cadenzas are quite challenging, with very fast alternating open and closed notes, with fast slurs into the closed notes. This requires good coordination with lips, right hand, and fingerings, but the effect is unusual and interesting. *Vuolle* is the cadenza for this piece, published separately as an unaccompanied work.

Range: g–c³

Duration: 15:29

Raff, Joachim (1822–1882) Germany

Romanze for Horn and Orchestra, op. 182, no. 1

Manuscript score and parts at the Fleisher Collection, Free Library of Philadelphia

Originally composed for horn or violoncello and piano, 1873, as the first of *Zwei Romanzen,* op. 182. First performance of the orchestrated version was in Wiesbaden, Germany on December 5, 1873, Karl Müller-Berghaus conductor, Zschernek soloist. A straightforward, lyrical piece in $\frac{4}{4}$, with traditional harmonies. In ABA form, the B section being a brief contrast in minor.

Range: c¹–g²

Duration: 4:00

See: Horn and keyboard

Raihala, Osmo Tapio (1964–) Finland

Concerto for French Horn

Music Finland, 2013, orchestra score only; available from raihala.com

Commissioned by Jukka Harju. Recommended work in the third International Uuno Klami Composition Competition, 2014.

Duration: 25:00

Rakowski, David (1958–) United States

David Rakowski has won numerous awards for his compositions and has been a finalist for the Pulitzer Prize. He is on the faculty at Brandeis University.

Locking Horns, for Horn and Chamber Orchestra (2001–2)
C.F. Peters, 2003, orchestra score only
   I. Tentative
   II. Vivace
   III. Slow and flexible
   IV. Theme and Variations: Poco allegro
   V. Allegro
Locking horns was commissioned by the New York ensemble Sequitur for hor-
   nist Dan Grabois, who premiered it and recorded it on Albany Records.
   This piece was the first-prize winner of the 2003 International Horn Society
   Competition. The solo horn begins as a member of the ensemble, gradually
   emerging as the soloist after musically battling (locking horns) with the
   horn in the ensemble. Their dialog continues throughout the piece, with
   the solo horn finally coming into its own. Challenging writing that is often
   angular, with wide legato leaps and intricate rhythmic figures.
Range: e–c^3
Duration: 18:00

Ramovš, Primož (1921–1999) Slovenia
Ramovš was a prolific composer of instrumental music, having written over four
hundred works. His compositional style changed throughout his life and became
increasingly avant-garde after 1960.

Apel, za rog in komorni orkester (Appel, pour cor et ensemble de chambre) (1963)
Drustvo slovenskih skladateljev (Society of Slovene Composers), 1968, orchestra
   score only
Premiered by hornist Jože Falout with the Ansambel Slavko Osterc. The title *Apel*
   means "call." This work is scored for solo horn, flute, clarinet, harp, and
   strings. In two sections that vary in tempo and harmonic speed, the horn
   writing is very accessible, with few extended techniques.
Range: e–b^2
Duration: 9:00

Raphling, Sam (1910–1988) United States
Rhapsody for French Horn Solo, Strings and Oboe
G. Schirmer, orchestra score; horn and piano version entitled *Sonata for French
   Horn and Piano,* Ricordi, 1961
In three short movements: Moderately lively—Slowly—Lively. The harmonic lan-
   guage is tonal and bright, infused with tinges of American folk song, rem-
   iniscent of Copland. The second movement is lyrical and features the oboe
   in dialogue with the horn. This is a very accessible work, suitable for the
   high school or early college player and above.
Range: e–a^2
Duration: 9:00
See: Horn and keyboard

Raukhverger, M. (Mikhail) (1901–1989) Russia

Kontŝert dliā valtorny s orkestrom (Concerto for Horn and Orchestra)
Sov. Kompozitor, 1989, piano reduction
>   I. Andante
>   II. Andantino
>   III. Allegro comodo

Published in an anthology of five horn concertos by Soviet composers entitled *Kontserty dlia mednykh dukhovykh instrumentov s orkestrom, Kontserty dlia valtornyvolume 4,* (Concertos for Brass Instruments and Orchestra, Vol. 4, Concertos for French Horn) that includes concertos by Aristakesian, Kolodub (for two horns), Raukhverger, Sat'yan [Satian], and Trubin. Composer and pianist, Raukhverger taught at the Moscow Conservatory for many years.

This piece is in three traditional movements and in contemporary tonal language. The first movement is lyrical, with a wide-ranging somber melody in the horn. The second movement, in $\frac{3}{4}$, develops an eighth-note motive based on fourths, and the final movement, the lightest in character of the three, is in a rhythmic $\frac{6}{8}$. The horn part is only moderately technical, with some quick chromatic writing, but it covers the full range of the horn, with several challenging passages extending above the staff.
Range: F♯–c³
Duration: 12:00

Raum, Elizabeth (1945–) Canada, born in the United States

Sherwood Legend (1996)
Cimarron Music Press, 2012, piano reduction
Written for Kurt Kellan, principal horn of the Calgary Philharmonic. Inspired by the Errol Flynn movie, *The Adventures of Robin Hood,* with its music score by Erich Korngold. In the program notes in the score, the composer calls this work "movie music without the movie, or programmatic music, or a tone poem." In three movements: 1. Swashbuckling hero—2. The pensive romantic—3. The unabashed scoundrel. This is romantic writing for the horn, very colorful and fun to play.
Range: c–b♭²
Duration: 24:00

Reger, Max (1873–1916) Germany

Scherzino for Horn and Strings (1899)
See: Horn and keyboard

Reinhardt, (Johann Christian?) Germany

Concerto ex Dis-Dur für Cornu concertato, 2 Violinen, Viola & Basso
Robert Ostermeyer, 1999, piano reduction and orchestra score
Known as no. 17a of the horn concerto manuscripts located at Lund University Library, in the Ms. Kat. Wenster Litt. I/1–17b. In three movements: Moder-

ato—Siciliano—Allegro ma non presto. This is a low-horn concerto for natural horn in E♭ with a few runs that extend into the high range. The outer
movements feature challenging acrobatic writing for the horn with wide
leaps down into the low range. In the middle-movement Siciliano the horn
alternates between playing a long melodic line and playing the bass line.
Range: B♭–b♭² (c–c³ for horn in E♭)
Duration: 9:00

Reise, Jay (1950–) United States

Concerto for Horn & 7 Instruments (2006)
J. Reise, 2006, full score
For horn, with oboe, clarinet, percussion, piano, violin, viola, and violoncello.
Commissioned and premiered by the Network for New Music, with Adam
Unsworth, horn, April 23, 2006. In three movements. The first has an ex-
tended section for horn alone, and is quite taxing, going up to high e♭³.
The second movement is marked "Quiet, distant, rhythms always distinct,"
with the horn moving through slow, slurred figures over a wide range. The
third movement is a driving Allegro moderato in ⅞, with intricate runs,
many technical passages, and a middle section that slows things down,
marked "Like a languid barcarolle." This is a demanding work, requiring
great virtuosity from the soloist.
Range: to e–e♭³
Duration: 25:00

Reissiger, Carl Gottlieb (1798–1859) Germany

Solo per il corno in F, für Horn und Orchester
H. Litolff's Verlag / C.F. Peters, 1980, piano reduction
Written for horn virtuoso Joseph Rudolf Lewy. A dramatic, operatic opening
section with ornaments, trills, and a wide range leads into a flowing major
section with a cadenza that ends the piece using material from the opening
section. According to editor Kurt Janetzky's preface, Reissiger's arrangement of the score indicates that this work can be performed with string
quartet or string orchestra, with the two flutes, two bassoons, and two
horns ad lib.
Range: c–c³
Duration: 8:17
See: Horn and keyboard

Ridout, Alan (1934–1996) United Kingdom

Concertino for Horn (in F) and Strings
Emerson Horn Editions, 1978, piano reduction
For string orchestra or string quartet. Ridout wrote a series of ten concertinos
with string orchestra for all of the orchestra wind instruments. Written for
Nigel Black, this is a very accessible work, in three movements, suitable for
the younger college player due to range and endurance required. Technical

passages lie well on the horn, with clever interplay between horn and strings (or piano) in the last movement.
Range: f♯–a²
Duration: 7:00

Riedt, Friedric Wilhelm (1710–1783) Germany
Riedt was a flutist in the court of King Friedrich the Great and later founded the Musikübenden Gesellschaft in Berlin.

Concerto a 5 ex dis corno, due violin, viola e bassus
Robert Ostermeyer, 1999, piano reduction and orchestra score
The Ostermeyer edition is taken from a manuscript located in the Landesbib-
        liothek Mecklenburg-Vorpommern in Schwerin. In one short movement
        that combines high florid writing above the staff with acrobatic runs in
        the mid-range. Trills, arpeggiated figures, and high tessitura make this a
        challenging work. Also ventures into the low range of the horn.
Range: B♭–b♭² (c–c³ for horn in E♭)
Duration: 5:00

Rihm, Wolfgang (1952–) Germany
New Grove describes Rihm as "among the most influential of European composers born in the decade after World War II. . . . a leading figure in the reorientation
of German music in the 1970s increasingly away from exclusively structuralist
concerns towards expressive immediacy and historical allusion."

Hornkonzert (2013–2014)
Universal Edition, orchestra score only
This exciting new addition to the horn repertoire was premiered August 19, 2014,
        by hornist Stefan Dohr with the Mahler Chamber Orchestra at the Lucerne
        Festival. In one continuous movement and in fluid tempos with legato ges-
        tures in the horn that move in and out of the texture, with dynamic con-
        trasts and occasional colorful effects of stopped writing, flutter tonguing,
        and glissandi. There is a very free improvisatory cadenza marked "sempre
        ppp poss., intimissimo." This is a virtuosic work that covers the entire range
        of the horn, requiring great control and endurance, particularly in the high
        tessitura.
Range: E–d³ (ossia E–c³)
Duration: 20:00

Rimmer, John (1939–) New Zealand
Rimmer taught at the University of Auckland and was composer in residence
with the Auckland Philharmonia, Dalewool Auckland Brass Band, and the Ma-
nukau City Symphony.

Hidden Treasures for Horn and Orchestra (2005)
Centre for New Zealand Music, 2005, orchestra score only
This work was commissioned by the New Zealand Symphony Orchestra, who
        premiered it April 26, 2006, at the Municipal Theatre in Napier, Edward

Allen, horn soloist. In contrasting sections, this intricate work liberally quotes the horn repertoire, reworking several ideas of the horn obbligato from Mahler's *Symphony No. 5* into a contemporary landscape. The orchestra is continuously active, at times providing layers of sound and at other times answering the horn or interjecting rhythmic punctuations. The horn section plays an important part, echoing the horn soloist on single repeated notes, just as in the Mahler symphony. Moderately difficult with challenging technical passages, but well paced with judicious breaks for the soloist.

Range: A–c^3
Duration: 11:00

Ristori, Emile (1893–1977) Switzerland

Concerto en La mineur
Brogneaux, 1949, piano reduction
    Allegro moderato
    Lento
    Allegro
Unabashedly romantic work, with colorful and dramatic orchestration reminiscent of film music, with quickly shifting moods and character within movements. Brief cadenza in the first movement. Challenging, but the diatonic writing in familiar key areas makes this an approachable work for the advanced college student and above.

Range: b–b^2
Duration: 19:25

Robbins, Gil (1931–2011) United States

Caprice for Horn and. . . .
Seesaw, 1979, full score
For horn, percussion, harp, and strings. A short one-movement work of medium difficulty, in several contrasting sections and traditional harmonic language. It opens in a flowing § and the final section is a fast Presto in ⁴₄, in counterpoint with the ensemble, with quick slurred octave leaps to high a^2.

Range: c–b^2
Duration: ca. 7:00

Roelstraete, Herman (1925–1985) Belgium

Romanza
CeBeDeM, 1987, full score, copy of manuscript
For horn and string orchestra. A short, flowing work in one movement, rhythmically straightforward in ⁴₄.

Range: a♭–f^2
Duration: 1:30

Rogers, Bernard (1893–1968) United States
American composer and teacher, served as editor at *Musical America,* and taught at the Cleveland Institute and the Hartt School of Music. He was on the faculty of the Eastman School of Music for many years and his pupils include David Diamond and Dominick Argento.

Fantasia, for Solo Horn in F, Kettle-drums, and String Orchestra (1952)
Presser, 1956, full score only
For hornist Morris Secon, who first performed the piece with the Rochester Philharmonic, February 11, 1955, Erich Leinsdorf conducting. This work is in one continuous movement, with outer sections of music based on a fanfare theme that alternates with the timpani. A lyrical middle section develops out of the fanfare motive. There are several instances of high b^2 held over several measures, but overall this is an accessible work. The full score is published and available in many libraries in the U.S.
Range: g♯–c^3
Duration: 11:00

Röllig Germany
For the two concertos listed below, only the last name "Röllig" appears on the manuscript, and it is unknown whether it is Christian August Röllig or Johann Georg Röllig (1710–1790).

Concerto in E flat Major for Horn and String Orchestra (Lund manuscript no. 14)
Birdalone Music, 1996, piano reduction and orchestra score; Robert Ostermeyer, 1999, piano reduction and orchestra score
This concerto is no. 14 of the eighteen manuscripts located at Lund University Library, in the Ms. Kat. Wenster Litt. I/1–17b. In three movements: Moderato—Siciliano—Tempo di menuetto. This is a challenging work that typifies high clarino-horn writing, and there are many opportunities for trills and embellishing the line. The title on the Ostermeyer edition is *Concerto ex Dis-Dur für Cornu concertato, 2 Violinen, Viola & Basso.*
Range: f^1–d^3 (g^1–e^3 for horn in E♭)
Duration: 9:30

Concerto in D Major for Horn and String Orchestra (Lund manuscript no. 15)
Birdalone Music, 1989, piano reduction and orchestra score; Robert Ostermeyer, 1999, piano reduction and orchestra score
This concerto is no. 15 of the eighteen manuscripts located at Lund University Library, in the Ms. Kat. Wenster Litt. I/1–17b. The concerto is in three movements: Allegro ma non molto—Siciliano—Allegro: Tempo di menuetto. Although still a very high part, full of clarino-horn writing, its upper-range requirements are not as strenuous as the composer's E♭ concerto, though the D major concerto is slightly more acrobatic, with arpeggiated figures in the first movement, and several octave leaps in the last movement.
Range: a–a^2 (c^1–c^3 for horn in D)
Duration: 10:30

Rollin, Robert (1947–) United States

Concerto Pastorale
Seesaw, 1983, horn and piano version is the composer's *Sonata Pastorale*
Commissioned by the Warren Chamber Orchestra and premiered October 30, 1982, William Slocum, horn soloist. The composer's preface states that "each movement is freely inspired by a different locale and its natural wildlife: the first movement, the Big Meadow area of the Blue Ridge Mountains inhabited by wild deer; the second, the deserted winter beach at Ocean City populated by gulls and sandpipers; and the third, the Blackwater Wildlife Refuge and Sanctuary near the Chesapeake Bay, where thousands of Canada geese find their winter homes." The first movement, "Blue Ridge Mountains," is expressive, marked Largo, and includes a very brief cadenza. The second movement, "Ocean City beach," is in an allegretto tempo, with running sixteenth notes in the bass instruments, gradually picked up by the entire string section, with the horn playing expressive triplet figures. The last movement, "Blackwater Refuge," is in a fast two with changing tempi. There are several opportunities for horn cadenzas.
Range: c–b^2
Duration: 14:00

Rom, Uri (1969–) Israel
Uri Rom worked for many years in Germany. He currently teaches at Buchmann-Mehta School of Music, Tel-Aviv University.

Rondo für Naturhorn und Orchester, Es-Dur
Edition Dohr, 2005, piano reduction and orchestra score
For horn in E♭. A short, clever rondo for contemporary natural horn, in $\frac{6}{8}$. Idiomatic writing for the natural horn, with many written high c^{3}s.
Range: B♭–b♭^{2} (c–c^3 for horn in E♭)
Duration: 5:00

Roper, Harrison (1932–) United States

Concertino
Touch of Brass, 1987, piano reduction
For horn and band. A three-movement concertino composed specifically to be accessible both musically and technically to the advancing high school student.
Range: a–a^2 (ossia a–g^2)
See: Horn and keyboard

Rosetti, Antonio (1750–1792) [also known as Franz Anton Rösler or Rössler]
Germany (Bohemia)
Rosetti was a double bassist and composer in the Oettingen-Wallerstein Court, then later in his career was employed by the Duke of Mecklenburg-Schwerin at Ludwigslust. He wrote over a dozen solo-horn concertos (the exact number is uncertain, due to various attributions and mis-attributions), and his double-horn concertos were played by the most famous horn duos of his era.

All Rosetti concertos for solo horn are in three-movement form; the second movement is often entitled "Romance," and the third movement is a rondo in either $\frac{3}{4}$ or $\frac{6}{8}$. Rosetti was writing for excellent horn players, including such prominent names as Giovanni Punto, Johannes and Carl Türrschmidt, Franz Zwierzina, and Josef Nagel, which can be evidenced by the level and sophistication of hand-horn technique he used and by the difficulty of his concertos. His liberal use of hand stopping showed off the technical abilities of the soloists, and also allowed him to venture further afield harmonically into different key areas, making these works inventive and full of variety and expression. Over the years, publishers and musicologists have identified the concertos using various numbering systems. The KaWe edition numbering (Concerto No. 1, Concerto No. 2 etc.) may be the most familiar to horn players, and was used to identify the concertos simply by number. With new editions and the relatively recent publication of Sterling Murray's catalog, *The music of Antonio Rosetti (Anton Rösler) ca. 1750–1792: a thematic catalog,* the Murray "C" numbers are quickly becoming the more common way to identify Rosetti's works, and will be used here. Another identifying number is the slightly older "K" number (also be referred to as the DTB number), which refers to Oskar Kaul's *Thematisches Verzeichnis der Instrumentalwerke von Anton Rosetti.* All editions listed are available as piano reductions.

Horn Concerto in D Minor C38 (ca. 1789–90)
Simrock, 1959 (Bernard Krol, ed.); Robert Ostermeyer, 2002
Murray C38
Kaul: III: 43
Written for horn in F. Based on an edition by publisher Spehr in Braunschweig
    ca. 1790. In three movements: Allegro molto—Adagio—Rondo. The horn
    opens in the written key of F, with a contrasting second theme in d minor.
    The last movement has many changes in character, more than the typical
    rondo, with sections of adagio in $\frac{3}{4}$ and a La Chasse in contrasting $\frac{6}{8}$. This
    and the very similar concerto C39 may be the only minor-key horn concertos of the eighteenth century.
Range: c–a^2
Duration: 20:49

Horn Concerto in D Minor C39 (ca. 1786)
Robert Ostermeyer, 2002
Written for horn in F. This concerto has many of the same themes as the first and
    third movements of Rosetti's D minor concerto C38. The second movement
    is completely different than that of C38, and the third-movement rondo
    lacks the adagio sections that are in C39. Robert Ostermeyer based this new
    edition on a print by Sieber that was published around 1786, and this may
    be an earlier version of the familiar D Minor concerto D38.
Range: c–a^2
Duration: ca. 18:00

Horn Concerto in E♭ Major C40 (ca. 1784–86)
KaWe, 1971 (Leloir, ed.); Hans Pizka Edition, 1985 (No. 117a Collection Leloir);
    Ostermeyer, 2001

Murray: C40

Kaul: III: 35

KaWe and Pizka editions: *Concerto No. 3*

Written for horn in E♭. In three movements: Allegro spiritoso—Adagio—Rondeau: Allegro non tanto. A challenging high-horn concerto written in the cor-alto style of the period. There are high scale passages in the opening movement and runs that extend well above the staff in the last movement.

Range: f¹–d³

Duration: 17:43

Horn Concerto in E♭ Major C41

KeWe, 1975; Robert Ostermeyer, 2004

Murray: C41

Kaul: III: 39

KaWe edition title: *Concerto No. 6 in E♭ Major*

In three movements: Allegro molto—Adagio non tanto—Rondeau: Allegretto. High-horn writing, with many ornaments similar to the E♭ concerto, C49, but in a cor-alto setting.

Range: d¹–c³

Duration: 17:00

Horn Concerto in E♭ Major C42

Hans Pizka Edition, 1979

Murray: C42

Kaul: III: 41

Pizka edition title: *Concerto per corno secundo*

In three movements: Allegro—Adagio—Rondeaux. Written for the cor-basse virtuoso, with quick technical passages in the midrange of the horn and wide downward leaps into the low range, requiring good flexibility. Quite possibly written for Franz Zwierzina

Range:B♭–f²

Duration: 10:00

Horn Concerto in E♭ Major C43 Q

Robert Ostermeyer, 2000

This work is identified as C43 Q by Sterling Murray in his thematic catalog, the Q indicating questionable authorship. Mozart's name appears on the manuscript, but Murray has identified Rosetti as the likely composer, based on the concerto's musical style and characteristics.

Horn Concerto in E♭ Major C47

Doblinger, 1974 (Bernhard Paumgartner, ed.)

Murray: C47

Kaul: III: 40

Doblinger edition title: *Concerto da camera no. 16.*

In three movements: Allegro moderato—Adagio—Rondo: Allegro. Edited from a set of manuscript parts in the library of the Mozarteum, Salzburg. This concerto stays, for the most part, in a more moderate range and is slightly less virtuosic than many of the other concertos. The last-movement rondo is in ⅜, which is also unlike other Rosetti horn concertos.

Range: b♭–b♭²
Duration: 14:56

Horn Concerto in E♭ Major C48 (ca. 1781)
KaWe, 1970 (Leloir, ed.); Robert Ostermeyer, 2002
Murray: C48
Kaul: III: 37
KaWe edition title: *Concerto No. 1 in E♭*
In three movements: Allegro—Romance, Adagio ma non tanto—Rondo: Allegretto. Scalar passages, similar to C40 (KaWe No. 3). Many ornamented passages similar to C49 (KaWe No. 2) including trills, turns, and grace notes. The KeWe edition includes a lengthy cadenza written by Edmund Leloir.

Range: e^1–c^3
Duration: 14:55

Horn Concerto in E♭ Major C49 (1779)
Amadeus, 2006 (Moesus, ed.); KaWe, 1965 (Leloir, ed.); International, 1960 (Chambers, ed.); Deutscher Verlag für Musik, 1969 (Damm, ed.); Eulenberg, 1978 (Päuler, ed.)
Murray: C49
Kaul: III: 36
KaWe edition title: *Concerto No. 2 in Mi♭*
In three movements: Allegro moderato—Romance, Adagio non tanto—Rondeau: Allegretto non troppo. Dedicated to "Monsieur Dürrschmidt," who was either Johann Türrschmidt, first horn in the Oettingen-Wallerstein orchestra until 1780, or more likely his son, low-horn virtuoso Carl Türrschmidt. This is perhaps the most popular Rosetti concerto among hornists, with an elegant opening movement, lyrical second movement with a contrasting minor section, and a third movement in ⅜ that is hunting music that still manages elegance with ornaments and grace notes and includes several opportunities for short "Eingang" cadenzas before each return of the rondo theme.

Range: f–b♭² (g–c^3 for horn in E♭)
Duration: 19:32

Horn Concerto in E Major C50 (ca. 1786)
KaWe, 1976; Robert Ostermeyer, 2003
Murray: C50
Kaul: III: 44
KaWe title: *Concerto No. 5 in E Major*
In three movements: Allegro—Adagio—Allegretto. Both modern editions available are based on a Pleyel edition of 1796–97. This piece is full of cor-basse writing and was quite possibly written for Franz Zwierzina. It includes low-horn "tricks" on the natural horn, such as diatonic scales down to written low c, which can only be implied on the hand horn, as these notes do not

speak well. Other cor-basse features are diatonic notes below written low c, fast arpeggiations and virtuosic octave leaps, and low notes, such as written low d♭, that are bent upward. There are many fast range changes and some dramatic sixteenth-note leaps of almost two octaves.

Range: F♯–f♯² (G–g² for horn in E)
Duration: 16:26

Horn Concerto in E Major C51
Simrock, 1964 (Jirí Stefan, ed.)
Murray: C51
Kaul: III: 42
For horn in E. The opening movement has flowing and elegant first and second themes with virtuosic and acrobatic sixteenth and triplet figures. This movement spans a range of over three octaves and also provides an opportunity for a cadenza. The second movement is an expressive Adagio in sounding E minor, with plenty of beautiful stopped colors on the natural horn. The third movement is a Rondo a la chasse in 𝄮 with grace notes in the main theme that add to its raucous nature. There are no less than five opportunities for a short "Eingang" cadenza before each return of the rondo theme.

Range: F♯–g♯² (G–a² for horn in E)
Duration: 18:00
Conflicting attributions, See: Punto, Giovanni *Concerto No. 1 in E.* Also appeared as Stamitz *Concerto in E♭* with some alterations. See: Stamitz, Karl.

Horn Concerto in E Major C52
Robert Ostermeyer, 2000
Murray: C52
Kaul: III: 45
Based on music recently discovered in the Monastery of Seitenstetten in Austria, this was originally identified as a concerto for two horns in E major by Giovanni Punto, with a missing first horn part. Robert Ostermeyer determined that this was actually a solo concerto for low horn. Through comparison with a set of incomplete orchestra parts (missing solo horn and first violin) by Rosetti, published in 1782 in Paris and now in the Bibliotheque Nationale, he determined that Rosetti was the actual composer of this work.
In three movements: Allegro moderato—Romance: Andantino—Rondo. This concerto features an extensive slow movement and a menuet at the end of the last movement. The character of the horn writing is similar to the E major concerto C51, including the second movement being in the tonic minor.

Range: B–g♯² (c–a² for horn in E)
Duration: 20:08

Horn Concerto in F major C53
KaWe, 1966
Murray: C53
Kaul: III: 38

KaWe title: *Concerto No. 4 in F Major*
For horn in F. In three movements: Allegro vivace—Romanza: Adagio non tanto
—Rondo: Allegretto. This is a rather showy low-horn piece, similar to other
Rosetti low-horn concertos, with wide leaps, although perhaps slightly less
acrobatic. It is also the most technically accessible among the concertos.
The KaWe edition has a lengthy cadenza by Edmond Leloir.
Range: f–b^2
Duration: 16:03

Horn Concerto in E♭ Major C54 Q
Robert Ostermeyer, 1999
This is identified as a double concerto, C54 Q in Sterling Murray's catalog. This
edition is based on music discovered in the Monastery of Melk in Austria,
and, as with the concerto C52, it was originally misidentified as a concerto
for two horns with a missing first horn part. The title reads *Corno 2do
prinzipale in Dis,* which was thought to be a second horn part of a double
concerto, but actually means concerto for low (second) horn.
In three movements: Allegro assai—Romance: Andante—Rondo: Allegretto. Cor-
basse writing, with wide leaps in the middle and low range. Again, Franz
Zwierzina comes to mind as the most likely horn soloist for whom this may
have been written.
Range: B♭–f^2 (c–g^2)
Duration: 14:00

Rosseau, Norbert (1907–1975) Belgium
Rosseau received his early musical training in Italy, where he lived from 1914–
1932 and was a violin virtuoso from an early age. After an injury, he turned to
composition and studied at the conservatory in Rome. He wrote in a wide range
of styles, from serial techniques to electronic and concrete music.

Concerto voor hoorn en orkest, op. 2.67 (1967)
CeBeDeM, 1998, piano reduction
In one continuous movement and beginning at a fast clip that never really lets
up. There are several lyrical sections, but the quick triplet figures drive this
work, with intricate writing in the accompaniment. There is an extensive
cadenza that concludes on a held high c^3, driving this contemporary work
to its grand conclusion.
Range: B–c^3
Duration: 14:00

Rossum, Frederik van (1939–) Belgium
Eloquences, pour cor et orchestre, op. 39
Cranz Contemporary Music, 1981, orchestra score only
In five movements: Exorde—Diatribe—Apologie—Allegorie—Peroraison. This
work expresses a wide range of characters, with colorful orchestration
throughout. The first movement opens with a tritone motive over string
glissandi, continuing with horn interjections back and forth. The second is

marked "Inesorabilmente," and moves quickly through changing meters, with the horn weaving an intricate chromatic line between winds, strings, and piano. The third is marked Quasi marche funebre ma con grandezza e dignita, and has the horn playing long, loud lines over the marching $\frac{4}{4}$ accompaniment. The fourth movement is a scherzo with glissandi, flutter tonguing, and trills, quite challenging for the horn, with leaps and fast passages over a few octaves. The final movement is somber, with the horn playing sustained passages over blocks of sound in the orchestra. Recorded by Francis Orval for the Queen Elisabeth International Music Competition 1980.

Range: D–d♭³
Duration: 17:00

Rota, Nino (1911–1979) Italy

Well known for his film music, particularly his collaboration with Federico Fellini and his award winning scores for *The Godfather* series, Rota was also a prolific composer of instrumental music.

Castel del Monte, Ballata per corno e orchestra (1974)
Ricordi, 1991, piano reduction
This ballade, named for the famous castle in southern Italy, was composed for
    hornist Domenico Ceccarosi, who premiered the work at the Corsi Internazionali di Lanciano on August 11, 1975. Its lyrical opening section leads
    into an Allegro organized around a dotted-triplet motive and reminiscent
    of the "Ride of the Valkyries" of Wagner. The third section is light, almost
    sardonic in character, with a passage of solo oboe that has the horn echoing
    motives from earlier sections. Lush and colorfully orchestrated, this is a
    very accessible work for the hornist, well paced with only modest demands
    on range.

Range: c–g²
Duration: 10:00

Andante sostenuto, per il concerto per corno e orchestra in re maggiore KV 412 di Wolfgang Amadeus Mozart
Schott, 2005; orchestra score only
A proposed slow movement for Mozart's *Horn concerto* K. 412. In $\frac{4}{4}$, written for
    horn in G.

Range: a–a² (g–g² for horn in G)
Duration: 5:00

Roth, Phillip (1853–1898) Germany

Concerto in fa
Edition KaWe, 1976 (Edmond Leloir, ed.), piano reduction
This work is based on a manuscript in the Regia Monacencis Bibliotheca (Bavarian State Library, Germany). In three movements: Allegro non troppo—
    Adagio—Polonaise. Characteristic nineteenth-century work with pleasing
    melodic writing and opportunities for the hornist to display virtuosity,

albeit within a relatively narrow range, considering the horn's capabilities. This work is moderately difficult, with extensive triplets in the first movement and sixteenth-note passages in the final movement.

Range: g^1–a^2

Duration: 15:00

Russell, Craig H. (1951–) United States

Rhapsody for Horn and Orchestra (1999, rev. 2006)
Craig Russell, 1999, 2006, piano reduction
1. Morning's Decisions
2. Dizzy Bird
3. Wistful Musing
4. Tito Machito
5. Flash

Dedicated to Michael Nowak and Richard Todd, this work was premiered with the San Luis Obispo Symphony, Richard Todd, horn, who also recorded it on the Naxos label. The first and third movements are similar, at a slow or moderate tempo., The composer indicates in the recording liner notes that both movements "pay spiritual homage to Samuel Barber's exquisite *Violin Concerto,* and share a melodic motive or two." The second and fourth movements are similar, in that both draw their inspiration from jazz greats: Dizzy Gillespie and Charlie "Bird" Parker in the bebop second movement, and Tito Puente and Machito in the Latin-jazz-styled fourth movement. The fifth movement is a ripping fast Perpetuo moto that the composer describes as "merciless." This is a challenging and virtuosic work, presenting a wide variety of musical ideas and styles, and requiring versatility from the soloist. The horn improvises in the second and fourth movements, the third movement has an extensive recitative for the horn, and the slow movements require control and thoughtful phrasing.

Range: G–d^3

Duration: 41:34

Sabatini, Guglielmo (ca. 1902–1967) United States

Classic Concerto for Solo Horn and Small Orchestra (after Borghi)
Cor Publishing Co., 1963, piano reduction
I. Largamente—Allegro moderato
II. Andante
III. Rondo finale

Written in traditional harmonic language and form, of medium difficulty with agile sixteenth-note passages in the first and last movements.

Range: B♭–b♭^{2}

Duration: 9:30

Elegia, for Solo Horn and Strings
Camara Music, 1960, piano reduction

In memoriam. This short work for horn and strings has plenty of room for expressive playing, with its legato phrasing building to declamatory *fortissimo* before returning to the main theme. Requires a bit of endurance for the return of the A section, as there are no opportunities for the horn player to rest, and the final phrase ends on a held high a².
Range: a–a²
Duration: 3:45

Sagvik, Stellan (1952–) Sweden
Bohuslänsk Concertino, op. 114d, *for Horn and Strings* (1982)
Pizzicato Helvetia, 2009, published as a score and six parts
    I. (Tune after Niklas Larsson, Liane)
    II. (Traditional tune)
    III. (Tune after Johan August Nilsson, Munkedal)
This is part of the composer's series of ten concertinos for wind instruments, which are all based on Swedish folk songs. For horn and strings or string quintet. Premiered by hornist Alexandru Marc, Filarmonica de Cluj/Tons. The first movement is pastoral and playful. The second movement, marked Contemplativo, is hymn-like, with horn in unison with strings, creating a spacious mood. The last movement begins in a largo tempo with a jaunty dotted-eighth figure that evolves into a faster rollicking tune. It stays in the horn's low and midrange, giving it a robust and earthy character.
Range: c♯–c³
Duration: 11:23

Saint-Saëns, Camille (1835–1921) France
Morceau de concert, op. 87 (1887, rev. 1893)
Durand, 1999; International, 1956; Faust Music, 2012 (Andrew Adams, Travis Bennett, ed.)—all piano reductions
Dedicated to Henri Chaussier. In three sections, this is a romantic work written for a later type of omnitonic horn developed by Henri Chaussier. This work includes a theme and variations first movement, a lyrical second movement that uses the low range and stopped horn, and a technical third movement with trills and wide range changes. This is a standard work in the repertoire and a good advanced student piece. The Faust Music edition is a new critical edition, based on an examination of both manuscripts—the manuscript for horn and piano and the manuscript for horn and orchestra, which was completed one month later.
Range: c–c³
Duration: 9:00

Romance pour cor, op. 36
Edition mf, 1988, orchestra score
Well-known work for horn and piano, this was also orchestrated for two flutes, oboe, two clarinets, bassoon, violins, viola, cello, and bass.
See: Horn and keyboard

Sallinen, Aulis (1935–) Finland

Sallinen trained at the Sibelius Academy, was manager of the Finnish Radio Symphony Orchestra, and eventually returned to the Sibelius Academy to teach composition. Winner of the Nordic Council Award and the Sibelius Prize, he is perhaps most known for his operas.

Concerto for Horn and Orchestra, Campane ed Arie (Bells and Arias), op. 82 (2002, rev. 2005)

Novello, 2006, piano reduction

The concerto was composed for the eighty-fifth birthday of K.H. Pentti and was premiered on October 10, 2003, by hornist Esa Tapani with the Helsinki Philharmonic Orchestra. The title of the concerto is a pun on "bells up" (a term for when hornists play with bells in the air) which manifests itself throughout the concerto. In two parts. Hunting calls open the first part, followed by a bell-like motive from the piccolo that is developed by the horn with long lines of wide and expressive intervals, leading into a cadenza. The slow opening tempo returns, with the horn line rising out of lush string colors. The second part is quick, with the horn trading off fast rhythmic passages with orchestral instruments. There is a middle section of piu lento with the horn in a contemplative mode trading back and forth with interjections of orchestral color. Stopped phrases lead back into a final rhythmic section, with a triumphant final passage, played bells up. This is a challenging and virtuosic work for the hornist.

Range: f♯–b♭^{2}

Duration: 22:00

Salminen, Susan (1957–) United States

Concerto for Horn and Brass Ensemble (1994)

Solid Wood Publishing, 1994, score and parts

    I. Pastorale, vivace

    II. Romanze

    III. Rondo

To Jack Herrick and the University of Northern Colorado Brass Ensemble. The composer wrote this work as her DM thesis at the University of Northern Colorado. In three movements in traditional forms, written in a tonal language with little chromaticism. The first movement has a cadenza, and the last movement is in $\frac{7}{4}$ with a few changing meters. There are several challenging passages above the staff, but, overall, this work is well paced for the soloist. There are multiphonics; glissandi, including one that spans four octaves; a few trills; and some stopped writing. The brass-ensemble writing is suited for college players who may be of varying levels.

Range: B♭–c^3

Duration: 9:33

Sansone, Lorenzo (1881–1975) United States, born in Italy

Instrument maker, music publisher, and orchestral hornist, Sansone taught at Juilliard from 1921–1946.

French Horn Concertino
Lorenzo Sansone, 1940, piano reduction
In three movements of only moderate difficulty, this tonal work is reminiscent of
late nineteenth-century writing for horn and piano, suitable for the student
hornist. The first movement, marked Allegro maestoso a capriccio, has
cadenza-like sections, and much room for expression. The second movement is an Andantino espressivo in $\frac{3}{4}$, and the third section is a light Rondo
in $\frac{3}{4}$.
Range: e–c^3 (ossia e–a^2)
Duration: 6:00

Sanz Sifre, Nicanor (1933–) Spain

Concierto núm. 1 en mi♭ mayor para trompa y piano
Boileau, 1976, piano reduction
  I. Lento—Allegro
  II. Romanza
  III. Rondo.
A dramatic work in traditional language and form, with virtuosic writing for the
horn soloist. The first and third movements have a cadenza.
Range: A–b♭^{2}
Duration: ca. 17:00

Sargon, Simon (1938–) United States, born in India

Questings: Concerto for Horn and Chamber Orchestra (1985–87)
Simon A. Sargon, 1990, piano reduction, available from the composer
  I. Concertato
  II. Pastorale
  III. Burlesque/Finale
For Gregory Hustis, who premiered the work in June 1991 at the International
Horn Society Symposium at the University of North Texas. The composer
explains in the score preface that the title refers to "the quest throughout
the compositions to regain the mood of peace and serenity with which it
opens." The horn begins with quiet calls over shimmering strings, "creating a vision of inner peace and tranquility." The first movement, Allegro,
interrupts this quiet mood with "restless agitation" between horn and orchestra, using bold and heroic motives in an energetic $\frac{3}{4}$. The second-movement pastorale opens quietly with the horn alone, followed by lyrical and
flowing themes. The third movement has the horn playing a straightforward tonal line, "but is constantly detoured into bitonality and dissonance
by the full orchestra." The piece concludes with a return to the opening material that began the quest. Written in contemporary tonal language, this is
a challenging work for the hornist, requiring good endurance, however the
overall pacing makes this an accessible work.
Range: e♭–d^3
Duration: 16:51

Sat'yan [Satian], Aram (1947–) Armenia

Metamorfoza dlia valtorny i strunnogo orkestra (Metamorphosis for Horn and String Orchestra)
Sov. Kompozitor, 1989, piano reduction
Published in an anthology of five horn concertos by Soviet composers, entitled
    *Kontserty dlia mednykh dukhovykh instrumentov s orkestrom, Kontserty
    dlia valtornyvolume 4,* (Concertos for Brass Instruments and Orchestra,
    Vol. 4, Concertos for French Horn) that includes concertos by Aristake-
    sian, Kolodub (for two horns), Raukhverger, Sat'yan [Satian], and Trubin.
    An expressive work in ABA form, with legato lines and a brief cadenza
    that leads to a piu mosso section before a return to the quiet opening
    material.
Range: G♯–b♭²
Duration: 8:00

Schibler, Armin (1920–1986) Switzerland

Prologue, invocation et danse, op. 47 (1956)
Ahn & Simrock, 1956, piano reduction
Written for the 1956 Geneva International Music Competition.
See: Horn and keyboard

Schickele, Peter (1935–) United States

Pentangle, Five Songs for French Horn and Orchestra (1976)
Theodore Presser, 1976, orchestra score only
    I. Cottonwood grove
    II. Tom on the town
    III. Noonsong
    IV. Ladies and gentlemen, the amazing and amusing Professor Presto
    V. The riddling knight
Commissioned by Thomas Bacon, who premiered the work February 15, 1976,
    with the West Shore Symphony, Muskegon, Michigan. Fused with folk-
    song and rock elements, jazz inflections, and jaunty folk melodies over
    walking bass lines. The third movement has multiphonics that are not an
    effect, but rather true melodic material. The fourth movement is a tribute to
    the magician, with theatrical surprises and items pulled out of the horn—
    confetti, silk scarves, a cloth rabbit, and flowers. The last movement is an
    adaptation of a traditional English ballad, with the horn soloist singing (al-
    though directions indicate a singer can handle the voice part if necessary).
    Colorful, creative, inventive, and a fun addition to both the horn repertoire
    and to classical music—which has a tendency to take itself too seriously.
    Challenges include some held high notes, double tonguing, multiphonics,
    but this is, overall, very accessible writing that is well paced for the horn
    soloist.
Range: B♭–c³
Duration: 25:00

Schmalz, Peter (1947–) United States

Dr. Peter Schmalz, hornist and director of the Osh Kosh West High School bands from 1972–2002, has written several works for horn.

Caduceus for Solo Horn and Band (1987)

Phoebus Publications, 1988, full score only

This piece is in one movement with contrasting sections of changing character and tempi: Reflectively—Motorically—Definitively—Energetically. The slow and lyrical opening section becomes increasingly energetic, with the horn in contrapuntal dialogue with the band, culminating in a cadenza for the horn. Well paced for the horn soloist.

Range: A♭–b²

Duration: 11:30

Schmidt, Hartmut (1946–) Austria, born in Germany

Konzert Nr. 1 für Alphorn (oder Naturhorn) und Streicher

Vogt & Fritz, 2003, full score

Written for alphorn in G or natural horn in G. Classic alphorn tones on open intervals that occur on the natural harmonic series. In three traditional movements written in the classical style: Allegro—Largo—Rondo. The final movement is in §. This would be quite challenging on the natural horn in G, as it would have many high c³s (high d³ on the valve horn in f), with octave leaps up to these notes.

Range: d–d³ (c–c³ for alphorn in G)

Duration: 17:40

Konzert Nr. 2 für Alphorn (oder Naturhorn) und Streicher (2000)

Vogt & Fritz, 2003, full score

Written for alphorn in G or natural horn in G. This work closely resembles the *Konzert Nr. 1 für Alphorn* above. It is also in three movements: Allegro—Largo—Rondo. Some sections of this piece use the same themes. The third-movement rondo has improvisatory sections for both strings and hornist and it incorporates a nursery rhyme.

Range: d–d³ (c–c³ for alphorn in G)

Duration: 16:00

Schmidt, Ole (1928–2010) Denmark

Concerto for Horn in F and Chamber Orchestra (1966)

Wilhelm Hansen, 1974, piano reduction

In two movements. The first features long extended lines for the horn in a largo tempo. The orchestra scoring is sparse at times, with interesting percussion writing, and an interlude reminiscent of Shostakovich. The second movement is in a fast three, with a slower, more playful middle section and some ethereal moments with horn over lush strings. Rhythmically straightforward, with quick passages, a cadenza in the second movement, wide leaps of fanfare figures, and glissandi.

Range: F–b²

Duration: 15:30

Schneider, Georg Abraham (1770–1839) Germany

Concerto pour le cor principale avec accompagnement de grand orchestre, op. 86
Manuscript score and parts at the Fleisher Collection, Free Library of Philadelphia
This work is from a set of "Combination Concertos," opp. 83–90 in F major, with
    identical thematic material, so that the expensive engraving of separate or-
    chestral parts could be avoided. Solo parts were composed, tailored to each
    specific instrument, but all have the same orchestral accompaniment. The
    composer wrote different solo parts for flute, clarinet, bassoon, horn, oboe,
    and bassethorn as well as two double concertos for flute/oboe and clarinet/
    bassoon.

Schneyder, Nikolaus (ca. 1989 fl.)
Both concertos discussed here were composed in 1989 in the style of the mid-eigh-
teenth-century baroque horn concertos. Both are idiomatically written in the
clarino range of the baroque era, but are not excessive, making these works quite
accessible for the modern hornist, with or without valves. A third concerto in Eb,
with the subtitle *Concerto a corno solo per la viola,* was written for horn player
and music publisher Viola Roth, and is currently unpublished.

Concerto in D Major for Horn and String Orchestra
Birdalone Music, 1992, score and parts
In the traditional three movements, fast-slow-fast, with trills and ornaments in-
    dicated throughout. Stylistically reminiscent of the mid-eighteenth-century
    English music of Thomas Arne and William Boyce.
Range: a–a^2 (c^1–c^3 for horn in D)

Concerto in Eb Major for Horn and String Orchestra
Birdalone Music, 1992, score and parts
In three movements: Moderato—Siciliano—Tempo di menuetto.
In a similar style to the concertos of Röllig and Graun from the Lund manuscript
    of baroque horn concertos.
Range: d^1–bb^2 (e^1–c^3 for horn in Eb)

Schoeck, Othmar (1886–1957) Switzerland

Concerto for Horn and String Orchestra, op. 65 (1951)
Boosey & Hawkes, 1952, piano reduction
This work is dedicated to Dr. Willy Abei. According to the program notes by
    Daniel Lienhard on Marie Louise Neunecker's recording on Koch, Schoeck
    said the concerto can be performed with a small string-chamber group. In
    three movements: Lebhaft energisch—Ruhig fliessand—Rondo: Ausserst
    schnell und leicht. The first movement is in sonata form with an energetic
    opening that gives way to a lyrical second theme. The second movement is
    scored with divisi violas and cellos, and exploits the horn's legato capabil-
    ities with long lines and poignant writing. The third-movement rondo is
    playful, humorous, and well crafted, in §. This idiomatic work is fun to play
    and is appropriate for the college-level player and above. The long lyrical
    lines and ubiquitous high notes require good endurance. This work has

appealed to many horn soloists, and has been recorded by Marie Louise Neunecker. Bruno Schneider, and Dennis Brain.

Range: a–c³
Duration: 17:22

Schollum, Robert (1913–1987) Austria

Dialog für Horn und Streichorchester (1958)
Verlag Doblinger, 1970, orchestra score only
This short work is written in the twelve-tone (dodecaphonic) style, using the intervals of fourths and fifths, in ABA form, and includes a cadenza. Angular writing, with wide intervals, suitable for the college-level hornist.

Range: A♭–f♯²
Duration: 4:00

Schonthal, Ruth (1924–2006) United States, born in Germany

Schonthal studied in Berlin, Sweden, Mexico City, and eventually made her way to Yale to study with Hindemith. *New Grove* states that "her music is expressionist, her forms ingenious."

Music for Horn and Orchestra (1978, arranged for horn and chamber orchestra 1979)
Furore Verlag, 1997, full score available, horn and piano version known as *Music for Horn and Piano*
The preface to this edition describes this work as "a wonderfully romantic-lyrical pastoral piece evoking the glow of the Alps. Very idiomatic for the horn, with some bitonality." In six short movements: Dolce e tranquillo—Allegro moderato—Moderato—Andante—Senza misure—Andante molto tranquillo. Full of pastoral, sweeping motives that utilize horn sixths and with expressive legato writing and wide intervals, reminiscent of yodeling. The fifth movement is unmeasured, with stopped writing and opportunities for expression. The movements are short, making things a bit less taxing, although a few passages in the final movement stay above the staff. Recorded on a now difficult to find vinyl LP, Meir Rimon, horn.

Range: e–b♭²
Duration: 11:00

Schuller, Gunther (1925–2015) United States

Orchestral-horn player, conductor, recording producer, writer, music publisher, and Pulitzer-prize-winning composer Gunther Schuller is also known to horn players for his book *Horn Technique.*

Concerto for Horn and Orchestra (1943–44)
Margun Music, 1982, orchestra score; second movement, *Nocturne,* published separately for horn and piano
Schuller played the premiere of this concerto with the Cincinnati Symphony, where he was principal horn, Eugene Goosens conducting. The first movement is marked Andante moderato, with romantic harmonic language and

beginning quietly in the low voices. It gains momentum for the dramatic entry of the soloist in a horn-call motive, which is developed throughout the movement in different tempi and character. The second movement, Nocturne is in a lento tempo, with a moody horn melody over syncopated strings and winds. The third-movement scherzo is full of changing meters and unexpected phrasing. There are several quasi-cadenzas for the horn that give the work a free character. The orchestration is thick, with many interesting voicings, such as pairs of bassoons and tuba solo in the last movement. The second movement, Nocturne, has been published for horn and piano.

Range: G–c³
Duration: 22:46

Concerto No. 2 for Horn and Orchestra (1975–76)
Associated Music Publishers, 1978, orchestra score only
Commissioned by and dedicated to Mario di Bonaventura; premiered in Budapest in 1978. In three movements: Vivace energico—Variations—Allegro moderato. This is from Schuller's mature period, and is an atonal work based on dodecaphonic writing. Virtuosic horn writing requiring dexterity and flexibility. Includes quarter-tone passages, glissandi, stopped writing, and flutter tonguing. This is a challenging work for both soloist and orchestra, with complex and intricate rhythmic writing. The final cadenza has aleatoric elements, where horn and orchestra are not strictly (vertically) coordinated.

Range: B–c♯³
Duration: 17:00

Schultz, Mark (1957–2015) United States

Dragons in the Sky, for horn and orchestra, or horn and wind ensemble (1989/1999)
JOMAR Press, 1999, full score
Winner of the 1990 International Horn Society Composition Competition, this work was originally scored for horn, percussion, and tape. A consortium of horn players and percussionists commissioned the two arrangements for orchestra and wind ensemble. The composer notes in the score preface that the music's inspiration comes from a battle depicted in J. R. R. Tolkien's *The Silmarillion.* The battle is between the kingdoms of the elves and the legions of the evil tyrant Morgoth, who "throws his winged dragons into the fray with 'thunder, lightning and a storm of fire' in a last, desperate attempt to win the day." In one movement. This work is dramatic and expressive. It opens with a forceful motive on repeated written C and moves into angular gestures and lyrical writing as the piece unfolds. There is an extensive cadenza, set off by a march-like ostinato figure in the low instruments, piano, harp, and percussion. The many timbral colors in the horn writing include stopped horn, scoops, flutter tonguing, and wah wah effects.

Range: F–c³
Duration: 13:00
See also: Jeff Snedeker, "New 'Dragons in the Sky': An Interview with Composer Mark Schultz," *The Horn Call* 29 (May 1999): 47–49

Pillars of Fire (1994)
JOMAR Press, 1994, full score
For horn and orchestra. Commissioned for Thomas Bacon by the Sarasota Mu-
    sic Festival. The opening is marked "Forceful, with great energy," with
    the horn soloist at the back of the stage between the two percussionists,
    first playing rhythmic patterns on the bass drum, then playing an open-
    ing horn-call motive of open fifths. Moving to the front of the stage, the
    soloist gets down to business as the piece evolves in a variety of contrast-
    ing characters, such as "dark, distant"—"crystalline, cantabile"—"forceful,
    brassy." There are unusual colorful effects, with orchestra musicians "play-
    ing" interesting objects, such as the winds playing tuned soda bottles and
    the string sections kneading noisy cellophane gift wrap and popping sheets
    of bubble wrap. The string players are also required to sing. Meanwhile,
    the horn soloist plays challenging and virtuosic gestures, punctuated with
    colorful contemporary effects such as trills, flutter tonguing, and making
    vowel sounds of *e-o-e-o* while playing. The piece ends quietly, with the horn
    soloist playing the bass drum in the distance, offstage.
Range: f♯–b²
Duration: 17:00

Schuman, William (1910–1992) United States

Three Colloquies for French Horn and Orchestra (1979)
Merion Music, T. Presser, 1980, piano reduction and orchestra score
    1. Rumination
    2. Renewal
    3. Remembrance
Commissioned and first performed by the New York Philharmonic, January 24,
    1980, Philip Myers, horn soloist, Zubin Mehta conducting. In three con-
    tinuous movements, the first begins slowly, and the horn moves in and out
    of the texture as it builds on a theme. Things grow more agitated, with
    increasing back-and-forth between percussion and the horn, then a retreat
    back into the texture with a relaxing of the mood. The second movement,
    "Renewal," is quick and rhythmic, beginning legierro, with dialogue be-
    tween trumpets and horn, then winds and horn. The middle section is a
    waltz-like Cantabile, then the scherzo resumes. The third movement, "Re-
    membrance," begins with a beautiful duet between the horn and solo cello,
    and the horn continues in this lyrical vein throughout the movement, trad-
    ing off lines with solo oboe, trumpet, strings, and other groups. The work
    closes with the horn's lyrical playing over tonal harmonies—jarring and
    beautiful after the dissonance that preceded it. Stamina, control with high
    entrances, the ability to project in the horn's middle and low range, and
    agility are all required of the horn player. While challenging for the hornist
    in many respects, this work is about the colors of the horn as it combines
    with the many different voices of the orchestra. Recorded by Philip Myers
    on *Works by Crumb and Schuman,* New World Records.
Range: F–c³
Duration: 24:00

Schuncke, Johann Christoph (1791–1856) Germany

Schuncke came from a family of horn players and was a hornist at the court of the Grand Duke of Baden in Karlsruhe.

Concertino pour le cor chromatique (ca. 1830)

Hofmeister, 2009 (Peter Damm, ed.), piano reduction and full score

This is an early work for the valve horn. In three continuous movements. The first opens with a short Adagio in the orchestra, followed by an Allegro con brio full of sixteenth-note passages in the horn that move through different key areas, fully exploiting the capabilities of the valve horn. This gives way to a lyrical Andante con moto in $\frac{6}{8}$, followed by an extensive third movement, marked Rondo allegretto, in $\frac{2}{4}$. This work shows what an excellent valve-horn player Schuncke was, with technical passages that move throughout the range of the horn and extend into the high range.

Range: f♯–c³

Duration: 14:00

Schwantner, Joseph (1943–) United States

Schwantner's compositional career has been marked by many awards, grants, and fellowships, including the Pulitzer Prize in 1979 and several Grammy nominations.

Beyond Autumn, Poem for Horn and Orchestra (1999)

Schott-Helicon, 1999, orchestra score only

Beyond Autumn was written for Gregory Hustis, who premiered it in September 1999 with the Dallas Symphony. It was commissioned by the International Horn Society and is dedicated to the memory of Jack Rossate, the composer's father-in-law. In one continuous movement. This work is full of atmosphere and emotional intensity. The somber tone is conveyed in the descriptive indications of different sections: misterioso, elegante e espressiveo, molto intense, con eloquenza, hauntingly, oscuro e lacrimoso (dark and tearful). Stamina and endurance are required for this work, yet it emphasizes the timbre of the horn against the orchestra, rather than the horn's technical capabilities. The solo horn begins offstage, playing several unmetered passages and gradually moves onstage, playing in front of the horn section, which is located in front of the orchestra. This staging accommodates the "serene chorale" in the middle of the piece, where the solo horn and horn section play in unison until the solo horn emerges from the group. Material from the opening returns, and the piece ends with a Recessional, with the horn moving offstage as it freely repeats the closing phrase.

Range: e–c³

Duration: 17:31

See also: William Scharnberg, "IHS Commissions a Major Work: 'Beyond Autumn' Poem for Horn and Orchestra by Joseph Schwantner," *The Horn Call* 30 (November 1999): 25–29

Schwartz, Elliott (1936–) United States
Elliott Schwartz is faculty emeritus at Bowdoin College and he has written several books on contemporary music. His compositions have been widely played in the United States and abroad and have been recorded.

Twilight Arrival for Horn and Wind Ensemble (2005)
American Composer's Alliance, 2005; wind ensemble score only
This is the second piece from the work *Summer's Journey* for wind ensemble. The
   first piece, entitled *Sunrise and Seascape,* is for solo flute and wind ensemble. The two pieces may be performed separately (with their own titles)
   or combined for *Summer's Journey.* Commissioned by nineteen wind ensembles through the World-Wide Concurrent Premieres and Commission
   Fund to celebrate the composer's seventieth year, it was inspired by a trip
   along the Maine coast and evokes images of dawn and dusk. It also references pieces with flute or horn in the title, such as Mozart's *Magic Flute*
   and Mahler's *Des Knaben Wunderhorn.* The horn moves in and out of the
   layers of texture and color, but returns to the opening three-note motive to
   pull the listener back in. This is a very accessible contemporary work for the
   horn soloist, with stopped writing and occasional flutter tonguing.
Range: c–g^2
Duration: 9:00 (total duration with both pieces is approximately 17:00)

Schwarz, Otto M. (1967–) Austria

Cape Horn
Mitropa Music, 2008, piano reduction
For horn and band. This is a bold and tuneful work, musically depicting the
   beauty as well as the perils of sailing around Cape Horn, the southernmost
   point of South America. It is written in the tonal language of film music,
   the composer's main genre. In three continuous sections. The first, marked
   Allegro, combines heroic motives, full of the sound of adventure. A contrasting elegy follows, beginning as a quasi-cadenza for the horn, followed
   by free and expressive writing. The third section brings back material in
   the character of the opening. Suitable for college-level players and above
   for both horn and ensemble. There are many ossia options for the soloist,
   accommodating different high-range abilities.
Range: c–c^3 (ossia c–b♭^{2} or ossia to c–a♭^{2})
Duration: 10:00

Schwertsik, Kurt (1935–) Austria
Schwertsik began his career as an orchestral hornist with the Niederösterre-
ichisches Tonkünstlerorchester and the Vienna Symphony Orchestra. He later
studied composition with Stockhausen and co-founded the contemporary ensemble Die Reihe. He currently teaches composition at the Vienna Hochschule
für Musik.

In keltischer Manier für Alphorn in Ges und kleines Orchestra, op. 27 (1975)
Boosey & Hawkes, full score only

This alphorn concerto is dedicated to "Herrn Direktor Ulrich Meyer." In four movements: Totenklage—Tanzfest—Idylle—Schlachtrufe. Each movement utilizes the horn's open tones to great effect, with declamatory statements, easygoing dance rhythms in alternating meters, and large slurs over the harmonic series. Although originally written for alphorn (and recorded on alphorn by hornist Robert Freund with the Pro Arte Orchester Graz), it is included here due to its interesting addition to the horn repertoire, and the horn's ability to play notes of the harmonic series that are not "in tune" with traditional western classical scales. The small orchestra is predominantly low-range instruments: cellos and basses, with oboe, alto and tenor saxophones, bassoons, horns, trombones, and percussion. Recently recorded by Nury Guarnaschelli, horn, with the ensemble Die Reihe on Phoenix Edition.

Range: c–a^2
Duration: 17:00

Sciarrino, Salvatore (1947–) Italy

Award-winning composer Sciarrino is a major figure in contemporary classical music whose works continue to be on the edge of "new" in new music.

Perturbazione in arrivo nel settore trombe, per corno e orchestra
Rai Trade, 2012, full score only
Dedicated to Christoph Walder, horn soloist who premiered the work with the Philharmonisches Orchester Cottbus, October 6, 2012. Detailed instructions are provided for all families of instruments, such as fingerings for the winds to achieve soft harmonics (bi-tonal chords) and the symbols for all of the noteheads. An intense work in two parts: A (prima dell'Eroica) and B (prima della Pastorale). It lays out a canvas of continuously changing sound that evokes nature with its rushing air and breezes. The horn part is virtuosic and demanding, with gestures on repeated pitches that change color as they dart in and out of the texture.

Range: c♯^{1}–d^3
Duration: 14:00

Searle, Humphrey (1915–1982) United Kingdom

Searle studied with Webern and was one of the first British composers to adopt the twelve-tone compositional technique.

Aubade, for Horn and Strings, op. 28 (1955)
Schott, 1956, piano reduction
Written for Dennis Brain and the Aldeburgh Festival in 1955, this is an intense work in three sections with lush orchestration in the strings. It opens quietly with the horn in wide legato leaps, gradually building in intensity and volume. The second section, Presto, is in § and gallops through the horn's ranges, ending on repeated high b^{2}s, before returning to the slow opening tempo. This piece requires endurance, solid high-range playing, and agility. Recorded by Barry Tuckwell.

Range: c–c^3
Duration: 7:00

Segers, Jan (1929–) Belgium

Essay for Horn and Symphonic Band (1979)
Scherzando, 1990s, full score; horn and piano version
Challenging work based on an atonal twelve-note series, presenting quickly changing moods and dynamic contrasts. Many varied gestures in the horn over constantly changing colors in the band make this an interesting work. There are alternate parts indicated for the extreme high notes.
Range: c–e♭³ (ossia c–b²)
Duration: 8:00

Seiber, Mátyás (1905–1960) United Kingdom, born in Hungary
Seiber settled in England in 1930 after completing studies in Hungary with Ko-dály and working in South Africa and Frankfurt.

Notturno for Horn and String Orchestra (1944)
Schott, 1952, arranged for horn and piano by Don Banks; Schott study score also available
"Written for Dennis Brain and dedicated to the memory of Brahms." This expressive work uses the full range of the horn with understated effect and has particularly beautiful writing in the middle to low range of the horn. The strings create an atmospheric backdrop to the horn's melodic lines while providing the counterpoint in the faster sections. A few challenges include a high b² held over several measures and a low G♭. Declamatory writing in the cadenza and quick sections require verve. Recorded by Sören Hermansson.
Range: G♭–b²
Duration: 8:00

Seidel, Jan (1908–1998) Czech Republic

Sinfonietta da caccia, concerto per corno ed orchestra (Lovecká symfonieta, koncert pro lesní roh a orchestra) (1965–66)
Editio Supraphon, Export, Artia, 1974, piano reduction
The title of this work translates to "Hunt Sinfonietta". In one continuous movement in two sections. After an orchestral introduction, the horn enters with agile horn figures in a fast ⅜. The second half is relaxed, beginning quietly, marked "La ninnananna della foresta" ("the lullaby of the forest") followed by hunting calls in the horn. There are descriptions in the score of each call—related to deer, sheep, birds, a love song. There is a final section entitled "Long live the forest and the hunt" before a coda that brings back the opening motives in ⅜. In a tonal harmonic language, with agile diatonic writing in a range that stays mostly in the treble-clef staff. There are several ossia for difficult phrases. Appropriate for the college player and above.
Range: B–b²
Duration: 15:00

Servais, Theo (1898–)

Cantilène sicilienne pour cor et piano (ou orchestre)
J. Maurer, 1971, piano reduction
For Monsieur Desire Malfait, professor of horn at the Conservatoire Tournai.
   Contrasting sections in ABA form, in traditional harmonic language. The
   outer sections are a flowing cantabile in ¾, the middle section is an easy-
   going Andantino in ⅜. Modest technical demands and range make this a
   suitable work for the high school or early college player.
Range: a–f♯
Duration: 5:00

Deuxième solo pour cor en fa avec accompagnement de piano ou d'orchestre
Schott, 1972, piano reduction
For Monsieur Adhémar Pluvinage, professor of horn at the Conservatoire Liége.
   In three movements: Allegro moderato—Andante—Allegro. Traditional
   diatonic language and writing for the horn, with a brief cadenza in the first
   movement. The last movement is a quick rondo in ⅜. Overall, this is a well-
   paced and suitable work for the intermediate horn player, with a refreshing
   variety of key areas in the second and third movements, including a section
   in B major (written key of F♯ for the horn).
Range: a–g² (ossia a–f♯²)
Duration: 13:00

Shebalin, Vissarion (1902–1963) Russia

Concertino for Horn and Orchestra, op. 14, no. 2 (1929–1930, rev. 1958)
Sov. kompozitor, 1960, full score; Chant du Monde, 2011, piano reduction by the
   composer (reprint of 1960 Sov. Kompozitor ed.)
   I. Andante cantabile—Allegro moderato
   II. Andante
   III. Vivo.
In three fairly short movements, written in tonal harmonic language, and firmly
   grounded in the romantic horn tradition, with lyrical melodies and soar-
   ing lines. The third movement is particularly virtuosic and quite challeng-
   ing for the soloist, with exciting agile writing and a cadenza.
Range: c–c³
Duration: 12:00

Short, Michael (1937–) United Kingdom

Apollo Concerto No. 5
Goodmusic, 2003, piano reduction
   I. Alla Marcia
   II. Adagio
   III. Vivace
The composer notes in the score that he wrote a series of "Apollo" concertos for
   different wind instruments in order to fill a gap in the repertoire for modern

concertos that are "light and accessible, playable by competent musicians, whether amateur or professional, and enjoyable for players and listeners alike." Written in a contemporary tonal language, this piece does venture above the staff, but is well paced for the soloist. The last movement features a jaunty motive in changing meters of $^{10}_8$ and $^{11}_8$, and a short cadenza.
Range: g–c^3
Duration: 15:00

Siebert, Friedrich (1906–1987) Germany

Scherzetto for Horn and Orchestra
Edition Eulenberg, 1966, score and ten parts; also for horn and piano
See: Horn and keyboard

Sierra, Roberto (1953–) United States

Concierto Evocativo for Horn and String Orchestra (1990)
Schirmer, 1990, piano reduction
Commissioned by Sören Hermansson who premiered the work December 14, 1990, with the Espoo City Symphony Orchestra, Finland. In three movements: Lento—Scherzando—Ritmico y enérgico. This work is full of interesting interplay and writing in both horn and string orchestra parts. Intense at times and full of variety and twists. There are long lyrical lines that hover around and above the staff and the piece features agile writing in the scherzando movement.
Range: A–c♯^{3} (ossia to c^3)
Duration: 17:00

Sikorski, Kazimierz (1895–1986) Poland
Composer and teacher, known for his symphonic works, concertos, chamber music, choral pieces, and as the teacher of many well-regarded Polish composers and musicians.

Concerto for Horn and Small Orchestra (1949)
Polskie Wydawnictwo Muzyczne, 1993, piano reduction
In three movements: Allegro—Lento sostenuto e molto cantabile—Rondo: Allegro giocoso. Written in contemporary tonal language. The first movement is full of energy, with a light eighth-note motive that propels things along to a contrasting cantabile second theme. The second movement is very expressive, developing a heartfelt cantabile horn line in counterpoint with strings. The last-movement rondo is light and quick, with a breezy pastoral character, in $^3_4$. This movement is fun to play, but is the most challenging of the three, with its agile writing at a quick tempo, grace note figures, and legato leaps.
Range: G–c^3
Duration: 17:33

Skolnik, Walter (1934–) United States

Cornucopia, for Solo Horn with String Orchestra (1968)
University Microfilms, 1969, orchestra score
1. Romanza
2. Scherzo
3. Arietta
4. Burlesca

Written under the auspices of the Music Educators National Conference's Contemporary Music Project for Creativity in Music Education Composers in Public Schools program for Nancy Schick and the Shawnee Mission (Kansas) East High School Orchestra. In four contrasting movements. The first and third are lyrical, the second is a spirited $\frac{6}{8}$, and the fourth is a quick $\frac{4}{4}$ marked Allegro energico, with syncopated rhythms. Suitable for the advanced high school through college-level player, for both soloist and ensemble.

Range: c–a^2
Duration: 8:00

Skroup, Dominik Josef (1766–1830) Germany (Bohemia)

Concerto in B♭ Major
Concertino, Panton, 1970, piano reduction

A straightforward work in one movement, at a moderato tempo in $\frac{4}{4}$ with a tuneful melody, a contrasting section in minor, and a cadenza. This appears to be transposed, since it is unlikely that it would have been written for horn in B♭ during this era and it is unclear where the manuscript for this work originated.

Range: c^1–g^2 (ossia to c^3)
Duration: 5:00

Sleeper, Thomas (1956–) United States

Concerto for Horn and Orchestra (2000)
Uroboros Music, 2000, orchestra score

For Stefan de Leval Jezierski. In three movements: Allegro—Andante ma non troppo, lusingando—Vivace. Each movement pays homage to a person in the composer's life. The first movement opens quietly, evolving into a march full of sardonic character, reminiscent of Shostakovich or Prokofiev. This is followed by contrasting material that shows off the horn's ability to play long sustained lines. The second movement is lyrical, with long, intense passages at *forte* volume. The driving last movement begins in $\frac{6}{8}$ and is full of changing meters, reworking material from the first and second movements. Not extreme in technical demands, but requires good long-range endurance from the hornist.

Range: g♯–c^3
Duration: 22:00

Smith, Kile (1956–) United States
Kile Smith is an active composer, music critic, classical-music radio show host, and former curator of the Fleisher Collection of Orchestral Music in Philadelphia.

Exsultet, for horn and string orchestra(2007)
Available from the composer, orchestra score only
    1. In the darkness, fire is kindled
    2. Procession
    3. Exsultet
Exsultet was written for hornist Jennifer Montone and the Philadelphia Classical Symphony, who premiered it March 2, 2007. The title comes from an ancient chant sung between Good Friday and Easter Sunday and is an "ecstatic yet profound utterance of joy." The piece is in three continuous movements and musically follows the vigil, first with an introspective and solemn "lighting of the candles," realized through long and slow lyrical lines in the horn. The second movement is a musical "Procession" into the sanctuary, and presents the music from the service, intoning "Lumen Christi" answered by "Deo gratias." The final movement, "Exsultet," begins at a fast tempo and works its way to an exuberant Estampie in a quick three, felt in one, with swirling fast passages in the horn. Challenges include wide-ranging legato writing and technical legato passages for the horn in the final movement.
Range: f♯–c³
Duration: 17:00

Smolanoff, Michael (1942–2013) United States

Essay for Horn and String Orchestra, op. 19
Piedmont Music, 1968, reduction for horn and organ, can be played on piano
See: Horn and keyboard

Soldh, Anders (1955–) Sweden

L'Intense Concerto, for Solo Horn and Concert Band
R. Martin, 2004, full score only
Dedicated to Jean-Pierre Denedese. This concerto lives up to its name. In three traditional movements. The first movement is a whipping Presto that changes meters, shifting from 7/8 to 6/8 to 3/4, this movement clips along at ♩ = 160. The second movement is an Adagio, the third movement a very fast 6/8.
Range: g–c³
Duration: 12:25

Soukup, Vladimír (1930–2012) Czech Republic

Konzert für Horn und Streicher
Bärenreiter-Alkor, full score only
Duration: 17:00

Spandau, Willem (1741–1806) Netherlands

Spandau was first horn in the electoral orchestra in The Hague and performed as a soloist. Charles Burney heard him perform in London and wrote about Spandau's excellent playing and his use of hand-horn technique.

Konzert Nr. 1 Es-Dur, für Horn Und Orchester

Hofmeister, 1998, piano reduction

Written for horn in E♭, this concerto is in the traditional three-movement form:
> Allegro vivace—Adagio—Allegro, la chasse. The tessitura is slightly higher than Mozart's concertos. Short cadenzas have been added by the editor.

Range: f–b♭² (g–c³ for horn in E♭)

Duration: 12:30

Sperger, Johannes (1750–1812) Czech Republic

Sperger was a famous double bass virtuoso who played in court orchestras in Hungary and Austria. A prolific composer, he is most known today for his eighteen concertos for double bass. He also wrote symphonies, concertos, and chamber music, including many works that feature wind instruments.

Concerto in Re maggiore per il corno primo e orchestra

Editions BIM, 1991, piano reduction and orchestra score

Three movements in the classical style, written for the corno di caccia, this work
> has many high passages above the staff, and challenging triplet writing in the highest range of the horn, more characteristic of the clarino writing of the baroque era than of its own. The slow second movement serves as an interlude in a $\frac{3}{4}$ Andante poco adagio, and the third movement is a $\frac{2}{4}$ in rondo form.

Range: e¹–e³ (g¹–g³ for horn in D)

Duration: 10:00

Concerto Es-Dur für Horn, SWV B26 (1786)

Robert Ostermeyer, 2005, piano reduction and orchestra score

A little-known work that is a significant addition to the classical horn repertoire,
> although rather extended for a classical concerto. This is a lighthearted concerto in the three-movement classical style. Like Sperger's horn concerto in D, it is full of many technical challenges in both range and quick passage-work, indicating that the horn players that Sperger was writing for—probably colleagues in his orchestra—were excellent players.

Range: d¹–f³ with ossia d¹–d³ (e¹–g³ with ossia e¹–e³ for horn in E♭)

Duration: 25:00

Stamitz, Karl (1745–1801) Germany

Concerto in E♭

Spurious. This work is a transposition of the Rosetti, *Concerto in E* (Murray C51),
> which is also attributed as Punto, *Concerto No. 1.* The second movement of the Stamitz concerto is transposed up into the cor-alto range. The other movements are the same as the versions by Rosetti/Punto, but are in E♭, along with several note differences. The practice of a soloist commission-

ing a work from a composer and considering it their own and publishing it under their name occurred occasionally in the eighteenth century, which might explain this concerto having been published in Paris under the name of Giovanni Punto, but the version that bears the name of Karl Stamitz is a bit more mysterious.

See: Rosetti, *Concerto in E* (Murray C51) and Punto, *Concerto No. 1*

Steinmüller, Joseph (1763–1808) Germany

Joseph Steinmüller came from a family of horn players; his father was hornist at Esterhazy, and his two younger brothers also played horn.

Concerto E-Dur für Horn und Orchester
Robert Ostermeyer, 2012, piano reduction and orchestra score
For horn in E. This edition is based on a 1798 publication by Johann Peter Spehr. Only the name Steinmüller is on the music from 1798, with an indication of op. 12. Robert Ostermeyer believes that it was the eldest brother who wrote this concerto. In three movements, typical of the classical style: Allegro con giusto—Romanze: Adagio—Rondo: Moderato. This concerto lies in the midrange of the horn, with only a few forays up into the high register. There are quick runs of sixteenth and triplet figures, making for more awkward fingering on the F horn, since the part is written for horn in E.
Range: B–b² (c–c³ for horn in E)
Duration: 20:00

Stekke, Léon (1904–1970) Belgium

Poème sylvèstre, op. 21
Brogneaux, 1943, piano reduction
For horn and orchestra or horn and piano. A single-movement piece in ABA form, opening with an Andante molto tranquillo, which is very free and rhythmically complex. A contrasting Allegro giocoso follows, more straightforward in its rhythms and textures. The piece ends with a return of the Andante tranquillo. Includes muted and stopped passages.
Range: A–b²

Stephenson, James M. (1969–) United States

Sounds Awakened, Concerto for French Horn and Orchestra (2012)
Stephenson Music, 2012, piano reduction
Co-commissioned by a group of hornists and their organizations: Gail Williams, Daniel Grabois (University of Wisconsin-Madison), Gregory Miller (University of Maryland School of Music), Seth Orgel (Louisiana State University), Erich Peterson (Grand Rapids Youth Symphony), Alexander Shuhan (gift from his father, George Shuhan), and Michelle Stebleton (Florida State University College of Music and Sigma Alpha Iota-Beta Alpha Chapter). Premiered on May 17, 2012, by Gail Williams, Barry Tuckwell conducting. The composer writes that the opening fanfare motive was inspired by Gail Williams' strength as a person and as a horn player. This recitative-like section

is followed by an intense and driving Allegro assai full of exciting runs of sextuplets for the horn soloist. The fast oscillating notes of the Allegro molto section were inspired by the composer's fascination with a "murmuration of starlings" flying at high speeds and maneuvering without running into each other. The second movement is lyrical and pensive, with wide legato leaps, and the third movement is virtuosic, bringing together material from the first two movements. A challenging work, requiring good endurance and excellent technical facility for the final movement. Notation is traditional, and the harmonic language is contemporary, tonal, and colorful.

Range: e–c^3
Duration: 14:30

Steptoe, Roger (1953–) United Kingdom, resides in France

Ballade for Horn and Chamber Orchestra (2010)
Editions BIM, 2010, piano reduction
Dedicated to Jeremy Mathez. In one continuous movement, made up of three
sections. The outer sections are slow and lyrical, the middle section is an
Allegro con spirito in §. There are two sections of "quasi-cadenza" for the
horn. This is an expressive work, full of changing character and would be
suitable for the advanced college student and above.

Range: e♭–c^3
Duration: 12:00

Stich, Johann Wenzel (Jan Václav) (1746–1803) Bohemia
See: Punto, Giovanni

Strauss, Franz (1822–1905) Germany
Horn player, composer, teacher, and father of Richard Strauss, Franz Strauss was
the principal horn of the Munich Court Opera Orchestra and taught at the Munich Academy.

Concerto, op. 8
Carl Fisher, 1937; Schirmer, 1977 (Barry Tuckwell, ed.)—both piano reductions
Franz Strauss premiered this work in 1865 in Munich, at the Odeon Concert Hall.
This is a standard concerto in the horn literature, particularly for the advanced high school player or early to intermediate college player. In three
continuous movements. Lyrical writing with good melodic lines, idiomatic
sixteenth-note writing, and brief cadenza passages make this an excellent
work for the advanced high school player through professional. Very well
paced.

Range: a–b♭^{2}
Duration: 13:00

Concerto No. 2 in E♭, op. 14
Hans Pizka Edition, 1979, piano reduction
Published only recently by Hans Pizka Edition, this work is very similar in style
and form to Franz Strauss' op. 8 concerto. It opens with a cadenza-like pas-

sage for the horn, giving way to a robust Allegro ma non troppo in $\frac{4}{4}$. The second movement begins with a straightforward horn line in minor, then the theme is repeated in a triumphant major. The final movement is almost exactly the same music as the first movement, changing slightly after the statement of the first theme, then ending with triplet passages. Technical challenges include several runs up to high b♭² and triplet passages, but overall the writing is idiomatic and lies well on the horn.

Range: f–b♭²
Duration: 15:00

Strauss, Richard (1864–1949) Germany

Horn Concerto No.1 in E♭, op. 11 (1882–1883, arranged for horn and piano 1883)
Universal, 2004; International, 1971; Cundy-Bettoney, 1939—all piano reductions
Written by Strauss at the age of nineteen for his father, the hornist Franz Strauss,
      principal horn in the Munich Court Orchestra and professor of music at
      the Königliche Musikschule. Full of idiomatic writing for the horn, this is
      one of the great works of the horn repertoire, with long, lyrical phrases and
      a heroic style that bring together the horn's most exciting characteristics
      in one piece. The orchestration is lovely and light, more characteristic of
      Mendelssohn than of Strauss' later style.
Range: f–b♭²
Duration: 15:00

Horn Concerto No.2 in E♭ (1942)
Boosey & Hawkes, 1950, piano reduction
A second concerto written by Strauss, toward the end of his life and sixty years
      after the first concerto. This is another great work that is a standard of the
      horn repertoire. In three continuous movements. The bold opening state-
      ment encapsulates and foreshadows what is to follow—romantic, heroic
      writing for the horn, with large octave leaps, long lines, and lithe passages
      that move quickly through the ranges of the horn. The second movement,
      Andante, is stunning, with a beautiful lyrical line. The final-movement
      rondo is full of acrobatic leaps, in $\frac{6}{8}$, reminiscent of the playful lines of
      Strauss' *Til Eulenspiegels Lustige Streiche*. This is a challenging work for the
      hornist, requiring great endurance, flexibility, and bravura.
Range: B♭–c³
Duration: 20:00

Šulek, Stjepan (1914–1986) Croatia

Šulek was a composer, conductor, violinist, and professor at the Zagreb Academy of Music for many years. *New Grove* calls him "an outstanding symphonist . . . along with Papandopulo, the leading personality of 20th-century Croatian music."

Konzert für Horn und Orchester (1972)
Editions Marc Reift, 1994, piano reduction
This concerto is in three traditional movements both in form and harmonic lan-
      guage. The first movement begins with an introductory horn call, going

back and forth between soloist and orchestra and leading into an Allegro organized around a moving triplet motive. The second movement, Intermezzo, is an expressive $\frac{3}{4}$, and the final movement is an Allegro in $\frac{4}{4}$ with changing tempi and moods ending with a cadenza. This piece requires flexibility and dexterity.

Range: F♯–c³

Duration: 15:00

Summer, Joseph, United States

The Silver Swan: a Fantasy for Orchestra, Harps, and Horn

Manuscript 1979, full score, located in the Fleisher Collection, Free Library of
    Philadelphia

Duration: ca. 10:00

Surtel, Maarten (1958–) Netherlands

"—del amor oscuro" versie voor hoorn en kamerorkest (1992, rev. 1993)

Donemus, 1992, orchestra score only

Originally composed for two ensembles (twenty-eight players) in 1988–1990, this
    version is for horn and large ensemble (with a battery of percussion), plus a
    smaller ensemble of violin, viola, and cello. The two ensembles play against
    each other at their own pace, coming together at fixed points. Adding to
    this aleatoric element is the horn soloist, who moves to three different positions on stage, playing complex gestures peppered with flutter tonguing,
    stopped effects, improvisatory moments, and extended techniques, such as
    blowing into the instrument without the mouthpiece. This is challenging
    writing for the hornist, requiring a good command of the ranges and flexibility. Endurance challenges include a series of held high b² passages, but
    there are also opportunities for the hornist to rest.

Range: B♭–c³

Duration: 10:00

Svane, Randall (1955–) United States

Horn Concerto (1990)

Randall Svane, 1990, orchestra score only

Premiered by David Jolley, horn, and the Colonial Symphony Orchestra, Madison, New Jersey, in May 1992, Yehuda Gilad, conductor. Begins "Boldly"
    with a quasi-cadenza in the horn over tremolo strings, followed by a moderately fast section, where the bold theme of the opening is expanded upon,
    alternating with cantabile sections in $\frac{3}{4}$. The second movement is contrasting, at a slow tempo; the third movement is rhythmic and driving, with the
    horn and orchestra answering each other in true *concertato* fashion before
    the horn plays a final cadenza.

Range: c–b²

Duration: 20:00

Sydeman, William Jay (1928–) United States

Concert Piece for Horn and Strings (1959)

Okra Music, 1968, full score; Subito Music

In two movements. The first is mostly lyrical with expressive writing in changing
    meters that alternates with more declamatory material. The second half
    is full of energy, with the horn in a continuing dialogue with the strings,
    picking up motives and playing off different lines, then emerging in its own
    solo voice before going back into the changing string texture. Contempo-
    rary harmonic language in traditional rhythmic notation. The horn has
    several muted passages. There are some technically demanding quick pas-
    sages and a few high entrances for the horn soloist.

Range: d♯–c³

Duration: 12:00

Székely, Endre (1912–1989) Hungary

Concerto per corno e orchestra, in memoriam Webern (1976)

Editio Musica Budapest, orchestra score only

For Ferenc Tarjáni, who commissioned this work. In four sections that grow in-
    creasingly animated, culminating in the third section of highly improvi-
    satory writing for the horn based only on groups of pitches. The orchestra
    provides a shifting backdrop of blocks of sound, often grouped by instru-
    ment family.

Range: E–d♯³ (ossia E–b²)

Duration: 10:00

Telemann, Georg Philipp (1681–1767) Germany

Concerto in D, TWV D8

Heinrichshofen Verlag, Pegasus, 1964 (Edmond Leloir, ed.); Schirmer, 1977 (Barry
    Tuckwell, ed.)—all piano reductions

Scored for horn and strings, the Heinricshoven Verlag is a clean edition, whereas
    the Schirmer edition has ornaments written very skillfully by Barry Tuck-
    well in the style of the period. In three movements: Vivace—Largo—Alle-
    gro. This work in high-baroque style is in the clarino range of the natural
    horn in D. The writing is typical of the solo-horn concerto of the period
    with fast articulated sixteenth-note passages, trills, and other ornaments.
    A rather short concerto, but due to the high tessitura it can be rather tax-
    ing. The second movement is lyrical, and the last movement is in a baroque-
    minuet style.

Range: e¹–b² (g¹–d³ for horn in D)

Duration: 8:40

Terzian, Alicia (1934–) Argentina

Carmen Criaturalis (1969/1971)

A. Terzian, full score

Scored for solo horn, string orchestra, cymbals, and vibraphone. Highly atmo-
    spheric and in one movement marked Lento. The horn begins as part of
    the texture, then gradually emerges, taking on its role as a solo part. Ex-
    perimental sounding, with the horn finding its way through the sounds,
    constantly varying its color with vibrato, stopped and open tones, bending
    pitches, and glissandi. Much of the writing hovers at the top of the treble
    staff, but there are many breaks for the soloist.
Range: c–b♭²
Duration: 9:00

Teyber, Anton (1756–1822) Austria
Teyber was court organist in Dresden and later was appointed court composer
in Vienna. He was from a family of musicians who were all acquainted with the
Mozarts.

Concerto per il corno
Verlag Doblinger, 1976, piano reduction
Teyber's association with the Mozarts could explain a long note-for-note quote
    from the Mozart horn quintet K. 407 in the first movement. In three move-
    ments that exemplify the form and elegant style of the classical concerto,
    this work puts the horn in a higher tessitura than many horn concertos of
    this time, including a run up to a high f³ in the last-movement rondo.
Range: f¹–f³
Duration: 14:00

2. Konzert Es-Dur, für Horn und Orchester
Robert Ostermeyer, 2000, piano reduction and orchestra score
For horn in E♭. A standard three-movement concerto of the early classical period:
    Allegro—Andantino—Allegro. Based on an autograph owned by the Ge-
    sellschaft der Musikfreunde in Vienna, the original title is *Concerto per il
    corno da caccia*. The writing for the horn is not as high as in the previous
    concerto, ascending only a few times to the written c³. Comparable in its
    technical demands, character, and frequency of stopped notes to Mozart's
    second and fourth concertos. In the manuscript, the last movement ends
    at measure 143, though the editor proposes that the composer did not leave
    the piece unfinished but merely assumed that the piece would end with the
    rondo theme repeated one more time, so this edition concludes the piece
    with one last statement of the theme. The middle movement is in the sub-
    dominant key of A♭ major, as in the third Mozart concerto.
Range: f–b♭² (g–c³ for horn in E♭)

Thatcher, Howard R. (1878–1973) United States
Composer, organist, and professor of music theory/harmony (1911–1953) at Peabody Institute in Baltimore, Maryland.

Concerto for Horn and Orchestra (1951)
Cor Publishing Company, 1961, piano reduction
Premiered March 9, 1952, Baltimore Symphony Orchestra with the composer
    conducting, Leigh Martinet, horn soloist. In three movements: Allegro con

brio—Andante non stentando—Allegro. This is a straightforward work in traditional forms and harmonic language and with a consistent phrase structure.

Range: g–g#^{2}
Duration: 12:00

Thomas, Augusta Read (1964–) United States

Silver Chants the Litanies, in Memoriam Luciano Berio (2003)
Schirmer, 2004, full score, a piano reduction is available for study purposes
Scored for winds, percussion, 2 pianos, harp and strings, it can be performed with orchestra, or with a smaller ensemble using single strings. Commissioned and premiered by the Meadows Wind Ensemble, Southern Methodist University, February 20, 2004, Greg Hustis, horn, Jack Delaney conducting. The title is taken from a poem by E. E. Cummings. This piece is full of quickly changing characters and moods for the horn, with sections marked: "Majestic," "Energetic and spry," "Elegant and spacious," "Playful," "Robust with zest," "Spirited," "Resonant and dreamy." The horn writing is fluid, and moves in and out of the texture with the changing colors of the orchestra. A challenging work with quick passages, dynamic changes in a contemporary idiom, and forays above the staff requiring control and endurance. Judicious breaks for the horn soloist make this an accessible work.

Range: b–c^3
Duration: 13:00

Thommessen, Olav Anton (1946–) Norway

Thommessen studied with Bernhard Heiden and Iannis Xenakis at Indiana University, then later worked with Piotr Perkowski, Werner Kaegi, and Otto Laske. He has been on the faculty of the Norwegian State Academy of Music since 1972.

Beyond Neon, Post-commercial Sound Sculptures for Horn and Large Symphony Orchestra, op. 41 (1981)
Edition Wilhelm Hansen, 1986, orchestra score only
Written for and dedicated to the Minnesota Orchestra, Neville Marriner, conductor, and horn soloist Kendall Betts. This is a one-movement work that puts the horn soloist firmly in the texture of the orchestra at the beginning of the piece. The horn line grows increasingly complex with gestures that have the horn soloist doubling with various instruments and groups. Weaving in and out of the texture, the horn emerges fully in an extended cadenza, then eventually returns back to the texture of the orchestra. Dexterity and good endurance are needed, as the horn must hold its own against the large orchestra.

Range: F–c#^{3}
Duration: 24:00

Tisné, Antoine (1932–1998) France

Tisné studied with Milhaud, Rivier, and Jolivet, and won the Prix de Rome and many other awards.

Voix, pour cor en fa et orchestre à cordes (1984)
Billaudot, 1986, piano reduction
Voix premiered March 10, 1987, with Daniel Catalanotti horn soloist with L'En-
    semble Orchestral de Paris, Tibor Varga, conductor. Dedicated to Daniel
    Bourgue. Based on the poem *Voix* by David Niemann. The text of the poem
    is printed in the music and organizes the piece into eight sections. Full
    of contemporary expressive elements, such as quarter tones, multiphonics,
    extremes in register, dramatic dynamic changes, sections of fast articu-
    lations, flutter tonguing, stopped writing, and glissandi. The piece is me-
    tered, with free sections that are left up to the performer and the conductor.
Range: G–c³
Duration: 20:00

Tomasi, Henri (1901–1971) France

Concerto, pour cor et orchestre (1954)
Alphonse Leduc, 1955, piano reduction
For Lucien Thévet. In three movements. The concerto opens with a relaxed Pas-
    torale in § that goes into a quick ¾ felt in one, developing motives of the
    opening then returning to the relaxed Pastorale. The second movement,
    "Nocturne (Cadence)," is cadenza-like writing with the horn playing
    freely over held chords in the orchestra. The third movement, "Final (Che-
    vauchée)," opens with a fast rising line in § with the hornist on a wild ride
    ("chevauchée") that never lets up. An exciting and challenging work that
    has become a standard in the horn repertoire, requiring technical facility,
    flexibility, stamina, and good command of the high range.
Range: g–c³
Duration: 16:15

Danse profane: no. 2 des "Cinq danses profanes et sacrées" (1959)
Alphonse Leduc, 1960
See: Horn and keyboard

Tomlinson, Ernest (1924–) United Kingdom
Tomlinson is known for his work in radio and television, his compositions of
British light music, and his conducting.

Rhapsody and Rondo for Horn and Orchestra (1957)
Mills Music, 1962, piano reduction
Commissioned by the BBC Light Music Festival, this work was premiered by Den-
    nis Brain at Royal Festival Hall on January 22, 1957, with the composer con-
    ducting. The Rhapsody's lyrical lines are free sounding and played rubato
    in the sonorous range at the top of the staff and above. The second-section
    rondo is lightning fast and playful, with the horn interrupting with a quote
    from the rondo of Mozart's *Horn Concerto No. 4,* a piece closely associated
    with Dennis Brain. This is a challenging work, requiring great technique, a
    light touch for the rondo, and good endurance and control in legato.
Range: c–d³
Duration: 11:00

Trubin, Boris (1930–) Russia

Kontsert dlīa valtorny s orkestrom (Concerto for Horn and Orchestra)
Sov. Kompozitor, 1989, piano reduction
Published in an anthology of five horn concertos by Soviet composers, entitled
  Kontserty dlia mednykh dukhovykh instrumentov s orkestrom, Kontserty
  dlia valtorny volume 4, (Concertos for Brass Instruments and Orchestra,
  Vol. 4, Concertos for French Horn) that includes concertos by Aristakesian,
  Kolodub (for two horns), Raukhverger, Sat'yan [Satian], and Trubin. The
  first movement is in a declamatory style and in contrasting sections that
  gain momentum as the movement progresses, ending in a fast ¾ felt in one.
  The second movement, marked Moderato, is in a flowing ⅜ and played with
  rubato. The final movement, Presto, is similar to the declamatory style of
  the first movement, with a driving eighth-note motive in ¼, with syncopated
  rhythms. This is a challenging work, with chromatic writing and sustained
  passages at a *forte* volume, requiring good long-range endurance.
Range: c♯–b²
Duration: 17:30

Tsontakis, George (1951–) United States
Tsontakis has won many prominent awards for his compositions, which have
been performed around the world. He is on the faculty at the Aspen Music School
and is the distinguished composer in residence at Bard College.

Shiver, for Horn Solo, Celesta, and Strings (2002)
Poco Forte Music, 2005, orchestra score only
Although this work is not yet published, a perusal score was available from Poco
  Forte Music on request. *Shiver* was commissioned and premiered by 20th
  Century Unlimited, in Santa Fe, New Mexico in March 2002 with horn soloist David Jolley. Composed during the aftermath of 9/11, the three movements of this work are an atmospheric journey of continuously changing
  character. Descriptive indications in the score such as "Haunting," "Distant & Simple," and "Gently Fluttering" give a sense of the first movement's
  character, with the horn often in the low range, building momentum, then
  returning to the opening tempo, marked "Mysteriously subdued." The
  second movement begins "Hypnotically steady; distant and aquatic" then
  builds to a section of impassioned cries, marked "Unleashed!" in the score.
  The final movement is "light and lilting," reaching a peaceful place with
  muted horn and celesta. There are a few extended techniques, including
  half-stopped writing, pitch bending, and expressive wide vibrato ('wob-
  ble"). Overall, this is a well-paced work for the horn soloist.
Range: B–b♭²
Duration: 20:00

Turner, Kerry (1960–) United States

Concerto for Low Horn in F and Chamber Orchestra (1995)
Editions BIM, 1996, piano reduction

In four movements. The first, marked Allegro and in $\frac{4}{4}$, opens with a dramatic glissando figure, followed by a folk-sounding Scots hymn, and a lyrical second theme. The slow second movement features a nostalgic tune in the horn over rich string harmonies, with novel use of a harpsichord. The third movement, marked Allegro scherzando, is scored for solo horn and winds, with playful changing meters and trading motives back and forth between the concertante wind group and horn solo. The fourth movement is a brisk Allegro, with agile sixteenth-note passages. This is an important addition to the horn repertoire that showcases the virtuosity of the low horn.

Range: G–g² (ossia F–g²)
Duration: 17:00

Concerto for Horn and Orchestra, "The Gothic" (2011)
Paddi's Prints, 2012, piano reduction
Commissioned by Karl Pituch, hornist, Leonard Slatkin, and the Detroit Symphony Orchestra, who premiered the work May 24, 2013. In four movements: Allegro vivo—Lento—Incantation—Allegro con brio. Opening with what the composer calls an "unmistakably Straussian flair," the first movement is heroic and virtuosic, with a contrasting lyrical theme. The second movement, Lento, features a haunting horn melody over muted strings, and the third movement is based on a Native American song, with the horn playing a twelve-tone obligato over the "Incantation," with a few half-valve glissandi and trills. The trumpets sound a fanfare, ushering in the fourth movement, which develops a fanfare motive with contrasting cantabile writing.

Range: d–c♯³ (ossia d–c³)
Duration: 20:00

Vandenbroek, Othon-Joseph (1758–1852) France, Born in the Netherlands
Vandenbroek was a hornist who taught at the Paris Conservatory, and is still known for his wind treatise *Traité général de tous les instruments a vent a l'usage des compositeurs*. Both concertos here were edited from the first editions that were published in 1787 by Boyer in Paris. Each manuscript indicated that they were performed by the author on the Concert Spirituel series in Paris. Both are in three traditional movements and written in the classical style.

Concerto for Horn in E♭ Major
Robert Ostermeyer, 2013, piano reduction and orchestra score
In three movements: Allegro assai—Romance—Rondeau en chasse.
Range: d¹–b♭² (e¹–c³ for horn in E♭)
Duration: 18:00

Concerto for Horn in F Major
Robert Ostermeyer, 2013, piano reduction and orchestra score
In three movements: Allegro maestoso—Adagio—Rondo de chasse.
Range: c¹–c³
Duration: 18:20

Van Doren, Theo (1898–1974) Belgium
See: Doren, Theo Van

Van Eechaute, Prosper
See: Eechaute, Prosper van

Van Keulen, Geert
See: Keulen, Geert van

Vasilenko, Sergei Nikiforovich (1872–1956) Russia
Vasilenko was a composer, conductor, and professor at the Moscow Conservatory.

Horn Concerto, op. 136 (1953)
Gos. muzykal'noe izd-vo, 1956, piano reduction
Written in tonal harmonic language. In three movements with contrasting sections. The first movement has the horn playing long legato lines, with opportunities for expressive playing, including a cadenza. The second movement is a flowing Andante in $\frac{3}{4}$, and the final movement alternates between $\frac{6}{8}$ and $\frac{3}{4}$, with a recurring playful theme.
Range: e–c³
Duration: 12:15

Veremans, Renaat (1894–1969) Belgium

Concerto for Horn (1964)
J. Maurer, 1965, piano reduction
    I. Allegro
    II. Andante sostenuto
    III. Allegro
Dedicated to Edm. Offermans. Traditional harmonic language and forms. This is a lyrical work in a style reminiscent of nineteenth-century romantic writing.
Range: c¹–c³
Duration: 14:00

Verrall, John (1908–2001) United States
Verrall studied composition with Donald Ferguson, R. O. Morris, and Zoltán Kodály, then, during summers at Tanglewood, with Aaron Copland, Roy Harris, and Frederick Jacobi. He was on the faculty at the University of Washington.

Rhapsody for Solo Horn and Strings (1979)
American Composers Alliance, 1979, full score
The composer notes in the preface that this piece makes several allusions to themes from the late works of Robert Schumann, "as points of departure to enter a world of fantasy prompted by the Romantic master." Written in a contemporary musical style and in one continuous movement of contrasting characters. There is a version of this piece for horn and piano, entitled *Eusebius Remembered,* written in three separate movements. The composer notes it is slightly different in both figuration and harmony.
Range: g–b²
Duration: 14:00

Vinter, Gilbert (1909–1969) United Kingdom

Hunter's Moon for Horn and Orchestra (1942)
Boosey & Hawkes, 1942, arranged for horn and piano
Now a staple in the horn repertoire, this was originally composed for horn and
   strings but is most often performed in the horn and piano arrangement. In
   ABA form, it begins with a characteristic hunting-horn motive in $\frac{6}{8}$, has an
   expressive Lento in the middle section, then returns to the $\frac{6}{8}$ material. Light
   and effective.
Range: G–b^2
Duration: 6:30
See: Horn and keyboard

Vito-Delvaux, Berthe di (1915–2005) Belgium
Studied at the Conservatoire Royal de Musique in Liège, and undertook composition studies with Léon Jongen in Brussels. Winner of many awards, including
the Prix de Rome (1943), she also taught at the Conservatoire Royal de Musique in
Liège. *New Grove* states that "although interested in contemporary music, in her
own works she remained faithful to her traditional musical upbringing, rejecting
serialism and atonality."

Concerto No. 1, op. 93, horn and orchestra (1963)
CeBeDeM, 1963, horn and piano reduction
Dedicated to Armand Lacroix.
Duration: 17:00

Concerto No. 2, op. 100, horn and orchestra (1965)
CeBeDeM, 1965, horn and piano reduction
Dedicated to Adhémar. Pluvinage.
Duration: 18:00

Vogel, Roger C. (1947–) United States
A prolific composer, Roger Vogel is on the faculty at the University of Georgia

Concerto for French Horn and String Orchestra (1980)
Dorn Publications, 1981, piano reduction
    I. Adagio—Allegro non troppo—Adagio—Allegro
    II. Larghetto con tenerezza
    III. Allegro.
Written in a contemporary expressive harmonic language with flowing gestures
   that take advantage of the horn's ability to sing. There are several technically challenging passages, but overall the horn writing is not extremely
   virtuosic. Good endurance is needed for sustaining long and expressive
   lines that often go above the staff. In several instances, the lower octave is
   indicated as an option.
Range: A♭–c^3 (ossia A♭–a^2)
Duration: 20:00

Wal-Berg (Voldemar Rosenberg) (1910–1994) France

Concertino für Horn und Orchester (1986)
Sikorski Musikverlage Hamburg, 1985, full score only
In three movements. The first movement, marked Vivo, is in one and in a traditional melodic style. The second movement is in three-part form, with outer sections in a very fast five and a slow middle section of Lento assai. The third movement, Vivo giocoso, is a spirited § with hemiola figures. This is an accessible work for the intermediate hornist.
Range: f–c³
Duration: 11:20

Wallach, Joelle (1946–) United States

In a Dark Time (the Eye Begins to See), Three Meditations for Horn and Piano or Chamber orchestra
Joelle Wallach, 2005, piano reduction, available from www.joellewallach.com
Commissioned by the 2006 Women's Brass Conference, where it was premiered by Laurel Bennert Ohlson. Inspired by the similarly titled poem by Theodore Roethke, all three movements are flowing and lyrical. Of medium difficulty, this is a well-paced work for the soloist.
Range: d–a♭²
Duration: 11:00

Watkins, Huw (1976–) United Kingdom
Watkins has received many awards and commissions for his work and is also an active pianist. Currently professor of composition at the Royal Academy of Music and composer in residence with Orchestra of the Swan in Stratford-upon-Avon.

Nocturne, for solo horn, 2 clarinets, and strings (2001–2002, rev. 2009)
Schott, 2009, full score only
This work was premiered March 10, 2002, David Jolley, horn, with the Cincinnati Chamber Orchestra, who commissioned the piece. Revised version premiered August 29, 2009, Presteigne Festival Orchestra, United Kingdom, Richard Watkins, horn. Flowing and lyrical, with wide ranging passages that are sometimes angular, and covering the full range of the horn. Clarinets add a pastoral color in counterpoint with the solo horn.
Range: B–c³
Duration: 10:00

Watkins, Michael Blake (1948–) United Kingdom

Horn Concerto (1974)
Novello & Company, 1975, full score only
Dedicated to "T. M. F." For strings and optional harp. In one continuous movement made up of five contrasting sections organized around a central cadenza. Stopped writing, wide leaps, and intricate technical passages make this a challenging work for the horn soloist.
Range: d♯–c³
Duration: 17:30

Weber, Carl Maria von (1786–1826) Germany

Concertino for Horn and Piano, op. 45 (1806, rev. 1815)

International, 1974 (John Cerminaro, ed.); Breitkopf & Härtel, 1974 (Henri Kling, ed.); Edition Peters, 1975 (Peter Damm, ed.); Schirmer, 1977 (Barry Tuckwell, ed.); KaWe, 1974 (Edmond Leloir, ed.); R. Lienau, 1950—all piano reductions

In four movements: Adagio, andante—Andante con moto, con fuoco—Cadenza, Adagio—Alla polacca.

Weber composed this work in 1806 at the age of nineteen for C. Dautrevaux, horn virtuoso in the court orchestra of Duke Eugen of Württemberg, Carlsruhe, Silesia, then later revised it for hornist Sebastian Rauch of Munich. The original 1806 version is lost. Written for horn in E, one of the more awkward keys for modern F-horn fingerings. After a brief Adagio of string tremolos, the horn enters with a melody in §. This is followed by a straightforward theme, marked Andante, followed by four variations with orchestral interludes between each. An involved Cadenza follows, ending with extensive multiphonic chords. The final movement, Alla polacca, incorporates music from the first theme. This virtuosic work, now a standard in the horn repertoire, pushed the technical limits of the early nineteenth-century horn, with pedal tones, multiphonics, wide leaps, and fast passages that quickly span the range of the horn. Most editions include alternate passages that keep the piece well within range of the cor-basse player of the period, giving alternate notes for every passage that ascends to c^3.

Range: F–e♭^{3} with ossias F–a^2 (F♯–e^3 with ossias F♯–b♭^{2} for horn in E)
Duration: 15:38

Weiner, Stanley (1925–1991) United States
Composer and violinist Weiner played with the Indianapolis Symphony and had a career as a violin soloist, mainly in Europe.

Concerto for Horn & String Orchestra (1967)
MCA Music, 1968, piano reduction by the composer
To Joseph Eger and Francis Orval. In three movements. The first is marked Allegro and is organized around a running triplet motive, ending with a cadenza. The second movement is quite active, with ornament-like groupings of notes in a slow tempo. The final movement is rhythmic, in § and §, marked Allegro molto vivace, with a few glissandi and trills. Some mixed meters and moderately chromatic, with challenging passages with repeated notes above the staff.

Range: A–c^3
Duration: 13:30

Weinzweig, John (1913–2006) Canada
Weinzweig studied composition at Eastman and taught in Toronto at the Royal Conservatory and at the University of Toronto.

Divertimento No. 7 for Horn and String Orchestra (1979, 1993 arranged for horn and piano by the composer)

John Weinzweig, 1993, horn and piano; available from the Canadian Music Centre

Written for hornist Eugene Rittich, who premiered it with the CBC Vancouver
Orchestra, March 31, 1980. The composer wrote a number of *divertimenti,*
many for the "neglected" instruments that don't have a great deal of solo
repertoire. The score preface explains that "in the short introduction the
horn presents a seminal motive of four notes that is to become a unifying element throughout the work. The form is an extended movement with
nine interconnected sections linked by horn solos, and alternating fast and
slow events." Special colorful effects include alternating open and closed
notes, quarter-tone oscillations, flutter tonguing, and glissandi. Some aleatoric writing, with challenging passages at some quick tempos. The piano
reduction of this work is shorter, an abbreviation of this piece.

Range: g♯–c³

Duration: 19:00 (horn and piano version 10:00)

Weismann, Julius (1879–1950) Germany

Conductor, pianist, and a prolific composer, Weismann studied composition with
Rheinberger, Herzogenberg, and Thuille.

Conzertino für Horn mit Begleitung von Kleinem Orchester, op. 118 (1935)

Richard Birnbach, 1936, piano reduction

The *Conzertino's* orchestration and harmonic language is romantic, while the solo
writing is light, engaging, and well written for the horn. In three traditional
movements, an Allegro moderato, an Andante tranquillo, and a light and
fast Allegro con spirito in ¾. Now reintroduced into the horn repertoire,
this well-crafted work was relatively unknown until recorded by Hermann
Baumann on *The Romantic Horn* (Arabesque) and Martin Hackleman on
Romanza (CBC Records).

Range: B♭–b♭²

Duration:15:00

Werder, Felix (1922–2012) Australia, born in Germany

Werder fled Nazi Germany to live in Australia, and he became a leading composer of the Australian musical avant-garde.

Cranach's Hunt for Horn and Orchestra (1975)

Australian Music Centre, full score only

To Alex Grieve. Notated in ¾ throughout, with contrasting sections delineated
with metronome markings to indicate the new tempo. There is some graphic
notation and a few sections of aleatoric writing. Challenging contemporary
writing for the horn soloist, with wide leaps, angular writing, and challenging gestures that jump up into the high range.

Range: g–c³

Duration: ca. 12:00

Werner, Fritz (1898–1977) Germany

Composer and conductor, noted for his work with the Heinrich Schütz Choir Heilbronn and his interpretations of Bach.

Concerto pour cor et orchestre à cordes, op. 54

Billaudot, 1975, piano reduction

For Hermann Baumann. This work follows traditional form and meter and is organized into three movements: Sostenuto, Allegro—Andantino—Allegro vivace e energico. The sostenuto opening features the horn alone, playing freely. There are a few instances of changing meters, muted horn, and stopped horn. Overall, this is an approachable work, with an emphasis on counterpoint and dialogue between horn and orchestra/piano.

Range: g–c^3

Duration: 15:00

Werner, Jean Jacques (1935–) France

Concerto pour cor, orchestre a cordes, piano et percussion (1962)

Editions Max Eschig, 1965, piano reduction

For Louis Courtinat. Premiered in 1966, Georges Barboteu, horn soloist, Orchestre de chambre de l'ORTF, (now the Orchestre Philharmonique de Radio France), with the composer conducting. The first movement, Allegro, in § features shifting rhythmic patterns that juxtapose motives in two and three. The second movement, Adagio, is expressive in its lyrical lines and dotted figures, followed by an Allegro giocoso in a quick and light ⅜.

Range: d–c^3

Duration: 15:00

Quatre bagatelles pour cor et orchestre à cordes (1987)

J.M. Fuzeau, 1988, piano reduction

    I. A capriccio e con anima

    II. Moto Perpetuo

    III. Pacato

    IV. Aperto

Duration: 17:00

Wessman, Harri (1949–) Finland

Concertino for Horn and String Orchestra, About Rain (Concertino käyrätorvelle ja jousiorkesterille) (1995)

Modus Musiikki, 1999, piano reduction

Wessman has written pieces for musicians of all ages and abilities. This is one of several concertinos written for the young soloist and is written for and dedicated to Jenni Kuronen, who premiered it in 1996. In three movements, the first two, "The sadness of rain," and "Rain song" are slow and introspective, and the third movement, "The joy of rain" is a fun Allegro in § with a back-and-forth between the horn and strings. The harmonic language is traditional, the scoring lush and romantic at times. This is a nice addition

to the concerto repertoire, particularly for the student player. The string parts are also suitable for a student orchestra. Recorded by Esa Tukia, horn, Oulu Symphony, Atso Almila conducting, MILS records.
Range: e–g²
Duration: 12:00

Whear, Paul W. (1925–) United States

Pastorale Lament for Horn and String Orchestra
Ludwig, 1971, piano reduction
Short, flowing work in one movement, with changing meters.
Range: c¹–a²
Duration: 5:30

Whettam, Graham (1927–2007) United Kingdom
Largely self taught, Whettam wrote many works for horn and was founder of Meriden Music. *New Grove* states that his style "owes much to Bartok and Mahler."

Concerto Ardente for Horn and String Orchestra (1992)
Meriden Music, 1996, piano reduction
Premiered by Richard Watkins, horn, at the Malvern Festival, 1993. Driving rhythms, quick dynamic changes, and often angular writing are characteristics of this challenging contemporary work. It does not venture into the low range of the horn, remaining solidly in the middle and upper ranges. The first movement has an extensive cadenza. The second movement is a Lento in three, beginning with muted horn and with alternating passages of *tranquillo* building to moments of *appassionato molto.* The final movement is extensive, with a middle section of muted horn and sixteenths and triplet sixteenths that require dexterity and good triple tonguing.
Range: b♭–c³
Duration: 24:00

Whitaker, Howard (1941–) United States
Howard Whitaker teaches composition at Wheaton College.

Fanfares, Concertino for Solo Horn and Brass Choir
Mentor Music, 1996, full score only
For Daniel Fackler. Scored for solo horn and four trumpets, four horns, three trombones, bass trombone, tuba, timpani, and percussion. This work is in two large sections, opening with a slow Maestoso ("like a recit."), with much opportunity for the horn to play expressively and freely over the brass instruments. This is followed by an Allegro, with the horn stepping aside to feature the brass ensemble. There is a brief return of the expressive horn line, with the piece finishing with an Allegro, and the horn ending on a high c♯³.
Range: b♭–c♯³

Wiedemann, Ludwig (?–1900)

Nocturno for Horn and Orchestra
Belwin, 1940, piano reduction
Short, lyrical work that stays mainly in the midrange of the horn. Traditional
   tonality, with a brief cadenza that goes up to a². Suitable for an intermediate
   horn student.
Range: g–a²
Duration: 3:30

Wiggins, Christopher (1956–) United Kingdom

Horn Concerto, op. 81 (1987–88)
Solid Wood Music (formerly Emerson Horn Editions), 1988, piano reduction and
   orchestra score
Christopher Wiggins has written many works for the horn. This is a bright and
   energetic work in five short movements, well paced, with the horn often
   venturing above the staff.
Range: e–c³
Duration: 14:15

Wilby, Philip (1949–) United Kingdom

Fantasie Concertant (2003)
Winwood Music, 2004, piano reduction
   1. Don Quixote's dream
   2. Burlesque
   3. Soliloquy
   4. Valse caprice
   5. Finale
For Lesley Howie. The publisher's website indicates that this was originally written with an accompaniment of brass band with a solo quintet of 2 cornets,
   euphonium, trombone, and tuba. The five movements are arranged around
   the central "Soliloquy" movement. This work features agile writing for the
   horn.
Range: G–b♭²

Wilder, Alec (1907–1980) United States

Alec Wilder studied privately at Eastman and was a songwriter and arranger
in New York. In the 1950s, he turned to writing opera, chamber music, works
for orchestra, musical theatre, and film. His close friendship with hornist John
Barrows (1913–1974) resulted in his composing a large number of pieces for horn.
With his distinctive voice and lyrical gifts that combine elements of jazz, popu-
lar, and classical music, his works have become standards in the horn literature.
Overall, his music is challenging, with angular melodies, chromatic writing, and
passages that extend into the high range, often at soft dynamics.
   See also: David Demsey and Ronald Prather, *Alec Wilder: A bio-bibliography*
(Westport, CT: Greenwood Press, 1993); and David Charles Calhoon, "The horn

music of Alec Wilder: A survey, with analysis of his *Sonata No. 1 for horn and piano*" (PhD thesis, University of Wisconsin Madison, 1992).

Concerto No. 2 for Horn and Chamber Orchestra (1960)
MarGun Music, distributed by G. Schirmer. Full score only
Also known as the *Concerto for French Horn and Chamber Orchestra (Comic)*.
Written for John Barrows who played the premiere August 4, 1961, with Yale University Chamber Orchestra. In four contrasting movements. The first movement is untitled, and moves at a fast clip in changing meters and with a jaunty eighth-and-sixteenth-note motive that trades off with other voices throughout the orchestra. The second and third movements are more lyrical, entitled "Romantic" and "Nostalgic," respectively. The fourth movement is similar to the first, at a fast tempo, entitled "Manic." In his survey of Alec Wilder's music for horn, David Calhoon points out that the first and fourth movements are harmonically adventurous, with the first movement using a twelve-tone melody in a tonal context, and the fourth movement using quartal harmonies, based on fourths.
Range: f♯–b♭^{2}
Duration: 15:00

Entertainment No. 4 for Horn and Chamber Orchestra (1972)
Margun Music, 1972, distributed by G. Schirmer, full score only
Written for Verne Reynolds. In five movements.
Range: c–a♭^{2}
Duration: 18:00

Five Love Songs for Horn and Chamber Orchestra (1979)
Israel Brass Woodwind Publications, 1985, piano reduction
For Morris Secon. Lyrical and flowing, with jazz/popular harmonic inflections and melodies that soar above the staff. Short songs that are wistful and nostalgic, these are quite beautiful and work very well in the horn and piano arrangement.
Range: B–c^3
Duration: 11:00

John Barrows, for Horn and Chamber Orchestra (1977)
Israel Brass Woodwind Publications, 1986, piano reduction
For Morris Secon, who premiered this work at the 1979 International Horn Society Workshop at Michigan State University, East Lansing. In four movements. The first is untitled, with a slow tempo of ♩=66. This is followed by movements marked "Romantically," "A piacere," and "Giocoso easy-playful." A flowing work, emphasizing Wilder's lyrical talents. Challenging for the hornist and requiring good endurance for the long, flowing lines. This is somber and dissonant writing within the context of tonal harmonic language.
Range: c–c^3
Duration: 12:00

Willi, Herbert (1956–) Austria

Äon, Konzert für Horn und Orchester 2007, aus dem Zyklus "Montafon"
Schott, 2008, orchestra score only
Composed for Stefan Dohr, who premiered the work on March 7, 2008, with
   the Radio Symphony Orchestra of Vienna. This work is part of a cycle of
   concertos by Willi. "Montafon" in the title refers to the Montafon Valley
   region in Austria. This work is in three movements. The first begins with
   solo horn against a string background and incorporates elements of jazz
   writing, alternating open and closed notes, and long horn lines. The second
   movement is Molto espressivo (dolce) with horn lines that evolve over a
   string background. The final movement is quick and rhythmic, with the
   horn weaving in and out of the texture.
Range: E–c³
Duration: 16:00

Williams, John (1932–) United States

Concerto for Horn and Orchestra (2003)
Hal Leonard, 2003, piano reduction
   I. Angelus, "Far far away, like bells, At evening pealing"
   II. The battle of the trees, "Swift oak . . . Stout guardian of the door"
   III. Pastorale, "There came a day at summer's full"
   IV. The hunt, "The hart loves the high wood"
   V. Nocturne, "The crimson day withdraws"
Dedicated to hornist Dale Clevenger who played the premiere on November 29,
   2003, with the Chicago Symphony Orchestra, the composer conducting.
   The first movement features the horn playing calls over bells sounding in
   the distance. The second movement is full of forceful writing in the horn,
   with the orchestra—particularly the percussion—joining in the fray. The
   third movement is a lightly orchestrated pastorale, with traditional wind
   combinations of horn with the double reeds of the orchestra. Tradition
   continues, with an attacca into the next movement, a boisterous hunt that
   features an extended cadenza. The final movement is the longest of the five,
   a contemplative winding down of sorts, with the horn playing over lush
   string writing that evokes nostalgia for wide open spaces and a simpler
   time. A technically demanding work that looks back on the long tradition
   of the horn.
Range: E–c♯³ (ossia A–c♯³)
Duration: 27:19

Wilson, Dana (1946–) United States

Concerto for Horn and Orchestra (or Wind Ensemble)
Dana Wilson, 2001, full score and piano reduction, available from the composer
Written for Gail Williams, who premiered the work with the Syracuse Sym-
   phony in 1997, then in 2002 premiered the version for wind ensemble with

the Ithaca College Wind Ensemble. The first movement, marked "Freely," opens with a fanfare, and a forceful eighth-note motive underpins the movement, as the solo horn develops the material of the rising opening statement, leading into a cadenza. The second movement, "Plaintively," features slow lyrical lines organized around falling seconds and rising thirds. The final movement, "With great energy," begins with an exchange between horn and percussion, with driving gestures that carry through the movement. This work has colorful effects such as flutter tonguing, upward scoops, pitch bends, alternating open and stopped notes. This is a technically demanding and virtuosic work for the hornist, with sustained high notes, wide leaps into the high range, and energetic passages that move through all ranges of the horn.

Range: B♭–b²
Duration: 18:48

Wilson, James (1922–2005) Ireland, born in England
A prolific, award-winning composer, Wilson taught composition at the Royal Irish Academy of Music, and was also for many years a course director of the Ennis/IMRO Composition Summer School.

Horn concerto, op. 23 for horn and orchestra (1967)
Contemporary Music Centre Ireland, 1993, piano reduction and orchestra score
Duration: 25:00

Winteregg, Steven (1952–) United States

Visions and Revelations for Horn and Orchestra (or horn and band) (1989)
Manuscript, 1989, full score, available from Lauren Keiser Music Publishing; a
    version for horn and band is also available.
Based on the vision of St. John, this one-movement work presents many contrast-
    ing moods and characters. Syncopated and driving sections contrast with
    moments of ethereal, contemplative writing, and colorful and effective use
    of percussion, piano, and harp. There is a short cadenza-like section of nat-
    ural horn writing, with closed notes and overtone glissandi. The horn writ-
    ing is challenging but well paced, with wide leaps, flutter tonguing, stopped
    writing, and glissandi.
Range: A–d³ (ossia A–b²)
Duration: 16:00

Witt, Friedrich (1770–1836) Germany
Witt was a composer and cellist in the orchestra of the Prince of Oettingen-
Wallerstein and later kapellmeister at the Würzburg theatre.

Concerto E-Dur für Horn und Orchester (1795)
Robert Ostermeyer, 2001, piano reduction and orchestra score
This concerto was written for Joseph Nagel, Witt's colleague who was first horn
    in the Oettingen-Wallerstein orchestra. In three movements. It is very
    much in the style of Rosetti, with whom Witt probably studied. The first

movement is an Allegro moderato in $\frac{4}{4}$, the second movement is an Adagio marked "Romance," and the third movement is a $\frac{3}{4}$ rondo. The range and fingering difficulties of the E-horn transposition on modern horn make this a challenging work.

Range: f♯–d♯^{3} (g–e^3 for horn in E)
Duration: 10:30

Wittell, Chester (1893–1988) United States

Wittell was a self-taught composer and pianist, played piano concertos with local orchestras, and composed and arranged over two hundred symphonies, overtures, concertos, and chamber music pieces.

Concerto in F major for Horn and Orchestra, op. 90 (1953)
McCoy's Horn Library, 2000, piano reduction
The preface to this edition indicates that Wittell considered his horn concerto "his finest composition." Written in traditional harmonic language and forms, this work is dedicated to Elwood Cauler, principal horn of the Lancaster Symphony.

Wolschina, Reinhard (1952–) Germany

3 Dialoge für Horn und 15 Solostreicher (1975)
Deutscher Verlag für Musik, 1980, full score only with horn part
For István Vincze. Notated in both traditional time signatures and unmeasured sections (free episodes) using duration, this is a challenging and expressive contemporary work with glissandi, flutter tonguing, and multiphonics.
Range: e♭–c^3
Duration: 15:00

Woltmann, Frederick (1908– 1965) United States

Poem for Horn and Strings (1936)
Score and parts available at the Fleisher Collection, Free Library of Philadelphia
Originally written for string quartet and horn. First performed by the Rochester Civic Orchestra, Rochester, New York, May 13, 1936, Richard Bales, conductor, Fred Klein, soloist. Short, lyrical work that features the horn in counterpoint with the strings, with a few changing meters. Very well paced for the horn soloist.
Range: b–g♯^{2}
Duration: 4:00

Rhapsody for Horn and Orchestra (1934)
Score and parts available at the Fleisher Collection, Free Library of Philadelphia
For Kurt Atterberg. Premiered December 12, 1935, Rochester Philharmonic Orchestra, Howard Hanson, conductor, Edward Murphy, horn soloist. A short, expressive work, the orchestra begins quietly, building until the horn enters *forte* on a brief declamatory theme that returns several times throughout the piece. There are contrasting sections of quickly changing character, including a brief dialogue with winds, and a quiet restatement

of the opening theme that ends the work. Well-paced work for the horn soloist, with only moderate demands on range and endurance.

Range: a–b²
Duration: 8:00

Yurko, Bruce (1951–) United States

Composer, conductor, and hornist. Yurko's works have been played by ensembles throughout the United States. He currently teaches composition and is director of the wind ensemble at Rowan University.

Concerto for Horn and Wind Ensemble (1975)
Bruce Yurko, full score, available from the composer
This work is dedicated to the composer's former horn teacher, Doug Hill, who premiered it May 21, 1976, at the University of Wisconsin Madison. In three continuous sections, the first is slow and lyrical, with the horn taking its motive from opening notes of the bells (chimes) of the first few bars. The second section is fast and features the horn interacting with an "articolato" motive in the ensemble, created by different rhythms that result in a swarming "sound cloud." The third section features the horn with a chorale backdrop, first played by flutes, then double reeds, and finally the muted brass. The solo-horn writing is quite demanding, with five cadenzas throughout the piece. There are lyrical passages, and fast wide leaps in both legato and declamatory styles that move through all of the ranges of the horn.

Range: F♯–c♯³
Duration: 18:00
See also: Ibrook Tower. "Bruce Yurko's concertos for wind ensemble (1973–1974), for horn and wind ensemble (1975), and for trombone and wind ensemble (1977)" (DMA thesis, University of Cincinnati, 1994).

Zador, Eugene (1894–1977) United States, born in Hungary

Like many composers who emigrated to the U.S. in the twentieth century, Zador settled in Hollywood and worked in the film industry. He orchestrated music for films, but his own compositions were opera, chamber works, orchestra and choral music, and songs.

Suite for Horn, Percussion and String Orchestra (1974)
Edition Eulenberg, 1975, piano reduction
    I. Prelude
    II. Fantasy
    III. March
    IV. Elegie
    V. Rondo-finale
In five short movements of contrasting character and written in modern tonal language with changing meters. Moderately technical, with agile writing and several passages extending up into the high range. There is an option to improvise a cadenza in the Rondo-finale.

Range: e♭–c³
Duration: 13:00

Zannas, Savvas (1952–) Greece

Composer, percussionist, and timpanist with the National Symphony Orchestra of ERT in Greece, Zannas has composed large-scale orchestral works and chamber music.

Concerto for Horn and String Orchestra (2008)
Panas Music, 2012, full score only
Dedicated to Antonis Lagos. In three movements. The first and second are played
    attacca. The first movement is in $\frac{4}{4}$, with sixteenth-note motives in horn
    and strings that drive the music forward. The second-movement Adagio
    features a five-note figure over two beats, and the energetic third movement
    brings back material from the second-movement Adagio. Good technique
    is required for the quick outer movements, and the tempo of the Adagio
    requires good control and endurance for sustaining long lines at a very
    slow tempo.
Range: f♯–b²
Duration: 18:00

Zbinden, Julien-François (1917–) Switzerland

Episodes for Horn and Strings, op. 95 (2000)
Editions BIM, 2000, piano reduction
Dedicated to Bruno Schneider and composed for the Philip Jones International
    Competition in Geubwiller, France, in 2001, this served as the final round
    piece for the competition. Organized into three sections played without
    break. The first episode begins slowly, opening lento sostenuto in the ac-
    companiment, and the horn enters with a brief cadenza. The episode gains
    momentum in the Andantino section, leading into the second episode, a
    slow, lyrical melody in $\frac{3}{4}$. The final episode is an Allegrissimo, with quick
    sixteenth-note and triplet passages, leading into a final cadenza full of an-
    gular writing with moderately wide intervals.
Range: d♯–c³
Duration: 12:00

Zdechlik, John (1937–) United States

Zdechlik is an active composer, performer, conductor, and clinician, who has written many works for concert band.

Concerto for French Horn and Band (1993)
Neil A. Kjos Music, 1996, full score only
    1. Giocoso
    2. Romance
    3. Allegro
Dedicated to Sarah Zdechlik and Miles Johnson. The edition lists two premieres
    of this work, first with Sarah Zdechlik at the University of Wisconsin Mad-
    ison in spring 1993; subsequently Sharon Moe performed the work with
    the Saint Olaf College Band in fall 1994. The first movement is rhythmic,
    in a rollicking $\frac{6}{8}$. The second movement develops a running sixteenth-note

and dotted eighth-sixteenth theme. The third movement, marked Allegro, features changes in character and tempos, with a cadenza that brings in material from the first two movements. This is a well-paced intermediate work, suitable for the college player.

Range: G–c³
Duration: 17:32

Žebeljan, Isidora (1967–) Serbia
Žebeljan is an award-winning composer and professor of composition at the Belgrade Music Academy.

Dance of the Wooden Sticks for Horn and String Orchestra (2008)
Ricordi, 2008, full score, for horn and string orchestra or string quintet
To Lisa Ford. This work was commissioned by the International Horn Society
    in 2008, as part of the Meir Rimon Commissioning Assistance Fund. It
    was premiered by hornist Boštjan Lipovšek and the Camerata Academ-
    ica Orchestra of Novi Sad, Serbia, conducted by Aleksandar Kojić, in the
    Novi Sad Synagogue in October 2010. This is an intricate work that incor-
    porates pastoral and folk elements in a contemporary style and harmonic
    language. It opens with a slow rubato horn line over strings that alternate
    between *natural* and *sul ponticello*. Continuously changing meters and
    intricate rhythmic figures continue to build in intensity throughout the
    piece, driving to the conclusion. A challenging work for both the string or-
    chestra and the hornist, with contemporary techniques of flutter tonguing,
    glissandi, trills, and stopped horn.

Range: e–c³
Duration: 7:00

Zeller, Georg (1857–?)

Concertino für Horn
Hans Pizka Edition, 1986, piano reduction
Following the form of a typical nineteenth-century concertino, this work is in
    one continuous movement, beginning with an expressive Andante in ⅜ fol-
    lowed by an Allegro in ¾. There are pleasing melodies and flourishes of vir-
    tuosity that may sound more difficult than they actually are. Modest range
    and well paced, with judicious breaks for the horn soloist.

Range: c–a²
Duration: 10:00

Zettler, Richard (1921–) Germany
Composer, conductor, educator, Zettler was solo trombonist with the Stuttgart
Radio Symphony for many years.

Concertino (1951)
Ries & Erler, 1966, piano reduction
In three movements that follow traditional fast-slow-fast form. Written in tonal
    harmonic language, with contrasting character within each movement. The

first movement is a theme with variations, the second is marked Andante sostenuto, and the final movement is in rondo form. The preface indicates that this piece could serve as a good study piece but could also be a welcome addition to the literature for every solo hornist. Suitable for the college-level player.

Range: e–c^3

Duration: 11:08

Zeuner, Charles (1795–1857) United States, born in Germany

Zeuner was a court musician, composer, and organist. He studied in Germany with Johann Nepomuk Hummel and Michael Gotthard Fischer before moving to Boston and, later, Philadelphia.

Variations pour le Cor, for Horn and Orchestra

Birdalone Music, 1997, arranged for horn and piano by Jeff Snedeker

This work features a theme with five variations, plus a final-movement Polacca. The original manuscript can be found in the Fleisher Collection of the Free Library of Philadelphia.

Range: g–g^2

Duration: 11:00

Zimmermann, Udo (1943–) Germany

Composer and conductor; founder and director of the Studio Neue Musik of the Dresden Staatsoper and Radio DDR; professor of composition at the Dresden Hochschule für Musik; and director of the Leipzig Opera and the Deutsche Oper, Berlin.

Nouveaux divertissements d'après Jean Philippe Rameau (1987)

VEB Deutscher Verlag für Musik, 1989, full score only

  I. Cadence ouverte vive et vertigineuse
  II. Dansant et charmant
  III. Ariette lyrique
  IV. Tambourin
  V. Très gai et rapide

Hornist Peter Damm premiered this work on June 1, 1988, with the Staatskapelle Dresden, and the composer conducting. Movements I, III, IV, and V are based on Rameau's opera *Castor et Pollux*. Movement II is based on the Fandango from Mozart's *Le Nozze di Figaro*. The first divertissement opens with a cadenza in contemporary harmonic language in the solo horn, then the orchestra surprises with a light and tonal entrance. This work has many surprises; it is witty and playful, as the horn and orchestra trade back and forth with highly tonal figures, gradually building up to atonal, complex, sometimes chaotic gestures. The somber third movement, Ariette lyrique, features beautiful horn lines over a grounded bass figure, with a free cadenza finishing the movement. The fifth movement is full of neo-baroque horn writing, with high d^3 and e^3 in the horn's extreme upper register.

Range: E♭–e^3

Duration: 22:45

Zupko, Ramon (1932–) United States
Zupko studied with Persichetti, Copland, and Leuning and taught for many years at Western Michigan University where he founded and directed the Studio for Electronic and Computer Music.

Prologue, Aria, and Dance, for French Horn and String orchestra (1961)
American Composers Alliance, 1968, full score, string parts available for purchase
In one movement of three continuous sections. The first section is a short, de-
    clamatory prologue, the second is a lyrical cantabile Aria and brings back
    some of the material of the prologue. The third section, "Dance," is an en-
    ergetic $\frac{3}{4}$, with some syncopated rhythms. Of medium difficulty, this work
    would be suitable for an advanced high school or college-level player. Writ-
    ten under the auspices of the Music Educators National Conference's Con-
    temporary Music Project for Creativity in Music Education, Composers in
    Public Schools program.
Range: $F–g^2$ (ossia $c\sharp–g^2$)
Duration: 9:00

Žuraj, Vito (1979–) Slovenia

Hawk-eye, Concerto for French Horn and Orchestra (2014)
Available from the composer, www.vitozuraj.com
Premiered February 27, 2014, Saar Berger, horn, with the Slovenian Philharmonic
    in Ljubljana, Slovenia, Matthias Pintscher conducting.
Duration: 15:00

Zwilich, Ellen Taaffe (1939–) United States
Pulitzer-Prize-winning composer Zwilich wrote several concertos for the more neglected instruments of the orchestra, including trumpet, trombone, bass trombone, oboe, horn, and bassoon.

Concerto for Horn and String Orchestra (1993)
Merion Music, Theodore Presser, 1995, piano reduction
The horn concerto was commissioned by Bravo! Colorado Music Festival, the
    Rochester Philharmonic, Orpheus Chamber Orchestra, and hornist David
    Jolley, who premiered the work, and later recorded it. The composer writes
    in the recording liner notes that although this piece is an "exploration of
    a wide range of expressive and dramatic capabilities of the horn . . . it can
    also be heard as a 'tone poem' with the horn cast as the 'hero.'" The piece is
    composed in one continuous movement divided into five sections. It opens
    slowly, with a somber horn line marked *mellow* then *broad* and finally
    brassy and free. Long lines in the horn give way to driving sixteenth notes,
    first in the strings, then exchanging this motive with the solo horn. An
    extended and virtuosic cadenza follows and incorporates material from the
    first section, adding expressive touches like bending pitches and stopped
    notes. The orchestra enters, in what feels like an accompanied recitative,
    transitioning into the next section of long lines for the horn, sometimes
    chant-like, that move in and out of unison with the strings. A muted call

of previously heard material ushers in the final section, a furious Allegro. Challenging for the hornist in range and technique, but well paced. An excellent addition to the horn-concerto repertoire.

Range: c–c^3

Duration: 14:10

See also: Terry Roberts, "Ellen Taaffe Zwilich Concerto for Horn and String Orchestra: An Overview and Analysis" (DM thesis, Florida State University, 2001).

Title Index

Name Index for Premieres, Commissions, and Dedications

Index—Music for Horn with Band, Wind Ensemble, or Brass Ensemble

Index—Music for Horn with Small Instrumental Ensemble

List of Composers by Nationality

The numbers after the composer's dates indicate the chapters in which that composer appears.

Albania

Peçi, Aleksandër (1951–) 2, 3

Argentina

Mindlin, Adolfo (1922–) 2
Matalon, Martin (1958–) 3

Rausch, Carlos (1924–) 1
Terzian, Alicia (1934–) 3

Armenia

Aristakesian, Emin Aspetovich (1936–1998) 3

Arutiunian, Aleksandr Grigori (1920–2012) 3
Sat'yan [Satian], Aram (1947–) 3

Australia

Banks, Don (1923–1980) 3
Bracegirdle, Lee (1952–)
   (born in United States) 3
Broadstock, Brenton (1952–) 3
Brumby, Colin (1933–) 3
Collins, Brendan 2
Cronin, Stephen (1960–) 3
Dixon, Michael Hugh (1961–)
   (born in New Zealand) 2
Dreyfus, George (1928–)
   (born in Germany) 2
Edwards, Ross (1943–) 3
Gordon, Christopher
   (1956–) 3
Henderson, Moya (1941–) 1

Hill, Alfred (1869–1960) 3
Holley, Alan (1954–) 1
Ledger, James (1966–) 3
Lovelock, William (1899–1986)
   (born in United Kingdom) 2
Morgan, David Sydney (1932–) 3
Paviour, Paul (1931–) (born in United
   Kingdom) 2
Reeder, Haydn (1944–) 2
Sitsky, Larry (1934–) 1
Stanhope, Paul (1969–) 1
Werder, Felix (1922–2012) (born in Ger-
   many) 3
Wilcher, Phillip (1958–) 2
Willmore, Alan (1935–1993) 2

Austria

Apostel, Hans Erich (1901–1972) (born in Germany) 1

Bischof, Rainer (1947–) 1

Bresgen, Cesar (1913–1988) (born in Germany) 3

De Pastel, Karen (1949–) (born in United States) 2

Dünser, Richard (1959–) 1

Eder, Helmut (1916–2005) 2

Einem, Gottfried von (1918–1996) 2

Fuchs (Fux), Peter (1753–1851) 3

Fürst, Paul Walter (1926–2013) 3

Hartzell, Eugene (1932–2000) (born in United States) 1, 2

Haydn, Franz Josef (1732–1809) 3

Haydn, Michael (1737–1806) 3

Hoffmeister, Franz Anton (1754–1812) 3

Kern, Frida (1891–1988) 2, 3

Krenek, Ernst (1900–1991) (worked in Austria and United States) 2

Krufft, Nicolaus von (1779–1818) 2

Leidesdorf, Maximilian Joseph (1787–1840) 2

Leitermeyer, Fritz (1925–2006) 1

Leschetizky, Theodor Hermann (1896–1948) 3

Lewy, Richard (1827–1883) 3

Ligeti, György (1923–2006) (born in Hungary) 3

Mozart, Leopold (1719–1787) 3

Mozart, Wolfgang Amadeus (1756–1791) 3

Neukomm, Sigismund von (1778–1858) 2

Opitz, Erich (1912–2001) 2

Pelinka, Werner (1952–) 2

Pilss, Karl (1902–1980) 2, 3

Proch, Heinrich (1809–1878) 2

Reiter, Albert (1905–1970) 2

Richter, Hans (1843–1916) 2

Schmidt, Hartmut (1946–) (born in Germany) 3

Schollum, Robert (1913–1987) 1, 3

Schwarz, Otto M. (1967–) 3

Schwertsik, Kurt (1935–) 3

Strauss, Johann (1825–1899) 2

Süssmayr, Franz Xaver (also Süßmayr) (1766–1803) 2

Teyber, Anton (1756–1822) 3

Wellesz, Egon (1885–1974) 1

Wildgans, Friedrich (1913–1965) 2

Willi, Herbert (1956–) 3

Belgium

Absil, Jean (1893–1974) 2

Barbier, René (1890–1981) 2, 3

Bertouille, Gérard (1898–1981) 3

Brusselmans, Michel (1886–1960) (resided in Paris) 3

Cabus, Noël Peter (1923–2000) 2

Chevreuille, Raymond (1901–1976) 2, 3

Constant, Franz (1910–1996) 2

Coppens, Claude A. (1936–) 1, 2

Crépin, Alain (1954–) 2

Dardenne, Jean (1951–) 2

DeBaar, Mathieu (1895–1954) 3

Doren, Theo Van (1898–1974) 3

Dupuis, Albert (1877–1967) 2

Eechaute, Prosper van (1904–1964) 3

Geert, Octaaf A. Van (1949–) 2

Gouders, Willy 1

Herberigs, Robert (1886–1974) 2, 3

Janssens, Robert (1939–) 2, 3

Jong, Marinus de (1891–1984) 3

Jongen, Joseph (1873–1953) 2

Keldermans, Raymond (1911–1984) 2

Kersters, Willem (1929–1998) 2

LeClerc, Michel (1914–1995) 2, 3

Leloir, Edmond (1912–2003) 2

Lenom, Clément (1865–1957) 2

Lonque, Armand (1908–1979) 2

Louël, Jean (1914–2005) 1, 2, 3

Maniet, René 3

Mengal, Jean-Baptiste (1792–1878) 2

Mengal, Martin Joseph (1784–1851) 2, 3

Meulemans, Arthur (1884–1966) 2, 3

Michel, Paul-Baudouin (1930–) 2

Moulaert, Raymond (1875–1962) 3

Orval, Francis (1944–) 1, 2

Orval, Jules-Louis (1913–2015) 1

Pauwels, Jean Englebert (1768–1804) 3

Poot, Marcel (1901–1988) 2

Pousseur, Henri (1929–2009) 1
Roelstraete, Herman (1925–1985) 3
Rosseau, Norbert (1907–1975) 3
Rossum, Frederik van (1939–) 2, 3
Ryelandt, Joseph (1870–1965) 2
Segers, Jan (1929–) 2, 3
Souffriau, Arsène (1926–) 2
Stekke, Léon (1904–1970) 2, 3

Van Doren, Theo (1898–1974) 3
Van Eechaute, Prosper (1904–1964) 2
Veremans, Renaat (1894–1969) 3
Vignery, Jane (Vignery, Jeanne Emilie Virginie) (1913–1974) 2
Vito-Delvaux, Berthe di (1915–2005) 3
Weiner, Stanley (1925–1991) (born in United States) 2, 3

Brazil

Blauth, Brenno (1931–1993) 2
Guarnieri, Camargo, (1907–1993) 1
Richter, Frederico (1932–) 2

Santoro, Claudio (1919–1989) 2
Siqueira, José (1907–1985) 2
Viana, Andersen (1962–) 2

Bulgaria

Karadimchev, Boris (1933–2014) 3

Kazandzhiev, Vasil (1934–) 2
Kostov, Georgi (1941–) 3

Canada

Archer, Violet (1913–2000) (born in the United States) 2
Armstrong, John Gordon (1952–) 1
Baker, Michael Conway (1937–) (born in United States) 2
Bauer, Robert P. (1950–) 1
Burdick, Richard O. (1961–) (born in United States) 1, 2, 3
Coulthard, Jean (1908–2000) 2
Crawford, Paul (1947–) 1
Fodi, John (1944–2009) (born in Hungary) 1
Forsyth, Malcolm (1936–2011) (born in South Africa) 2
Freedman, Harry (1922–2005) (born in Poland) 1
Gellman, Steven (1947–) 1
Hétu, Jacques (1938–2010) 3
Kaplin, David (1923–) 2
Klein, Lothar (1932–2004) (born in Germany) 1

Knudson, Elizabeth (1981–) 3
Lauber, Anne (1943–) 2
Morawetz, Oskar (1917–2007) (born in Czech Republic) 2
Morel, François (1926–) 2
O'Neill, Charles (1882–1964) 2
Pilon, Daniel (1957–) 1
Raum, Elizabeth (1945–) (born in United States) 1, 2, 3
Raum, Erika (1972–) 1
Saint-Marcoux, Micheline Coulombe (1938–1985) 1
Schudel, Thomas (1937–) (born in United States) 2
Smallman, Jeff (1965–) 2
Swan, John D. (1937–) 2
Sweete, Don 2
Weinzweig, John(1913–2006) 2, 3
Wuensch, Gerhard (1925–1980) (born in Austria) 2

China

He, Jianjun (1958–) 2

Cuba

Puentes, José A. Pérez (1951–) 2

Croatia

Bjelinski, Bruno (1909–1992) 3
Kelemen, Milko (1924–) 3
Lhotka, Fran (1883–1962) (born

in Czech Republic) 2
Miletić, Miroslav (1925–) 3
Šulek, Stjepan (1914–1986) 3

Czech Republic

Bartoš, Jan Zdeněk (1908–1981) 2
Blažek, Zdeněk (1905–1988) 2
Bořkovec, P. (1894–1972) 2
Ceremuga, Josef (1930–2005) 2
Domažlický, František (1913–1997) 3
Dvořáček, Jiří (1928–2000) 2
Feld, Jindrick (Jindřich) (1925–2007) 2
Filas, Juraj (1955–) (born Kosice, Slovak
   Republic) 3
Flosman, Oldrich (1925–1998) 3
Fried, Alexej (1922–2011) 1
Hlobil, Emil (1901–1987) 2
Havlik, Jiří (1956–) 3
Hybler, Martin (1977–) 3
Jirko, Ivan (1926–1978) 3

Kalabis, Viktor (1923–2006) 1, 2
Kofroň, Jaroslav (1921–1966) 2
Kricka, Jaroslav (1882–1969) 3
Labor, Josef (1842–1924) 2
Laburda, Jirí (1931–) 3
Pauer, Jiří (1919–2007) 3
Rychlík, Jan (1916–1964) 2
Seidel, Jan (1908–1998) 3
Šesták, Zdeněk (1925–) 2
Slavický, Klement (1910–1999) 1, 2
Slavický, Milan (1947–2009) 1
Soukup, Vladimír (1930–2012) 3
Sperger, Johannes (1750–1812) 3
Vacek, Milos (1928–2012) 2
Vojaček, Hynek (1825–1916) 2

Denmark

Bentzon, Niels Viggo (1919–2000) 1, 2
Børresen, Hakon (1876–1954) 3
Høeberg, Georg (1872–1950) 2
Kayser, Leif (1919–2001) 3

Lindorff-Larsen, Eilert (1902–1983) 3
Lorentzen, Bent (1935–) 3
Nielsen, Carl (1865–1931) 2
Schmidt, Ole (1928–2010) 3

Estonia

Pärt, Arvo (1935–) 2

Sisask, Urmas (1960–) 2

Finland

Aho, Kalevi (1949–) 1
Almila, Atso (1953–) 1
Haapanen, Perttu (1972–) 1
Kaipainen, Jouni (1956–) 3
Kilpiö, Lauri (1974–) 1
Lindberg, Magnus (1958–) 3
Meriläinen, Usko (1930–2004) 1

Raihala, Osmo Tapio (1964–) 1, 3
Rechberger, Herman (1947–)
   (born in Austria) 1
Sallinen, Aulis (1935–) 3
Salonen, Esa-Pekka (1958–) 1, 2
Wessman, Harri (1949–) 2, 3

France

Agobet, Jean-Louis (1968–) 2, 3
Ameller, André (1912–1990) 2
Amy, Gilbert (1936–) 2

Ancelin, Pierre (1934–2001) 2
Arrieu, Claude (1903–1990) 2
Aubain, Jean (1928–) 2, 3

Aubin, Francine (1938–) 3
Aubin, Tony (1907–1981) 2
Auclert, Pierre (1905–1975) 2
Bachelet, Alfred (1864–1944) 2
Balay, Guillaume (1871–1943) 2
Barboteu, Georges (1926–2006) (born in
    Algeria) 1, 2, 3
Barraine, Elsa (1910–1999) 2
Baumgartner, Jean Paul (1932–2012) 3
Berghmans, José (1921–1992) 2, 3
Bernaud, Alain (1932–) 2
Berthelot, René (1903–1999) 2
Berthomieu, Marc (1906–1991) 1
Beydon, Jean-Olivier (1956–) 2
Bigot, Eugène (1888–1965) 2
Bigot, Pierre (1932–2008) 2
Bitsch, Marcel (1921–2011) 2
Blanc, Adolphe (1828–1885) 2
Bleuse, Marc (1937–) 1
Bloch, André (1873–1960) 2
Boieldieu, François-Adrien (1775–1834) 2
Boisseau, Jean-Thierry (1949–) 1, 2
Bonneau, Paul (1918–1995) 2
Boucard, Marcel (1892–1976) 2
Boulard, Frederic (1967–) 1
Bourrel, Yvon (1932–) 2
Bousquet, Francis (1890–1942) 2
Boutry, Roger (1932–) 2
Bozza, Eugène (1905–1991) 2
Brémond, François (1844–1925) 2
Brenet, Thérèse (1935–) 2
Brouquières, Jean (1923–1994) 2
Brown, Charles (1898–1988) 2, 3
Bruneau, Alfred (1857–1934) 2, 3
Busser, Henri (1872–1973) 2, 3
Campo, Régis (1968–) 1
Canavesio, Adrien (b. 1913) 2
Canteloube, Joseph (1879–1957) 2
Capdevielle, Pierre (1906–1969) 2
Carles, Marc (1933–) 2
Carrière, G. L. 2
Castérède, Jacques (1926–2014) 2, 3
Cecconi-Botella, Monic (1936–) 2
Cellier, Alexandre (1883–1968) 2
Chabrier, Emmanuel (1841–1894) 3
Chailley, Jacques (1910–1999) 2
Charpentier, Jacques (1933–) 2, 3
Charron, Jacques (1954–) 2, 3
Chaussier, Henri (1854–1914) 2
Chevillard, Camille (1859–1923) 2

Clapisson, Louis (1808–1866) 2
Clergue, Jean (1896–1969) 2
Clérisse, Robert (1899–1973) 2
Coiteux, Francis (1944–) 2
Colomer, Blas María (1833–1917) (born in
    Spain) 2
Constant, Marius (1925–2004) (born in
    Romania) 3
Coriolis, Emmanuel de (1907–1977) 2
Corret, A. (ca. early 19th cent.) 2
Corrette, Michel (1707–1795) 3
Cosma, Edgar (1925–2006) (born in Ro-
    mania) 2, 3
Couson, Laurent 2
Couturier, Jean-Louis (1963–) 2
Crepy, Bernard de (1939–) 2
Damase, Jean-Michel (1928–2013) 2, 3
Daucé, Edouard (1893–1967) 2
Dauprat, Louis Francois (1781–1868) 2, 3
Dautremer, Marcel (1906–1978) 2
Decruck, Fernande (1896–1954) 2
Defaye, Jean-Michel (1932–) 2
Delerue, Georges (1925–1992) 2, 3
Delgiudice, Michel (1924–) 2
Delmas, Marc (1885–1931) 2
Demar, Johann Sebastian (1763–1832)
    (born in Germany) 3
Demessieux, Jeanne (1921–1968) 2
Demillac, Francis-Paul (1917–) 2
Depelsenaire, Jean-Marie (1914–1986) 2
Désenclos, Albert (1912–1971) 2
Desportes, Yvonne (1907–1993) 2
de Vienne, Bernard (1957–) 1
Devienne, François (1759–1803) 3
Devogel, Jacques (1926–1995) 2
Domnich, Heinrich (1767–1844) (born in
    Germany) 3
Dubost, André (1935–) 1
Dubois, Pierre Max (1930–1995) 2, 3
Dubois, Theodore (1837–1924) 2, 3
Duclos, Renè (1899–1964) 2, 3
Dukas, Paul (1865–1935) 2, 3
Durand, Philippe (1956–) 1
Duvernoy, Frédéric (1765–1838) 2, 3
Eler, André-Frédéric (1764–1821) 3
Escaich, Thierry (1965–) 2
Fasce, Albert (1930–) 2
Florentz, Jean-Louis (1947–2004) 1
Francaix, Jean (1912–1997) 2, 3
Gabaye, Pierre (1930–2000) 2

Gabelles, Gustave Ferdinand Elie
   (1883–1969) 2
Gagnebin, Henri (1886–1977) 2
Gallay, Jacques François (1795–1864) 1, 2, 3
Gallon, Noël (1891–1966) 2
Gantchoula, Philippe (1956–) 2
Garaudé, Alexis de (1779–1852) 2
Gartenlaub, Odette (1922–2014) 2
Gastinel, Gérard (1949–) 1, 2
Gillet, Bruno (1936–) 2
Girard, Anthony (1959–) (born in
   United States) 2
Gotkovsky, Ida (1933–) 2, 3
Gounod, Charles (1818–1893) 2
Gousset, Bruno (1958–) 2
Guérinel, Lucien (1930–) 1, 3
Guilbert, Robert (18?–1952) 2
Guillou, René (1903–1958) 2
Guillonneau, Christian (1958–) 2
Hakim, Naji (1955–) (born in Lebanon) 2
Hasquenoph, Pierre (1922–1982) 3
Hérold, Ferdinand (1791–1833) 2
Holstein, Jean-Paul (1939–) 2
Houdy, Pierrick (1929–) 2
Hulin, Eric (1961–) 2
d'Indy, Vincent (1851–1931) 2, 3
Jadin, Louis-Emmanuel (1768–1853) 2
Jemain, Joseph (1864–1954)
Jevtic, Ivan (1947–) (born in Serbia) 3
Jollet, Jean-Clément (1954–) 2
Joubert, Claude-Henry (1948–) 2
Kastel, Fabrice (1966–) 2
Koechlin, Charles (1867–1950) 1, 2, 3
Lacour, Guy (1932–2013) 2
Lamy, Fernand (1881–1966) 2
Lancen, Serge (1922–2005) 2
Le Flem, Paul (1881–1984) 2
Lefebvre, Charles (1843–1917) 2
Lefebvre, Claude (1931–2012) 1
Lejet, Edith (1941–) 1
Lemeland, Aubert (1932–) 2
Leroux, Xavier (1863–1919) 2
Leroy, Camille (1949–) 2
Lersy, Roger (1920–2004) 2
Lesaffre, Charles (1949–) 2
Lézé, Jean-François (1971–) 2
Litaize, Gaston (1909–1991) 2
Louvier, Alain (1945–) 2
Luigini, Alexandre (1850–1906) 2
Mallié, Loïc (1947–) 2

Marc, Edmond (1939–) 2
Marechal, Henri (1842–1924) 2
Mari, Pierrette (1929–) 2
Martelli, Henri (1895–1980) 2
Massenet, Jules (1842–1912) 2
Maurat, Edmond (1881–1972) 2
Mazellier, Jules (1879–1959) 2
Méreaux, Max (1946–) 2
Meunier, Gérard (1928–) 2
Mignion, Rene (1907–1981) 2
Mihalovici, Marcel (1898–1985) (born in
   Romania) 2
Mohr, Jean-Baptiste (1823–1891) 2
Montbrun, Raymond Gallois (1918–1994) 2
Mourey, Colette (1954–) 2
Moyse, Louis (1912–2007) 2
Murgier, Jacque (1912–1986) 2
Murail, Tristan (1947–) 3
Naulais, Jèrôme (1951–) 1, 2
Nedellec, Patrick (1946–) 2
Niverd, Lucien (1879–1967) 2
Pascal, Andrè (1932–2001) 2
Pascal, Claude (1921–) 1, 2
Passani, Emile (1905–1974) 2, 3
Pauset, Brice (1965–) 2
Pernoo, Jacques (1921–2003) 2
Pessard, Emile (1843–1917) 2
Petit, Pierre (1922–2000) 1, 2
Pichaureau, Claude (1940–) 2
Planel, Robert (1908–1994) 2
Poulenc, Francis (1899–1963) 2
Presle, Jacques de la (1888–1969) 2
Proust, Pascal (1959–) 1, 2
Pugno, Stéphane-Raoul (1852–1914) 2
Pyncou, Samuel 2
Rateau, Johanne Michel (1938–) 2
René, Charles (1863–1935) 2
Roger, Denise (1924–2005) 1
Rossignol, Bruno (1958–) 1, 2
Rougeron, Philippe (1928–) 2
Rueff, Jeanine (1922–1999) 2
Saint-Saëns, Camille (1835–1921) 2, 3
Samuel-Rousseau, Marcel (1882–1955) 2
Sancan, Pierre (1916–2008) 2
Santamaria, Gaëtan (1957–) 2
Schmitt, Florent (1870–1958) 2
Selmer-Collery, Jules (1902–1988) 2
Sieber, Georges Julien (1775–1847) 2
Stefanelli, Matthieu (1985–) 2
Tisné, Antoine (1932–1998) 1, 2, 3

Tomasi, Henri (1901–1971) 2, 3
Tosi, Daniel (1953–) 2
Vallée, Georges Robert (1897–1976) 2
Vallier, Jacques (1922–) 2
Vidal, Paul (1863–1931) 2
Vienne, Bernard de (1957–) 1

Voirpy, Alain (1955–) 1
Wal-Berg (Voldemar Rosenberg) (1910–1994)
Weber, Alain (1930–) 2
Wehage, Paul (1963–) (born in United
   States) 1
Werner, Jean-Jacques (1935–) 1, 2, 3

Germany

Abel, Karl Friedrich (1723–1787) 3
Agthe, Friedrich Wilhelm (1794–1830) 3
Allers, Hans-Günther (1935–) 2, 3
Ambrosius, Hermann (1897–1983) 2
Arends, Michael (1939–) 2
Arnecke, Jörn (1973–) 1
Aschenbrenner, Johannes (1903–1964) 3
Backofen, Johann Georg Heinrich
   (1768–1839) 3
Baumann, Hermann (1934–) 1
Beethoven, Ludwig von (1770–1827) 2
Berg, Stephen A. (1945–) (born in
   United States) 2
Bieler, Helmut (1940–) 1
Blume, Hermann (1891–1967) 3
Blumer, Theodor (1881–1964) 3
Bödecker, Louis (1845–1889) 2
Braun, Gerhard (1932–) 1
Bredemeyer, Reiner (1929–1995) 1
Bruns, Victor (1904–1996) 1
Büttner, Max (1879–1948) 2
Cilensek, Johann (1913–1998) 3
Czerny, Karl (1791–1857) 2
Danzi, Franz (1763–1826) 2, 3
Dietrich, Albert (1829–1908) 2, 3
Dimmler, Franz Anton (1753–1827) 3
Dolorko, Ratko (1959–) 2
Draeseke, Felix (1835–1913) 2
Driessler, Johannes (1921–1998) 3
Eichborn, Hermann Ludwig (1847–1918) 2
Eisner, Carl (1802–1874) 2
Eschmann, Johann Carl (1826–1882) 2
Fesca, Friedrich Ernst (1789–1826) 3
Fick, Peter Joachim (d. 1743) 3
Finke, Fidelio (1891–1968) 2
Förster, Christoph (1693–1745) 3
Franz, Oscar (1843–1886) 2
Frehse, Albin (1878–1973) 2, 3
Fridl (Friedl, Friedel), Carl 3
Fries, Albin (1955–) 2
Gabler, Egon (1876–1959) 3

Gehra, August (Heinrich?) (1715–1785) 3
Genzmer, Harald (1909–2007) 2, 3
Gerster, Ottmar (1897–1969) 3
Gillmann, Kurt (1889–1974) 3
Goldhammer, Siegmund (1932–) 3
Gottwald, Heinrich (1821–1876) 2
Graap, Lothar (1933–) 2
Graef, Friedemann (1949–) 1
Grahl, Kurt (1947–) 2
Graun, Carl Heinrich (1703/4–1750) 3
Graun, Johann Gottlieb (1702/3–1771) 3
Gropp, Helmut (1899–1972) 2
Grüger, Vincent (1962–) 1
Grunelius, Wilhelm von (1942–) 1
Gugel, Heinrich (1743–1802) 2
Haag, Hanno (1939–2005) 3
Haas, Joseph (1879–1960) 2
Hampel, Anton Joseph (ca. 1710–1771) 3
Hauser, Ernst 2
Heider, Werner (1930–) 1, 3
Helmschrott, Robert Maximilian (1938–) 2
Herchet, Jörg (1943–) 1, 3
Hespos, Hans-Joachim (1938–) 1
Hessenberg, Kurt (1908–1994) 2
Hindemith, Paul (1895–1963) (worked in
   United States) 2, 3
Hlouschek, Theodor (1923–2010) (born in
   Czech Republic) 1, 2
Hofmann, Wolfgang (1922–2003) 2
Holler, Georg Augustin (1744–1814) 3
Hummel, Bertold (1925–2002) 1, 2, 3
Kanefzky, Franz (1964–) 1
Kalkbrenner, Friedrich (1785–1849) 2
Kalliwoda, Johann Wenzel (1801–1866)
   (Bohemia) 2, 3
Kaminski, Heinrich (1886–1946) 2
Kampe, Gordon (1976–) 2
Kellner, Johann Andreas (1724–1785) 3
Kiel, Clemens August (1813–1871) 3
Kirchner, Volker David (1942–) 2, 3
Klebe, Giselher (1925–2009) 2

Steinmüller, Joseph (1763–1808) 3
Stich, Johann Wenzel (Jan Václav)
    (1746–1803) (Punto, Giovanni)
    (Bohemia) 3
Stockhausen, Karlheinz (1928–2007) 1
Strauss, Franz (1822–1905) 2, 3
Strauss, Richard (1864–1949) 2, 3
Suttner, Josef (1881–1974) (born in Czech
    Republic) 2
Telemann, Georg Philipp (1681–1767) 3
Thieriot, Ferdinand (1838–1919) 2
Thistle, Robert (1945–) (born in United
    States) 2
Thurner, Friedrich Eugen (1785–1827) 2
Wasielewski, W.J. von (1822–1896) 2

Weber, Carl Maria von (1786–1826) 3
Weinhart, Christoph (1958–) 1, 2
Weismann, Julius (1879–1950) 3
Werner, Fritz (1898–1977) 3
Werner, Jacob (1938–2006) 2
Widmann, Jörg (1973–) 1
Wirth, Adam (1846?–1879) 2
Witt, Friedrich (1770–1836) 3
Wolschina, Reinhard (1952–) 1, 3
Zapff, Oskar (1862–1920) 2
Zehm, Fredrich (1923–2007) 2
Zenger, Max (1837–1911) 2
Zettler, Richard (1921–) 3
Zimmermann, Udo (1943–) 3
Zobel, Emely (1964–1996) 1

Greece

Xanthoulis, Nikos (1962–) 2

Zannas, Savvas (1952–) 3

Hungary

Bakki, József (1940–1981) 2
Bozay, Attila (1939–1999) 3
Dávid, Gyula (1913–1977) 3
Dubrovay, László (1943–) 1
Durkó, Zsolt (1934–1997) 2, 3
Hidas, Frigyes (1928–2007) 3
Kocsár, Miklós (1933–) 1, 2, 3
Láng, István (1933–) 1, 3

Nagy, Zsolt (1957–) 1, 2
Sári, József (1935–) 1
Soproni, József (1930–) 2
Szabo, Csaba (1936–2003) 2
Székely, Endre (1912–1989) 3
Zador, Eugene (1894–1977)
    (worked in United
    States) 3

Ireland

Wilson, Ian (1964–) 1

Wilson, James (1922–2005) (born in
    England) 3

Israel

Bertini, Gary (1927–2005) (born in Rus-
    sia) 3
Braun, Yehezkel (1922–2014) 1, 2, 3
Graziani, Yitzhak (1924–2003) (born in
    Bulgaria) 2, 3
Kogan, Lev (1927–2007) (born in Russia)
    1, 2, 3
Mishori, Yaacov (1937–) 1

Reinhardt, Bruno (1929–) (born in Ro-
    mania) 1
Rom, Uri (1969–) 2, 3
Rooth, Laszlo (1919–) (born in Ro-
    mania) 2
Sheriff, Noam (1935–) 1
Stutschewsky, Joachim (1891–1982) (born
    in the Ukraine) 1

Italy

Belloli, Agostino (1778–1839) 3

Belloli, Luigi (1770–1817) 3

Bergonzi, Benedetto (1790–1840) 2
Bonnard, Giulio (1885–1972) 2
Campolieti, Luigi (1905–1975) 2
Ceccarossi, Domenico (1910–1997) 1
Cherubini, Luigi (1760–1842) (resided in
   France) 2, 3
Chillemi, Salvatore (1935–) 2
Chiti, Gian Paolo (1939–) 1, 2
Cortese, Luigi (1899–1976) 2
Cossetto, Emil (1918–2006) 2
De Angelis, Ugalberto (1932–1982) 3
Donatoni, Franco (1927–2000) 1
Ferrari, Giorgio (1925–2010) 1, 2
Gentile, Ada (1947–) 1
Ghidoni, Armando (1959–) 2
Lucidi, Marco (1962–) 1

Mercadante, Saverio (1795–1870) 3
Montico, Mario (1885–1959) 3
Prosperi, Carlo (1921–1990) 2
Puzzi, Giovanni (1792–1876)
   (worked in United
   Kingdom) 2
Rossari, Gustavo (1827–1881) 2
Rossini, Gioacchino (1792–1868) 1, 2
Rota, Nino (1911–1979) 3
Saglietti, Corrado Maria (1957–) 2
Scelsi, Giacinto (1905–1988) 1
Sciarrino, Salvatore (1947–) 3
Sinigaglia, Leone (1868–1944) 2
Spontini, Gaspare (1774–1851) 2
Tutino, Marco (1954–) 1
Viozzi, Giulio (1912–1984) 2

Japan

Hoshina, Hiroshi (1936–) 3
Hosokawa, Toshio (1955–) 3

Ikebe, Shin'ichirō (1943–) 1

Latvia

Altmanis, Alvils (1950–) 2

Vasks, Peteris (1946–) 2

Lithuania

Dvarionas, Balys (1904–1972) 3

Netherlands

Andriessen, Jurriaan (1925–1996) 1
Badings, Henk (1907–1987) 2
Booren, Jo van den (1935–) 1
Bree, Johannes Bernadus van (1801–1857) 3
Coenen, Johannes Meinardus (1824–1899) 2
De Wolf, J. E. (b. 1908) 2
Dragstra, Willem (1956–) 2
Eisma, Will (1929–) (born in Indonesia) 3
Flothuis, Marius (1914–2001) 1, 3
Hekster, Walter (1937–2012) 2
Henkemans, Hans (1913–1995) 3
Hutschenruyter, Wouter, Jr. (1859–1943) 2, 3
Hutschenruyter, Wouter Sr. (1796–1878) 3
Ketting, Otto (1935–2012) 1, 2, 3
Keulen, Geert van (1943–) 3
Koetsier, Jan (1911–2006) 2, 3
Laman, Wim (1946–)
Loevendie, Theo (1930–) 3

Mengelberg, Karel (1902–1984) 3
Meijering, Chiel (1954–) 2
Mulder, Herman (1894–1989) 2
Namavar, Reza (1980–) 3
Poelman, Alex (1981–) 3
Ponjee, Ted (1953–) 2
Raxach, Enrique (1932–) (born in
   Spain) 2
Roo, Paul de (1957–) 2
Rossum, Hans van (1958–) 2
Ruijters, René (1955–) 2
Schouwman, Hans (1902–1967) 2
Spandau, Willem (1741–1806) 3
Steup, Hendrik C. (1778–1827) 2
Surtel, Maarten (1958–) 3
Vandenbroek, Othon-Joseph (1758–1852)
   resided in France 3
Wagemans, Peter-Jan (1952–) 1

New Zealand

Abbott, Clifford (1916–1994) 2
Biddington, Eric (1953–) 2, 3
Grenfell, Maria (1969–) 2

Hamilton, David (1955–) 3
Rimmer, John (1939–) 3
Sarcich, Paul (1951–) 2

Norway

Berge, Sigurd (1929–2002) 1
Böttcher, Eberhard (1934–) (born in
    Germany) 3
Brevik, Tor (1932–) 1
Kvam, Oddvar S. (1927–) 1
Kvandal, Johan (1919–1999) 1, 2

Madsen, Trygve (1940–) 1, 2, 3
Nystedt, Knut (1915–2014) 1, 3
Olsen, Sparre (1903–1984) 1, 3
Plagge, Wolfgang (1960–) 1, 2
Schjelderup-Ebbe, Dag (1926–2013) 2
Thommessen, Olav Anton (1946–) 3

Philippines

Molina, Antonio (1894–1980)

Poland

Kilar, Wojciech (1932–2013)
Machala, Kazimierz (1948–) 3
Moss, Piotr (1949–)

Penderecki, Krzysztof (1933–) 1, 3
Sikorski, Kazimierz (1895–1986) 3

Portugal

Almeida, Antonio Victorino D' (1940–) 2
Carrapatoso, Eurico (1962–) 2

Marques, Telmo (1963–) 2
Vieira, Fátima (1974–) 1

Russia

Agababov, Arkadi (1940–) 2
Aladov, Nikolaï (1890–1972) 2
Anisimov, Boris Ivanovich (1907–
    1997) 2
Buyanovsky, Vitaly [Buianovskii, Vitalii]
    (1928–1993) 1, 2
Chemberdzhi Yekaterina [Chemberdgi,
    Ekaterina] (1960–) 3
Glazunov, Alexander (1865–1936) 2
Gedike [Goedicke], Aleksandr Fyodor-
    ovich (1877–1957) 3
Gliere, Rheinhold (1875–1956) 2, 3
Gubaidulina, Sofia (1931–) (resides in
    Germany) 2
Karaev, Kara (1918–1982) 2
Komarovsky, A. [Anatoli] (1909–1955) 3
Krivitsky, David [Krivitskii, David Isaa-
    kovich] (1937–2010) 3

Kryukov [Kriukov], Vladimir, (1902–
    1960) 2, 3
Levitin, Yury Abramovich (1912–1993) 3
Makarov, Evgenii Petrovich (1912–
    1985) 2
Miroshnikov, Oleg. (1925–) 2
Pakhmutova, Aleksandra (1929–) 2
Peskin, Vladimir (1906–1988)
Raukhverger, M. (Mikhail) (1901–1989) 3
Scherbachev, Vladimir(1887–1952) 2
Scriabin, Aleksandr Nikolayevich
    (1872–1915) 2
Shebalin, Vissarion (1902–1963) 3
Tcherepnin, Nicholas (also Tschérépnine,
    Nicholai) (1873–1945) 2
Trubin, Boris (1930–) 3
Vasilenko, Sergei Nikiforovich (1872–
    1956) 3

Serbia

Grgin, Ante (1945–) 2
Jevtic, Ivan (1947–) resides in France 3

Žebeljan, Isidora (1967–) 3

Slovenia

Globokar, Vinko (1934–) 1
Gregorc, Jurij (1916–1985) 3
Habe, Tomaž (1947–) 3
Kantušer, Božidar (1921–1999) 2
Krek, Uroš (1922–2008) 3

Lebic, Lojze (1934–) 1
Merkù, Pavle (1927–) (born in Italy) 1
Petrić, Ivo (1931–) 1, 2, 3
Ramovš, Primož (1921–1999) 2, 3
Žuraj, Vito (1979–) 1, 3

Spain

Bertran, Moisès (1967–) 2
Blanquer, Amando (1935–2005) 2, 3
Boliart, Xavier (1948–) 2
Bretón, Tomás (1850–1923) 2
Brotons, Salvador (1959–) 1, 2, 3
Casablancas, Benet (1956–) 3
Colomer, Juan J. (1966–) 2
Echevarria, Victorino (1898–1965) 2
Egea, J. Vincent (1961–) 2
Font, Luis (?–1911) 2

Lázaro, José Villena (1941–) 1
Llàcer Plà, Francisco (1918–2002) 2
Meseguer Llopis, Juan Bautista (1959–) 2
Monjo, Didac (1949–) 2
Muneta, Jesús María (1939–) 2
Pérez, Raúl (1969–) 1
Peron-Cano, Carlos (1976–) 2
Sanz Sifre, Nicanor (1933–) 3
Valero Castells, Andrés (1973–) 1
Zarzo Pitarch, Vicente (1938–) 1

Sweden

Alfvén, Hugo (1872–1960) 2
Andersson, B. Tommy (1964–) 3
Atterberg, Kurt (1887–1974) 3
Böttcher, Eberhard (1934–) (born in
Germany) 3
Crusell, Bernhard (1775–1838) (born in
Finland) 2, 3
Eklund, Hans (1927–1999) 3
Frumerie, Gunnar de (1908–1987) 3
Hallnäs, Eyvind (1937–) 3
Hermanson, Åke (1923–1996) 1
Hjorth, Daniel (1973–) 1
Karkoff, Maurice (1927–2013) 1

Koch, Erland von (1910–2009) 1
Körling, August (1842–1919) 2
Larsson, Lars-Erik (1908–1986) 3
Lundberg, Staffan (1952–) 1, 2
Lundquist, Torbjörn (1920–2000) 3
Malmlöf-Forssling, Carin (1916–2005) 1
Maros, Miklós (1943–) (born in Hungary) 1
Mellnäs, Arne (1933–2002) 1
Perder, Kjell (1954–) 1
Rabe, Folke (1935–) 1, 3
Sagvik, Stellan (1952–) 3
Soldh, Anders (1955–) 3
Sylvan, Sixten (1914–2001) 2

Switzerland

Arter, Matthias (1964–) 1
Baratto, Paolo (1926–2008) 2
Beck, Conrad (1901–1989) 2
Burkhard, Willy (1900–1955) 2
Darbellay, Jean-Luc (1946–) 1, 2, 3
Derungs, Gion Antoni (1935–2012) 3

Diethelm, Caspar (1926–1997) 1
Frischknecht, Hans Eugen (1939–) 1
Godel, Didier (1945–) 2
Haselbach, Josef (1936–2002) 2
Hess, Willy (1906–1997) 2, 3
Holliger, Heinz (1939–) 1

Isoz, Etienne (1905–1986) (born in
  Hungary) 2
Jarrell, Michael (1958–) 1
Kelterborn, Rudolf (1931–) 1
Kling, Henri (1842–1918) (born in France) 2, 3
Knüsel, Alfred (1941–) 1
Longinotti, Paolo (1913–1963) 2
Leutwiler, Toni (1923–2009) 3
Meier, Jost (1939–) 3
Mersson, Boris (1921–2013) (born in Ger-
  many) 2
Moret, Norbert (1921–1998) 3
Perrin, Jean (1920–1989) 2
Piantoni, Louis (1885–1958) 2
Quadranti, Luigi (1941–) 1

Reichel, Bernard (1901–1992) 2
Richards, Scott (1951–) (born in Scot-
  land) 1
Ristori, Emile, (1893–1977) 2, 3
Roth, Michel (1976–) 1
Sack, Theodor (1910–1989) 2
Schibler, Armin (1920–1986) 2, 3
Schlaepfer, Jean-Claude (1961–) 1
Schoeck, Othmar (1886–1957) 3
Semini, Carlo Florindo (1914–2004) 2
Sturzenegger, Kurt (1949–) 1, 2
Sturzenegger, Christophe (1976–) 1, 2
Székely, Erik (1927–) 2
Vuataz, Roger (1898–1988) 2
Zbinden, Julien-François (1917–) 1, 2

Uganda

Tamusuza, Justinian (1951–) 1

Ukraine

Akimenko, Fedir (1876–1945) 2

United Kingdom

Abbott, Alan (1926–) 2
Arnold, Malcolm (1921–2006) 1, 3
Ayres, Richard (1965–) 3
Bainbridge, Simon (1952–) 3
Ball, Christopher (1936–) 3
Barton-Armstrong, John (1923–2010) 2
Baker, Ernest (1912–1992) 2
Bax, Arnold E. Trevor (1883–1953) 2
Bayliss, Colin (1948–) 3
Bennett, Richard Rodney (1936–2012) 2, 3
Berkeley, Michael (1948–) 3
Bishop, Jeffrey (1943–) 2
Bissill, Richard (1960–) 1, 2
Bourgeois, Derek (1941–) 1
Bowen, York (1884–1961) 2, 3
Bowers, Timothy (1954–) 2
Bradford-Anderson, Muriel 2
Brightmore, Victor (1902–1994) 2
Broadbent, Nigel (1952–) 2
Bunting, Christopher (1924–2005) 2
Bush, Alan (1900–1995) 2
Butt, James (1929–2003) 1, 2, 3
Butterworth, Arthur (1923–2014) 3
Butterworth, Neil (1934–) 2

Butler, Martin (1960–) 1
Carr, Gordon (1943–) 2
Carse, Adam (1878–1958) 2
Catelinet, Philip Bramwell (1910–1995) 2
Charlton, Alan (1970–) 1
Cliff, Tony 3
Clews, Eileen (1935–) 2
Cooke, Arnold (1906–2005) 2
Criswell, J. Patrick 2
Cruft, Adrian (1921–1987) 3
Davies, Alison (1956–) 1
Davies, Peter Maxwell (1934–) 1, 3
Davis, Lizzie 2
Dawes, Julian (1942–) 2
Denwood, Russell (1950–) 2
Dodgson, Stephen (1924–2013) 1
Downes, Andrew (1950–) 2
Duck, Leonard (1916–2002) 2
Dunhill, Thomas Frederick (1877–1946) 2
East, Harold (1947–) (born in Canada) 2
Firsova, Elena (1950–) (born in Russia) 3
Fox, Adrienne (1941–) 2
Francis, Alun (1943–) 1, 3
Fricker, Peter Racine (1920–1990) 2

Frith, John (1947–) 2
Fujikura, Dai (1977–) (born in Japan) 3
Garland, Chris 2
Gibbs, Christopher (1938–) 2
Gipps, Ruth (1921–1999) 2, 3
Godfrey, Philip (1964–) 2
Gough, Christopher (1991–) 1, 2
Gould, Janetta (1926–) 2
Graham, Peter, (1958–) 2
Graves, Richard (1926–2002) 2
Gregson, Edward (1945–) 2, 3
Gwilt, David (1932–) 2
Halstead, Anthony (1945–) 1
Hamilton, Iain (1922–2000) 2, 3
Hanmer, Ronald (1917–1994) 2
Hardy, Mabel (1875–1971) 2
Harris, Paul (1956–) 2
Head, Michael (1900–1976) 2
Hedges, Anthony (1931–) 1, 3
Hoddinott, Alun (1929–2008) 2, 3
Holloway, Robin (1943–)
Howarth, Frank (1905–1994) (worked in
    Canada) 2
Humphries, John (ca. 1707–ca. 1740) 3
Jacob, Gordon (1895–1984) 3
Jacques, Michael (1944–) 2
James, Ifor (1931–2004) 2
Johns, Terence 2
Kelly, Bryan (1934–) 2
Kennaway, Lamont 2
Kershaw, Richard (1946–) 2
Knussen, Oliver (1954–) 3
Lane, Liz (1964–) 1
Lawrence, Peter (1954–) 2
Ledbury, Oliver (1963–) 2
LeFanu, Nicola (1947–) 3
Lewis, Anthony (1915–1983) 3
Lipkin, Malcolm (1932–) 3
Lloyd Webber, William (1914–1982) 2
Longstaff, Edward (1965–) 2
Lutyens, Elisabeth, (1906–1983) 2, 3
Lyon, David (1938–) 1, 3
Martland, Steve (1959–2013) 3
Mason, Benedict (1955–) 3
Mathias, William (1934–1992) 3

Matthews, Colin (1946–) 3
McCabe, John (1939–2015) 2, 3
McGuire, Edward (1948–) (Scotland) 1
Musgrave, Thea (1928–) (born Scotland,
    resides in United States) 2, 3
Noble, Harold (1903–1998) 2
Northcott, Bayan (1940–) 3
Olive, Vivienne (1950–) (resides in Ger-
    many) 1
Orr, Robin (1909–2006) 2
Parsons, Alan (1931–) 2
Patterson, Paul (1947–) 3
Pitfield, Thomas (1903–1999) 2
Potter, Cipriani (1792–1871) 2
Powers, Anthony (1953–) 3
Procter-Gregg, Humphrey (1895–1980) 2
Randall, Anthony (1937–) 2
Reeman, John (1946–) 2
Ridout, Alan (1934–1996) 2, 3
Ridgeon, John (1944–) 2
Roddie, Matthew (1974–) (Scotland) 1
Roe, Betty (1930–) 2
Searle, Humphrey (1915–1982) 3
Seiber, Mátyás (1905–1960) (born in
    Hungary) 3
Short, Michael (1937–) 3
Simaku, Thomas (1958–) (born in
    Albania) 2
Solomons, David W. (1953–) 1, 2
Steptoe, Roger (1953–) (resides in
    France) 1, 3
Stevenson, Ronald (1928–) (Scotland) 2
Stringer, John (1967–) 2
Stroud, Richard (1982–) 1
Tomlinson, Ernest (1924–) 3
Vass, George (1957–) 1
Vinter, Gilbert (1909–1969) 2, 3
Warren, Norman (1934–) 2
Watkins, Huw (1976–) 3
Watkins, Michael Blake (1948–) 3
Whettam, Graham (1927–2007) 2, 3
Wiggins, Christopher D. (1956–) 1, 2, 3
Wilby, Philip (1949–) 1, 2, 3
Wilson, Thomas (1927–2001) (Scotland) 1
Woolfenden, Guy (1937–) 2

United States

Actor, Lee (1952–) 3
Adams, Leslie (1932–) 2

Adler, Samuel (1928–) (born in Ger-
    many) 1, 2, 3

Agrell, Jeffrey (1948–) 1, 2

Albert, Thomas (1949–) 2

Albright, William (1944–1998) 2

Alexander, Josef (1907–1990) 2

Amis, Kenneth (1970–) (born in Bermuda) 2

Amram, David (1930–) 1, 3

Amrhein, Karen (1970–) 2

Andersen, Arthur Olaf (1880–1958) 2

Aprahamian, Maia (1935–2011) 2

Arnn, John 2

Atkinson, Condit (1928–2009) 2

Avalon, Robert (1955–2004) 2

Babbitt, Milton (1916–2011) 1

Bach, Jan (1937–) 1, 2, 3

Bach, P. D. Q. (1742–1807) (Peter Schickele) 3

Bacon, Ernst (1898–1990) 2

Balmages, Brian (1975–) 3

Bakaleinikoff, Vladimir (1885–1953) (born in Russia) 2

Baksa, Robert (1938–) 2

Baldwin, Daniel (1978–) 1, 2

Barnes, Arthur P. (1930–) 2

Barnett, Carol E. (1949–) 2, 3

Baron, Maurice (1899–1964) (born in France) 2

Barrows, John R. (1913–1974) 2

Basler, Paul (1963–) 1, 2, 3

Bassett, Leslie (1923–) 2

Báthory-Kitsz, Dennis (1949–) 1

Beckel, James (1948–) 2, 3

Becker, John J. (1886–1961) 3

Beckler, Stanworth R. (1923–) 2

Benjamin, Thomas (1940–) 2

Bennett, David D. (1892–1990) 2, 3

Benson, Warren (1924–2005) 2

Bernstein, Leonard (1918–1990) 2

Bertolozzi, Joseph (1959–) 3

Bestor, Charles (1924–) 3

Beversdorf, Thomas (1924–1981) 2

Black, Daniel (1979–) 1, 3

Blaha, Joseph L. (1951–) 2

Blank, Allan (1925–2013) 1

Boerma, Scott (1964–) 3

Borroff, Edith (1925–) 2

Bowder, Jerry Lee (1928–2005) 2

Boysen, Andrew Jr. (1968–) 2

Boziwick, George (1954–) 1

Branscombe, Gena (1881–1977) (born in Canada) 2

Briggs, Kendall Durelle (1959–) 2

Brings, Allen (1934–) 1

Broughton, Bruce (1945–) 2, 3

Brouwer, Margaret (1940–) 1, 2

Brown, Richard E. (1947–) 2

Busler-Blais, Lydia (1969) 2

Buss, Howard J. (1951–) 1, 2

Butts, Carrol M. (1924–1980) 2

Cacavas, John (1930–2014) 2

Cacioppo, Curt (1951–) 1

Caliendo, Christopher (1960–) 2

Callabro, Louis (1926–1991) 2

Callaway, Ann (1945–) 2

Campanelli, Richard (1949–) 2

Carter, Elliott (1908–2012) 1, 3

Cazden, Norman (1914–1980) 2

Chaffin, Lon W. (1957–) 2

Chajes, Julius (1910–1985) (born in Poland) 2

Chandler, Hugh (1956–) 2

Chasalow, Eric (1955–) 1, 3

Cheslock, Louis (1898–1981) 3

Cheung, Anthony (1982–) 3

Childs, Barney (1926–2000) 1

Cioffari, Richard (1947–) 2

Clearfield, Andrea (1960–) 2

Coakley, Donald (1934–) 2

Cohen, Fred (1958–) 3

Cohen, Sol B. (1891–1988) 2

Collorafi, James (James Nicholas) (1957–) 2, 3

Constantinides, Dinos (1929–) (born in Greece) 2

Cooman, Carson P. (1982–) 1, 2, 3

Cope, David (1941–) 1, 2

Coscia, Silvio (1899–1977) 2

Cox, Philip W. L. (1883–?) 2

Craft, Jonathan (1986–) 2

Cunningham, Michael G. (1937–) 2

Custer, Calvin (1939–1998) 2

Danburg, Russell (1909–1994) 2

David, Avram (1930–2004) 1

Danner, Gregory (1958–) 2

Davison, John H. (1938–1999) 2

Deason, David (1945–) 1

De Lamarter, Eric (1880–1953) 2

Dennison, Sam (1926–2005) 3

Dickson, John (1963–) 2

Diercks, John (1927–) 2

Dillon, Lawrence (1959–) 3

Di Lorenzo, Anthony (1967–) 2, 3
Dishinger, R. C. (1941–) 2
Donato, Anthony (1909–1990) 2
Dvorak, Robert James, (1919–) 2
Dzubay, David (1964–) 1
Edelson, Edward (1932–) 2
Edstrom, Brent (1964–) 2
Effinger, Cecil (1914–1990) 2
Ehle, Robert C. 2
Epstein, David (1930–2002) 2
Eversole, James (1929–) 3
Ewazen, Eric, (1954–) 2, 3
Faith, Richard (1926–) 2
Faust, Randall E. (1947–) 1, 2, 3
Fennelly, Brian (1937–) 2
Fine, Elaine (1959–) 2
Finko, David (1936–) (born in Russia) 2
Flory, Neil (1970–) 1
Fossa, Matthew 2
Fox, Frederick (1931–2011) 3
Frackenpohl, Arthur (1924–) 1, 2, 3
Frangkiser, Carl (1894–1967) 2
Freund, Don (1947–) 1
Friedman, Stanley (1951–) 1, 3
Fuchs, Kenneth (1956–) 3
Gardner, Randy C. (1952–) 1
Garfield, Bernard (1924–) 2
Garlick, Antony (1927–2000) 2
Garrop, Stacy L. (1969–) 1
Gates, Crawford M. (1921–) 2
George, Thom Ritter (1942–) 3
Ghezzo, Dinu (1941–2011) (born in
    Romania) 1
Gillespie, Don (1942–) 2
Gillingham, David R. (1947–) 2, 3
Godfrey, Daniel (1949–) 3
Gomez, Alice (1960–) 1
Goossen, Frederic (1927–2011) 1
Grabois, Daniel (1964–) 1
Grant, James (1954–) 1, 2
Grant, Parks (1910–1988) 3
Greer, Lowell (1950–) 1
Gryč, Stephen (1949–) 1
Haddad, Don (1935–) 2, 3
Hagen, Daron (1961–) 3
Hailstork, Adolphus C. (1941–) 2
Hannay, Roger (1930–2006) 3
Harmon, John (1935–) 2
Harris, Floyd O. (1913–2007) 2

Hartley, Walter S. (1927–) 2
Haugland, A. Oscar (1922–2013) 2, 3
Hauser, Eric (1891–1964) 2
Hayes, Joseph (1919–2011) 2
Heiden, Bernhard (1910–2000) (born in
    Germany) 2, 3
Henry, Otto (1933–) 1
Henslee, Kenneth C. (1941–) 1
Hermann, Ralph (1914–1994) 3
Hersch, Michael (1971–) 3
Heuser, David (1966–) 1
Higdon, Jennifer (1962–) 2
Hilfiger, John Jay (1948–) 2
Hill, Douglas (1946–) 1, 2
Hilliard, Quincy C. (1954–) 2
Hindemith, Paul (1895–1963) (born in
    Germany) 2, 3
Hodkinson, Sydney (1934–) (born in
    Canada) 1
Holab, William (1958–) 1
Holcombe, Bill (1924–2010) 2
Holliday, Kent (1940–) 2
Holmes, Paul (1923–) 2
Horvit, Michael (1932–) 2
Hoss, Wendell (1892–1980) 2
Hovhaness, Alan (1911–2000) 3
Huggler, John (1921–1993) 3
Hughes, Mark (1934–1972) 2
Hurrell, Clarence Elmer (1912–1975) 2
Hutcheson, Jere (1938–) 2
Jacobs, Mark Eliot (1960–) 2
Jacobson, Harvey 2
Jalbert, Pierre (1967–) 3
Johnson, Tom (1939–) (resides in France) 1
Jones, Wendal (1932–2013) 2
Jones, Samuel (1935–) 3
Jordahl, Robert (1926–2008) 2
Kaefer, John F. (1976–) 2
Kallstrom, Michael J. (1956–) 1
Kaminsky, Laura (1956–) 1
Kauder, Hugo (1888–1972) (born in Czech
    Republic) 1, 2, 3
Kaun, Bernhard (1899–1980) (born in
    Germany) 3
Kavanaugh, Patrick (1954–) 1
Keegan, Mike 1
Keim, Aaron 2
Kelley, Daniel 2
Kibbe, Michael (1945–) 1

Kimmell, Jack Normain (1932–) 2

Kinney, Gordon J. (1905–1981) 2

Klauss, Noah (1901–1977) 2

Knight, Morris (1933–) 2

Koch, Frederick (1923–2005) 2

Kohn, Karl (1926–) (born in Austria) 2

Kopke, Paul (1918–2000) 2

Korn, Peter Jona (1922–1998) (born in Germany) 3

Kraft, Leo (1922–2014) 3

Kraft, William (1923–) 1, 3

Kreisler, Alexander von (1893–1969) (born in Russia) 2

Krenek, Ernst (1900–1991) (worked in Austria and United States) 2

Kurka, Robert (1921–1957) 3

Lane, Richard (1933–2004) 2

Lansky, Paul (1944–) 2

Lazarof, Henri (1932–2013) (born in Bulgaria) 1, 3

Leclaire, Dennis (1950–) 2

Lees, Benjamin (1924–2010) 3

Le Siege, Annette (1945–) 1, 2

Levy, Frank (1930–) 2

Lewis, Robert Hall (1926–1996)

Lieberson, Peter (1946–2011) 3

Lockwood, Normand (1906–2002) 3

London, Edwin (1929–2013) 3

Lotzenhiser, George W. (1923–) 2

Lowe, Laurence (1956–) 2

Lu, Wayne (1970–) 1, 2

Machala, Kazimierz (1948–) (born in Poland) 3

Maganini, Quinto (1897–1974) 2

Maggio, Robert 2

Maltby, R. (1914–1991) 2

Marshall, Pamela (1954–) 1

Martin, Robert (1952–) 1

Maslanka, David (1943–) 2

Matchett, Steve (1957–) 1

McKay, George Frederick (1899–1970) 2

McKinley, William Thomas (1938–2015) 3

McTee, Cindy (1953–) 2

McQuade Dewhirst, Michelle (1973–) 3

Miller, Brett 2

Miller, J. Greg (1984–) 1, 2

Molyneux, Garth E. (1958–) 2

Moylan, William (1956–) 2

Muelbe, William (1888–1966) 2

Mueller, Otto (1870–1960) (born in Germany) 2, 3

Musgrave, Thea (1928–) (born Scotland) 2, 3

Nagel, Jody (1960–) 1, 2, 3

Naigus, James (1987–) 1, 2

Nelhybel, Vaclav (1919–1996) (born in Czech Republic) 2

Nelson, Paul (1929–2008) 3

Nicholas, James (James Collorafi) (1957–) 1, 2, 3

Norden, Hugo (1909–1986) 2, 3

Nowlin, Ryan (1978–) 2

Nyquist, Morine (b. 1909) 2

Oldberg, Arne (1874–1962) 2, 3

Olson, Judith (1940–) 2

Onofrio, Marshall 2

Osborne, Chester, G. (1915–1987) 2

Ostransky, Leroy (1918–1993) 2

Ott, Joseph (1929–1990) 2

Panos, Alexander (1980–) 2

Pehrson, Joseph (1950–) 2, 3

Pellegrini, Ernesto (1932–) 2

Perrini, Nicholas J. (1932–) 2

Persichetti, Vincent (1915–1987) 1

Phan, P. Q. (1963–) (born in Vietnam) 3

Phillips, Craig (1961–) 2

Piacquadio, Peter (1945–) 2, 3

Pinkham, Daniel (1923–2006) 2

Plog, Anthony (1947–) (worked in Germany) 1, 2, 3

Ployhar, James D. (1926–2007) 2

Poole, Reid (1919–2006) 2

Pope, Conrad (1951–) 1

Porter, Quincy (1897–1966) 2

Presser, William (1916–2004) 1, 2

Puts, Kevin (1972–) 3

Raheb, Jeff 1

Rakowski, David (1958–) 3

Raphling, Sam (1910–1988) 1, 2, 3

Read, Gardner (1913–2005) 2

Reise, Jay (1950–) 3

Reynolds, Verne (1926–2011) 1, 2

Richards, Paul (1969–) 2

Richmond, Jeffrey W. (1981–) 2

Richardson, Mark (1962–) 2

Robbins, Gil (1931–2011) 3

Robin, Greg (1976–) 1

Robinson, Marty (1969–) 1

Rodriguez, Robert Xavier (1946–) 2

Rogers, Bernard (1893–1968) 3
Rollin, Robert (1947–) 2, 3
Roper, Harrison (1932–) 2, 3
Rosenthal, Irving 1
Rosner, Arnold (1945–2013) 1, 2
Ross, Walter (1936–) 2
Ruesink, Linda (1964–) 2
Russell, Craig H. (1951–) 3
Sabatini, Guglielmo (ca. 1902–1967) 2, 3
Sain, James (1959–) 1
Salminen, Susan (1957–) 2, 3
Sampson, David (1951–) 2
Sanders, Bernard Wayne (1957–) (works in Germany) 2
Sanders, Robert Levine (1906–1974) 2
Sansone, Lorenzo (1881–1975) (born in Italy) 3
Sargon, Simon (1938–) (born in India) 2, 3
Scarmolin, Anthony Louis (1890–1969) (born in Italy) 2
Scheurer, Rolf (1918–2006) 2
Schickele, Peter (1935–) 2, 3
Schmalz, Peter (1947–) 2, 3
Schmidt, William (1926–2009) 2
Schnyder, Daniel (1961–) (born in Switzerland) 1, 2
Schonthal, Ruth (1924–2006) (born in Germany) 2, 3
Schuller, Gunther (1925–2015) 2, 3
Schultz, Mark (1957–2015) 1, 2, 3
Schuman, William (1910–1992) 3
Schwantner, Joseph (1943–) 3
Schwartz, Elliott (1936–) 3
Schwartz, George W. (1918–2010) 2
Shaw, Lowell (1930–) 1
Sibbing, Robert (1929–) 2
Sichel, John A. 2
Sierra, Roberto (1953–) 3
Silver, Sheila (1946–) 1
Sims, Ezra (1928–2015) 1
Skolnik, Walter (1934–) 2, 3
Sleeper, Thomas (1956–) 1, 3
Smith, Kile (1956–) 3
Smith, Leonard B. (1915–2002)
Smolanoff, Michael (1942–2013) 2, 3
Snedeker, Jeffrey (1958–) 1
Solomon, Edward S. 2
Songer, Lewis 1
Stacy, William Barney (1944–) 1

Stanton, Harry (1945–) 2
Stein, Leon (1910–2002) 1
Steiner, Gitta (1932–1990) 2
Stephenson, James M. (1969–) 1, 2, 3
Stevens, Halsey (1908–1989) 2
Stewart, Don (1935–) 2
Stirling, Ian (1919–2002) 2
Stokes, Harvey J. (1957–) 2
Story, Brian S. (1955–) 2
Stout, Gordon (1952–) 1
Summer, Joseph 3
Svane, Randall (1955–) 3
Sydeman, William Jay (1928–) 2, 3
Tautenhahn, Gunther (1938–2014) (born in Lithuania) 1, 2
Terwilliger, Eric (1954–) (resides in Germany) 1
Thatcher, Howard R. (1878–1973) 3
Thomas, Augusta Read (1964–) 3
Thompson, Bruce A. (1937–) 1, 2
Tillotson, Natalie 2
Tsontakis, George (1951–) 3
Turner, Kerry (1960–) (works in Luxembourg) 1, 2, 3
Turok, Paul (1929–2012) 2
Uber, David (1921–2007) 1, 2
Valenti, Michael (1942–) 2
VanderCook, Hale Ascher (1864–1949) 2
Varner, Tom (1957–) 1
Verrall, John (1908–2001) 2, 3
Vogel, Roger C. (1947–) 1, 3
Vollrath, Carl (1931–) 2
Wall, Robert 2
Wallach, Joelle (1946–) 2, 3
Washburn, Robert (1928–2013) 2
Weigel, Eugene (1910–1998) 2
Wessel, Mark (1894–1973) 2
Whear, Paul W. (1925–) 2, 3
Whitaker, Howard (1941–) 3
White, John (1931–) 2
Wigglesworth, Frank (1918–1996) 1
Wilder, Alec (1907–1980) 1, 2, 3
Williams, Edgar Warren (1949–) 1
Williams, John (1932–) 3
Wilson, Dana (1946–) 1, 2, 3
Winkler, Peter (1943–) 2
Winter, James H. (1919–2006) 2
Winteregg, Steven (1952–) 1, 2, 3
Wittell, Chester (1893–1988) 2, 3

Wolber, Gary (1968–) 2
Wolff, Christian (1934–) 2
Woltmann, Frederick (b. 1908–1965) 3
Woodman, James (1957–) 2
Woodson, Thomas C. (1954–) 1
Wright, Maurice (1949–) 1
Yancich, Milan (1921–2007) 1
Young, Scott (1970–) 2
Yurko, Bruce (1951–) 3

Zádor, Eugene (1894–1977) (born in
  Hungary) 2
Zdechlik, John P. (1937–) 2, 3
Zeuner, Charles (1795–1857) (born in
  Germany) 2, 3
Zinn, William (1924–)
Zucker, Laurel (1955–) 2
Zupko, Ramon (1931–) 3
Zwilich, Ellen Taaffe (1939–) 3

LINDA DEMPF is Music and Media Librarian at the College of New Jersey. She holds an MLS from Indiana University Bloomington, and a DM in Horn from Indiana University's Jacobs School of Music. She performs on the natural horn with period instrument ensembles throughout the United States.

RICHARD SERAPHINOFF is Professor of Horn at the Indiana University Jacobs School of Music and the Historical Performance Institute. He has performed and recorded regularly on natural horn with many period instrument ensembles throughout the country. Seraphinoff has presented numerous recitals and master classes at workshops and universities around the United States and in Europe, is a maker of early horn reproductions, and has authored several articles about the natural horn.

CPSIA information can be obtained
at www.ICGtesting.com
Printed in the USA
BVHW03*1401120318
510356BV00010B/294/P

9 780253 019295